2012

GOVERNMENTAL GAAP PRACTICE MANUAL

ERIC S. BERMAN

.CCH

a Wolters Kluwer business

ISBN: 978-0-8080-2635-8

Portions of this work were published in a previous edition.

Printed in the United States of America

Governmental GAAP Practice Manual

By Eric S. Berman

Financial professionals who work with state and local governments must stay current with emerging governmental standards, understand how accounting transactions should be reported, and prepare accurate and complete financial statements or face some unfortunate consequences. This one-of-a-kind hands-on tool shows state and local government accountants and auditors how to apply generally accepted accounting principles (GAAP) to state and local governments in a practical step-by-step approach. The approach in CCH's *Governmental GAAP Practice Manual* is explained in plain English and supported by practical, straightforward journal entries and examples common in the everyday government environment.

CCH's *Governmental GAAP Practice Manual* is organized sequentially so that readers can start at the beginning and follow how a typical governmental entity posts accounting transactions and ultimately creates its financial statements in accordance with generally accepted accounting principles. Readers can focus on a particular topic, read the relevant material, determine the appropriate journal entries, and follow the remaining chapters as they show in a step-by-step manner the preparation of the annual financial statements. For example, readers interested in how the information accounted for in Internal Service Funds is presented in a governmental entity's financial statements, can start with Chapter 8 (Internal Service Funds), go to Chapter 13 (Developing Information for Fund Financial Statements), proceed to Chapter 14 (Developing Information for Government-Wide Financial Statements), and see the end result in Chapter 16 (Basic Financial Statements).

2012 Edition

The 2012 edition has been updated with the very latest information on the following pronouncements that have the following implementation dates:

Implementation Period for Financial Statements	Pronouncement	Title
Periods Beginning after June 15, 2010	GASB-54	Fund Balance Reporting and Governmental Fund Type Definitions
	GASB-59	Financial Instruments Omnibus
Periods Beginning after June 15, 2011	GASB-57[a]	OPEB Measurements by Agent Employers and Agent Multiple-Employer Plans

Periods Beginning after December 15, 2011	GASB-60	Accounting and Financial Reporting for Service Concession Arrangements
	GASB-62	Codification of Accounting and Financial Reporting Guidance Contained in Pre-November 30, 1989 FASB and AICPA Pronouncements
Periods Beginning after June 15, 2012	GASB-61	The Financial Reporting Entity: Omnibus, an amendment of GASB Statements No. 14 and No. 34

[a] Only relating to the provisions of timing and frequency of measurements of other postemployment benefit plans actuarial valuations first used to report in plan financial statements. The remainder of the provisions are already implemented.

The *Governmental GAAP Practice Manual* is designed to serve as a practical tool for applying the basic requirements of GAAP in the preparation of state and local government financial statements. The accounting and financial reporting illustrations included here show how to apply the most common transactions encountered by a general-purpose government. The focus of this publication is on the conversion process necessary to take typical state and local government financial transactions and generate the financial statements required by GAAP. It is not intended to provide illustrations of the application of all GASB and applicable FASB pronouncements. A discussion of all GASB and applicable FASB pronouncements can be found in CCH's *Governmental GAAP Guide*.

CCH Learning Center

CCH's goal is to provide you with the clearest, most concise, and up-to-date accounting and auditing information to help further your professional development, as well as a convenient method to help you satisfy your continuing professional education requirements. The CCH Learning Center* offers a complete line of self-study courses covering complex and constantly evolving accounting and auditing issues. We are continually adding new courses to the library to help you stay current on all the latest developments. The CCH Learning Center courses are available 24 hours a day, seven days a week. You'll

---

get immediate exam results and certification. To view our complete accounting and auditing course catalog, go to: **http:/cch.learningcenter.com.**

Accounting Research Manager™

Accounting Research Manager is the accounting industry's largest and most comprehensive online database, providing easy access to objective and insightful government, accounting, auditing, and SEC information. While other research tools simply summarize the authoritative literature, leaving you to decipher often-complex information, Accounting Research Manager goes the extra mile to give you the clearest possible picture. We bring clarity to your government and financial reporting research.

The *Accounting Research Manager Government Library* provides one-stop access to governmental authoritative and proposal stage literature, including:

- **GASB (Governmental Accounting Standards Board)** Statements & Interpretations, Technical Bulletins, Implementation Guides & related proposal stage literature

- **GAO (Government Accountability Office)** Governmental Auditing Standards, Financial Audit Manual

- **OMB (Office of Management and Budget)** Circulars, Compliance Supplements

The Government Library also offers in-depth, interpretive guidance. Users can access our government titles that include the *Governmental GAAP Guide, Governmental GAAP Practice Manual, Knowledge-Based Audits™ of State and Local Governments with Single Audits,* and the *Governmental GAAP Update Service.*

Learn more about Accounting Research Manager by visiting **www.accountingresearchmanager.com.**

11/11

Contents

Preface

Generally accepted accounting and financial reporting principles applicable to state and local governments are fundamentally different from those applicable to nongovernment entities. In its desire to establish accounting and reporting standards that make governmental financial reports more relevant to users, the Governmental Accounting Standards Board (GASB) established two sets of financial statements: fund financial statements, which focus on individually significant funds, and government-wide financial statements, which attempt to provide insight into the overall financial position and activities of the governmental reporting entity.

The dual presentation approach added a significant degree of complexity to an already challenging financial reporting model. This financial reporting model poses a variety of challenges to both those who prepare and those who read governmental financial statements; however, the major implementation problem facing preparers of governmental financial statements was to develop an approach that seamlessly produces the two distinct levels of financial statements.

Most governmental entities are expected to solve this problem by using a worksheet approach to convert fund financial statement information to the government-wide financial statements. The purpose of this book is to demonstrate in a detailed manner how a governmental entity can apply the complex standards established by GASB through a worksheet approach.

This practice manual is a companion to CCH's *Governmental GAAP Guide,* which provides current information on accounting and reporting standards.

The Structure of This Book

The fundamental issue for understanding how to apply the accounting and financial reporting standards established by the GASB is the development of a clear understanding of the relationship between the modified accrual basis of accounting and current financial resources measurement focus (as used at the fund financial statement level for governmental funds) and the accrual basis of accounting and economic resources measurement focus (as used at the fund financial statement level for proprietary and fiduciary funds, and the government-wide financial statement level for governmental activities and business-type activities). Chapter 1 of the *Governmental GAAP Practice Manual* provides a detailed analysis of the interrelationship of the two bases of accounting and measurement focuses. Numerous transactions that governmental entities experience must first be recorded on the modified accrual basis and current financial resources focus (for presentation in the governmental fund financial statements) and then converted to the accrual basis and economic resources focus (for presentation in the government-wide financial statements). Included in Chapter 1 is a comprehensive checklist of transactions and events that typically require a worksheet conversion entry. An understanding of these entries will provide a governmental accountant with a basis for analyzing unique and complex transactions and then converting their initial recording on the modified accrual basis to the accrual basis.

Starting in Chapter 2 is a comprehensive illustration that continues through the remaining chapters of the book. For governmental funds, a variety of transactions are illustrated and journalized in Chapter 2 through Chapter 6, which result in a year-end trial balance for each individual fund based on the modified accrual basis of accounting and current financial resources measurement focus. For this year's edition, all of these chapters have been updated for implementation of GASB-54, (Fund Balance Reporting and Governmental Fund Type Definitions). In Chapter 14 these trial balances are used as the basis for developing the information needed to prepare the fund financial statements, as adjusted for the implementation of GASB-54. Chapter 16 illustrates the worksheet methodology for converting the information related to governmental funds (modified accrual basis and current financial resources focus) to information that is needed for the governmental activities column of the government-wide financial statements (accrual basis and economic resources focus).

A similar approach is used for proprietary funds (Chapter 7 and Chapter 8) and fiduciary funds (Chapter 9 through Chapter 13): Illustrative entries are developed for each of the funds, and the resulting trial balances become the basis for preparing fund financial statements (Chapter 13) and the business-type activities column of the government-wide financial statements (Chapter 14). However, because proprietary fund financial statements and the business-type activities column in the government-wide financial statements are presented on the same basis of accounting and measurement focus (accrual basis and economic resources focus), generally a conversion is not necessary for these funds and activities. In addition, because fiduciary funds are not presented in the government-wide financial statements, a conversion is not needed.

In Chapter 16 the basic financial statements (including the fund financial statements and government-wide statements) are prepared based on the information developed in Chapter 13 and Chapter 14.

Chapter 17 provides a discussion of note disclosure concepts and a listing of the required note disclosures applicable to state and local government financial statements.

Chapter 18 discusses and develops information related to management's discussion and analysis and other required supplementary information. Chapter 19 illustrates combining financial statements that are presented as part of supplementary information included in a governmental entity's Comprehensive Annual Financial Report.

Chapter 20 provides the preparers of financial statements with an in-depth review of the statistical section of the CAFR.

Finally, in the 2012 edition of the *Governmental GAAP Practice Manual*, Practice Alerts have been added at key points throughout the book. This highlighted feature discusses matters that have not been finalized in the standard-setting process but are on the horizon and will impact your practice or your financial statement preparation practice. To gauge importance:

- Practice Alerts indicate new GASB standards being implemented currently or in the next few years and proposed standards that have been exposed or areas of practice that are being researched.

- Practice Points discuss GASB standards previously implemented but still new enough to require reminders and best practices.

- Observations provide further explanatory and observational text to assist in implementing a standard or that provides an alternative point of view.

How to Use This Text

This text is structured so that it may be used in a number of ways. For a thorough understanding of how to implement the standards established by GASB, the reader can read the entire text beginning with the first chapter and ending with the final chapter. The sequential reading of all of the chapters serves as an excellent professional development course for new accounting professionals who have been hired by a governmental entity and need to be fully immersed in governmental financial reporting.

The text can also be read with an emphasis on a single chapter. Furthermore, a cluster of chapters can be read depending on the needs of the reader. Throughout the book, transactions are labeled with ID numbers so readers can refer from financial statements back to worksheet and journal entries (e.g. "JE02.51A" refers to worksheet entry "51A" in Chapter 2). For example: a governmental accountant interested in understanding how the accounts related to Internal Service Funds are to be integrated into both the fund financial statements and the government-wide financial statements will find that a careful study of Chapter 8, "Internal Service Funds," provides a complete foundation for understanding this fund's role in governmental financial reporting. A reader concerned with understanding the basis for the conversion from the modified accrual basis to the accrual basis will find a thorough reading of Chapter 1, "Overview," to be an excellent foundation for understanding the issue. A reader confused about how specific governmental funds are tweaked in order to create the governmental activities column of the government-wide financial statement will find in the section on governmental funds (Chapter 2 through Chapter 6) and Chapter 14 ("Developing Information for Government-Wide Financial Statements") a clear explanation of the interrelationship of accounts in governmental funds and amounts reported in the government-wide financial statements.

The emphasis of the *Governmental GAAP Practice Manual* is on the process of preparing financial statements. That is, the specific accounting transactions are straightforward—and there is a strategy to avoid getting bogged down in GASB standards that are complex in and of themselves. Once the conversion process, as clearly described in this text, is understood, more complicated accounting and reporting issues can easily be handled by referring to the GASB standards discussed in this text's companion work, the *Governmental GAAP Guide*. In writing these two companion books, it is my desire to provide governmental accountants with a highly effective and efficient approach that can help them in their day-to-day responsibilities.

Acknowledgments

The writing of this book was made possible by the efforts of a number of dedicated people. Tony Powell and many others at CCH provided the much-needed editorial support that makes any professional book an accurate and readable work. I would also like to say thanks to my partners, co-workers, friends, and especially my family for the necessary support to complete this edition.

Although many individuals played an important role in the preparation of the *Governmental GAAP Practice Manual*, any errors or omissions are the responsibility of the author. The *Governmental GAAP Practice Manual* continues to evolve as new pronouncements are issued and as I strive to better explain governmental accounting and reporting standards. If you have suggestions for improving the quality of the material, please send them to the editor:

Tony Powell
CCH, a Wolters Kluwer business
76 Ninth Avenue, Ste. 724
New York, NY 10011
tony.powell@wolterskluwer.com

Eric S. Berman
Pasadena, California

About the Author

Eric S. Berman, CPA, has over 20 years of governmental accounting and auditing experience and is a Quality Control Partner and Principal with Brown Armstrong Certified Public Accountants of Bakersfield, California. Eric manages the firm's Pasadena, California, office. Prior to joining Brown Armstrong, he was a Deputy Comptroller for the Commonwealth of Massachusetts from 1999 to 2010, and the Chief Financial Officer of the Massachusetts Water Pollution Abatement Trust from 1994 to 1999. Eric is a licensed CPA in Massachusetts and also holds practice privileges (with attest) in California. He obtained an M.S. in Accountancy from Bentley University. Eric represents the Association of Government Accountants (AGA) for the Government Accounting Standards Advisory Council to GASB and chairs the AGA's Financial Management Standards Board. He also is the past chair of the American Institute of Certified Public Accountants (AICPA) Governmental Performance and Accountability Committee and was also a member of the AICPA's State and Local Government Expert Panel. Eric is frequently called upon to consult and train state and local governments throughout the country on governmental accounting and auditing.

PART I.
INTRODUCTION

CHAPTER 1
OVERVIEW

CONTENTS

INTRODUCTION

The financial reporting model for a state or local government's annual financial statements established by GASB-34 (Basic Financial Statements—and Management's Discussion and Analysis—for State and Local Governments), which requires that a governmental entity present in its general purpose external financial statements both fund financial statements and government-wide financial statements.

The purpose of this reporting model is, in part, to make governmental financial reporting more consistent with and responsive to the fundamental concepts adopted in GASB Concept Statement No. 1 (GASB:CS-1) (Objectives of Financial Reporting). GASB:CS-1 identifies the following primary user groups of governmental financial reports:

- Citizens of the governmental entity
- Direct representatives of the citizens (legislatures and oversight bodies)
- Investors, creditors, and others involved in the lending process

GASB:CS-1 identifies accountability as the paramount objective of financial reporting by state and local governments. Accountability is based on the transfer of responsibility for resources or actions from the citizenry to another party, such as the management of a governmental entity. Financial reporting should communicate adequate information to user groups to enable them to assess the performance of those parties empowered to act in the place of the citizenry.

The assessment of accountability is fulfilled in part when financial reporting enables user groups to determine to what extent current-period expenses are financed by current-period revenues. This reporting objective is based on the concept of interperiod equity, which is based on the idea that the citizenry, as a group, that benefits from an expense should pay for it. For this reason, financial reporting should provide a basis for determining whether, during a reporting period, (1) a surplus was created (a benefit to the future citizenry), (2) a deficit was incurred (a burden to the future citizenry), (3) a surplus from a previous reporting period was used to finance current expenses (a benefit to the current citizenry), (4) a deficit from a previous reporting period was satisfied with current revenues (a burden to the current citizenry), or (5) current, and only current, expenses were financed by using current and only current revenues (achievement of interperiod equity).

Financial reporting by a state or local government should also provide a basis for user groups to determine whether (1) the governmental entity obtained and used resources consistent with the legally adopted budget and (2) finance-related legal and contractual requirements have been met. A budget reflects a myriad of public policies adopted by a legislative body and generally has the force of law as its basis for authority. The legally adopted budget is an important document in establishing and assessing the accountability of those responsible for the management of a governmental entity. While finance-related legal and contractual requirements are not as fundamental as the legally adopted budget, they nonetheless provide a basis for accountability, and financial reporting should demonstrate that this accountability either has or has not been achieved with respect to the requirements.

The basis of accounting and measurement focus are fundamental to providing a financial reporting model that can help user groups to determine whether a governmental entity has demonstrated fiscal accountability. Governmental fund financial statements are presented on modified accrual accounting concepts and the flow of current financial resources. Generally, governmental accounting standards interpret the flow of current financial resources applied on a modified accrual basis to mean that revenues, and the resulting assets, are accrued at the end of the year only if the revenues are earned and the receivables are expected to be collected in time to pay for fund liabilities in existence at the end of the period. Expenditures and the related fund liabilities are accrued when they are expected to be paid out of revenues recognized during the current period. Proprietary and fiduciary funds are reported on the accrual basis of accounting and economic resources measurement focus. GASB-34 added accrual basis accounting and economic resources measurement focus for governmental funds activities on an entity-wide basis in the government-wide statement of net assets and statement of activities.

The standards established by GASB-34 apply to external financial reports prepared by state and local governments. The standards focus on general-purpose governments that are prepared by states, cities, counties, towns, and villages.

Public colleges and universities must follow the guidance established by GASB-35 (Basic Financial Statements—and Management's Discussion and Analysis—for Public Colleges and Universities). GASB-35 requires that, in general, public colleges and universities use the same accounting and financial reporting standards that are used by all other governmental entities under the standards established by GASB-34. Specifically, public colleges and universities that issue separate financial reports should observe the guidance established in GASB-34 (pars. 134–138) for special-purpose governmental entities.

The material in CCH's *Governmental GAAP Practice Manual* is presented in a sequential fashion so that the reader can start from Chapter 2 and follow how a typical governmental entity can post typical accounting transactions and ultimately create its financial statements based on generally accepted accounting principles (GAAP) applicable to state and local governments. However, readers can also focus on a particular topic, read that material, determine the appropriate journal entries, and then follow the remaining chapters that result in the preparation of the financial statements. For example, if a reader is interested in how the information accounted for in Internal Service Funds is presented in a governmental entity's annual financial statements, he or she can start with Chapter 8 "Internal Service Funds," then go to Chapter 13, "Developing Information for Fund Financial Statements," then proceed to Chapter 14, "Developing Information for Government-Wide Financial Statements," and, review detailed financial statements in Chapter 16, "Basic Financial Statements." Chapters 2 through 6 review governmental fund activities in depth and have been updated for the implementation of GASB-54 (Fund Balance Reporting and Governmental Fund Type Definitions).

Application Issue

One of the more complex application issues in governmental accounting and financial reporting is the development of procedures that facilitate the presentation of the two levels of financial statements (the fund financial statements and the government-wide financial statements). Many governmental entities address this application issue by using a worksheet approach to convert fund financial statement information into government-wide financial statements. The purpose of this book is to demonstrate in a detailed step-by-step manner how an accountant or auditor can apply GAAP for state and local governments using a worksheet approach in the development of these financial statements.

One of the unique aspects of GAAP for state and local governmental entities is the presentation of two levels of reporting:

1. Fund financial statements

2. Government-wide financial statements

Fund-based financial statements must be included in a governmental entity's financial report in order to demonstrate that restrictions imposed by statutes, regulations, or contracts have been followed. Certain fund financial statements have a short-term emphasis, and in the case of governmental type funds they generally measure and account for cash and "other assets that can easily be converted to cash." GAAP requires that fund financial reporting be focused on significant (or "major") funds by reporting the entity's General Fund and other *major* funds in separate columns in the fund financial statements and the remaining *nonmajor* funds aggregated in a single column. Governmental type funds are presented on the modified accrual basis of accounting and current financial resources measurement focus, and proprietary and fiduciary funds are reported on the accrual basis of accounting and economic resources measurement focus.

Government-wide financial statements were established by GASB-34 in order to provide a basis for determining (1) the extent to which current services provided by an entity were financed with current revenues and (2) the degree to which a governmental entity's financial position has changed during the fiscal year. In order to achieve these objectives, government-wide financial statements include a statement of net assets and a statement of activities. Government-wide financial statements are based on a flow of all economic resources applied on the accrual basis of accounting. The flow of economic resources refers to all assets available to the governmental unit for the purpose of providing goods and services to the public. When the flow of economic resources and the accrual basis of accounting are combined, they provide the foundation for generally accepted accounting principles used by business enterprises in that essentially all assets and liabilities, both current and long-term, are reported in the government-wide financial statements.

Modified Accrual Basis of Accounting and Current Financial Resources Measurement Focus

Recognized as GAAP for governmental type funds, the modified accrual basis of accounting uses elements of both cash and accrual concepts. Revenues are recorded when they are both measurable and available to finance current expenditures of the government. Revenue is considered available when it is collectible during the current period, or the actual collection will occur either during the current period or after the end of the period but in time to pay current year expenditures and liabilities.

The flow of current financial resources measurement focus applied on a modified accrual basis is a narrow interpretation of what constitutes assets and liabilities for an accounting entity (a governmental fund). Assets comprise only current financial resources, such as cash and claims to cash, investments, receivables, inventory, and other, similar current financial assets. Liabilities comprise governmental fund liabilities, which are normally expected to be liquidated with current financial resources.

Governmental funds generally record a liability when it is expected that the liability will be paid from revenues recognized during the current period. These definitions have been interpreted by many practitioners to mean that accruals can be made only when the related cash flow is collected or paid "shortly" after the end of the fiscal accounting period.

GASBI-6 (Recognition and Measurement of Certain Liabilities and Expenditures in Governmental Fund Financial Statements (an interpretation of NCGA Statements 1, 4, and 5; NCGA Interpretation 8; and GASB Statements No. 10, 16, and 18)) was issued in March 2000 in order to address some of these issues. The GASB describes the Interpretation as exactly that—an interpretation. The Interpretation is not an attempt to change the standards that are the basis for the preparation of fund financial statements, but rather its purpose is "to improve the comparability, consistency and objectivity of financial reporting in governmental fund financial statements by providing a common, internally consistent interpretation of standards affecting the recognition of certain fund liability and expenditures, in areas where practice differences have occurred or could occur."

The GASBI-6 Interpretation addresses what is meant by "shortly" in the context of the accrual of liabilities related to future expenditures. Liabilities that are normally expected to be paid with current financial resources should be presented as a fund liability, while liabilities that have been incurred but that will not be paid with current financial resources should be considered "general long-term liabilities." General long-term liabilities are presented in the government-wide financial statements (statement of net assets) and not in a governmental fund balance sheet.

The basic guidance for determining when a governmental fund should accrue an expenditure/liability is found in NCGA-1 (par. 70), which states that "most expenditures and transfers out are measurable and should be recorded when the related liability is incurred." GASBI-6 (par. 12) expands on this general guidance by noting the following:

> Governmental fund liabilities and expenditures that should be accrued include liabilities that, once incurred, normally are paid in a timely manner and in full from current financial resources—for example, salaries, professional services, supplies, utilities, and travel.

These transactions give rise to fund liabilities that are considered mature liabilities because they are "normally due and payable in full when incurred." However, GASBI-6 points out that there are several significant exceptions to this general guidance established in NCGA-1. Specifically, NCGA-1 (pars. 9–11) states that "unmatured long-term indebtedness" should not be reported as a fund liability (except for debts that are related to proprietary and trust funds). Unmatured long-term indebtedness is defined as "the portion of general long-term indebtedness that is not yet due for payment," and it includes debts such as the following:

1. Formal debt agreements such as bonds and notes

2. Liabilities not "normally expected to be liquidated with expendable available financial resources"

3. Other commitments that are not current liabilities properly recorded in governmental funds

GASBI-6 (par. 12) points out that the three specified categories listed above are exceptions to the general rule that a liability is recorded as a fund liability and "in the absence of an explicit requirement to do otherwise, a government should accrue a governmental fund liability and expenditure in the period in which the government incurs the liability."

Unlike commercial enterprises, much of the revenue received by governments is not based on an exchange or exchange-like transaction (the selling of a product or service and receiving something of approximate equal value), but rather arises from the entity's taxing powers or as grants from other governmental entities or individuals (nonexchange transactions). Nonexchange transactions are accounted for based on the standards established by GASB-33 (Accounting and Financial Reporting for Nonexchange Transactions).

PRACTICE ALERT: GASB is researching whether changes are warranted for reporting the current financial resources measurement focus applied on a modified accrual basis. So far GASB has identified six accounting and financial reporting issues that stem from these three basic project elements:

1. What messages are financial statements conceptually attempting to convey? (In other words, what is the story that the financial statements attempt to communicate, or what questions should be answered by reading different financial statements and financial statements prepared using different measurement focuses? For example, the statement of cash flows answers the question, "What happened to cash during the year?"

2. What is the relationship among objectives of financial reporting (user needs), financial statements, measurement focuses, and measurement attributes at the conceptual level?

3. How does when an element is recognized affect the meaning that is to be conveyed by a particular financial statement?

4. What are the fundamental recognition criteria necessary to report an element in a financial statement?

5. What measurement attribute(s) best conveys the message(s) intended for financial statements? What is the role of historical cost and fair value information in conveying these messages? Is the same measurement attribute applicable in all measurement focuses?

6. Should the application of fair value be different for the statement of net assets and the statement of activities? How does fair value relate to the cost of service model of the statement of activities?

Assuming that current financial resources are closer to cash basis financial statements than now, a challenge presents itself. In cash basis financial statements, external receivables and payables do not exist as of the balance sheet date, because cash has not been transferred outside the government. This also limits the amount of inflows and outflows during a current period to cash transactions. Therefore, equity at the end of a period truly is cash. But governments sign contracts that last longer than one period. Shouldn't the financial position of a government take that into account? Is this the right message that should be conveyed in a financial statement?

To address these questions, the GASB has tentatively concluded that current financial resource financial statements must convey, at a minimum, the following messages:

- What were the current financial resources and claims against current financial resources of the entity at the reporting date?
- What was the balance of current financial resources at the reporting date that was available for spending?
- What were the amounts and sources of inflows and outflows of current financial resources during the reporting period?

The project's current timeline includes a preliminary views document that is slated to be issued during 2011, with a final concepts statement to be issued sometime in 2012.

Accrual Basis of Accounting and Economic Resources Measurement Focus

The accrual basis of accounting is used by commercial enterprises to prepare their financial statements. Generally, under this accounting basis, revenues are recognized when earned and expenses are recorded when incurred for activities related to exchange and exchange-like activities.

The flow of economic resources measurement focus refers to the reporting of all of the net assets available to the governmental unit for the purpose of providing goods and services to the public. When the flow of economic resources and the accrual basis of accounting are combined, they provide the foundation for generally accepted accounting principles used by proprietary and fiduciary funds and business-type activities. This approach recognizes the deferral and capitalization of certain expenditures and the deferral of certain revenues.

When the flow of economic resources is applied on an accrual basis for a fund, all assets and liabilities, both current and long-term, are presented in the fund's balance sheet or statement of net assets. The following is a summary of the key differences between this approach and the current financial resources measurement focus as it applies to individual governmental funds:

- Capital assets are recorded in the fund's balance sheet or statement of net assets net of accumulated depreciation (amortization in the case of intangible assets).
- Long-term debts are recorded in the fund's balance sheet or statement of net assets.
- The fund's equity represents the net assets (total assets minus total liabilities) available to the fund rather than fund balance.

The accrual basis of accounting and economic resources measurement focus is used to prepare proprietary fund, fiduciary fund, and government-wide financial statements.

Fund Financial Statements

GASB-34 (par. 63) identifies the following as fund types that are to be used to record a governmental entity's activities during an accounting period:

Governmental Funds (Emphasizing Major Funds)

- General Fund
- Special Revenue Funds
- Capital Projects Funds
- Debt Service Funds
- Permanent Funds

Proprietary Funds

- Enterprise Funds (emphasizing major funds)
- Internal Service Funds

Fiduciary Funds and Similar Component Units

- Pension (and other employee benefit) Trust Funds
- Investment Trust Funds
- Private-Purpose Trust Funds
- Agency Funds

Two new fund types, namely Permanent Fund and Private-Purpose Trust Funds, were defined by GASB-34. Permanent Funds are to be used to report resources that are legally restricted to the extent that only earnings and no principal (corpus) may be used for purposes that support the reporting government's programs (i.e., for the benefit of the public). For example, a fund established to maintain a city park in perpetuity but only through the earnings of the fund is an example of a Permanent Fund. Private-Purpose Trust Funds are to be used to account for trust arrangements under which principal and income benefit individuals, private organizations, and other governments and that are not accounted for in other fiduciary funds (Pension Trust Funds, Investment Trust Funds, and Agency Funds) (GASB-34, par. 65).

PRACTICE ALERT: GASB-54 (Fund Balance Reporting and Governmental Fund Type Definitions), issued in February 2009, became effective for financial statements for periods beginning after June 15, 2010. The new definitions in GASB-54 provide that governmental funds of a particular type either should be used (i.e., required) or are used (i.e., discretionary) for all activities that meet its criteria. If use of a fund type is generally discretionary, specific situations under which a fund of that type should be used are identified either in the definitions in GASB-54 (i.e., debt service funds) or by requirements established in other authoritative pronouncements (i.e., special revenue and capital projects funds). The fund balance classification section of GASB-54 defines the terminology "restricted," "committed," and "assigned."

OBSERVATION: GASB-54 modified the definitions of governmental fund types. Specifically, special revenue funds are defined as those funds used to account for and report the proceeds of specific revenue sources that are restricted or committed to expenditure for specified purposes other than debt service or capital projects. Therefore, a stabilization arrangement would meet the criteria to be reported as a separate special revenue fund only if the fund's resources are derived from a specific restricted or committed revenue source, specifically restricted or committed for that stabilization purpose.

Government-Wide Financial Statements

The focus of government-wide financial statements is on the overall financial position and activities of the government as a whole. These financial statements are constructed around the concept of a primary government as defined by GASB-14 (The Financial Reporting Entity) (as amended by GASB-39 and now GASB-61) and therefore encompass the primary government and its component units except for fiduciary funds of the primary government and component units that are fiduciary in nature. Financial statements of fiduciary funds are not presented in the government-wide financial statements but are included in the fund financial statements (GASB-34, par. 13).

GASB-34 requires that government-wide financial statements be formatted following these guidelines (GASB-34, pars. 14 and 15):

- Separate rows and columns should be used to distinguish between the primary government's governmental activities and businesslike activities
- A total column should be used for the primary government
- Separate rows and columns should distinguish between the total primary government (governmental activities plus businesslike activities) and its discretely presented component units
- A total column may be used for the reporting entity (primary government and discretely presented component units), but this is optional
- A total column may be used for prior-year information, but this is optional

Governmental activities should be accounted for and reported based on all applicable GASB pronouncements, NCGA pronouncements, and the following pronouncements issued on or before November 30, 1989, unless they conflict with GASB or NCGA pronouncements (GASB-34, par. 17):

- Financial Accounting Standards Board (FASB) Statements and Interpretations
- Accounting Principles Board (APB) Opinions
- Accounting Research Bulletins (ARBs) of the Committee on Accounting Procedure

Prior to GASB-34, pronouncements of the FASB, the APB, and the Committee on Accounting Procedures have not, for the most part, been applied to information presented in governmental funds. The GASB decided that government-wide financial statements must be prepared by applying these pronouncements issued on or before November 30, 1989 (unless they conflict with GASB pronouncements), on a retroactive basis (with exceptions discussed in paragraph 146 of GASB-34). Pronouncements issued by the FASB after November 30, 1989, do not have to be followed in the preparation of financial statements for governmental activities in the government-wide financial statements.

Business-type activities must follow either Alternative 1 or Alternative 2 as described in GASB-20 (Accounting and Financial Reporting for Proprietary Funds and Other Governmental Entities that Use Proprietary Fund Accounting). Under Alternative 1, governmental entities using proprietary fund accounting must follow (1) all GASB pronouncements and (2) FASB Statements and Interpretations, APB Opinions, and Accounting Research Bulletins (ARBs) issued on or before November 30, 1989 except those that conflict with a GASB pronouncement. Under Alternative 2, governmental entities using proprietary fund accounting must follow (1) all GASB pronouncements and (2) all FASB Statements and Interpretations, APB Opinions, and ARBs no matter when issued except those that conflict with a GASB pronouncement. Unlike Alternative 1, Alternative 2 has no cutoff date for determining the applicability of FASB pronouncements.

PRACTICE ALERT: GASB-62 (Codification of Accounting and Financial Reporting Guidance Contained in Pre-November 30, 1989 FASB and AICPA Pronouncements) is an omnibus statement that supersedes the provisions of GASB-20 by incorporating into GASB's literature all FASB Statements and Interpretations, APB Opinions, and ARBs no matter when issued except those that conflict with a GASB pronouncement. GASB-62 also incorporates all AICPA pronouncements. It is effective for periods beginning after December 15, 2011. All the provisions of the aforementioned standards are incorporated into CCH's *Governmental GAAP Guide*; so little if any change from this edition is expected due to any upcoming promulgation. However, certain items such as governmental combinations that have guidance contained in APB Opinion No. 16, are being researched by GASB and were not included in GASB-62.

Methodology for Preparing Governmental Financial Statements

The remainder of the chapters of this book are based on a comprehensive example that begins at the transaction point and ends with the preparation of the basic financial statements and selected disclosures. For governmental type funds, a variety of transactions are illustrated and journalized in Chapter 2 through Chapter 6, which results in a year-end trial balance for each individual fund based on the modified accrual basis of accounting and current financial resources measurement focus, along with entries required to implement GASB-54.

NOTE: The transactions illustrated in these chapters are routine. There is no attempt to illustrate every type of transaction that could be processed through a particular fund. The emphasis throughout this book is the conversion process and not a comprehensive analysis of GASB pronouncements. A discussion of all GASB pronouncements can be found in CCH's *Governmental GAAP Guide.*

In Chapter 13, these trial balances are used as the basis for developing the information needed to prepare the fund financial statements.

Chapter 14 illustrates a worksheet methodology for converting the information related to governmental funds (modified accrual basis/current financial resources focus) to information that is needed for the governmental activities column of the government-wide financial statements (accrual basis of accounting/economic resources focus).

A similar approach is used for proprietary funds (Chapter 7 and Chapter 8) and fiduciary funds (Chapter 9 through Chapter 12) in that illustrative entries are developed for each of the funds and the resulting trial balances become the basis for preparing fund financial statements (Chapter 13) and the business-type activities column of the government-wide financial statements (Chapter 14). However, the specific process for developing the information for proprietary funds and fiduciary funds is somewhat different from that used for governmental funds. Proprietary funds are already reported on an accrual basis/economic resources focus, thus there is no need to develop a worksheet approach that converts from the modified accrual to the accrual basis of accounting and current financial resources measurement focus, but there is a need to merge certain balances related to Internal Service Funds in order to present business-type activities in a manner required by GAAP. Also, fiduciary fund information is presented only in the fund financial statements. GAAP prohibits the presentation of the information in the government-wide financial statements.

In Chapter 16, the basic financial statements as required by GAAP are prepared based on the information created in Chapter 13 and Chapter 14. Finally, Chapters 17–20, using the information illustrated in previous chapters, presents management's discussion and analysis, note disclosure requirements, and other required supplementary information mandated by GAAP. Chapter 17, "Notes to The Financial Statements," provides a summary listing of note disclosure requirements applicable to state and local government financial statements. A comprehensive presentation and disclosure checklist is provided in the companion book, CCH's *Governmental GAAP Guide*, to facilitate the required financial reporting and disclosure.

Elements of Governmental Financial Statements and Recognition Measurement Attributes

The 2006 GASB white paper *Why Governmental Accounting and Financial Reporting Is—and Should Be—Different* makes a persuasive argument that public sector accounting is fundamentally different from accounting outside the public sector. For this reason the elements reported within the financial statements of states and local governments and their measurement and recognition criteria deserve different consideration. To provide the framework for establishing accounting principles related to the elements of financial statements and their measurement and recognition within the financial statements, the GASB has issued GASB

Concepts Statement No. 4 (Elements of Financial Statements) (GASB:CS-4) and placed on its agenda a project for another proposed Concepts Statement (Measurement and Recognition Attributes).

GASB:CS-4 sets new definitions for seven elements of historically based financial statements of state and local governments as follows:

- Elements of the Financial Position Statement
    1. Assets
    2. Liabilities
    3. Deferred Outflow of Resources
    4. Deferred Inflow of Resources
    5. Net Position
- Elements of the Resources Flow Statements
    6. Inflow of Resources
    7. Outflow of Resources

The GASB definitions of the elements are based upon the inherent characteristics of each element, and they are linked by a common definition feature in that they are based on the concept of measuring and reporting *resources*. The definitions of the elements apply to an entity that is a governmental unit (that is, a legal entity) and are applicable to any measurement focus under which financial statements may be prepared, for example, economic resources, current financial resources, and cash resources measurement focuses.

With the completion of GASB:CS-4 and GASB Concepts Statement No. 5 (Services Efforts and Accomplishments Reporting (an Amendment to GASB Concepts Statement No. 2)), the GASB has now turned its attention to a Concepts Statement project entitled "Measurement and Recognition Attributes." This conceptual framework project has two primary objectives: (1) to develop recognition criteria for whether information should be reported in state and local governmental financial statements (measurement) and when that information should be reported (recognition) and (2) to consider the measurement attributes (e.g., historical cost or fair value) that conceptually should be used in governmental financial statements. This project will ultimately lead to a sixth Concepts Statement.

PRACTICE ALERT: GASB CS-4, introduced deferred inflows and deferred outflows of resources to governmental accounting in June 2007. Deferred inflows and outflows of resources are either acquisitions or consumptions of resources, respectively, that are applicable to future periods. GASB has issued an exposure draft titled "Financial Reporting of Deferred Outflows of Resources, Deferred Inflows of Resources, and Net Position," proposes a Statement of Net Position (instead of a Statement of Net Assets) that would incorporate the Deferred Outflows and Inflows of Resources. Net position would include three elements: (1) net investment in capital assets, (2) restricted net position, and (3) unrestricted net position. A new accounting equation would also be implemented. Net Position would be the sum of assets and deferred outflows of resources reduced by liabilities and deferred inflows of resources (deferred positions presented separately from assets and liabilities). If approved, the statement would be effective for periods beginning after June 15, 2011. However, for governments that have deferred inflows and outflows of resources associated with hedging derivatives, implementation of the standard upon approval may provide more clarity.

WORKSHEET CONVERSION ENTRY CHECKLIST

Perhaps the major implementation problem facing those who prepare governmental financial statements based on the standards established by GAAP for state and local governments is the development of procedures that facilitate the presentation of the two levels of financial statements. Most governmental entities are expected to address this application issue by maintaining their accounting systems for governmental funds on the current financial resources measurement focus and modified accrual basis or budgetary/statutory basis, which will be the basis for preparing the governmental type fund financial statements, and then using a worksheet approach to convert from the modified accrual basis and current financial resources measurement focus to the accrual basis and economic resource measurement focus in order to prepare the government-wide financial statements. That approach is illustrated throughout this book.

The GASB's *Comprehensive Implementation Guide* raised the question of whether the accounting records for governmental funds should include the adjustment necessary to report governmental activities on an accrual basis because it is usually assumed that financial statements should be derived from account balances in the accounting records. The formal accounting records should *not* include adjustments of this nature. Governmental funds are typically accounted for on a cash, modified accrual, or budgetary basis of accounting, and, if necessary, worksheet adjustments are made to convert these balances to a GAAP basis (modified accrual) for financial reporting purposes. The modified accrual based financial statements are the basis for preparing the fund financial statements required by GAAP. Once the governmental funds have been converted to the modified accrual basis, they are combined for internal purposes and various worksheet conversion adjustments are made to convert them to an accrual basis for reporting governmental activities in the government-wide financial statements.

There are innumerable transactions that a governmental entity could experience that would first have to be recorded on the modified accrual basis and current financial resources measurement focus (for presentation in the governmental fund financial statements) and then converted to the accrual basis and economic resources measurement focus (for presentation in the governmental activities column of the government-wide financial statements). The following checklist has been developed to identify and illustrate typical transactions that will require a worksheet conversion entry. An understanding of these entries will provide a governmental accountant with the basis to analyze transactions that are uncommon and properly convert their initial recording on the modified accrual basis to the accrual basis.

The components of the worksheet conversion entry checklist are as follows.

Long-Term Debt and Related Transactions

☐ Issuance of long-term debt: current transactions
☐ Issuance of long-term debt: previous year's balances
☐ Debt service transactions
☐ Deep discount debt
☐ Zero-coupon bonds
☐ Discount bonds (less than 20%)
☐ Advance refundings of debt
☐ Early extinguishments of debt (nonrefunding)

Capital Assets and Related Transactions

☐ Capital expenditures: current period transactions
☐ Capital assets: previous year's balances
☐ Capital leases: current period transactions
☐ Capital leases: previous year's balances
☐ Leasehold improvements
☐ Gains/losses related to capital asset dispositions
☐ Nonmonetary exchanges (trade-ins)
☐ Donations of capital assets from outside parties (nonexchange transaction)
☐ Donations of capital asset to outside parties
☐ Gains and losses related to capital asset dispositions
☐ Impairment of capital assets
☐ Maintenance and preservation costs
☐ Changes in accounting principles
☐ Changes in accounting estimates

Noncurrent Monetary Assets

☐ Long-term non-interest-bearing notes receivable
☐ Lease payments receivable

Operating and Other Transactions

☐ Accrual of expenses: current period transactions
☐ Accrual of expenses: previous year's balances
☐ Accrual of revenues: current period transactions
☐ Accrual of revenues: previous year's balances
☐ Extraordinary items
☐ Special items

Reclassification Entries

☐ Merging Internal Service Funds

☐ Eliminations of transfers and the identification of internal balances

☐ Terminology and format

OBSERVATION: The emphasis of the discussion in this chapter is on governmental type funds (General Fund, Special Revenue Funds, Capital Projects Funds, Debt Service Funds, and Permanent Funds) rather than proprietary funds because the presentation basis for proprietary funds is accrual accounting and economic resource measurement focus, which is the same basis and focus for the government-wide financial statements. Also, fiduciary funds are not discussed in this chapter, because these funds are presented in the fund financial statements but are not incorporated into the government-wide financial statements.

ANALYSIS OF YEAR ENDED JUNE 30, 20X2

The worksheet conversion entries that would be typical for items included in the worksheet conversion entry checklist is presented in this section. The guidance on how each component would be handled in a typical government environment is also presented. The following analysis assumes, unless otherwise stated, that the worksheet conversion entry is made for the year ended June 30, 20X2.

Issuance of Debt

Generally, liabilities that do not consume current financial resources of a governmental fund are not reported at the fund financial statement level. For example, the proceeds from the issuance of debt are recorded as an other financing source in a governmental fund rather than as a fund liability. On the other hand, in the government-wide financial statements, the debt must be presented as a liability related to governmental activities. To illustrate the conversion process required to convert from the modified accrual basis of accounting to the accrual basis, assume that 5%, 10-year general obligation bonds with a maturity value of $1,000,000 are sold on September 1, 20X1 at a price ($975,878) to yield 6%. The following entry is made to record the issuance of the debt in a governmental fund (modified accrual basis):

	Debit	Credit
Cash	957,878	
Discount on long-term debt issued (other uses of financial resources)	42,122	
Bonds payable		1,000,000

In the governmental fund financial statements, the issuance of the debt is presented on the statement of revenues, expenditures, and changes in fund balances as an "other source of financial resources," but the amount is not presented in the balance sheet at the fund statement level. In order to convert the transaction from a modified accrual basis to an accrual basis, the following conversion worksheet entry is made at the end of the year:

	Debit	Credit
Long-term debt issues (other sources of financial resources)	1,000,000	
Discount on long-term debt issued (other uses of financial resources)		42,122
Bonds payable		957,878

The above entry records the net proceeds as bonds payable. It is also acceptable to create a separate discount account (contra liability account) and record the maturity value of the debt in a separate account for the government-wide financial statements.

The effect of the worksheet entry is to report the transaction as a long-term general obligation in the government-wide financial statements (governmental activities column).

Issuance of Long-Term Debt: Previous Year's Balances

In addition to current year debt transactions, the previous year's balance of long-term debt outstanding must be considered. These amounts do not appear on the current year-end trial balance for governmental funds, but they must appear on the government-wide financial statements because they are obligations of the governmental entity. The worksheet conversion entry reduces the beginning "net asset" balance. For example, assume that a governmental entity had bonds payable outstanding at the end of the previous year of $45,000,000 (originally issued at par). The following worksheet entry is made to establish the beginning balances related to the governmental activities column in the statement of net assets:

	Debit	Credit
Net assets	45,000,000	
Bonds payable		45,000,000

The beginning balance of the "Net Assets" account is based on the beginning balance for the governmental entity's "Fund Balance" account. The Fund Balance amount is adjusted through the worksheet entries in order to convert it from a modified accrual amount (Fund Balance) to an accrual amount (Net Assets).

It should be noted that the worksheet entry must be based on the amortized balance of the debt. That is, if the bonds were issued at a discount or premium, an amortization schedule must be made in order to determine the amount of the book value of the debt outstanding as of the end of the previous year.

Debt Service Transactions

NCGA-1 points out that most expenditures are measurable and should be recorded when the related fund liability is incurred. One of several exceptions to this generalization is the treatment of interest and principal payments for general long-term indebtedness. Interest and principal on long-term debt are not recorded as expenditures as they accrue, but rather when they become due and payable. However, for the government-wide financial statements, debt service payments are reflected as reductions to outstanding debt (principal repayments) and interest expense. Debt service transactions that should be considered include the following:

- Interest paid during the year

- Principal repaid during the year

- Amortization of discount/premium

Interest Paid During the Year

The amount of interest expenditure recorded during the year will seldom be equal to the accrual-based interest expense that must be reflected in the government-wide financial statements. For example, assume that a governmental entity had the following general obligation bonds outstanding as of the end of the previous year and issued $7,000,000 on April 1, 20X2. All of the bonds were originally issued at par:

Maturing Value	Stated Interest Rate	Interest Payment Date	Interest Expenditures (Modified Accrual)	Interest Expense (Accrual)
$20,000,000	5%	March 1	$1,000,000	$1,000,000
15,000,000	6%	August 1	900,000	900,000
10,000,000	5.5%	December 1	550,000	550,000
7,000,000	5%	April 1	-0-	87,500
Total			$2,450,000	$2,537,500

In order to record the additional interest expense for the year ended June 30, 20X2, the following worksheet entry is made:

	Debit	Credit
Interest expense/expenditure ($2,537,500 – $2,450,000)	87,500	
Interest payable		87,500

The GASB's *Comprehensive Implementation Guide* makes the following observations about reporting interest expense on the statement of activities: (1) interest expense related to a capital lease is not a direct expense of the function that uses the capital assets subject to the lease. The use of a capital lease is just another financing option and should be evaluated like any other borrowing arrangement. And (2) under most circumstances, no interest on general long-term liabilities is reported as a direct expense; therefore, using the caption "interest on long-term debt" is sufficient to indicate that all interest expense is indirect. The amount of total interest expense must either be determinable on the face of the statement of activities or be disclosed in a note to the financial statements.

Principal Repaid During the Year

If long-term debt has been repaid during the year, the principal repayment is recorded as an expenditure in the fund financial statements, and a worksheet conversion entry is necessary to convert the principal payment from an expenditure to a reduction of the governmental entity's general debt. For example, if a $10,000,000 general obligation bonds matures during the year, its retirement is recorded in a governmental fund as follows:

	Debit	Credit
Expenditures—principal	10,000,000	
Cash		10,000,000

In order to convert this transaction to an accrual basis, the following worksheet conversion entry is made:

	Debit	Credit
Bonds payable	10,000,000	
Expenditures—principal		10,000,000

Amortization of Discount/Premium

When a governmental entity issues debt at a discount or premium, the discount/premium is ignored in recording interest expenditures in a governmental fund; however, the discount/premium must be amortized annually in order to report interest on an accrual basis in the government-wide financial statements. For example, the following bond amortization schedule would be prepared for the $1,000,000 bonds that were issued at a discount in the previous section (Issuance of Debt):

Date	Cash	6% Interest	Amortization	Book Value
9/1/X1	$ —	$ —	$ —	$957,878
9/1/X2	50,000	57,473	7,473	$965,351
9/1/X3	50,000	57,921	7,921	973,272
9/1/X4	50,000	58,396	8,396	981,668
9/1/X5	50,000	58,900	8,900	990,568
9/1/X6	50,000	59,432	9,432	1,000,000
Total	$250,000	$292,122	$42,122	

Based on the above amortization schedule, no interest would be recorded during the fiscal year ended June 30, 20X2. However, in order to convert the transaction to an accrual basis, the following worksheet entry is made:

	Debit	Credit
Interest expense/expenditure ($57,473×10/12)	47,894	
Interest payable ($50,000×10/12)		41,667
Bonds payable		6,227

The credit to the account "Bonds Payable" represents the amortization of the discount for the partial year. If a separate discount is created, the credit would be to the discount account.

Deep-Discount Debt

Governmental activities should be accounted for and reported based on all applicable GASB pronouncements, NCGA pronouncements, and the following pronouncements issued on or before November 30, 1989, unless they conflict with GASB or NCGA pronouncements (GASB-34, par. 17) until GASB-62 is implemented for periods beginning after December 15, 2011:

- Financial Accounting Standards Board (FASB) Statements and Interpretations
- Accounting Principles Board (APB) Opinions
- Accounting Research Bulletins (ARBs) of the Committee on Accounting Procedure

Generally, a governmental entity must apply the FASBs, APBs, and ARBs on a retroactive basis; however, the GASB did provide exceptions to this requirement. One of those exceptions applies to debt discounts and premiums. The standards established by APB-12 (Omnibus Opinion—1967) and APB-21 (Interest on Receivables and Payables) require that discounts and premiums related to debt (and receivables) be amortized as part of interest expense (and income). The GASB states that the standards established by these two APB Opinions may be applied on a prospective basis; that is, the standards apply only to debt issuances that occur on or after the effective date of GASB-34.

However, the discount/premium amortization exception does not apply to deep-discount or zero-coupon debt. GAAP defines zero-coupon debt as debt that is "originally sold at far below par value and pays no interest until it matures," and deep-discount debt is defined as "debt that is sold at a discount of 20 percent or more from its face or par value at the time it is issued."

Zero-Coupon Bonds

To illustrate discount/premium amortization exception, assume that a governmental entity issued zero-coupon bonds three years ago (6/30/W8) that have a maturity value of $1,000,000. The bonds were sold at a yield of 6% and the following amortization schedule applies to the debt:

Date	Cash	6% Interest	Amortization	Book Value
6/30/W8	$—	$—	$—	$ 747,260
6/30/W9	0	44,836	44,836	792,096
6/30/X0	0	47,526	47,526	839,622
6/30/X1	0	50,377	50,377	889,999
6/30/X2	0	53,400	53,400	943,399
6/30/X3	0	56,601	56,601	1,000,000
	$—	$252,740	$252,740	

As of the year ended June 30, 20X2, there has only been one entry in the governmental fund, and that was for the receipt of the proceeds. However, in order to convert the information from a modified accrual to an accrual basis, the following worksheet conversion entry is made as of June 30, 20X2:

	Debit	Credit
Interest expense/expenditure (see amortization schedule)	53,400	
Net assets	889,999	
Bonds payable		943,399

When the bonds mature on June 30, 20X3, the governmental fund will report an expenditure of $1,000,000 ($747,260 principal payment + $252,740 interest). In order to convert that transaction from a modified accrual to an accrual basis, the following worksheet conversion entry is made as of June 30, 20X3:

	Debit	Credit
Interest expense/expenditure (see amortization schedule)	56,601	
Net assets	943,399	
Bonds payable		1,000,000
Bonds payable	1,000,000	
Interest expense/expenditure		252,740
Expenditures—principal		747,260

OBSERVATION: The first worksheet conversion entry accrues interest for the year and the second entry reduces the debt to zero. These entries are shown separately for illustrative purposes, but they may be combined in practice.

Discount Bonds (Less than 20%)

As noted earlier, for bonds with a discount of less than 20% that were issued prior to the governmental entity's adoption of GASB-34, there is no requirement to take the discount amortization into consideration to determine interest expense on the government-wide financial statements. (However, amortization applies to all bonds issued at a discount after the adoption of GASB-34.) For example, assume that the example described earlier is changed to assume that the bonds were issued on June 30, 20W8 (before the adoption of GASB-34 by the entity). The amortization schedule for the debt is reproduced as follows with the new dates:

Date	Cash	6% Interest	Amortization	Book Value
6/30/W8	$—	$—	$—	$ 957,878
6/30/W9	50,000	57,473	7,473	965,351
6/30/X0	50,000	57,921	7,921	973,272
6/30/X1	50,000	58,396	8,396	981,668
6/30/X2	50,000	58,900	8,900	990,568
6/30/X3	50,000	59,432	9,432	1,000,000
Total	$250,000	$292,122	$42,122	

There is no requirement to amortize the discount, because it amounts to only 4.2% ($42,122/$1,000,000). If the assumption continues that GASB-34 standards had not been adopted in 20W8 when the bonds were issued, the amount of interest expenditure recorded in the governmental fund for the year ended June 30, 20X2 would be $50,000. There would be no requirement to reflect the discount amortization (interest expense) on the government-wide financial statements; however, a worksheet conversion entry would be made as of June 30, 20X2 to record the original proceeds of the debt as follows:

	Debit	Credit
Net assets	957,878	
Bonds payable		957,878

OBSERVATION: The amount of the debt presented on the government-wide financial statements does not change from the initial issuance proceeds because the discount is not amortized.

When the debt is retired on 6/30/X3, expenditures of $1,050,000 ($1,000,000 principal payment + $50,000 interest) will be recorded in the appropriate governmental fund and the following worksheet conversion entries will be made to convert the information from a modified accrual basis to an accrual basis:

	Debit	Credit
Net assets	957,878	
Bonds payable		957,878
Bonds payable	957,878	
Interest expense/expenditure (the total amount of discount)	42,122	
Expenditures—principal		1,000,000

The amount of interest expense reflected on the government-wide financial statements must include the discount because it was not accrued for in previous years.

OBSERVATION: If the amount of interest expense is materially distorted in the year the bonds are retired, the nature of the distortion should be explained in a note to the financial statements.

Advance Refundings of Debt

An advance refunding of debt occurs when a governmental entity issues new debt and uses the proceeds to retire currently existing debt. In the fund financial statements, the advance refunding is reported as an "other financing source"/ "other financing use" transaction; however, in the government-wide financial statements, the transaction must be converted to an accrual-based presentation. That is, the old debt is removed and the new debt is established. In addition, the difference between the book value of the old debt and its reacquisition price is reported on the government-wide financial statements as a decrease (contra liability) or increase (valuation account) to the book value of the new debt issued to finance the advance refunding. Subsequently, the difference (deferral) is amortized over the original remaining life of the old debt or the life of the new debt, whichever is less.

For example, assume that the following amortization schedule represents bonds outstanding as of July 1, 20X1:

Date	Cash	6% Interest	Amortization	Book Value
6/30/W8	$—	$—	$—	$957,878
6/30/W9	50,000	57,473	7,473	965,351
6/30/X0	50,000	57,921	7,921	973,272
6/30/X1	50,000	58,396	8,396	981,668
6/30/X2	50,000	58,900	8,900	990,568
6/30/X3	50,000	59,432	9,432	1,000,000
Total	$250,000	$292,122	$42,122	

On July 1, 20X1, the governmental entity decides to take advantage of lower interest rates and issues new debt at par that has a maturity value of $1,100,000 and a maturity date of 5 years. In order to retire the old debt, the governmental entity must pay (based on the terms of the original bond agreement) existing bondholders $1,100,000.

The following entries are made in the appropriate governmental fund to issue the new debt and retire the old debt:

	Debit	Credit
Cash	1,100,000	
Other financing source—bonds issued		1,100,000
Other financing use—payment to refunded debt escrow agent	1,100,000	
Cash		1,100,000

In order to convert the transaction from a modified accrual basis to an accrual basis for presentation in the government-wide financial statements, the following worksheet conversion entry is made at the end of the fiscal year ended June 30, 20X2:

	Debit	Credit
Other financing source—bonds issued	1,100,000	
Bonds payable (new debt)		1,100,000
Bonds payable (old debt)	981,668	
Deferred loss on early retirement of debt	118,332	
Other financing use—payment to refund debt escrow agent		1,100,000

The entry above assumes that the governmental entity made a worksheet conversion entry that reflected all of the debt outstanding at the beginning of the year, including the debt retired during the year.

The "deferred loss on early retirement of debt" is presented in the government-wide financial statements as an offset to the new debt and is amortized over 2 years (which is remaining life of the old debt at retirement because its life is less than the 5-year life of the newly issued debt). For this reason, the following conversion worksheet entry is made as of June 30, 20X2 to record the amortization:

	Debit	Credit
Interest expense ($118,332/2 years)	59,166	
Deferred loss on early retirement of debt		59,166

Early Extinguishments of Debt (Nonrefunding)

In some instances, a governmental entity retires debt early and uses internal resources as the basis for repayment of the debt rather than proceeds from the issuance of new debt (nonrefunding). Under this strategy, an expenditure (rather than an other financing use account) is used to record the transaction in the appropriate governmental fund; however, in the government-wide financial statements, the transaction must be converted to an accrual basis by removing the debt and recording an extraordinary gain or loss.

To illustrate an early extinguishment of debt that does not involve refunding, assume that a governmental entity retires debt that has a book value of $981,668 for a reacquisition price of $1,100,000. The following entry is made in the governmental fund that finances the retirement:

	Debit	Credit
Expenditures—principal	1,100,000	
Cash		1,100,000

At the end of the year, the following worksheet conversion entry is made to report the early retirement on an accrual basis in the government-wide financial statements:

	Debit	Credit
Bonds payable	981,668	
Extraordinary loss on early retirement of debt	118,332	
Expenditures—principal		1,100,000

Capital Expenditures: Current Period Transactions

When capital assets are acquired by a governmental entity, payments related to acquisitions are recorded as expenditures at the fund statement level. However, in order to convert the fund financial statement information from a modified accrual basis to an accrual basis for the preparation of the government-wide financial statements, the expenditure is capitalized and any related depreciation expense is reported.

To illustrate the conversion of capital expenditures to an accrual basis, assume that on July 1, 20X1 a governmental entity constructed a building at a cost of $5,000,000. The estimated useful life of the building is 25 years with no residual value. The construction cost of the building would be recorded in the appropriate governmental fund as follows:

	Debit	Credit
Expenditures—capital outlays	5,000,000	
Cash		5,000,000

In order to report the capital assets illustrated in this example in the government-wide financial statement as required by GAAP, the following work-sheet conversion entry is made:

	Debit	Credit
Buildings	5,000,000	
Expenditures—capital outlays		5,000,000

In this example, the depreciation expense on the building is assumed to be related to general government expenses for purposes of classification on the statement of activities. In order to reflect depreciation expense, the following worksheet conversion entry is made:

	Debit	Credit
Expenses—general government ($5,000,000/25 years)	200,000	
Accumulated depreciation—building		200,000

GAAP requires a governmental entity to report all of its capital assets in the statement of net assets, based on their original historical cost plus ancillary charges such as transportation, installation, and site preparation costs. Capital assets include such items as (1) land and land improvements, (2) buildings and building improvements, (3) vehicles, (4) infrastructure assets, and (5) works of art, historical treasures, and other, similar assets. Capital assets should be presented in the statement of net assets at historical cost less accumulated depreciation. A single amount (net of accumulated depreciation) may be presented on the face of the financial statement, in which case accumulated depreciation and the major categories of capital assets (land, buildings, equipment, infrastructure, etc.) must be reported in a note (GASB-34, pars. 18–22). Intangible assets are also included, if applicable, net of accumulated amortization. Amortization occurs on intangible capital assets that have definite lives. For the purpose of the entries below, intangible assets can be substituted for the assets as described because they are presented similarly.

Capital Assets: Previous Year's Balances

In addition to current year transactions, previous years' transactions are analyzed to determine how permanent balances (statement accounts) that appeared on last year's accrual-based financial statements affect the current year's government-wide financial statements. As shown earlier, worksheet conversion entries arising from this analysis are made through the beginning balance of net assets.

For example, assume that a governmental entity had the following capital assets at the beginning of the year:

	Cost	Accumulated Depreciation
Land	$100,000,000	—
Buildings (60% depreciated)	400,000,000	$240,000,000
Equipment (70% depreciated)	200,000,000	140,000,000
Total	$700,000,000	$380,000,000

Based on the above analysis, the following worksheet conversion entry would be made to establish the beginning balances related to the governmental activities column in the statement of net assets:

	Debit	Credit
Land	100,000,000	
Buildings	400,000,000	
Equipment	200,000,000	
Accumulated depreciation—buildings		240,000,000
Accumulated depreciation—equipment		140,000,000
Net assets		320,000,000

Capital Leases: Current Period Transactions

Rather than purchase a capital asset directly from a vendor, a governmental entity may lease the item. If the agreement is considered a capitalized lease as defined in NCGA-5 (Accounting and Financial Reporting Principles for Lease Agreements of State and Local Governments) and FAS-13 (Accounting for Leases), the transaction is accounted for in the appropriate governmental fund as both an issuance of debt and a capital expenditure (both of which were discussed in previous sections). Thus, in order to convert the fund financial statements from a modified accrual basis to an accrual basis for the preparation of the government-wide financial statements, the expenditure must be capitalized, any related depreciation expense must be recorded, and the debt must be recognized along with the accrual of any related interest expense.

To illustrate the capitalization of a lease, assume a governmental entity leases office equipment that has an economic life of 5 years and no residual value. Lease payments of $50,000 are to be made in five annual installments beginning on July 1, 20X1. The governmental entity's incremental borrowing rate is 10%. The capitalized value of the lease is $208,493 ($50,000 × 4.16986) and the following amortization schedule applies to the agreement. (The equipment is part of general government overhead costs.)

Date	Cash	10% Interest	Amortization	Book Value
7/1/X1	$—	$—	$—	$208,493
7/1/X1	50,000	0	50,000	158,493
7/1/X2	50,000	15,849	34,151	124,342
7/1/X3	50,000	12,434	37,566	86,776
7/1/X4	50,000	8,678	41,322	45,454
7/1/X5	50,000	4,546	45,454	0
	$250,000	$41,507	$208,403	

The execution of the lease would be recorded in the governmental by making the following entry:

	Debit	Credit
Expenditures—general government	208,493	
Other financing sources—capitalized leases		208,493
Expenditures—general government	50,000	
Cash		50,000

In the governmental fund financial statements, the issuance of the debt component of the lease is presented on the statement of revenues, expenditures, and changes in fund balances as an other financing source, but the amount is not presented in the balance sheet as a liability at the fund statement level. Likewise, the capital expenditure component of the lease is presented as an expenditure. In order to convert the transaction from a modified accrual basis to an accrual basis, the following worksheet conversion entries are prepared:

	Debit	Credit
Other financing sources—capitalized leases	208,493	
Expenditures—general government		208,493
(To reverse other financing source and expenditure)		
Equipment—capitalized leases	208,493	
Lease obligation payable—due within one year		208,493
(To record capital asset and related obligation)		
Lease obligation payable	50,000	
Expenditures—general government		50,000
(To record initial payment as a reduction to the lease obligation rather than an expenditure)		
Expenses—general government	41,699	
Accumulated depreciation—capitalized leases		41,699
($208,493/5 years)		
(To record depreciation on the capital lease)		
Interest expenses	15,849	
Interest payable (amount due on 7/1/X2 per amortization schedule)		15,849
(To accrue interest on the lease obligation for the year)		

PRACTICE ALERT: Lease accounting has been codified in GASB-62. No update to current GAAP is contained within the standard, but preparers should refer to GASB-62 rather than the former FASB-13, as amended, for further lease accounting information.

Capital Leases: Previous Year's Balances

In addition to capital lease agreements executed in the current year, the governmental entity must also consider those signed in previous years. The lease payments in the current period are accounted for as expenditures in the appropriate governmental fund, but at the end of the year, worksheet conversion entries are made to (1) recognize the obligation and the capital asset at the beginning of the year, (2) reduce the obligation by payments made during the current year (net of interest expense), and (3) record depreciation on the capital lease.

For example, assume that a governmental entity made a $20,000 payment during the current year (fiscal year ended June 30, 20X2) based on a lease agreement signed on June 30, 20X0. The amortization schedule for the lease agreement is as follows:

Date	Cash	8% Interest	Amortization	Book Value
6/30/X0	$—	$—	$—	$99,854
6/30/X0	20,000	0	20,000	79,854
6/30/X1	20,000	6,388	13,612	66,242
6/30/X2	20,000	5,299	14,701	51,541
6/30/X3	20,000	4,123	15,877	35,664
6/30/X4	20,000	2,853	17,147	18,517
6/30/X5	20,000	1,483	18,517	0
	$120,000	$20,146	$99,854	

The current lease payment is recorded in the appropriate governmental fund during the June 30, 20X2 year as follows assuming the equipment was used for general government purposes:

	Debit	Credit
Expenditures—general government	14,701	
Expenditures—interest	5,299	
Cash		20,000

In order to convert this payment from a modified accrual basis to an accrual basis, the following worksheet conversion entries are made at the end of the year assuming the capital lease was 20% depreciated as of the beginning of the year:

	Debit	Credit
Leased capital assets	99,854	
Net assets		79,883
Accumulated depreciation ($99,854 × 20%)		19,971
(To record the book value of the capital lease as of the beginning of the year)		
Net assets	66,242	

Lease obligations payable		66,242
(To record obligation as of the beginning of the year)		
Lease obligations payable	14,701	
Expenditures—general government		14,701
(To record the lease payment as a reduction to the principal obligation) (note that the interest recorded for the year is the same under the modified and accrual methods)		
Expenses—general government	19,971	
Accumulated depreciation—capital leases		19,971
(To record depreciation on the capital lease)		

Leasehold Improvements

When a lessee makes improvements to a capital asset, the expenditure should be reported as a capital leasehold improvement and depreciated over the remaining life of the lease or the life of the improvement, whichever is less. Leasehold improvements are recorded in the appropriate governmental fund as expenditures, but at the end of the year the transaction must be converted to an accrual basis by capitalizing the improvement and recognizing the related depreciation.

For example, assume that on the first day of the current year a governmental entity makes a $500,000 improvement to a building it is leasing. The improvement is expected to have an economic life of about 12 years but the remaining life of the lease is 10 years. The improvement cost would be recorded in the appropriate governmental fund as follows:

	Debit	Credit
Expenditures—general government	500,000	
Cash		500,000

In order to convert the transaction to an accrual basis, the following worksheet conversion entry would be made at the end of the year:

	Debit	Credit
Leasehold improvements	500,000	
Expenditures—general government		500,000
Expenses—general government ($500,000/10 years)	50,000	
Accumulated depreciation—leasehold improvements		50,000

Gains and Losses Related to Capital Asset Dispositions

When a governmental entity sells or abandons capital assets, any proceeds from the disposition are recorded in a governmental fund as either another source of financial resources or a special item based on professional judgment. At the end of the year, the transaction is converted to an accrual basis, with any related gain or loss reflected in the government-wide financial statements. For example, assume that land and a building that had been used as a fire station are sold for $400,000. The land and building's original cost were $50,000 and $700,000, respectively. The building is 70% depreciated. The following entry is made to record the transaction in the governmental fund that received the proceeds from the disposition:

	Debit	Credit
Cash	400,000	
Other financing sources—disposition of capital assets		400,000

The following worksheet conversion entry is made at the end of the year:

	Debit	Credit
Accumulated depreciation ($700,000 × 70%)	490,000	
Other financing sources—disposition of capital assets	400,000	
Land		50,000
Building		700,000
Gain on sale of capital assets		140,000

The gain on the sale of capital assets may be reported as a program revenue for the public safety program (fire protection) or it could be argued that the amount should be related to general government programs. It is also possible that the gain could be reported as a special item; however, it is unlikely that the gain would be considered extraordinary, because most governmental entities sell or abandon many of their capital assets at some point in time. In any case, professional judgment must be used to classify the gain on the governmental entity's government-wide financial statements.

Nonmonetary Exchanges (Trade-Ins)

A governmental entity may trade in a variety of capital assets as partial payment for new capital assets. The accounting for nonmonetary exchanges of capital assets, which is based on APB-29 (Accounting for Nonmonetary Transactions), is classified as follows:

- Exchange of dissimilar capital assets
- Exchange of similar capital assets with a loss
- Exchange of similar capital assets with a gain (no boot involved)
- Exchange of similar capital assets with a gain (boot involved)

Exchange of Dissimilar Capital Assets

When dissimilar capital assets are exchanged in a nonmonetary transaction, any gain or loss related to the transaction is reflected in the government-wide financial statements. The gain or loss is determined by comparing the fair value of the exchange (either the fair value of the asset received or the fair value of the asset given up—theoretically they should be the same) with the book value of the asset(s) given up.

For example, assume that on the first day of the current year a governmental entity exchanges a used vehicle that had an original cost of $40,000 and is 60%

depreciated for machinery. The fair value of the vehicle is $20,000. The gain or loss on the exchange is determined as follows:

Fair value of exchange		$20,000
Book value of asset given up:		
Cost	$40,000	
Accumulated depreciation ($40,000 × 60%)	(24,000)	16,000
Gain on nonmonetary exchange		$ 4,000

The nonmonetary exchange is not recorded in a governmental fund, because it does not involve current financial resources; however, the following worksheet conversion entry is made to reflect the exchange in the government-wide financial statements at the end of the year:

	Debit	Credit
Machinery	20,000	
Accumulated depreciation—vehicles	24,000	
Vehicles		40,000
Gain on exchange of capital assets		4,000

Professional judgment must be used to determine whether the gain on the exchange of a capital asset is reported as a special item or as program revenue. Special items are discussed later in this chapter.

Exchange of Similar Capital Assets with a Loss

When similar capital assets are exchanged in a nonmonetary transaction, any loss related to the transaction is reflected in the government-wide financial statements. For example, assume that a governmental entity exchanges equipment with an original cost of $40,000 and 60% depreciated for similar equipment. The transferred equipment has a fair value of $14,000. The loss on the exchange is determined as follows:

Fair value of exchange		$14,000	$14,000
Book value of asset given up:			
Cost		$40,000	
Accumulated depreciation ($40,000 × 60%)		(24,000)	16,000
Loss on nonmonetary exchange			$ 2,000

The nonmonetary exchange is not recorded in a governmental fund, because it does not involve current financial resources; however, the following worksheet conversion entry is made to reflect the exchange in the government-wide financial statements:

	Debit	Credit
Machinery	14,000	
Accumulated depreciation—vehicles	24,000	
Loss on exchange of capital assets	2,000	
Vehicles		40,000

For financial reporting purposes, the loss would be classified as either a program expense or a special item. The management of the governmental entity must make that determination.

Special accounting rules apply when exchanges of assets are made between reporting units within the same financial reporting entity. GASB-48 (Sales and Pledges of Receivables and Future Revenues and Intra-Entity Transfers of Assets and Future Revenues) provides guidance on these types of exchanges or transfers of capital assets.

Exchange of Similar Capital Assets with a Gain (No Boot Involved)

When similar capital assets are exchanged in a nonmonetary transaction and there is no boot involved, any gain related to the transaction is deferred. Boot is defined as cash or some other monetary asset (such as a notes receivable). For example, consider the previous illustration but assume that the value of the asset transferred asset is $19,000. The gain on the exchange is determined as follows:

Fair value of exchange		$19,000
Book value of asset given up:		
Cost	$40,000	
Accumulated depreciation ($40,000 × 60%)	(24,000)	16,000
Gain on nonmonetary exchange		$ 3,000

The nonmonetary exchange is not recorded in a governmental fund, because it does not involve current financial resources; however, the following worksheet conversion entry is made to reflect the exchange in the government-wide financial statements:

	Debit	Credit
Machinery	16,000	
Accumulated depreciation—vehicles	24,000	
Vehicles		40,000

It should be noted that the newly acquired machinery is not recorded at fair value ($19,000), because the $3,000 gain is not reflected in the government-wide financial statements. In effect, the gain is indirectly recognized in the government-wide financial statements because depreciation expense will be understated by $3,000 over the life of the asset.

Exchange of Similar Capital Assets with a Gain (Boot Involved)

When similar capital assets are exchanged in a nonmonetary transaction and boot is involved, no gain is recognized if the governmental entity does not receive boot. If boot is received, then a portion of the gain is recognized.

To illustrate the payment of boot, assume that a governmental entity exchanges equipment with an original cost of $70,000 that is 40% depreciated for similar equipment. The fair value of the asset received is $60,000 and the governmental entity pays boot (cash) of $10,000 to the other party. The gain on the exchange is determined as follows:

Fair value of exchange	$60,000	
Book value of asset given up:		
Cost	$70,000	
Accumulated depreciation ($70,000 × 40%)	(28,000)	
	42,000	
Cash	10,000	52,000
Gain on nonmonetary exchange		$ 8,000

The following entry is made in a governmental fund to record the exchange because current financial resources are expended (assuming the machinery is related to general governmental services):

	Debit	Credit
Expenditures—general government	10,000	
Cash		10,000

At the end of the year, the following worksheet conversion entry is made to report the nonmonetary exchange on an accrual basis in the government-wide financial statements:

	Debit	Credit
Equipment (new)	52,000	
Accumulated depreciation	28,000	
Equipment (old)		70,000
Expenditures—general government		10,000

To illustrate the receipt of boot, assume that a governmental entity exchanges equipment with an original cost of $70,000 that is 40% depreciated for similar equipment. The fair value of the equipment received is $60,000 and the governmental entity also receives boot (cash) of $10,000 from the other party. The gain on the exchange is determined as follows:

Fair value of exchange ($60,000 + $10,000)	$70,000	
Book value of asset given up:		
Cost	$70,000	
Accumulated depreciation ($70,000 × 40%)	(28,000)	42,000
Gain on nonmonetary exchange		$28,000

The following entry is made in the governmental fund that receives the boot:

	Debit	Credit
Cash	10,000	
Other financing sources—disposition of capital assets		10,000

In some instances a special item would be recorded rather than other financing sources—disposition of capital assets. Special items are discussed below.

At the end of the year a worksheet conversion entry is made to report the nonmonetary exchange on an accrual basis in the government-wide financial statements. Although the gain is $28,000, APB-29 requires that the following formula be used to determine the portion of the gain that can be recognized:

$$\frac{\text{Boot}}{\text{Fair Value of Exchange}} \times \text{Gain} = \text{Recognized Gain}$$

$$\frac{10{,}000}{70{,}000} \times 28{,}000 = 4{,}000 \text{ (recognized gain)}$$

The gain determined above is recognized in the following year-end worksheet conversion entry:

	Debit	Credit
Other financing sources—disposition of capital assets	10,000	
Equipment (new)	36,000	
Accumulated depreciation	28,000	
Equipment (old)		70,000
Gain on exchange of capital assets		4,000

As discussed earlier, the gain—based on professional judgment—would be classified as either program revenue or a special item in the government-wide financial statements.

PRACTICE ALERT: GASB-62 does not change the above presentations formerly related to APB-29.

Donations of Capital Assets from Outside Parties

When a governmental entity receives as a donation a capital asset, the receipt is not recorded in a governmental fund, because current financial resources are not involved; however, the transaction must be reflected in the government-wide financial statements based on the fair value of the donated property (GASB-34, par. 18).

To illustrate this concept, assume that an individual donates land ($1,000,000) and a building ($3,500,000) to a governmental entity. The property is to be used as a health center in a disadvantaged neighborhood. As stated above, the transaction is not recorded in a governmental fund, but the following worksheet conversion entry is made at the end of the year:

	Debit	Credit
Land	1,000,000	
Building	3,500,000	
Program revenues—capital grants and contributions		4,500,000

> **OBSERVATION:** The donation is recorded as program revenues; however, it could be recorded as an extraordinary item if it is both infrequent and nonoperating.

The building would be depreciated over its estimated economic life.

Donations of Capital Assets to Outside Parties

A governmental entity may donate capital assets to an external party. Again, because the transaction does not involve current financial resources, it is not recorded in a governmental fund. At the end of the year, a worksheet conversion entry must be made to reflect the transaction in the government-wide financial statements, based on the fair value of the donated property.

For example, assume that a state gives land and a building to a municipality to be used as a drug rehabilitation center. The land and building's original cost were $400,000 and $900,000, respectively. The building is 80% depreciated and the total fair value of the property at the donation date is $90,000. The following worksheet conversion entry is to be made by the state at the end of the year:

	Debit	Credit
Expenses—health and welfare	90,000	
Extraordinary loss on donation of capital assets	490,000	
Accumulated depreciation ($900,000 × 80%)	720,000	
Land		400,000
Building		900,000

Professional judgment would be used to determine whether the difference between the fair value of the asset donated and its book value should be recorded as an extraordinary loss. If the two criteria (infrequent and non-operating) are not satisfied, then the difference could be reported as (1) a program expense for health and welfare or perhaps as a general government expense or (2) a special item.

Gains and Losses Related to Capital Asset Dispositions

When a governmental entity sells or abandons capital assets, proceeds from the disposition are recorded in the appropriate governmental fund as either another source of financial resources or a special item based on professional judgment. At the end of the year, the transaction is converted to an accrual basis with any related gain or loss reflected in the government-wide financial statements. For example, assume that land and a building that had been used as fire station is sold for $400,000. The land and building's original cost were $50,000 and $700,000, respectively. The building is 70% depreciated. The following entry is made to record the transaction in the governmental fund that received the proceeds from the disposition:

	Debit	Credit
Cash	400,000	
Other financing sources—disposition of capital assets		400,000

The following worksheet conversion entry is made at the end of the year:

	Debit	Credit
Accumulated depreciation ($700,000 × 70%)	490,000	
Other financing sources—disposition of capital assets	400,000	
Land		50,000
Building		700,000
Gain on sale of capital assets		140,000

The gain on sale of the capital asset may be reported as a program revenue for public safety program (fire protection) or it could be argued that the amount should be related to general government programs. It is also possible that the gain could be reported as a special item; however, it is unlikely that the gain would be considered extraordinary, because most governmental entities sell or abandon many of their capital assets at some point in time. In any case, professional judgment must be used to classify the gain on the governmental entity's government-wide financial statements.

Impairment of Capital Assets

A governmental entity may be involved in an impairment of a capital asset that is destroyed, and, because the asset is necessary to the governmental entity's operating activities, then replaced. The impairment is recorded separately from an inflow into a governmental fund when cash (or a claim that meets the definition of availability) is received from insurance proceeds. GASB-42 requires that insurance recoveries be separately reported from any gains or losses or restoration activity. Insurance recoveries reported in subsequent years would be reported as a program revenue, nonoperating revenue, or an extraordinary item, whichever is appropriate.

To illustrate this concept, assume that fire destroys a governmental entity's administrative building. The original cost of the building was $4,000,000 and is 40% depreciated. The governmental entity has fire insurance on the property and receives $3,000,000 from the insurance provider. The governmental entity constructs a new building at a cost of $5,200,000. The following entries are made to record the involuntary conversion and the insurance proceeds in the appropriate governmental funds:

	Debit	Credit
Cash	3,000,000	
Extraordinary item—proceeds from fire insurance policy		3,000,000
(To record the fire insurance proceeds)		
Expenditures—capital outlays	5,200,000	
Cash		5,200,000
(To record the construction of a new building)		

At the end of the year, the following worksheet conversion entry is made to reflect the involuntary conversion in the government-wide financial statements:

	Debit	Credit
Extraordinary item—proceeds from fire insurance	3,000,000	
Accumulated depreciation ($4,000,000 × 40%)	1,600,000	
Building		4,000,000
Extraordinary gain—involuntary conversion of capital assets		600,000
(To remove the capital assets destroyed and to record an extraordinary gain on the impairment of a capital asset)		
Buildings	5,200,000	
Expenditures—capital outlays		5,200,000
(To reclassify capital expenditures)		

Maintenance and Preservation Costs

Maintenance costs are normal costs that allow a capital asset to be used in a normal manner over its originally expected economic life. Preservation costs are defined in the GASB's *Comprehensive Implementation Guide* as costs "that extend the useful life of an asset beyond its original estimated useful life, but do not increase the capacity or efficiency of the asset."

Maintenance costs and preservation costs are reported as expenditures in a governmental fund, but in the government-wide financial statements maintenance costs are expensed and preservation costs are capitalized. To illustrate the accounting for these costs, assume that a governmental entity incurs maintenance cost of $100,000 and preservation costs (related to a building) of $250,000. The building is used for general government services.

The costs are recorded in the appropriate governmental fund by making the following entry:

	Debit	Credit
Expenditures—general government	350,000	
Cash		350,000

At the end of the year, the following worksheet conversion entry is made to reflect the transaction in the government-wide financial statements:

	Debit	Credit
Buildings	250,000	
Expenditures—general government		250,000

Changes in Accounting Principles

When a governmental entity changes an accounting principle, the effect of the change is not reported in the entity's operating statement but instead is displayed as an adjustment to the beginning balance of its fund net asset account in the government-wide financial statements. (Generally, a change in an accounting principle will not be shown in a governmental fund, because there is no effect on current financial resources.)

The amount of the adjustment is the difference between (1) the actual beginning balance in the net asset account and (2) the assumed beginning balance in the net asset account, assuming that the new accounting principle had always been used by the governmental entity. The analysis of the difference between the two amounts always focuses on the balances at the beginning of the year in which the change is made no matter when the actual decision to make the change is made (GASB-34, par. 309).

To illustrate a change in an accounting principle, assume that a governmental entity changes its method of computing depreciation for the year ended June 30, 20X2 from an accelerated method to the straight-line method. The following balances apply to the beginning of the fiscal year:

	Actual Balance Accelerated Method	Recomputed Balance Straight-Line Method
Accumulated depreciation as of July 1, 20X1	$12,400,000	$9,200,000

The change in the method of computing depreciation expense does not affect any governmental fund, but the following worksheet entry is made at the end of the year to reflect the change in the government-wide financial statements:

	Debit	Credit
Accumulated depreciation ($12,400,000 – $9,200,000)	3,200,000	
Cumulative effect of a change in an accounting principle		3,200,000

The cumulative effect from the change is presented at the bottom of the statement of activities in the governmental activities column as follows (except for the cumulative effect amount, all other amounts are assumed):

	Governmental Activities
Change in net assets	$ 7,000,000
Net assets—beginning balance before restatement	450,000,000
Add: Cumulative effect of a change in an accounting principle (See Note X)	3,200,000
Net assets—beginning balance after restatement	453,200,000
Net assets—ending balance	$460,200,000

If the government-wide financial statements are presented on a comparative basis, the previous year's financial statements are restated to reflect the change in the method used to compute depreciation expense in order to satisfy the consistency standard.

In general, the accounting for a change in an accounting principle is based on the standards established by APB-20 (Accounting Changes) with an exception. APB-20 general solution is to require that the effects from changes in accounting principles be presented on a commercial enterprise's income statement (with some exceptions) and therefore affects the computation of net income. However, GAAP requires that the effects be presented as an adjustment to the beginning balance of net assets rather than as the change in net assets (the equivalent of net income for a commercial enterprise). The GASB states that "the exception taken to the requirements of Opinion 20 is appropriate because it was intended to avoid the manipulation of 'earnings per share' by commercial enterprises" and there is no equivalent EPS number for a governmental entity.

PRACTICE ALERT: GASB-62 does not change the above presentations formerly related to APB-20.

Changes in Accounting Estimates

A change in an accounting estimate is accounted for in a prospective manner. That is, a change in estimate does not require a cumulative effect adjustment similar to the one described in the previous section. For governmental fund financial statements the change in an accounting estimate may result in an adjustment to a balance sheet account (usually an asset) so that the account will reflect an amount that is compatible with the flow of current financial resources concept. For example, if a governmental entity believes that the estimated amount of uncollectible accounts related to property taxes receivable is understated, the new estimated percentage is reflected in the current financial statements by decreasing revenue and increasing the allowance account.

In government-wide financial statements a variety of assets and liabilities may be affected by changes in accounting estimates. For example, the life of a capital asset may change, the amount of an asset's residual value may change, or the estimated liability related to compensated absences may decrease or increase.

While all changes in accounting estimates are treated on a prospective basis, the effect of a change is dependent on the related asset or liability. For example, if it is estimated that for the last three years the provision for compensated absences has been understated by about 1% for each year, the total understatement for the 3-year period (3%) is charged to the expense and related obligation. On the other hand, if the life of a depreciable asset has changed, the change is folded into the government-wide financial statements by taking the un-depreciated cost (net of estimated residual value) and depreciating that amount over the remaining life of the property. To illustrate, assume a governmental entity purchased a building for $22,000,000 (with a residual value of $2,000,000) and an estimated economic life of 40 years. The asset is depreciated for 5 years and then it is estimated that the remaining life of the building is only 20 years. In the sixth year, the depreciating expense for each of the next 15 years is recomputed as follows:

Original cost of building	$22,000,000
Less: estimated residual value	(2,000,000)
Depreciable cost	20,000,000
Depreciation for 5 years ($20,000,000 × 5/40 years)	(2,500,000)
Remaining depreciable cost at the beginning of the 6th year	17,500,000
New depreciation rate (1/20 years)	× 5%
Annual depreciation expense for years 6 through 25	$875,000

Because accounting changes do not require a cumulative effects adjustment, there is no worksheet conversion entry to be made in order to convert the modified accrual financial statements to an accrual basis.

The change in the estimated economic life of a depreciable asset does not result in an adjustment to the governmental fund financial statements, because it does not change the estimated value of a current financial resource.

Long-Term Noninterest Bearing Notes Receivable

A governmental entity may enter into a transaction that involves the receipt of a long-term noninterest note receivable. The receipt of the note would not be reported in a governmental fund's statement of revenues, expenditures, and change in fund balance, because the transaction does not represent current financial resources. The transaction may or may not affect the entity's balance sheet, depending on the accounting method used. That is, the governmental entity could either not record a receivable or record a receivable but simultaneously establish a fund balance reserve. Either method is acceptable.

In the government-wide financial statements, the notes must be recorded after imputing interest as formerly required by APB-21, now codified in GASB-62. The discount rate used to impute interest should be based on the credit risk related to the other party to the note.

To illustrate the accounting for a long-term noninterest bearing note receivable, assume that on July 1, 20X1 a governmental entity sells land to the county for $5,000,000. The original cost of the land is $2,000,000. The county signs a 3-year, noninterest bearing note. Based on the credit rating of the county, its incremental borrowing rate is estimated to be 6%. The present value of the note is $4,198,100 ($5,000,000×.83962) and the following amortization schedule relates to the note:

Date	Cash	6% Interest	Amortization	Book Value
7/1/X1	$—	$—	$—	$4,198,100
6/30/X2	0	251,886	251,886	4,449,986
6/30/X3	0	266,999	266,999	4,716,985
6/20/X4	0	283,015	283,015	5,000,000
	$0	$801,900	$801,900	

Using the second accounting alternative described above (recording the note and a reserve), the governmental entity makes the following entry in the governmental fund that will eventually receive the proceeds from the sale of the land:

	Debit	Credit
Long-term notes receivable	4,198,100	
Fund balance—reserved for long-term notes		4,198,100

PRACTICE ALERT: To convert to GASB-54 presentation, if the note proceeds are required to be reinvested in a program by a bond covenant, a granting agency, a lawsuit or some other party external to the government, the balance must be restricted. If the program's enabling statute or a similar law dictates where the funds will be ultimately used, the balance would be committed. If management has the ability to direct where the balance is utilized or if the fund is a special revenue fund, the balance would be assigned. Otherwise the balance would be unassigned. In the above, assume that the loan must be utilized upon repayment for new small business loans in accordance a federal grant agreement. The conversion entry for GASB-54 would be as follows (assuming that systems are not converted to originally post the entry in the proper place):

	Debit	Credit
Fund balance—reserved for long-term notes	4,198,100	
Fund balance—restricted for long-term notes		4,198,100

At June 30, 20X2, the following worksheet conversion entry is made to restate the transaction on an accrual basis, assuming the GASB-54 entry above:

	Debit	Credit
Fund balance—restricted for long-term notes	4,198,100	
Land		2,000,000
Gain on sale of land		2,198,100
(To record the sale of the land and remove the fund balance reservation)		
Long-term notes receivable	251,886	
Interest revenue (see amortization schedule)		251,886
(To accrue interest on the noninterest bearing note)		

The standards originally established by APB-21 do not have to be applied on a retroactive basis. They need only be applied to receivables and payables that originate during the year in which the standards established by GASB-34 are implemented by a governmental entity (GASB-34, par. 146).

PRACTICE ALERT: GASB-62 does not change the above presentations formerly set out in APB-21 and which requires imputation of interest.

Lease Payments Receivable

A governmental entity may lease property to another party that creates an in-substance sale that must be accounted for based on the standards established by NCGA-5 and formerly FAS-13, as codified by GASB-62. The specific accounting for the lessor (governmental entity) depends upon whether the lease is a sales-type lease or a direct financing lease. When the governmental entity (lessor) is involved in an in-substance sale of property and the sales price is greater than the book value of the asset leased to the other party (lessee), the sales-type lease method must be used. If the governmental entity is simply functioning as a financing entity, the direct financing lease method is used.

Sales-Type Lease

In order to illustrate the accounting for sales-type lease, assume that a governmental entity leases used heavy-duty equipment to the county government. The equipment originally cost $1,000,000 and is 65% depreciated. The estimated fair value of the equipment is $431,213 and has a remaining estimated economic life of 5 years. The property was leased to the county on July 1, 20X1, and five annual payments of $100,000 (beginning on July 1, 20X1) are to be made by the county government. The lease payments are based on an 8% interest rate (implicit interest rate) and the amortization schedule for the lease agreement is as follows:

Date	Cash	8% Interest	Amortization	Book Value
7/1/X1	$—	$—	$—	$431,213
7/1/X1	100,000	0	0	331,213
7/1/X2	100,000	26,497	73,503	257,710
7/1/X3	100,000	20,617	79,383	178,327
7/1/X4	100,000	14,266	85,734	92,593
7/1/X5	100,000	7,407	92,593	0
	$500,000	$68,787	$331,213	

The following entry is made in the appropriate governmental fund to record the lease transaction on July 1, 20X1:

	Debit	Credit
Cash	100,000	
Long-term lease payments receivable	331,213	
Other financing sources—disposition of capital asset		100,000
Fund balance reserved for long-term lease payments		331,213

PRACTICE ALERT: To convert to GASB-54 presentation, if the note payments were originally funded by a program through a bond covenant, a granting agency, a lawsuit, or some other party external to the government, the balance must be restricted. If the program's enabling statute or a similar law dictates how the funds will be ultimately used, the balance would be committed. If management has the ability to direct where the balance is utilized, or if the fund is a special revenue fund, the balance would be assigned. Otherwise the balance would be unassigned. In the above, assume that the loan was funded from a federal grant agreement for small business loans. The conversion entry for GASB-54 would be as follows (assuming that systems are not converted to originally post the entry in the proper place):

	Debit	Credit
Fund balance—reserved for long-term lease payments	331,213	
Fund balance—restricted for long-term lease payments		331,213

PRACTICE POINT: It would also be acceptable to record only the $100,000 cash flow.

At the end of the fiscal year, the following worksheet conversion entries are made to reflect the lease transaction in the government-wide financial statement on an accrual basis assuming the GASB-54 entry above:

	Debit	Credit
Fund balance restricted for long-term lease payments	331,213	
Other financing sources—disposition of capital asset	100,000	
Accumulated depreciation—equipment	650,000	
Equipment		1,000,000
Gain on disposition of capital assets		81,213
(To reflect the sales-type lease on an accrual basis)		
Interest receivable (see amortization schedule)	26,497	
Interest revenue		26,497
(To accrue interest earned during the year)		

Direct Financing Lease

In a direct financing lease, the lessor (the governmental entity) does not have a gain or loss on the in-substance sale of property but simply acts as a financing agent in the agreement. To illustrate this approach, assume that the governmental entity in the above example decides to finance the purchase of the heavy-duty equipment for the county government. The purchase is made from a vendor, the governmental entity pays the vendor the fair value of the property ($431,213), and it then leases the property to the county government based on the lease terms described for a sales-type lease. The financing was part of a program mandated by a federal grant award.

The direct financing lease would be recorded in the appropriate governmental fund at the date the lease is executed by making the following entry in accordance with GASB-54:

	Debit	Credit
Other financing uses—execution of lease agreement	431,213	
Long-term lease payments receivable	331,213	
Cash (payment to vendor)		431,213
Fund balance restricted for long-term lease payments		331,213
(To record lease agreement)		
Cash (receipt from county government)	100,000	
Other financing sources—receipt of lease payments		100,000
(To record initial lease receipt)		

At the end of the fiscal year, the following worksheet conversion entries are made to reflect the lease transaction in the government-wide financial statement on an accrual basis:

	Debit	Credit
Fund balance restricted for long-term lease payments	331,213	
Other financing sources—receipt of lease payments	100,000	
Other financing uses—execution of lease agreement		431,213
(To reflect the direct financing lease on an accrual basis)		
Interest receivable	26,497	
Interest revenue		26,497
(To accrue interest earned during the year)		

Accrual of Expenses: Current Period Transactions

The basic guidance for determining when a governmental fund should accrue an expenditure/liability is found in NCGA-1 (par. 70), which states that "most expenditures and transfers out are measurable and should be recorded when the related liability is incurred." GASBI-6 (Recognition and Measurement of Certain Liabilities and Expenditures in Governmental Fund Financial Statements) expands on this general guidance by noting the following:

> Governmental fund liabilities and expenditures that should be accrued include liabilities that, once incurred, normally are paid in a timely manner and in full from current financial resources—for example, salaries, professional services, supplies, utilities, and travel.

These transactions give rise to fund liabilities that are considered mature liabilities because they are "normally due and payable in full when incurred."

Although NCGA-1 implies that a fund liability should be recorded when the obligation is incurred, one of the most important concepts that forms the basis for preparing the financial statements of a governmental fund is that liabilities are recorded only when they are normally expected to be liquidated with expendable available financial resources. As described in GASBI-6, this exception to the broad accrual assumption is based on the same guidance established for formal debt agreements as described in a previous section. That is, "governments, in general, are normally expected to liquidate liabilities with expendable available financial resources to the extent that the liabilities mature (come due for payment) each period." In order to apply this broad generalization to current practice, GASBI-6 notes that "a series of specific accrual modifications have been established pertaining to the reporting of certain forms of long-term indebtedness." Two of the exceptions deal with operating expenditures, namely debts that arise from compensated absences policies, and claims and judgments. For these two operating expenditures, only the portion of the estimated future payments that will use expendable available financial resources should be reported as a current expenditure on the operating statement and fund liability on the balance sheet. However, if these liabilities meet the general conditions of a contingency (probable incurrence and subject to a reasonable estimation), they must be accrued for the government-wide financial statements.

To illustrate this approach, assume that a governmental entity's legal department evaluates several claims from third parties related to the police department activities and has made the following analysis:

	Amount of Claim	Reasonable Estimate of Eventual Payment
Claim #1	$12,000,000	$1,900,000
Claim #2	5,000,000	800,000
Claim #3	4,000,000	200,000
Claim #4	2,000,000	100,000
Total	$23,000,000	$3,000,000

The legal staff of the governmental entity determines it is probable that all of the claims will have to be paid, but the estimate of the loss is about $3,000,000; however, the staff believes that these payments will not be made until sometime during the next budgetary period at the earliest.

FAS-5 (Accounting for Contingencies) requires that a loss contingency be accrued if it is subject to reasonable estimation and it is probable that a liability was incurred (or an asset was impaired). This event represents a loss contingency of $3,000,000, but because the loss will not use current expendable financial resources, the estimated losses are not reported in a governmental fund. However, at the end of the fiscal year, the following worksheet conversion entry is made to reflect the loss contingencies in the government-wide financial statements:

	Debit	Credit
Expenses—public safety	3,000,000	
Claims payable		3,000,000

PRACTICE ALERT: GASB-62 does not change the above presentations formerly set out in FAS-5, with the exception of pollution remediation contingencies, for which standards are promulgated under GASB-49.

Accrual of Expenses: Previous Year's Balances

When operating expenses are reflected in the government-wide financial statements because of a worksheet conversion entry, care must be taken so that the expense is not reported twice if the item is reported in a governmental fund as an expenditure in the following year. For example, assume that Claims #3 and #4 discussed in the previous section are settled during the next year for $900,000 (the fiscal year ended June 30, 20X2). In addition, at the end of the fiscal year, the following analysis is made by the legal department:

	Amount of Claim	Reasonable Estimate of Eventual Payment
Claim #1	$12,000,000	$1,900,000
Claim #2	5,000,000	800,000
Claim #5	6,000,000	300,000
Claim #6	2,400,000	250,000
Total	$25,400,000	$3,250,000

The actual claims paid would be recorded in the appropriate governmental fund as follows:

	Debit	Credit
Expenditures—public safety	900,000	
Cash		900,000

The following worksheet conversion entry is made at the end of 20X2 to present the claims obligation on the statement of net assets at an accrual amount:

	Debit	Credit
Expenses—public safety	1,150,000	
Net assets (beginning balance)	3,000,000	
Expenditures—public safety		900,000
Claims payable		3,250,000

The debit to net assets assumes that the beginning point in the worksheet is the governmental fund's balance, which does not have the $3,000,000 accrual from the last period.

Accrual of Revenues: Current Period Transactions

GASB-33 (Accounting and Financial Reporting for Nonexchange Transactions) provides accounting and reporting standards for the following four categories of nonexchange transactions:

1. Derived tax revenues
2. Imposed nonexchange revenues
3. Government-mandated nonexchange transactions
4. Voluntary nonexchange transactions

The standards established by GASB-33 retain fundamental criteria for revenue recognition that applies to the modified accrual basis of accounting, namely, that revenue is to be recorded when it is both available and measurable. NCGA-1 defines available as "collectible within the current period or soon enough thereafter to be used to pay liabilities of the current period." Revenue is measurable when it is subject to reasonable estimation.

In preparing government-wide financial statements, the same standards established by GASB-33 should be used to determine when revenue related to nonexchange transactions should be recognized except that the availability criterion does not have to be satisfied. Thus, nonexchange transactions need to be analyzed at the end of the accounting period to identify those that require a worksheet adjustment to convert from the modified accrual to the accrual basis of accounting.

To illustrate the accrual of operating revenue, assume that at June 30, 20X1 a municipality has property taxes receivable (net) of $3,000,000 of which $2,600,000 is considered available as defined by NCGA-1 and satisfies the criteria established by GASB-33 for imposed nonexchange revenues. Assuming the municipality has already recorded property taxes at the full levied amount (net of estimated write-offs), the following entry is made in the appropriate governmental fund:

	Debit	Credit
General revenues—property taxes	400,000	
Property taxes receivable		400,000
($3,000,000–$2,600,000)		

However, at the end of the period, a worksheet conversion entry is made for the $400,000 as follows, because the availability criterion does not have to be satisfied in order to reflect revenue in the government-wide financial statements:

	Debit	Credit
Property taxes receivable ($3,000,000 – $2,600,000)	400,000	
General revenues—property taxes		400,000

Accrual of Revenues: Previous Year's Balances

When operating revenues are reflected in the government-wide financial statements because of a worksheet conversion entry, care must be taken so that the revenue is not reported twice if the item is reported in a governmental fund as revenue in the following year. For example, in the previous illustration, the property taxes that were reflected in the government-wide financial statements as of June 30, 20X2 will be collected during the following accounting period and recorded as revenue in the appropriate governmental fund under the modified accrual basis of accounting. This fact must be taken into consideration when property tax revenue is accrued as of June 30, 20X3.

To illustrate, assume that as of June 20, 20X3 the municipality has property taxes receivable (net) of $3,400,000 of which $3,100,000 is considered available. The municipality makes the following entry in the appropriate governmental fund:

	Debit	Credit
General revenues—property taxes	300,000	
Property taxes receivable		300,000
($3,400,000–$3,100,000)		

In addition, the following worksheet conversion entry is made to recognize the $300,000 as revenue during the current period (20X3) reported on the accrual basis of accounting but net of the accrual ($400,000) that was made during the previous year (20X2):

	Debit	Credit
Property taxes receivable	300,000	
General revenues—property taxes	100,000	
Net assets (beginning balance)		400,000

Extraordinary Items

GASB-34 incorporates the definition of extraordinary items (unusual in nature and infrequent in occurrence) as formerly provided in APB-30 (Reporting the Results of Operations—Reporting the Effects of Disposal of a Segment of a Business, and Extraordinary, Unusual and Infrequently Occurring Events and Transactions) into the preparation of both governmental fund and government-wide financial statements; however, extraordinary items are reported in a governmental fund only if the item increases or decreases current financial resources during the year. When an event or transaction is reported as extraordinary in both sets of financial statements, the amounts are generally not the same, because in the fund financial statements only the amount that affects current financial resources is reported and in the government-wide financial statements the amount of the gain or loss determined on an accrual basis is reported (GASB-34, par. 55). GASB-62 also contains a section on extraordinary and special items.

The GASB's *Comprehensive Implementation Guide* notes that an event is unusual in nature if it "possesses a high degree of abnormality" and therefore is not related to the entity's normal operations. An event is infrequent in occurrence if it is not expected to occur again in the foreseeable future. Both of these concepts must be applied in the context of the characteristics of a particular entity, and their application is highly judgmental. Thus, what is considered unusual or infrequent for one governmental entity might not be for another. There is no list of extraordinary items, because that determination must be made on a case-by-case basis using professional judgment. The GASB's *Guide* states that the following may qualify as extraordinary items: (1) Costs related to an environmental disaster caused by a large chemical spill due to a train derailment in a small city; (2) Significant damage to the community or destruction of government facilities by natural disaster (tornado, hurricane, flood, earthquake, and so forth) or terrorist act (geographic location of the government may determine if a weather-related natural disaster is infrequent); and (3) a large bequest to a small government by a private citizen.

To illustrate the accounting for an extraordinary item, assume that a governmental entity had several pieces of road equipment destroyed by a flash flood.

The equipment had an original cost of $3,400,000 and was 20% depreciated. The equipment was fully insured, which resulted in proceeds of $2,500,000. The extraordinary item is reflected in the governmental fund that receives the insurance proceeds by making the following entry:

	Debit	Credit
Cash	2,500,000	
Extraordinary item—proceeds from casualty loss		2,500,000

To convert the extraordinary item from a modified accrual basis to an accrual basis for presentation in the government-wide financial statements, the following worksheet conversion entry is made:

	Debit	Credit
Extraordinary item—proceeds from casualty loss	2,500,000	
Accumulated depreciation ($3,400,000 × 20%)	680,000	
Extraordinary loss—flood damage	220,000	
Equipment		3,400,000

PRACTICE POINT: As shown above, it is possible to have an extraordinary item that results in an increase to fund balance in a governmental fund on the modified accrual basis and an extraordinary loss on the accrual-basis government-wide financial statements or vice versa.

Special Items

Unlike APB-30, the GASB identifies a new classification, "special items," which are described as "significant transactions or other events within the control of management that are either unusual in nature or infrequent in occurrence" but not both. Special items are reported separately and before extraordinary items. If a significant transaction or other event occurs but is not within the control of management and that item is either unusual or infrequent, the item is not reported as a special item, but the nature of the item must be described in a note to the financial statements (GASB-34, par. 56). As previously discussed, GASB-62 also contains a section on special items.

The GASB's *Comprehensive Implementation Guide* states that the following may qualify as special items: (1) Sales of certain general governmental capital assets, (2) special termination benefits resulting from workforce reductions due to the sale of utility operations, (3) early-retirement program offered to all employees, and (4) significant forgiveness of debt. An item can only satisfy the criteria for either an extraordinary item or a special item, but not both. For example, if an item is both unusual and infrequent it must be reported as an extraordinary item irrespective of whether it was subject to management control.

Special items may be reported in both a governmental fund and the government-wide financial statements; however, like extraordinary items, they are reported in a governmental fund only if the item increases or decreases current financial resources during the year.

To illustrate the accounting for a special item, assume that the management of a governmental entity decides to sell vacant land (with a historical cost basis of $200,000) to a commercial developer for $130,000 (its estimated fair value). The governmental entity has several vacant lots and over the past several years has sold the property to encourage development in the downtown area. The management believes the sales are unusual in nature (that is, nonoperating), but since they are frequent they are not considered extraordinary. The special item would be reflected in the appropriate governmental fund by making the following entry:

	Debit	Credit
Cash	130,000	
Special item—proceeds from sale of land		130,000

To convert the special item from a modified accrual basis to an accrual basis for presentation in the government-wide financial statements, the following worksheet conversion entry is made:

	Debit	Credit
Special item—proceeds from sale of land	130,000	
Special item—loss on sale of land	70,000	
Land		200,000

PRACTICE ALERT: GASB-62 does not change the above presentations. GASB-34 defines "special items" as significant transactions that are in the control of management that are either unusual in nature or infrequent in occurrence.

Merging Internal Service Funds

GASB-34 introduced a number of changes to the governmental financial reporting model. In the past, Internal Service Funds were an integral part of the financial reporting model, and although GASB-34 continues with this type of proprietary fund, the nature of how Internal Service Funds are reported in the new model is significantly different.

The financial statements of all Internal Service Funds are combined into a single column and are presented to the right of the Enterprise Funds. Thus, the major fund reporting concept established by GASB-34 does not apply to Internal Service Funds.

At the government-wide reporting level, Internal Service Funds and similar activities are eliminated to avoid doubling-up expenses and revenues in preparing the government activities column of the statement of activities. The effect of this approach is to adjust activities in an Internal Service Fund to a break-even balance. That is, if the Internal Service Fund had a "net profit" for the year there should be a pro rata reduction in the charges made to the funds that used the Internal Service Fund's services for the year. Likewise, a net loss would require a pro rata adjustment that would increase the charges made to the various participating funds. After making these eliminations, any residual balances related to the Internal Service Fund's assets, liabilities, and net assets are generally reported in the governmental activities column in the statement of net assets.

To illustrate the merging of an Internal Service Fund's accounts in the government-wide financial statements, assume that the following pre-closing trial balances for governmental funds exist at the end of a governmental entity's fiscal year:

Pre-Closing Trial Balance for Government Activities

	Debit	Credit
Assets	16,000	
Liabilities		6,000
Program revenues		39,000
Program A expenses	10,000	
Program B expenses	20,000	
Interest expense	4,000	
Investment income		1,000
Net assets		4,000
Totals	50,000	50,000

These amounts include all governmental funds (General Fund, Special Revenue Funds, Capital Projects Funds, Debt Service Funds, and Permanent Funds) adjusted from a modified accrual basis (as presented in the fund-level financial statements) to an accrual basis (which is the basis required in the government-wide financial statements).

Pre-Closing Trial Balance for Government Activities

	Debit	Credit
Assets	4,000	
Liabilities		2,000
Revenues		5,000
Expenses	4,500	
Net assets		1,500
Totals	8,500	8,500

OBSERVATION: The Internal Service Fund balances are reported on an accrual basis at the fund financial statement level.

The activities accounted for in the Internal Service Fund resulted in a "net profit" of $500 ($5,000 − $4,500), which means that the operating expenses listed in the pre-closing trial balance of government activities are overstated by $500. In order to merge the residual amounts of the Internal Service Fund into the government-activities column of the reporting entity, the following worksheet adjustments are made:

	Pre-Closing Trial Balance for Governmental Activities		Eliminations Based on Internal Service Residual Balances		Pre-Closing Trial Balance for Government Activities Including Internal Service Residual Balances	
	Debit	Credit	Debit	Credit	Debit	Credit
Assets	16,000	—	4,000	—	20,000	—
Liabilities	—	6,000	—	2,000	—	8,000
Program revenues	—	39,000	—	—	—	39,000
Program A expenses	10,000	—	—	300	9,700	—
Program B expenses	20,000	—	—	200	19,800	—
Interest expense	4,000	—	—	—	4,000	—
Investment income	—	1,000	—	—	—	1,000
Net assets	—	4,000	—	1,500	—	5,500
	50,000	50,000	4,000	4,000	53,500	53,500

It is assumed that during the year the Internal Service Fund's activities were provided to Program A (60%) and Program B (40%), which were reported in governmental funds.

Once the governmental activities have been adjusted to include residual values (including assets, liabilities, net assets, and operating activities), the statement of net assets and statement of activities must be formatted to reflect the standards established by GASB-34.

The government-wide financial statements are divided into governmental activities and business-type activities. Generally, as illustrated above, the activities conducted by an Internal Service Fund are related to governmental activities and, therefore, the residual amounts of the Internal Service Fund are merged with other governmental funds and presented in the governmental activities column of the government-wide financial statements. However, the activities of an Internal Service Fund must be analyzed to determine whether they are governmental or business-type in nature or both. If the activities are business-type in nature the residual amounts must be merged with the business-type activities in the government-wide financial statements. In addition, the operating accounts (depreciation expenses, investment income, etc.) reported by the Internal Service Fund must be analyzed to determine whether they should be used to compute the "net profit or loss" that is the basis for allocation to the governmental or business-type activities. These issues are discussed in Chapter 8, "Internal Service Funds."

Eliminations of Transfers and the Identification of Internal Balances

GASB-34 classifies transfers within and among governmental funds, proprietary funds, and fiduciary funds as follows (GASB-34, par. 112):

- Reciprocal interfund activity
  - — Interfund loans
  - — Interfund services provided and used
- Nonreciprocal interfund activity
  - — Interfund transfers
  - — Interfund reimbursements

Interfund Loans (Reciprocal Interfund Activity)

Loans that are expected to be repaid are to be reported as interfund receivables by the lender fund and interfund payables by the borrower fund and are not eliminated at the fund financial statement level.

At the government-wide financial statement level, interfund loans are eliminated if the loan is between governmental funds. For example, a loan between the General Fund and a Special Revenue Fund is eliminated. However, a loan between a governmental fund and an Enterprise Fund is not eliminated but is reclassified as an *internal balance*. Internal balances are reported on the face of the statement of net assets in both the governmental activities column and the business-type activities column; however, the amounts will equal and are offset when the total column for the primary government is prepared.

For example, if there was a $1,000,000 loan from the General Fund to an Enterprise Fund, the following worksheet conversion entry would be made to prepare government-wide financial statements:

	Debit	Credit
Due to General Fund	1,000,000	
Internal balance		1,000,000
Internal balance	1,000,000	
Due from Enterprise Fund		1,000,000

The first entry is made on the worksheet that combines all governmental funds (converting from modified accrual to accrual) and the second entry is made on the worksheet that combines all Enterprise Funds for the preparation of the government-wide financial statements.

Interfund Service Provided and Used (Reciprocal Interfund Activity)

Interfund receivables/payables may arise from an operating activity (that is, the sale of goods and services) between funds rather than in the form of a loan arrangement. If the interfund operating activity is recorded at an amount that approximates the fair value of the goods or services exchanged, the provider/seller fund records the activity as revenue and the user/purchaser fund records an expenditure/expense. These nominal accounts are not eliminated at the fund financial statement level. Likewise, any unpaid balance at the end of the period is reported as an interfund receivable/payable at the fund financial statement level.

At the government-wide financial statement level, interfund receivables and payables between a governmental fund and an Enterprise Fund are eliminated through the use of an internal balance account as explained in the previous section. However, the revenue and expense related to the transaction are not eliminated at the government-wide financial statement level.

If the interfund activity is between two governmental funds, the activity and resulting balances are accounted for in a manner similar to the approach discussed earlier for Internal Service Funds if the amounts are material.

Interfund Transfers (Nonreciprocal Interfund Activity)

Interfund transfers are a type of nonreciprocal transaction that represents interfund activities whereby the two parties to the event do not receive equivalent cash, goods, or services. Governmental funds report transfers of this nature as other financing uses and other financial sources. Transfers and the related amounts that are due to other funds and due from other funds are not eliminated at the fund financial statement level.

At the government-wide financial statement level, transfers within the governmental fund group and the related amounts due to other funds and due from other funds are eliminated. For example, assume that the total transfers from the General Fund to a Capital Projects Funds were $250,000 but only $200,000 had been transferred at the end of the year. The following worksheet conversion entries are made in order to prepare the government-wide financial statements:

	Debit	Credit
Transfers in—from General Fund	250,000	
Transfers out—to Capital Projects Fund		250,000
Due to Capital Projects Fund	50,000	
Due from General Fund		50,000

If the transfer is between a governmental fund and an Enterprise Fund, the transfers are not eliminated and any residual due to/due from amount outstanding at the end of the year is reclassified as an internal balance (described earlier).

Interfund Reimbursements (Nonreciprocal Interfund Activity)

A fund may incur an expenditure or expense that will subsequently be reimbursed by another fund. Reimbursements are reported only once, in the governmental fund that is eventually responsible for the item. There are no eliminations at either the fund financial statement level; however, if a governmental fund reimburses an Enterprise Fund (or vice versa) and there is an amount due to/due from that is outstanding at the end of the year, that amount would be reclassified as an internal balance.

For example, assume that the General Fund paid $100,000 of expenses for an Enterprise Fund and at the end of the year only $80,000 of the payment had been reimbursed. During the year, the two funds make the following entries to record the transactions:

	Debit	Credit
General Fund		
Due from Enterprise Fund	100,000	
Cash		100,000

Cash	80,000	
Due from Enterprise Fund		80,000
Enterprise Fund		
Expense	100,000	
Due to General Fund		100,000
Due to General Fund	80,000	
Cash		80,000

At the fund financial statement level, there would be no eliminations; however, at the government-wide financial statement level, the following worksheet conversion entry is made:

	Debit	Credit
Internal balance	20,000	
Due from Enterprise Fund		20,000
Due to General Fund	20,000	
Internal balance		20,000

The first entry is made on the worksheet that combines all governmental funds (converting from modified accrual to accrual basis) for presentation of balances in the governmental activities column of the government-wide financial statements and the second entry is made on the worksheet that combines all Enterprise Funds for the preparation of the business-type activities column on the government-wide financial statements.

PRACTICE ALERT: On the future GASB technical agenda is a proposed Concepts Statement entitled "Measurement and Recognition." This conceptual framework project has two primary objectives: (1) to develop recognition criteria for whether information should be reported in state and local governmental financial statements (measurement) and when that information should be reported (recognition) and (2) to consider the measurement attribute or measurement attributes (e.g., historical cost or fair value) that conceptually should be used in governmental financial statements. This project ultimately will lead to a sixth Concepts Statement.

TERMINOLOGY AND FORMAT

Governmental Funds Financial Statements

A governmental fund's balance sheet is prepared using the "balance sheet format," in which assets equal liabilities plus fund balances. The balance sheet reports the governmental entity's current financial resources and the claims to those resources for each major governmental fund and for the nonmajor funds. A total column is used to combine all of the major funds and nonmajor funds (GASB-34, par. 83).

PRACTICE POINT: Although the focus of presenting governmental funds has changed from a fund-type orientation to a major / nonmajor fund format, the balance sheet is essentially prepared in the same manner as previously required by NCGA-1, with the exception of segregating fund balances in accordance with GASB-54.

The balance-sheet-format operating statement for governmental funds measures the flow of current financial resources and therefore essentially follows the current standards used to prepare governmental financial statements. The operating statement has columns for each major fund, one for all (combined) nonmajor funds, and a total column, as illustrated in the following (GASB-34, par. 86):

	General Fund	Major Fund # 1	Nonmajor Funds	Total
Revenues (detailed)	$XXX	$XXX	$XXX	$XXX
Expenditures (detailed)	XXX	XXX	XXX	XXX
Excess (deficiency) of revenues over (under) expenditures	XXX	XXX	XXX	XXX
Other financing sources and uses, including transfers (detailed)	XXX	XXX	XXX	XXX
Special and extraordinary items (detailed)	XXX	XXX	XXX	XXX
Net change in fund balance	XXX	XXX	XXX	XXX
Fund balances (all types)—beginning of period	XXX	XXX	XXX	XXX
Fund balances (all types)—end of period	$XXX	$XXX	$XXX	$XXX

NCGA-1 illustrates three distinct formats that can be used to prepare the statement of revenues, expenditures, and changes in fund balances for governmental funds; however, GASB-34 mandates that the above format be observed (GASB-34, par. 86).

Government-Wide Financial Statements

GASB-34 *recommends* that the statement of net assets be formatted so that the net asset amount of the reporting entity is formed by subtracting total liabilities from total assets. The category "net assets" as recommended would replace the "fund equity" section previously used by governmental entities.

In addition, the following broad guidelines are to be followed in the preparation of the statement of net assets:

- Assets and liabilities are presented in the statement of net assets based on their relative liquidity.

- Capital assets (net of depreciation) are presented based on their original historical cost (including capitalized interest costs, if applicable) plus ancillary charges such as transportation, installation, and site preparation costs (capital assets include infrastructure assets).

- Three components of net assets, namely (1) invested in capital assets, net of related debt, (2) restricted net assets, and (3) unrestricted net assets are presented.

OBSERVATION: The GASB concluded that if the unspent portion of the capital related debt was considered "capital related," the "invested in capital assets, net of related debt" component of net assets would be understated because there would be no capital assets to offset the debt. On the other hand, including the unspent proceeds with capital assets would not be appropriate. The GASB agreed that a practical solution would be to allocate that portion of the "capital related" debt to the component of net assets that includes the unspent proceeds; for example, "restricted net assets—capital projects." The GASB stated that they did not believe that this implies that the debt is "payable" from restricted assets but, rather, is merely consistent with the philosophy of "net" assets. Many large general-purpose governments such as states construct assets and issue debt for municipalities or entities that are part of the government's reporting entity. In these cases, debt would be issued, but assets would not be present, resulting in a negative investment in capital assets, net of related debt.

The format for the government-wide statement of activities is significantly different from any operating statement currently used in governmental financial reporting. The focus of the statement of activities is on the *net cost* of various activities provided by the governmental entity. The statement begins with a column that identifies the cost of each governmental activity. Another column identifies the revenues that are specifically related to the classified governmental activities. The difference between the expenses and revenues related to specific activities computes the net cost or benefits of the activities, which "identifies the extent to which each function of the government draws from the general revenues of the government or is self-financing through fees and intergovernmental aid."

GASB-34 identifies the following as specific classifications that are to be used to prepare the statement of activities:

- Program Revenues
  — Charges for services
  — Operating grants and contributions
  — Capital grants and contributions
- General revenues
- Contributions to Permanent Funds
- Special Items
- Extraordinary Items
- Transfers

In addition, the following broad guidelines are to be followed in the preparation of the statement of activities:

- Expenses are presented by major function (at a minimum, each functional program should include direct expenses).

- Depreciation expense is reported as a direct expense of the specific functional categories if the related capital asset can be identified with the functional category.

- Depreciation expense related to capital assets that are not identified with a particular functional category may be presented as a separate line item.

- Interest expense on general long-term debt is generally considered an indirect expense and is not to be allocated as a direct expense to specific functional categories but instead is presented as a single line item.

GASB-34 does not require infrastructure assets that are part of a network or subsystem of a network (referred to as eligible infrastructure assets) to be depreciated under certain conditions. This method is referred to as the "modified approach." If the modified approach is used, the implementation issues have far more to do with engineering concepts than financial reporting. CCH's *Governmental GAAP Practice Manual* assumes that the governmental entity depreciates all of its infrastructure assets.

As stated above, the format of the statement of activities is significantly different from other operating statements and is not compatible with the conventional accounting spreadsheet structure. In CCH's *Governmental GAAP Practice Manual,* the conventional spreadsheet structure is used (because of its convenience and simplicity) and the completed worksheet is then reformatted to create a statement of activities consistent with the standards established by GASB-34.

COMPREHENSIVE ILLUSTRATION

The remainder of this book is structured around a comprehensive illustration based on the fictional City of Centerville, which has the following funds.

Governmental Funds

- The General Fund

- Special Revenue Funds

  — *Center City Special Services District* This fund provides special services, such as street maintenance, street cleaning, and similar services to approximately six square blocks of the business district. Businesses in this area pay a special service fee restricted for these services.

  — *Local Fuel Tax Fund* This fund receives a share of the fuel taxes collected by the state government. The fuel tax receipts are legally required to be used to maintain and repair the City's streets and highways.

- Capital Projects Funds

  — *Easely Street Bridge Project* This fund accounts for the construction of a bridge that will relieve traffic congestion between the downtown district and the east end of Centerville.

— *Bland Street Drainage Project* This fund accounts for construction work to mitigate flooding problems on one of the City's major thoroughfares.

— *West End Recreation Center Project* This fund accounts for construction activities related to a recreational facility for pre-teen and teenage students.

- Debt Service Funds

  — *Senior Citizens' Center Bonds* This fund is used to service serial bonds ($10,000,000) that were issued to build the Centerville Senior Citizens' Center.

  — *Easely Street Bridge Bonds* This fund is used to service two bonds instruments ($2,000,000 and $10,000,000) that partially finance the construction of a new bridge.

  — *Bland Street Drainage Bonds* This fund is used to service serial bonds ($4,900,000) that were issued to finance the Bland Street drainage project.

  — *West End Recreation Center Bonds* This fund is used to service bonds ($3,000,000) that were issued to finance the construction of the recreation center.

- Permanent Funds

  — *City Cemetery Fund* This fund accounts for a public cemetery that was endowed by contributions from interested individuals. Only the investment earnings from the permanent endowment can be used to preserve and maintain the cemetery.

Proprietary Funds

- Enterprise Funds

  — *Centerville Toll Bridge* The toll bridge was constructed several years ago and provides access across the Centerville River from the downtown area to a primarily residential section of the city.

  — *Centerville Utilities Authority* This Authority provides sewer services to the citizens, businesses, and other institutions of the City. A blended component unit.

  — *Centerville Parking Authority* This Authority owns and manages parking garages and lots in downtown Centerville. A blended component unit.

  — *Centerville Municipal Airport* This regional airport serves the City and several smaller communities in three adjacent counties.

- Internal Service Funds

  — *Communications and Technology Support Center* This fund provides a variety of communication and computer support services to all of the City's governmental and proprietary funds.

— *Fleet Management Unit*   This fund provides a motor pool to all of the City's governmental funds and to some other governmental units that are not part of the City's reporting entity. The unit provides no services to Enterprise Funds.

— *Special Services Support Center*   This fund provides support services exclusively for the Centerville Municipal Airport.

Fiduciary Funds

- Pension Trust Funds

  — *City of Centerville Pension Trust Fund*   The City's defined benefits pension agreement is administered by the State Public Employees Retirement Fund (SPERF) and is reported by the City in this trust fund.

- Private-Purpose Trust Funds

  — *Scholarship Trust Fund*   This fund accounts for an endowment arrangement whereby needy students are assisted with their higher education expenditures.

- Agency Funds

  — *Community Support Fund*   This fund is used to distribute certain state grants to various not-for-profit organizations.

PRACTICE POINT: For a discussion of the identification of a major fund in the City of Centerville comprehensive illustration, see the section titled "Identifying a Major Fund," in Chapter 13, "Developing Information for Fund Financial Statements."

PART II.
GOVERNMENTAL FUNDS

CHAPTER 2
THE GENERAL FUND

CONTENTS

NATURE OF GENERAL FUNDS

An entity's General Fund is used to account for a governmental unit's current operations by recording inflows and outflows of financial resources. Current inflows are typically from revenue sources such as property taxes, income taxes, sales taxes, fines, and penalties. Current outflows are generally related to the unit's provision for various governmental services such as health and welfare, streets, public safety, and general governmental administration. Every state or local government must have a General Fund.

The definition of the General Fund continues to be based on the description established by NCGA-1 (Governmental Accounting and Financial Reporting Principles).

PRACTICE ALERT: GASB-54 (Fund Balance Reporting and Governmental Fund Type Definitions), is effective for periods beginning after June 15, 2010. GASB-54 makes significant changes to fund balance classifications as well as clarifies and makes changes to the definitions of governmental fund types. The new definitions in GASB-54 provide that governmental funds of a particular type either should be used (i.e., required) or are used (i.e., discretionary) for all activities that meet its criteria. If use of a fund type is generally discretionary, specific situations under which a fund of that type should be used are identified either in the definitions in GASB-54 (i.e., debt service funds) or by requirements established in other authoritative pronouncements (i.e., special revenue and capital projects funds). The fund balance classification section of GASB-54 defines the terminology "restricted," "committed," and "assigned."

The fund balance discussions in this chapter are based on the classifications and definitions discuss the changes applicable under GASB-54. Practice Alerts that discuss the changes to the standards as a result of implementation of GASB-54 have been added throughout this edition of CCH's *Governmental GAAP Practice Manual*.

Below is the General Fund and the remaining Governmental fund type definitions (italicized words indicate major changes):

Fund Type	Pre GASB-54 Definition (periods beginning before June 15, 2010)	Post GASB-54 Definition (periods beginning after June 15, 2010)
General Fund	To account for all financial resources except those required to be reported in another fund.	To account for and report all financial resources not accounted for *and reported* in another fund.
Special Revenue Funds	To account for the proceeds of specific revenue sources (other than trusts for individuals, private organizations, or other governments or for major capital projects) that are *legally* restricted to expenditure for specified purpose.	To account for and report the proceeds of specific revenue sources that are restricted or committed to expenditure for specified purposes other than debt service or capital projects.
Capital Project Funds	To account for financial resources to be used for the acquisition or construction of *major* capital facilities (*other than those financed by proprietary funds or that are in trust funds for individuals, private organizations, or other governments*).	To account for and report financial resources that are restricted, committed, or assigned to expenditure for capital outlays, including the acquisition or construction of capital facilities or other capital assets.
Debt Service Funds	To account for the accumulation of resources for, and the payment of, general long-term debt principal and interest.	To account for and report financial resources that are restricted, committed, or assigned to expenditure for principal and interest.
Permanent Funds	To account for resources that are legally restricted to the extent that only earnings, and not principal, may be used for the purposes that support the reporting government's programs—that is, for the benefit of the government or its citizenry.	To account for and report resources that are restricted to the extent that only earnings, and not principal, may be used for purposes that support the reporting government's programs—that is, for the benefit of the government or its citizenry.

MEASUREMENT FOCUS AND BASIS OF ACCOUNTING

The modified accrual basis and flow of current financial resources are used to prepare the financial statements of a General Fund. The flow of current financial resources applied on a modified accrual basis is a narrow interpretation of what constitutes revenues, expenditures, assets, and liabilities of a governmental entity.

PRACTICE ALERT: The GASB is in the midst of a lengthy project deliberating the current financial resources model used by the governmental funds. Upon issuance of a final standard, the standards of revenue and expenditure recognition could change. A preliminary views document is expected in 2011, followed by an Exposure Draft sometime in the fall of 2011. As this edition of CCH's *Governmental GAAP Practice Manual* went to press, it appears that GASB is headed toward publishing a concepts statement rather than a full standard.

Revenue Recognition

Most governmental entities are involved in a number of nonexchange and exchange (and exchange-like) transactions. What distinguishes a nonexchange transaction from an exchange transaction is that in a nonexchange transaction a government "either gives value (benefit) to another party without directly receiving equal value in exchange or receives value (benefit) from another party without directly giving equal value in exchange" (GASB-33, par. 7).

In a nonexchange transaction two parties are the provider of the resources and the receiver of the resources. A state or local government could be either the provider or the receiver of the resources in a nonexchange transaction. GASB-33 (Accounting and Financial Reporting for Nonexchange Transactions) provides accounting and reporting standards for the following four categories of nonexchange transactions:

1. Derived tax revenues

2. Imposed nonexchange revenues

3. Government-mandated nonexchange transactions

4. Voluntary nonexchange transactions

In general, revenue related to a nonexchange transaction should be recognized when the revenue is both measurable and available. Measurable means that the expected asset flow is subject to reasonable estimation, while available means that the resources are realizable within the current accounting period, or shortly after the end of the period but in time to pay liabilities of the current accounting period.

In practice, the period of collectability has generally ranged from thirty days to as much as a year. GASB-38 (Certain Financial Statement Note Disclosures) does not attempt to define the availability criterion in a more restricted manner, but it does require a governmental entity to specifically disclose what period of time is used to implement the standard. For example, the disclosure requirement could be met by simply stating "the city considers receivables collected within sixty days after year-end to be available and recognizes them as revenues of the current year."

When a governmental entity is involved in an exchange transaction, the revenue is recognized when it is earned, assuming that the timing of the receipt of the resources satisfies the availability criterion.

OBSERVATION: For a discussion of revenue recognition criteria, see the chapter titled "Revenues: Nonexchange and Exchange Transactions" in CCH's *Governmental GAAP Guide.*

The detail guidance established by GASB-33 applies to both fund financial statements and government-wide financial statements except that revenues do not have to be *available* to accrue revenue for government-wide financial statements.

Expenditure Recognition

NCGA-1, paragraph 70, states that "most expenditures and transfers out are measurable and should be recorded when the related liability is incurred." GASBI-6 (Recognition and Measurement of Certain Liabilities and Expenditures in Governmental Fund Financial Statements) expands on this general guidance by noting the following:

> Governmental fund liabilities and expenditures that should be accrued include liabilities that, once incurred, normally are paid in a timely manner and in full from current financial resources—for example, salaries, professional services, supplies, utilities, and travel [GASBI-6, par. 12].

These transactions give rise to fund liabilities that are considered mature liabilities because they are "normally due and payable in full when incurred." However, GASBI-6 points out that there are several significant exceptions to the general guidance established in NCGA-1. Specifically, NCGA-1 states that "unmatured long-term indebtedness" should not be reported as a fund liability (except for debts that are related to proprietary and trust funds). Unmatured long-term indebtedness is defined as "the portion of general long-term indebtedness that is not yet due for payment," and includes debts such as the following (NCGA-1, pars. 9–11):

- Formal debt agreements such as bonds and notes
- Liabilities not "normally expected to be liquidated with expendable available financial resources"
- Other commitments that are not current liabilities properly recorded in governmental funds

GASBI-6 points out that the three specified categories listed above are exceptions to the general rule that a liability is recorded as a fund liability and "in the absence of an explicit requirement to do otherwise, a government should accrue a governmental fund liability and expenditure in the period in which the government incurs the liability" (GASBI-6, par. 12).

For a discussion of expenditure/liabilities recognition criteria, see the chapter titled "Expenses/Expenditures: Nonexchange and Exchange Transactions" in CCH's *Governmental GAAP Guide.*

The accounting for expenditures/liabilities continues to be recorded based on the standards established by GASBI-6 (Recognition and Measurement of Certain Liabilities and Expenditures in Governmental Fund Financial Statements).

Other Financing Uses and Sources

A General Fund may be involved in transactions that reduce or increase current financial resources but because of the nature of the transactions the items are not identified as revenues or expenditures. Examples of these transactions include the proceeds from the sale of debt, payments to bond refunding escrow agents, proceeds from the sale of capital assets (if considered immaterial amounts, they may be reported as miscellaneous revenue), and transfers (discussed below). Other financing sources and uses should be reported on the General Fund's statement of revenues, expenditures, and changes in fund balances after the excess (deficiency) of revenues over expenditures.

Interfund Billings and Activities

Interfund transfers represent interfund activities whereby the two parties to the transaction do not receive equivalent cash, goods, or services. A General Fund should report transfers of this nature in their activity statements as other financing uses (Transfers Out) and other financial sources of funds (Transfers In). Any resulting balances at the end of the accounting period should be reported as amounts due to and due from other funds.

Based on the standards established by GASB-34, there is no differentiation between operating transfers and residual equity transfers. There are simply transfers. No transfers can be reported as adjustments to a fund's beginning equity balance as previously allowed (GASB-34, par. 112).

Loans among funds should be reported as interfund receivables by the lender fund and interfund payables by the borrower fund. That is, the proceeds from interfund loans should not be reported as *other financing sources or uses* in the General Fund's operating statement. If a loan or a portion of a loan is not expected to be repaid *within a reasonable time,* the interfund receivable/payable should be reduced by the amount not expected to be repaid, and that amount should be reported as an interfund transfer by both funds that are a party to the transfer.

Interfund receivables/payables may arise from an operating activity (that is, the sale of goods and services) between funds rather than in the form of a loan arrangement. If the interfund operating activity is recorded at an amount that approximates the fair value of the goods or services exchanged, the provider/seller fund should record the activity as revenue and the user/purchaser fund should record an expenditure/expense. Any unpaid balance at the end of the period should be reported as an interfund receivable/payable in the General Fund. "Interfund services provided and used" replaces the previous term "quasi-external transactions." However, except for changes in terminology, GASB-34 did not change the essential manner by which reciprocal interfund activity is reported [GASB-34, par. 112a(2)].

PRACTICE ALERT: Many governments do not allow the payable of interfund balances beyond one fiscal year. Some governments also routinely transfer balances between enterprise funds and the general fund to fund operations beyond the normal allocation of overhead costs. Unusual transfers or the recognition of an allowance against a long-term balance of an interfund receivable could be signs of financial distress. Large interfund, nonroutine transactions are indicative of heightened audit risk.

Reimbursements

The General Fund may incur an expenditure that will subsequently be reimbursed by another fund. Reimbursements should be recorded only once in order to avoid double counting the item and should be presented as an expenditure of the fund that is responsible for the payment [GASB-34, par. 112b(2)].

Reporting Fund Balances under GASB-54

GASB Statement No. 54 (Fund Balance Reporting and Governmental Fund Type Definitions) was issued in an effort to improve the consistency in reporting fund balance components, enhance fund balance presentation, improve the usefulness of fund balance information, and clarify the definitions of the governmental fund types. The results of a GASB project research revealed that fund balance was one of the most widely used elements of financial information in state and local government financial statements while at the same time being one of the most misunderstood and misapplied elements. The requirements of GASB-54 became effective for financial statements for periods beginning after June 15, 2010.

Fund balance information is used by taxpayers, bond analysts, research groups, oversight agencies, government managers, and legislators in key decision-making regarding a government's available liquid resources for repaying debt, reducing taxes, adding or expanding programs or projects, and enhancing its financial position. The GASB began research when concerns were raised by certain financial statement users that there was substantial variation in the information governments were reporting about fund balance in their governmental funds, resulting primarily from a difference in understanding among financial statement preparers as to the definitions of reserved and unreserved fund balances and confusion over the difference between reserved fund balances and restricted net assets.

The classification requirements in GASB-54 should improve financial reporting by providing fund balance categories and classifications that are more easily understood. For example, elimination of the reserved component of fund balance in favor of a restricted classification should improve consistency between information reported in the government-wide statements and in the governmental fund financial statements and reduce some of the previous confusion about the relationship between reserved fund balance and restricted net assets. User understanding should also be enhanced through the consistent classification of the spendable portion of fund balance based on the relative strength of the constraints that control the purposes for which specific amounts can be spent, including amounts that are restricted, committed, assigned, and unassigned.

Fund Balance Classifications

GASB-54 introduces entirely new terminology and classification of fund balances in governmental funds to replace the previous classifications of "reserved, unreserved, designated and undesignated." In addition to identifying the portion of fund balance that is not spendable, the new standards establish a hierarchy of fund balance classifications based primarily on the extent to which a government is bound to observe spending constraints imposed upon how resources reported in governmental funds may be used. For example, GASB-54 distinguishes fund balance between

- Amounts that are considered nonspendable because they are not available for current use (such as fund balance associated with inventories, long-term receivables, and permanent fund principal), and

- Amounts that are available for use but are classified based on the relative strength of the constraints that control the purposes for which specific amounts can be spent. Beginning with the most binding constraints, these classifications are

  — Restricted;

  — Committed;

  — Assigned; and

  — Unassigned.

Nonspendable Fund Balance

Amounts that cannot be spent because they are either (1) not in spendable form (e.g. inventories, prepaid amounts, long-term loans and notes receivables, property held for resale) or (2) legally or contractually required to be maintained intact (e.g. the corpus or principal of a permanent fund).

Although long-term loans and notes receivables and property held for resale are generally reported as part of nonspendable fund balance, if the use of the proceeds from collection of the receivables or sale of the properties is restricted, committed, or assigned, they should be included in those appropriate fund balance classifications rather than the nonspendable classification.

The amount that should be reported as nonspendable fund balance must be determined first before classifying any remaining amounts by level of constraint (i.e. restricted, committed, or assigned).

PRACTICE POINT: GASB-54 states that amounts for the two categories of nonspendable fund balance [i.e. (1) not in spendable form and (2) legally or contractually to be retained intact] may be presented separately or in the aggregate on the face of the governmental fund's balance sheet. If displayed in the aggregate, the notes to the financial statement should present the separate amounts. GASB-54 contains examples of both separate and aggregated displays.

OBSERVATION: GASB-54 brings consistency between reporting restricted fund balance in governmental funds and restricted net asset for governmental activities in the government-wide statement of net assets pursuant to GASB-34; however, there are still some differences. For example, GASB-34 requires net assets required to held in perpetuity (i.e. permanent fund principal) to be reported as part of "restricted net assets." Under GASB-54, such amounts are classified as "nonspendable" fund balance.

Restricted Fund Balance

Amounts that are constrained for a specific purpose through restrictions of external parties (e.g. creditors, grantors, contributors, or laws or regulations of other governments) or by constitutional provision or enabling legislation (i.e. amounts that can be spent only for specific purposes pursuant to a state law, grant agreement, or donor agreement), pursuant to the definition of "restricted" in paragraph 34 of GASB-34, as amended by GASB-46.

The term "enabling legislation" as used in GASB-54 also means legislation that authorizes a government to assess, levy, charge, or otherwise mandate payment of resources from external resource providers and includes a legally enforceable requirement that the resources be used only for the specific purposes defined in the legislation.

GASB-54 states that restricted fund balance may be displayed on the face of the governmental fund's balance sheet in the aggregate or in a manner that distinguishes between the major restricted purposes. If restricted fund balance displayed in the aggregate, the notes to the financial statement should present the separate amounts for specific purposes.

Committed Fund Balance

Committed fund balance is amounts that are constrained for specific purposes imposed by formal action of the government's highest level of decision-making authority (i.e. amounts that have been committed by a governing body's legislation, ordinance, or resolution for a specific purpose, such as an amount from specific park and recreation revenues committed by a governing body's resolution to be used only for park maintenance)

Committed fund balances cannot be used for other purposes unless the government uses the same action (i.e. legislation, ordinance, or resolution) that it took to originally commit the amounts. The authorization specifying the purposes of the committed amounts should have the consent of both the legislative and executive branches of the government. Also, the formal action by the government's highest level of decision-making authority to commit resources should occur prior to the end of the reporting period, although the actual amount committed may be determined in a subsequent period.

Fund balance "committed" by legislation is distinguished from fund balance "restricted" by enabling legislation by the fact that amounts committed by legislation may be deployed for other purposes with appropriate due process by the government, such as through changes in legislation, ordinance, or resolution. Constraints imposed on the use of committed fund balances are imposed by the government "separate" from the enabling legislation that authorized the raising of the underlying revenue. Therefore, compliance with the constraints imposed on the resources that commit the government to spend the amounts for specific purposes is not considered "legally enforceable."

GASB-54 states that committed fund balance may be displayed on the face of the governmental fund's balance sheet in the aggregate or in a manner that distinguishes between the major commitments. If the committed fund balance is displayed in the aggregate, the notes to the financial statement should present the separate amounts for specific purposes.

Assigned Fund Balance

Assigned fund balance is amounts that are constrained by the government's intent to be used for a specific purpose but are neither restricted nor committed. Intent should be expressed by (1) the governing body itself or (2) a body (e.g. a budget or finance committee) or official to which the governing body has delegated the authority to assign amounts to be used for specific purposes (i.e. these amounts are intended to be used by the government for specific purposes but do not meet the criteria to be classified as restricted or committed, such as an amount set aside by management to fund a projected budgetary deficit in a subsequent year's budget).

"Assigned" fund balance is distinguished from "committed" fund balance by the fact that committed amounts must be constrained by the government's highest level of decision-making authority and assigned amounts do not require this level of authority to place the assignment or remove it. For example, management of a government may be authorized by a governing body to designate fund balances for a specific purpose, such as an amount set aside to fund accrued compensated absences for terminated employees, without formal action by the governing body itself. The amounts associated with this designation by management would meet the criteria to be reported as assigned fund balances. Assigned fund balances are similar to the unreserved—designated fund balances reported prior to GASB-54.

Assigned fund balances include all remaining amounts not reported as nonspendable, restricted, or committed in all governmental funds (i.e. special revenue, capital project, debt service, and permanent funds) other than the general fund. By reporting particular amounts that are not restricted or committed in a special revenue, capital projects, or debt service fund, a government has in essence assigned those amounts to the purposes of the respective funds. Assignment within the general fund conveys that the intended use of those amounts is for a specific purpose that is narrower than the general purposes of the government itself. However, governments should not report an assignment for an amount to a specific purpose if the assignment would result in a deficit in unassigned fund balance.

GASB-54 states that assigned fund balance may be displayed on the face of the governmental fund's balance sheet in the aggregate or in a manner that distinguishes between the major assignments. If the assigned fund balance is displayed in the aggregate, the notes to the financial statement should present the separate amounts for specific purposes.

Unassigned Fund Balance

Unassigned fund balance is the residual classification for a government's general fund and includes all amounts that are not constrained as reported in the other classifications.

Although any governmental fund may report amounts that are nonspendable, restricted, committed, or assigned or any combination of these four classifications, only the general fund can report a positive unassigned amount. In other governmental funds, if expenditures incurred for specific purposes exceed the amounts restricted, committed, or assigned to those purposes, the government should first reduce any assigned amounts within the fund and then, if there are no further assigned amounts to reduce, it should report the negative residual amount as "negative unassigned" fund balances. This means that a negative residual amount *should not be reported* for restricted, committed, or assigned balances in any fund.

PRACTICE ALERT: Similar to the treatment of net assets pursuant to GASB-34, the government should develop and apply an accounting policy to determine the classification of unrestricted fund balances as to whether it considers committed, assigned, or unassigned amounts have been spent when an expenditure is incurred for purposes for which amounts in any of those unrestricted classifications could be used. GASB-54 states that if a government does not establish such a policy, it should consider that committed amounts are reduced first, followed by assigned amounts, and then unassigned amounts.

Disclosure Requirements

GASB-54 requires that governments disclose the following information about their fund balance classification policies and procedures and other related information in the notes to the financial statements:

- For committed fund balance: (1) the government's highest level of decision-making authority and (2) the formal action that is required to be taken to establish (and modify or rescind) a fund balance commitment.

- For assigned fund balance: (1) the body or official authorized to assign amounts to a specific purpose and (2) the policy established by the governing body pursuant to which that authorization is given.

- For all the classification of fund balances: (1) whether the government considers restricted or unrestricted amounts to have been spent when an expenditure is incurred for purposes for which both restricted and unrestricted fund balance is available and (2) whether committed, assigned, or unassigned amounts are considered to have been spent when an expenditure is incurred for purposes for which amounts in any of those unrestricted fund balance classifications could be used.

- For nonspendable fund balance displayed in the aggregate on the face of the balance sheet, the notes should disclose amounts for the two nonspendable components, if applicable. If restricted, committed, or assigned fund balances are displayed in the aggregate, specific purposes information not displayed on the face of the balance sheet should be disclosed.

- For established stabilization arrangements, even if an arrangement does not meet the criteria to be classified as restricted or committed, the government should disclose the following information in the notes to the financial statements:

—The authority for establishing stabilization arrangements (for example, by statute or ordinance);

—The requirements for additions to the stabilization amount;

—The conditions under which stabilization amounts may be spent; and

—The stabilization balance, if not apparent on the face of the financial statements.

- If a governing body has formally adopted a minimum fund balance policy (for example, specifying a percentage of annual revenue or some other amount in lieu of separately setting aside stabilization amounts), the government should describe in the notes to its financial statements the established policy that sets forth the minimum amount.

- Encumbrances should be disclosed in the notes to the financial statements as commitments of government by major funds and nonmajor funds in the aggregate for funds that use encumbrance accounting.

PRACTICE ALERT: Documenting how a government distinguishes between "assigned," "committed," and "restricted" is vitally important for a successful implementation of GASB-54. These policies should be included in the government's summary of significant accounting policies in the notes to the basic financial statements.

Stabilization Arrangements

Many state and local governments have established and reported "rainy day," "budget or revenue stabilization," "working capital needs," or "contingencies or emergencies" and similar amounts within fund balances as reserves or designations. Such amounts are generally restricted or committed as to use for meeting emergency needs, stabilizing financial position when revenue shortfalls are experienced or for other, similar purposes. Recognizing the considerable diversity in practice as to how these amounts were reported, the GASB issued GASB-54, which states that the authority to establish stabilization arrangements and set aside such resources should come from constitution, charter, statute, ordinance, resolution provisions and contain provisions that the resources may be expended only under certain circumstances exist as defined in the formal action document. The formal action that imposes the spending parameters or criteria should indentify and describe the circumstances that qualify as an appropriate use of the stabilization resources, and they should be such that they would not be expected to occur routinely.

PRACTICE ALERT: GASB-54 points out that a stabilization amount that can be accessed "in the case of emergency" would not qualify to be classified within the committed category because the circumstances or conditions that prescribes its use (i.e. what exactly constitutes an emergency) are not sufficiently detailed. Similarly, an amount set aside to "offset an anticipated revenue shortfall" would not qualify as a restricted or committed fund balance stabilization arrangement unless the shortfall was quantified and was of such magnitude to distinguish it from other revenue shortfalls that routinely occur.

GASB-54, paragraphs 20 and 21, treats a qualifying stabilization as a specific purpose, allowing the amounts constrained to be reported as a restricted or committed fund balance in the general fund if they meet certain criteria, based on the source of the constraint on their use. However, "stabilization" is regarded as a specific purpose only if circumstances or conditions that signal the need for stabilization are identified in sufficient detail and are not expected to occur routinely. Amounts related to stabilization arrangements that do not meet the criteria to be reported as restricted or committed fund balances should be reported as "unassigned" fund balance within the general fund.

If a government has not established a stabilization amount pursuant to the proposed criteria but has formally established a minimum fund balance requirement, then the minimum fund balance requirement is reported as unassigned fund balance in the general fund and is required to be disclosed in the notes to the financial statements.

GASB-54 modified the definitions of governmental fund types. Specifically, special revenue funds are defined as those funds used to account for and report the proceeds of specific revenue sources that are restricted or committed to expenditure for specified purposes other than debt service or capital projects. Therefore, a stabilization arrangement would meet the criteria to be reported as a separate special revenue fund only if the fund's resources are derived from a specific restricted or committed revenue source, specifically restricted or committed for that stabilization purpose.

Transition Issues

The requirements of GASB-54 are effective for financial statements for periods beginning after June 15, 2010. There is a provision in GASB-54 that requires retroactive restatement of fund balance for all prior periods presented; however, for the statistical section, financial statement preparers may choose to report this information prospectively. If the previous year's information is not restated, preparers should explain the nature of the differences in the prior year's information.

PRACTICE ALERT: Even if a statistical section is not restated, the management's discussion and analysis section is also required supplementary information. Analysis of fund balances for governmental funds will be difficult if a restatement for at least the prior period is not done. Many governments present five years of fund balances as part of the analysis. In that case, ideally, all five years should be restated. Any restatement in the management's discussion and analysis should also be presented in the statistical section and in a restatement note to the basic financial statements.

FINANCIAL REPORTING AT FUND LEVEL

The balances and activities of the General Fund are presented in the following financial statements at the fund financial statement level:

- Balance Sheet
- Statement of Revenues, Expenditures, and Changes in Fund Balances

Transactions and accounts recorded in the General Fund continue to be based on standards established by various NCGA and GASB Statements and Interpretations that were outstanding before the issuance of GASB-34 because GASB-54 did not affect transactional details beyond fund balances.

These two fund financial statements include all of the governmental funds (General Fund, Special Revenue Funds, Capital Projects Funds, Debt Service Funds, and Permanent Funds). A governmental entity should present the financial statements of its governmental and proprietary fund, but the basis for reporting these funds is not by fund type but rather by major funds (GASB-34, par. 74).

The focus of reporting governmental funds and proprietary funds is that major funds are reported for these fund types; however, combined financial statements for fund types are not reported (GASB-34, par. 75).

A fund is considered a major fund if both of the following two criteria are satisfied (GASB-34, pars. 75 and 76):

1. Total assets, liabilities, revenues, or expenditures/expenses of the governmental (enterprise) fund are equal to or greater than 10% of the corresponding element total (assets, liability, and so forth) for all funds that are considered governmental funds (enterprise funds).

2. The same element that met the 10% criterion in (1) is at least 5% of the corresponding element total for all governmental and enterprise funds combined.

The General Fund is always considered a major fund and therefore must be presented in a separate column.

GASB-34 requires that a budgetary comparison schedule be prepared for the General Fund. This schedule is discussed in Chapter 18, "Management's Discussion and Analysis and Other Required Supplementary Information" (GASB-34, par. 70).

FINANCIAL REPORTING AT GOVERNMENT-WIDE LEVEL

The fund-based financial statements as described above are included in a governmental entity's financial report in order to demonstrate that restrictions imposed by statutes, regulations, or contracts have been followed. These financial statements have a short-term emphasis and generally measure and account for cash and "other assets that can easily be converted to cash."

On the other hand, government-wide financial statements were established by GASB-34 in order to provide a basis for determining (1) the extent to which current services provided by the entity were financed with current revenues and

(2) the degree to which a governmental entity's financial position has changed during the fiscal year. In order to achieve these objectives, government-wide financial statements include a statement of net assets and a statement of activities. Government-wide financial statements are based on a flow of all economic resources applied on the accrual basis of accounting. The flow of economic resources refers to all assets available to the governmental unit for the purpose of providing goods and services to the public. When the flow of economic resources and the accrual basis of accounting are combined, they provide the foundation for generally accepted accounting principles used by business enterprises in that essentially all assets and liabilities, both current and long-term, are reported in the government-wide financial statements.

The government-wide financial statements include a statement of net assets and a statement of activities with columns for governmental activities and business-type activities. For the most part, balances presented for governmental funds are converted from the modified accrual basis to the accrual basis of accounting and reported in the governmental activities column. Enterprise Funds are presented as business-type activities.

Perhaps the major implementation problem faced by those who prepare governmental financial statements based on the standards established by GASB-34 was the development of system procedures that facilitate the presentation of the two levels of financial statements. Most governmental entities solved this problem by maintaining their accounting systems on a modified accrual basis or (budgetary/statutory basis), which is the basis for preparing the fund financial statements, and then using a worksheet approach to convert from the modified accrual basis to the accrual basis in order to prepare the government-wide financial statements. This approach is adopted in this text.

For the most part, this approach requires that the General Fund's ending trial balance (which is on a modified accrual basis) be adjusted to reflect accrual balances; however, when a governmental entity has Internal Service Funds these latter funds must be merged into a governmental fund. Internal Service Funds and similar activities should be eliminated to avoid doubling-up expenses and revenues in preparing the government activities column of the statement of activities. The effect of this approach is to adjust activities in an Internal Service Fund to a break-even balance. That is, if the Internal Service Fund had a "net profit" for the year, there should be a pro rata reduction in the charges made to the funds that used the Internal Service Fund's services for the year. Likewise, a net loss requires a pro rata adjustment that increases the charges made to the various participating funds. After making these eliminations, any residual balances related to the Internal Service Fund's assets, liabilities, and net assets should generally be reported in the governmental activities column in the statement of net assets.

ILLUSTRATIVE TRANSACTIONS

Note: The transactions presented here assume that internal systems are *not* redesigned for GASB-54. Therefore conversion entries are used. In the 2013 edition of *CCH's Governmental GAAP Practice Manual*, beginning balances will be presented in GASB-54 format. Governments that do not redesign their internal accounting systems for GASB-54 will have to restate using adjusting entries similar to those contained in this section. The conversion entries to GASB-54 and assumptions are presented after JE02.49 as JE02.G54-1, JE02.G54-2, and so on.

In order to illustrate accounting and financial reporting standards that should be observed for the General Fund, assume that the City of Centerville had the following trial balance for the fund at July 1, 20X1:

	Trial Balance	
Accounts	**Debit**	**Credit**
Cash	$15,200,000	
Interest receivable	20,000	
Property taxes receivable	1,400,000	
Allowance for uncollectible property taxes		$ 1,000,000
Investments in marketable debt securities	300,000	
Investments in marketable equity securities	2,200,000	
Interest in equity investment pool	1,800,000	
Interest in short-term fixed income investment pool	1,500,000	
Inventories	12,000	
Accounts payable		8,320,000
Deferred revenue—property taxes		245,000
Due to other funds—Internal Service Fund— Communications and Technology Support Center		70,000
Due to other funds—Internal Service Fund—Fleet Management Unit		22,000
Fund balance—reserved for inventories		12,000
Fund balance—reserved for encumbrances		10,000
Fund balance		12,753,000
Totals	$22,432,000	$22,432,000

Note that the fund balance entries above are *not* GASB-54 compliant; however, they show what will likely be present in most trial balances for the year of conversion.

This section presents illustrative transactions and entries for the General Fund during the fiscal year ended June 30, 20X2.

When it is not obvious how expenditures of the General Fund should be allocated, the following assumption is made:

Governmental Activity	**Allocation Assumption**
General government	60%
Public safety	20%
Streets	10%
Recreation and parks	5%
Health and welfare	5%
Total	100%

GASB-34 generally did not change the manner of accounting for transactions that are recorded in the General Fund.

Transaction JE02.01—Accounts payable of $8,320,000 from the previous year was paid:

Accounts	Debit	Credit
Accounts payable	8,320,000	
Cash		8,320,000

Also, the encumbrance ($10,000) from the previous year was reversed, vouchered (general government expenditures), and paid:

Accounts	Debit	Credit
Fund balance—reserve for encumbrances	10,000	
Fund balance		10,000
Encumbrances	10,000	
Reserve for encumbrances		10,000
Expenditures—general government	10,000	
Accounts payable		10,000
Accounts payable	10,000	
Cash		10,000
Reserve for encumbrances	10,000	
Encumbrances		10,000

PRACTICE ALERT: Reserves are not GASB-54 compliant; however, for the purpose of this *Practice Manual*, the reserves are presented because it is likely that governmental operations will not change. Conversion entries are presented later in this chapter.

Many General Funds journalize their budgets. Because budgetary entries are reversed at the end of the period and have no effect on a General Fund's statement of revenues, expenditures, and changes in fund balances, these entries are not illustrated in this example. For a discussion of journalizing budgetary information see the chapter titled "Governmental Funds" in CCH's *Governmental GAAP Guide*.

Paragraph 92 of NCGA-1 requires that a governmental entity disclose the method used to account for encumbrances. When NCGA-1 was issued, governmental accounting standards with respect to encumbrances were in transition in that previously some governmental entities had treated encumbrances as expenditures and some had not. Current generally accepted accounting principles require that encumbrances not be reported as expenditure/liabilities, and for that reason GASB-38 (Certain Financial Statement Note Disclosures) eliminates the disclosure requirement established by NCGA-1, since there are no acceptable alternatives for the treatment of encumbrances.

Transaction JE02.02—Interest and investment income accrued at the end of the previous year was collected during the year:

Accounts	Debit	Credit
Cash	20,000	
Interest receivable		20,000

Transaction JE02.03—Property taxes receivable of $400,000 at the beginning of the year was collected and the balance ($1,000,000) was written off:

Accounts	Debit	Credit
Cash	400,000	
Allowance for uncollectible property taxes	1,000,000	
Property taxes receivable		1,400,000

Transaction JE02.04—The town levied property taxes of $100,000,000. It is expected that 10% of the amount levied will be uncollectible:

Accounts	Debit	Credit
Property taxes receivable	100,000,000	
General revenues—property taxes		90,000,000
Allowance for uncollectible property taxes		10,000,000

Nonexchange revenues (such as property taxes) continue to be recorded and the accounting continues to be performed based on the standards established by GASB-33 (Accounting and Financial Reporting for Nonexchange Transactions).

The GASB's *Comprehensive Implementation Guide* emphasizes the point that all taxes are considered general revenues rather than program revenues and presents the following illustrations (in each case the tax revenue is reported as general revenue): (1) A county government imposes a separate sales tax, the proceeds of which are required to be used for public safety or health and welfare programs (because of the restrictions on use, these taxes are not "discretionary" revenues); (2) a city levies a special tax that is restricted for use within a specific program or function (a separate property tax levied to pay debt service costs, for example); and (3) a county government has enacted a transient occupancy (hotel/motel) tax, a percentage of which is required to be used for "tourism" programs in the county. (The county has significant tourism activity and reports it as a separate function in its statement of activities. The county maintains that the revenue comes from "those who directly benefit from the goods or services of the program" and, consequently, that it should be reported as charges for services.)

The GASB's *Comprehensive Implementation Guide* notes that special assessment activities provided by a governmental entity are generally characterized by their narrow scope and the method by which they are financed. For financial reporting purposes, operating special assessments revenues are not considered general revenues like property taxes. Operating special assessments are program revenues (charges for services) because they are assessed against the specific parties entitled to the specific service.

Transaction JE02.05—Property taxes collected in advance in the previous year are applied to current property tax billings:

Accounts	Debit	Credit
Deferred revenue—property taxes	245,000	
Property taxes receivable		245,000

OBSERVATION: Some governmental entities use the deferred revenue account to report receivables that are not expected to be collected within a short period of time after the end of the year. This illustration uses deferred revenue only for cash received from property owners before the period in which the revenue can be recognized.

PRACTICE ALERT: The GASB is in the midst of a project delineating between what is a deferred revenue and a deferred inflow of resources.

Transaction JE02.06—Property tax collections totaled $87,000,000:

Accounts	Debit	Credit
Cash	87,000,000	
Property taxes receivable		87,000,000

Transaction JE02.07—Additional investments of $200,000 and $500,000 were transferred to the Equity Investment Pool and Short-Term Fixed Income Investment Pool, respectively. Both of the funds are Investment Trust Funds:

Accounts	Debit	Credit
Interest in Equity Investment Pool	200,000	
Interest in Short-Term Fixed Income Investment Pool	500,000	
Cash		700,000

Transaction JE02.08—The City leased office equipment that has an economic life of 5 years and no residual value. Lease payments of $100,000 are to be made in five annual installments beginning on August 1, 20X1. The City's incremental borrowing rate is 8%. The capitalized value of the lease is computed as follows.

$100,000 \times (n = 4; i = 8\%)$ 3.31213 =	$331,213
First payment on first day of contract =	100,000
Total present value	$431,213

The following amortization schedule applies to the lease:

Date	Cash	Interest	Amortization	Book Value
8/1/X1	$—	$—	$—	$431,213
8/1/X1	100,000	$—	$—	331,213

Date	Cash	Interest	Amortization	Book Value
8/1/X2	100,000	26,497	73,503	257,710
8/1/X3	100,000	20,617	79,383	178,327
8/1/X4	100,000	14,266	85,734	92,593
8/1/X5	100,000	7,407	92,593	-0-
	$500,000	$68,787	$331,213	

The equipment is part of the general government overhead costs, and the lease transaction is recorded in the General Fund as follows:

Accounts	Debit	Credit
Expenditures—general government	431,213	
Other financing sources—capitalized leases		431,213
Expenditures—general government	100,000	
Cash		100,000

In addition, payments of $1,500,000 for capital lease agreements signed in a previous year totaled $1,500,000. The following amortization schedule applies to these items:

Date	Cash	Interest	Amortization	Book Value
6/30/X0	$—	$—	$—	$7,818,540
6/30/X0	1,500,000	$—	$—	6,318,540
6/30/X1	1,500,000	379,112	1,120,888	5,197,652
6/30/X2	1,500,000	311,859	1,188,141	4,009,512
6/30/X3	1,500,000	240,571	1,259,429	2,750,083
6/30/X4	1,500,000	165,005	1,334,995	1,415,088
6/30/X5	1,500,000	84,913*R	1,415,088	-0-
	$9,000,000	$1,181,460	$6,318,540	

* R = rounding

The equipment is used for various governmental activities, and the lease payment is recorded as follows:

Accounts	Debit	Credit
Expenditures—general government ($1,188,141 × 60%)	712,885	
Expenditures—public safety ($1,188,141 × 20%)	237,628	
Expenditures—streets ($1,188,141 × 10%)	118,814	
Expenditures—recreation and parks ($1,188,141 × 5%)	59,407	
Expenditures—health and welfare ($1,188,141 × 5%)	59,407	
Expenditures—interest	311,859	
Cash		1,500,000

PRACTICE POINT: The accounting for capital leases continues to be performed based on the standards established by NCGA-5 (Accounting and Financial Reporting Principles for Lease Agreements of State and Local Governments).

Transaction JE02.09—The state government approved unrestricted operating grants for various localities for the fiscal year ended June 30, 20X2. The City's share of the grant is $24,000,000, to be paid in four equal installments. The last installment ($6,000,000) does not meet the definition of "available" resources, but the terms of the grant satisfy the accrual standards as established by GASB-33 and is therefore reported as revenue in the government-wide financial statements:

Accounts	Debit	Credit
Intergovernmental grants receivable	18,000,000	
General revenues—unrestricted grants		18,000,000

The availability criterion requires that resources only be recorded as revenue if those resources are expected to be collected or otherwise realized in time to pay liabilities reported in the governmental fund at the end of the accounting period. In practice, the period of collectability has generally ranged from thirty days to as much as a year. GASB-38 does not attempt to define the availability criterion in a more restricted manner, but it does require a governmental entity to specifically disclose what period of time is used to implement the standard. For example, the disclosure requirement could be met by simply stating "the city considers receivables collected within sixty days after year-end to be available and recognizes them as revenues of the current year" (GASB-38, par. 7).

Transaction JE02.10—A purchase order for $50,000 for office supplies is signed:

Accounts	Debit	Credit
Encumbrances	50,000	
Reserve for encumbrances		50,000

NCGAI-6 (Notes to the Financial Statements Disclosure), paragraph 4, requires that construction and other significant commitments by governmental entities be disclosed in a note. The AICPA's *State and Local Governments—Audit and Accounting Guide* defines "commitments" as "existing arrangements to enter into future transactions or events, such as long-term contractual obligations with suppliers for future purchases at specified prices and sometimes at specified quantities." Commitments should be evaluated to determine whether they give rise to encumbrances that must be reported by governmental funds.

Transaction JE02.11—The supplies ordered in Transaction JE02.10 are received. All supplies are used for general governmental purposes. The consumption method is used to account for supplies (see above notes on GASB-54):

Accounts	Debit	Credit
Reserve for encumbrances	50,000	
Encumbrances		50,000

Accounts	Debit	Credit
Inventories	50,000	
Accounts payable		50,000

Based on the standards established by NCGA-1 either the consumption method or the purchase method may be used to account for inventories/supplies at the fund financial statement level; however, the consumption method must be used to prepare the government-wide financial statements.

Transaction JE02.12—The liability arising from the supplies received in Transaction JE02.11 is paid:

Accounts	Debit	Credit
Accounts payable	50,000	
Cash		50,000

Transaction JE02.13—The City received dividends of $40,000 from investments held in marketable equity securities:

Accounts	Debit	Credit
Cash	40,000	
Interest and investment income		40,000

Transaction JE02.14—Withdrawals of $550,000 and $20,000 were made from the Equity Investment Pool and the Short-Term Fixed Income Investment Pool (both Investment Trust Funds), respectively:

Accounts	Debit	Credit
Cash	570,000	
Interest in Equity Investment Pool		550,000
Interest in Short-Term Fixed Income Investment Pool		20,000

PRACTICE POINT: The accounting for investments continues to be based on the standards established by GASB-31 (Accounting and Financial Reporting for Certain Investments and for External Investment Pools).

Transaction JE02.15—An operating grant of $2,000,000 was received from the state to be used to promote recreational activities:

Accounts	Debit	Credit
Cash	2,000,000	
Program revenues—operating grants (recreation and parks)		2,000,000

Governmental entities may receive pass-through grants, which are defined by GASB-24 (Accounting and Financial Reporting for Certain Grants and Other Financial Assistance) as "grants and other financial assistance received by a governmental entity to transfer to or spend on behalf of a secondary recipient." A "secondary recipient" is "the individual or organization, government or otherwise, that is the ultimate recipient of a pass-through grant, or another recipient organization that passes the grant through to the ultimate recipient." GASB-24 requires that cash pass-through grants generally be recorded simultaneously as revenue and expenditures in a governmental fund or revenue and expenses in a proprietary fund. Only in those instances when the recipient government functions as a cash conduit should a pass-through grant be accounted for in an Agency Fund. The AICPA's *State and Local Governments—Audit and Accounting Guide* states that when a governmental entity receives a fee related to the administration of pass-through grants, the fee should be recorded as revenue.

Transaction JE02.16—On November 1, a purchase order for $900,000 for various vehicles for the following governmental programs was signed (the vehicles have estimated useful lives of 3 years and no residual values):

General government	$100,000
Police activities	300,000
Streets department	400,000
Parks department	100,000
Total payments	$900,000

Accounts	Debit	Credit
Encumbrances	900,000	
Reserve for encumbrances		900,000

Transaction JE02.17—On December 1, the vehicles ordered in the previous transaction were received:

Accounts	Debit	Credit
Reserve for encumbrances	900,000	
Encumbrances		900,000
Expenditures—general government	100,000	
Expenditures—public safety	300,000	
Expenditures—streets	400,000	
Expenditures—recreation and parks	100,000	
Accounts payable		900,000

Transaction JE02.18—On December 15, the vendor was paid for the vehicles received on December 1:

Accounts	Debit	Credit
Accounts payable	900,000	
Cash		900,000

Transaction JE02.19—On December 31, the City purchased $500,000 of investments for the City's debt securities portfolio:

Accounts	Debit	Credit
Investments in debt securities	500,000	
Cash		500,000

Transaction JE02.20—The City received three of the four installments ($18,000,000) of the state operating grant accrued in a previous transaction:

Accounts	Debit	Credit
Cash	18,000,000	
Intergovernmental grants receivable		18,000,000

Transaction JE02.21—During the year the City had the following capital asset transactions.

The following capital assets were sold:

	Original Cost	Accumulated Depreciation	Proceeds	Loss on Sale of Asset
Buildings (related to general administrative activities)	$ 7,000,000	$2,000,000	$4,500,000	500,000
Equipment (related to general administrative activities)	1,400,000	1,000,000	200,000	200,000
Vehicles (related to public safety activities)	3,200,000	3,000,000	100,000	100,000
Total	$11,600,000	$6,000,000	$4,800,000	$800,000

The dispositions are recorded as follows:

Accounts	Debit	Credit
Cash	4,800,000	
Other financing sources—disposition of capital assets		4,800,000

Based on the standards established by NCGA-1 (Governmental Accounting and Financial Reporting Principles) the disposition of a capital asset is only recorded to the extent that cash (or near cash) is received; however, a gain or loss on the disposition must be recorded in order to prepare the government-wide financial statements.

The following equipment was acquired for cash:

	Cost	Depreciation for Current Year
General government	$2,000,000	$170,000
Public safety	1,300,000	110,000
Streets	700,000	95,000
Recreation and parks	500,000	40,000
Health and welfare	200,000	22,000
Total	$4,700,000	$437,000

The authorization, voucher, and payment of the expenditures are recorded as follows:

Accounts	Debit	Credit
Encumbrances	4,700,000	
Reserve for encumbrances		4,700,000

Accounts	Debit	Credit
Reserve for encumbrances	4,700,000	
Encumbrances		4,700,000
Expenditures—general government	2,000,000	
Expenditures—public safety	1,300,000	
Expenditures—streets	700,000	
Expenditures—recreation and parks	500,000	
Expenditures—health and welfare	200,000	
Accounts payable		4,700,000
Accounts payable	4,700,000	
Cash		4,700,000

In addition, the state gave the City several acres of land for development as a system of parks. The land has an estimated appraisal value of $20,000,000, and this type of gift from the state is considered unusual and non-operating (an extraordinary item).

No entry is made for the land received as a gift from the state because it does not represent expendable financial resources. The land will be reported in the government-wide financial statements as an extraordinary item.

GASB-34 established two new categories for governmental fund operating statements and for government-wide financial statements, namely extraordinary items and special items. GASB-34 incorporates the definition of "extraordinary items" (unusual in nature and infrequent in occurrence) as provided in APB-30 (Reporting the Results of Operations—Reporting the Effects of Disposal of a Segment of a Business, and Extraordinary, Unusual and Infrequently Occurring Events and Transactions) (GASB-34, par. 55). Unlike APB-30, the GASB identifies a new classification, "special items," which are described as "significant transactions or other events within the control of management that are either unusual in nature or infrequent in occurrence." Special items should be reported separately and before extraordinary items. If a significant transaction or other event occurs but is not within the control of management and that item is either unusual or infrequent, the item is not reported as a special item, but the nature of the item must be described in a note to the financial statements (GASB-34, par. 56).

Transaction JE02.22—The City received a contribution of $50,000 from a corporation to support the City's obesity awareness program:

Accounts	Debit	Credit
Cash	50,000	
Program revenues—operating contributions (health and welfare)		50,000

Transaction JE02.23—The City received a capital grant of $500,000 from the state for the purchase of police vehicles:

Accounts	Debit	Credit
Cash	500,000	
Program revenues—capital grants (public safety)		500,000

Transaction JE02.24—The City signed a purchase order for the acquisition of $520,000 of police vehicles:

Accounts	Debit	Credit
Encumbrances	520,000	
Reserve for encumbrances		520,000

Transaction JE02.25—The City received dividends of $30,000 from investments held in marketable equity securities:

Accounts	Debit	Credit
Cash	30,000	
Interest and investment income		30,000

Transaction JE02.26—On May 1, the City received the police vehicles ordered in a previous transaction. The vehicles have an estimated economic life of 3 years and have nominal residual values:

Accounts	Debit	Credit
Reserve for encumbrances	520,000	
Encumbrances		520,000
Expenditures—public safety	520,000	
Accounts payable		520,000

Transaction JE02.27—The City paid the invoice for the police vehicles received on May 1. The purchase was financed from the capital grant received on March 1 ($500,000) and from general resources:

Accounts	Debit	Credit
Accounts payable	520,000	
Cash		520,000

Transaction JE02.28—The City received $300,000 of property tax receipts that apply to the next fiscal year:

Accounts	Debit	Credit
Cash	300,000	
Deferred revenues—property taxes		300,000

Transaction JE02.29—The City signed a purchase order for $25,000 for office supplies:

Accounts	Debit	Credit
Encumbrances	25,000	
Reserve for encumbrances		25,000

Transaction JE02.30—During the fiscal year the following cash payments were made for the following expenditures:

General government	$20,000,000
Public safety	12,000,000
Streets	9,000,000
Recreation and parks	5,000,000
Health and welfare	7,000,000
Education (payment to school district—a component unit)	32,000,000
Total payments	$85,000,000

Accounts	Debit	Credit
Expenditures—general government	20,000,000	
Expenditures—public safety	12,000,000	
Expenditures—streets	9,000,000	
Expenditures—recreation and parks	5,000,000	
Expenditures—health and welfare	7,000,000	
Expenditures—education (component unit)	32,000,000	
Cash		85,000,000

Based on the standards established by GASBI-6 expenditures should continue to be recorded on an accrual basis except with respect to the expenditures identified in the Interpretation.

Expenditures presented in the statement of revenues, expenditures, and changes in fund balances should continue to be classified consistent with the standards discussed in NCGA-1 (par. 110–16).

Transaction JE02.31—During the fiscal year the following cash receipts were received:

Charges for events held by Parks Department	$125,000
Fines related to police activities	200,000
Fees charged by Streets Department	150,000
Licenses and permits collected by the various governmental agencies (receipts are related to general government activities)	50,000
Total collections	$525,000

Accounts	Debit	Credit
Cash	525,000	
Program revenues—charges for services (recreation and parks)		125,000
Program revenues—charges for services (public safety)		200,000

Accounts	Debit	Credit
Program revenues—charges for services (streets)		150,000
Program revenues—charges for services (general government)		50,000

In some instances a state law prohibits the use of fines for particular purposes (for example, public safety expenses and other expenses that are related to the generation of the fine revenue). Even though the uses of the fine revenues (or in general, all charges for services) are somewhat limited, the GASB's *Comprehensive Implementation Guide* states that they are nonetheless program revenues and not general revenues.

The size or importance of a program's revenue does not change the character of the revenue for classification purposes on the statement of activities. For example, the GASB's *Comprehensive Implementation Guide* notes that the fact that a community that has a substantial amount of fines and those fines are used to fund a variety of programs does not make the fine revenue a general revenue item. The GASB's *Guide* notes that "the net cost of a function or program is the difference between (1) expenses and (2) the charges, fees, and fines that derive directly from it and the grants and contributions that are restricted to it." A particular function might generate a "profit" that can be used in a variety of ways. That fact does not make the revenue general revenue.

Transaction JE02.32—Franchise taxes collected during the year amounted to $1,300,000:

Accounts	Debit	Credit
Cash	1,300,000	
General revenues—franchise taxes		1,300,000

PRACTICE POINT: The accounting for nonexchange revenues (such as franchise taxes) continues to be performed based on the standards established by GASB-33.

Transaction JE02.33—During the year contributions of $7,000,000 were made to the State Public General Employees Retirement Fund ($4,200,000), State Public Safety Officers Retirement Fund ($2,100,000), and State Postemployment Health-care Benefits Fund ($700,000):

Accounts	Debit	Credit
Expenditures—general government ($7,000,000 × 60%)	4,200,000	
Expenditures—public safety ($7,000,000 × 20%)	1,400,000	
Expenditures—streets ($7,000,000 × 10%)	700,000	
Expenditures—recreation and parks ($7,000,000 × 5%)	350,000	
Expenditures—health and welfare ($7,000,000 × 5%)	350,000	
Cash		7,000,000

PRACTICE ALERT: The GASB has recently released two exposure drafts, titled "Accounting and Financial Reporting by Employers for Pension Benefits and Financial Reporting for Defined Benefit Pension Plans" and "Note Disclosures for Defined Contribution Plans." Both contain major changes in how defined benefit plans are accounted for and reported, and they represent the culmination of years of work and hearings. The expenditures recognized might not change dramatically, but their calculation will should the provisions of "Accounting and Financial Reporting by Employers for Pension Benefits" be approved as exposed. Pension expenditures would be recognized as work is performed for active employees and plan changes would be based upon expected remaining service lives of active employees. Chapter 13 of the CCH's *Governmental GAAP Guide* contains a thorough review of the provisions of the exposure drafts.

Transaction JE02.34 (Adjustment)—The General Fund's interest in the Equity Investment Pool is replaced based on the ending-year balances in the Investment Trust Fund:

Accounts	Debit	Credit
Cash	388,000	
Investment in short-term instruments	24,000	
Investments in equity securities	1,359,600	
Dividends receivable	2,800	
Interest receivable	800	
Other receivable	2,400	
Other assets	1,200	
Expenditures—general government	98,000	
Interest expense	2,800	
Accounts payable		8,800
Demand loan payable to bank		30,000
Change in fair value of investments		366,400
Dividend income (interest and investment revenue)		20,800
Interest income (interest and investment revenue)		3,600
Interest in Equity Investment Pool		1,450,000

The General Fund's interest in the Short-Term Fixed Income Investment Pool is replaced based on the ending year balances in the Investment Trust Fund:

Accounts	Debit	Credit
Cash	697,000	
Investment in short-term instruments	1,301,000	
Interest receivable	14,000	
Other receivable	12,000	
Other assets	4,000	
Expenditures—general government	25,000	
Interest expense	3,000	
Change in fair value of investments	94,000	

Accounts	Debit	Credit
Accounts payable		3,000
Demand loan payable to bank		45,000
Interest income (interest and investment revenue)		122,000
Interest in Short-Term Fixed Income Investment Pool		1,980,000

The above two entries are based on the analysis in Chapter 11, "Investment Trust Funds and Individual Investment Accounts."

Transaction JE02.35 (Adjustment)—The investments in the debt securities portfolio had a net decrease in fair value of $150,000 and the investments in the equity securities portfolio had a net increase in fair value of $240,000:

Accounts	Debit	Credit
Investments in marketable equity securities	240,000	
Investments in debt securities		150,000
Change in fair value of investments (revenue)		90,000

The GASB's *Comprehensive Implementation Guide* points out that losses related to changes in the fair value of investment subject to the standards established by GASB-31 should be reported as an offset to program revenues when the earnings from the investments are restricted for a specific purpose. If no restriction exists, the losses are reported as a loss in the general revenue section of the statement of activities.

GASB-31 requires that certain investments be reported at fair value. Specifically, GASB-31 requires that the following investments be reported at fair value: (1) marketable equity securities (including unit investment trusts and closed-end mutual funds), (2) marketable option contracts, (3) marketable stock warrants, (4) marketable stock rights, (5) interest-bearing investment contracts (with some exceptions), (6) debt securities (with some exceptions), (7) open-end mutual funds, and (8) investment pools and 2a7-like pools. GASB-31 does not establish accounting standards for investments in securities that it does not specifically list. The AICPA's *State and Local Governments—Audit and Accounting Guide* states that generally, those investments should be reported "at original cost when acquired and that any purchased discount or premium from the investment's face or maturity value [be] accreted or amortized to investment income over the life of the investment in a systematic and rational manner." For example, if a governmental entity acquires nonmarketable equity securities, the investment is recorded at cost in subsequent periods (irrespective of its change in fair value) unless there is a decline in its fair value that is other than temporary.

Transaction JE02.36 (Adjustment)—The City's Legal Department notes that a $5,000,000 claim was raised during the year by an individual based on alleged personal and property damages caused by a police vehicle. It is believed that it is *probable* that the claim will have to be paid but the estimate of the loss is about $300,000. It is also believed that the claim will be settled during the latter part of next year. This claim represents a loss contingency of $300,000, but since the loss will not use current expendable financial resources it is not accrued in the General Fund. The amount will be reported in the governmental activities column of the government-wide financial statements, as shown later in the chapter.

Estimated claims and judgments of $2,000,000 were outstanding as of the beginning of the year and two of the claims (related to public safety activities) were settled for $400,000. The payment is recorded as follows:

Accounts	Debit	Credit
Expenditures—public safety	400,000	
Cash		400,000

The balance of the estimated unsettled claims at the beginning of the year ($1,600,000) is expected to be settled during the next 2 to 5 years. The accounting for loss contingencies (such as claims and judgments) continues to be performed based on the standards established by NCGA-4 (Accounting and Financial Reporting Principles for Claims and Judgments and Compensated Absences).

Transaction JE02.37 (Adjustment)—Compensated absences paid during the year totaled $60,000, which was included in Transaction JE02.30. Compensated absences earned by employees during the year amounted to $220,000. The $220,000 amount will not use current expendable financial resources, so it is not reflected in the fund financial statements. (As illustrated later, the $220,000 will be reported in the government-wide financial statements.)

Transaction JE02.38 (Adjustment)—Property taxes receivable from specific residents of $9,000,000 is identified as uncollectible:

Accounts	Debit	Credit
Allowance for uncollectible property taxes	9,000,000	
Property taxes receivable		9,000,000

Transaction JE02.39 (Adjustment)—After additional analysis the allowance for uncollectible accounts is increased by $1,000,000. This is a change in an accounting estimate:

Accounts	Debit	Credit
General revenues—property taxes	1,000,000	
Allowance for uncollectible property taxes		1,000,000

The GASB's *Comprehensive Implementation Guide* points out that GASB-33 (pars. 16 and 18) requires that derived taxes and imposed nonexchange revenues (which are both general revenues) be reported net of estimated refunds and estimated uncollectible amounts, respectively. The GASB's *Guide* also notes that uncollectible exchange transaction revenues related to governmental activities on the statement of activities should be recorded net of any uncollectible amounts. That is, a bad debts expense account should not be used for presentation purposes.

Transaction JE02.40 (Adjustment)—It is expected that the remaining balance of property taxes receivable (net of the allowance) will be collected during the next fiscal year. Approximately 70% of that amount will not be collected in time to pay existing liabilities, thus not satisfying the availability criterion:

Accounts	Debit	Credit
General revenues—property taxes ($2,000,000 × 70%)	1,400,000	
Property taxes receivable		1,400,000

	Property Taxes Receivable	Allowance for Uncollectible/ Doubtful Accounts	Revenue
Beginning balance	$ 1,400,000	$ 1,000,000	—
Collections and write-offs	(1,400,000)	(1,000,000)	—
Application of deferred taxes received in the previous year	(245,000)	—	—
Amounts recognized at levy date	100,000,000	10,000,000	$90,000,000
Receivables collected	(44,000,000)	—	—
Receivables collected	(43,000,000)	—	—
Specific write-offs	(9,000,000)	(9,000,000)	—
Change in estimate	—	1,000,000	(1,000,000)
Balances—accrual basis	3,755,000	2,000,000	89,000,000
Receivables estimated to be collected in the next fiscal year but not in time to pay existing liabilities ($2,000,000 × 70%)	(1,400,000)	—	(1,400,000)
Balance—modified accrual basis	$ 2,355,000	$ 2,000,000	$87,600,000

Transaction JE02.41 (Adjustment)—The City uses the consumption method to account for supplies. At the end of the year, $17,000 of inventories was on hand. The amount of supplies consumed during the year was $45,000 ($12,000 + $50,000 – $17,000):

Accounts	Debit	Credit
Expenditures—general government ($45,000 × 60%)	27,000	
Expenditures—public safety ($45,000 × 20%)	9,000	
Expenditures—streets ($45,000 × 10%)	4,500	
Expenditures—recreation and parks ($45,000 × 5%)	2,250	
Expenditures—health and welfare ($45,000 × 5%)	2,250	
Inventories		45,000
Fund balance	5,000	
Fund balance—reserved for inventories		5,000

The fund balance entries above are *not* GASB-54 compliant; however, they show what will likely be present in most trial balances for the year of conversion.

Inventories or supplies are accounted for in governmental funds by using either the consumption method or the purchase method. A governmental entity may (but is not required to) account for inventories or supplies based on the guidance established by ARB-43 (Restatement and Revision of Accounting Research Bulletins, Chapter 4, Inventory Pricing). ARB-43 requires that inventories or supplies be subjected to the lower of cost or market test for possible write-down. That is, if the replacement cost of inventories or supplies is less than the cost of the items (using FIFO, LIFO, or the average cost method), a write-down is required. The AICPA's *State and Local Governments—Audit and Accounting Guide* points out that if a governmental entity does not chose to follow ARB-43 with respect to the lower of cost or market method, it should nonetheless write down inventories or supplies if they are affected by physical deterioration or obsolescence. This requirement applies to the use of either the consumption method or the purchase method. The purchase method could be affected by the need for a write-down because NCGA-1, paragraph 73, requires that a governmental fund record inventories or supplies when a significant amount of inventories or supplies exits at the end of the year. Under this circumstance a write-down would require a reduction both in the asset balance and the reserve fund balance for inventory or supplies.

Transaction JE02.42 (Adjustment)—The following charges, fees, and permits apply to activities that occurred during the current fiscal year, but approximately 60% will be collected in time to pay existing liabilities:

Charges for events held by Parks Department	$10,000
Fines related to police activities	2,000
Fees charged by public health activities	4,000
Licenses and permits collected by the various governmental agencies (receipts are related to general government activities)	5,000
Total collections	$21,000

Accounts	Debit	Credit
Other receivables ($21,000 × 60%)	12,600	
Program revenues—charges for services (recreation and parks) ($10,000 × 60%)		6,000
Program revenues—charges for services (public safety) ($2,000 × 60%)		1,200
Program revenues—charges for services (health and welfare) ($4,000 × 60%)		2,400
Program revenues—charges for services (general government) ($5,000 × 60%)		3,000

Transaction JE02.43 (Adjustment)—The encumbrance ($25,000) incurred on June 25th is outstanding at the end of the year, but the City intends to honor the encumbrance and reappropriate funds to pay for the commitment in the next fiscal year (see Transaction JE02.29):

Accounts	Debit	Credit
Reserve for encumbrances	25,000	
Encumbrances		25,000
Fund balance	25,000	
Fund balance—reserve for encumbrances		25,000

Transaction JE02.44 (Adjustment)—The following expenditures are recognized at the end of the year based on the modified accrual basis of accounting:

General government	$600,000
Public safety	30,000
Streets	20,000
Recreation and parks	10,000
Health and welfare	5,000
Total	$665,000

Accounts	Debit	Credit
Expenditures—general government	600,000	
Expenditures—public safety	30,000	
Expenditures—streets	20,000	
Expenditures—recreation and parks	10,000	
Expenditures—health and welfare	5,000	
Accounts payable		665,000

Transaction JE02.45 (Adjustment)—Interest and investment income of $23,000 is accrued at the end of the year:

Accounts	Debit	Credit
Interest receivables	23,000	
Interest and investment revenue		23,000

Transaction JE02.46—The following transfers were made to various funds during the year:

Special Revenue Fund—Center City Special Services Fund	$ 75,000
Capital Projects Fund—Easely Street Bridge	1,000,000
Capital Projects Fund—Bland Street Drainage Project	600,000
Capital Projects Fund—West End Recreation Center Project	300,000
Debt Service Fund—Senior Citizens' Center Bonds	1,300,000
Debt Service Fund—Easely Street Bridge Bonds	220,000
Debt Service Fund—Bland Street Drainage Bonds	1,100,000
Debt Service Fund—West End Recreation Center Bonds	700,000
Internal Service Fund—Communications and Technology Support Center	40,000
Enterprise Fund—Centerville Toll Bridge	50,000
Enterprise Fund—Centerville Parking Authority	90,000
Total	$5,475,000

Accounts	Debit	Credit
Transfers out—Special Revenue Fund—Center City Special Services Fund	75,000	
Transfers out—Capital Projects Fund—Easely Street Bridge	1,000,000	
Transfers out—Capital Projects Fund—Bland Street Drainage Project	600,000	
Transfers out—Capital Projects Fund—West End Recreation Center Project	300,000	
Transfers out—Debt Service Fund—Senior Citizens' Center Bonds	1,300,000	
Transfers out—Debt Service Fund—Easely Street Bridge Bonds	220,000	
Transfers out—Debt Service Fund—Bland Street Drainage Bonds	1,100,000	
Transfers out—Debt Service Fund—West End Recreation Center Bonds	700,000	
Transfers out—Internal Service Fund— Communications and Technology Support Center	40,000	
Transfers out—Enterprise Fund—Centerville Toll Bridge	50,000	
Transfers out—Enterprise Fund—Centerville Parking Authority	90,000	
Cash		5,475,000

PRACTICE POINT: Various interfund transfers occur within most governmental reporting entities. GASB-38 (Certain Financial Statement Note Disclosures) requires certain disclosures for both interfund balances outstanding at the end of the year and transfers made during the year.

Transaction JE02.47—A transfer of $50,000 from an Internal Service Fund (Fleet Management Unit) was received by the General Fund:

Accounts	Debit	Credit
Cash	50,000	
Transfers in—Internal Service Fund—Fleet Management Unit		50,000

Transaction JE02.48—During the year, the Communications and Technology Support Center (an Internal Service Fund) billed the General Fund $4,500,000 for services performed. The General Fund made payments of $4,400,000:

Accounts	Debit	Credit
Expenditures—general government ($4,500,000 × 60%)	2,700,000	
Expenditures—public safety ($4,500,000 × 20%)	900,000	
Expenditures—streets ($4,500,000 × 10%)	450,000	
Expenditures—recreation and parks		

Accounts	Debit	Credit
($4,500,000 × 5%)	225,000	
Expenditures—health and welfare		
($4,500,000 × 5%)	225,000	
Cash		4,400,000

Due to other funds—Internal Service Fund—
      Communications and Technology Support
      Center
		100,000

Transaction JE02.49—During the year, the Fleet Management Unit (an Internal Service Fund) billed the General Fund $4,700,000 for services performed. The General Fund made payments of $4,650,000 during the year:

Accounts	Debit	Credit
Expenditures—general government		
($4,700,000 × 60%)	2,820,000	
Expenditures—public safety		
($4,700,000 × 20%)	940,000	
Expenditures—streets ($4,700,000 × 10%)	470,000	
Expenditures—recreation and parks		
($4,700,000 × 5%)	235,000	
Expenditures—health and welfare		
($4,700,000 × 5%)	235,000	
Cash		4,650,000
Due to other funds—Internal Service Fund— Fleet Management Unit		50,000

Transaction JE02.50—During the year the following Enterprise Funds made loans to the General Fund:

Centerville Utilities Authority	$2,000,000
Centerville Municipal Airport	400,000
Total	$2,400,000

Accounts	Debit	Credit
Cash	2,400,000	
Due to other funds—Enterprise Fund— Centerville Utilities Authority		2,000,000
Due to other funds—Enterprise Fund— Centerville Municipal Airport		400,000

After the transactions for the year are posted the year-end trial balance (June 30, 20X2) before the conversion for GASB-54, for the City's General Fund appears as follows:

Accounts	Adjusted Trial Balance	
	Debit	Credit
Cash	$10,045,000	
Interest receivable	37,800	
Dividends receivable	2,800	
Property taxes receivable	2,355,000	
Allowance for uncollectible property taxes		$ 2,000,000
Other receivables	27,000	
Investments in short-term instruments	1,325,000	
Investments in marketable debt securities	650,000	
Investments in marketable equity securities	3,799,600	
Inventories	17,000	
Other assets	5,200	
Accounts payable		676,800
Demand loan payable to bank		75,000
Deferred revenue—property taxes		300,000
Due to other funds—Internal Service Fund—Communications and Technology Support Center		170,000
Due to other funds—Internal Service Fund—Fleet Management Unit		72,000
Due to other funds—Enterprise Fund—Centerville Utilities Authority		2,000,000
Due to other funds—Enterprise Fund—Centerville Municipal Airport		400,000
Fund balance—reserved for inventories		17,000
Fund balance—reserved for encumbrances		25,000
Fund balance		12,733,000
Program revenues—charges for services (general government)		53,000
Program revenues—operating grants (recreation and parks)		2,000,000
Program revenues—charges for services (recreation and parks)		131,000
Program revenues—charges for services (health and welfare)		2,400
Program revenues—operating contributions (health and welfare)		50,000
Program revenues—charges for services (health and welfare)		150,000
Program revenues—capital grants (public safety)		500,000
Program revenues—charges for services (public safety)		201,200
General revenues—property taxes		87,600,000
General revenues—franchise taxes		1,300,000
General revenues—unrestricted grants		18,000,000
Miscellaneous revenue		4,800,000
Interest and investment revenue		239,400

Accounts	Adjusted Trial Balance	
	Debit	Credit
Change in fair value of investments		362,400
Expenditures—general government	33,824,098	
Expenditures—public safety	18,036,628	
Expenditures—streets	11,863,314	
Expenditures—recreation and parks	6,481,657	
Expenditures—health and welfare	8,076,657	
Expenditures—interest	317,659	
Expenditures—education (component unit)	32,000,000	
Other financing sources—capitalized leases		431,213
Transfers in—Internal Service Fund—Fleet Management Unit		50,000
Transfers out—Special Revenue Fund—Center City Special Services Fund	75,000	
Transfers out—Capital Projects Fund—Easely Street Bridge	1,000,000	
Transfers out—Capital Projects Fund—Bland Street Drainage Project	600,000	
Transfers out—Capital Projects Fund—West End Recreation Center Project	300,000	
Transfers out—Debt Service Fund—Senior Citizens' Center Bonds	1,300,000	
Transfers out—Debt Service Fund—Easely Street Bridge Bonds Bridge Bonds	220,000	
Transfers out—Debt Service Fund—Bland Street Drainage Bonds	1,100,000	
Transfers out—Debt Service Fund—West End Recreation Center Bonds	700,000	
Transfers out—Internal Service Fund— Communications and Technology Support Center	40,000	
Transfers out—Enterprise Fund—Centerville Toll Bridge	50,000	
Transfers out—Enterprise Fund—Centerville Parking Authority	90,000	
Totals	$134,339,413	$134,339,413

The worksheet that summarizes the foregoing journal entries for the General Fund for the year-end trial balance (on a modified accrual basis) is presented in Appendix 2A.

GASB-54 CONVERSION ENTRIES

The following balances are key for a proper GASB-54 conversion in the conversion year:

Fund balance—reserved for inventories	17,000
Fund balance—reserved for encumbrances	25,000
Fund balance	12,733,000

However, other information is needed to properly convert the beginning balances and the ending balances. This information may include the following:

Nonspendable Balances	Any balances of inventory and long term receivables
Restricted Balances	Any balances from bond proceeds, grants, and other external restrictions or due to enabling statutes
Committed Balances	Any passed budgets and other commitments made by the highest level of decision making.
Assigned Balances	Any long-term contracts signed or where management intends to fund a program.

In accordance with GASB-54 the beginning balances as of July 1, 20X1 were:

Fund balance—reserved for inventories	12,000
Fund balance—reserved for encumbrances	10,000
Fund balance	12,753,000

To reclass the beginning balances, the following entries are needed:

Transaction JE02.G54-1 (reclass) The reserve for inventory pursuant to GASB-54, par. 6 is nonspendable. Therefore the following reclass is needed:

Accounts	Debit	Credit
Fund balance—reserved for inventories	12,000	
Fund balance—non-spendable		12,000

Transaction JE02.G54-2 (reclass) Because there is a beginning balance reserved for encumbrances, because JE02.02 relieved the previous encumbrance for general government, the following reclass is needed, assuming that management has signed a contract that is unpaid at year end and the contract was not lapsed:

Accounts	Debit	Credit
Fund balance—reserved for encumbrances	10,000	
Fund balance—assigned—general government		10,000

Transaction JE02.G54-3 (reclass) Because there is a large beginning balance in fund balance, assuredly some of the balance is either committed or assigned or even restricted. Assume that the City passed a budget for fiscal year X1–X2 on June 18, 20X1, the following amounts would then be restricted, committed, or assigned from the June 30, 20X1 balance:

Restricted for Health and Welfare due to federal grant funding	$240,000
Restricted for Parks and Recreation due to federal grant funding	80,000
Restricted for Education (component unit) due to base level funding	55,000
Budgeted for Economic Stabilization due to budget holding back a percentage of revenues in reserve (committed)	210,000
Budgeted for Public Safety (committed)	110,000
Additional amounts budgeted for Education (component unit) above base level funding (committed)	50,000
Additional amounts budgeted for Health and Welfare (committed)	75,000
Additional summer personnel contracts signed by management for Parks and Recreation	50,000
Total Restrictions, Commitments and Assignments	$870,000

The remainder is unassigned; therefore the following needs to be reclassed as of July 1, 20X1:

Accounts	Debit	Credit
Fund balance	12,753,000	
Fund balance—Restricted—Health and Welfare		240,000
Fund balance—Restricted—Parks and Recreation		80,000
Fund balance—Restricted—Education (component unit)		55,000
Fund balance—Committed—Economic Stabilization		210,000
Fund balance—Committed—Public Safety		110,000
Fund balance—Committed—Education (component unit)		50,000
Fund balance—Committed—Health and Welfare		75,000
Fund balance—Assigned—Parks and Recreation		50,000
Fund balance—Unassigned		11,833,000

Therefore, the adjusted beginning balance after these entries in accordance with GASB-54 would be as follows:

Accounts	Trial Balance Debit	Trial Balance Credit
Cash	$15,200,000	
Interest receivable	20,000	
Property taxes receivable	1,400,000	
Allowance for uncollectible property taxes		$1,000,000
Investments in marketable debt securities	300,000	
Investments in marketable equity securities	2,200,000	
Interest in equity investment pool	1,800,000	
Interest in short-term fixed income investment pool	1,500,000	
Inventories	12,000	
Accounts payable		8,320,000
Deferred revenue—property taxes		245,000
Due to other funds—Internal Service Fund—Communications and Technology Support Center		70,000
Due to other funds—Internal Service Fund—Fleet Management Unit		22,000
Fund balance—nonspendable		12,000
Fund balance—Restricted—Health and Welfare		240,000
Fund balance—Restricted—Parks and Recreation		80,000
Fund balance—Restricted—Education (component unit)		55,000
Fund balance—Committed—Economic Stabilization		210,000
Fund balance—Committed—Public Safety		110,000
Fund balance—Committed—Education (component unit)		50,000
Fund balance—Committed—Health and Welfare		75,000

	Trial Balance	
Accounts	**Debit**	**Credit**
Fund balance—Assigned—Parks and Recreation		50,000
Fund balance—Assigned—General Government		10,000
Fund balance—Unassigned		11,833,000
Totals	$22,432,000	$22,432,000

Adjustments of the main journal entries would be as follows:

JE02.1 The debit to fund balance—reserve for encumbrances would be replaced by a debit to fund balance—assigned—general government. The credit to fund balance would be replaced by a credit to fund balance—unassigned.

As spending occurs throughout the year and encumbrances are established, the credits to the various assigned, committed, and restricted fund balances would be debited to establish encumbrances in the particular order of spending that the City established by policy. Once the various fund balances are debited, encumbrances and reserves for encumbrances would be established. Ultimately, it is likely that most of the restricted, committed, and assigned balances would be spent, and if they were unspent at the end of the year, they would close as part of the closing process to fund balance—unassigned. The recording of new restrictions, commitments, and assignments would occur with the budget passage, external restriction establishment, or enabling legislation process. Note that the fund balance committed for economic stabilization in this example was not spent; it was closed and reestablished in the GASB-54 journal entry below.

JE02.41 The debit to fund balance would be reflected as a debit to fund balance unassigned and the credit to fund balance—reserved for inventories would be reflected as a credit to fund balance—nonspendable for $5,000

JE02.43 (Adjustment) The fund balance debit for $25,000 would be reflected as a debit to fund balance—unassigned and the credit to fund balance—reserve for encumbrances because there is no detail behind the purchase; so. for the general government it would be reflected as a fund balance assigned—general government credit for $25,000.

Transaction JE02.G54-4 At the end of the year, if a budget is passed, then various restrictions, commitments, and assignments may occur. In this case, we are assuming that the City established the 20X3 budget before year end at a 5% across-the-board increase. Therefore the following restrictions, commitments, and assignments need to occur, including a new fund balance assignment for public safety for $20,500:

Restricted for Health and Welfare due to federal grant funding	$252,000
Restricted for Parks and Recreation due to federal grant funding	84,000
Restricted for Education (component unit) due to base level funding	57,750
Budgeted for Economic Stabilization due to budget holding back a percentage of revenues in reserve (committed) (reestablished)	210,000
Budgeted for Public Safety (committed)	115,500

Additional amounts budgeted for Education (component unit) above base level funding (committed)	52,500
Additional amounts budgeted for Health and Welfare (committed)	78,750
Additional summer personnel contracts signed by management for Parks and Recreation	52,500
Additional overtime costs anticipated and assigned by management to public safety	20,500
Total Restrictions, Commitments, and Assignments	$923,500

Accounts	Debit	Credit
Fund balance-unassigned	923,500	
Fund balance—Restricted—Health and Welfare		252,000
Fund balance—Restricted—Parks and Recreation		84,000
Fund balance—Restricted—Education (component unit)		57,750
Fund balance—Committed—Economic Stabilization		210,000
Fund balance—Committed—Public Safety		115,500
Fund balance—Committed—Education (component unit)		52,500
Fund balance—Committed—Health and Welfare		78,750
Fund balance—Assigned—Parks and Recreation		52,500
Fund balance—Assigned—Public Safety		20,500

Therefore, once these adjustments are made, the fund balance portion of the closing (June 30, 20X2) trial balance for the general fund in accordance with GASB-54 should be as follows:

FUND BALANCE SECTION ONLY	PARTIAL Trial Balance	
Accounts	Debit	Credit
Fund balance—nonspendable—inventories		17,000
Fund balance—Restricted—Health and Welfare		252,000
Fund balance—Restricted—Parks and Recreation		84,000
Fund balance—Restricted—Education (component unit)		57,750
Fund balance—Committed—Economic Stabilization		210,000
Fund balance—Committed—Public Safety		115,500
Fund balance—Committed—Education (component unit)		52,500
Fund balance—Committed—Health and Welfare		78,750
Fund balance—Assigned—General Government		25,000
Fund balance—Assigned—Parks and Recreation		52,500

FUND BALANCE SECTION ONLY	PARTIAL Trial Balance	
Accounts	Debit	Credit
Fund balance—Assigned—Public Safety		20,500
Fund balance—Unassigned		11,809,500

FUND FINANCIAL STATEMENTS

At the fund financial statement level, a governmental fund must prepare a statement of revenues, expenditures, and changes in fund balances and a balance sheet. Based on the adjusted trial balances created above, the following financial statements reflect the balances and activities of the General Fund (Appendix 2B).

NCGA-1 illustrates three distinct formats that can be used to prepare the statement of revenues, expenditures, and changes in fund balances for governmental funds; however, GASB-34 eliminated two of the options and only the format illustrated below can be used (GASB-34, par. 86).

The formatting of the balance sheet at the fund financial statement level was not changed by GASB-34.

General Fund
Statement of Revenues, Expenditures, and
Changes in Fund Balances
June 30, 20X2

REVENUES

Property taxes	$ 87,600,000
Franchise taxes	1,300,000
Intergovernmental grants	20,500,000
Charges for services	537,600
Contributions	50,000
Interest and investment revenue	239,400
Change in fair value of investments	362,400
Total revenues	110,589,400

EXPENDITURES

Current:

General government	33,824,098
Public safety	18,036,628
Streets	11,863,314
Recreation and parks	6,481,657
Health and welfare	8,076,657
Education (component unit)	32,000,000
Interest	317,659
Total expenditures	110,600,013
Excess (deficiency) of revenues over expenditures	(10,613)

OTHER FINANCING SOURCES (USES):

Disposition of capital assets	4,800,000
Execution of capital leases	431,213
Transfers in	50,000
Transfers out	(5,475,000)
Total other financing sources and uses	(193,787)
Net change in fund balances	(204,400)
Fund balances—beginning	12,775,000
Fund balances—ending	$12,570,600

PRACTICE ALERT: GASB-54 does not require the presentation of deseg-regated fund balances in the statement of revenues, expenditures, and changes in fund balances. To do so would not be GAAP and, furthermore, would probably cause separate columns for separate classes of fund balances similar to not-for-profit financial statements. All surplus or deficit closes to Fund balance—unassigned.

General Fund
Balance Sheet
June 30, 20X2

ASSETS

Cash	$10,045,000
Property taxes receivable (net)	355,000
Other receivables	67,600
Investments	5,774,600
Inventories	17,000
Other assets	5,200
Total assets	$16,264,400

LIABILITIES AND FUND BALANCES

Liabilities:

Accounts payable	$ 676,800
Demand loans payable	75,000
Due to other funds	2,642,000
Deferred revenue	300,000
Total liabilities	3,693,800

Fund Balances:

Nonspendable—inventories	17,000
Fund balance—Restricted—Health and Welfare	252,000
Fund balance—Restricted—Parks and Recreation	84,000
Fund balance—Restricted—Education (component unit)	57,750
Fund balance—Committed—Economic Stabilization	210,000
Fund balance—Committed—Public Safety	115,500

LIABILITIES AND FUND BALANCES

Fund balance—Committed—Education (component unit)	52,500
Fund balance—Committed—Health and Welfare	78,750
Fund balance—Assigned—General Government	25,000
Fund balance—Assigned—Parks and Recreation	52,500
Fund balance—Assigned—Public Safety	20,500
Fund balance—Unassigned	11,605,100
Total Fund balances	12,570,600
Total liabilities and fund balances	$16,264,400

The General Fund financial statements are not reported separately in the governmental entity's financial report, but they are used in Chapter 13, "Developing Information for Fund Financial Statements."

CONVERTING TO GOVERNMENT-WIDE FINANCIAL STATEMENTS

As noted earlier, government-wide financial statements are reported on the accrual basis of accounting. Generally, most governments will work from their governmental fund financial statements trial balances (which are on a modified accrual basis), and through the use of worksheet entries convert to accrual based financial statements. In order to convert the transactions that were recorded in the General Fund from a modified accrual basis to an accrual basis, the following worksheet entries are made.

GASB-34 introduced the concept of accrual based financial statements for governmental activities. For most governmental entities, the conversion of the General Fund from a modified accrual basis to an accrual basis is an important part of developing government-wide financial statements. The focus of government-wide financial statements is on the overall financial position and activities of the government as a whole. These financial statements are constructed around the concept of a primary government as defined by GASB-14 (The Financial Reporting Entity) and therefore encompass the primary government and its component units except for fiduciary funds of the primary government and component units that are fiduciary in nature (GASB-34, par. 13).

PRACTICE ALERT: GASB-61 (The Financial Reporting Entity: Omnibus, an amendment of GASB Statements No. 14 and No. 34), released in December of 2010, modifies certain requirements for inclusion of component units in the financial reporting entity. For organizations that previously were required to be included as component units by meeting GASB-14's (as amended by GASB-39) fiscal dependency criterion, a financial benefit or burden relationship would also need to be present between the primary government and that organization for it to be included in the reporting entity as a component unit. Further, for organizations that do not meet the financial accountability criteria for inclusion as component units but that, nevertheless, should be included because the primary government's management determines that it would be misleading to exclude them, GASB-61 clarifies the manner in which that determination should be made and the types of relationships that generally should be considered in making the determination. GASB-61 also amends the criteria for reporting component units as if they were part of the primary government (that is, blending) in certain circumstances. Finally, GASB-61 also clarifies the reporting of equity interests in legally separate organizations. It requires a primary government to report its equity interest in a component unit as an asset. A more thorough discussion of GASB-61's changes can be founds in CCH's *Governmental GAAP Guide*.

Current Transactions

Worksheet entries to convert from the modified accrual basis to the accrual basis are made for the following transactions that occurred during the year:

- Capital lease (Worksheet Entries JE02.51A and JE02.51B)
- Unrestricted operating grant (Worksheet Entry JE02.52)
- Capital assets acquired (Worksheet Entries JE02.53A, JE02.53B, JE02.53D, and JE02.53C)
- Capital assets sold (Worksheet Entry JE02.54)
- Depreciation expense (Worksheet Entry JE02.55)
- Extraordinary item (Worksheet Entry JE02.56)
- Accrual for claims/assessments and compensated absences (Worksheet Entry JE02.57A, JE02.57B, and JE02.57C)
- Property tax revenue accrual (Worksheet Entry JE02.58)
- Program revenue accruals (Worksheet Entry JE02.59)

PRACTICE ALERT: GASB-54 does not affect the conversion entries to convert from the modified accrual to the full accrual basis of accounting except that some governments may want to show the five elements of fund balance rather than starting the conversion entries with the total fund balance.

Capital Lease (Worksheet Entries JE02.51A and JE02.51B)

Rather than purchase a capital asset directly from a vendor, a governmental entity may lease the item. If the agreement is considered a capitalized lease as defined in NCGA-5 (Accounting and Financial Reporting Principles for Lease Agreements of State and Local Governments), the transaction is accounted for in a governmental fund as both an issuance of debt and a capital expenditure. Thus, in order to convert the fund financial statements from a modified accrual basis to an accrual basis for the preparation of the government-wide financial statements, the expenditure must be capitalized, any related depreciation expense must be recorded, and the debt must be recognized along with the accrual of any related interest expense.

As shown in Transaction JE02.08, the City entered into a lease on August 1, 20X0. In order to convert from a modified accrual basis to an accrual basis, the following worksheet entries are made at the end of the year:

JE02.51A	Other financing sources—capitalized leases	431,213	
	Expenditures—general government		431,213
	(To reverse other financing source and expenditure)		
	Leased capital assets	431,213	
	Lease obligation payable		431,213
	(To record capital asset and related obligation)		
	Lease obligation payable	100,000	
	Expenditures—general government		100,000
	(To record initial payment as a reduction to the lease obligation rather than an expenditure)		
	Expenses—general government	79,058	
	Accumulated depreciation—leased capital assets ($431,213 × 1/5 × 11/12)		79,058
	(To record depreciation on the capital lease)		
	Interest expense	24,290	
	Interest payable ($26,497 × 11/12)—(see the original amortization schedule)		24,290
	(To accrue interest on the lease obligation)		

If in the previous year interest expense was also accrued, the previous accrual would have to be omitted from the current year's statement of activities (debiting net assets and crediting interest expense) because the interest would have been recorded in the current year under the modified accrual basis of accounting. In this illustration it is assumed no accrual was made in the previous year.

Also in Transaction JE02.08, a $1,500,000 lease payment was made for capital leases executed in a previous year. In order to convert this payment from a modified accrual basis to an accrual basis, the following worksheet entries are made at the end of the year:

JE02.51B	Lease obligation payable (see the original amortization schedule)	1,188,141	
	Expenditures—general government		712,885
	Expenditures—public safety		237,628
	Expenditures—streets		118,814
	Expenditures—recreation and parks		59,407
	Expenditures—health and welfare		59,407
	(To record lease payments as a reduction to the principal obligation and an increase to interest expense rather than as an expenditure)		

Unrestricted Operating Grant (Worksheet Entry JE02.52)

GASB-33 (Accounting and Financial Reporting for Nonexchange Transactions) establishes revenue recognition criteria for nonexchange transactions, including operating grants (voluntary nonexchange transactions). As noted in Transaction JE02.09, the fourth installment ($6,000,000) of the unrestricted operating grant is not recorded as revenue under the modified accrual basis but is considered revenue under the accrual basis of accounting. Thus, the following worksheet entry is made:

Accounts	Debit	Credit
JE02.52 Intergovernmental grants receivable	6,000,000	
General revenues—unrestricted grants		6,000,000
(To accrue grant revenue that was not subject to accrual under the modified accrual method)		

PRACTICE POINT: If in the previous year grant revenue was also accrued, the previous accrual would have to be omitted from the current year's statement of activities (by debiting revenue and crediting net assets) because it would have been recorded in the current year under the modified accrual basis of accounting. In this illustration it is assumed no accrual was made in the previous year.

PRACTICE ALERT: Under the provisions of GASB-54, if the grant was revenue sharing from one level of government to another, then, indeed, the related fund balance would be unrestricted. However, if there were restrictive terms on the grant award, the portion of the fund balance available for expenditure in the general fund would be restricted.

GASB-33 establishes accounting standards for reporting subsequent contravention of eligibility requirements or purpose restrictions for intergovernmental grants. Situations covered by GASB-33 relate to circumstances whereby subsequent events indicate that resources will not be transferred in a manner originally anticipated under a grant or that resources previously transferred will have to be returned. This circumstance usually arises because (1) eligibility requirements related to a government-mandated transaction or a voluntary nonexchange transaction are no longer being satisfied or (2) the recipient will not satisfy a purpose restriction within the time period specified by the intergovernmental grant. The AICPA's *State and Local Governments—Audit and Accounting Guide* states that a similar situation arises when grant revenues are subject to a grant audit and the possibility of an adjustment has arisen. Under this development, the recipient governmental entity should consider whether a loss contingency arises based on the standards established by FAS-5 (Accounting for Contingencies) to determine whether a liability should be reported (or netted against a related receivable) or a note disclosure should be made.

PRACTICE ALERT: GASB-62 (Codification of Accounting and Financial Reporting Guidance Contained in Pre-November 30, 1989 FASB and AICPA Pronouncements) contains the FAS-5 contingency standards. Upon implementation for periods beginning after December 15, 2011, reference would be made to GASB-62.

Capital Assets Acquired (Worksheet Entries JE02.53A, JE02.53B, JE02.53D, and JE02.53C)

When capital assets are acquired by a governmental entity, payments related to acquisitions are recorded as expenditures at the fund statement level. However, in order to convert the fund financial statements from a modified accrual basis to an accrual basis for the preparation of the government-wide financial statements, the expenditure must be capitalized and any related depreciation expense must be recorded. Based on an analysis of Transactions JE02.17, JE02.21, and JE02.26, the following worksheet entries are made.

A governmental entity may establish a policy whereby capital acquisitions that are less than an established amount are accounted for as an expense rather than capitalized. The GASB's *Comprehensive Implementation Guide* addresses the question of whether the threshold amount applies to the purchase of a group of assets (such as the acquisition of 100 computers) as well as to an individual asset (such as the acquisition of a single computer). There is no pronouncement that addresses this issue; however, the general rule of materiality should apply. That is, it is acceptable to expense capital assets acquired as a group as long as the financial statements are not materially misstated.

In order to compute depreciation expense on assets, a governmental entity may use "any established depreciation method." There is no list of acceptable depreciation methods. In order for a depreciation method to be acceptable, it must meet the general conditions of being both "systematic" and "rational." Under the composite depreciation method, similar (such as all buildings) or dissimilar assets (such as roads, bridges, tunnels, and so forth) are combined in order to form a single historical cost basis for computing depreciation and accounting for the disposition of capital assets. The composite depreciation method, which is illustrated in GASB-34 in the context of infrastructure assets, can also be used to compute depreciation expense for other capital assets; however, the method should not be applied across classes of assets.

Analysis of vehicles purchased on December 1, 20X1 (Transaction JE02.17)

	Accounts	Debits	Credits
JE02.53A	Vehicles	900,000	
	Expenditures—general government		100,000
	Expenditures—public safety		300,000
	Expenditures—streets		400,000
	Expenditures—recreation and parks		100,000
	(To capitalize payments for capital assets that were accounted for as expenditures)		
JE02.53B	Expenses—general government ($175,000 × 1/9)	19,445	
	Expenses—public safety ($175,000 × 3/9)	58,333	
	Expenses—streets ($175,000 × 4/9)	77,778	
	Expenses—recreation and parks ($175,000 × 1/9)	19,444	
	Accumulated depreciation—vehicles ($900,000 × 1/3 × 7/12)		175,000

Accounts	Debits	Credits
(To record depreciation expense)		
Analysis of equipment purchased (Transaction JE02.21)		
JE02.53D Equipment	4,700,000	
Expenditures—general government		2,000,000
Expenditures—public safety		1,300,000
Expenditures—streets		700,000
Expenditures—recreation and parks		500,000
Expenditures—health and welfare		200,000
(To capitalize payments for capital assets that were accounted for as expenditures)		
Expenses—general government (See details of Transaction JE02.21)	170,000	
Expenses—public safety	110,000	
Expenses—streets	95,000	
Expenses—recreation and parks	40,000	
Expenses—health and welfare	22,000	
Accumulated depreciation—equipment		437,000
(To record depreciation expense)		
Analysis of vehicles purchased on May 1, 20X2 (Transaction JE02.26)		
JE02.53C Vehicles	520,000	
Expenditures—public safety		520,000
(To capitalize payments for capital assets that were accounted for as expenditures)		
Expenses—public safety	28,889	
Accumulated depreciation—vehicles ($520,000 $\times$ 1/3 $\times$ 2/12)		28,889
(To record depreciation expense)		

Capital Assets Sold (Worksheet Entry JE02.54)

As described in Transaction JE02.21, the City sold a variety of capital assets during the year. Under the modified accrual basis only the cash proceeds ($4,800,000) are recorded as other financing sources—disposition of capital assets. In order to convert to the accrual basis, the following worksheet entry is made:

Accounts	Debits	Credits
JE02.54 Accumulated depreciation—buildings	2,000,000	
Accumulated depreciation—equipment	1,000,000	
Accumulated depreciation—vehicles	3,000,000	
Other financing sources—disposition of capital assets	4,800,000	
Expenses—general government (loss on sale of assets) ($500,000 + $200,000)	700,000	
Expenses—public safety (loss on sale of assets)	100,000	
Buildings		7,000,000
Equipment		1,400,000

Vehicles		3,200,000

(To remove the net book value and record the
related gain/loss on the sale of capital assets
for the year)

Depreciation Expense (Worksheet Entry JE02.55)

In addition, to the depreciation expense recorded in the previous worksheet entries, depreciation expense on capital assets acquired in previous years is as follows:

Buildings	$ 8,000,000
Equipment	1,500,000
Vehicles	22,000,000
Leased capital assets	1,200,000
Infrastructure assets	700,000
Total	$33,400,000

In this example all of the depreciation related to infrastructure assets is allocated to streets activities.

In order to record depreciation expense in the government-wide financial statements, the following entry is made:

	Accounts	Debits	Credits
JE02.55	Expenses—general government ($32,700,000 × 60%)	19,620,000	
	Expenses—public safety ($32,700,000 × 20%)	6,540,000	
	Expenses—streets ($32,700,000 × 10%) + $700,000	3,970,000	
	Expenses—recreation and parks ($32,700,000 × 5%)	1,635,000	
	Expenses—health and welfare ($32,700,000 × 5%)	1,635,000	
	Accumulated depreciation—buildings		8,000,000
	Accumulated depreciation—equipment		1,500,000
	Accumulated depreciation—vehicles		22,000,000
	Accumulated depreciation—leased capital assets		1,200,000
	Accumulated depreciation—infrastructure assets		700,000
	(To record depreciation expense)		

The GASB's *Comprehensive Implementation Guide* points out that the estimated useful life of an asset is the period of time that the governmental entity believes the asset will be used in its activities. The GASB's *Guide* notes that factors relevant to making this determination include the following: (1) The asset's present state of condition, (2) how the asset will be used, (3) maintenance policy, and (4) relevant service and technology demands. The GASB's *Guide* notes that the estimated useful life relates to the expected experience of the governmental entity. The experience of other governmental entities is relevant only if the expected experience is anticipated to be the same. The GASB's *Guide* notes that there is not a generally accepted schedule of useful lives that can be used to determine depreciation expense for governmental entities. Although informal schedules or guidance may be provided by professional organizations, it is the responsibility of management to determine the estimated useful lives of capital assets.

The Internal Revenue Service's schedule of lives for property classes related to the Modified Accelerated Cost Recovery System is not based on the actual estimated economic lives of assets. The GASB's *Guide* suggests that the following be used to estimate the useful lives of depreciable assets: (1) General guidelines obtained from professional or industry organizations, (2) information for comparable assets of other governments, and (3) internal information. These sources should be considered starting points and modified based on the specific characteristics and expected use of the newly acquired capital asset. The GASB's *Guide* notes that in general, the lives of capital assets should be reviewed each year; however, from a practical point of view a governmental entity reviews only those lives that may have changed because some of the following events occurred during the current year: (1) Property replacement policies changed, (2) preventive maintenance policies changed, and (3) unexpected technological changes occurred. If a governmental entity concludes that the life of a capital asset should be changed, APB-20 (Accounting Changes) requires that its undepreciated cost (less the revised residual value) be allocated over the remaining life of the asset. This is a change in an accounting estimate.

GAAP does not require that infrastructure assets that are part of a network or subsystem of a network (referred to as eligible infrastructure assets) be depreciated if certain conditions relating to the asset management system and the documentation of the condition level of the infrastructure are met. The illustration in this book assumes that the governmental entity depreciates all of its infrastructure assets (GASB-34, par. 23).

Extraordinary Item (Worksheet Entry JE02.56)

GASB-34 incorporates the definition of extraordinary items (unusual in nature and infrequent in occurrence) as provided in APB-30 (Reporting the Results of Operations—Reporting the Effects of Disposal of a Segment of a Business, and Extraordinary, Unusual and Infrequently Occurring Events and Transactions).

PRACTICE ALERT: GASB-62 contains the APB-30 standards applicable to governments. Upon implementation for periods beginning after December 15, 2011, reference would be made to GASB-62.

The donation of land to the City (Transaction JE02.21) by the state is considered by the City to be an extraordinary item and is recorded on the accrual basis as follows:

	Accounts	Debits	Credits
JE02.56	Land	20,000,000	
	Extraordinary item—donation of land by the state		20,000,000
	(To record the receipt of land as an extraordinary item)		

Accrual for Claims/Assessments and Compensated Absences (Worksheet Entries JE02.57A, JE02.57B, and JE02.57C)

The basic guidance for determining when a governmental fund should accrue an expenditure/liability is found in NCGA-1 (par. 70), which states that "most expenditures and transfers out are measurable and should be recorded when the related liability is incurred." GASBI-6 (Recognition and Measurement of Certain Liabilities and Expenditures in Governmental Fund Financial Statements) expands on this general guidance by noting the following:

> Governmental fund liabilities and expenditures that should be accrued include liabilities that, once incurred, normally are paid in a timely manner and in full from current financial resources—for example, salaries, professional services, supplies, utilities, and travel.

These transactions give rise to fund liabilities that are considered mature liabilities because they are "normally due and payable in full when incurred."

Based on the standards established by GASBI-6 (Recognition and Measurement of Certain Liabilities and Expenditures in Governmental Fund Financial Statements)expenditures should continue to be recorded on an accrual basis except with respect to the expenditures identified in the Interpretation. Two of the exceptions identified in GASBI-6 are the accounting for compensated absences and loss contingencies.

As described in Transactions (Adjustments) JE02.36 and JE02.37, a claim of $300,000 and compensated absences of $220,000 must be accrued as follows:

Analysis of legal claims			
JE02.57A	Expenses—public safety	300,000	
	Claims payable		300,000
	(To accrue claims expense at year end)		

Analysis of compensated absences			
	Accounts	Debits	Credits
	Expenses—general government (60% × $220,000)	132,000	
	Expenses—public safety (20%)	44,000	
	Expenses—streets (10%)	22,000	
	Expenses—recreation and parks (5%)	11,000	
	Expenses—health and welfare (5%)	11,000	
	Compensated absences payable		220,000
	(To accrue compensated absences expense at year end)		

In addition, a claim of $400,000 was paid during the year (Transaction JE02.36) and charged to public safety expenditures. On an accrual basis that amount is charged to the claims payable account, not the expenditures account, as follows:

Accounts	Debit	Credit
JE02.57B Claims payable	400,000	
Expenditures—public safety		400,000
(To record payments of claims during the year as a reduction to the related obligation rather than as an expenditure)		

Also, compensated absences of $60,000 were paid during the year (Transaction JE02.37) and charged to various activities. On an accrual basis, that amount is charged to the compensated absences payable account as follows:

Accounts	Debits	Credits
JE02.57C Compensated absences payable	60,000	
Expenditures—general government ($60,000 × 60%)		36,000
Expenditures—public safety ($60,000 × 20%)		12,000
Expenditures—streets ($60,000 × 10%)		6,000
Expenditures—recreation and parks ($60,000 × 5%)		3,000
Expenditures—health and welfare ($60,000 × 5%)		3,000
(To record payments of compensated absences during the year as a reduction to the related obligation rather than as an expenditure)		

Like commercial enterprises, governmental entities are exposed to a variety of risks that can result in losses. GASB-10 (Accounting and Financial Reporting for Risk Financing and Related Insurance Issues) establishes the following guidelines to determine when claims and judgments are considered loss contingencies that should be accrued: (1) On the basis of information available before the financial statements are issued, it is probable (likely to occur) that an asset has been impaired or a liability has been incurred as of the date of the financial statements and (2) the loss can be reasonably estimated. The accrual of a loss in a current period implies that an event will occur in a subsequent period that will substantiate the recognition of the accrual. FAS-5 (Accounting for Contingencies) (after December 15, 2011, GASB-62,) establishes the broad principles that are the basis for the guidance established in GASB-10. Although there are innumerable examples of loss contingencies for governmental entities, the AICPA's *State and Local Governments—Audit and Accounting Guide* lists the following as examples of loss contingencies that should be evaluated for possible accrual: (1) Contractual actions (such as claims for delays or inadequate specifications on contracts), (2) guarantees of other entities' debt, (3) unemployment compensation claims, (4) property tax appeals, (5) tax refund claims, and (6) refunds of nonexchange revenues when the recipient government does not satisfy a provider's requirements. These last three items should be evaluated in the context of GASB-33 (Accounting and Financial Reporting for Nonexchange Transactions).

Arbitrage involves the simultaneous purchase and sale of the same or essentially the same securities with the object of making a profit on the spread between two markets. In the context of governmental finance, arbitrage describes the strategy of issuing tax-exempt debt and investing the proceeds in debt securities that have a higher rate of return; however, state and local governments are subject to rules and regulations established by the Internal Revenue Code and the U.S. Treasury that, under certain conditions, create an arbitrage rebate to be paid to the federal government. In general, the state or local government should use the guidance established in GAAP to determine whether an arbitrage liability must be recognized. The AICPA's *State and Local Governments—Audit and Accounting Guide* requires that the arbitrage analysis be made annually "to determine whether it is material and thus should be reported in the financial statements."

Property Tax Revenue Accrual (Worksheet Entry JE02.58)

As noted in the analysis that supports Transaction JE02.40 (Adjustment), an additional amount ($1,400,000) of property taxes is earned based on accrual accounting. In order to record this amount the following worksheet entry is made:

JE02.58	Property taxes receivable	1,400,000	
	General revenues—property taxes		1,400,000
	(To accrue property taxes that were not subject to accrual under the modified accrual basis)		

OBSERVATION: If in the previous year property tax revenue was also accrued, the previous year's accrual would have to be omitted from the current year's statement of activities (by debiting revenue and crediting net assets) because it would have been recorded in the current year under the modified accrual basis of accounting. In this illustration, for simplicity, it is assumed no accrual was made in the previous year.

Program Revenue Accruals (Worksheet Entry JE02.59)

As explained in Transaction JE02.42 (Adjustment), certain charges, fees, and permits were not accrued under the modified accrual basis of accounting. The following worksheet entry is needed to recognize those revenue items that should be accrued:

JE02.59	Other receivables ($21,000 × 40%)	8,400	
	Program revenues—charges for services (recreation and parks) ($10,000 × 40%)		4,000
	Program revenues—charges for services (public safety) ($2,000 × 40%)		800
	Program revenues—charges for services (health and welfare) ($4,000 × 40%)		1,600

Program revenues—charges for services (general government) ($5,000 × 40%)	2,000
(To accrue revenue related to service charges that were not subject to accrual under the modified accrual basis)	

PRACTICE POINT: If in the previous year program revenue was also accrued, the previous year's accrual would have to be omitted from the current year's statement of activities (by debiting revenue and crediting net assets) as explained above.

Beginning of Year Balances

Worksheet entries to convert from the modified accrual basis to the accrual basis are made for the following accounts based on their beginning of the year balances:

- Capital assets (Worksheet Entry JE02.60)
- Long-term debt (Worksheet Entry JE02.61)
- Compensated absences and claims/judgements (Worksheet Entry JE02.62)

Capital Assets (Worksheet Entry JE02.60)

The following capital assets were held by the City at the beginning of the year:

	Cost	Accumulated Depreciation
Land and improvements	$105,000,000	
Construction in progress	2,050,000	
Buildings	220,000,000	$75,000,000
Equipment	19,000,000	7,000,000
Vehicles	75,000,000	39,000,000
Leased capital assets	7,818,540	2,500,000
Infrastructure assets	20,000,000	12,000,000

To convert the fund financial statements to an accrual basis, the following worksheet entry is made:

	Accounts	Debits	Credits
JE02.60	Land and improvements	105,000,000	
	Construction in progress	2,050,000	
	Buildings	220,000,000	
	Equipment	19,000,000	
	Vehicles	75,000,000	
	Leased capital assets	7,818,540	
	Infrastructure assets	20,000,000	
	Accumulated depreciation—buildings		75,000,000
	Accumulated depreciation—equipment		7,000,000

Accounts	Debits	Credits
Accumulated depreciation—vehicles		39,000,000
Accumulated depreciation—leased capital assets		2,500,000
Accumulated depreciation—infrastructure assets		12,000,000
Net assets		313,368,540
(To record capital assets held at the beginning of the year)		

The GASB's *Comprehensive Implementation Guide* notes that construction in progress is a capital asset and should be reported in the statement of net assets with other assets that are not being depreciated (such as land).

The GASB's *Guide* points out that land improvements must be evaluated to determine whether they are subject to depreciation. That is, costs that are permanent in nature are not subject to depreciation. For example, grading cost incurred to prepare a site for the construction of a building is generally considered a permanent improvement and would be reported as part of the carrying value (historical cost) of the land, and therefore would not be depreciated. Costs that are not permanent should be depreciated. For example, paving a parking lot is not permanent and would be reported as a land improvement subject to depreciation.

Long-Term Debt (Worksheet Entry JE02.61)

As shown in Transaction JE02.08, the City executed a capital lease in a previous year and the balance according to the amortization schedule at the beginning of the year is $5,197,652. To convert this lease to an accrual amount as of the beginning of the year, the following entry is made:

JE02.61

	Debits	Credits
Net assets	5,197,652	
Lease obligations payable		5,197,652
(To record a capital lease outstanding at the beginning of the year)		

Other long-term liabilities as of the beginning of the year are accrued in Chapter 4, "Capital Projects Funds," and Chapter 5, "Debt Service Funds."

Compensated Absences and Claims/Judgments (Worksheet Entry JE02.62)

Liabilities not reported in the fund financial statements that were related to compensated absences and claims/judgements had beginning balances of $4,500,000 and $2,000,000, respectively To convert the fund financial statements to an accrual basis for these liabilities the following worksheet entry is made:

	Accounts	Debits	Credits
JE02.62	Net Assets	6,500,000	
	Compensated absences payable		4,500,000

Accounts	Debits	Credits
Claims and judgements payable		2,000,000
(To record compensated absences and claims and judgements outstanding at the beginning of the year)		

The GASB's *Comprehensive Implementation Guide* states that a governmental entity must make an estimate of compensated absences that may be paid within one year based on factors such as (1) historical experience, (2) budgeted amounts, and (3) personnel policies concerning the length of accumulation.

The GASB's *Comprehensive Implementation Guide* states that when a governmental entity accounts for its risk financing activities in its General Fund (modified accrual based accounting) the liability/expense related to claims should be reported on an accrual basis as defined in GASB-10 (Accounting and Financial Reporting for Risk Financing and Related Insurance Issues), paragraphs 53-57, in the government-wide financial statements.

After the foregoing worksheet entries are prepared, the adjusted trial balances (on an accrual basis) for the General Fund would appear as follows as of June 30, 20X2:

Accounts	Adjusted Trial Balance Debit	Adjusted Trial Balance Credit
Cash	$ 10,045,000	
Property taxes receivable (net)	1,755,000	
Other receivables	76,000	
Investments	5,774,600	
Inventories	17,000	
Other Assets	5,200	
Intergovernmental grants receivable	6,000,000	
Land and improvements	125,000,000	
Construction in progress	2,050,000	
Buildings	213,000,000	
Equipment	22,300,000	
Vehicles	73,220,000	
Leased capital assets	8,249,753	
Infrastructure assets	20,000,000	
Accumulated depreciation—buildings		$ 81,000,000
Accumulated depreciation—equipment		7,937,000
Accumulated depreciation—vehicles		58,203,889
Accumulated depreciation—leased capital assets		3,779,058
Accumulated depreciation—infrastructure assets		12,700,000
Accounts payable		676,800
Demand loan payable to bank		75,000
Interest payable		24,290
Due to other funds		2,642,000
Deferred revenue		300,000

Accounts	Adjusted Trial Balance	
	Debit	Credit
Claims payable		1,900,000
Compensated absences payable		4,660,000
Lease obligation payable		4,340,724
Net assets		314,445,888
General revenue—property taxes		89,000,000
Franchise taxes		1,300,000
Intergovernmental grants—General revenues—unrestricted grants		26,500,000
Program revenues/charges for services (general government)		55,000
Program revenues/charges for services (recreations and parks)		135,000
Program revenues/charges for services (public safety)		202,000
Program revenues/charges for services (health and welfare)		4,000
Program revenues/charges for services (streets)		150,000
Contributions		50,000
Interest and investment revenue		239,400
Other financing sources—disposition of capital assets		0
Change in fair value of investments		362,400
General government expenditures/expenses	51,164,503	
Public safety expenditures/expenses	22,448,222	
Streets expenditures/expenses	14,803,278	
Recreation and parks expenditures/expenses	7,524,694	
Health and welfare expenditures/expenses	9,482,250	
Interest expense	341,949	
Education (component unit)	32,000,000	
Extraordinary item—donation of land by the state		20,000,000
Execution of capital leases		
Transfers in		50,000
Transfers out	5,475,000	
Total	$630,732,449	$630,732,449

The worksheet to convert from a modified accrual basis to an accrual basis is presented in Appendix 2C. (Appendix 2D is the adjusted trial balance for the General Fund.) This accrual based trial balance for the General Fund is used in Chapter 14, "Developing Information for Government-Wide Financial Statements," in order to prepare the government-wide financial statements.

APPENDIX 2A: WORKSHEET FOR SUMMARIZING CURRENT TRANSACTIONS AND ADJUSTMENTS: MODIFIED ACCRUAL BASIS

Accounts	Trial Balance Debit	Trial Balance Credit	Adjustments Debit (JE)	Adjustments Debit	Adjustments Credit (JE)	Adjustments Credit	Adjusted Trial Balance Debit	Adjusted Trial Balance Credit	Operating Statement Debit	Operating Statement Credit	Balance Sheet Debit	Balance Sheet Credit
Cash	15,200,000	—	JE02.02	20,000	JE02.01	8,320,000	10,045,000	—	—	—	10,045,000	—
	—	—	JE02.03	400,000	JE02.07	700,000	—	—	—	—	—	—
	—	—	JE02.06	87,000,000	JE02.08	100,000	—	—	—	—	—	—
	—	—	JE02.13	40,000	JE02.12	50,000	—	—	—	—	—	—
	—	—	JE02.14	570,000	JE02.18	900,000	—	—	—	—	—	—
	—	—	JE02.15	2,000,000	JE02.19	500,000	—	—	—	—	—	—
	—	—	JE02.22	50,000	JE02.21	4,700,000	—	—	—	—	—	—
	—	—	JE02.23	500,000	JE02.27	520,000	—	—	—	—	—	—
	—	—	JE02.28	30,000	JE02.30	85,000,000	—	—	—	—	—	—
	—	—	JE02.31	300,000	JE02.33	7,000,000	—	—	—	—	—	—
	—	—	JE02.32	525,000	JE02.46	5,475,000	—	—	—	—	—	—
	—	—	JE02.47	1,300,000	JE02.48	4,400,000	—	—	—	—	—	—
	—	—	JE02.50	50,000	JE02.49	4,650,000	—	—	—	—	—	—
	—	—	JE02.20	2,400,000	JE02.01	10,000	—	—	—	—	—	—
	—	—	JE02.21	18,000,000	JE02.08	1,500,000	—	—	—	—	—	—
	—	—	JE02.36	4,800,000	JE02.36	400,000	—	—	—	—	—	—
	—	—	JE02.34	388,000		—	—	—	—	—	—	—
	—	—	JE02.34	697,000		—	—	—	—	—	—	—
Interest receivable	20,000	—	JE02.45	23,000	JE02.02	20,000	37,800	—	—	—	37,800	—
	—	—	JE02.34	800		—	—	—	—	—	—	—
	—	—	JE02.34	14,000		—	—	—	—	—	—	—

Account	Balance	Debit postings	Credit postings	Balance	Balance
Dividends receivable	—	JE02.34 2,800	—	2,800	2,800
Property taxes receivable	1,400,000	JE02.04 100,000,000	JE02.03 1,400,000; JE02.05 245,000; JE02.06 87,000,000; JE02.38 9,000,000; JE02.40 1,400,000	2,355,000	2,355,000
Allowance for uncollectible property taxes	1,000,000	JE02.03 1,000,000; JE02.38 9,000,000	JE02.04 10,000,000; JE02.39 1,000,000	2,000,000	2,000,000
Other receivables	—	JE02.42 12,600; JE02.34 2,400; JE02.34 12,000	—	27,000	27,000
Intergovernmental grants receivable	—	JE02.09 18,000,000	JE02.20 18,000,000	—	—
Investment in short-term instruments	—	JE02.34 24,000; JE02.34 1,301,000	—	1,325,000	1,325,000
Investments in marketable debt securities	300,000	JE02.19 500,000	JE02.35 150,000	650,000	650,000
Investments in marketable equity securities	2,200,000	JE02.34 1,359,600; JE02.35 240,000	—	3,799,600	3,799,600
Interest in equity investment pool	1,800,000	JE02.07 200,000; JE02.14 550,000; JE02.34 1,450,000	—	—	—

Account	Balance		Adj. Ref (Dr)	Amount	Adj. Ref (Cr)	Amount	Net Position Dr	Net Position Cr
Interest in short-term fixed-income investment pool	1,500,000	—	JE02.07	500,000	JE02.14	20,000	—	—
					JE02.34	1,980,000		
Inventories	12,000	—	JE02.11	50,000	JE02.41	45,000	17,000	—
Other assets	—	—	JE02.34	1,200		—	5,200	—
			JE02.34	4,000				
Accounts payable	8,320,000	—	JE02.01	8,320,000	JE02.11	50,000	—	676,800
			JE02.12	50,000	JE02.17	900,000		
			JE02.18	900,000	JE02.26	520,000		
			JE02.27	520,000	JE02.44	665,000		
			JE02.01	10,000	JE02.01	10,000		
			JE02.21	4,700,000	JE02.21	4,700,000		
					JE02.34	8,800		
					JE02.34	3,000		
Demand	—	—			JE02.34	30,000	—	75,000
					JE02.34	45,000		
Deferred revenue—property taxes	245,000	—	JE02.05	245,000	JE02.28	300,000	—	300,000
Due to other funds—Internal Service Fund—Communications and Technology Support Center	70,000	—			JE02.48	100,000	—	170,000
Due to other funds—Internal Service Fund—Fleet Management Unit	22,000	—			JE02.49	50,000	—	72,000
Due to other funds—Enterprise Fund—Centerville Utilities Authority	—	—			JE02.50	2,000,000	—	2,000,000

Account		Adjustments (Dr.)		Adjustments (Cr.)	Adjusted	
Due to other funds—Enterprise Fund—Centerville Municipal Airport	—	—	—	—	—	—
Reserve for encumbrances	—	JE02.11 50,000	— JE02.50 400,000	—	400,000	400,000
	—	JE02.17 900,000	JE02.10 50,000	—	—	—
	—	JE02.26 520,000	JE02.16 900,000	—	—	—
	—	JE02.21 4,700,000	JE02.24 520,000	—	—	—
	—	JE02.43 25,000	JE02.29 25,000	—	—	—
	—	JE02.01 10,000	JE02.01 10,000	—	—	—
	—		JE02.21 4,700,000	—	—	—
Fund balance—reserved for inventories	—	12,000	— JE02.41 5,000	—	17,000	17,000
Fund balance—reserved for encumbrances	—	10,000 JE02.01	JE02.43 10,000	—	25,000	25,000
	—	12,753,000 JE02.41	JE02.01 5,000	—	12,733,000	12,733,000
Fund balance—	—	JE02.43	25,000	—	—	—
Program revenues—charges for services (general government)	—	—	JE02.31 50,000	53,000	53,000	—
	—	—	JE02.42 3,000	—	—	—
Program revenues—operating grants (recreation and parks)	—	—	JE02.15 2,000,000	2,000,000	2,000,000	—
Program revenues—charges for services (recreation and parks)	—	—	JE02.31 125,000	131,000	131,000	—
	—	—	JE02.42 6,000	—	—	—

Account							Adjustments				
Program revenues—charges for services (health and welfare)	—	—	—	—	—	—	JE02.42	2,400	2,400	2,400	—
Program revenues—operating contributions (health and welfare)	—	—	—	—	—	—	JE02.22	50,000	50,000	50,000	—
Program revenues—charges for services (streets)	—	—	—	—	—	—	JE02.31	150,000	150,000	150,000	—
Program revenues—capital grants (public safety)	—	—	—	—	—	—	JE02.23	500,000	500,000	500,000	—
Program revenues—charges for services (public safety)	—	—	—	—	—	—	JE02.31	200,000	201,200	201,200	—
							JE02.42	1,200			
General revenues—property taxes	—	—	JE02.39	1,000,000	JE02.04	90,000,000	87,600,000	87,600,000	—
			JE02.40	1,400,000					
General revenues—franchise taxes	—	—	—	—	—	—	JE02.32	1,300,000	1,300,000	1,300,000	—
General revenues—unrestricted grants	—	—	—	—	—	—	JE02.09	18,000,000	18,000,000	18,000,000	—
Interest and investment revenue	—	—	—	—	—	—	JE02.13	40,000	239,400	239,400	—
							JE02.25	30,000			
							JE02.45	23,000			

Account	Ref.	Amount	Ref.	Amount		
Change in fair value of investments	— JE02.34	20,800				
	— JE02.34	3,600				
	— JE02.34	122,000				
	JE02.34 94,000 JE02.34	366,400		362,400		362,400
	— JE02.35	90,000				
Expenditures—general government	JE02.08	431,213		33,824,098		33,824,098
	JE02.08	100,000				
	JE02.17	100,000				
	JE02.30	20,000,000				
	JE02.33	4,200,000				
	JE02.41	27,000				
	JE02.44	600,000				
	JE02.48	2,700,000				
	JE02.49	2,820,000				
	JE02.01	10,000				
	JE02.21	2,000,000				
	JE02.08	712,885				
	JE02.34	98,000				
	JE02.34	25,000				
Expenditures—public safety	JE02.17	300,000		18,036,628		18,036,628
	JE02.30	12,000,000				
	JE02.26	520,000				
	JE02.33	1,400,000				
	JE02.41	9,000				
	JE02.44	30,000				

**Expenditures—
streets**

JE02.48	900,000		
JE02.49	940,000		
JE02.21	1,300,000		
JE02.08	237,628		
JE02.36	400,000		
JE02.17	400,000	11,863,314	11,863,314
JE02.30	9,000,000		
JE02.33	700,000		
JE02.41	4,500		
JE02.44	20,000		
JE02.48	450,000		
JE02.49	470,000		
JE02.21	700,000		
JE02.08	118,814		

**Expenditures—
recreation and parks**

JE02.17	100,000	6,481,657	6,481,657
JE02.30	5,000,000		
JE02.33	350,000		
JE02.41	2,250		
JE02.44	10,000		
JE02.48	225,000		
JE02.49	235,000		
JE02.21	500,000		
JE02.08	59,407		

Account								
Expenditures—health and welfare	JE02.30	7,000,000			8,076,657		8,076,657	
	JE02.33	350,000						
	JE02.41	2,250						
	JE02.44	5,000						
	JE02.48	225,000						
	JE02.49	235,000						
	JE02.21	200,000						
	JE02.08	59,407						
Encumbrances	JE02.10	50,000	JE02.11	50,000				
	JE02.16	900,000	JE02.17	900,000				
	JE02.24	520,000	JE02.26	520,000				
	JE02.29	25,000	JE02.43	25,000				
	JE02.01	10,000	JE02.01	10,000				
	JE02.21	4,700,000	JE02.21	4,700,000				
Expenditures—interest	JE02.08	311,859			317,659		317,659	
	JE02.34	2,800						
	JE02.34	3,000						
Expenditures—education (component unit)	JE02.30	32,000,000			32,000,000		32,000,000	
Other financing sources—capitalized leases			JE02.08	431,213		431,213		431,213
Other financing sources—disposition of capital assets			JE02.21	4,800,000		4,800,000		4,800,000
Transfers in—Internal Service Fund—Fleet Management Unit			JE02.47	50,000		50,000		50,000

Account	Ref				
Transfers Out—Special Revenue Fund—Center City Special Services Fund	JE02.46	75,000	—	75,000	75,000
Transfers Out—Capital Projects Fund—Easely Street Bridge	JE02.46	1,000,000	—	1,000,000	1,000,000
Transfers Out—Capital Projects Fund—Bland Street Drainage Project	JE02.46	600,000	—	600,000	600,000
Transfers Out—Capital Projects Fund—West End Recreation Center Project	JE02.46	300,000	—	300,000	300,000
Transfers Out—Debt Service Fund—Senior Citizens' Center Bonds	JE02.46	1,300,000	—	1,300,000	1,300,000
Transfers Out—Debt Service Fund—Easely Street Bridge Bonds	JE02.46	220,000	—	220,000	220,000
Transfers Out—Debt Service Fund—Bland Street Drainage Bonds	JE02.46	1,100,000	—	1,100,000	1,100,000

Account		Ref						
Transfers Out—Debt Service Fund—West End Recreation Center Bonds	—	JE02.46	700,000	—	700,000	—	700,000	—
Transfers Out—Internal Service Fund—Communications and Technology Support Center	—	JE02.46	40,000	—	40,000	—	40,000	—
Transfers Out—Enterprise Fund—Centerville Toll Bridge	—	JE02.46	50,000	—	50,000	—	50,000	—
Transfers out—Enterprise Fund—Centerville Parking Authority	—	JE02.46	90,000	—	90,000	—	90,000	—
Totals	22,432,000		397,081,413	134,339,413	116,075,013	115,870,613	18,264,400	18,468,800
Net increase (decrease)					(204,400)	115,870,613	18,264,400	(204,400)

APPENDIX 2B: GENERAL FUND: STATEMENT OF REVENUES, EXPENDITURES, AND CHANGES IN FUND BALANCES AND BALANCE SHEET

General Fund
Statement of Revenues, Expenditures, and Changes in Fund Balances
June 30, 20X1

REVENUES

Property taxes	$ 87,600,000
Franchise taxes	1,300,000
Intergovernmental grants	20,500,000
Charges for services	537,600
Contributions	50,000
Interest and investment revenue	239,400
Change in fair value of investments	362,400
Total revenues	110,589,400

EXPENDITURES

Current:

General government	33,824,098
Public safety	18,036,628
Streets	11,863,314
Recreation and parks	6,481,657
Health and welfare	8,076,657
Education (component unit)	32,000,000
Interest	317,659
Total expenditures	110,600,013
Excess (deficiency) of revenues over expenditures	(10,613)

OTHER FINANCING SOURCES (USES):

Disposition of capital assets	4,800,000
Execution of capital leases	431,213
Transfers in	50,000
Transfers out	(5,475,000)
Total other financing sources and uses	(193,787)
Net change in fund balances	(204,400)
Fund balances—beginning	12,775,000
Fund balances—ending	$ 12,570,600

General Fund
Balance Sheet
June 30, 20X1

ASSETS

Cash	$10,045,000
Property taxes receivable (net)	355,000
Other receivables	67,600
Investments	5,774,600
Inventories	17,000
Other assets	5,200
Total assets	$16,264,400

LIABILITIES AND FUND BALANCES

Liabilities:

Accounts payable	$ 676,800
Demand loans payable	75,000
Due to other funds	2,642,000
Deferred revenue	300,000
Total liabilities	3,693,800

FUND BALANCES:

Reserved for inventories	17,000
Reserved for encumbrances	25,000
Unreserved	12,528,600
Total fund balances	12,570,600
Total liabilities and fund balances	$16,264,400

APPENDIX 2C: WORKSHEET TO CONVERT FROM MODIFIED ACCRUAL BASIS TO ACCRUAL BASIS

Accounts	Modified Accrual Trial Balance Debit	Credit	Adjustments	Debit		Credit	Accrual Trial Balance Debit	Credit
Cash	10,045,000	—					10,045,000	—
Property taxes receivable (net)	355,000	—	JE02.58	1,400,000		—	1,755,000	—
Other receivables	67,600	—	JE02.59	8,400		—	76,000	—
Investments	5,774,600	—				—	5,774,600	—
Inventories	17,000	—				—	17,000	—
Other assets	5,200	—				—	5,200	—
Intergovernmental grants receivable	—	—	JE02.52	6,000,000		—	6,000,000	—
Land and improvements	—	—	JE02.56	20,000,000		—	125,000,000	—
			JE02.60	105,000,000		—		
Construction in progress	—	—	JE02.60	2,050,000		—	2,050,000	—
Buildings	—	—	JE02.60	220,000,000	JE02.54	7,000,000	213,000,000	—
Equipment	—	—	JE02.53D	4,700,000	JE02.54	1,400,000	22,300,000	—
			JE02.60	19,000,000				
Vehicles	—	—	JE02.53A	900,000	JE02.54	3,200,000	73,220,000	—
			JE02.53C	520,000				
			JE02.60	75,000,000				
Leased capital assets	—	—	JE02.51A	431,213		—	8,249,753	—
			JE02.60	7,818,540				
Infrastructure assets	—	—	JE02.60	20,000,000		—	20,000,000	—
Accumulated depreciation—buildings	—	—	JE02.54	2,000,000	JE02.55	8,000,000	—	81,000,000
					JE02.60	75,000,000		—

Account		Debit ref	Debit	Credit ref	Credit		Balance
Accumulated depreciation—equipment	—	JE02.54	1,000,000	JE02.53D	437,000	—	7,937,000
	—			JE02.55	1,500,000	—	—
Accumulated depreciation—vehicles	—	JE02.54	3,000,000	JE02.60	7,000,000	—	58,203,889
	—			JE02.53B	175,000	—	—
	—			JE02.53C	28,889	—	—
	—			JE02.55	22,000,000	—	—
	—			JE02.60	39,000,000	—	—
Accumulated depreciation—leased capital assets	—			JE02.51A	79,058	—	3,779,058
	—			JE02.55	1,200,000	—	—
	—			JE02.60	2,500,000	—	—
Accumulated depreciation—infrastructure assets	—			JE02.55	700,000	—	12,700,000
	—			JE02.60	12,000,000	—	—
Accounts payable	676,800					—	676,800
Demand loan payable to bank	75,000					—	75,000
Interest payable	—			JE02.51A	24,290	—	24,290
Due to other funds	2,642,000					—	2,642,000
Deferred revenue	300,000					—	300,000
Claims payable	—	JE02.57B	400,000	JE02.57A	300,000	—	1,900,000
	—			JE02.62	2,000,000	—	—
Compensated absences payable	—	JE02.57C	60,000	JE02.57A	220,000	—	4,660,000
	—			JE02.62	4,500,000	—	—
Lease obligation payable	—	JE02.51A	100,000	JE02.51A	431,213	—	4,340,724
	—	JE02.51B	1,188,141	JE02.61	5,197,652	—	—
Fund balance/net assets	12,775,000	JE02.61	5,197,652	JE02.60	313,368,540	—	314,445,888
		JE02.62	6,500,000			—	—
General revenue—property taxes	87,600,000			JE02.58	1,400,000	—	89,000,000
Franchise taxes	1,300,000					—	1,300,000

Intergovernmental grants—general revenues—unrestricted grants	20,500,000	—		JE02.52	6,000,000	26,500,000
Program revenues/charges for services (general government)	53,000			JE02.59	2,000	55,000
Program revenues/charges for services (recreations and parks)	131,000			JE02.59	4,000	135,000
Program revenues/charges for services (public safety)	201,200			JE02.59	800	202,000
Program revenues/charges for services (health and welfare)	2,400			JE02.59	1,600	4,000
Program revenues/charges for services (streets)	150,000				—	150,000
Contributions	50,000				—	50,000
Interest and investment revenue	239,400				—	239,400
Change in fair value of investments	362,400				—	362,400
General government expenditures/expenses	33,824,098	JE02.51A 79,058	JE02.51A 431,213			51,164,503
		JE02.53B 19,445	JE02.51A 100,000			
		JE02.53D 170,000	JE02.51B 712,885			
		JE02.54 700,000	JE02.53A 100,000			
		JE02.55 19,620,000	JE02.53D 2,000,000			
		JE02.57A 132,000	JE02.57C 36,000			
Public safety expenditures/expenses	18,036,628	JE02.53B 58,333	JE02.51B 237,628			22,448,222
		JE02.53C 28,889	JE02.53A 300,000			
		JE02.53D 110,000	JE02.53C 520,000			
		JE02.54 100,000	JE02.53D 1,300,000			
		JE02.55 6,540,000	JE02.57B 400,000			
		JE02.57A 300,000	JE02.57C 12,000			
		JE02.57A 44,000	—			

Account		Debit adjustment	Credit adjustment	
Streets expenditures/expenses	11,863,314	JE02.53B 77,778	JE02.51B 118,814	14,803,278
	—	JE02.53D 95,000	JE02.53A 400,000	—
	—	JE02.55 3,970,000	JE02.53D 700,000	—
	—	JE02.57A 22,000	JE02.57C 6,000	—
Recreation and parks expenditures/expenses	6,481,657	JE02.53B 19,444	JE02.51B 59,407	7,524,694
	—	JE02.53D 40,000	JE02.53A 100,000	—
	—	JE02.55 1,635,000	JE02.53D 500,000	—
	—	JE02.57A 11,000	JE02.57C 3,000	—
Health and welfare expenditures/expenses	8,076,657	JE02.53D 22,000	JE02.51B 59,407	9,482,250
	—	JE02.55 1,635,000	JE02.53D 200,000	—
	—	JE02.57A 11,000	JE02.57C 3,000	—
Interest expenditures/expense	317,659	JE02.51A 24,290	—	341,949
Education (component unit)	32,000,000	—	—	32,000,000
Extraordinary item—donation of land by the state	—	—	JE02.56 20,000,000	20,000,000
Other financing sources—disposition of capital assets	—			—
Execution of capital leases	—	JE02.54 4,800,000	—	—
Transfers in	431,213	JE02.51A 431,213	—	—
Transfers out	50,000	—	—	50,000
	5,475,000			5,475,000
Total	132,339,413	542,969,396	542,969,396	630,732,449

APPENDIX 2D: GENERAL FUND: ADJUSTED TRIAL BALANCE

Accounts	Adjusted Trial Balance Debit	Credit
Cash	$ 10,045,000	
Property taxes receivable (net)	1,755,000	
Other receivables	76,000	
Investments	5,774,600	
Inventories	17,000	
Other assets	5,200	
Intergovernmental grants receivable	6,000,000	
Land and improvements	125,000,000	
Construction in progress	2,050,000	
Buildings	213,000,000	
Equipment	22,300,000	
Vehicles	73,220,000	
Leased capital assets	8,249,753	
Infrastructure assets	20,000,000	
Accumulated depreciation—buildings		$ 81,000,000
Accumulated depreciation—equipment		7,937,000
Accumulated depreciation—vehicles		58,203,889
Accumulated depreciation—leased capital assets		3,779,058
Accumulated depreciation—infrastructure assets		12,700,000
Accounts payable		676,800
Demand loan payable to bank		75,000
Interest payable		24,290
Due to other funds		2,642,000
Deferred revenue		300,000
Claims payable		1,900,000
Compensated absences payable		4,660,000
Lease obligation payable		4,340,724
Fund balance/net assets		314,445,888
General revenue—property taxes		89,000,000
Franchise taxes		1,300,000
Intergovernmental grants—general revenues— unrestricted grants		26,500,000
Program revenues/charges for services (general government)		55,000
Program revenues/charges for services (recreations and parks)		135,000

Program revenues/charges for services (public safety)		202,000
Program revenues/charges for services (health and welfare)		4,000
Program revenues/charges for services (streets)		150,000
Contributions		50,000
Interest and investment revenue		239,400
Miscellaneous revenue		
Change in fair value of investments		362,400
General government expenditures/expenses	51,164,503	
Public safety expenditures/expenses	22,448,222	
Streets expenditures/expenses	14,803,278	
Recreation and parks expenditures/expenses	7,524,694	
Health and welfare expenditures/expenses	9,482,250	
Interest expense	341,949	
Education (component unit)	32,000,000	
Extraordinary item—donation of land by the state		20,000,000
Other financing sources—disposition of capital assets		0
Execution of capital leases		0
Transfers in		50,000
Transfers out	5,475,000	
Total	$630,732,449	$630,732,449

CHAPTER 3
SPECIAL REVENUE FUNDS

CONTENTS

NATURE OF SPECIAL REVENUE FUNDS

NCGA-1 states that the purpose of a Special Revenue Fund is to account for the proceeds of specific revenue sources (other than for major capital projects) that are legally restricted to expenditures for specified purposes. For example, the following circumstances could be the basis for reporting activities in a Special Revenue Fund:

- Gasoline taxes are to be used only for road maintenance

- Lottery proceeds are to be used only for a drug prescription plan for elderly citizens

- Personal property taxes are to be used only for educational purposes

GASB-34 revised the fund structure for state and local governments. One of the changes was the elimination of Expendable Trust Funds, which previously had been used to account for resources for which both the principal and earnings could be expended. Resources that were previously accounted for in an Expendable Trust Fund are generally now reported in a Special Revenue Fund (GASB-34, par. 63).

A Special Revenue Fund may include resources that are unrestricted (for example, a transfer from the General Fund) and resources that are restricted (for example, revenues from a state-shared motor fuel tax that must be used for street repair and maintenance). Because the resources (cash) are available for both restricted and unrestricted uses, a revenue flow assumption must be made by the governmental entity to identify whether unrestricted or restricted resources are used first. The GASB's *Comprehensive Implementation Guide* states that either approach is acceptable; however, the financial statements must disclose which accounting policy has been adopted.

The GASB's *Comprehensive Implementation Guide* states that when resources or an activity benefits both the government and private parties, two separate funds (Special Revenue Fund and Private-Purpose Trust Fund) should be used unless one of the two activities is a nonmajor activity, in which case the predominant activity would determine which fund type would be used. In some circumstances a fund's principal or income benefits a discretely presented component unit. The GASB's *Guide* points out that a discretely presented component unit is part of the financial reporting entity; so, it is not an "individual, private organization or other government" and, therefore, the resources should be reported in a Special Revenue Fund.

GASB-24 (Accounting and Financial Reporting for Certain Grants and Other Financial Assistance) requires that a state government account for the distribution of food stamp benefits as revenue and expenditures in either a General Fund or a Special Revenue Fund (GASB-24, par. 6).

When a governmental entity has a component unit that is blended into its financial statements, the General Fund of the component unit must be reported as a Special Revenue Fund of the primary government (GASB-14, par. 54).

NCGA-1 makes the point that a Special Revenue Fund should be used only when it is legally mandated. In many instances, it may be possible to account for restricted resources directly in the General Fund if these restricted resources are used to support expenditures that are usually made from the General Fund.

PRACTICE ALERT: GASB-54 (Fund Balance Reporting and Governmental Fund Type Definitions), which is effective for periods beginning after June 15, 2010, makes significant changes to fund balance classifications as well as clarifies and makes changes to the definitions of governmental fund types. The new definitions in GASB-54 provide that governmental funds of a particular type either should be used (i.e., required) or are used (i.e., discretionary) for all activities that meet its criteria. If use of a fund type is generally discretionary, specific situations under which a fund of that type should be used are identified either in the definitions in GASB-54 (i.e., debt service funds) or by requirements established in other authoritative pronouncements (i.e., special revenue and capital projects funds). The fund balance classification section of GASB-54 defines the terminology "restricted," "committed," and "assigned."

OBSERVATION: GASB-54 modifies the definitions of governmental fund types. Specifically, special revenue funds are defined as those funds used to account for and report the proceeds of specific revenue sources that are restricted or committed to expenditure for specified purposes other than debt service or capital projects. Therefore, a stabilization arrangement would meet the criteria to be reported as a separate special revenue fund only if the fund's resources are derived from a specific restricted or committed revenue source specifically restricted or committed for that stabilization purpose. For some governments, the updated definition will be more restrictive than current practice, whereas for governments that strictly follow the pre-GASB-54 definition, the GASB-54 definition will be less restrictive.

PRACTICE ALERT: Because the definition of special revenue funds has narrowed slightly under GASB-54, there could be an instance where a special revenue fund should be part of the General Fund. If that is the case, then the General Fund beginning fund balance must be restated for the reclassified special revenue fund activity. However, for all governmental fund, the overall beginning fund balance would not change.

PRACTICE POINT: Some legislative bodies may call what in reality is a special revenue fund a "trust" within legislation and vice versa. Care must be taken to delineate between funds with trust documents and funds with enabling legislation that meets the definition of a special revenue fund in GASB-54.

MEASUREMENT FOCUS AND BASIS OF ACCOUNTING

The modified accrual basis and flow of current financial resources are used to prepare the financial statements of Special Revenue Funds. The same accounting principles that are used to measure revenues, expenditures, assets, and liabilities of a General Fund are also used to account for those items in a Special Revenue Fund. These accounting principles are discussed in Chapter 2, "The General Fund," and are not repeated here.

FINANCIAL REPORTING AT FUND LEVEL

The balances and activities of Special Revenue Funds are presented in the following financial statements at the fund financial statement level:

- Balance Sheet
- Statement of Revenues, Expenditures, and Changes in Fund Balances

The two fund financial statements listed above include all of the governmental funds (General Fund, Special Revenue Funds, Capital Projects Funds, Debt Service Funds, and Permanent Funds), and these funds are reported based on the concept of a major fund as defined by GAAP.

GAAP requires that a budgetary comparison schedule be prepared for each major Special Revenue Fund that has a legally adopted annual budget. This schedule is discussed in Chapter 18, "Management's Discussion and Analysis and Other Required Supplementary Information," in the context of the General Fund. For this illustration it is assumed that none of the Special Revenue Funds legally adopt an annual budget (GASB-34, par. 130).

> **PRACTICE ALERT:** Implementation of GASB-54 will require segregation of fund balance into "non-expendable," "restricted," "committed," and "assigned" balances for special revenue funds. If expenditures incurred for specific purposes exceed the amounts restricted, committed, or assigned to those purposes, the government should first reduce any assigned amounts within the fund and then, if there are no further assigned amounts to reduce, report the negative residual amount as "negative unassigned" fund balances. This means that a negative residual amount *should not be reported* for restricted, committed, or assigned balances in any fund.

FINANCIAL REPORTING AT GOVERNMENT-WIDE LEVEL

The fund-based financial statements as described above are included in a governmental entity's financial report in order to demonstrate that restrictions imposed by statutes, regulations, or contracts have been followed. Balances in the fund financial statements are converted from a modified accrual basis to an accrual basis in order to create the basic information for the government-wide financial statements. For the most part this approach requires that all of the Special Revenue Funds combined ending trial balance (which is on a modified accrual basis) be adjusted to reflect accrual balances. This conversion is illustrated later in this chapter.

ILLUSTRATIVE TRANSACTIONS

Note: The transactions presented here assume that internal systems are *not* redesigned for GASB-54. Therefore conversion entries are used. In the 2013 edition of the CCH *Governmental GAAP Practice Manual*, beginning balances will be presented in GASB-54 format. Governments that do not redesign their internal accounting systems for GASB-54 will have to restate using adjusting entries similar to those contained in this section. The conversion entries to GASB-54 and assumptions are presented after JE03.18 and as JE03.G54-1, JE03.G54-2, and so on.

In order to illustrate accounting and financial reporting standards that should be observed for Special Revenue Funds, assume that the City of Centerville has the following Special Revenue Funds:

- Center City Special Services District

- Local Fuel Tax Fund

Special Revenue Funds

Special revenue funds are defined as follows:

Fund Type	Pre GASB-54 Definition (periods beginning before June 15, 2010)	Post GASB-54 Definition (periods beginning after June 15, 2010)
Special Revenue Funds	To account for the proceeds of specific revenue sources (other than trusts for individuals, private organizations, or other governments or for major capital projects) that are legally restricted to expenditure for specified purpose.	To account for and report the proceeds of specific revenue sources that are restricted or committed to expenditure for specified purposes other than debt service or capital projects.

One of the most common areas of confusion regarding the reporting of reserved fund balances involves the reporting of fund balances of governmental funds when the entire fund balance is restricted for a specified purpose, such as a motor fuel tax fund whose resources are required by law to be used for street and highway maintenance. Many financial statement preparers and users were unsure as to whether the fund balance of this type fund should be reported as reserved or unreserved because of the nature of its restriction. A significant majority of the financial statement users interviewed during GASB's Fund Balance Reporting and Governmental Fund Type Definitions project did not understand that a legal segregation reservation of fund balance for restricted resources is narrower in scope than the fund that the resources are reported in. In other words, the available fund balance of, say, a motor fuel tax fund should not be reported as a reserved fund balance within the fund.

Center City Special Services Fund

The Center City Special Services District (CCSSD) provides special services, such as street maintenance, street cleaning, and similar services to approximately six square blocks of the business district. Businesses in this area pay a special service fee that is approximately 5% of their property tax bill. The trial balance for this fund at the beginning of the fiscal year is as follows:

Accounts	Trial Balance Debit	Trial Balance Credit
Cash	$30,000	
Other receivables	14,500	
Property taxes receivable	50,000	
Allowance for uncollectible property taxes		$40,000
Accounts payable		26,000
Deferred revenue—property taxes		12,000
Fund balance		16,500
Totals	$94,500	$94,500

The fund balance entries above are *not* GASB-54 compliant; however, they show what will likely be present in most trial balances for the year of conversion.

This section presents illustrative transactions and entries for the fund during the fiscal year ended June 30, 20X2.

Transaction JE03.01—Accounts payable and accrued expenses of $26,000 from the previous year were paid:

Accounts	Debit	Credit
Accounts payable	26,000	
Cash		26,000

Transaction JE03.02—Accrued interest receivable from the previous year was received:

Accounts	Debit	Credit
Cash	14,500	
Other receivables		14,500

Transaction JE03.03—Property taxes receivable of $10,000 at the beginning of the year were collected and the balance ($40,000) was written off:

Accounts	Debit	Credit
Cash	10,000	
Allowance for uncollectible property taxes	40,000	
Property taxes receivable		50,000

Transaction JE03.04—The Center City Special Services District levied property taxes of $3,000,000. It is expected that 10% of the amount levied will be uncollectible:

Accounts	Debit	Credit
Property taxes receivable	3,000,000	
General revenues—property taxes		2,700,000
Allowance for uncollectible property taxes		300,000

All taxes are considered to be general revenues (for presentation on the statement of activities) even if they are restricted to a particular program or activity (GASB-34, par. 52).

The accounting for nonexchange revenues (such as property taxes) continues to be performed based on the standards established by GASB-33 (Accounting and Financial Reporting for Nonexchange Transactions).

Transaction JE03.05—Property taxes collected in the previous year are applied to current property tax billings:

Accounts	Debit	Credit
Deferred revenue—property taxes	12,000	
Property taxes receivable		12,000

Some governmental entities use the deferred revenue account to report receivables that are not expected to be collected within a short period of time after the end of the year. This illustration uses deferred revenue only for cash received from property owners before the period in which the revenue can be recognized.

Transaction JE03.06—Property tax collections totaled $2,610,000 for the year:

Accounts	Debit	Credit
Cash	2,610,000	
Property taxes receivable		2,610,000

Transaction JE03.07—The City received $10,000 of property tax receipts that apply to the next fiscal year:

Accounts	Debit	Credit
Cash	10,000	
Deferred revenues—property taxes		10,000

Transaction JE03.08—Property taxes receivable from specific business enterprises of $270,000 are identified as uncollectible:

Accounts	Debit	Credit
Allowance for uncollectible property taxes	270,000	
Property taxes receivable		270,000

Transaction JE03.09—After additional analysis the allowance for uncollectible accounts is increased by $30,000. This is an accounting change in estimate:

Accounts	Debit	Credit
General revenues—property taxes	30,000	
Allowance for uncollectible property taxes		30,000

Transaction JE03.10—Government expenditures of $2,750,000 were incurred, of which $2,700,000 was paid. Of the total expenditures, 20% are allocated to general government and 80% to street programs:

Accounts	Debit	Credit
Expenditures—general government ($2,750,000 × 20%)	550,000	
Expenditures—streets ($2,750,000 × 80%)	2,200,000	
Cash		2,700,000
Accounts payable		50,000

PRACTICE POINT: Expenditures presented in the statement of revenues, expenditures, and changes in fund balances should continue to be classified consistent with the standards discussed in NCGA-1 (par. 110–116).

Transaction JE03.11—The General Fund made a transfer of $75,000 to subsidize the activities of the Center City Special Services District:

Accounts	Debit	Credit
Cash	75,000	
Transfers in—General Fund		75,000

Transaction JE03.12—Interest and penalties of $18,000 were assessed during the year, of which $3,000 was collected. The balance is expected to be collected in time to pay current liabilities of the fund:

Accounts	Debit	Credit
Cash	3,000	
Other receivables	15,000	
Miscellaneous revenue		18,000

After the transactions for the year are posted, the year-end trial balance (June 30, 20X2) before the conversion for GASB-54 for the Center City Special Services District appears as follows:

	Adjusted Trial Balance	
Accounts	**Debit**	**Credit**
Cash	$ 26,500	
Other receivables	15,000	
Property taxes receivable	108,000	
Allowance for uncollectible property taxes		$ 60,000
Accounts payable		50,000
Deferred revenue—property taxes		10,000
Fund balance		16,500
General revenues—property taxes		2,670,000
Miscellaneous revenue		18,000
Expenditures—general government	550,000	
Expenditures—streets	2,200,000	
Transfers in—General Fund		75,000
Totals	$2,899,500	$2,899,500

PRACTICE ALERT: Absent any other information, the only reclass to implement GASB-54 will be to reclass the beginning fund balance to fund balance—assigned. The net surplus or deficit would also close to fund-balance-assigned until a negative fund balance is generated. If no other committed or restricted balances are available, the negative fund balance would be unassigned. If a budget or enabling legislation was passed, then a balance may be committed.

The worksheet that summarizes the foregoing journal entries for the year-end trial balance is presented in Appendix 3A.

Local Fuel Tax Fund

The Local Fuel Tax Fund (LFTF) receives a share of the fuel taxes collected by the state government. The fuel tax receipts are to be used to maintain and repair streets and highways. The trial balance for this fund at the beginning of the fiscal year is presented as follows:

Accounts	Trial Balance	
	Debit	Credit
Cash	$25,000	
Other receivables	3,000	
Accounts payable		$15,000
Fund balance		13,000
Totals	$28,000	$28,000

The fund balance entries above are *not* GASB-54 compliant; however, they show what will likely be present in most trial balances for the year of conversion.

This section presents illustrative transactions and entries for the fund during the fiscal year ended June 30, 20X2.

Transaction JE03.13—Accounts payable of $15,000 from the previous year were paid:

Accounts	Debit	Credit
Accounts payable	15,000	
Cash		15,000

Transaction JE03.14—Accrued interest receivable from the previous year was collected:

Accounts	Debit	Credit
Cash	3,000	
Other receivables		3,000

Transaction JE03.15—During the year the state transferred $4,500,000 of motor fuel taxes to the City. The funds may be spent on either operating or capital expenditures:

Accounts	Debit	Credit
Cash	4,500,000	
Program revenues—operating grants (streets)		4,500,000

Transaction JE03.16—Government expenditures of $4,200,000 were incurred, of which $4,175,000 were paid. Of the total expenditures, 5% are allocated to general government and 95% to streets programs:

Accounts	Debit	Credit
Expenditures—general government ($4,200,000 × 5%)	210,000	
Expenditures—streets ($4,200,000 × 95%)	3,990,000	
Cash		4,175,000
Accounts payable		25,000

Transaction JE03.17—Interest income of $6,000 was earned during the year, of which $4,000 was collected. The balance is expected to be collected in time to pay current liabilities of the fund:

Accounts	Debit	Credit
Cash	4,000	
Other receivables	2,000	
Interest revenue		6,000

Transaction JE03.18—During the year, $300,000 was transferred to the Bland Street Drainage Project (Capital Projects Fund):

Accounts	Debit	Credit
Transfers out—Capital Projects Fund (Bland Street Drainage)	300,000	
Cash		300,000

After the transactions for the year are posted, the year-end trial balance (June 30, 20X2) for the Local Fuel Tax Fund, before the conversion to GASB-54 format appears as follows:

	Adjusted Trial Balance	
Accounts	Debit	Credit
Cash	$ 42,000	
Other receivables	2,000	
Accounts payable		$ 25,000
Fund balance		13,000
Program revenues—operating grants (streets)		4,500,000
Interest revenue		6,000
Expenditures—general government	210,000	
Expenditures—streets	3,990,000	
Transfers out—Capital Projects Fund (Bland Street Drainage)	300,000	
Totals	$4,544,000	$4,544,000

PRACTICE ALERT: Similarly to the Central City Special Services District, absent any other information, the only reclass to implement GASB-54 will be to reclass the beginning fund balance to fund balance—assigned. The net surplus or deficit would also close to fund balance—assigned until a negative fund balance is generated. If no other assigned balances are available, the negative fund balance would be unassigned. If a budget or enabling legislation was passed, then a balance may be committed.

(See Appendix 3B.) The worksheet that summarizes the foregoing journal entries for the year-end trial balance is presented in Appendix 3C.

FUND FINANCIAL STATEMENTS

At the fund financial statement level a governmental fund must prepare a statement of revenues, expenditures, and changes in fund balances and a balance sheet. Based on the adjusted trial balances created above, the following preliminary financial statements reflect the combined balances and activities of the two Special Revenue Funds. These financial statements are prepared to facilitate the preparation of the fund financial statements illustrated in Chapter 13, "Developing Information for Fund Financial Statements."

PRACTICE POINT: NCGA-1 illustrates three distinct formats that can be used to prepare the statement of revenues, expenditures, and changes in fund balances for governmental funds; however, GASB-34 eliminated two of the options and only the format illustrated below can be used (GASB-34, par. 86).

Special Revenue Funds
Balance Sheet
June 30, 20X2
(Before conversion to GASB 54)

	Center City Special Services Fund	Local Fuel Tax Fund	Total
ASSETS			
Cash	$26,500	$42,000	$68,500
Other receivables	15,000	2,000	17,000
Property taxes receivable (net)	48,000	—	48,000
Total assets	$89,500	$44,000	$133,500
LIABILITIES AND FUND BALANCES			
Liabilities:			
Accounts payable	$50,000	$25,000	$75,000
Deferred revenue— property taxes	10,000	—	10,000
Total liabilities	60,000	25,000	85,000
Fund balances:			
Fund balance—reserved	29,500	19,000	48,500
Total liabilities and fund balances	$89,500	$44,000	$133,500

GASB-54 CONVERSION ENTRIES

The following balances are key for a proper GASB-54 conversion in the conversion year:

Fund balance—reserved –Central City Special Services District	16,500
Fund balance—reserved –Local Fuel Tax Fund	13,000

However, other information is needed to properly convert the beginning balances and the ending balances. This information may include the following:

Nonspendable Balances	Any balances of inventory and long-term receivables.
Restricted Balances	Any balances from bond proceeds, grants, and other external restrictions or due to enabling statutes.
Committed Balances	Any passed budgets or other commitments made by the highest level of decision making.

To reclass the beginning balances, the following entries are needed:

Transaction JE03.G54-1 (reclass) Undesignated balances in special revenue funds are generally assigned balances.

Accounts	Debit	Credit
Fund balance—reserved –Central City Special Services District	16,500	
Fund balance—assigned –Central City Special Services District		16,500

For the Local Fule Tax Fund:

Accounts	Debit	Credit
Fund balance—reserved –Local Fuel Tax Fund	13,000	
Fund balance—assigned –Local Fuel Tax fund		13,000

Assume that Central City doesn't budget for these funds and no other commitments or restrictions exist.

Special Revenue Funds
Statement of Revenues, Expenditures, and
Changes in Fund Balances
June 30, 20X2

	Center City Special Services Fund	Local Fuel Tax Fund	Total
REVENUES			
Property taxes	$2,670,000	—	$2,670,000
Program revenues—operating grants (street)	—	$4,500,000	4,500,000
Interest	—	6,000	6,000
Miscellaneous	18,000	—	18,000
Total revenue	2,688,000	4,506,000	7,194,000
EXPENDITURES			
General government	550,000	210,000	760,000
Streets	2,200,000	3,990,000	6,190,000
Total expenditures	2,750,000	4,200,000	6,950,000
Excess (deficiency) of revenues over expenditures	(62,000)	306,000	244,000
OTHER FINANCING SOURCES (USES)			
Transfers in—General Fund	75,000	—	75,000

Special Revenue Funds
Statement of Revenues, Expenditures, and
Changes in Fund Balances
June 30, 20X2

	Center City Special Services Fund	Local Fuel Tax Fund	Total
REVENUES			
Transfers out—Capital Projects Fund (Bland Street Drainage)	—	(300,000)	(300,000)
Total other financing sources and uses	75,000	(300,000)	(225,000)
Net change in fund balances	13,000	6,000	19,000
Fund balances—beginning	16,500	13,000	29,500
Fund balances—ending	$ 29,500	$ 19,000	$ 48,500

PRACTICE ALERT: GASB-54 does not require the presentation of desegregated fund balances in the statement of revenues, expenditures, and changes in fund balances. To do so would not be GAAP and, furthermore, would probably cause separate columns for separate classes of fund balances similar to not-for-profit financial statements. All surplus closes to Fund balance—assigned. Annual deficits would close to Fund balance—assigned unless no positive balances are available in assigned balances. If deficit balances still exist after lowering all positive balances to zero, the remainder would be labeled fund deficit—unassigned.

The combined financial statements for the Special Revenue Funds are not reported separately in the governmental entity's financial report, but they are used later in Chapter 13, "Developing Information for Fund Financial Statements."

CONVERTING TO GOVERNMENT-WIDE FINANCIAL STATEMENTS

Government-wide financial statements are reported on the accrual basis of accounting. Generally most governments work from their governmental fund financial statements (which are on a modified accrual basis) and through the use of worksheet entries convert to accrual based financial statements.

In order to illustrate the conversion of the Special Revenue Funds from a modified accrual to an accrual basis, it is assumed that both funds are due an operating grant from the state government and that the characteristics of the grants satisfy the revenue recognition criteria established by GASB-33, except the resources will not be available to pay current expenditures of the funds.

If it is assumed that the Center City Special Services District is entitled to a $50,000 restricted operating state grant, the following entry is needed to convert the fund financial statements from a modified accrual basis to an accrual basis:

Accounts	Debit	Credits
JE03.19 Intergovernmental grants receivable	50,000	
Program revenues—operating grants (streets)		50,000
(To accrue grant revenue that was not subject to accrual under the modified accrual method)		

If it is assumed that the Local Fuel Tax Fund is entitled to a $20,000 restricted operating state grant and all eligibility requirements are met for the grant, the following entry is needed to convert the financial statements from a modified accrual basis to an accrual basis:

Accounts	Debit	Credit
JE03.20 Intergovernmental grants receivable	20,000	
Program revenues—operating grants (streets)		20,000
(To accrue grant revenue that was not subject to accrual under the modified accrual method)		

After these worksheet entries are prepared, the combined adjusted trial balances (on an accrual basis) for the Special Revenue Funds are as follows as of June 30, 20X2:

	CCSSD	LFTF	Total
Cash	$ 26,500	$42,000	$68,500
Other receivables	15,000	2,000	17,000
Property taxes receivable	108,000	—	108,000
Intergovernmental grants receivable	50,000	20,000	70,000
Allowance for uncollectible property taxes	(60,000)	—	(60,000)
Accounts payable	(50,000)	(25,000)	(75,000)
Deferred revenue—property taxes	(10,000)	—	(10,000)
Net Assets	(16,500)	(13,000)	(29,500)
General revenues—property taxes	(2,670,000)	—	(2,670,000)
Program revenues—operating grants	(50,000)	(4,520,000)	(4,570,000)
Miscellaneous revenues	(18,000)	—	(18,000)
Interest revenue	—	(6,000)	(6,000)
Expenditures—general government	550,000	210,000	760,000
Expenditures—streets	2,200,000	3,990,000	6,190,000
Transfers out—Capital Projects Fund (Bland Street Drainage)	—	300,000	300,000
Transfers in—General Fund	(75,000)	—	(75,000)
Totals	$ 0	$ 0	$ 0

These accrual based trial balances are used in Chapter 13, "Developing Information for Fund Financial Statements," in order to prepare the government-wide financial statements.

APPENDIX 3A: WORKSHEET FOR SUMMARIZING CURRENT TRANSACTIONS: CENTER CITY SPECIAL SERVICES DISTRICT FUND

Accounts	Trial Balance Debit	Trial Balance Credit	Adjustments Debit Ref	Adjustments Debit	Adjustments Credit Ref	Adjustments Credit	Adjusted Trial Balance Debit	Adjusted Trial Balance Credit	Operating Statement Debit	Operating Statement Credit	Balance Sheet Debit	Balance Sheet Credit
Cash	30,000	—	JE03.02	14,500	JE03.01	26,000	26,500	—	—	—	26,500	—
			JE03.03	10,000	JE03.10	2,700,000	—	—	—	—	—	—
			JE03.06	2,610,000		—	—	—	—	—	—	—
			JE03.07	10,000		—	—	—	—	—	—	—
			JE03.11	75,000		—	—	—	—	—	—	—
			JE03.12	3,000		—	—	—	—	—	—	—
Other receivables	14,500	—	JE03.12	15,000	JE03.02	14,500	15,000	—	—	—	15,000	—
Property taxes receivable	50,000	—	JE03.04	3,000,000	JE03.03	50,000	108,000	—	—	—	108,000	—
					JE03.05	12,000	—	—	—	—	—	—
					JE03.06	2,610,000	—	—	—	—	—	—
					JE03.08	270,000	—	—	—	—	—	—
Allowance for uncollectible property taxes	—	40,000	JE03.03	40,000	JE03.04	300,000	—	60,000	—	—	—	60,000
			JE03.08	270,000	JE03.09	30,000	—	—	—	—	—	—
Accounts payable	—	26,000	JE03.01	26,000	JE03.10	50,000	—	50,000	—	—	—	50,000

Account	Ref.									
Deferred revenue—property taxes	JE03.05 / JE03.07	—	12,000	12,000	10,000	10,000	—	—	—	10,000
Fund balance		—	16,500	—	—	16,500	—	—	—	16,500
General revenues—property taxes	JE03.09 / JE03.04	—	30,000	2,700,000	2,670,000	2,670,000	—	—	—	—
Miscellaneous revenue	JE03.12	—	—	18,000	18,000	18,000	—	—	—	—
Expenditures—general government	JE03.10	—	550,000	—	550,000	—	550,000	—	—	—
Expenditures—streets	JE03.10	—	2,200,000	—	2,200,000	—	2,200,000	—	—	—
Transfers in—General Fund	JE03.11	—	—	75,000	75,000	75,000	—	75,000	—	—
Totals		94,500	8,865,500	8,865,500	2,899,500	2,899,500	2,750,000	2,763,000	149,500	136,500
Net increase (decrease)		94,500	—	—	13,000	—	13,000	—	—	13,000
		94,500			2,763,000	2,763,000			149,500	149,500

APPENDIX 3B: SPECIAL REVENUE FUNDS: BALANCE SHEET AND STATEMENT OF REVENUES, EXPENDITURES, AND CHANGES IN FUND BALANCES

Special Revenue Funds
Balance Sheet
June 30, 20X2

	Center City Special Services Fund	Local Fuel Tax Fund	Total
ASSETS			
Cash	$26,500	$42,000	$68,500
Other receivables	15,000	2,000	17,000
Property taxes receivable (net)	48,000	—	48,000
Total assets	$89,500	$44,000	$133,500
LIABILITIES AND FUND BALANCES			
Liabilities:			
Accounts payable	$50,000	$25,000	$75,000
Deferred revenue—property taxes	10,000	—	10,000
Total liabilities	60,000	25,000	85,000
Fund balances:			
Fund balance—assigned	29,500	19,000	48,500
Total liabilities and fund balances	$89,500	$44,000	$133,500

Special Revenue Funds
Statement of Revenues, Expenditures, and Changes in Fund Balances
June 30, 20X2

	Center City Special Services Fund	Local Fuel Tax Fund	Total
REVENUES			
Property taxes	$2,670,000	—	$2,670,000
Program revenues—operating grants (street)	—	$4,500,000	4,500,000
Interest	—	6,000	6,000
Miscellaneous	18,000	—	18,000
Total revenue	2,688,000	4,506,000	7,194,000
EXPENDITURES			
General government	550,000	210,000	760,000
Streets	2,200,000	3,990,000	6,190,000
Total expenditures	2,750,000	4,200,000	6,950,000
Excess (deficiency) of revenues over expenditures	(62,000)	306,000	244,000

OTHER FINANCING SOURCES (USES)

Transfers in—General Fund	75,000	—	75,000
Transfers out—Capital Projects Fund (Bland Street Drainage)	—	(300,000)	(300,000)
Total other financing sources and uses	75,000	(300,000)	(225,000)
Net change in fund balances	13,000	6,000	19,000
Fund balances—beginning	16,500	13,000	29,500
Fund balances—ending	$29,500	$19,000	$48,500

APPENDIX 3C: WORKSHEET FOR SUMMARIZING CURRENT TRANSACTIONS: LOCAL FUEL TAX FUND

Accounts	Trial Balance Debit	Trial Balance Credit	Adjustments Debit	JE	Adjustments Credit	JE	Adjusted Trial Balance Debit	Adjusted Trial Balance Credit	Operating Statement Debit	Operating Statement Credit	Balance Sheet Debit	Balance Sheet Credit
Cash	25,000	—	3,000	JE03.14	15,000	JE03.13	42,000	—	—	—	42,000	—
			4,500,000	JE03.15	4,175,000	JE03.16						
			4,000	JE03.17	300,000	JE03.18						
Other receivables	3,000	—	2,000	JE03.17	3,000	JE03.14	2,000	—	—	—	2,000	—
Accounts payable	—	15,000	15,000	JE03.13	25,000	JE03.16	—	25,000	—	—	—	25,000
Fund balance	—	13,000	—		—		—	13,000	—	—	—	13,000
Program revenues—operating grants (street)	—	—	—		4,500,000	JE03.15	—	4,500,000	—	4,500,000	—	—
Interest revenue	—	—	—		6,000	JE03.17	—	6,000	—	6,000	—	—
Expenditures—general government	—	—	210,000	JE03.16	—		210,000	—	210,000	—	—	—
Expenditures—streets	—	—	3,990,000	JE03.16	—		3,990,000	—	3,990,000	—	—	—
Transfers out—Capital Projects Fund (Bland Street Drainage)	—	—	300,000	JE03.18	—		300,000	—	300,000	—	—	—
Totals	28,000	28,000	9,024,000		9,024,000		4,544,000	4,544,000	4,500,000	4,506,000	44,000	38,000
Net increase (decrease)									6,000	—	—	6,000
									4,506,000	4,506,000	44,000	44,000

APPENDIX 3D: SPECIAL REVENUE FUNDS: COMBINED ADJUSTED TRIAL BALANCES

	CCSSD	LFTF	Total
Cash	$ 26,500	$ 42,000	$ 68,500
Other receivables	15,000	2,000	17,000
Property taxes receivable	108,000	—	108,000
Intergovernmental grants receivable	50,000	20,000	70,000
Allowance for uncollectible property taxes	(60,000)	—	(60,000)
Accounts payable	(50,000)	(25,000)	(75,000)
Deferred revenue—property taxes	(10,000)	—	(10,000)
Fund balance	(16,500)	(13,000)	(29,500)
General revenues—property taxes	(2,670,000)	—	(2,670,000)
Program revenues— operating grants	(50,000)	(4,520,000)	(4,570,000)
Miscellaneous revenues	(18,000)	—	(18,000)
Interest revenue	—	(6,000)	(6,000)
Expenditures—general government	550,000	210,000	760,000
Expenditures—streets	2,200,000	3,990,000	6,190,000
Transfers out—Capital Projects Fund (Bland Street Drainage)	—	300,000	300,000
Transfers in—General Fund	(75,000)	—	(75,000)
Totals	$ 0	$ 0	$ 0

CHAPTER 4
CAPITAL PROJECTS FUNDS

CONTENTS

NATURE OF CAPITAL PROJECTS FUNDS

A Capital Projects Fund is used to account for major capital expenditures, such as the construction of civic centers, libraries, and general administrative services buildings. The acquisition of other capital assets, such as machinery, furniture, and vehicles, is usually accounted for in the fund responsible for the financing of the expenditure. The purpose of a Capital Projects Fund, as previously defined by NCGA-1, was

> to account for financial resources to be used for the acquisition or construction of major capital facilities (other than those financed by proprietary funds or in trust funds for individuals, private organizations, or other governments). (Capital outlays financed from general obligation bonds proceeds should be accounted for through a Capital Projects Fund.)

GASB-54 redefines capital projects funds as funds that

> are used to account for and report financial resources that are restricted, committed, or assigned to expenditure for capital outlays, including the acquisition or construction of capital facilities and other capital assets. Capital projects funds exclude those types of capital-related outflows financed by proprietary funds or for assets that will be held in trust for individuals, private organizations, or other governments.

The major difference is that the major capital facilities are not the only items funded by capital projects funds. Governments fund police cars, information technology, and other non-facility items through the use of capital projects funds. Hence, the expansion.

PRACTICE ALERT: Large governments may fund and build projects for smaller governments, deeding the project over to the smaller government upon completion. Because a capital asset is not being constructed that would ultimately be recorded on the larger government's books, either an agency fund or a special revenue fund may be used (if funded by federal grants, a special revenue fund may be preferable). The smaller government may use a capital projects fund on their books if they send monies to the larger government and receive the capital asset in exchange.

A separate Capital Projects Fund is usually established when the acquisition or construction of a capital project extends beyond a single fiscal year and the financing sources are provided by more than one fund, or the capital asset is financed by specifically designated resources. Specifically designated resources may arise from the issuance of general governmental bonds, receipts of grants from other governmental units, designation of a portion of tax receipts, or a combination of these and other financing sources. A Capital Projects Fund is to be used when mandated by law or stipulated by regulations or covenants related to the financing source. For control purposes, it also may be advantageous to use a separate Capital Projects Fund even though one is not legally required.

MEASUREMENT FOCUS AND BASIS OF ACCOUNTING

The modified accrual basis and flow of current financial resources are used to prepare the financial statements of a Capital Projects Fund. These concepts are discussed in Chapter 2, "The General Fund."

As noted above, resources to finance the construction of a capital asset may come from a variety of sources. Grants (either government-mandated or voluntary nonexchange transactions) received from another government are reported as revenue when the standards established by GASB-33 (Accounting and Financial Reporting for Nonexchange Transactions) are satisfied. Proceeds from the issuance of debt are recorded as other financing sources when the proceeds are available to the governmental entity. Transfers from the General Fund or other intergovernmental transfers are reported in the entity's financial statements based on the guidance provided by GASB-34 (par. 112).

PRACTICE POINT: Care must be taken in the recording of proceeds of long-term debt. Treasury practices may only account for the net receipt of cash proceeds from the issuance of the debt. However, the par amount of the debt may be different. For example, assume $100,000,000 in bonds are sold at a premium of 2% (at 102). Bond issuance costs are $500,000. Assume accrued interest is $0. The following calculation, then, would determine the amount of bonds to be allocated to fund capital projects:

Bonds at Par	$ 100,000,000
Original Issue Premium	2,000,000
Subtotal	102,000,000
Bond Issuance Costs	(500,000)
Net Proceeds to be allocated to fund capital projects	$101,500,000

In this example, the $101,500,000 would be allocated to bondable accounts while the $2,000,000 and $500,000 would be amortized over the life of the outstanding debt. The $100,000,000 needs to be included on the government-wide financial statements as part of outstanding long-term debt.

GASB-34 required that the *proceeds* from the sale of long-term debt be reported as an other financing source and that any related discount or premium, and/or debt issuance costs be separately reported. Taken literally, that cannot be accomplished, since the term *proceeds* generally means that any discount or premium and the related cost is netted against the face amount of the debt. GASB-37 (Basic Financial Statements—and Management's Discussion and Analysis—for State and Local Governments: Omnibus) points out that GASB-34 should have referred to the "face amount" of the debt and not to the proceeds. Under the clarified language, if debt with a face amount of $1,000,000 was issued for $1,050,000, the financial statements of the Capital Projects Fund would present two elements of the transactions, namely (1) long-term debt issued of $1,000,000 and (2) a premium on long-term debt issued of $50,000.

Furthermore, some governments bond in a consolidated fashion, and some bond in advance of expenditures and others in arrears. Each alternative has its own positive and negative aspects with regard to the Internal Revenue Code provisions on governmental bonds (IRC Section 146). Generally the recording of expenditures of a Capital Projects Fund is limited to payments or commitments to pay contractors and payments of support services (usually classified as general government expenditures). Commitments (liabilities) to pay contractors should be recorded as expenditures of the current budgetary period if they are normally expected to be liquidated with expendable available financial resources as defined by GASBI-6 (Recognition and Measurement of Certain Liabilities and Expenditures in Governmental Fund Financial Statements).

In many instances, a Capital Projects Fund will have excess cash, which will be temporally invested. Temporary investments and the related revenue are reported in the fund's financial statements based on the guidance provided by

GASB-31 (Accounting and Financial Reporting for Certain Investments and for External Investment Pools).

FINANCIAL REPORTING AT FUND LEVEL

The balances and activities of Capital Projects Funds are presented in the following two financial statements at the fund financial statement level:

1. Balance Sheet

2. Statement of Revenues, Expenditures, and Changes in Fund Balances

Transactions and accounts recorded in Capital Projects Funds continue to be based on standards established by various NCGA/GASB Statements and Interpretations that were outstanding before the issuance of GASB-34.

PRACTICE ALERT: GASB-54 (Fund Balance Reporting and Governmental Fund Type Definitions), effective for periods beginning after June 15, 2010, makes significant changes to fund balance classifications as well as clarifies and makes changes to the definitions of governmental fund types. The new definitions in GASB-54 provide that governmental funds of a particular type either should be used (i.e., required) or are used (i.e., discretionary) for all activities that meet its criteria. If use of a fund type is generally discretionary, specific situations under which a fund of that type should be used are identified either in the definitions in GASB-54 (i.e., debt service funds) or by requirements established in other authoritative pronouncements (i.e., special revenue and capital projects funds). The fund balance classification section of GASB-54 defines the terminology "restricted," "committed," and "assigned."

Capital Projects Fund Type

As previously mentioned, the capital projects fund type is defined as follows:

Fund Type	Pre GASB-54 Definition	Post GASB-54 Definition
Capital Project Funds	To account for financial resources to be used for the acquisition or construction of major capital facilities (other than those financed by proprietary funds or in trust funds for individuals, private organizations, or other governments).	To account for and report financial resources that are restricted, committed, or assigned to expenditure for capital outlays, including the acquisition or construction of capital facilities or other capital assets.

The two Capital Projects Funds financial statements include all of the governmental funds (General Fund, Special Revenue Funds, Capital Projects Funds, Debt Service Funds, and Permanent Funds), and these funds are reported based on the concept of a major fund as defined by GASB-34.

PRACTICE POINT: A significant aspect of reporting governmental funds and proprietary funds is that major funds are reported for these funds; however, combined financial statements for fund types are not reported. Fund financial statements must present in a separate column a (major) fund that satisfies both of the following criteria: (1) total assets, liabilities, revenues, or expenditures/expenses of the governmental/enterprise fund are equal to or greater than 10% of the corresponding total (assets, liabilities, and so forth) for all funds that are considered governmental funds/enterprise funds and (2) total assets, liabilities, revenues, or expenditures/expenses of the governmental fund/enterprise fund are equal to or greater than 5% of the corresponding total for all governmental and enterprise funds combined (GASB-34, pars. 74–76). In establishing these criteria, the GASB intended that a major fund arise when a particular element (assets for example) of a fund meets both the 10% threshold and the 5% threshold. Some preparers have read the requirement to mean that a major fund arises when one element (assets for example) satisfies the 10% threshold and another element (revenues, for example) satisfies the 5% threshold. GASB-37 amended GASB-34 to make clear the GASB's original intent: That is, a single element must satisfy both criteria.

FINANCIAL REPORTING AT GOVERNMENT-WIDE LEVEL

The fund-based financial statements as described above are included in a governmental entity's financial report in order to demonstrate that restrictions imposed by statutes, regulations, or contracts have been followed. Balances in these fund financial statements are converted from a modified accrual basis to an accrual basis in order to create the basic information for the government-wide financial statements.

For the most part, this approach requires that all of the Capital Projects Funds' combined ending trial balances (which are on a modified accrual basis) be adjusted to reflect accrual balances. Briefly, this means that all capital expenditures for the current period are converted to a specific asset (building, infrastructure, etc.) and proceeds from the issuance of debt are converted from an other source of financial resources to long-term debt. This conversion is illustrated later in this chapter.

OBSERVATION: The GASB concluded that if the unspent portion of the capital related debt was considered "capital related," the "invested in capital assets, net of related debt" component of net assets would be understated because there would be no capital assets to offset the debt. On the other hand, including the unspent proceeds with capital assets would not be appropriate. The GASB agreed that a practical solution would be to allocate that portion of the "capital related" debt to the component of net assets that includes the unspent proceeds; for example, "restricted net assets—capital projects." The GASB stated that they did not believe that this implies that the debt is "payable" from restricted assets but, rather, is merely consistent with the philosophy of "net" assets.

ILLUSTRATIVE TRANSACTIONS

Note: The transactions presented here assume that internal systems are *not* redesigned for GASB-54. Therefore conversion entries are used. In the 2013 edition of the CCH *Governmental GAAP Practice Manual*, beginning balances will be presented in GASB-54 format. Governments that do not redesign their internal accounting systems for GASB-54 will have to restate using adjusting entries similar to those contained in this section. The conversion entries to GASB-54 and assumptions are presented after JE04.24 and are presented as JE04.G54-1, JE04.G54-2, and so on.

In order to illustrate accounting and financial reporting standards that are observed for Capital Projects Funds, assume that the City of Centerville has the following Capital Projects Funds:

- Easely Street Bridge Project
- Bland Street Drainage Project
- West End Recreation Center Project

Easely Street Bridge Project

The Easely Street Bridge Project is being constructed to relieve traffic congestion between the downtown district and the east end of Centerville. Its trial balance for the beginning of the fiscal year is as follows:

	Trial Balance	
Accounts	Debit	Credit
Cash	$122,000	
Temporary investments	620,000	
Accounts payable		$ 26,000
Fund balance		716,000
Totals	$742,000	$742,000

The fund balance entries above are *not* GASB-54 compliant; however, they show what will likely be present in most trial balances for the year of conversion.

This section presents illustrative transactions and entries for the project during the fiscal year ended June 30, 20X2.

GASB-34 generally did not change the manner of accounting for transactions that are recorded in Capital Projects Funds.

Transaction JE04.01 —Accounts payable of $26,000 from the previous year were paid:

Accounts	Debit	Credit
Accounts payable	26,000	
Cash		26,000

Transaction JE04.02—During the year interest revenue of $30,000 was earned and received:

Accounts	Debit	Credit
Cash	30,000	
Interest revenue		30,000

Transaction JE04.03—Capital expenditures of $11,100,000 were incurred and paid during the year:

Accounts	Debit	Credit
Expenditures—capital outlays	11,100,000	
Cash		11,100,000

GASB-34 originally required that the cost of constructing a capital asset include certain interest costs as described in FAS-34 (Capitalization of Interest Cost). These costs would be part of the capital asset amount that is reported in the government-wide financial statements and would be included in the basis for computing depreciation expense. GASB-37 (Basic Financial Statements—and Management's Discussion and Analysis—for State and Local Governments: Omnibus) revises GASB-34 by stating that the cost basis of a capital assets does not include interest costs incurred during the construction of a capital asset related to governmental activities. However, the elimination of the provisions of FAS-34 does not apply to the capitalization of interest costs incurred by Enterprise Funds and, therefore, interest is capitalized and reported for business-type activities.

Transaction JE04.04—General government expenditures of $495,000 were incurred, of which $400,000 were paid:

Accounts	Debit	Credit
Expenditures—general government	495,000	
Cash		400,000
Accounts payable		95,000

PRACTICE POINT: Based on the standards established by GASBI-6, expenditures should continue to be recorded on an accrual basis except with respect to the expenditures identified in the Interpretation.

Transaction JE04.05—On October 1, 20X1, bonds with a maturity value of $10,000,000 were issued for $9,328,956. The bonds had a stated interest rate of 7% and were sold at an effective interest rate of 8%. Interest is paid annually:

Accounts	Debit	Credit
Cash	9,328,956	
Discount on long-term debt issued (other uses of financial resources)	671,044	
Long-term debt issued (other sources of financial resources)		10,000,000

GASB-34 originally required that the *proceeds* from the sale of long-term debt be reported as an other financing source and that any related discount or premium, and/or debt issuance costs be separately reported. Taken literally, that cannot be accomplished since the term *proceeds* generally means that any discount or premium and the related cost is netted against the face amount of the debt. The GASB's *Comprehensive Implementation Guide* points out that GASB-34 should have referred to the "face amount" of the debt and not to the proceeds.

GASB-37 amends GASB-34 by substituting the term "proceeds" with "face amount."

Transaction JE04.06—A capital grant of $1,250,000 was received from the state government:

Accounts	Debit	Credit
Cash	1,250,000	
Program revenues—capital grants and contributions (streets)		1,250,000

Transaction JE04.07—Additional temporary investments of $75,000 were made during the year:

Accounts	Debit	Credit
Temporary investments	75,000	
Cash		75,000

Transaction JE04.08—The General Fund made a transfer of $1,000,000 to help fund the project:

Accounts	Debit	Credit
Cash	1,000,000	
Transfers in—General Fund		1,000,000

After the transactions for the year are posted, the year-end trial balance (June 30, 20X2) for the Easely Street Bridge Capital Project appears as follows before conversion to GASB-54:

Accounts	Adjusted Trial Balance Debit	Credit
Cash	$ 129,956	
Temporary investments	695,000	
Accounts payable		$95,000
Fund balance		716,000
Program revenues—capital grants (street)		1,250,000
Interest revenue		30,000
Expenditures—capital outlays (streets)	11,100,000	
Expenditures—general government	495,000	
Long-term debt issued (other sources of financial resources)		10,000,000
Discount on long-term debt issued (other uses of financial resources)	671,044	
Transfers in—General Fund		1,000,000
Totals	$13,091,000	$13,091,000

PRACTICE ALERT: Absent any other information, the only reclass to implement GASB-54 will be to reclass the beginning fund balance to fund balance—assigned. The net surplus or deficit would also close to fund balance—assigned until a negative fund balance is generated. If no other committed or restricted balances are available, the negative fund balance would be unassigned. If a budget or enabling legislation was passed, then a balance may be committed.

The worksheet that summarizes the foregoing journal entries for the Easely Street Bridge Capital Project for the year-end trial balance is presented in Appendix 4A.

Bland Street Drainage Project

The Bland Street Drainage Project is being constructed to mitigate flooding problems. Its trial balance for the beginning of the fiscal year is as follows:

	Trial Balance	
Accounts	Debit	Credit
Cash	$ 127,000	
Temporary investments	42,000	
Accounts payable		$ 33,000
Fund balance		136,000
Totals	$ 169,000	$ 169,000

This section presents illustrative transactions and entries for the project during the fiscal year ended June 30, 20X2.

Transaction JE04.09—Accounts payable of $33,000 from the previous year were paid:

Accounts	Debit	Credit
Accounts payable	33,000	
Cash		33,000

Transaction JE04.10—During the year, interest revenue of $4,000 was earned and received:

Accounts	Debit	Credit
Cash	4,000	
Interest revenue		4,000

Transaction JE04.11—Capital expenditures of $1,500,000 were incurred and paid during the year:

Accounts	Debit	Credit
Expenditures—capital outlays	1,500,000	
Cash		1,500,000

A governmental entity's capital assets are reported in the government-wide financial statements. Footnote 64 to GASB-34 notes that a government that has the primary responsibility for maintaining a particular infrastructure asset should report the asset in its financial statements. The GASB's *Comprehensive Implementation Guide* makes it clear that footnote 64 applies only to situations in which the ownership of a particular asset is uncertain. Generally, ambiguity of ownership would only arise for infrastructure assets such as highways. The GASB's *Guide* also addresses whether title and ownership are one and the same. Public assets are unique in that although title is held by the governmental entity's citizens, numerous other parties and entities have the right to use the property. Nonetheless, the governmental entity that holds title to an asset should generally report the asset in its financial statements. The GASB's *Guide* notes that one exception to this generalization occurs when a lessee reports a capitalized lease based on the standards established by NCGA-5 (Accounting and Financial Reporting Principles for Lease Agreements of State and Local Governments).

In many instances capital assets purchased by state or local governments are financed or partially financed by federal awards, and the federal government could retain a reversionary interest in the asset. The GASB's *Comprehensive Implementation Guide* states that such assets (even though the federal government retains a reversionary interest in the asset's salvage value) should be reported by the state or local government because "the state or local government is the party that uses the assets in its activities and makes the decisions regarding when and how the assets will be used and managed." Except in the case of certain infrastructure assets (where the modified approach is used), depreciation expense should be recorded for these assets.

Transaction JE04.12—General government expenditures of $97,000 were incurred, of which $70,000 were paid:

Accounts	Debit	Credit
Expenditures—general government	97,000	
Cash		70,000
Accounts payable		27,000

Transaction JE04.13—A capital grant of $750,000 was received from the federal government:

Accounts	Debit	Credit
Cash	750,000	
Program revenues—capital grants and contributions (streets)		750,000

Transaction JE04.14—Additional temporary investments of $20,000 were made during the year:

Accounts	Debit	Credit
Temporary investments	20,000	
Cash		20,000

Transaction JE04.15—The General Fund made a transfer of $600,000 to help fund the project:

Accounts	Debit	Credit
Cash	600,000	
Transfers in—general fund		600,000

Transaction JE04.16—During the year, $300,000 was received from the Local Fuel Tax Fund (Special Revenues Fund):

Accounts	Debit	Credit
Cash	300,000	
Transfers in—special revenue fund (local fuel tax fund)		300,000

After the transactions for the year are posted, the year-end trial balance (June 30, 20X2) for the Bland Street Drainage Project appears as follows:

	Adjusted Trial Balance	
Accounts	Debit	Credit
Cash	$158,000	
Temporary investments	62,000	
Accounts payable		$27,000
Fund balance		136,000
Program revenues—capital grants and contributions (street)		750,000
Interest revenue		4,000
Expenditures—capital outlays (streets)	1,500,000	
Expenditures—general government	97,000	
Transfers in—general fund		600,000
Transfers in—special revenue fund (local fuel tax fund)		300,000
Totals	$1,817,000	$1,817,000

PRACTICE ALERT: Similarly to above, absent any other information, the only reclass to implement GASB-54 will be to reclass the beginning fund balance to fund balance—assigned. The net surplus or deficit would also close to fund balance—assigned until a negative fund balance is generated. If no other committed or restricted balances are available, the negative fund balance would be unassigned. If a budget was passed or enabling legislation, then a balance may be committed.

The worksheet that summarizes the foregoing journal entries for the Bland Street Drainage Capital Project for the year-end trial balance is presented in Appendix 4B.

West End Recreation Center Project

Construction on the West End Recreation Center was started during the current year in order to provide recreational activities to pre-teen and teenage students. Prior to the current year, funds were accumulated in the fund before actual construction was begun. The West End Recreation Center Project Fund's trial balance for the beginning of the fiscal year is as follows:

	Trial Balance	
Accounts	Debit	Credit
Cash	$500,000	
Temporary investments	22,000	

	Trial Balance	
Accounts	**Debit**	**Credit**
Accounts payable		$13,000
Fund balance		509,000
Totals	$522,000	$522,000

Transaction JE04.17—Accounts payable of $13,000 from the previous year were paid:

Accounts	**Debit**	**Credit**
Accounts payable	13,000	
Cash		13,000

Transaction JE04.18—During the year interest revenue of $2,000 was earned and received:

Accounts	**Debit**	**Credit**
Cash	2,000	
Interest revenue		2,000

Transaction JE04.19—Capital expenditures of $1,300,000 were incurred and paid during the year:

Accounts	**Debit**	**Credit**
Expenditures—capital outlays	1,300,000	
Cash		1,300,000

Transaction JE04.20—General government expenditures of $25,000 were incurred, of which $20,000 were paid:

Accounts	**Debit**	**Credit**
Expenditures—general government	25,000	
Cash		20,000
Accounts payable		5,000

Transaction JE04.21—On December 31, 20X1, serial bonds of $3,000,000 were issued at par. The bonds mature at a rate of $500,000 every six months beginning on June 30, 20X2. Interest of 12% is due semiannually beginning on June 30, 20X2:

Accounts	**Debit**	**Credit**
Cash	3,000,000	
Long-term debt issued (other sources of financial resources)		3,000,000

NCGA-1 mandates that the principal repayment and interest related to long-term debt be recorded when the amounts are due and payable (cash basis); however, governmental accounting standards do not address when proceeds from the issuance of long-term debt should be recorded. The AICPA's *State and Local Governments—Audit and Accounting Guide* states that debt proceeds should be recorded "in the period debt instruments are issued, that is, on the closing date." When debt is issued in one year but the proceeds are actually received shortly after the end of the year, a receivable should be recorded in the year in which the debt is issued.

PRACTICE POINT: Due to federal tax rules, for consolidated sales of debt in arrears, bond proceeds are often not allocated until six months after closing, in order to gain assurance that expenditures are eligible to be bonded. If the proceeds are unallocated at year-end, they cannot be included as part of invested in capital assets, net of related debt, because the capital assets have not yet been identified

Transaction JE04.22—A capital grant of $450,000 was received from the state government:

Accounts	Debit	Credit
Cash	450,000	
Program revenues—capital grants and contributions (recreation and parks)		450,000

Transaction JE04.23—Additional temporary investments of $2,900,000 were made during the year:

Accounts	Debit	Credit
Temporary investments	2,900,000	
Cash		2,900,000

Transaction JE04.24—The General Fund made a transfer of $300,000 to help fund the project:

Accounts	Debit	Credit
Cash	300,000	
Transfers in—general fund		300,000

After the transactions for the year are posted, the year-end trial balance (June 30, 20X2) for the West End Recreation Center Capital Project appears as follows:

	Adjusted Trial Balance	
Accounts	Debit	Credit
Cash	$19,000	
Temporary investments	2,922,000	
Accounts payable		$5,000
Fund balance		509,000
Program revenues—capital grants and contributions (recreation and parks)		450,000
Interest revenue		2,000
Expenditures—capital outlays (recreation and parks)	1,300,000	
Expenditures—general government	25,000	
Long-term debt issued		3,000,000
Transfers in—general fund		300,000
Totals	$4,266,000	$4,266,000

The worksheet that summarizes the foregoing journal entries for the West End Recreation Center Capital Project for the year-end trial balance is presented in Appendix 4C.

FUND FINANCIAL STATEMENTS

Before Conversion to GASB-54

At the fund financial statement level, a governmental fund must prepare a statement of revenues, expenditures, and changes in fund balances and a balance sheet. Based on the adjusted trial balances created above, the following preliminary financial statements reflect the balances and activities of the three Capital Projects Funds. These financial statements are prepared to facilitate the preparation of the fund financial statements illustrated in Chapter 13, "Developing Information For Fund Financial Statements." (See Appendixes 4D and 4E.)

Capital Projects Funds
Balance Sheet
June 30, 20X2

	Easely Street Bridge Project	Bland Street Drainage Project	West End Recreation Center Project	Total
ASSETS				
Cash	$129,956	$158,000	$19,000	$306,956
Temporary investments	695,000	62,000	2,922,000	3,679,000
Total assets	$824,956	$220,000	$2,941,000	$3,985,956
LIABILITIES AND FUND BALANCES				
Liabilities:				
Accounts payable	$95,000	$27,000	$5,000	$127,000
Total liabilities	95,000	27,000	5,000	127,000
Fund balances:				
Fund balance— unreserved	729,956	193,000	2,936,000	3,858,956
Total liabilities and fund balances	$824,956	$220,000	$2,941,000	$3,985,956

GASB-54 CONVERSION ENTRIES

The following balances are key for a proper GASB-54 conversion in the conversion year:

Fund balance—Easily Street Bridge Project	716,000
Fund balance—Bland Street Drainage Project	136,000
Fund balance—West End Recreation Center Project	509,000

However, other information is needed to properly convert the beginning balances and the ending balances. This information may include the following:

Nonspendable Balances	Any balances of inventory and long-term receivables.
Restricted Balances	Any balances from bond proceeds, grants, and other external restrictions or due to enabling statutes.
Committed Balances	Any passed budgets or other commitments made by the highest level of decision making.

To reclass the beginning balances, the following entries are needed.

Transaction JE04.G54-1 (reclass) Undesignated balances in capital projects funds are generally assigned balances.

Accounts	Debit	Credit
Fund balance—reserved –Easily Street Bridge Project	716,000	
Fund balance—assigned –Easily Street Bridge Project		716,000

For the Bland Street Drainage Project:

Accounts	Debit	Credit
Fund balance—reserved –Bland Street Drainage Project	136,000	
Fund balance—assigned –Bland Street Drainage Project		136,000

For the West End Recreation Center Project

Accounts	Debit	Credit
Fund balance—reserved –West End Recreation Center Project	509,000	
Fund balance—assigned –West End Recreation Center Project		509,000

Assume that Central City doesn't budget for these funds and no other commitments or restrictions exist.

Capital Projects Funds
Statement of Revenues, Expenditures, and
Changes in Fund Balances
June 30, 20X2

	Easely Street Bridge Project	Bland Street Drainage Project	West End Recreation Center Project	Total
REVENUES				
Program revenues—capital grants (street)	$1,250,000	$750,000	—	$2,000,000

Capital Projects Funds
Statement of Revenues, Expenditures, and
Changes in Fund Balances
June 30, 20X2

	Easely Street Bridge Project	Bland Street Drainage Project	West End Recreation Center Project	Total
Program revenues—capital grants and contributions (recreation and parks)	—	—	$450,000	450,000
Interest	30,000	4,000	2,000	36,000
Total revenue	1,280,000	754,000	452,000	2,486,000
EXPENDITURES				
General government	495,000	97,000	25,000	617,000
Capital outlays	11,100,000	1,500,000	1,300,000	13,900,000
Total expenditures	11,595,000	1,597,000	1,325,000	14,517,000
Excess (deficiency) of revenues over expenditures	(10,315,000)	(843,000)	(873,000)	(12,031,000)
OTHER FINANCING SOURCES (USES)				
Long-term debt issued	10,000,000	—	3,000,000	13,000,000
Discount on long-term debt issued	(671,044)	—	—	(671,044)
Transfers in	1,000,000	900,000	300,000	2,200,000
Total other financing sources and uses	10,328,956	900,000	3,300,000	14,528,956
Net change in fund balances	13,956	57,000	2,427,000	2,497,956
Fund balances—beginning	716,000	136,000	509,000	1,361,000
Fund balances—ending	$729,956	$193,000	$2,936,000	$3,858,956

PRACTICE ALERT: GASB-54 does not require the presentation of desegregated fund balances in the statement of revenues, expenditures, and changes in fund balances. To do so would not be GAAP and, furthermore, would probably cause separate columns for separate classes of fund balances similar to not-for-profit financial statements. All surplus closes to Fund balance—assigned. Annual deficits would close to Fund balance—assigned unless no positive balances are available in assigned balances. If deficit balances still exist after lowering all positive balances to zero, the remainder would be labeled fund deficit—unassigned.

The combined financial statements for the Capital Projects Funds are not reported separately in the governmental entity's financial report, but they are used in Chapter 13, "Developing Information for Fund Financial Statements."

GOVERNMENT-WIDE FINANCIAL STATEMENTS

Government-wide financial statements are reported on the accrual basis of accounting. Generally, most governments work from their governmental fund financial statements (which are on a modified accrual basis) and through the use of worksheet entries convert to accrual based financial statements.

In order to convert the transactions that were recorded in the Capital Projects Funds from a modified accrual basis to an accrual basis the following worksheet entries are made.

Easely Street Bridge Project

The capital expenditure on the bridge is converted from an expenditure to a capital asset (infrastructure assets) by making the following worksheet entry:

	Accounts	Debit	Credit
JE04.25	Construction-in-progress	11,100,000	
	Expenditures—capital outlays		11,100,000
	(To record the construction of a capital asset and reverse the recognition of the related expenditure)		

The issuance of debt is converted from net source of financial resources to a liability by making the following worksheet entry:

	Accounts	Debit	Credit
JE04.26	Long-term debt issued (other sources of financial resources)	10,000,000	
	Discount on long-term debt issued (other uses of financial resources)		671,044
	Bonds payable		9,328,956
	(To record the issuance of long-term debt and reverse the recognition of other sources of financial resources)		

The conversion entry to accrue interest expense including the effects of the amortization of bond discount is made in Chapter 5, "Debt Service Funds."

Bland Street Drainage Project

The capital expenditure on the Bland Street drainage project is converted from an expenditure to a capital asset (infrastructure assets) by making the following worksheet entry:

	Accounts	Debit	Credit
JE04.27	Construction-in-progress	1,500,000	
	Expenditures—capital outlays		1,500,000
	(To record the construction of a capital asset and reverse the recognition of the related expenditure)		

West End Recreation Center Project

The capital expenditure on the recreation center is converted from an expenditure to a building (other capital assets) by making the following worksheet entry:

Accounts	Debit	Credit
JE04.28 Construction-in-progress	1,300,000	
Expenditures—capital outlays		1,300,000
(To record the construction of a capital asset and reverse the recognition of the related expenditure)		

The issuance of debt is converted from a source of financial resources to a liability by making the following worksheet entry:

Accounts	Debit	Credit
JE04.29 Long-term debt issued (other sources of financial resources)	3,000,000	
Bonds payable		3,000,000
(To record the issuance of long-term debt and reverse the recognition of other sources of financial resources)		

The serial bonds in this example are due in $500,000 installments every six months. The long-term liabilities will be allocated between the amounts due within one year and beyond one year in Chapter 16, "Basic Financial Statements."

After the foregoing entries are prepared, the adjusted trial balances (on an accrual basis) for the three Capital Projects Funds appear as follows as of June 30, 20X1 (see Appendix 4F):

Adjusted Trial Balance

Accounts	Easely Street Bridge Project Debits (Credits)	Bland Street Drainage Project Debits (Credits)	West End Recreation Center Project Debits (Credits)	Total Debits (Credits)
Cash	$ 129,956	$ 158,000	$ 19,000	$ 306,956
Temporary investments	695,000	62,000	2,922,000	3,679,000
Construction-in-progress	11,100,000	1,500,000	1,300,000	13,900,000
Accounts payable	(95,000)	(27,000)	(5,000)	(127,000)
Bonds payable	(9,328,956)	—	(3,000,000)	(12,328,956)
Net Assets	(716,000)	(136,000)	(509,000)	(1,361,000)
Program revenues—capital grants (street)	(1,250,000)	(750,000)	—	(2,000,000)
Program revenues—capital grants and contributions (recreation and parks)	—	—	(450,000)	(450,000)
Interest revenue	(30,000)	(4,000)	(2,000)	(36,000)

Adjusted Trial Balance

Accounts	Easely Street Bridge Project Debits (Credits)	Bland Street Drainage Project Debits (Credits)	West End Recreation Center Project Debits (Credits)	Total Debits (Credits)
Expenditures—general government	495,000	97,000	25,000	617,000
Transfers in	(1,000,000)	(900,000)	(300,000)	(2,200,000)
Totals	$ -0-	$ -0-	$ -0-	$ -0-

This combined trial balance on the accrual basis is used in Chapter 14, "Developing Information for Government-Wide Financial Statements."

APPENDIX 4A: WORKSHEET FOR SUMMARIZING CURRENT TRANSACTIONS: EASELY STREET BRIDGE PROJECT

Accounts	Trial Balance Debit	Trial Balance Credit	Adjustments Ref	Adjustments Debit	Adjustments Ref	Adjustments Credit	Adjusted Trial Balance Debit	Adjusted Trial Balance Credit	Operating Statement Debit	Operating Statement Credit	Balance Sheet Debit	Balance Sheet Credit
Cash	122,000	—	JE04.02	30,000	JE04.01	26,000	129,956	—	—	—	129,956	—
			JE04.05	9,328,956	JE04.03	11,100,000	—	—	—	—	—	—
			JE04.06	1,250,000	JE04.04	400,000	—	—	—	—	—	—
			JE04.08	1,000,000	JE04.07	75,000	—	—	—	—	—	—
Temporary investments	620,000	—	JE04.07	75,000		—	695,000	—	—	—	695,000	—
Accounts payable	—	26,000	JE04.01	26,000	JE04.04	95,000	—	95,000	—	—	—	95,000
Fund balance—	—	716,000		—		—	—	716,000	—	—	—	716,000
Program revenues— capital grants and contributions (Street)	—	—		—	JE04.06	1,250,000	—	1,250,000	—	1,250,000	—	—
Interest revenue	—	—		—	JE04.02	30,000	—	30,000	—	30,000	—	—
Expenditures—capital outlays (streets)	—	—	JE04.03	11,100,000		—	11,100,000	—	11,100,000	—	—	—

Account	Encumbrances Dr	Encumbrances Cr	Trial Balance Dr	Trial Balance Cr	Adjustments Dr	Adjustments Cr	Operating Statement Dr	Operating Statement Cr	Balance Sheet Dr	Balance Sheet Cr
Expenditures—general government	—	—	—	—	**JE04.04** 495,000	—	495,000	—	—	—
Long-term debt issued (other sources of financial resources)	—	—	—	—	—	**JE04.05** 10,000,000	—	10,000,000	—	—
Discount on long-term debt issued (other uses of financial resources)	—	—	—	—	**JE04.05** 671,044	—	671,044	—	—	—
Transfers in—General Fund	—	—	—	—	—	**JE04.08** 1,000,000	—	1,000,000	—	—
Totals	742,000	742,000	23,976,000	23,976,000	13,091,000	13,091,044	12,266,044	12,280,000	824,956	811,000
Net increase (decrease)							13,956			13,956
							12,280,000	12,280,000	824,956	824,956

APPENDIX 4B: WORKSHEET FOR SUMMARIZING CURRENT TRANSACTIONS: BLAND STREET DRAINAGE PROJECT

Accounts	Trial Balance		Adjustments				Adjusted Trial Balance		Operating Statement		Balance Sheet	
	Debit	Credit	(ref)	Debit	(ref)	Credit	Debit	Credit	Debit	Credit	Debit	Credit
Cash	127,000	—	JE04.10	4,000	JE04.09	33,000	158,000	—	—	—	158,000	—
			JE04.13	750,000	JE04.11	1,500,000						
			JE04.15	600,000	JE04.12	70,000						
			JE04.16	300,000	JE04.14	20,000						
Temporary investments	42,000	—	JE04.14	20,000		—	62,000	—	—	—	62,000	—
Accounts payable	—	33,000	JE04.09	33,000	JE04.12	27,000	—	27,000	—	—	—	27,000
Fund balance—	—	136,000		—			—	136,000	—	—	—	136,000
Program revenues—capital grants and contributions (street)	—	—		—	JE04.13	750,000	—	750,000	—	750,000	—	—
Interest revenue	—	—		—	JE04.10	4,000	—	4,000	—	4,000	—	—

Account											
Expenditures—capital outlays (streets)	—	—	JE04.11	1,500,000	—	—	1,500,000	—	1,500,000	—	—
Expenditures—general government	—	—	JE04.12	97,000	—	—	97,000	—	97,000	—	—
Transfers in—General Fund	—	—		—	JE04.15	600,000	—	600,000	—	600,000	—
Transfers in—special revenue fund (local fuel tax fund)	—	—		—	JE04.16	300,000	—	300,000	—	300,000	—
Totals	169,000	169,000		3,304,000		3,304,000	1,817,000	1,817,000	1,597,000	1,654,000	220,000
											163,000
Net increase (decrease)									57,000	—	—
											57,000
	169,000	169,000		3,304,000		3,304,000	1,817,000	1,817,000	1,654,000	1,654,000	220,000
											220,000

APPENDIX 4C: WORKSHEET FOR SUMMARIZING CURRENT TRANSACTIONS: WEST END RECREATION CENTER CAPITAL PROJECT

Accounts	Trial Balance Debit	Trial Balance Credit	Adjustments Debit	Adjustments Credit	Adjusted Trial Balance Debit	Adjusted Trial Balance Credit	Operating Statement Debit	Operating Statement Credit	Balance Sheet Debit	Balance Sheet Credit
Cash	500,000	—	JE04.18 2,000 JE04.21 3,000,000 JE04.22 450,000 JE04.24 300,000	JE04.17 13,000 JE04.19 1,300,000 JE04.20 20,000 JE04.23 2,900,000	19,000	—	—	—	19,000	—
Temporary investments	22,000	—	JE04.23 2,900,000	—	2,922,000	—	—	—	2,922,000	—
Accounts payable	—	13,000	JE04.17 13,000	JE04.20 5,000	—	5,000	—	—	—	5,000
Fund balance	—	509,000	—	—	—	509,000	—	—	—	509,000
Program revenues—capital grants and contributions (recreation and parks)	—	—	—	JE04.22 450,000	—	450,000	—	450,000	—	—
Interest revenue	—	—	—	JE04.18 2,000	—	2,000	—	2,000	—	—

			JE						
Expenditures—capital outlays (recreation and parks)	—	—	JE04.19	1,300,000	—	1,300,000	—	—	—
Expenditures—general government	—	—	JE04.20	25,000	—	25,000	—	—	—
Long-term debt issued	—	3,000,000	JE04.21	—	3,000,000	—	3,000,000	—	—
Transfers in—General Fund	—	300,000	JE04.24	300,000	300,000	300,000	—	—	—
Totals	522,000	7,990,000		4,266,000	4,266,000	1,325,000	3,752,000	2,427,000	2,941,000
Net increase (decrease)	—	—		—	—	2,427,000	—	514,000	—
	522,000	7,990,000		4,266,000	4,266,000	3,752,000	3,752,000	2,941,000	2,941,000

APPENDIX 4D: CAPITAL PROJECTS FUNDS: BALANCE SHEET AND STATEMENT OF REVENUES, EXPENDITURES, AND CHANGES IN FUND BALANCES

Capital Projects Funds
Balance Sheet
June 30, 20X2

	Easely Street Bridge Project	Bland Street Drainage Project	West End Recreation Center Project	Total
ASSETS				
Cash	$129,956	$158,000	$ 19,000	$ 306,956
Temporary investments	695,000	62,000	2,922,000	3,679,000
Total assets	$824,956	$220,000	$2,941,000	$3,985,956
LIABILITIES AND FUND BALANCES				
Liabilities:				
Accounts payable	$ 95,000	$ 27,000	$ 5,000	$ 127,000
Total liabilities	95,000	27,000	5,000	127,000
Fund balances:				
Fund balance—assigned	729,956	193,000	2,936,000	3,858,956
Total liabilities and fund balances	$824,956	$220,000	$2,941,000	$3,985,956

Capital Projects Funds
Statement of Revenues, Expenditures, and Changes in Fund Balances
June 30, 20X2

	Easely Street Bridge Project	Bland Street Drainage Project	West End Recreation Center Project	Total
REVENUES				
Program revenues—capital grants (street)	$1,250,000	$750,000	—	$2,000,000

Program revenues—capital grants and contributions (recreation and parks)	—	—	$450,000	450,000
Interest	30,000	4,000	2,000	36,000
Total revenue	1,280,000	754,000	452,000	2,486,000

EXPENDITURES

General government	495,000	97,000	25,000	617,000
Capital outlays	11,100,000	1,500,000	1,300,000	13,900,000
Total expenditures	11,595,000	1,597,000	1,325,000	14,517,000
Excess (deficiency) of revenues over expenditures	(10,315,000)	(843,000)	(873,000)	(12,031,000)

OTHER FINANCING SOURCES (USES)

Long-term debt issued	10,000,000	—	3,000,000	13,000,000
Discount on long-term debt issued	(671,044)	—	—	(671,044)
Transfers in	1,000,000	900,000	300,000	2,200,000
Total other financing sources and uses	10,328,956	900,000	3,300,000	14,528,956
Net change in fund balances	13,956	57,000	2,427,000	2,497,956
Fund balances— beginning	716,000	136,000	509,000	1,361,000
Fund balances— ending	$ 729,956	$ 193,000	$2,936,000	$ 3,858,956

APPENDIX 4E: CAPITAL PROJECTS FUNDS: WORKSHEET TO CONVERT FROM MODIFIED ACCRUAL TO ACCRUAL BASIS

	Modified Accrual Basis		Adjustments	Accrual Basis
Cash	306,956		—	306,956
Temporary investments	3,679,000		—	3,679,000
Construction in progress	—	JE04.25	11,100,000	13,900,000
	—	JE04.27	1,500,000	
	—	JE04.28	1,300,000	
Accounts payable	(127,000)		—	(127,000)
Bonds payable	—	JE04.26	(9,328,956)	(12,328,956)
	—	JE04.29	(3,000,000)	
Fund balance—reserved	(1,361,000)		—	(1,361,000)
Program revenues—capital grants (street)	(2,000,000)		—	(2,000,000)
Program revenues—capital grants and contributions (recreation and parks)	(450,000)		—	(450,000)
Interest	(36,000)		—	(36,000)
General government	617,000		—	617,000
Capital outlays	13,900,000	JE04.25	(11,100,000)	0
	—	JE04.27	(1,500,000)	
	—	JE04.28	(1,300,000)	
Long-term debt issued	(13,000,000)	JE04.26	10,000,000	0
	—	JE04.29	3,000,000	
Discount on long-term debt issued	671,044		(671,044)	0
Transfers in	(2,200,000)		—	(2,200,000)
Total	0		0	0

APPENDIX 4F: CAPITAL PROJECTS FUNDS: ADJUSTED TRIAL BALANCES

	Adjusted Trial Balance			
	Easely Street Bridge Project	Bland Street Drainage Project	West End Recreation Center Project	Total
Accounts	Debits (Credits)	Debits (Credits)	Debits (Credits)	Debits (Credits)
Cash	$ 129,956	$ 158,000	$ 19,000	$ 306,956
Temporary investments	695,000	62,000	2,922,000	3,679,000
Construction-in-progress	11,100,000	1,500,000	1,300,000	13,900,000
Accounts payable	(95,000)	(27,000)	(5,000)	(127,000)
Bonds payable	(9,328,956)	—	(3,000,000)	(12,328,956)
Fund balance	(716,000)	(136,000)	(509,000)	(1,361,000)
Program revenues—capital grants (street)	(1,250,000)	(750,000)	—	(2,000,000)
Program revenues—capital grants and contributions (recreation and parks)	—	—	(450,000)	(450,000)
Interest revenue	(30,000)	(4,000)	(2,000)	(36,000)
Expenditures—general government	495,000	97,000	25,000	617,000
Transfers in	(1,000,000)	(900,000)	(300,000)	(2,200,000)
Totals	$ -0-	$ -0-	$ -0-	$ -0-

CHAPTER 5
DEBT SERVICE FUNDS

CONTENTS

NATURE OF DEBT SERVICE FUNDS

A Debt Service Fund may be created to account for resources that will be used to service general long-term debt. General long-term debt includes noncurrent bonds and notes, as well as other noncurrent liabilities that might arise from capitalized lease agreements and other long-term liabilities not created by the issuance of a specific debt instrument.

MEASUREMENT FOCUS AND BASIS OF ACCOUNTING

The modified accrual basis and flow of current financial resources are used to prepare the financial statements of a Debt Service Fund. These concepts are discussed in Chapter 2, "The General Fund."

The resources that flow into a Debt Service Fund may come from a variety of sources, including taxes specifically levied to service a particular debt issue, special assessments levied against certain property owners, transfers from other funds (usually the General Fund), any premium or accrued interest created when the related debt was issued, and any excess funds remaining in the related Capital Projects Fund when the capital asset is completed.

Taxes or special assessments levied specifically to service a particular debt issuance are recorded as revenue in the Debt Service Fund. Levies and assessments not specifically identified for the purpose of servicing a particular debt issuance are recorded as revenue in the fund that is responsible for the tax or assessment (usually the General Fund), and the eventual movement from that fund to the Debt Service Fund is reported as a transfer. Premiums, accrued interest, or excess funds remaining after construction received by the Debt Service Fund are also reported as transfers.

Prior to the issuance of GASB-34, transfers were identified as operating or residual equity transfers. GASB-34 eliminated these distinctions and all are referred to simply as transfers. Furthermore, no transfer can be reported as an adjustment to the beginning balance of the fund balance of any fund (GASB-34, par. 112).

Generally, the recording of expenditures of a Debt Service Fund is limited to payments servicing debt (both principal repayments and interest) and payments of support services (usually classified as general government expenditures). Interest and principal on long-term debt are not recorded as expenditures as they accrue, but rather when they become due and payable. For example, if a governmental entity issues a 30-year bond, the liability would not be reported as a fund liability until the debt is actually due and payable, which would be thirty years after issuance.

Current accounting standards provide for an exception to the basic concept that general long-term indebtedness is not reported as an expenditure until the amount becomes due and payable. For example, when funds have been transferred to the Debt Service Fund during the fiscal year in anticipation of making debt service payments "shortly" after the end of the period, it is acceptable to accrue the related liability in the Debt Service Fund as an expenditure in the year the transfer is made.

Prior to the issuance of GASBI-6 (Recognition and Measurement of Certain Liabilities and Expenditures in Governmental Fund Financial Statements), there was a considerable amount of confusion about what is meant by "shortly." The Interpretation states that "shortly" means "early in the following year;" however, the period of time after the end of the year cannot be greater than one month (GASBI-6, pars. 9 and 13).

FINANCIAL REPORTING AT FUND LEVEL

The balances and activities of Debt Service Funds are presented in the following two financial statements at the fund financial statement level:

1. Balance Sheet
2. Statement of Revenues, Expenditures, and Changes in Fund Balances

Transactions and accounts recorded in Debt Service Funds continue to be based on standards established by various NCGA and GASB Statements and Interpretations that were outstanding before the issuance of GASB-34.

PRACTICE ALERT: GASB-54 (Fund Balance Reporting and Governmental Fund Type Definitions), effective for periods beginning after June 15, 2010, makes significant changes to fund balance classifications as well as clarifies and makes changes to the definitions of governmental fund types. The new definitions in GASB-54 provide that governmental funds of a particular type either should be used (i.e., required) or are used (i.e., discretionary) for all activities that meet its criteria. If use of a fund type is generally discretionary, specific situations under which a fund of that type should be used are identified either in the definitions in GASB-54 (i.e., debt service funds) or by requirements established in other authoritative pronouncements (i.e., special revenue and capital projects funds). The fund balance classification section of GASB-54 defines the terminology "restricted," "committed," and "assigned."

Debt Service Fund Types

Debt service fund types are defined as follows:

Fund Type	Pre GASB-54 Definition	Post GASB-54 Definition
Debt Service Funds	To account for the accumulation of resources for, and the payment of, general long-term debt principal and interest.	To account for and report financial resources that are restricted, committed, or assigned to expenditure for principal and interest.

The GASB-54 states that debt service funds should be used to report resources if they are legally mandated or are being accumulated for principal and interest maturing in future years. This new definition for debt service funds is not significantly different from the current definition and is likely to result in little or no change in current practice.

The aforementioned two fund financial statements include all of the governmental funds (General Fund, Special Revenue Funds, Capital Projects Funds, Debt Service Funds, and Permanent Funds), and these funds are reported based on the concept of a major fund as defined by GASB-34.

PRACTICE POINT: Ideally proceeds and escrow fund balances of crossover refunding bond transactions should also be shown in debt service funds. In these transactions, prior bonds are legally defeased through the refunding transaction. However, because the proceeds are not escrowed properly or are not invested in direct obligations of the U.S. government (especially state and local government securities [SLGS]), obligations guaranteed by the U.S. government or securities backed by the U.S. government and (or the escrow is not funded sufficiently to pay the entirety of the principal and interest of the refunded debt), the transactions cannot be considered a defeasance for accounting purposes. Therefore ideally the balance of the debt and the payments on the debt should be reported in debt service funds.

FINANCIAL REPORTING AT GOVERNMENT-WIDE LEVEL

The fund-based financial statements as described above are included in a governmental entity's financial report in order to demonstrate that restrictions imposed by statutes, regulations, or contracts have been followed. Balances in these fund financial statements are converted from a modified accrual basis to an accrual basis in order to create the basic information for the government-wide financial statements.

For the most part, this approach requires that all of the Debt Service Funds combined ending trial balances (which are on a modified accrual basis) be adjusted to reflect accrual balances. Briefly, this means that all debt outstanding at the end of the period must be reported as a liability and that interest (including the amortization of any discount or premium accounts) must be reported on an accrual basis. This conversion is illustrated later in this chapter.

ILLUSTRATIVE TRANSACTIONS

Note: The transactions presented assume that internal systems are *not* redesigned for GASB-54. Therefore conversion entries are used. In the 2013 edition of the CCH *Governmental GAAP Practice Manual*, beginning balances will be presented in GASB-54 format. Governments that do not redesign their internal accounting systems for GASB-54 will have to restate using adjusting entries similar to those contained in this section. The conversion entries to GASB-54 and assumptions are presented after JE05.24 as JE05.G54-1, JE05.G54-2, and so on.

In order to illustrate accounting and financial reporting standards that are observed for Debt Service Funds, assume that the City of Centerville has the following Debt Service Funds:

- Senior Citizens' Center Bonds
- Easely Street Bridge Bonds
- Bland Street Drainage Bonds
- West End Recreation Center Bonds

PRACTICE POINT: Many governments sell consolidated debt that incorporates a number of bond authorizations instead of, say, the Senior Citizens' Center, Easely Street Bridge, Bland Street, and West End Recreation Center bonds, named above. Accounting for consolidated bonds is similar to what is contained here except allocations to capital spending occur from one series of bonds to many authorizations instead of from one series of bonds for one authorization.

Senior Citizens' Center Bonds

The Senior Citizens' Center Debt Service Fund is used to service serial bonds ($10,000,000) that were issued to build the Centerville Senior Citizens' Center. The fund's trial balance for the beginning of the fiscal year is as follows.

GASB-34 generally did not change the manner of accounting for transactions that are recorded in Debt Service Funds.

Accounts	Trial Balance Debit	Credit
Cash	$14,000	
Temporary investments	5,000	
Accounts payable		$6,000
Fund balance		13,000
Totals	$19,000	$19,000

The fund balance entry above and in all the debt service fund illustrations contained in this chapter are *not* GASB-54 compliant; however, they show what will likely be present in most trial balances for the year of conversion.

This section presents illustrative transactions and entries for the fund during the fiscal year ended June 30, 20X2.

Transaction JE05.01—Accounts payable of $6,000 from the previous year were paid:

Accounts	Debit	Credit
Accounts payable	6,000	
Cash		6,000

Transaction JE05.02—During the year interest revenue of $4,000 was earned and received:

Accounts	Debit	Credit
Cash	4,000	
Interest revenue		4,000

PRACTICE POINT: Investments of bond proceeds happen regularly. However, care must be taken by treasurers to invest bond proceeds so that if investment revenues are greater than the bond yield and are not spent for eligible capital purposes, a yield-reduction payment representing the interest earnings between the bond yield and the investment yield may be due to the Internal Revenue Service. Debt service funds may hold these payments and related escrow accounts.

Transaction JE05.03—During the year, $750,000 of the revenue bonds for the senior citizens' center were paid. In addition, $500,000 of interest was paid:

Accounts	Debit	Credit
Expenditures—principal	750,000	
Expenditures—interest ($10,000,000 × 5%)	500,000	
Cash		1,250,000

Based on the standards established by GASBI-6, expenditures should continue to be recorded on an accrual basis except with respect to the expenditures identified in the Interpretation. One exception is that debt service payments are to be recorded when "due and payable."

Transaction JE05.04—General government expenditures of $9,000 were incurred, of which $7,000 was paid:

Accounts	Debit	Credit
Expenditures—general government	9,000	
Cash		7,000
Accounts payable		2,000

Transaction JE05.05—Additional temporary investments of $15,000 were made during the year:

Accounts	Debit	Credit
Temporary investments	15,000	
Cash		15,000

Transaction JE05.06—The General Fund made a transfer of $1,300,000 to service the debt and interest payments:

Accounts	Debit	Credit
Cash	1,300,000	
Transfers in—General Fund		1,300,000

After the transactions for the year are posted, the year-end trial balance (June 30, 20X2) for the Senior Citizens' Center Bonds Debt Service Fund appears as follows:

	Adjusted Trial Balance	
Accounts	Debit	Credit
Cash	$ 40,000	
Temporary investments	20,000	
Accounts payable		$ 2,000
Fund balance		13,000
Interest revenue		4,000
Expenditures—general government	9,000	
Expenditures—principal	750,000	
Expenditures—interest	500,000	
Transfers in—General Fund		1,300,000
Totals	$1,319,000	$1,319,000

PRACTICE ALERT: Absent any other information, the only reclass to implement GASB-54 will be to reclass the beginning fund balance to fund balance—assigned. The net surplus or deficit would also close to fund balance—assigned until a negative fund balance is generated. If no other committed or restricted balances are available, the negative fund balance would be unassigned. If a budget or enabling legislation was passed, then a balance may be committed.

The worksheet that summarizes the foregoing journal entries for the Senior Citizens' Center Bonds Debt Service Fund for the year-end trial balance is presented in Appendix 5A.

Easely Street Bridge Bonds

The Easely Street Bridge Debt Service Fund is used to service the two bond instruments ($2,000,000 and $10,000,000) that are partially financing the construction of the new bridge. Its trial balance for the beginning of the fiscal year is as follows:

Accounts	Trial Balance	
	Debit	Credit
Cash	$25,000	
Temporary investments	12,000	
Accounts payable		$5,000
Fund balance		32,000
Totals	$37,000	$37,000

This section presents illustrative transactions and entries for the fund during the fiscal year ended June 30, 20X2.

Transaction JE05.07—Accounts payable of $5,000 from the previous year were paid:

Accounts	Debit	Credit
Accounts payable	5,000	
Cash		5,000

Transaction JE05.08—During the year interest revenue of $1,000 was earned and received:

Accounts	Debit	Credit
Cash	1,000	
Interest revenue		1,000

Transaction JE05.09—During the year $200,000 of interest payments were made on the 10%, 5-year bonds that were issued to yield 9%:

Accounts	Debit	Credit
Expenditures—interest ($2,000,000 × 10%)	200,000	
Cash		200,000

Transaction JE05.10—General government expenditures of $11,000 were incurred, of which $8,000 was paid:

Accounts	Debit	Credit
Expenditures—general government	11,000	
Cash		8,000
Accounts payable		3,000

Transaction JE05.11—Additional temporary investments of $5,000 were made during the year:

Accounts	Debit	Credit
Temporary investments	5,000	
Cash		5,000

Transaction JE05.12—The General Fund made a transfer of $220,000 to service the debt and interest payments:

Accounts	Debit	Credit
Cash	220,000	
Transfers in—General Fund		220,000

After the transactions for the year are posted, the year-end trial balance (June 30, 20X2) for the Easely Street Bridge Debt Service Fund appears as follows:

Accounts	Adjusted Trial Balance Debit	Credit
Cash	$28,000	
Temporary investments	17,000	
Accounts payable		$3,000
Fund balance		32,000
Interest revenue		1,000
Expenditures—general government	11,000	
Expenditures—interest	200,000	
Transfers in—General Fund		220,000
Totals	$256,000	$256,000

The worksheet that summarizes the foregoing journal entries for the Easely Street Bridge Debt Service Fund for the year-end trial balance is presented in Appendix 5B.

Bland Street Drainage Bonds

The Bland Street Drainage Debt Service Fund is used to service the serial bonds ($4,900,000) that were issued to finance the project. Its trial balance for the beginning of the fiscal year is as follows:

Accounts	Trial Balance Debit	Credit
Cash	$15,000	
Temporary investments	21,000	
Accounts payable		$4,000
Fund balance		32,000
Totals	$36,000	$36,000

This section presents illustrative transactions and entries for the fund during the fiscal year ended June 30, 20X2.

Transaction JE05.13—Accounts payable of $4,000 from the previous year were paid:

Accounts	Debit	Credit
Accounts payable	4,000	
Cash		4,000

Transaction JE05.14—During the year interest revenue of $3,000 was earned and received:

Accounts	Debit	Credit
Cash	3,000	
Interest revenue		3,000

Transaction JE05.15—During the year, $700,000 of the serial bonds for the Bland Street Drainage Project Center were paid. In addition, $294,000 of interest was paid:

Accounts	Debit	Credit
Expenditures—principal	700,000	
Expenditures—interest ($4,900,000 × 6%)	294,000	
Cash		994,000

Transaction JE05.16—General government expenditures of $15,000 were incurred, of which $12,000 was paid:

Accounts	Debit	Credit
Expenditures—general government	15,000	
Cash		12,000
Accounts payable		3,000

Transaction JE05.17—Additional temporary investments of $3,000 were made during the year:

Accounts	Debit	Credit
Temporary investments	3,000	
Cash		3,000

Transaction JE05.18—The General Fund made a transfer of $1,100,000 to service the debt and interest payments:

Accounts	Debit	Credit
Cash	1,100,000	
Transfers in—General Fund		1,100,000

After the transactions for the year are posted, the year-end trial balance (June 30, 20X2) for the Bland Street Drainage Debt Service Fund appears as follows:

	Adjusted Trial Balance	
Accounts	Debit	Credit
Cash	$105,000	
Temporary investments	24,000	
Accounts payable		$ 3,000
Fund balance		32,000
Interest revenue		3,000
Expenditures—general	15,000	
Expenditures—principal	700,000	
Expenditures—interest	294,000	
Transfers in—General Fund		1,100,000
Totals	$1,138,000	$1,138,000

The worksheet that summarizes the foregoing journal entries for the Bland Street Drainage Debt Service Fund for the year-end trial balance is presented in Appendix 5C.

West End Recreation Center Bonds

The West End Recreation Center Debt Service Fund is used to service the bonds ($3,000,000) that were issued to finance the project. The fund's trial balance for the beginning of the fiscal year is as follows:

	Trial Balance	
Accounts	Debit	Credit
Cash	$27,000	
Temporary investments	3,000	
Accounts payable		$2,000
Fund balance		28,000
Totals	$30,000	$30,000

This section presents illustrative transactions and entries for the fund during the fiscal year ended June 30, 20X2.

Transaction JE05.19—Accounts payable of $2,000 from the previous year were paid:

Accounts	Debit	Credit
Accounts payable	2,000	
Cash		2,000

Transaction JE05.20—During the year, interest revenue of $1,000 was earned and received:

Accounts	Debit	Credit
Cash	1,000	
Interest revenue		1,000

Transaction JE05.21—During the year, $500,000 of the serial bonds for the Bland Street Drainage Project Center were paid. In addition, $180,000 of interest was paid:

Accounts	Debit	Credit
Expenditures—principal	500,000	
Expenditures—interest ($3,000,000 × 12% × 6/12)	180,000	
Cash		680,000

Transaction JE05.22—General government expenditures of $7,000 were incurred, of which $6,000 were paid:

Accounts	Debit	Credit
Expenditures—general government	7,000	
Cash		6,000
Accounts payable		1,000

Transaction JE05.23—Additional temporary investments of $3,000 were made during the year:

Accounts	Debit	Credit
Temporary investments	3,000	
Cash		3,000

Transaction JE05.24—The General Fund made a transfer of $700,000 to service the debt and interest payments:

Accounts	Debit	Credit
Cash	700,000	
Transfers in—General Fund		700,000

After the transactions for the year are posted, the year-end trial balance (June 30, 20X2) for the West End Recreation Center Debt Service Fund appears as follows:

Accounts	Adjusted Trial Balance	
	Debit	Credit
Cash	$37,000	
Temporary investments	6,000	
Accounts payable		$1,000
Fund balance		28,000
Interest revenue		1,000
Expenditures—general government	7,000	
Expenditures—principal	500,000	
Expenditures—interest	180,000	
Transfers in—General Fund		700,000
Totals	$730,000	$730,000

The worksheet that summarizes the foregoing journal entries for the West End Recreation Center Debt Service Fund for the year-end trial balance is presented in Appendix 5D.

FUND FINANCIAL STATEMENTS

Before the Conversion to GASB-54

At the fund financial statement level, a governmental fund prepares a statement of revenues, expenditures, and changes in fund balances and a balance sheet. Based on the adjusted trial balances created above, the following financial statements reflect the balances and activities of the Debt Service Funds. These financial statements are prepared to facilitate the preparation of the fund financial statements illustrated in Chapter 13, "Developing Information for Fund Financial Statements." (See Appendixes 5E and 5F.)

The formatting of the balance sheet at the fund financial statement level was not changed by GASB-34.

Debt Service Funds
Balance Sheet
June 30, 20X2

	Senior Citizens' Center Bonds	Easely Street Bridge Bonds	Bland Street Drainage Bonds	West End Recreation Center Bonds	Total
ASSETS					
Cash	$40,000	$28,000	$105,000	$37,000	$210,000
Temporary investments	20,000	17,000	24,000	6,000	67,000
Total assets	$60,000	$45,000	$129,000	$43,000	$277,000
LIABILITIES AND FUND BALANCES					
Liabilities:					
Accounts payable	$2,000	$3,000	$3,000	$1,000	$9,000

Debt Service Funds
Balance Sheet
June 30, 20X2

	Senior Citizens' Center Bonds	Easely Street Bridge Bonds	Bland Street Drainage Bonds	West End Recreation Center Bonds	Total
Total liabilities	2,000	3,000	3,000	1,000	9,000
Fund balances:					
Fund balance— reserved	58,000	42,000	126,000	42,000	268,000
Total liabilities and fund balances	$60,000	$45,000	$129,000	$43,000	$277,000

GASB-54 CONVERSION ENTRIES

The following balances are key for a proper GASB-54 conversion in the conversion year:

Fund balance—Senior Citizens' Center Bonds	13,000
Fund balance—Easely Street Bridge Bonds	32,000
Fund balance—Bland Street Drainage Bonds	32,000
Fund balance—West End Recreation Center Bonds	28,000

However, other information is needed to properly convert the beginning balances and the ending balances. This information may include he following:

Nonspendable Balances	Any balances of inventory and long-term receivables.
Restricted Balances	Any balances from bond proceeds, grants, and other external restrictions or due to enabling statutes.
Committed Balances	Any passed budgets or other commitments made by the highest level of decision making.

To reclass the beginning balances, the following entries are needed.

Transaction JE05.G54-1 (reclass) Reserved balances in debt service funds are generally restricted balances.

Accounts	Debit	Credit
Fund balance—reserved –Senior Citizens' Center Bonds	13,000	
Fund balance—restricted –Senior Citizens' Center Bonds		13,000

For the Easely Street Bridge Bonds:

Accounts	Debit	Credit
Fund balance—reserved –Easely Street Bridge Project	32,000	
Fund balance—restricted –Easely Street Bridge Project		32,000

For the Bland Street Drainage Bonds:

Accounts	Debit	Credit
Fund balance—reserved –Bland Street Drainage Bonds	32,000	
Fund balance—restricted –Bland Street Drainage Bonds		32,000

For the West End Recreation Center Bonds:

Accounts	Debit	Credit
Fund balance—reserved –West End Recreation Center Bonds	28,000	
Fund balance—restricted –West End Recreation Center Bonds		28,000

Assume that Central City doesn't budget for these funds and no other commitments or restrictions exist.

PRACTICE ALERT: Should funds be accumulated in excess of amounts needed to fund debt service, if the funds are being accumulated because of an act's enabling legislation, those amounts would continue to be restricted. Should the excess be due to an act of the highest level of decision-making authority in the government, those amounts would be committed. Otherwise amounts would be assigned. Should amounts needed for debt service be in excess of the amounts in fund balance, then potentially a negative unassigned amount would exist should no assigned amounts exist.

Debt Service Funds
Balance Sheet
June 30, 20X2

	Senior Citizens' Center Bonds	Easely Street Bridge Bonds	Bland Street Drainage Bonds	West End Recreation Center Bonds	Total
REVENUES					
Interest	$4,000	$1,000	$3,000	$1,000	$9,000
Total revenue	4,000	1,000	3,000	1,000	9,000
EXPENDITURES					
General government	9,000	11,000	15,000	7,000	42,000
Principal	750,000	—	700,000	500,000	1,950,000
Interest	500,000	200,000	294,000	180,000	1,174,000
Total expenditures	1,259,000	211,000	1,009,000	687,000	3,166,000
Excess (deficiency) of revenues over expenditures	(1,255,000)	(210,000)	(1,006,000)	(686,000)	(3,157,000)
OTHER FINANCING SOURCES (USES)					
Transfers in	1,300,000	220,000	1,100,000	700,000	3,320,000

Debt Service Funds
Balance Sheet
June 30, 20X2

	Senior Citizens' Center Bonds	Easely Street Bridge Bonds	Bland Street Drainage Bonds	West End Recreation Center Bonds	Total
Total other financing sources and uses	1,300,000	220,000	1,100,000	700,000	3,320,000
Net change in fund balances	45,000	10,000	94,000	14,000	163,000
Fund balances—beginning	13,000	32,000	32,000	28,000	105,000
Fund balances—ending	$58,000	$42,000	$126,000	$42,000	$268,000

PRACTICE ALERT: GASB-54 does not require the presentation of deseg-regated fund balances in the statement of revenues, expenditures, and changes in fund balances. To do so would not be GAAP and, furthermore, would probably cause separate columns for separate classes of fund balances similar to not-for-profit financial statements. All surplus closes to Fund balance—assigned. Annual deficits would close to Fund balance—assigned unless no positive balances are available in assigned balances. If deficit balances still exist after lowering all positive balances to zero, the remainder would be labeled fund deficit—unassigned.

The **combined** financial statements for the Debt Service Funds are not reported separately in the governmental entity's financial report, but they are used in Chapter 13, "Developing Information for Fund Financial Statements."

CONVERTING TO GOVERNMENT-WIDE FINANCIAL STATEMENTS

Government-wide financial statements are reported on the accrual basis of accounting. Generally, most governments work from their governmental fund financial statements (which are on a modified accrual basis) and through the use of worksheet entries convert to accrual based financial statements.

In order to convert the transactions that were recorded in the Debt Service Funds from a modified accrual basis to an accrual basis, the following worksheet entries are made.

Debt Outstanding at the Beginning of the Year

The following balances of capital debt issues were outstanding at the beginning of the current year:

Revenue bonds—Senior Citizens' Center Bonds—5% serial bonds, interest is paid annually on June 30th $10,000,000

Easely Street Bridge Project—5-year bonds, 10% bonds, interest is paid annually on June 30th 2,064,791

Bland Street Drainage Project—6% serial bonds, interest is paid annually on
   June 30th   4,900,000

Total $16,964,791

The following worksheet entry is made to record the debt outstanding at the beginning of the year, since it does not appear on the fund financial statements:

Accounts	Debit	Credit
JE05.25 Fund balance—restricted—Senior Citizens' Center Bonds	10,000,000	
Fund balance—restricted—Easely Street Bridge Bonds	2,064,791	
Fund balance—restricted—Bland Street Drainage Bonds	4,900,000	
Revenue bonds payable (Senior Citizens' Center Bonds)		10,000,000
Bonds payable (Easely Street Bridge Bonds)		2,064,791
Bonds payable (Bland Street Drainage Bonds)		4,900,000
(To record debt that was outstanding at the beginning of the year)		

Senior Citizens' Center Bonds

The principal repayment of $750,000 through the Senior Citizens' Center Bond Fund is converted from an expenditure to a reduction of debt by making the following worksheet entry:

Accounts	Debit	Credit
JE05.26 Revenue bonds payable	750,000	
Expenditures—principal		750,000
(To record payments during the year as reductions to debt obligations rather than as expenditures)		

The bonds payment date is June 30th of each year, therefore, the cash expenditure for interest for the debt ($500,000) is equal to the interest expense on an accrual basis for the year and no adjustment is needed to convert interest to an accrual basis.

Easely Street Bridge Bonds

The Easely Street Bridge Bond Fund has the following debt instruments outstanding:

- 10%, 5-year bonds that were issued to yield 9%.
- 7%, 8-year bonds that were issued to yield 8%

The 5-year bonds were issued on June 30, 20X0 and pay interest annually. The amortization schedule for the bonds is as follows:

Date	Cash	Interest	Premium Amortization	Book Value
6/30/X0	$—	$—	$—	$2,077,790
6/30/X1	200,000	187,001	12,999	2,064,791
6/30/X2	200,000	185,831	14,169	2,050,622
6/30/X3	200,000	184,556	15,444	2,035,178
6/30/X4	200,000	183,166	16,834	2,018,344
6/30/X5	200,000	181,656R	18,344	2,000,000
	$1,000,000	$922,210	$77,790	

R = rounding

On a modified accrual basis, the amount of interest expenditure recognized in the fund financial statements must be adjusted to include the amortization of the bond premium for the year, as shown in the following worksheet entry:

Accounts	Debit	Credit
JE05.27 Bonds payable	14,169	
Interest expense		14,169
(To record the amortization of bond premiums for the year)		

The 10-year bonds were issued on October 1, 20X1 and pay interest annually. The amortization schedule for the bonds is as follows:

Date	Cash	Interest	Amortization	Book Value
10/1/X1	$—	$—	$—	$9,328,956
10/1/X2	700,000	746,316	(46,316)	9,375,272
10/1/X3	700,000	750,022	(50,022)	9,425,294
10/1/X4	700,000	754,024	(54,024)	9,479,318
10/1/X5	700,000	758,345	(58,345)	9,537,663
10/1/X6	700,000	763,013	(63,013)	9,600,676
10/1/X7	700,000	768,054	(68,054)	9,668,730
10/1/X8	700,000	773,498	(73,498)	9,742,228
10/1/X9	700,000	779,378	(79,378)	9,821,606
10/1/Y0	700,000	785,729	(85,729)	9,907,335
10/1/Y1	700,000	792,665R	(92,665)	10,000,000
	$7,000,000	$7,671,044	$(671,044)	

R = rounding

Because the 10-year bonds were issued during the current year and interest is not payable until October 1, 20X3, the following worksheet entry is made to report the interest on an accrual basis for the government-wide financial statements:

Accounts	Debit	Credit
JE05.28 Interest expense ($746,316 × 9/12)	559,737	
Interest payable ($700,000 × 9/12)		525,000

Accounts	Debit	Credit
Bonds payable ($46,316 × 9/12)		34,737
(To accrue interest for the year)		

If in the previous year interest expense was also accrued, the previous accrual would have to be omitted from the current year's statement of activities (debiting net assets and crediting interest expense) because the interest would have been recorded in the current year under the modified accrual basis of accounting. In this illustration, since the bonds were issued in the current year, there was no interest accrual at the end of the previous year.

Bland Street Drainage Bonds

The principal repayment of $700,000 made through the Bland Street Drainage Bond Fund is converted from an expenditure to a reduction of debt by making the following worksheet entry:

	Accounts	Debit	Credit
JE05.29	Bonds payable	700,000	
	Expenditures—principal		700,000
	(To record payments during the year as reductions to the debt obligation rather than as expenditures)		

The bonds' interest payment date is June 30th of each year, therefore the cash expenditure for interest for the debt ($294,000) is equal to the interest expense on an accrual basis for the year.

West End Recreation Center Bonds

The principal repayment of $500,000 made through the West End Recreation Center Bond Fund is converted from an expenditure to a reduction of debt by making the following worksheet entry:

	Accounts	Debit	Credit
JE05.30	Bonds payable	500,000	
	Expenditures—principal		500,000
	(To record payments during the year as reductions to the debt obligation rather than as expenditures)		

The bond interest payment date is June 30th of each year; therefore the cash expenditure for interest for the debt ($180,000) is equal to the interest expense on an accrual basis for the year.

After these entries are prepared, the adjusted trial balances (on an accrual basis) for the four funds would appear as follows as of June 30, 20X2 (see Appendix 5G):

Adjusted Trial Balance

Accounts	Senior Citizens' Center Bonds Debits (Credits)	Easely Street Bridge Bonds Debits (Credits)	Bland Street Drainage Bonds Debits (Credits)	West End Recreation Center Bonds Debits (Credits)	Totals Debits (Credits)
Cash	$ 40,000	$ 28,000	$ 105,000	$ 37,000	$ 210,000
Temporary investments	20,000	17,000	24,000	6,000	67,000
Accounts payable	(2,000)	(3,000)	(3,000)	(1,000)	(9,000)
Interest payable	—	(525,000)	—	—	(525,000)
Revenue bonds payable	(9,250,000)	—	—	—	(9,250,000)
Bonds payable	—	(2,085,359)	(4,200,000)	500,000	(5,785,359)
Net Assets	9,987,000	2,032,791	4,868,000	(28,000)	16,859,791
Interest revenue	(4,000)	(1,000)	(3,000)	(1,000)	(9,000)
Expenditures— general government	9,000	11,000	15,000	7,000	42,000
Expenditures— interest	500,000	745,568	294,000	180,000	1,719,568
Transfers in	(1,300,000)	(220,000)	(1,100,000)	(700,000)	(3,320,000)
Totals	$ -0-	$ -0-	$ -0-	$ -0-	$ -0-

The balance in the long-term liability account for the West End Recreation Center Bond Fund has a debit balance because the debt was issued during the current period and the long-term debt was recorded in a worksheet entry in Chapter 4, "Capital Projects Funds." These balances will be offset in Chapter 14, "Developing Information for Government-Wide Financial Statements."

This combined trial balance on the accrual basis is used in Chapter 14, "Developing Information for Government-Wide Financial Statements," in order to prepare the government-wide financial statements.

APPENDIX 5A: WORKSHEET FOR SUMMARIZING CURRENT TRANSACTIONS: SENIOR CITIZENS' CENTER BONDS

Accounts	Trial Balance Debit	Trial Balance Credit	Adjustments Debit		Adjustments Credit		Adjusted Trial Balance Debit	Adjusted Trial Balance Credit	Operating Statement Debit	Operating Statement Credit	Balance Sheet Debit	Balance Sheet Credit
Cash	14,000	—	JE05.02	4,000	JE05.01	6,000	40,000	—	—	—	40,000	—
			JE05.06	1,300,000	JE05.03	1,250,000						
			JE05.04	—	JE05.04	7,000						
			JE05.05	—	JE05.05	15,000						
Temporary investments	5,000	—	JE05.05	15,000		—	20,000	—	—	—	20,000	—
Accounts payable	—	6,000	JE05.01	6,000	JE05.04	2,000	—	2,000	—	—	—	2,000
Fund balance	—	13,000		—		—	—	13,000	—	—	—	13,000
Interest revenue	—	—		—	JE05.02	4,000	—	4,000	—	4,000	—	—
Expenditures—general government	—	—	JE05.04	9,000		—	9,000	—	9,000	—	—	—
Expenditures—principal	—	—	JE05.03	750,000		—	750,000	—	750,000	—	—	—
Expenditures—interest	—	—	JE05.03	500,000		—	500,000	—	500,000	—	—	—
Transfers in—General Fund	—	—		—	JE05.06	1,300,000	—	1,300,000	—	1,300,000	—	—
Totals	19,000	19,000		2,584,000		2,584,000	1,319,000	1,319,000	1,259,000	1,304,000	60,000	15,000
Net increase (decrease)									45,000			45,000
									1,304,000	1,304,000	60,000	60,000

APPENDIX 5B: WORKSHEET FOR SUMMARIZING CURRENT TRANSACTIONS: EASELY STREET BRIDGE BONDS

Accounts	Trial Balance Debit	Trial Balance Credit	Adjustments Debit (ref)	Adjustments Debit	Adjustments Credit (ref)	Adjustments Credit	Adjusted Trial Balance Debit	Adjusted Trial Balance Credit	Operating Statement Debit	Operating Statement Credit	Balance Sheet Debit	Balance Sheet Credit
Cash	25,000	—	JE05.08	1,000	JE05.07	5,000	28,000	—	—	—	28,000	—
			JE05.12	220,000	JE05.09	200,000						
					JE05.10	8,000						
					JE05.11	5,000						
Temporary investments	12,000	—	JE05.11	5,000			17,000	—	—	—	17,000	—
Accounts payable	—	5,000	JE05.07	5,000	JE05.10	3,000	—	3,000	—	—	—	3,000
Fund balance	—	32,000					—	32,000	—	—	—	32,000
Interest revenue	—	—			JE05.08	1,000	—	1,000	—	1,000	—	—
Expenditures—general government	—	—	JE05.10	11,000			11,000	—	11,000	—	—	—
Expenditures—interest	—	—	JE05.09	200,000			200,000	—	200,000	—	—	—
Transfers in—General Fund	—	—			JE05.12	220,000	—	220,000	—	220,000	—	—
Totals	37,000	37,000		442,000		442,000	256,000	256,000	211,000	221,000	45,000	35,000
Net increase (decrease)									10,000	—	—	10,000
									221,000	221,000	45,000	45,000

APPENDIX 5C: WORKSHEET FOR SUMMARIZING CURRENT TRANSACTIONS: BLAND STREET DRAINAGE BONDS

Accounts	Trial Balance Debit	Trial Balance Credit	Adjustments Debit (ref)	Adjustments Debit	Adjustments Credit (ref)	Adjustments Credit	Adjusted Trial Balance Debit	Adjusted Trial Balance Credit	Operating Statement Debit	Operating Statement Credit	Balance Sheet Debit	Balance Sheet Credit
Cash	15,000	—	JE05.14	3,000	JE05.13	4,000	105,000	—	—	—	105,000	—
			JE05.18	1,100,000	JE05.15	994,000						
					JE05.16	12,000						
					JE05.17	3,000						
Temporary investments	21,000	—	JE05.17	3,000	JE05.16	3,000	24,000	—	—	—	24,000	—
Accounts payable	—	4,000	JE05.13	4,000	JE05.16	3,000	—	3,000	—	—	—	3,000
Fund balance	—	32,000					—	32,000	—	—	—	32,000
Interest revenue	—	—			JE05.14	3,000	—	3,000	—	3,000	—	—
Expenditures—general	—	—	JE05.16	15,000			15,000	—	15,000	—	—	—
Expenditures—principal	—	—	JE05.15	700,000			700,000	—	700,000	—	—	—
Expenditures—interest	—	—	JE05.15	294,000			294,000	—	294,000	—	—	—
Transfers in—general fund	—	—			JE05.18	1,100,000	—	1,100,000	—	1,100,000	—	—
Totals	36,000	36,000		2,119,000		2,119,000	1,138,000	1,138,000	1,009,000	1,103,000	129,000	35,000
Net increase (decrease)									94,000			94,000
									1,103,000	1,103,000	129,000	129,000

APPENDIX 5D: WORKSHEET FOR SUMMARIZING CURRENT TRANSACTIONS: WEST END RECREATION CENTER BONDS

Accounts	Trial Balance Debit	Trial Balance Credit	Adjustments Ref	Adjustments Debit	Adjustments Ref	Adjustments Credit	Adjusted Trial Balance Debit	Adjusted Trial Balance Credit	Operating Statement Debit	Operating Statement Credit	Balance Sheet Debit	Balance Sheet Credit
Cash	27,000	—	JE05.20 JE05.24	1,000 700,000	JE05.19 JE05.21 JE05.22 JE05.23	2,000 680,000 6,000 3,000	37,000	—	—	—	37,000	—
Temporary investments	3,000	—	JE05.23	3,000		—	6,000	—	—	—	6,000	—
Accounts payable	—	2,000	JE05.19	2,000	JE05.22	1,000	—	1,000	—	—	—	1,000
Fund balance	—	28,000		—		—	—	28,000	—	—	—	28,000
Interest revenue	—	—		—	JE05.20	1,000	—	1,000	—	1,000	—	—
Expenditures—general government	—	—	JE05.22	7,000		—	7,000	—	7,000	—	—	—
Expenditures—principal	—	—	JE05.21	500,000		—	500,000	—	500,000	—	—	—
Expenditures—interest	—	—	JE05.21	180,000		—	180,000	—	180,000	—	—	—
Transfers in—general fund	—	—		—	JE05.24	700,000	—	700,000	—	700,000	—	—
Totals	30,000	30,000		1,393,000		1,393,000	730,000	730,000	687,000	701,000	43,000	29,000
Net increase (decrease)									14,000	—	—	14,000
									701,000	701,000	43,000	43,000

APPENDIX 5E: DEBT SERVICE FUNDS: BALANCE SHEET AND STATEMENT OF REVENUES, EXPENDITURES, AND CHANGES IN FUND BALANCES

Debt Service Funds
Balance Sheet
June 30, 20X2

	Senior Citizens' Center Bonds	Easely Street Bridge Bonds	Bland Street Drainage Bonds	West End Recreation Center Bonds	Total
ASSETS					
Cash	$40,000	$28,000	$105,000	$37,000	$210,000
Temporary investments	20,000	17,000	24,000	6,000	67,000
Total assets	$60,000	$45,000	$129,000	$43,000	$277,000
LIABILITIES AND FUND BALANCES					
Liabilities:					
Accounts payable	$ 2,000	$ 3,000	$ 3,000	$ 1,000	$ 9,000
Total liabilities	2,000	3,000	3,000	1,000	9,000
Fund balances:					
Fund balance— restricted	58,000	42,000	126,000	42,000	268,000
Total liabilities and fund balances	$60,000	$45,000	$129,000	$43,000	$277,000

Debt Service Funds
Statement of Revenues, Expenditures, and Changes in Fund Balances
June 30, 20X2

	Senior Citizens' Center Bonds	Easely Street Bridge Bonds	Bland Street Drainage Bonds	West End Recreation Center Bonds	Total
REVENUES					
Interest	$ 4,000	$ 1,000	$ 3,000	$ 1,000	$ 9,000
Total revenue	4,000	1,000	3,000	1,000	9,000

EXPENDITURES

General government	9,000	11,000	15,000	7,000	42,000
Principal	750,000	—	700,000	500,000	1,950,000
Interest	500,000	200,000	294,000	180,000	1,174,000
Total expenditures	1,259,000	211,000	1,009,000	687,000	3,166,000
Excess (deficiency) of revenues over expenditures	(1,255,000)	(210,000)	(1,006,000)	(686,000)	(3,157,000)

OTHER FINANCING SOURCES (USES)

Transfers in	1,300,000	220,000	1,100,000	700,000	3,320,000
Total other financing sources and uses	1,300,000	220,000	1,100,000	700,000	3,320,000
Net change in fund balances	45,000	10,000	94,000	14,000	163,000
Fund balances— beginning	13,000	32,000	32,000	28,000	105,000
Fund balances— ending	$ 58,000	$ 42,000	$ 126,000	$ 42,000	$ 268,000

APPENDIX 5F: DEBT SERVICE FUNDS: WORKSHEET TO CONVERT FROM MODIFIED ACCRUAL TO ACCRUAL BASIS

	Modified Accrual Basis		Adjustments	Accrual Basis
Cash	210,000		—	210,000
Temporary investments	67,000		—	67,000
Accounts payable	(9,000)		—	(9,000)
Interest payable	—	JE05.28	(525,000)	(525,000)
Revenue bonds payable	—	JE05.25	(10,000,000)	(9,250,000)
	—	JE05.26	750,000	
Bonds payable	—	JE05.25	(6,964,791)	(5,785,359)
	—	JE05.27	14,169	
	—	JE05.28	(34,737)	
	—	JE05.29	700,000	
	—	JE05.30	500,000	
Fund balance—reserved	(105,000)	JE05.25	16,964,791	16,859,791
Interest	(9,000)		—	(9,000)
General government	42,000		—	42,000
Principal	1,950,000	JE05.26	(750,000)	0
	—	JE05.29	(700,000)	
	—	JE05.30	(500,000)	
Interest	1,174,000	JE05.27	(14,169)	1,719,568
	—	JE05.28	559,737	
Transfers in	(3,320,000)		—	(3,320,000)
Total	0		0	0

APPENDIX 5G: DEBT SERVICE FUNDS: ADJUSTED TRIAL BALANCES (ACCRUAL BASIS)

Accounts	Senior Citizens' Center Bonds Debits (Credits)	Easely Street Bridge Bonds Debits (Credits)	Bland Street Drainage Bonds Debits (Credits)	West End Recreation Center Bonds Debits (Credits)	Totals Debits (Credits)
Cash	$ 40,000	$ 28,000	$ 105,000	$ 37,000	$ 210,000
Temporary investments	20,000	17,000	24,000	6,000	67,000
Accounts payable	(2,000)	(3,000)	(3,000)	(1,000)	(9,000)
Interest payable	—	(525,000)	—	—	(525,000)
Revenue bonds payable	(9,250,000)	—	—	—	(9,250,000)
Bonds payable	—	(2,085,359)	(4,200,000)	500,000	(5,785,359)
Fund balance	9,987,000	2,032,791	4,868,000	(28,000)	16,859,791
Interest revenue	(4,000)	(1,000)	(3,000)	(1,000)	(9,000)
Expenditures—general government	9,000	11,000	15,000	7,000	42,000
Expenditures—interest	500,000	745,568	294,000	180,000	1,719,568
Transfers in	(1,300,000)	(220,000)	(1,100,000)	(700,000)	(3,320,000)
Totals	$ -0-	$ -0-	$ -0-	$ -0-	$ -0-

CHAPTER 6
PERMANENT FUNDS

CONTENTS

NATURE OF PERMANENT FUNDS

GAAP states that a Permanent Fund "should be used to report resources that are legally restricted to the extent that only earnings, and not principal, may be used for purposes that support the reporting government's programs—that is, for the benefit of the government or its citizenry." For example, a governmental entity may receive resources from other parties, including individuals, private organizations and other governments, whereby the earnings generated from the investment of the resources can only be used in a way specified by the donor and the beneficiary of the use of those resources must be the governmental entity or its citizenry (GASB-34, par. 65).

Permanent Funds are different from Private-Purpose Funds in that the latter fund type is used when resources (the principal, the earnings, or both) are to be used for the benefit of individuals, private organizations, or other governments. Permanent Funds are classified as a governmental fund type and Private-Purpose Funds are considered fiduciary funds.

Prior to the issuance of GASB-34 there was no Permanent Fund category.

MEASUREMENT FOCUS AND BASIS OF ACCOUNTING

Since Permanent Funds (which are in effect public-purpose trust funds) are governmental funds, the modified accrual basis and flow of current financial resources are used to prepare their financial statements. These concepts are discussed in Chapter 2, "The General Fund."

Based on the standards established by GASB-34, public-purpose trust funds, previously presented as Nonexpendable Trust Funds, are now presented as Permanent Funds and, therefore, as noted above, reported on a modified accrual basis of accounting. This approach was taken for two reasons. The GASB believes that even though a public-purpose trust fund might initially appear to be appropriately classified in the fiduciary fund category, these funds are created for the benefit of the governmental entity rather than for external parties. Thus, it is more appropriate for them to be considered governmental funds (at the fund financial statement reporting level) and governmental activities (at the government-wide financial statement reporting level). Furthermore, the GASB acknowledges that technically the resources held by a Permanent Fund should be accounted for on the accrual basis (rather than the modified accrual basis); however, based on research it appears that public-purpose trust funds that are nonexpendable predominantly account for financial resources and for this reason "revenue recognition is generally consistent between the accrual and modified accrual bases." If the GASB had not adopted this approach, it would have been necessary to classify public-purpose nonexpendable trust funds as proprietary funds and then require that their activities be presented in the governmental activities of the government-wide financial statements. That reporting strategy would have required another reconciling item between the proprietary fund financial statements and the government-wide financial statements, thus adding one more element of complexity to an already complex reporting model.

GASB-34 notes that in some instances net assets may be restricted on a permanent basis (in perpetuity). Under this circumstance, the restricted net assets must be subdivided into expendable and nonexpendable restricted net assets at the government-wide financial reporting level (GASB-34, par. 35).

In some instances the mandated purpose of specific resources to be accounted for in a separate fund are such that it is not readily apparent which fund type should be used for financial reporting purposes. For example the GASB's *Comprehensive Implementation Guide* notes that a governmental entity might need to account for financial resources that are legally restricted by enabling legislation but that a minimum balance (nonexpendable) defined by the legislation must be maintained in the fund. The nonexpendable portion of the fund description suggests that a Permanent Fund should be used, although the legal restriction characteristic suggests that a Special Revenue Fund is appropriate. The GASB's *Guide* notes that either fund type could be used under this circumstance. If a Permanent Fund is used, the portion of the fund that is expendable should be identified as unreserved; however, if a Special Revenue Fund is used, the portion of the fund that is not expendable should be identified as a reserved fund balance.

The resources that flow into a Permanent Fund include contributions from external parties as well as transfers within the governmental entity (usually the General Fund) and earnings generated by the resources once they are invested. Contributions from external parties are considered voluntary nonexchange transactions and are accounted for based on the standards established by GASB-33 (Accounting and Financial Reporting for Nonexchange Transactions). Resources received by a Permanent Fund from another fund are accounted for as transfers as required by GASB-34. Investment income that arises from resources invested by a Permanent Fund is accounted for and reported in the financial statements based on the standards established by GASB-31 (Accounting and Financial Reporting for Certain Investments and for External Investment Pools).

Under previous governmental GAAP, a transfer from a governmental fund to a fund similar to a Permanent Fund would have been accounted for as a residual equity transfer. GASB-34 eliminates the concepts of operating and residual equity transfers in that all transfers are simply reported as transfers. Furthermore, no transfer can be reported as an adjustment to the beginning balance of any fund (GASB-34, par. 112).

Expenditures of a Permanent Fund are recorded on the modified accrued basis of accounting. These expenditures are limited to the activities specifically identified in the donor agreement, legislative statute, or ordinance that created the fund. These expenditures are reported to conform to the level of detail presented in the governmental entity's operating statement. For example, the expenditures are generally classified as general government, education, public safety, and the like.

FINANCIAL REPORTING AT FUND LEVEL

The balances and activities of Permanent Funds are presented in the following two financial statements at the fund financial statement level:

1. Balance Sheet

2. Statement of Revenues, Expenditures, and Changes in Fund Balances

Permanent Fund financial statements are no different from other governmental funds and are based on standards established by various NCGA and GASB Statements and Interpretations that were outstanding before the issuance of GASB-34.

PRACTICE ALERT: GASB-54 (Fund Balance Reporting and Governmental Fund Type Definitions), effective for periods beginning after June 15, 2010, makes significant changes to fund balance classifications as well as clarifies and makes changes to the definitions of governmental fund types. The new definitions in GASB-54 provide that governmental funds of a particular type either should be used (i.e., required) or are used (i.e., discretionary) for all activities that meet its criteria. If use of a fund type is generally discretionary, specific situations under which a fund of that type should be used are identified either in the definitions in GASB-54 (i.e., debt service funds) or by requirements established in other authoritative pronouncements (i.e., special revenue and capital projects funds). The fund balance classification section of GASB-54 defines the terminology "restricted," "committed," and "assigned."

Permanent Funds

Permanent funds are defined as follows:

Fund Type	Pre GASB-54 Definition	Post GASB-54 Definition
Permanent Funds	To account for resources that are legally restricted to the extent that only earnings, and not principal, may be used for the purposes that support the reporting government's programs that is, for the benefit of the government or its citizenry.	To account for and report resources that are restricted to the extent that only earnings, and not principal, may be used for purposes that support the reporting government's programs that is, for the benefit of the government or its citizenry.

Permanent funds should not include private-purpose trust funds. GASB-54's new definition of the permanent fund type incorporates only minor wording changes in the interest of consistency with the other definitions used in the governmental funds.

The aforementioned two fund financial statements include all of the governmental funds (General Fund, Special Revenue Funds, Capital Projects Funds, Debt Service Funds, and Permanent Funds), and these funds are reported based on the concept of a major fund as established by GASB-34.

FINANCIAL REPORTING AT GOVERNMENT-WIDE LEVEL

The fund-based financial statements described above are included in a governmental entity's financial report in order to demonstrate that restrictions imposed by statutes, regulations, or donor contracts have been followed. Balances in these fund financial statements are converted from a modified accrual basis to an accrual basis in order to create the basic information for the government-wide financial statements. For the most part this approach requires that all of the Permanent Funds' combined ending trial balances (which are on a modified accrual basis) be adjusted to reflect accrual balances, if necessary. Because of the nature of Permanent Funds, there may be few, if any, adjustments needed for this conversion.

ILLUSTRATIVE TRANSACTIONS

Note: The transactions presented assume that internal systems are not redesigned for GASB-54. Therefore conversion entries are used. In the 2013 edition of the CCH *Governmental GAAP Practice Manual*, beginning balances will be presented with beginning balances in GASB-54 format. Governments that do not redesign their internal accounting systems for GASB-54 will have to restate using adjusting entries similar those contained in this section. The conversion entries to GASB-54 and assumptions are presented after JE06.06 and are presented as JE06.G54-1, JE06.G54-2, and so on.

This section presents illustrative transactions and entries for the Permanent Fund during the fiscal year ended June 30, 20X2. In the current illustration, the expenditures related to the purpose of the Permanent Fund are recorded directly in the Permanent Fund. Alternatively, the expendable portion of the fund balance could be transferred to another fund (usually the General Fund or a Special Revenue Fund), in which case that fund would report the expenditures.

In order to illustrate accounting and financial reporting standards that are followed for a Permanent Fund, assume that the City of Centerville has a Cemetery Fund that was created several years ago by a few families that have been part of the community for many generations. Only the investment earnings from the permanent endowment received can be used to help preserve and maintain the Centerville Cemetery, a public cemetery. The trial balance for the beginning of the fiscal year is as follows:

Accounts	Trial Balance	
	Debit	Credit
Cash	$13,000	
Investment in debt securities	215,000	
Accounts payable		$6,000
Fund balance		222,000
Totals	$228,000	$228,000

The fund balance entry above and in all the debt service fund illustrations contained in this chapter are *not* GASB-54 compliant; however, they show what will likely be present in most trial balances for the year of conversion.

Transaction JE06.01—Accounts payable of $6,000 from the previous year were paid:

Accounts	Debit	Credit
Accounts payable	6,000	
Cash		6,000

Transaction JE06.02—During the year interest and investment revenue of $30,000 was earned and received:

Accounts	Debit	Credit
Cash	30,000	
Interest and Investment Revenue (program revenue—operating grants and contributions [general government])		30,000

The transaction is reported as interest and investment revenue at the fund financial statement level; however, because the earnings are restricted to a particular activity they are reported at the government-wide financial statement level as program revenue related to general government activities.

The GASB's *Comprehensive Implementation Guide* notes that GASB-34 points out that when the earnings of a Permanent Fund are required to be used for a specific purpose but are not distributed in the current year, those earnings (even though they are not distributed or spent) should be reported as program revenues.

Transaction JE06.03—Maintenance expenditures related to the cemetery of $35,000 were incurred, of which $31,000 was paid:

Accounts	Debit	Credit
Expenditures—general government	35,000	
Cash		31,000
Accounts payable		4,000

Based on the standards established by GASBI-6 (Recognition and Measurement of Certain Liabilities and Expenditures in Governmental Fund Financial Statements), expenditures for the newly created Permanent Funds should continue to be recorded on an accrual basis except with respect to the expenditures identified in the Interpretation.

Transaction JE06.04—Additional contributions of $22,000 to the permanent endowment of the fund were received from private citizens during the year:

Accounts	Debit	Credit
Cash	22,000	
Revenue—permanent endowment additions		22,000

GASB-34 notes that when a governmental entity receives contributions to its term and permanent endowments or to permanent fund principal, those contributions should be reported as separate items in the lower portion of the statement of activities. These receipts are not considered to be program revenues (such as program-specific grants), because in the case of term endowments there is an uncertainty of the timing of the release of the resources from the term restriction and in the case of permanent contributions the principal can never be expended (GASB-34, par. 53).

PRACTICE POINT: Transactions JE06.02 through JE06.04 note that $30,000 in investment earnings were received during the year and $31,000 in cash was expended during the year, with $22,000 in permanent additions received. Although it would seem that the fund is spending corpus, GASB's *Comprehensive Implementation Guidance* (pars. 6.31.3 and 7.37.1) allows for spending of amounts of investments at fair value above basis if the differential is accounted for as "undistributed investment income"; however, no such designation is required. Furthermore, this situation could occur if there was undistributed investment income from prior years.

GASB-34 requires that the following disclosures be made for donor-restricted endowments: (1) the amount of net appreciation on investments related to donor-restricted endowments that are available for expenditure and how that appreciation is reported in net assets, (2) the state law that establishes how net appreciation may be spent by the governmental entity, and (3) the investment-spending policy that is, the rate of endowment investments that may be authorized for expenditure) (GASB-34, par. 121).

GASB-34 requires that when net assets are restricted on a permanent basis (in perpetuity), the restricted net assets section of the statement of net assets (government-wide financial statement) must be subdivided into expendable and nonexpendable amounts.

Transaction JE06.05—Additional investments of $25,000 in bonds for the year were made:

Accounts	Debit	Credit
Investments in debt securities	25,000	
Cash		25,000

Transaction JE06.06—At the end of the year the portfolio of debt securities had increased in value by $4,000:

Accounts	Debit	Credit
Investments in debt securities	4,000	
Interest and Investment Revenue (program revenue—operating grants and contributions [general government])		4,000

Investments and related revenue continue to be accounted for in accordance with the standards established by GASB-31 (Accounting and Financial Reporting for Certain Investments and for External Investment Pools).

After the transactions for the year are posted, the year-end trial balance (June 30, 20X2) for the Cemetery Fund appears as follows:

	Adjusted Trial Balance	
Accounts	Debit	Credit
Cash	$3,000	
Investment in debt securities	244,000	
Accounts payable		$4,000
Fund balance		222,000
Interest and investment revenue (program revenue—operating grants and contributions [general government])		34,000
Expenditures—general government	35,000	
Revenue—permanent endowment additions		22,000
Totals	$282,000	$282,000

PRACTICE ALERT: Absent any other information, the only reclass to implement GASB-54 will be to reclass the beginning fund balance to fund balance—assigned. The net surplus or deficit would also close to fund balance—assigned until a negative fund balance is generated. If no other committed or restricted balances are available, the negative fund balance would be unassigned. If a budget or enabling legislation was passed, then a balance may be committed.

PRACTICE POINT: As discussed above, had interest and investment revenue exceeded expenditures, the differential could have been reclassed to "undistributed investment income," although no such designation is required. This reclassification would allow a segregation of restricted fund balance amounts related to corpus. Upon implementation of GASB-54, the undistributed investment income would be included as part of "restricted," "committed," or "assigned" fund balance.

The worksheet that summarizes the foregoing journal entries for the Centerville Cemetery Permanent Fund for the year-end trial balance is presented in Appendix 6A.

FUND FINANCIAL STATEMENTS

At the fund financial statement level, a governmental fund must prepare a statement of revenues, expenditures, and changes in fund balances and a balance sheet. Based on the adjusted trial balances created above, the following financial statements reflect the balances and activities of the Permanent Fund (see Appendix 6B):

Permanent Fund
Balance Sheet
June 30, 20X2

ASSETS	
Cash	$3,000
Investments in debt securities	244,000
Total Assets	$247,000
LIABILITIES AND FUND BALANCES	
Liabilities:	
Accounts payable	$4,000
Total Liabilities	4,000
Fund balance	
Fund balance	243,000
Total Liabilities and Fund Balances	$247,000

GASB-54 CONVERSION ENTRIES

The following balances are key for a proper GASB-54 conversion in the conversion year.

Fund balance—Permanent Fund	222,000

However, other information is needed to properly convert the beginning balances and the ending balances. This information may include the following:

Nonspendable Balances	Any balances of inventory and long-term receivables.
Restricted Balances	Any balances from bond proceeds, grants, and other external restrictions or due to enabling statutes.
Committed Balances	Any passed budgets or other commitments made by the highest level of decision making.

> **PRACTICE ALERT:** Most likely, amounts in permanent funds will be non-spendable fund balances. However, if any undistributed interest earnings are in a permanent fund as of fiscal year end, a case could be made that those funds would be restricted.

To reclass the beginning balances, the following entries are needed.

Transaction JE06.G54-1 (reclass) Reserved balances in permanent funds are generally nonspendable balances.

Accounts	Debit	Credit
Fund balance—reserved—permanent fund	222,000	
Fund balance—nonspendable—permanent fund		222,000

Permanent Funds
Statement of Revenues, Expenditures, and Changes
in Fund Balances
June 30, 20X2

REVENUES

Interest and investment revenue (Program Revenue—Operating Grants and Contributions [General Government])	$34,000
Revenue—permanent endowment additions	22,000
Total Revenue	56,000

EXPENDITURES

General government	35,000
Total Expenditures	35,000
Excess (deficiency) of revenues over expenditures	21,000
Fund balances—beginning	222,000
Fund balances—ending	$243,000

The financial statements for the Permanent Fund are not reported separately in the governmental entity's financial report, but they are used in Chapter 13, "Developing Information for Fund Financial Statements."

GOVERNMENT-WIDE FINANCIAL STATEMENTS

Government-wide financial statements are reported on the accrual basis of accounting. Generally most governments work from their governmental fund financial statements (which are on a modified accrual basis) and through the use of worksheet entries convert to accrual based financial statements.

There are no adjustments needed to convert the above Permanent Fund from a modified accrual basis to an accrual basis (see Appendix 6C).

APPENDIX 6A: WORKSHEET FOR SUMMARIZING CURRENT TRANSACTIONS: CENTERVILLE CEMETERY

Accounts	Trial Balance Debit	Trial Balance Credit	Adjustments (ref)	Adjustments Debit	Adjustments (ref)	Adjustments Credit	Adjusted Trial Balance Debit	Adjusted Trial Balance Credit	Operating Statement Debit	Operating Statement Credit	Balance Sheet Debit	Balance Sheet Credit
Cash	13,000	—	JE06.02 JE06.04	30,000 22,000	JE06.01 JE06.03 JE06.05	6,000 31,000 25,000	3,000	—	—	—	3,000	—
Investment in debt securities	215,000	—	JE06.05 JE06.06	25,000 4,000		—	244,000	—	—	—	244,000	—
Accounts payable	—	6,000	JE06.01	6,000	JE06.03	4,000	—	4,000	—	—	—	4,000
Fund balance	—	222,000		—		—	—	222,000	—	—	—	222,000
Interest and investment revenue (program revenue—operating grants and contributions [general government])	—	—		—	JE06.02 JE06.06	30,000 4,000	—	34,000	—	34,000	—	—
Expenditures—general government	—	—	JE06.03	35,000		—	35,000	—	35,000	—	—	—
Revenue—permanent endowment additions	—	—		—	JE06.04	22,000	—	22,000	—	22,000	—	—
Totals	228,000	228,000		122,000		122,000	282,000	282,000	35,000	56,000	247,000	226,000
Net increase (decrease)									21,000	—	—	21,000
									56,000	56,000	247,000	247,000

APPENDIX 6B: PERMANENT FUNDS: BALANCE SHEET AND STATEMENT OF REVENUES, EXPENDITURES, AND CHANGES IN FUND BALANCES

Permanent Fund
Balance Sheet
June 30, 20X2

ASSETS

Cash	$ 3,000
Investments in debt securities	244,000
Total Assets	$247,000

LIABILITIES AND FUND BALANCES

Liabilities:	
Accounts payable	$ 4,000
Total Liabilities	4,000
Fund balances:	
Fund balance, nonspendable	243,000
Total Liabilities and Fund Balances	$247,000

Permanent Funds
Statement of Revenues, Expenditures, and Changes in Fund Balances
June 30, 20X2

REVENUES

Interest and investment revenue (program revenue—operating grants and contributions [general government])	$ 34,000
Revenue—permanent endowment additions	22,000
Total Revenue	56,000

EXPENDITURES

General government	35,000
Total Expenditures	35,000
Excess (deficiency) of revenues over expenditures	21,000
Fund balances—beginning	222,000
Fund balances—ending	$243,000

APPENDIX 6C: NO ADJUSTMENTS

There are no adjustments needed to convert Permanent Funds from a modified accrual basis to an accrual basis.

PART III.
PROPRIETARY FUNDS

CHAPTER 7
ENTERPRISE FUNDS

CONTENTS

NATURE OF ENTERPRISE FUNDS

An Enterprise Fund is a proprietary fund that is generally used to account for governmental activities that are similar to activities that may be performed by a commercial enterprise. For example, an Enterprise Fund can be used to account for transit systems, solid-waste landfills, toll roads, hospitals, and other activities that charge a fee in order to recover operational costs.

More specifically, an Enterprise Fund *may* be used to "report any activity for which a fee is charged to external users for goods or services." However, GAAP states that an Enterprise Fund *must* be used to account for an activity if any one of the following three criteria is satisfied (GASB-34, par. 67):

1. The activity is financed with debt that is secured *solely* by a pledge of the net revenues from fees and charges of the activity.

2. Laws or regulations require that the activity's costs of providing services, including capital costs (such as depreciation or capital debt ser-

vice), be recovered with fees and charges, rather than with taxes or similar revenues.

3. The pricing policies of the activity establish fees and charges designed to recover its costs, including capital costs (such as depreciation or debt service).

The criteria established by GASB-34 are different from the standards that were previously used to determine when an Enterprise Fund should be used by a governmental entity. The GASB believes that the establishment of the criteria listed above reduce the degree of subjectivity that is used by governmental entities in determining when an Enterprise Fund should be used.

Some financial statement preparers raised the question about whether the criteria listed above apply to activities that are currently accounted for in Internal Service Funds. GASB-34 takes the position that an Enterprise Fund, not an Internal Service Fund, must be used when external users are the predominant participants in the fund. GASB-37 (Basic Financial Statements—and Management's Discussion and Analysis—for State and Local Governments: Omnibus) reemphasizes this point by adding a footnote to paragraph 67 that states, "the focus of these criteria is on fees charged to external users."

GASB-34 (footnote 34) requires that a state's unemployment compensation fund be reported as an Enterprise Fund. In addition, paragraph 391 (Basis for Conclusions) points out that "the Board concluded that unemployment compensation benefit plans should be reported as Enterprise Funds similar to public entity risk pools." GASB-10 (Accounting and Financial Reporting for Risk Financing and Related Insurance Issues) provides financial accounting and reporting standards for public entity risk pools. The GASB's *Comprehensive Implementation Guide* raises the issue of whether unemployment compensation funds are required to follow all of the accounting and reporting standards established by GASB-10. The intention of footnote 34 of GASB-34 was not to extend the standards established by GASB-10 to unemployment compensation funds but, rather, to point out that the unemployment compensation funds are similar to public entity risk pools in that they involve risk-retention operations.

GASB-34 requires that an Enterprise Fund be used to account for activities when laws or regulations require that the activity's costs of providing services be recovered with fees and charges rather than with taxes or similar revenues. This criterion is the basis for the GASB concluding that a state's unemployment compensation program is to be reported in an Enterprise Fund. However, administrative costs should not be accounted for in the Enterprise Fund but, rather, accounted for in the state's General Fund, unless legal requirements identify another fund (other than the General Fund) to be used. The GASB's *Comprehensive Implementation Guide* points out that accounting for administrative costs in the Enterprise Fund is inconsistent with the purpose of an Enterprise Fund because an unemployment compensation program's strategy is to fund unemployment benefits through charges levied on employers.

The GASB's *Comprehensive Implementation Guide* raises the issue of whether special assessment debt for which a governmental entity is "not obligated in any manner" should be reported in an Enterprise Fund based on the first criterion listed in paragraph 67 of GASB-34 (the activity is financed with debt that is secured solely by a pledge of the net revenues from fees and charges of the activity). The GASB's *Guide* points out that the arrangement whereby a governmental entity simply collects amounts from property owners to service debt issued to finance the construction or enhancement of a capital asset is not an "activity" that would require the use of an Enterprise Fund. Paragraph 19 of GASB-6 (Accounting and Financial Reporting for Special Assessments) describes a typical debt-financed special assessment arrangement whereby the collection of payments from property owners is accounted for in an Agency Fund when a governmental entity is not obligated in any manner for repayment of the debt.

The second and third criteria refer to the establishment of a pricing policy that recovers costs, including depreciation expense or debt service. In some situations, the activity might be responsible for little or no debt. The GASB's *Comprehensive Implementation Guide* states that under this circumstance the criteria are still met when debt service requirements (if any) are used to establish the pricing policy. There is no implied assumption that there is equality between the depreciation expense and the debt service on capital debt for a particular activity.

A governmental entity may be created to provide loans to special interest groups (e.g., veterans), other governmental entities (e.g., public universities) or not-for-profit organizations (e.g., hospitals). Usually, the purpose of establishing a public finance authority is to lower the special interest groups' cost of borrowing funds. The authority providing the loan can borrow at a lower rate than the individual parties can on their own. Based on the nature of this financing arrangement, finance authorities are usually accounted for as Enterprise Funds. In many instances, a public finance authority purchases or constructs a capital asset, retains title to the capital asset, and leases the asset to another party. However, in some instances public finance authorities are not directly involved in loan arrangements, because conduit debt obligations are issued. GASBI-2 (Disclosure of Conduit Debt Obligations) defines "conduit debt obligations" as "certain limited-obligation revenue bonds, certificates of participation, or similar debt instruments issued by a state or local governmental entity for the express purpose of providing capital financing for a specific third party that is not a part of the issuer's financial reporting entity." Conduit debt transactions are arranged so that payments required by the other entity (through mortgage or lease payments) are equal to the mortgage payment schedule related to the original debt entered into by the public finance authority. However, the public finance authority involved in conduit debt may incur administrative expenses related to the debt and may charge the other party a fee for its services. The AICPA's Audit and Accounting Guide *State and Local Governments* points out that fees and administrative expenses related to conduit debt should be reported on the authority's financial statements as revenue and expenses, respectively.

State Lotteries

State lotteries usually satisfy one or more of these conditions and therefore are accounted for in Enterprise Funds. For many lottery games, a fixed percentage of ticket sales must be paid out as winnings. The AICPA's Audit and Accounting Guide *State and Local Governments* points out that lottery prize costs under this (or similar) payout arrangements are subject to accrual based on their relationship to total ticket sales and that accrual might be appropriate under conditions such as the following: (1) prizes have been won and claimed but have not been paid, (2) prizes have been won but not claimed, and (3) games are in progress at the end of the year. (Alternatively, some lotteries are accounted for as governmental funds. Those that are governmental funds use a rationale that they are mainly cash flow mechanisms for the government rather than an entity that meets the aforementioned criteria for an enterprise fund.)

Some lotteries allow a winner to either take an immediate lump-sum payment or receive payments over a specified period of time. If the lottery winner chooses to receive the winnings over a period of time and the state purchases an annuity from an insurance company in the name of the winner, The AICPA's Audit and Accounting Guide *State and Local Governments* points out that no related liability or asset should be reported on the state's financial statements. When the state does not purchase an annuity in the name of the winner, the liability should be presented at its present value. When determining the liability to be discounted, the amount should include amounts won as well as amounts won but not yet claimed and amounts that will be won and claimed for games in progress at the end of the year. Also, the state may decide to finance the periodic payments to the winner by "purchasing U.S. Treasury securities matched in timing and amount to the future payments." Under this arrangement, the investment in securities should be reported as an asset on the state's financial statements. The lottery liability and the investment cannot be offset against one another. When the state has financed the periodic payments to the lottery winner through the purchase of an annuity from an insurance company, the state should consider whether a contingent liability should be disclosed in its financial statements.

OBSERVATION: Even though GASB-62 (Codification of Accounting and Financial Reporting Guidance Contained in Pre-November 30, 1989 FASB and AICPA Pronouncements) addresses most types of enterprise fund activities, curiously, one of the few activities that is not codified from AICPA or FASB standards relates to state lotteries.

MEASUREMENT FOCUS AND BASIS OF ACCOUNTING

The accrual basis of accounting and the flow of economic resources are used to prepare the financial statements of an Enterprise Fund. Generally, under the flow of economic resources, measurement focus and accrual basis of accounting, revenues are recognized when earned and expenses are recorded when incurred when these activities are related to exchange and exchange-like activities. In addition, long-lived assets (such as buildings and equipment) are capitalized and depreciated, and all debt is reported in the fund (GASB-34, par. 16).

Generally, activities accounted for in Enterprise Funds are characterized as business-type activities. Business-type activities must follow either Alternative 1 or Alternative 2 as described in GASB-20 (Accounting and Financial Reporting for Proprietary Funds and Other Governmental Entities That Use Proprietary Fund Accounting). Under Alternative 1, governmental entities using proprietary fund accounting must follow (1) all GASB pronouncements and (2) FASB Statements and Interpretations, APB Opinions, and Accounting Research Bulletins (ARBs) issued on or before November 30, 1989, except those that conflict with a GASB pronouncement. Under Alternative 2, governmental entities using proprietary fund accounting must follow (1) all GASB pronouncements and (2) all FASB Statements and Interpretations, APB Opinions, and ARBs, no matter when issued, except those that conflict with a GASB pronouncement. Unlike Alternative 1, Alternative 2 has no cutoff date for determining the applicability of FASB pronouncements.

PRACTICE ALERT: GASB-62 (Codification of Accounting and Financial Reporting Guidance Contained in Pre-November 30, 1989 FASB and AICPA Pronouncements) is an omnibus statement that supersedes the provisions of GASB-20 by incorporating into GASB's literature all FASB Statements and Interpretations, APB Opinions, and ARBs no matter when issued except those that conflict with a GASB pronouncement. GASB-62 statement also incorporates all AICPA pronouncements. It is effective for periods beginning after December 15, 2011. All the provisions of the aforementioned standards are incorporated into CCH's *Governmental GAAP Guide*; so, little if any change to this edition is expected from any upcoming promulgation. However, certain items such as governmental combinations that have guidance contained in APB Opinion No. 16, are being researched by GASB and were not included in GASB-62.

Prior to the issuance of GASB-34, an Enterprise Fund could account for depreciation expense in the conventional manner or depreciation expense could be closed at the end of the year directly to the fund's contributed capital account that was created when a restricted grant, entitlement, or shared revenue was provided to acquire the related capital asset. GASB-34 prohibits the latter method of accounting for depreciation expense (GASB-34, par. 103).

NCGA-1 allowed for certain transfers to an Enterprise Fund to be accounted as an equity or fund balance transaction (residual equity transfer). Current GAAP does not allow for residual equity transfer in that all transfers must be reported on an Enterprise Fund's operating statement (GASB-34, par. 112).

FINANCIAL REPORTING AT FUND LEVEL

The balances and activities of Enterprise funds are presented in the following three financial statements at the fund financial statement level:

1. Statement of Net Assets (or Balance Sheet)
2. Statement of Revenues, Expenses, and Changes in Fund Net Assets (or Fund Equity)
3. Statement of Cash Flows

These three fund financial statements include all of the proprietary funds (Enterprise Funds and Internal Service Funds). The financial statements of Enterprise Funds are presented at the fund financial statement reporting level based on the major fund concept; however, the financial statements of Internal Service Funds are all combined into a single column and the major fund criteria are not used.

PRACTICE ALERT: At the time of this publication, GASB is in the process of deliberating a proposed standard titled "Financial Reporting of Deferred Outflows of Resources, Deferred Inflows of Resources, and Net Position." Should the draft be accepted as exposed, the current statement of net assets would transition to a statement of net position for periods beginning after June 15, 2011, with earlier application encouraged. The updated formula for a statement of net position would be assets, plus deferred outflows of resources, less liabilities, less deferred inflows of resources, equals net position. Because of the issues of presentation of the fair value of derivative hedges, it is speculated that the new statement of net position will be approved with minimal changes. For the remainder of this chapter, and for that matter, this volume, where the term "net assets" is presented, if a fair value of a derivative hedge is also presented, a statement of net position is synonymous with a statement of net assets.

PRACTICE POINT: The focus of reporting governmental funds and Enterprise Funds is that major funds are reported for these funds; however, combined financial statements for fund types are not required to be reported (GASB-34, par. 75).

A fund is considered a major fund if both of the following two criteria (GASB-34, pars. 75 and 76) are satisfied:

1. Total assets, liabilities, revenues, or expenditures/expenses of the governmental/enterprise fund are equal to or greater than 10% of the corresponding element total (assets, liability, and so forth) for all funds that are considered governmental funds/enterprise funds.

2. The same element that met the 10% criterion in (1) is at least 5% of the corresponding element total for all governmental and enterprise funds combined.

In establishing the above two criteria, the GASB intended that a major fund arises when a particular element (assets, for example) of a fund meets both the 10% threshold and the 5% threshold. Some preparers read the requirement to mean that a major fund arises when one element (assets, for example) satisfies the 10% threshold and another element (revenues, for example) satisfies the 5% threshold. GASB-37 clarifies the GASB's original intent. That is, a single element must satisfy both criteria.

Proprietary funds must prepare a statement of cash flows based on the guidance established by GASB-9 (Reporting Cash Flows of Proprietary and Nonexpendable Trust Funds and governmental Entities that Use Proprietary

Fund Accounting), except the statement of cash flows should be formatted based on the direct method in computing cash flows from operating activities. Prior to the issuance of GASB-34, the statement of cash flows could be prepared based on either the direct or indirect method (GASB-34, par. 105).

GASB-34 requires reconciliation between the governmental statement of net assets and statement of changes in net assets and business-type activities. Often, there is no need for this reconciliation because both sets of financial statements are based on the same measurement focus and basis of accounting. When there are differences between the two sets of financial statements, the differences must be reconciled on the face of the proprietary fund financial statements. GASB-34 notes that a reconciling item could arise when the transactions and perhaps residual assets and liabilities of an Internal Service Fund are related to business-type activities (GASB-34, par. 104).

FINANCIAL REPORTING AT GOVERNMENT-WIDE LEVEL

Government-wide financial statements were established by GASB-34 in order to provide a basis for determining (1) the extent to which current services provided by the entity were financed with current revenues and (2) the degree to which a governmental entity's financial position has changed during the fiscal year. In order to achieve these objectives, government-wide financial statements include a statement of net assets and a statement of activities. Government-wide financial statements are based on a flow of all economic resources applied on the accrual basis of accounting. The flow of economic resources refers to all assets available to the governmental unit for the purpose of providing goods and services to the public.

Perhaps the major implementation problem faced by those who prepare governmental financial statements is the development of system procedures that facilitate the presentation of the two levels of financial statements. However, because there are generally no or few reconciling items between totals reported for Enterprise Funds on the proprietary fund financial statements and totals reported in the government-wide financial statements for businesses-type activities, the conversion of the information from a fund financial statement format to a business-type activities format can be relatively straightforward.

For the most part, this approach requires that the Enterprise Funds' ending trial balances (which are already on an accrual basis) be adjusted to reflect Internal Service Fund activities, if any. That is, Internal Service Funds and similar activities related to business-type activities are eliminated to avoid doubling-up expenses and revenues in preparing the business-type activities column of the statement of activities. The effect of this approach is to adjust activities in an Internal Service Fund to a break-even balance. For example, if the Internal Service Fund had a "net profit" for the year, there is a pro rata reduction in the charges made to the funds that used the Internal Service Fund's services for the year. Likewise, a net loss requires a pro rata adjustment that increases the charges made to the various Enterprise Funds. After making these eliminations, any residual balances related to the Internal Service Fund's assets, liabilities, and net assets are reported in the business-type activities column in the statement of net assets (as demonstrated in Chapter 8, "Internal Service Funds").

PRACTICE POINT: If an internal service fund is in any way funded by charges to federal funds, the federal government may monitor and approve the rate-setting and cost-allocation process of an internal service fund in accordance with White House Office of Management and Budget Circular A-87 (Cost Principles for State, Local, and Indian Tribal Governments). If an internal service fund generates a "net profit" for the year, a reduction in charges needs to be made for the following year in a roll-forward fashion to mitigate the potential of overcharging the federal government.

GASB-34 requires that business-type activities be separately reported at least by segment on the statement of activities (government-wide financial statement). The GASB's objective for reporting disaggregated information in the business-type activities section of the statement of activities was not to identify segment information but rather to have a separate presentation for activities that are *different*. In order to better achieve this objective, GASB-37 amends GASB-34 by requiring that the statement of activities present "activities accounted for in Enterprise Funds by different identifiable activities," which is described the following way: "An activity within an Enterprise Fund is identifiable if it has a specific revenue stream and related expenses and gains and losses that are accounted for separately."

ILLUSTRATIVE TRANSACTIONS

In order to illustrate accounting and financial reporting standards that are observed for Enterprise Funds, assume that the City of Centerville has the following Enterprise Funds:

- Centerville Toll Bridge
- Centerville Parking Authority
- Centerville Utilities Authority
- Centerville Municipal Airport

Centerville Toll Bridge

The Centerville Toll Bridge (CTB) was constructed several years ago and provides access across the Centerville River from the downtown area to a primarily residential section of the city. The fund's trial balance for the beginning of the fiscal year is as follows:

	Trial Balance	
Accounts	Debit	Credit
Cash	$ 220,000	
Interest receivable	4,500	
Temporary investments	33,000	

Accounts	Trial Balance	
	Debit	Credit
Supplies	26,000	
Construction in progress	40,000	
Land and improvements	100,000	
Superstructure	1,400,000	
Accumulated depreciation—superstructure		$ 650,000
Buildings	250,000	
Accumulated depreciation—buildings		120,000
Equipment	40,000	
Accumulated depreciation—equipment		25,000
Vehicles	800,000	
Accumulated depreciation—vehicles		270,000
Accounts payable and accrued expenses		26,000
Due to other funds—Communications and Technology Center		4,000
Compensated absences liability		7,000
Claims and judgements payable		25,000
Notes payable		40,000
Bonds payable		100,000
Net assets		1,646,500
Totals	$2,913,500	$2,913,500

This section presents illustrative transactions and entries for the CTB during the fiscal year ended June 30, 20X2.

Transaction JE07.01—Accounts payable and accrued expenses of $26,000 from the previous year were paid:

Accounts	Debit	Credit
Accounts payable and accrued expenses	26,000	
Cash		26,000

Transaction JE07.02—Accrued interest receivable from the previous year was received:

Accounts	Debit	Credit
Cash	4,500	
Interest receivable		4,500

Transaction JE07.03—During the year, cash tolls collected from customers totaled $4,750,000:

Accounts	Debit	Credit
Cash	4,750,000	
Charges for services		4,750,000

Transaction JE07.04—The following operating expenses were incurred during the year, of which $4,150,000 were paid in cash:

Personal services	$2,400,000
Contractual services	1,200,000
Repairs and maintenance	400,000
Other supplies and expenses	200,000
Total	$4,200,000

Accounts	Debit	Credit
Personal services expenses	2,400,000	
Contractual services expenses	1,200,000	
Repairs and maintenance expenses	400,000	
Other supplies and expenses	200,000	
Cash		4,150,000
Accounts payable and accrued expenses		50,000

Transaction JE07.05—During the year, interest and investment revenue of $30,000 was earned, of which $27,000 was received in cash:

Accounts	Debit	Credit
Cash	27,000	
Interest receivable	3,000	
Interest and investment revenue		30,000

PRACTICE POINT: The accounting for investments continues to be recorded based on the standards established by GASB-31 (Accounting and Financial Reporting for Certain Investments and for External Investment Pools).

Transaction JE07.06—The following capital assets were purchased during the year for cash:

Land and improvements	$ 40,000
Equipment	30,000
Vehicles	120,000
Total	$190,000

Accounts	Debit	Credit
Land and improvements	40,000	
Equipment	30,000	
Vehicles	120,000	
Cash		190,000

Transaction JE07.07—During the year, a building under construction (construction in progress) was completed at a total cost of $170,000 (after incurring additional costs of $130,000 for the current year) and new construction costs of $70,000 were incurred on a new unfinished project:

Accounts	Debit	Credit
Construction in progress	130,000	
Cash		130,000
Building	170,000	
Construction in progress		170,000
Construction in progress	70,000	
Cash		70,000

The GASB's *Comprehensive Implementation Guide* points out that the modified approach may be applied to eligible infrastructure assets accounted for as either governmental or business-type activities. For example, an Enterprise Fund that owns a toll road (which is an infrastructure asset) could use the modified approach. In that case, the Enterprise Fund should use the modified approach in the preparation of both the government-wide and fund financial statements. In addition, an Enterprise Fund that depreciated eligible infrastructure assets before the standards established by GASB-34 were adopted can use the modified approach for those assets.

Transaction JE07.08—The following assets were sold or abandoned during the year. The cash proceeds were $50,000:

	Original Cost	Accumulated Depreciation
Buildings	$ 90,000	$ 70,000
Equipment	15,000	12,000
Vehicles	85,000	65,000
Total	$190,000	$147,000

Accounts	Debit	Credit
Cash	50,000	
Accumulated depreciation—buildings	70,000	
Accumulated depreciation—equipment	12,000	
Accumulated depreciation—vehicles	65,000	
Buildings		90,000
Equipment		15,000
Vehicles		85,000
Miscellaneous revenue—gain on sale of assets		7,000

Transaction JE07.09—During the year, a portion of the notes payable ($10,000), a portion of the bonds payable ($20,000), and interest expense of $6,000 were paid:

Accounts	Debit	Credit
Notes payable	10,000	
Bonds payable	20,000	
Interest expense	6,000	
Cash		36,000

Transaction JE07.10—Compensated absences of $1,000 were paid during the year and additional costs of $2,000 were accrued:

Accounts	Debit	Credit
Personal services expenses	2,000	
Compensated absences liability		1,000
Cash		1,000

Transaction JE07.11—Claims and judgements of $8,000 were paid during the year and additional costs of $10,000 were accrued:

Accounts	Debit	Credit
Insurance claims and expenses	10,000	
Claims and judgements payable		2,000
Cash		8,000

Transaction JE07.12—Depreciation expense recognized during the year was as follows:

Superstructure	$ 28,000
Buildings	25,000
Equipment	6,000
Vehicles	280,000
Total	$339,000

Accounts	Debit	Credit
Depreciation expense	339,000	
Accumulated depreciation—superstructure		28,000
Accumulated depreciation—buildings		25,000
Accumulated depreciation—equipment		6,000
Accumulated depreciation—vehicles		280,000

GAAP does not require that infrastructure assets that are part of a network or subsystem of a network (referred to as "eligible infrastructure assets") be depreciated if certain conditions relating to the asset management system and the documentation of the condition level of the infrastructure are met. CCH's *Governmental GAAP Guide* explains these conditions. Generally, infrastructure assets are related to governmental rather than business-type activities; however, if an Enterprise Fund has eligible infrastructure assets, the fund may choose not to depreciate the assets. The illustration in this book assumes that the governmental entity's Enterprise Funds depreciate all eligible infrastructure assets (GASB-34, par. 23).

Transaction JE07.13—An operating grant of $100,000 and a capital grant of $250,000 were received from the state government:

Accounts	Debit	Credit
Cash	350,000	
Operating grants and contributions		100,000
Capital grants and contributions		250,000

PRACTICE POINT: The accounting for nonexchange revenues (such as operating and capital grants) continues to be recorded based on the standards established by GASB-33 (Accounting and Financial Reporting for Nonexchange Transactions).

Transaction JE07.14—Other operating revenues earned and received during the year amounted to $20,000 and other operating expenses incurred and paid during the year amounted to $30,000:

Accounts	Debit	Credit
Cash	20,000	
Operating revenues—miscellaneous		20,000
Operating expenses—miscellaneous	30,000	
Cash		30,000

GASB-34 notes that an important element of the statement of revenues, expenses, and changes in fund net assets is that there must be a differentiation between operating revenues and nonoperating revenues, and operating expenses and nonoperating expenses, based on policies established by the governmental entity. Those policies are disclosed in the entity's summary of significant accounting policies and applied consistently from period to period. GASB-34 states that, in general, differentiations between operating and nonoperating transactions should follow the broad guidance established by GASB-9 (Reporting Cash Flows of Proprietary and Nonexpendable Trust Funds and governmental Entities that Use Proprietary Fund Accounting). For example, transactions related to (1) capital and related financing activities, (2) noncapital financing activities, (3) investing activities, and (4) nonexchange revenues, such as tax revenues, would generally be considered nonoperating transactions for purposes of preparing the statement of revenues, expenses, and changes in net assets (GASB-34, par. 102).

Transaction JE07.15—Additional temporary investments of $25,000 were purchased during the year:

Accounts	Debit	Credit
Temporary investments	25,000	
Cash		25,000

Transaction JE07.16—An operating grant (transfer) of $50,000 was received from the General Fund:

Accounts	Debit	Credit
Cash	50,000	
Transfers in—General Fund		50,000

Transaction JE07.17—During the year, the Communications and Technology Support Center (Internal Service Fund) billed the CTB $80,000 for services performed. The CTB made payments of $66,000:

Accounts	Debit	Credit
Contractual services expenses	80,000	
Cash		66,000
Due to other funds—Internal Service Fund—Communications and Technology Support Center		14,000

Interfund receivables/payables may arise from an operating activity (that is the sale of goods and services) between funds rather than in the form of a loan arrangement. If the interfund operating activity is recorded at an amount that approximates the fair value of the goods or services exchanged, the provider/seller fund should record the activity as revenue and the user/purchaser fund should record an expenditure/expense. "Interfund services provided" and "interfund services used" replace the previous term "quasi-external transactions." However, except for changes in terminology, GASB-34 did not change the essential manner by which reciprocal interfund activity is reported (GASB-34, par. 112).

Transaction JE07.18—Supplies of $32,000 were on hand at the end of the year:

Accounts	Debit	Credit
Inventories	6,000	
Other supplies and expenses		6,000

PRACTICE POINT: Inventories/supplies can only be accounted for in an Enterprise Fund based on the consumption method.

After the transactions for the year are posted, the year-end trial balance (June 30, 20X2) for the Centerville Toll Bridge appears as follows:

	Adjusted Trial Balance	
Accounts	Debit	Credit
Cash	$ 739,500	
Interest receivable	3,000	
Temporary investments	58,000	
Supplies	32,000	
Construction in progress	70,000	
Land and improvements	140,000	
Superstructure	1,400,000	
Accumulated depreciation—superstructure		$ 678,000
Buildings	330,000	
Accumulated depreciation—buildings		75,000
Equipment	55,000	
Accumulated depreciation—equipment		19,000
Vehicles	835,000	
Accumulated depreciation—vehicles		485,000
Accounts payable and accrued expenses		50,000

Accounts	Adjusted Trial Balance	
	Debit	Credit
Due to other funds—Communications and Technology Center		18,000
Compensated absences liability		8,000
Claims and judgements payable		27,000
Notes payable		30,000
Bonds payable		80,000
Net assets		1,646,500
Charges for services		4,750,000
Interest and investment revenue		30,000
Miscellaneous revenue—gain on sale of assets		7,000
Operating grants and contributions		100,000
Capital grants and contributions		250,000
Operating revenues—miscellaneous		20,000
Personal services expenses	2,402,000	
Contractual services expenses	1,280,000	
Repairs and maintenance expenses	400,000	
Other supplies and expenses	194,000	
Insurance claims and expenses	10,000	
Depreciation expense	339,000	
Interest expense	6,000	
Operating expenses—miscellaneous	30,000	
Transfers in—General Fund		50,000
Totals	$8,323,500	$8,323,500

The worksheet that summarizes the foregoing journal entries for the CTB's year-end trial balance is presented in Appendix 7A.

Centerville Utilities Authority

The Centerville Utilities Authority (CUA) provides sewer services to citizens, businesses, and other institutions of Centerville. The fund's trial balance for the beginning of the fiscal year is as follows:

Accounts	Trial Balance	
	Debit	Credit
Cash	$2,970,000	
Interest receivable	15,000	
Accounts receivable	6,000,000	
Allowance for doubtful accounts		$ 300,000
Temporary investments	40,000	
Due from other governments Supplies	54,000	
Construction in progress	1,500,000	
Land and improvements	4,000,000	
Distribution and collection systems	45,000,000	

Accounts	Trial Balance Debit	Trial Balance Credit
Accumulated depreciation—distribution and collection systems		41,000,000
Buildings	13,000,000	
Accumulated depreciation—buildings		10,920,000
Equipment	6,500,000	
Accumulated depreciation—equipment		2,380,000
Vehicles	1,400,000	
Accumulated depreciation—vehicles		800,000
Accounts payable and accrued expenses		1,100,000
Due to other funds—Internal Service Fund— Communications and Technology Support Center		15,000
Compensated absences liability		75,000
Claims and judgements payable		220,000
Notes payable		250,000
Bonds payable		7,400,000
Net assets		16,019,000
Totals	$80,479,000	$80,479,000

This section presents illustrative transactions and entries for the CUA during the fiscal year ended June 30, 20X2.

Transaction JE07.19—Accounts payable and accrued expenses of $1,100,000 from the previous year were paid:

Accounts	Debit	Credit
Accounts payable and accrued expenses	1,100,000	
Cash		1,100,000

Transaction JE07.20—Accrued interest receivable from the previous year was received:

Accounts	Debit	Credit
Cash	15,000	
Interest receivable		15,000

Transaction JE07.21—During the year, customers were billed $36,000,000 for services provided and cash collections on account amounted to $34,000,000:

Accounts	Debit	Credit
Cash	34,000,000	
Accounts receivable	2,000,000	
Charges for services		36,000,000

Governmental entities that provide utility services (such as water, sewer, and gas) may require deposits from customers, or a government may charge developers and/or customers system development fees (tap fees). A customer deposit is usually required to be paid before a service is turned on. When the service is terminated, the deposit is returned to the customer. Utility services are usually accounted for as Enterprise Funds. The AICPA's Audit and Accounting Guide *State and Local Governments* points out that receipt of customer deposits should be recorded as a liability and should continue to be reported as such until they are "applied against unpaid billings or refunded to customers." The AICPA Audit Guide also notes the initial receipt of a customer's system development fee should be recorded as a liability and recognized as revenue using the general guidance related to either an exchange transaction or a nonexchange transaction. In an exchange transaction, the governmental entity and the other party to the transaction exchange cash, goods, or services that are essentially of the same value. An Enterprise Fund should recognize revenue related to an exchange transaction on an accrual basis, meaning that revenue is considered realized when (1) the earnings process is complete or virtually complete and (2) an exchange has taken place. A nonexchange transaction arises when the transfer of goods or services between two parties is not of equal value. When a customer's system development fee is considered to be a nonexchange transaction, it must be accounted for based on the guidance established by GASB-33. Professional judgment must be used in the context of a particular transaction to determine its character.

PRACTICE ALERT: Many utilities must follow regulatory accounting procedures. GASB-62 (Codification of Accounting and Financial Reporting Guidance Contained in Pre-November 30, 1989 FASB and AICPA Pronouncements) contains the provisions of the former FAS-71 applicable to public utilities. GASB-62 is an omnibus statement that supersedes the provisions of GASB-20 by incorporating into GASB's literature all FASB Statements and Interpretations, APB Opinions, and ARBs no matter when issued except those that conflict with a GASB pronouncement. GASB-62 statement also incorporates all AICPA pronouncements. It is effective for periods beginning after December 15, 2011. All the provisions of the aforementioned standards are incorporated into CCH's *Governmental GAAP Guide*; so, little if any change from this edition is expected due to any upcoming promulgation. However, certain items such as governmental combinations that have guidance contained in APB Opinion No. 16, are being researched by GASB and were not included in GASB-62.

Bad debts expense of $150,000 (classified as other supplies and expenses for the period) was recorded during the year and customer accounts of $80,000 were written off:

Accounts	Debit	Credit
Other supplies and expenses	150,000	
Accounts receivable		80,000
Allowance for doubtful accounts		70,000

Transaction JE07.22—The following operating expenses were incurred during the year, of which $30,000,000 was paid in cash:

Personal services	$22,000,000
Contractual services	11,000,000
Repairs and maintenance	700,000

Accounts	Debit	Credit
Other supplies and expenses	600,000	
Total	$34,300,000	

Accounts	Debit	Credit
Personal services expenses	22,000,000	
Contractual services expenses	11,000,000	
Repairs and maintenance expenses	700,000	
Other supplies and expenses	600,000	
Cash		30,000,000
Accounts payable and accrued expenses		4,300,000

Transaction JE07.23—During the year, interest and investment revenue of $400,000 was earned, of which $350,000 was received in cash:

Accounts	Debit	Credit
Cash	350,000	
Interest receivable	50,000	
Interest and investment revenue		400,000

Transaction JE07.24—The following capital assets were purchased during the year for cash:

	Debit	Credit
Land and improvements	$1,200,000	
Distribution and collection systems	1,300,000	
Equipment	1,200,000	
Vehicles	750,000	
Total	$4,450,000	

Accounts	Debit	Credit
Land and improvements	1,200,000	
Distribution and collection systems	1,300,000	
Equipment	1,200,000	
Vehicles	750,000	
Cash		4,450,000

Transaction JE07.25—During the year, a building under construction (construction in progress) was completed at a cost of $2,200,000 (after incurring additional costs of $700,000) and new construction costs of $200,000 were incurred on a new unfinished project:

Accounts	Debit	Credit
Construction in progress	700,000	
Cash		700,000
Building	2,200,000	
Construction in progress		2,200,000
Construction in progress	200,000	
Cash		200,000

Transaction JE07.26—The following assets were sold or abandoned during the year. The cash proceeds were $500,000:

	Original Cost	Accumulated Depreciation
Buildings	$ 750,000	$ 600,000
Equipment	3,100,000	2,800,000
Vehicles	490,000	330,000
Total	$4,340,000	$3,730,000

Accounts	Debit	Credit
Cash	500,000	
Miscellaneous expenses (loss on sale of assets)	110,000	
Accumulated depreciation—buildings	600,000	
Accumulated depreciation—equipment	2,800,000	
Accumulated depreciation—vehicles	330,000	
Buildings		750,000
Equipment		3,100,000
Vehicles		490,000

Transaction JE07.27—During the year, a portion of the notes payable ($40,000), a portion of the bonds payable ($1,700,000), and interest expense of $450,000 were paid. In addition, bonds of $2,000,000 and notes of $120,000 were issued during the year:

Accounts	Debit	Credit
Notes payable	40,000	
Bonds payable	1,700,000	
Interest expense	450,000	
Cash		2,190,000

Accounts	Debit	Credit
Cash	2,120,000	
Bonds payable		2,000,000
Notes payable		120,000

Transaction JE07.28—Compensated absences of $13,000 were paid during the year and additional costs of $22,000 were accrued:

Accounts	Debit	Credit
Personal services expenses	22,000	
Compensated absences liability		9,000
Cash		13,000

Transaction JE07.29—Claims and judgements of $12,000 were paid during the year and additional costs of $21,000 were accrued:

Accounts	Debit	Credit
Insurance claims and expenses	21,000	
Claims and judgements payable		9,000
Cash		12,000

Transaction JE07.30—Depreciation expense recognized during the year was as follows:

Distribution and collection systems	$1,200,000
Buildings	625,000
Equipment	920,000
Vehicles	280,000
Total	$3,025,000

Accounts	Debit	Credit
Depreciation expense	3,025,000	
Accumulated depreciation—distribution and collection systems		1,200,000
Accumulated depreciation—buildings		625,000
Accumulated depreciation—equipment		920,000
Accumulated depreciation—vehicles		280,000

Transaction JE07.31—A capital grant of $1,250,000 was received from the state government:

Accounts	Debit	Credit
Cash	1,250,000	
Capital grants and contributions		1,250,000

Transaction JE07.32—Other operating revenues earned and received during the year amounted to $10,000 and other operating expenses incurred and paid during the year amounted to $5,000:

Accounts	Debit	Credit
Cash	10,000	
Operating revenues—miscellaneous		10,000
Operating expenses—miscellaneous	5,000	
Cash		5,000

Transaction JE07.33—Additional temporary investments of $15,000 were purchased during the year:

Accounts	Debit	Credit
Temporary investments	15,000	
Cash		15,000

Transaction JE07.34—A loan of $2,000,000 was made to the General Fund:

Accounts	Debit	Credit
Due from other funds—General Fund	2,000,000	
Cash		2,000,000

Transaction JE07.35—During the year, the Communications and Technology Support Center (Internal Service Fund) billed the CUA $220,000 for services performed. The CUA made payments of $200,000:

Accounts	Debit	Credit
Contractual services expenses	220,000	
Cash		200,000
Due to other funds—Internal Service Fund— Communications and Technology Support Center		20,000

Transaction JE07.36—A loan of $100,000 was made to another government:

Accounts	Debit	Credit
Due from other governments	100,000	
Cash		100,000

The GASB's *Comprehensive Implementation Guide* discusses the question of how a governmental entity should report a "payment in lieu of taxes" from an Enterprise Utility Fund to its General Fund. The nature of the payment must be examined to determine whether it approximates a fair value exchange. If the interfund operating activity is recorded at an amount that approximates the fair value of the goods or services exchanged, the General Fund (provider/seller fund) should record the activity as revenue and the Enterprise Utility Fund (user/purchaser fund) should record an expenditure/expense. It is unlikely that this type of transaction would involve an exchange of services of equivalent value, because of the indirect nature of the services provided through the General Fund. For this reason, it is probable that the payment would be treated as a transfer out by the Enterprise Utility Fund and transfer in by the General Fund.

Transaction JE07.37—Supplies of $75,000 were on hand at the end of the year:

Accounts	Debit	Credit
Inventories	21,000	
Other supplies and expenses		21,000

After the transactions for the year are posted, the year-end trial balance (June 30, 20X2) for the CUA appears as follows:

	Adjusted Balance	
Accounts	Debit	Credit
Cash	$ 230,000	
Interest receivable	50,000	
Accounts receivable	7,920,000	
Allowance for doubtful accounts		$ 370,000
Temporary investments	55,000	
Due from other funds—General Fund	2,000,000	

Accounts	Adjusted Balance	
	Debit	Credit
Due from other governments	100,000	
Supplies	75,000	
Construction in progress	200,000	
Land and improvements	5,200,000	
Distribution and collection systems	46,300,000	
Accumulated depreciation—distribution and collection systems		42,200,000
Buildings	14,450,000	
Accumulated depreciation—buildings		10,945,000
Equipment	4,600,000	
Accumulated depreciation—equipment		500,000
Vehicles	1,660,000	
Accumulated depreciation—vehicles		750,000
Accounts payable and accrued expenses		4,300,000
Due to other funds—Internal Service Fund—Communications and Technology Support Center		35,000
Compensated absences liability		84,000
Claims and judgements payable		229,000
Notes payable		330,000
Bonds payable		7,700,000
Net assets		16,019,000
Charges for services		36,000,000
Interest and investment revenue		400,000
Capital grants and contributions		1,250,000
Operating revenues—miscellaneous		10,000
Personal services expenses	22,022,000	
Contractual services expenses	11,220,000	
Repairs and maintenance expenses	700,000	
Other supplies and expenses	729,000	
Insurance claims and expenses	21,000	
Depreciation expense	3,025,000	
Interest expense	450,000	
Operating expenses—miscellaneous	5,000	
Miscellaneous expenses—loss on sale of assets	110,000	
Totals	$121,122,000	$121,122,000

The worksheet that summarizes the foregoing journal entries for the CUA's year-end trial balance is presented in Appendix 7B.

Centerville Parking Authority

The Centerville Parking Authority (CPA) owns and manages parking garages and parking lots in downtown Centerville. Its trial balance for the beginning of the fiscal year is as follows:

Accounts	Trial Balance	
	Debit	**Credit**
Cash	$ 150,000	
Interest receivable	1,000	
Temporary investments		
Supplies	20,000	
Construction in progress	150,000	
Land and improvements	3,000,000	
Buildings	2,400,000	
Accumulated depreciation—buildings		$ 1,300,000
Equipment	120,000	
Accumulated depreciation—equipment		75,000
Vehicles	90,000	
Accumulated depreciation—vehicles		32,000
Accounts payable and accrued expenses		4,000
Due to other funds—Communications and Technology Center		7,000
Compensated absences liability		4,000
Claims and judgements payable		5,000
Notes payable		10,000
Bonds payable		500,000
Net assets		3,994,000
Totals	$5,931,000	$5,931,000

This section presents illustrative transactions and entries for the CPA during the fiscal year ended June 30, 20X2.

Transaction JE07.38—Accounts payable and accrued expenses of $4,000 from the previous year were paid:

Accounts	Debit	Credit
Accounts payable and accrued expenses	4,000	
Cash		4,000

Transaction JE07.39—Accrued interest receivable from the previous year was received:

Accounts	Debit	Credit
Cash	1,000	
Interest receivable		1,000

Transaction JE07.40—During the year, parking revenue collected from customers totaled $1,500,000:

Accounts	Debit	Credit
Cash	1,500,000	
Charges for services		1,500,000

Transaction JE07.41—The following operating expenses were incurred during the year, of which $5,700,000 was paid in cash:

Personal services	$5,400,000
Contractual services	300,000
Repairs and maintenance	50,000
Other supplies and expenses	40,000
Total	$5,790,000

Accounts	Debit	Credit
Personal services expenses	5,400,000	
Contractual services expenses	300,000	
Repairs and maintenance expenses	50,000	
Other supplies and expenses	40,000	
Cash		5,700,000
Accounts payable and accrued expenses		90,000

Transaction JE07.42—During the year, interest and investment revenue of $10,000 was earned, of which $7,000 was received in cash:

Accounts	Debit	Credit
Cash	7,000	
Interest receivable	3,000	
Interest and investment revenue		10,000

Transaction JE07.43—The following capital assets were purchased during the year for cash:

Land and improvements	$120,000
Equipment	30,000
Vehicles	25,000
Total	$175,000

Accounts	Debit	Credit
Land and improvements	120,000	
Equipment	30,000	
Vehicles	25,000	
Cash		175,000

Transaction JE07.44—During the year, a parking lot under construction (construction in progress) was completed at a total cost of $160,000 (after incurring additional costs of $10,000 for the current year) and new construction costs of $15,000 were incurred on a new unfinished project:

Accounts	Debit	Credit
Construction in progress	10,000	
Cash		10,000
Land and land improvements	160,000	

Accounts	Debit	Credit
Construction in progress		160,000
Construction in progress	15,000	
Cash		15,000

Transaction JE07.45—The following assets were sold or abandoned during the year. The land and improvements represent a parking lot that was sold for $5,000,000 to a local real estate developer. The other capital assets were sold for $5,000:

	Original Cost	Accumulated Depreciation
Land and improvements	$1,500,000	
Equipment	10,000	$ 7,000
Vehicles	13,000	12,000
Total	$1,523,000	$19,000

Accounts	Debit	Credit
Cash	5,005,000	
Accumulated depreciation—equipment	7,000	
Accumulated depreciation—vehicles	12,000	
Land and improvements		1,500,000
Equipment		10,000
Vehicles		13,000
Miscellaneous revenue—gain on sale of assets		1,000
Special item—gain on sale of parking lot		3,500,000

PRACTICE POINT: GASB-34 defines a "special item" as "significant transactions or other events within the control of management that are either unusual in nature or infrequent in occurrence." Special items should be reported separately and before extraordinary items. If a significant transaction or other event occurs but is not within the control of management and that item is either unusual or infrequent, the item is not reported as a special item, but the nature of the item must be described in a note to the financial statements (GASB-34, par. 56). These definitions are further explained in GASB-62.

Transaction JE07.46—During the year, a portion of the notes payable ($10,000) and interest expense of $27,000 were paid. In addition, notes payable of $30,000 were issued during the year:

Accounts	Debit	Credit
Notes Payable	10,000	
Interest expense	27,000	
Cash		37,000

Accounts	Debit	Credit
Cash	30,000	
Notes Payable		30,000

Transaction JE07.47—Compensated absences of $1,000 were paid during the year and additional costs of $2,000 were accrued:

Accounts	Debit	Credit
Personal services expenses	2,000	
Compensated absences liability		1,000
Cash		1,000

Transaction JE07.48—Claims and judgements of $1,000 were paid during the year and additional costs of $3,000 were accrued:

Accounts	Debit	Credit
Insurance claims and expenses	3,000	
Claims and judgements payable		2,000
Cash		1,000

Transaction JE07.49—Depreciation expense recognized during the year was as follows:

Buildings	$ 90,000
Equipment	15,000
Vehicles	12,000
Total	$117,000

Accounts	Debit	Credit
Depreciation expense	117,000	
Accumulated depreciation—buildings		90,000
Accumulated depreciation—equipment		15,000
Accumulated depreciation—vehicles		12,000

Transaction JE07.50—Other operating revenues earned and received during the year amounted to $22,000 and other operating expenses incurred and paid during the year amounted to $3,000:

Accounts	Debit	Credit
Cash	22,000	
Operating revenues—miscellaneous		22,000
Operating expenses—miscellaneous	3,000	
Cash		3,000

Transaction JE07.51—Additional temporary investments of $5,000 were purchased during the year:

Accounts	Debit	Credit
Temporary investments	5,000	
Cash		5,000

Transaction JE07.52—A transfer of $90,000 was received from the General Fund:

Accounts	Debit	Credit
Cash	90,000	
Transfers in—General Fund		90,000

Transaction JE07.53—During the year, the Communications and Technology Support Center (Internal Service Fund) billed the CPA $100,000 for services performed. The CPA made payments of $90,000:

Accounts	Debit	Credit
Contractual services expenses	100,000	
Cash		90,000
Due to other funds—Internal Service Fund—Communications and Technology Support Center		10,000

Transaction JE07.54—Supplies of $24,000 were on hand at the end of the year:

Accounts	Debit	Credit
Inventories	4,000	
Other supplies and expenses		4,000

After the transactions for the year are posted, the year-end trial balance (June 30, 20X2) for the CPA appears as follows:

	Adjusted Trial Balance	
Accounts	**Debit**	**Credit**
Cash	$ 764,000	
Interest receivable	3,000	
Temporary investments	5,000	
Supplies	24,000	
Construction in progress	15,000	
Land and improvements	1,780,000	
Buildings	2,400,000	
Accumulated depreciation—buildings		$1,390,000
Equipment	140,000	
Accumulated depreciation—equipment		83,000
Vehicles	102,000	
Accumulated depreciation—vehicles		32,000
Accounts payable and accrued expenses		90,000
Due to other funds—Communications and Technology Center		17,000
Compensated absences liability		5,000
Claims and judgements payable		7,000
Notes payable		30,000
Bonds payable		500,000
Net assets		3,994,000
Charges for services		1,500,000
Interest and investment revenue		10,000

Accounts	Adjusted Trial Balance Debit	Credit
Miscellaneous revenue—gain on sale of assets		1,000
Operating revenues—miscellaneous		22,000
Personal services expenses	5,402,000	
Contractual services expenses	400,000	
Repairs and maintenance expenses	50,000	
Other supplies and expenses	36,000	
Insurance claims and expenses	3,000	
Depreciation expense	117,000	
Interest expense	27,000	
Operating expenses—miscellaneous	3,000	
Special item—gain on sale of parking lot		3,500,000
Transfers out—General Fund		90,000
Totals	$11,271,000	$11,271,000

The worksheet that summarizes the foregoing journal entries for the CPA's year-end trial balance is presented in Appendix 7C.

Centerville Municipal Airport

The Centerville Municipal Airport (CMA) is a regional airport that serves the City and several smaller communities in the three adjacent counties. The fund's balance for the beginning of the fiscal year is as follows:

Accounts	Trial Balance Debit	Credit
Cash	$ 1,150,000	
Interest receivable	55,000	
Temporary investments	10,000,000	
Accounts receivable	5,000,000	
Due from other funds—General Fund Due from other governments Supplies	50,000	
Construction in progress	25,000,000	
Land and improvements	10,000,000	
Runways and tarmacs	27,000,000	
Accumulated depreciation—runways and tarmacs		$ 6,500,000
Buildings	30,000,000	
Accumulated depreciation—buildings		6,500,000
Equipment	7,000,000	
Accumulated depreciation—equipment		4,300,000
Vehicles	2,300,000	
Accumulated depreciation—vehicles		1,900,000
Accounts payable and accrued expenses		3,400,000
Due to other funds—Communications and Technology Center		25,000

Accounts	Trial Balance	
	Debit	Credit
Due to other funds—Internal Service Fund—Special Services Support Center		77,000
Compensated absences liability		125,000
Claims and judgements payable		120,000
Notes payable		4,500,000
Revenue bonds payable—Terminal A		12,000,000
Revenue bonds payable—Terminal B		4,500,000
Net assets		73,608,000
Totals	$117,555,000	$117,555,000

This section presents illustrative transactions and entries for the CMA during the fiscal year ended June 30, 20X2.

Transaction JE07.55—Accounts payable and accrued expenses of $3,400,000 from the previous year were paid:

Accounts	Debit	Credit
Accounts payable and accrued expenses	3,400,000	
Cash		3,400,000

Transaction JE07.56—Accrued interest receivable from the previous year was received:

Accounts	Debit	Credit
Cash	55,000	
Interest receivable		55,000

Transaction JE07.57— Airlines were billed $175,000,000 during the year for services provided and cash collections on account amounted to $165,000,000. In addition, during the year lessees were billed for $52,000,000 and cash collections on account amounted to $49,000,000. These rental revenues are used as security for revenue bonds for Terminal A ($30,000,000) and Terminal B ($22,000,000):

Accounts	Debit	Credit
Cash	165,000,000	
Accounts receivable	10,000,000	
Charges for services		175,000,000
Cash	49,000,000	
Accounts receivable	3,000,000	
Charges for services—rental income—security for Terminal A revenue bonds		30,000,000
Charges for services—rental income—security for Terminal B revenue bonds		22,000,000

Transaction JE07.58—The following operating expenses were incurred during the year, of which $191,000,000 were paid in cash:

Personal services		$161,000,000
Contractual services		30,000,000
Repairs and maintenance		2,100,000
Other supplies and expenses		1,800,000
Total		$194,900,000

Accounts	Debit	Credit
Personal services expenses	161,000,000	
Contractual services expenses	30,000,000	
Repairs and maintenance expenses	2,100,000	
Other supplies and expenses	1,800,000	
Cash		191,000,000
Accounts payable and accrued expenses		3,900,000

Transaction JE07.59—During the year, interest and investment revenue of $1,200,000 was earned, of which $1,000,000 was received in cash:

Accounts	Debit	Credit
Cash	1,000,000	
Interest receivable	200,000	
Interest and investment revenue		1,200,000

Transaction JE07.60—The following capital assets were purchased during the year for cash:

Land and improvements		$3,200,000
Runways and tarmac		500,000
Equipment		2,300,000
Vehicles		1,100,000
Total		$7,100,000

Accounts	Debit	Credit
Land and improvements	3,200,000	
Runways and tarmac	500,000	
Equipment	2,300,000	
Vehicles	1,100,000	
Cash		7,100,000

Transaction JE07.61—During the year, a building under construction (construction in progress) was completed at a cost of $3,200,000 (after incurring additional costs of $400,000) and new construction costs of $1,300,000 were incurred on a new unfinished project:

Accounts	Debit	Credit
Construction in progress	400,000	
Cash		400,000
Building	3,200,000	

Accounts	Debit	Credit
Construction in progress		3,200,000
Construction in progress	1,300,000	
Cash		1,300,000

Transaction JE07.62—The following assets were sold or abandoned during the year. The cash proceeds were $420,000:

	Original Cost	Accumulated Depreciation
Equipment	$2,100,000	$1,600,000
Vehicles	900,000	715,000
Total	$3,000,000	$2,315,000

Accounts	Debit	Credit
Cash	420,000	
Expenses—loss on sale of assets	265,000	
Accumulated depreciation—equipment	1,600,000	
Accumulated depreciation—vehicles	715,000	
Equipment		2,100,000
Vehicles		900,000

Transaction JE07.63—During the year, additional notes payable of $3,200,000 were issued and revenue bonds related to Terminal A ($2,000,000) and Terminal B ($500,000) were paid off. Interest expense of $1,220,000 was paid:

Accounts	Debit	Credit
Cash	3,200,000	
Notes payable		3,200,000
Revenue bonds payable—Terminal A	2,000,000	
Revenue bonds payable—Terminal B	500,000	
Interest expense	1,220,000	
Cash		3,720,000

A governmental entity may issue general obligation bonds whose proceeds are used to construct capital assets reported in an Enterprise Fund. If the debt is directly related to and expected to be paid from the Enterprise Fund, both the capital asset and the debt are reported in the business-type activities column of the statement of net assets. However, the GASB's *Comprehensive Implementation Guide* points out that if the Enterprise Fund is not expected to service the debt, the debt is reported in the governmental activities column and the capital asset is reported in the business-type activities column of the statement of net assets. The GASB's *Guide* notes that if a discretely presented component unit is the recipient of the capital asset, the component unit reports the capital assets, but it reports the obligation only if it is "legally obligated to repay it" because the GASB views transactions with discretely presented component units as external transactions. If the debt is not reported by the discretely presented component unit, the primary government uses the capital debt balance to compute its unrestricted net assets because the debt was not issued to purchase capital assets of the primary government but, rather, for the component unit. However, if the primary government decides to report an optional total column for the reporting entity (which includes the primary government and the discretely presented component unit), the capital debt is used to compute the amount reported as net assets invested in capital assets (net of related debt) in the reporting entity's total column. Under this circumstance, amounts for unrestricted net assets and net assets invested in capital assets (net of related debt) are not determined by adding across the relevant rows. For this reason, the face of the financial statement or a note to the financial statements must explain why the amounts are reclassified for presentation in the final reporting entity's column.

Transaction JE07.64—Compensated absences of $17,000 were paid during the year and additional costs of $25,000 were accrued:

Accounts	Debit	Credit
Personal services expenses	25,000	
Compensated absences liability		8,000
Cash		17,000

Transaction JE07.65—Claims and judgements of $25,000 were paid during the year and additional costs of $100,000 were accrued:

Accounts	Debit	Credit
Insurance claims and expenses	100,000	
Claims and judgements payable		75,000
Cash		25,000

Transaction JE07.66—Depreciation expense recognized during the year was as follows:

Runways and tarmacs	$1,300,000
Buildings	1,200,000
Equipment	450,000
Vehicles	420,000
Total	$3,370,000

Accounts	Debit	Credit
Depreciation expense	3,370,000	
Accumulated depreciation—runways and tarmacs		1,300,000
Accumulated depreciation—buildings		1,200,000
Accumulated depreciation—equipment		450,000
Accumulated depreciation—vehicles		420,000

Transaction JE07.67—A capital grant of $2,000,000 was authorized by the state government. As of the end of the year, $1,700,000 of the amount had been collected:

Accounts	Debit	Credit
Cash	1,700,000	
Due from other governments	300,000	
Capital grants and contributions		2,000,000

Transaction JE07.68—Other operating revenues earned and received during the year amounted to $60,000 and other operating expenses incurred and paid during the year amounted to $70,000:

Accounts	Debit	Credit
Cash	60,000	
Operating revenues—miscellaneous		60,000
Operating expenses—miscellaneous	70,000	
Cash		70,000

Transaction JE07.69—Additional temporary investments of $50,000 were purchased during the year:

Accounts	Debit	Credit
Temporary investments	50,000	
Cash		50,000

Transaction JE07.70—A loan of $400,000 was made to the General Fund:

Accounts	Debit	Credit
Due from other funds—General Fund	400,000	
Cash		400,000

Transaction JE07.71—During the year, the Communications and Technology Support Center (Internal Service Fund) billed the CMA $600,000 for services performed. The CMA made payments of $540,000:

Accounts	Debit	Credit
Contractual services expenses	600,000	
Cash		540,000
Due to other funds—Internal Service Fund—Communications and Technology Support Center		60,000

Transaction JE07.72—During the year, the Special Services Support Center (Internal Service Fund) billed the CMA $2,950,000 for services performed. The CMA made payments of $2,600,000:

Accounts	Debit	Credit
Contractual services expenses	2,950,000	
Cash		2,600,000
Due to other funds—Internal Service Fund—Special Services Support Center		350,000

Transaction JE07.73—Supplies of $55,000 were on hand at the end of the year:

Accounts	Debit	Credit
Inventories	5,000	
Other supplies and expenses		5,000

After the transactions for the year are posted, the year-end trial balance (June 30, 20X2) for the Centerville Municipal Airport appears as follows:

	Adjusted Trial Balance	
Accounts	**Debit**	**Credit**
Cash	$10,963,000	
Interest receivable	200,000	
Temporary investments	10,050,000	
Accounts receivable	18,000,000	
Due from other funds—General Fund	400,000	
Due from other governments	300,000	
Supplies	55,000	
Construction in progress	23,500,000	
Land and improvements	13,200,000	
Runways and tarmacs	27,500,000	
Accumulated depreciation—runways and tarmacs		$ 7,800,000
Buildings	33,200,000	
Accumulated depreciation—buildings		7,700,000
Equipment	7,200,000	
Accumulated depreciation—equipment		3,150,000
Vehicles	2,500,000	
Accumulated depreciation—vehicles		1,605,000
Accounts payable and accrued expenses		3,900,000
Due to other funds—Communications and Technology Center		85,000
Due to other funds—Internal Service Fund—Special Services Support Center		427,000
Compensated absences liability		133,000
Claims and judgements payable		195,000
Notes payable		7,700,000
Revenue bonds payable—Terminal A		10,000,000
Revenue bonds payable—Terminal B		4,000,000
Net assets		73,608,000
Charges for services		175,000,000
Charges for services—rental income—security for Terminal A revenue bonds		30,000,000
Charges for services—rental income—security for Terminal B revenue bonds		22,000,000
Interest and investment revenue		1,200,000
Capital grants and contributions		2,000,000
Operating revenues—miscellaneous		60,000
Personal services expenses	161,025,000	
Contractual services expenses	33,550,000	
Repairs and maintenance expenses	2,100,000	
Other supplies and expenses	1,795,000	
Insurance claims and expenses	100,000	

Accounts	Adjusted Trial Balance	
	Debit	Credit
Depreciation expense	3,370,000	
Interest expense	1,220,000	
Operating expenses—miscellaneous	70,000	
Expenses—loss on sale of assets	265,000	
Totals	$350,563,000	$350,563,000

The worksheet that summarizes the foregoing journal entries for the CMA's year-end trial balance is presented in Appendix 7D.

FUND FINANCIAL STATEMENTS

At the fund financial statement level, Enterprise Funds are presented in the proprietary funds along with the Internal Service Funds. Proprietary funds prepare a statement of net assets (or balance sheet), statement of revenues, expenses, and changes in fund net assets (or fund equity) and statement of cash flows. Based on the adjusted trial balances created above, the following financial statements reflect the balances and activities of all the Enterprise Funds.

PRACTICE POINT: The statement of net assets may be presented in either one of the following formats: (1) net assets format, where assets less liabilities equal net assets or (2) balance sheet format, where assets equal liabilities plus net assets (GASB-34, pars. 97 and 98).

Until GASB-62 is adopted by a government (transition will occur for periods beginning after December 15, 2011) business-type activities must follow either Alternative 1 or Alternative 2, as described in GASB-20 (Accounting and Financial Reporting for Proprietary Funds and Other Governmental Entities that Use Proprietary Fund Accounting). Under Alternative 1, governmental entities using proprietary fund accounting must follow (1) all GASB pronouncements and (2) FASB Statements and Interpretations, APB Opinions, and Accounting Research Bulletins (ARBs) issued on or before November 30, 1989, except those that conflict with a GASB pronouncement. Under Alternative 2, governmental entities using proprietary fund accounting must follow (1) all GASB pronouncements and (2) all FASB Statements and Interpretations, APB Opinions, and ARBs, no matter when issued, except those that conflict with a GASB pronouncement. Unlike Alternative 1, Alternative 2 has no cutoff date for determining the applicability of FASB pronouncements. The GASB's *Comprehensive Implementation Guide* raises the question about the presentation of comprehensive income for those governmental entities that use Alternative 2. FAS-130 (Reporting Comprehensive Income) requires that certain unrealized gains and losses (such as the change in the fair value of investments in certain marketable securities) be reported as a component of stockholders' equity and not as an element on the operating statement. The GASB's *Guide* notes that the concept of comprehensive income does not apply to proprietary funds, because governmental financial reporting standards do not allow for items to bypass a governmental entity's operating statement. For example, investments in marketable securities must be accounted for on a fair value basis, with any unrealized gain or loss presented on the entity's operating statement. All of the unrealized gains and losses identified in FASB pronouncements that are reported in stockholders' equity must be presented as either revenue or an expense on a proprietary fund's statement of revenues, expenses, and changes in fund net assets (as well as in the statement of activities). These alternatives become moot when GASB-62 is adopted by a government.

The GASB's *Guide* points out that GASB-34 only requires that operating and nonoperating expenses be "detailed." There is no requirement pertaining to how the expenses are to be classified. One entity could use a functional or program classification scheme, while another could present expenses by their nature.

In the preparation of the statement of net assets, notes payable were assumed to be associated with the acquisition of capital assets and the current and noncurrent portions of certain liabilities were assumed. Also, certain assumptions were made in determining the amount of restricted net assets. (See Appendix 7E.)

Enterprise Funds
Statement of Net Assets
June 30, 20X2

	Centerville Toll Bridge	Centerville Utilities Authority	Centerville Parking Authority	Centerville Municipal Airport	Total
ASSETS					
Current assets:					
Cash	$ 739,500	$ 230,000	$ 764,000	$10,963,000	$12,696,500
Interest receivable	3,000	50,000	3,000	200,000	256,000
Accounts receivable (net)	—	7,550,000	—	18,000,000	25,550,000
Due from other funds	—	2,000,000	—	400,000	2,400,000
Due from other governments	—	100,000	—	300,000	400,000
Temporary investments	58,000	55,000	5,000	10,050,000	10,168,000
Supplies	32,000	75,000	24,000	55,000	186,000
Total current assets	832,500	10,060,000	796,000	39,968,000	51,656,500
Noncurrent assets:					
Construction in progress	70,000	200,000	15,000	23,500,000	23,785,000
Land and improvements	140,000	5,200,000	1,780,000	13,200,000	20,320,000
Superstructure	1,400,000	—	—	—	1,400,000

	Centerville Toll Bridge	Centerville Utilities Authority	Centerville Parking Authority	Centerville Municipal Airport	Total
Distribution and collection systems	—	46,300,000	—	—	46,300,000
Runways and tarmacs	—	—	—	27,500,000	27,500,000
Buildings	330,000	14,450,000	2,400,000	33,200,000	50,380,000
Equipment	55,000	4,600,000	140,000	7,200,000	11,995,000
Vehicles	835,000	1,660,000	102,000	2,500,000	5,097,000
Less accumulated depreciation	(1,257,000)	(54,395,000)	(1,505,000)	(20,255,000)	(77,412,000)
Total noncurrent assets	1,573,000	18,015,000	2,932,000	86,845,000	109,365,000
Total assets	$ 2,405,500	$28,075,000	$3,728,000	$126,813,000	$161,021,500
LIABILITIES					
Current liabilities:					
Accounts payable and accrued expenses	$ 50,000	$ 4,300,000	$ 90,000	$ 3,900,000	$ 8,340,000
Due to other funds	18,000	35,000	17,000	512,000	582,000
Compensated absences	3,000	21,000	2,000	15,000	41,000
Claims and judgements	5,000	17,000	4,000	25,000	51,000
Notes payable	10,000	70,000	30,000	—	110,000
Revenue bonds— Terminal A	—	—	—	2,000,000	2,000,000
Revenue bonds— Terminal B	—	—	—	500,000	500,000
Bonds payable	20,000	850,000	—	—	870,000
Total current liabilities	106,000	5,293,000	143,000	6,952,000	12,494,000
Noncurrent liabilities:					
Compensated absences	5,000	63,000	3,000	118,000	189,000
Claims and judgments	22,000	212,000	3,000	170,000	407,000
Notes payable	20,000	260,000	—	7,700,000	7,980,000
Revenue bonds— Terminal A	—	—	—	8,000,000	8,000,000
Revenue bonds— Terminal B	—	—	—	3,500,000	3,500,000
Bonds payable	60,000	6,850,000	500,000	—	7,410,000
Total noncurrent liabilities	107,000	7,385,000	506,000	19,488,000	27,486,000
Total liabilities	$ 213,000	$12,678,000	$ 649,000	$ 26,440,000	$39,980,000

	Centerville Toll Bridge	Centerville Utilities Authority	Centerville Parking Authority	Centerville Municipal Airport	Total
NET ASSETS					
Invested in capital assets, net of related debt	$ 1,463,000	$ 9,985,000	$2,402,000	$ 69,145,000	$ 82,995,000
Restricted	622,000	5,250,000	595,000	30,895,000	37,362,000
Unrestricted	107,500	162,000	82,000	333,000	684,500
Total net assets	$2,192,500	$15,397,000	$3,079,000	$100,373,000	$121,041,500

Enterprise Funds
Statement of Revenues, Expenses, and Changes in Fund
Net Assets For the Year Ended June 30, 20X2

	Centerville Toll Bridge	Centerville Utilities Authority	Centerville Parking Authority	Centerville Municipal Airport	Total
OPERATING REVENUES					
Charges for services	$4,750,000	$36,000,000	$1,500,000	$175,000,000	$217,250,000
Charges for services— rental income— security for Terminal A revenue bonds	—	—	—	30,000,000	30,000,000
Charges for services— rental income— security for Terminal B revenue bonds	—	—	—	22,000,000	22,000,000
Miscellaneous	20,000	10,000	22,000	60,000	112,000
Total operating revenues	4,770,000	36,010,000	1,522,000	227,060,000	269,362,000
OPERATING EXPENSES					
Personal services	2,402,000	22,022,000	5,402,000	161,025,000	190,851,000
Contractual services	1,280,000	11,220,000	400,000	33,550,000	46,450,000
Repairs and maintenance	400,000	700,000	50,000	2,100,000	3,250,000
Other supplies and expenses	194,000	729,000	36,000	1,795,000	2,754,000
Insurance claims and expenses	10,000	21,000	3,000	100,000	134,000
Depreciation	339,000	3,025,000	117,000	3,370,000	6,851,000
Miscellaneous	30,000	5,000	3,000	70,000	108,000
Total operating expenses	4,655,000	37,722,000	6,011,000	202,010,000	250,398,000
Operating income (loss)	115,000	(1,712,000)	(4,489,000)	25,050,000	18,964,000

	Centerville Toll Bridge	Centerville Utilities Authority	Centerville Parking Authority	Centerville Municipal Airport	Total
NONOPERATING REVENUES (EXPENSES)					
Interest and investment revenue	30,000	400,000	10,000	1,200,000	1,640,000
Interest	(6,000)	(450,000)	(27,000)	(1,220,000)	(1,703,000)
Operating grants and contributions	100,000	—	—	—	100,000
Miscellaneous	7,000	(110,000)	1,000	(265,000)	(367,000)
Total nonoperating revenue (expenses)	131,000	(160,000)	(16,000)	(285,000)	(330,000)
Income (loss) before capital contributions and transfers	246,000	(1,872,000)	(4,505,000)	24,765,000	18,634,000
Capital contributions	250,000	1,250,000	—	2,000,000	3,500,000
Transfers in	50,000	—	90,000	—	140,000
Special item—gain on sale of parking lot	—	—	3,500,000	—	3,500,000
Change in net assets	546,000	(622,000)	(915,000)	26,765,000	25,774,000
Total net assets— beginning	1,646,500	16,019,000	3,994,000	73,608,000	95,267,500
Total net assets—ending	$2,192,500	$ 15,397,000	$3,079,000	$100,373,000	$121,041,500

Enterprise Funds
Statement of Cash Flows
For the Year Ended June 30, 20X2

	Centerville Toll Bridge	Centerville Utilities Authority	Centerville Parking Authority	Centerville Municipal Airport	Total
CASH FLOWS FROM OPERATING ACTIVITIES					
Receipts from customers	$4,750,000	$34,000,000	$1,500,000	$214,000,000	$254,250,000
Payments to suppliers	(1,806,000)	(12,112,000)	(345,000)	(36,425,000)	(50,688,000)
Payments to employees	(2,371,000)	(19,013,000)	(5,361,000)	(158,017,000)	(184,762,000)
Internal activity— payments to other funds	(66,000)	(200,000)	(90,000)	(3,140,000)	(3,496,000)
Other receipts (payments)	(18,000)	5,000	19,000	(10,000)	(4,000)
Net cash provided by operating activities	489,000	2,680,000	(4,277,000)	16,408,000	15,300,000

	Centerville Toll Bridge	Centerville Utilities Authority	Centerville Parking Authority	Centerville Municipal Airport	Total
CASH FLOWS FROM NON-CAPITAL FINANCING ACTIVITIES					
Subsidies and transfers from (to) other funds and state government	150,000	—	90,000	—	240,000
CASH FLOWS FROM CAPITAL AND RELATED FINANCING ACTIVITIES					
Proceeds from the issuance of capital debt	—	2,120,000	—	3,200,000	5,320,000
Capital contributions	250,000	1,250,000	30,000	1,700,000	3,230,000
Acquisitions of capital assets	(390,000)	(5,350,000)	(200,000)	(8,800,000)	(14,740,000)
Proceeds from sale of capital assets	50,000	500,000	5,005,000	420,000	5,975,000
Principal paid on capital debt	(30,000)	(1,740,000)	(10,000)	(2,500,000)	(4,280,000)
Interest paid on capital debt	(6,000)	(450,000)	(27,000)	(1,220,000)	(1,703,000)
Net cash (used) by capital and related financing activities	(126,000)	(3,670,000)	4,798,000	(7,200,000)	(6,198,000)
CASH FLOWS FROM INVESTING ACTIVITIES					
Loans to other funds	—	(2,000,000)	—	(400,000)	(2,400,000)
Loans to other governments	—	(100,000)	—	—	(100,000)
Interest and dividends	31,500	365,000	8,000	1,055,000	1,459,500
Purchase of investments	(25,000)	(15,000)	(5,000)	(50,000)	(95,000)
Net cash provided (used) by investing activities	6,500	(1,750,000)	3,000	605,000	(1,135,500)
Net increase (decrease) in cash	519,500	(2,740,000)	614,000	9,813,000	8,206,500
Balances—beginning of year	220,000	2,970,000	150,000	1,150,000	4,490,000
Balances—end of year	$739,500	$230,000	$ 764,000	$10,963,000	$12,696,500

	Centerville Toll Bridge	Centerville Utilities Authority	Centerville Parking Authority	Centerville Municipal Airport	Total
Reconciliation of operating income (loss) to net cash provided (used) by operating activities:					
Operating income (loss)	$115,000	$(1,712,000)	$(4,489,000)	$25,050,000	$18,964,000
Adjustments:					
Depreciation expense	339,000	3,025,000	117,000	3,370,000	6,851,000
Change in assets and liabilities:					
Receivables, net	—	(1,850,000)	—	(13,000,000)	(14,850,000)
Inventories	(6,000)	(21,000)	(4,000)	(5,000)	(36,000)
Accounts and accrued liabilities	41,000	3,238,000	99,000	993,000	4,371,000
Net cash provided (used) by operating activities	$489,000	$2,680,000	$(4,277,000)	$16,408,000	$15,300,000

As noted earlier in this chapter, an Enterprise Fund must use the direct method in displaying cash flows from operating activities.

A proprietary fund's statement of revenues, expenses, and changes in fund net assets must differentiate between operating revenues and nonoperating revenues, and operating expenses and nonoperating expenses based on policies established by the governmental entity. GASB-34 (par. 102) states that, in general, differentiations between operating and nonoperating transactions should follow the broad guidance established by GASB-9. GASB-34 points out that nonoperating revenues should include tax revenues, certain nonexchange fees, and interest. In addition, The AICPA's Audit and Accounting Guide *State and Local Governments* states that the following should be considered nonoperating revenues: (1) revenues from appropriations between primary governments and their component units, (2) contributions, (3) grants, (4) entitlements, (5) shared revenues for operating purposes, and (6) shared revenues that can be used for either operating purposes or capital expenditures.

The combined financial statements for the Enterprise Funds are used in Chapter 13, "Developing Information for Fund Financial Statements."

CONVERTING TO GOVERNMENT-WIDE FINANCIAL STATEMENTS

Government-wide financial statements are reported on the accrual basis of accounting. Generally, most governments work from their proprietary fund financial statements and through the use of worksheet entries convert to accrual based financial statements. Because proprietary funds are presented on an accrual basis, often there is no need to make worksheet entries to convert the information from a fund basis to a government-wide basis; however, the residual balances and the activities of Internal Service Funds must be analyzed to determine how they are to be merged into the government-wide financial statements. This consolidation process is illustrated in Chapter 14, "Developing Information for Government-Wide Financial Statements."

The GASB's *Comprehensive Implementation Guide* states that the operating/nonoperating format required for an Enterprise Fund at the fund reporting level is not required for the "business-activities" portion of the statement of activities. Thus, the results of operations of an Enterprise Fund must be reformatted in order to identify direct expenses (both operating and nonoperating), program revenues (including charges for services, operating and capital grants, and contributions), general revenues (unrestricted grants and contributions, and investment earnings), special items, extraordinary items, and transfers.

APPENDIX 7A: WORKSHEET FOR SUMMARIZING CURRENT TRANSACTIONS: CENTERVILLE TOLL BRIDGE

Accounts	Trial Balance Debit	Trial Balance Credit	Adjustments Debit		Adjustments Credit		Adjusted Trial Balance Debit	Adjusted Trial Balance Credit	Operating Statement Debit	Operating Statement Credit	Balance Sheet Debit	Balance Sheet Credit
Cash	220,000	—	JE07.02	4,500	JE07.01	26,000	739,500	—	—	—	739,500	—
		—	JE07.03	4,750,000	JE07.04	4,150,000	—		—	—	—	—
		—	JE07.05	27,000	JE07.06	190,000	—		—	—	—	—
		—	JE07.08	50,000	JE07.07	130,000	—		—	—	—	—
		—	JE07.13	350,000	JE07.07	70,000	—		—	—	—	—
		—	JE07.14	20,000	JE07.09	36,000	—		—	—	—	—
		—	JE07.16	50,000	JE07.10	1,000	—		—	—	—	—
		—		—	JE07.11	8,000	—		—	—	—	—
		—		—	JE07.14	30,000	—		—	—	—	—
		—		—	JE07.15	25,000	—		—	—	—	—
		—		—	JE07.17	66,000	—		—	—	—	—
Interest receivable	4,500	—	JE07.05	3,000	JE07.02	4,500	3,000	—	—	—	3,000	—
Temporary investments	33,000	—	JE07.15	25,000		—	58,000	—	—	—	58,000	—
Supplies	26,000	—	JE07.18	6,000		—	32,000	—	—	—	32,000	—
Construction in progress	40,000	—	JE07.07	130,000	JE07.07	170,000	70,000	—	—	—	70,000	—
	—		JE07.07	70,000			—		—	—	—	—

Account	Dr	Cr	Adj. ref	Adj. Dr	Adj. ref	Adj. Cr	Dr	Cr			Dr	Cr
Land and improvements	100,000	—	JE07.06	40,000	—	—	140,000	—	—	—	140,000	—
Superstructure	1,400,000	—	—	—	—	—	1,400,000	—	—	—	1,400,000	—
Accumulated depreciation—superstructure	—	650,000	—	—	JE07.12	28,000	—	678,000	—	—	—	678,000
Buildings	250,000	—	JE07.06	170,000	JE07.08	90,000	330,000	—	—	—	330,000	—
Accumulated depreciation—buildings	—	120,000	JE07.08	70,000	JE07.12	25,000	—	75,000	—	—	—	75,000
Equipment	40,000	—	JE07.06	30,000	JE07.08	15,000	55,000	—	—	—	55,000	—
Accumulated depreciation—equipment	—	25,000	JE07.08	12,000	JE07.12	6,000	—	19,000	—	—	—	19,000
Vehicles	800,000	—	JE07.06	120,000	JE07.08	85,000	835,000	—	—	—	835,000	—
Accumulated depreciation—vehicles	—	270,000	JE07.08	65,000	JE07.12	280,000	—	485,000	—	—	—	485,000
Accounts payable and accrued expenses	—	26,000	JE07.01	26,000	JE07.04	50,000	—	50,000	—	—	—	50,000
Due to other funds—Communications and Technology Center	—	4,000	—	—	JE07.17	14,000	—	18,000	—	—	—	18,000
Compensated absences liability	—	7,000	—	—	JE07.10	1,000	—	8,000	—	—	—	8,000

Account	Trial Balance Dr	Trial Balance Cr	Adjustments Dr	Adjustments Cr	Adjusted Balance Dr	Adjusted Balance Cr	Statement Dr	Statement Cr
Claims and judgements payable	—	25,000	—	JE07.11 2,000	—	27,000	—	27,000
Notes payable	—	40,000	JE07.09 10,000	—	—	30,000	—	30,000
Bonds payable	—	100,000	JE07.09 20,000	—	—	80,000	—	80,000
Net assets	—	1,646,500	—	—	—	1,646,500	—	1,646,500
Charges for services	—	—	—	JE07.03 4,750,000	—	4,750,000	—	4,750,000
Interest and investment revenue	—	—	—	JE07.05 30,000	—	30,000	—	30,000
Miscellaneous revenue—gain on sale of assets	—	—	—	JE07.08 7,000	—	7,000	—	7,000
Operating grants and contributions	—	—	—	JE07.13 100,000	—	100,000	—	100,000
Capital grants and contributions	—	—	—	JE07.13 250,000	—	250,000	—	250,000
Operating revenues—miscellaneous	—	—	—	JE07.14 20,000	—	20,000	—	20,000
Personal services expenses	—	—	JE07.04 2,400,000; JE07.10 2,000	—	2,402,000	—	2,402,000	—
Contractual services expenses	—	—	JE07.04 1,200,000; JE07.17 80,000	—	1,280,000	—	1,280,000	—

Account											
Repairs and maintenance expenses	—	JE07.04	400,000		—	400,000	400,000	400,000	—	—	—
Other supplies and expenses	—	JE07.04	200,000	JE07.18	6,000	194,000	194,000	194,000	—	—	—
Insurance claims and expenses	—	JE07.11	10,000		—	10,000	10,000	10,000	—	—	—
Depreciation expense	—	JE07.12	339,000		—	339,000	339,000	339,000	—	—	—
Interest expense	—	JE07.09	6,000		—	6,000	6,000	6,000	—	—	—
Operating expenses—miscellaneous	—	JE07.14	30,000		—	30,000	30,000	30,000	—	—	—
Transfers in—General Fund	—		—	JE07.16	50,000	—	50,000	—	50,000	—	—
Totals	2,913,500		10,715,500		50,000	8,323,500	8,323,500	4,661,000	5,207,000	3,662,500	3,116,500
Net increase (decrease)								546,000	—	—	546,000
								5,207,000	5,207,000	3,662,500	3,662,500

APPENDIX 7B: WORKSHEET FOR SUMMARIZING CURRENT TRANSACTIONS: CENTERVILLE UTILITIES AUTHORITY

Accounts	Trial Balance Debit	Trial Balance Credit	Adjustments Debit		Adjustments Credit		Adjusted Trial Balance Debit	Adjusted Trial Balance Credit	Operating Statement Debit	Operating Statement Credit	Balance Sheet Debit	Balance Sheet Credit
Cash	2,970,000	—	JE07.20	15,000	JE07.19	1,100,000	230,000	—	—	—	230,000	—
			JE07.21	34,000,000	JE07.16	30,000,000						
			JE07.23	350,000	JE07.24	4,450,000						
			JE07.26	500,000	JE07.25	700,000						
			JE07.27	2,120,000	JE07.25	200,000						
			JE07.31	1,250,000	JE07.27	2,190,000						
			JE07.32	10,000	JE07.28	13,000						
					JE07.29	12,000						
					JE07.32	5,000						
					JE07.33	15,000						
					JE07.35	200,000						
					JE07.34	2,000,000						
					JE07.36	100,000						
Interest receivable	15,000	—	JE07.23	50,000	JE07.20	15,000	50,000	—	—	—	50,000	—
Accounts receivable	6,000,000	—	JE07.21	2,000,000	JE07.21	80,000	7,920,000	—	—	—	7,920,000	—
Allowance for doubtful accounts	—	300,000		—	JE07.21	70,000	—	370,000	—	—	—	370,000
Temporary investments	40,000	—	JE07.33	15,000		—	55,000	—	—	—	55,000	—

Account	Balance	Ref.	Debit	Ref.	Credit	Balance Dr	Balance Cr
Due from other funds—General Fund	—	JE07.34	2,000,000	—	—	2,000,000	—
Due from other governments	—	JE07.36	100,000	—	—	100,000	—
Supplies	54,000	JE07.37	21,000	—	—	75,000	—
Construction in progress	1,500,000	JE07.25	700,000	JE07.25	2,200,000	200,000	—
	—	JE07.25	200,000	—	—	—	—
Land and improvements	4,000,000	JE07.24	1,200,000	—	—	5,200,000	—
Distribution and collection systems	45,000,000	JE07.24	1,300,000	—	—	46,300,000	—
Accumulated depreciation—distribution and collection systems	41,000,000	—	—	JE07.30	1,200,000	—	42,200,000
Buildings	13,000,000	JE07.25	2,200,000	JE07.26	750,000	14,450,000	—
Accumulated depreciation—buildings	10,920,000	JE07.26	600,000	JE07.30	625,000	—	10,945,000
Equipment	6,500,000	JE07.24	1,200,000	JE07.26	3,100,000	4,600,000	—
Accumulated depreciation—equipment	2,380,000	JE07.26	2,800,000	JE07.30	920,000	—	500,000
Vehicles	1,400,000	JE07.24	750,000	JE07.26	490,000	1,660,000	—
Accumulated depreciation—vehicles	800,000	JE07.26	330,000	JE07.30	280,000	—	750,000

Accounts payable and accrued expenses	—	1,100,000	JE07.19 1,100,000	JE07.22 4,300,000	4,300,000	—	—	4,300,000
Due to other funds—Internal Service Fund—Communications and Technology Support Center	—	15,000	—	JE07.35 20,000	35,000	—	—	35,000
Compensated absences liability	—	75,000	—	JE07.28 9,000	84,000	—	—	84,000
Claims and judgements payable	—	220,000	—	JE07.29 9,000	229,000	—	—	229,000
Notes payable	—	250,000	JE07.27 40,000	JE07.27 120,000	330,000	—	—	330,000
Bonds payable	—	7,400,000	JE07.27 1,700,000	JE07.27 2,000,000	7,700,000	—	—	7,700,000
Net assets	—	16,019,000	—	—	16,019,000	—	—	16,019,000
Charges for services	—	—	—	JE07.21 36,000,000	36,000,000	36,000,000	—	—
Interest and investment revenue	—	—	—	JE07.23 400,000	400,000	400,000	—	—
Capital grants and contributions	—	—	—	JE07.31 1,250,000	1,250,000	1,250,000	—	—
Operating revenues—miscellaneous	—	—	—	JE07.32 10,000	10,000	10,000	—	—
Personal services expenses	—	—	JE07.22 22,000,000 / JE07.28 22,000	—	22,022,000	—	22,022,000	—

Account											
Contractual services expenses	—	—	JE07.22 11,000,000; JE07.35 220,000	—	11,220,000	—	11,220,000	—	—	—	—
Repairs and maintenance expenses	—	—	JE07.22 700,000	—	700,000	—	700,000	—	—	—	—
Other supplies and expenses	—	—	JE07.22 600,000; JE07.21 150,000	JE07.37 21,000	729,000	—	729,000	—	—	—	—
Insurance claims and expenses	—	—	JE07.29 21,000	—	21,000	—	21,000	—	—	—	—
Depreciation expense	—	—	JE07.30 3,025,000	—	3,025,000	—	3,025,000	—	—	—	—
Interest expense	—	—	JE07.27 450,000	—	450,000	—	450,000	—	—	—	—
Operating expenses—miscellaneous	—	—	JE07.32 5,000	—	5,000	—	5,000	—	—	—	—
Miscellaneous expenses—loss on sale of assets	—	—	JE07.26 110,000	—	110,000	—	110,000	—	—	—	—
Totals	80,479,000	80,479,000	94,854,000	94,854,000	121,122,000	121,122,000	38,282,000	37,660,000	82,840,000	82,840,000	83,462,000
Net increase (decrease)							(622,000)	—			(622,000)
							37,660,000	37,660,000	82,840,000	82,840,000	82,840,000

APPENDIX 7C: WORKSHEET FOR SUMMARIZING CURRENT TRANSACTIONS: CENTERVILLE PARKING AUTHORITY

Accounts	Trial Balance Debit	Trial Balance Credit	Adjustments Debit		Adjustments Credit		Adjusted Trial Balance Debit	Adjusted Trial Balance Credit	Operating Statement Debit	Operating Statement Credit	Balance Sheet Debit	Balance Sheet Credit
Cash	150,000	—	JE07.39	1,000	JE07.38	4,000	764,000	—	—	—	764,000	—
			JE07.40	1,500,000	JE07.41	5,700,000	—		—	—	—	—
			JE07.42	7,000	JE07.43	175,000	—		—	—	—	—
			JE07.45	5,005,000	JE07.44	10,000	—		—	—	—	—
			JE07.46	30,000	JE07.44	15,000	—		—	—	—	—
			JE07.50	22,000	JE07.46	37,000	—		—	—	—	—
			JE07.52	90,000	JE07.47	1,000	—		—	—	—	—
					JE07.48	1,000	—		—	—	—	—
					JE07.50	3,000	—		—	—	—	—
					JE07.51	5,000	—		—	—	—	—
					JE07.53	90,000	—		—	—	—	—
Interest receivable	1,000	—	JE07.42	3,000	JE07.39	1,000	3,000	—	—	—	3,000	—
Temporary investments	—	—	JE07.51	5,000	—	—	5,000	—	—	—	5,000	—
Supplies	20,000	—	JE07.54	4,000	—	—	24,000	—	—	—	24,000	—
Construction in progress	150,000	—	JE07.44	10,000	JE07.44	160,000	15,000	—	—	—	15,000	—

Account	Debit	Credit	Ref.	Debit	Credit	Ref.	Debit	Credit
Land and improvements	3,000,000	—	JE07.44	15,000	—	—	—	—
Buildings	2,400,000	—	JE07.43 / JE07.44	1,300,000	120,000 / 160,000	JE07.45	1,500,000	1,780,000
Accumulated depreciation—buildings	—	—	—	—	—	—	—	1,390,000
Equipment	120,000	—	JE07.43	75,000	30,000 / 10,000	JE07.49 / JE07.45	90,000	2,400,000
Accumulated depreciation—equipment	—	—	JE07.45 / JE07.43	—	15,000 / 13,000	JE07.49 / JE07.45	83,000	140,000
Vehicles	90,000	—	JE07.45 / JE07.43	75,000	7,000 / 25,000	JE07.49 / JE07.45	102,000	102,000
Accumulated depreciation—vehicles	—	—	JE07.45	32,000	12,000	JE07.49	32,000	32,000
Accounts payable and accrued expenses	—	—	JE07.38	4,000	4,000	JE07.41	90,000	90,000
Due to other funds—Communications and Technology Center	—	—	—	7,000	—	JE07.53	10,000	17,000
Compensated absences liability	—	—	JE07.47	4,000	1,000	JE07.47	5,000	5,000
Claims and judgments payable	—	—	JE07.48	5,000	2,000	JE07.48	7,000	7,000

Notes payable	—	10,000	JE07.46	30,000			30,000	—	—	30,000
Bonds payable	—	500,000					500,000	—	—	500,000
Net assets	—	3,994,000					3,994,000	—	—	3,994,000
Charges for services	—	—	JE07.40	1,500,000			1,500,000	—	—	1,500,000
Interest and investment revenue	—	—	JE07.42	10,000			10,000	—	—	10,000
Miscellaneous revenue—gain on sale of assets	—	—	JE07.45	1,000			1,000	—	—	1,000
Operating revenues—miscellaneous	—	—	JE07.50	22,000			22,000	—	—	22,000
Personal services expenses	—	—	JE07.41	5,400,000	JE07.47	2,000	5,402,000	—	—	—
Contractual services expenses	—	—	JE07.41	300,000	JE07.53	100,000	400,000	—	—	—
Repairs and maintenance expenses	—	—	JE07.41	50,000			50,000	—	—	—
Other supplies and expenses	—	—	JE07.41	40,000	JE07.54	4,000	36,000	—	—	—
Insurance claims and expenses	—	—	JE07.48	3,000			3,000	—	—	—
Depreciation expense	—	—	JE07.49	117,000			117,000	—	—	—
Interest expense	—	—	JE07.46	27,000			27,000	—	—	—

Operating expenses—miscellaneous	—	—	JE07.50	3,000	—	3,000	—	3,000	—	—	—
Special item—gain on sale of parking lot	—	—	—	—	JE07.45	3,500,000	—	3,500,000	—	3,500,000	—
Transfers in—General Fund	—	—	—	—	JE07.52	90,000	—	90,000	—	90,000	—
Totals	5,931,000	5,931,000		13,102,000	13,102,000	11,271,000	11,271,000	6,038,000	5,123,000	5,233,000	6,148,000
Net increase (decrease)								(915,000)	—	—	(915,000)
								5,123,000	5,123,000	5,233,000	5,233,000

APPENDIX 7D: WORKSHEET FOR SUMMARIZING CURRENT TRANSACTIONS: CENTERVILLE MUNICIPAL AIRPORT

Accounts	Trial Balance Debit	Trial Balance Credit	Adjustments Debit (ref)	Adjustments Debit	Adjustments Credit (ref)	Adjustments Credit	Adjusted Trial Balance Debit	Adjusted Trial Balance Credit	Operating Statement Debit	Operating Statement Credit	Balance Sheet Debit	Balance Sheet Credit
Cash	1,150,000	—	JE07.56	55,000	JE07.55	3,400,000	10,963,000	—	—	—	10,963,000	—
		—	JE07.57	165,000,000	JE07.58	191,000,000	—	—	—	—	—	—
		—	JE07.57	49,000,000	JE07.60	7,100,000	—	—	—	—	—	—
		—	JE07.59	1,000,000	JE07.61	400,000	—	—	—	—	—	—
		—	JE07.62	420,000	JE07.61	1,300,000	—	—	—	—	—	—
		—	JE07.63	3,200,000	JE07.63	3,720,000	—	—	—	—	—	—
		—	JE07.67	1,700,000	JE07.64	17,000	—	—	—	—	—	—
		—	JE07.68	60,000	JE07.65	25,000	—	—	—	—	—	—
		—		—	JE07.68	70,000	—	—	—	—	—	—
		—		—	JE07.69	50,000	—	—	—	—	—	—
		—		—	JE07.70	400,000	—	—	—	—	—	—
		—		—	JE07.71	540,000	—	—	—	—	—	—
		—		—	JE07.72	2,600,000	—	—	—	—	—	—
Interest receivable	55,000	—	JE07.59	200,000	JE07.56	55,000	200,000	—	—	—	200,000	—
Temporary investments	10,000,000	—	JE07.69	50,000		—	10,050,000	—	—	—	10,050,000	—
Accounts receivable	5,000,000	—	JE07.57	10,000,000	JE07.57	18,000,000	18,000,000	—	—	—	18,000,000	—
		—	JE07.57	3,000,000		—	—	—	—	—	—	—

Account	Beginning Balance	Adjustments — Debit	Adjustments — Credit	Adjusted — Debit	Adjusted — Credit	Statement — Debit	Statement — Credit
Due from other funds—General Fund	—	JE07.70 400,000	—	400,000	—	400,000	—
Due from other governments	—	JE07.67 300,000	—	300,000	—	300,000	—
Supplies	50,000	JE07.73 5,000	—	55,000	—	55,000	—
Construction in progress	25,000,000	JE07.61 400,000 JE07.61 1,300,000	JE07.61 3,200,000	23,500,000	—	23,500,000	—
Land and improvements	10,000,000	JE07.60 3,200,000	—	13,200,000	—	13,200,000	—
Runways and tarmacs	27,000,000	JE07.60 500,000	—	27,500,000	—	27,500,000	—
Accumulated depreciation—runways and tarmacs	6,500,000	—	JE07.66 1,300,000	—	7,800,000	—	7,800,000
Buildings	30,000,000	JE07.61 3,200,000	—	33,200,000	—	33,200,000	—
Accumulated depreciation—buildings	6,500,000	—	JE07.66 1,200,000	—	7,700,000	—	7,700,000
Equipment	7,000,000	JE07.60 2,300,000	JE07.62 2,100,000	7,200,000	—	7,200,000	—
Accumulated depreciation—equipment	4,300,000	JE07.62 1,600,000	JE07.66 450,000	—	3,150,000	—	3,150,000
Vehicles	2,300,000	JE07.60 1,100,000	JE07.62 900,000	2,500,000	—	2,500,000	—

Accumulated depreciation—vehicles	—	1,900,000	JE07.62 715,000	JE07.66 420,000	—	1,605,000	—	—	1,605,000
Accounts payable and accrued expenses	—	3,400,000	JE07.55 3,400,000	JE07.58 3,900,000	—	3,900,000	—	—	3,900,000
Due to other funds—Communications and Technology Center	25,000			— JE07.71 60,000	—	85,000	—	—	85,000
Due to other funds—Internal Service Fund—Special Services Support Center	77,000			— JE07.72 350,000	—	427,000	—	—	427,000
Compensated absences liability	125,000			— JE07.64 8,000	—	133,000	—	—	133,000
Claims and judgements payable	120,000			— JE07.65 75,000	—	195,000	—	—	195,000
Notes payable	4,500,000			— JE07.63 3,200,000	—	7,700,000	—	—	7,700,000
Revenue bonds payable—Terminal A	12,000,000	JE07.63 2,000,000		—	—	10,000,000	—	—	10,000,000
Revenue bonds payable—Terminal B	4,500,000	JE07.66 500,000		—	—	4,000,000	—	—	4,000,000

Net assets	73,608,000	—	—	73,608,000	—	—	73,608,000
Charges for services	—	JE07.57 175,000,000	175,000,000	175,000,000	175,000,000	—	—
Charges for services—rental income—security for Terminal A revenue bonds	—	JE07.57 30,000,000	30,000,000	30,000,000	30,000,000	—	—
Charges for services—rental income—security for Terminal B revenue bonds	—	JE07.57 22,000,000	22,000,000	22,000,000	22,000,000	—	—
Interest and investment revenue	—	JE07.59 1,200,000	1,200,000	1,200,000	1,200,000	—	—
Capital grants and contributions	—	JE07.67 2,000,000	2,000,000	2,000,000	2,000,000	—	—
Operating revenues—miscellaneous	—	JE07.68 60,000	60,000	60,000	60,000	—	—
Personal services expenses	—	JE07.58 161,000,000 JE07.64 25,000	161,025,000	161,025,000	−161,025,000	—	—
Contractual services expenses	—	JE07.58 30,000,000 JE07.71 600,000 JE07.72 2,950,000	33,550,000	33,550,000	33,550,000	—	—

Repairs and maintenance expenses	—	JE07.58	2,100,000	—	—	2,100,000	2,100,000	—	2,100,000	—
Other supplies and expenses	—	JE07.58	1,800,000	JE07.73	5,000	1,795,000	1,795,000	—	1,795,000	—
Insurance claims and expenses	—	JE07.65	100,000	—	—	100,000	100,000	—	100,000	—
Depreciation expense	—	JE07.66	3,370,000	—	—	3,370,000	3,370,000	—	3,370,000	—
Interest expense	—	JE07.63	1,220,000	—	—	1,220,000	1,220,000	—	1,220,000	—
Operating expenses—miscellaneous	—	JE07.68	70,000	—	—	70,000	70,000	—	70,000	—
Miscellaneous expenses—loss on sale of assets	—	JE07.62	265,000	—	—	265,000	265,000	—	265,000	—
Totals	117,555,000		458,105,000		350,563,000	350,563,000	203,495,000	230,260,000	147,068,000	120,303,000
Net increase (decrease)							26,765,000	230,260,000	147,068,000	26,765,000

APPENDIX 7E: ENTERPRISE FUNDS: STATEMENT OF NET ASSETS; STATEMENT OF REVENUES, EXPENSES, AND CHANGES IN FUND NET ASSETS; AND STATEMENT OF CASH FLOWS

Enterprise Funds
Statement of Net Assets
June 30, 20X2

	Centerville Toll Bridge	Centerville Utilities Authority	Centerville Parking Authority	Centerville Municipal Airport	Total
ASSETS					
Current assets:					
Cash	$ 739,500	$ 230,000	$ 764,000	$10,963,000	$12,696,500
Interest receivable	3,000	50,000	3,000	200,000	256,000
Accounts receivable (net)	—	7,550,000	—	18,000,000	25,550,000
Due from other funds	—	2,000,000	—	400,000	2,400,000
Due from other governments	—	100,000	—	300,000	400,000
Temporary investments	58,000	55,000	5,000	10,050,000	10,168,000
Supplies	32,000	75,000	24,000	55,000	186,000
Total current assets	832,500	10,060,000	796,000	39,968,000	51,656,500
Noncurrent assets:					
Construction in progress	70,000	200,000	15,000	23,500,000	23,785,000
Land and improvements	140,000	5,200,000	1,780,000	13,200,000	20,320,000
Superstructure	1,400,000	—	—	—	1,400,000
Distribution and collection systems	—	46,300,000	—	—	46,300,000
Runways and tarmacs	—	—	—	27,500,000	27,500,000
Buildings	330,000	14,450,000	2,400,000	33,200,000	50,380,000
Equipment	55,000	4,600,000	140,000	7,200,000	11,995,000
Vehicles	835,000	1,660,000	102,000	2,500,000	5,097,000
Less accumulated depreciation	(1,257,000)	(54,395,000)	(1,505,000)	(20,255,000)	(77,412,000)
Total noncurrent assets	1,573,000	18,015,000	2,932,000	86,845,000	109,365,000
Total assets	2,405,500	28,075,000	3,728,000	126,813,000	161,021,500
LIABILITIES					
Current liabilities:					
Accounts payable and accrued expenses	50,000	4,300,000	90,000	3,900,000	8,340,000
Due to other funds	18,000	35,000	17,000	512,000	582,000
Compensated absences	3,000	21,000	2,000	15,000	41,000
Claims and judgements	5,000	17,000	4,000	25,000	51,000
Notes payable	10,000	70,000	30,000	—	110,000

	Centerville Toll Bridge	Centerville Utilities Authority	Centerville Parking Authority	Centerville Municipal Airport	Total
Revenue bonds—Terminal A	—	—	—	2,000,000	2,000,000
Revenue bonds—Terminal B	—	—	—	500,000	500,000
Bonds payable	20,000	850,000	—	—	870,000
Total current liabilities	106,000	5,293,000	143,000	6,952,000	12,494,000
Noncurrent liabilities:					
Compensated absences	5,000	63,000	3,000	118,000	189,000
Claims and judgements	22,000	212,000	3,000	170,000	407,000
Notes payable	20,000	260,000	—	7,700,000	7,980,000
Revenue bonds—Terminal A	—	—	—	8,000,000	8,000,000
Revenue bonds—Terminal B	—	—	—	3,500,000	3,500,000
Bonds payable	60,000	6,850,000	500,000	—	7,410,000
Total noncurrent liabilities	107,000	7,385,000	506,000	19,488,000	27,486,000
Total liabilities	213,000	12,678,000	649,000	26,440,000	39,980,000
NET ASSETS					
Invested in capital assets, net of related debt	1,463,000	9,985,000	2,402,000	69,145,000	82,995,000
Restricted	622,000	5,250,000	595,000	30,895,000	37,362,000
Unrestricted	107,500	162,000	82,000	333,000	684,500
Total net assets	$2,192,500	$15,397,000	$3,079,000	$100,373,000	$121,041,500

Enterprise Funds
Statement of Revenues, Expenses, and Changes in Fund Net Assets
For the Year Ended June 30, 20X2

	Centerville Toll Bridge	Centerville Utilities Authority	Centerville Parking Authority	Centerville Municipal Airport	Total
OPERATING REVENUES					
Charges for services	$4,750,000	$36,000,000	$1,500,000	$175,000,000	$217,250,000
Charges for services—rental income—security for Terminal A revenue bonds	—	—	—	30,000,000	30,000,000
Charges for services—rental income—security for Terminal B revenue bonds	—	—	—	22,000,000	22,000,000
Miscellaneous	20,000	10,000	22,000	60,000	112,000
Total operating revenues	4,770,000	36,010,000	1,522,000	227,060,000	269,362,000
OPERATING EXPENSES					
Personal services	2,402,000	22,022,000	5,402,000	161,025,000	190,851,000
Contractual services	1,280,000	11,220,000	400,000	33,550,000	46,450,000
Repairs and maintenance	400,000	700,000	50,000	2,100,000	3,250,000
Other supplies and expenses	194,000	729,000	36,000	1,795,000	2,754,000
Insurance claims and expenses	10,000	21,000	3,000	100,000	134,000

	Centerville Toll Bridge	Centerville Utilities Authority	Centerville Parking Authority	Centerville Municipal Airport	Total
Depreciation	339,000	3,025,000	117,000	3,370,000	6,851,000
Miscellaneous	30,000	5,000	3,000	70,000	108,000
Total operating expenses	4,655,000	37,722,000	6,011,000	202,010,000	250,398,000
Operating income (loss)	115,000	(1,712,000)	(4,489,000)	25,050,000	18,964,000

NONOPERATING REVENUES (EXPENSES)

	Centerville Toll Bridge	Centerville Utilities Authority	Centerville Parking Authority	Centerville Municipal Airport	Total
Interest and investment revenue	30,000	400,000	10,000	1,200,000	1,640,000
Interest	(6,000)	(450,000)	(27,000)	(1,220,000)	(1,703,000)
Operating grants and contributions	100,000	—	—	—	100,000
Miscellaneous	7,000	(110,000)	1,000	(265,000)	(367,000)
Total nonoperating revenue (expenses)	131,000	(160,000)	(16,000)	(285,000)	(330,000)
Income (loss) before capital contributions and transfers	246,000	(1,872,000)	(4,505,000)	24,765,000	18,634,000
Capital contributions	250,000	1,250,000	—	2,000,000	3,500,000
Transfers in	50,000	—	90,000	—	140,000
Special item—gain on sale of parking lot	—	—	3,500,000	—	3,500,000
Change in net assets	546,000	(622,000)	(915,000)	26,765,000	25,774,000
Total net assets—beginning	1,646,500	16,019,000	3,994,000	73,608,000	95,267,500
Total net assets—ending	$2,192,500	$15,397,000	$3,079,000	$100,373,000	$121,041,500

Enterprise Funds
Statement of Cash Flows
For the Year Ended June 30, 20X2

	Centerville Toll Bridge	Centerville Utilities Authority	Centerville Parking Authority	Centerville Municipal Airport	Total
CASH FLOWS FROM OPERATING ACTIVITIES					
Receipts from customers	$4,750,000	$34,000,000	$1,500,000	$214,000,000	$254,250,000
Payments to suppliers	(1,806,000)	(12,112,000)	(345,000)	(36,425,000)	(50,688,000)
Payments to employees	(2,371,000)	(19,013,000)	(5,361,000)	(158,017,000)	(184,762,000)
Internal activity—payments to other funds	(66,000)	(200,000)	(90,000)	(3,140,000)	(3,496,000)
Other receipts (payments)	(18,000)	5,000	19,000	(10,000)	(4,000)
Net cash provided by operating activities	489,000	2,680,000	(4,277,000)	16,408,000	15,300,000
CASH FLOWS FROM NONCAPITAL FINANCING ACTIVITIES					
Subsidies and transfers from (to) other funds and state government	150,000	—	90,000	—	240,000

	Centerville Toll Bridge	Centerville Utilities Authority	Centerville Parking Authority	Centerville Municipal Airport	Total
CASH FLOWS FROM CAPITAL AND RELATED FINANCING ACTIVITIES					
Proceeds from the issuance of capital debt	—	2,120,000	—	3,200,000	5,320,000
Capital contributions	250,000	1,250,000	30,000	1,700,000	3,230,000
Acquisitions of capital assets	(390,000)	(5,350,000)	(200,000)	(8,800,000)	(14,740,000)
Proceeds from sale of capital assets	50,000	500,000	5,005,000	420,000	5,975,000
Principal paid on capital debt	(30,000)	(1,740,000)	(10,000)	(2,500,000)	(4,280,000)
Interest paid on capital debt	(6,000)	(450,000)	(27,000)	(1,220,000)	(1,703,000)
Net cash (used) by capital and related financing activities	(126,000)	(3,670,000)	4,798,000	(7,200,000)	(6,198,000)
CASH FLOWS FROM INVESTING ACTIVITIES					
Loans to other funds	—	(2,000,000)	—	(400,000)	(2,400,000)
Loans to other governments	—	(100,000)	—	—	(100,000)
Interest and dividends	31,500	365,000	8,000	1,055,000	1,459,500
Purchase of investments	(25,000)	(15,000)	(5,000)	(50,000)	(95,000)
Net cash provided (used) by investing activities	6,500	(1,750,000)	3,000	605,000	(1,135,500)
Net increase (decrease) in cash	519,500	(2,740,000)	614,000	9,813,000	8,206,500
CASH FLOWS FROM NONCAPITAL FINANCING ACTIVITIES					
Balances—beginning of year	220,000	2,970,000	150,000	1,150,000	4,490,000
Balances—end of year	$739,500	$ 230,000	$ 764,000	$10,963,000	$12,696,500
Reconciliation of operating income (loss) to net cash provided (used) by operating activities:					
Operating income (loss)	$115,000	$(1,712,000)	$(4,489,000)	$25,050,000	$18,964,000
Adjustments:					
Depreciation expense	339,000	3,025,000	117,000	3,370,000	6,851,000
Change in assets and liabilities:					
Receivables, net	—	(1,850,000)	—	(13,000,000)	(14,850,000)
Inventories	(6,000)	(21,000)	(4,000)	(5,000)	(36,000)
Accounts and accrued liabilities	41,000	3,238,000	99,000	993,000	4,371,000
Net cash provided (used) by operating activities	$489,000	$ 2,680,000	$(4,277,000)	$16,408,000	$15,300,000

CHAPTER 8
INTERNAL SERVICE FUNDS

CONTENTS

NATURE OF INTERNAL SERVICE FUNDS

GAAP states that Internal Service Funds may be used to report "any activity that provides goods or services to other funds, departments, or agencies of the primary government and its component units, or to other governments, on a cost reimbursement basis." An Internal Service Fund should be used only when the reporting government itself is the *predominant participant* in the fund. When transactions with other governmental entities represent the predominant portion of the activity, an Enterprise Fund is used (GASB-34, par. 68).

MEASUREMENT FOCUS AND BASIS OF ACCOUNTING

The accrual basis of accounting and the flow of economic resources are used to prepare the financial statements of an Internal Service Fund. Under the flow of economic resources measurement focus and accrual basis of accounting, revenues are recognized when earned and expenses are recorded when incurred when these activities are related to exchange and exchange-like activities. In addition, long-lived assets (such as buildings and equipment) are capitalized and depreciated, and all debt is reported in the fund (GASB-34, par. 16).

In some instances an Internal Service Fund may provide services or goods to fiduciary funds. The GASB's *Comprehensive Implementation Guide* states that in determining whether the services are predominantly provided to internal parties (therefore an Internal Service Fund is appropriate) or predominantly provided to external parties (therefore an Enterprise Fund is appropriate), the activities with fiduciary funds should be considered internal. However, in folding the activities into the government-wide financial statements, activities with fiduciary funds should be treated as external transactions. Under this circumstance, the external sales and related cost of sales should not be used to determine the net profit or loss amount that is the basis for adjusting the expenses incurred in the governmental column of the statement of activities.

As discussed in Chapter 7, "Enterprise Funds," the Enterprise fund type can follow either Alternative 1 or Alternative 2 as described in GASB-20 (Accounting and Financial Reporting for Proprietary Funds and Other Governmental Entities That Use Proprietary Fund Accounting). Prior to the issuance of GASB-34, there was some confusion about whether Internal Service Funds were subject to the two alternatives established by GASB-20. The GASB clarified the issue by stating that "the option should not apply to Internal Service Funds" (GASB-34, par. 423).

PRACTICE ALERT: GASB-62 (Codification of Accounting and Financial Reporting Guidance Contained in Pre-November 30, 1989 FASB and AICPA Pronouncements) is an omnibus statement that supersedes the provisions of GASB-20 by incorporating into GASB's literature all FASB Statements and Interpretations, APB Opinions, and ARBs no matter when issued except those that conflict with a GASB pronouncement. The omnibus statement also incorporates all AICPA pronouncements. It is effective for periods beginning after December 15, 2011. All the provisions of the aforementioned standards are incorporated into CCH's *Governmental GAAP Guide*; so, little if any change from this edition is expected due to any upcoming promulgation. However, certain items such as governmental combinations that have guidance contained in APB Opinion No. 16, are being researched by GASB and were not included in GASB-62.

As part of a self-insurance strategy, a state or local government may establish a separate Internal Service Fund (Self-Insurance Fund) to account for the payment of claims and judgements. The recognition of a loss contingency in a Self-Insurance Internal Service Fund arising from claims and judgements is governed by accounting and reporting standards currently established by FAS-5

(Accounting for Contingencies) until GASB-62 is implemented. GASB-34 does change the option of using a Self-Insurance Internal Service Fund.

PRACTICE POINT: For internal service fund activities that are reimbursed out of federal funds, Office of Management and Budget (OMB) Circular A-87 places stringent requirements on what can be charged as an "allowable cost," with an emphasis on consistent accounting no matter what the source of funds is. Complete coverage of OMB Circular A-87 from an auditing perspective is found in CCH's *Knowledge-Based Audits*™ *of State and Local Governments with Single Audits.*

FINANCIAL REPORTING AT THE FUND LEVEL

The balances and activities of Internal Service Funds are presented in the following three financial statements at the fund financial statement level:

1. Statement of net assets (or balance sheet)
2. Statement of revenues, expenses, and changes in fund net assets (or fund equity)
3. Statement of cash flows

An Internal Service Fund's statement of net assets is presented based on the guidance established in GASB-34. The statement of net assets may be presented in either one of the following formats: (1) net assets format, where assets less liabilities equal net assets, or (2) balance sheet format, where assets equal liabilities plus net assets (GASB-34, pars. 97 and 98).

These three fund financial statements include all of the proprietary funds (Internal Service Funds and Enterprise Funds). The financial statements of all Internal Service Funds are combined into a single column and are presented to the right of the Enterprise Funds. The Internal Service Funds column and the Enterprise Funds total column should not be added together in the proprietary fund financial statements.

The focus of reporting governmental funds and proprietary funds is that major funds are reported for these funds; however, the major fund concept does not apply to Internal Service Funds (GASB-34, par. 75).

Proprietary funds must prepare a statement of cash flows based on the guidance established by GASB-9, except the statement of cash flows should be formatted based on the direct method in computing cash flows from operating activities. Prior to the issuance of GASB-34, the statement of cash flows could be prepared based on either the direct or indirect method (GASB-34, par. 105).

GASB-34 requires a reconciliation between the government-wide financial statements (statement of net assets and statement of changes in net assets) and the governmental fund activities; however, no reconciliation is needed for the Internal Service Fund column, because the Internal Service Fund financial statements are merged with governmental activities and/or business-type activities for presentation on the government-wide financial statements (GASB-34, par. 104).

PRACTICE ALERT: Even though GASB-54's implementation will dramatically change governmental fund balance presentation, the merger of an internal service fund's financial statements into the governmental activities of a government will have minimal effect on the presentation of fund balances under GASB-54 because the internal service fund's revenues and expenses "close" to the paying and receiving funds. Any balances remaining are presented as "due to" and "due from" funds, which will raise or decline fund balances.

FINANCIAL REPORTING AT THE GOVERNMENT-WIDE LEVEL

Government-wide financial statements are divided into governmental activities and business-type activities. Generally, the activities conducted by an Internal Service Fund are related to governmental activities, and therefore the residual amounts of the Internal Service Funds are consolidated with other governmental funds and presented in the governmental activities column of the government-wide financial statements. However, the activities of an Internal Service Fund must be analyzed to determine whether they are governmental or business-type in nature or both. If the activities are business-type in nature, the residual amounts are consolidated with the business-type activities in the government-wide financial statements.

Internal Service Funds are eliminated to avoid doubling-up expenses and revenues in preparing the governmental activities column of the statement of activities. The effect of this approach is to adjust activities in an Internal Service Fund to a break-even balance. That is, if the Internal Service Fund had a "net profit" for the year, there should be a pro rata reduction in the charges made to the funds that used the Internal Service Fund's services for the year. Likewise, a net loss would require a pro rata adjustment that would increase the charges made to the various participating funds.

ILLUSTRATIVE TRANSACTIONS

In order to illustrate accounting and financial reporting standards that should be observed for Internal Service Funds, assume that the City of Centerville has the following three Internal Service Funds:

1. Communications and Technology Support Center
2. Fleet Management Unit
3. Special Services Support Center

Communications and Technology Support Center

The Communications and Technology Support Center (CTSC) provides a variety of communication and computer support services to all of the City's governmental and proprietary funds. The fund's trial balance for the beginning of the fiscal year is as follows:

Accounts	Trial Balance	
	Debit	Credit
Cash	$ 260,000	
Interest receivable	3,000	
Due from other funds—General Fund	70,000	
Due from other funds—Centerville Municipal Airport	25,000	
Due from other funds—Centerville Utilities Authority	15,000	
Due from other funds—Centerville Parking Authority	7,000	
Due from other funds—Centerville Toll Bridge	4,000	
Temporary investments	15,000	
Inventories	7,000	
Land and improvements	2,300,000	
Buildings	1,400,000	
Accumulated depreciation—buildings		$ 350,000
Equipment	5,500,000	
Accumulated depreciation—equipment		1,200,000
Vehicles	120,000	
Accumulated depreciation—vehicles		55,000
Accounts payable and accrued expenses		15,000
Compensated absences liability		4,000
Claims and judgements payable		12,000
Notes payable		1,500,000
Net assets		6,590,000
Totals	$ 9,726,000	$9,726,000

This section presents illustrative transactions and entries for the CTSC during the fiscal year ended June 30, 20X2.

GASB-34 generally did not change the manner of accounting for transactions that are recorded in Internal Service Funds.

Transaction JE08.01—Accounts payable and accrued expenses of $15,000 from the previous year were paid:

Accounts	Debit	Credit
Accounts payable and accrued expenses	15,000	
Cash		15,000

Transaction JE08.02—Accrued interest receivable from the previous year was received:

Accounts	Debit	Credit
Cash	3,000	
Interest receivable		3,000

Transaction JE08.03—During the year, the following billings and cash collections were made from the various funds serviced by the CTSC:

Fund Name	Billings	Cash Collections
General Fund	$4,500,000	$4,400,000
Centerville Municipal Airport	600,000	540,000
Centerville Utilities Authority	220,000	200,000
Centerville Parking Authority	100,000	90,000
Centerville Toll Bridge	80,000	66,000
Total	$5,500,000	$5,296,000

Accounts	Debit	Credit
Cash	5,296,000	
Due from other funds—General Fund	100,000	
Due from other funds—Centerville Municipal Airport	60,000	
Due from other funds—Centerville Utilities Authority	20,000	
Due from other funds—Centerville Parking Authority	10,000	
Due from other funds—Centerville Toll Bridge	14,000	
Charges for services		5,500,000

Transaction JE08.04—The following operating expenses were incurred during the year, of which $7,200,000 was paid in cash:

Personal services	$4,800,000
Contractual services	1,300,000
Repairs and maintenance	1,100,000
Other supplies and expenses	50,000
Total	$7,250,000

Accounts	Debit	Credit
Personal services expenses	4,800,000	
Contractual services expenses	1,300,000	
Repairs and maintenance expenses	1,100,000	
Other supplies and expenses	50,000	
Cash		7,200,000
Accounts payable and accrued expenses		50,000

Transaction JE08.05—During the year, interest and investment revenue of $5,000 was earned, of which $4,000 was received in cash:

Accounts	Debit	Credit
Cash	4,000	
Interest receivable	1,000	
Interest and investment revenue		5,000

PRACTICE POINT: The accounting for investments continues to be recorded based on the standards established by GASB-31 (Accounting and Financial Reporting for Certain Investments and for External Investment Pools).

Transaction JE08.06—The following capital assets were purchased during the year for cash:

Land and improvements	$400,000
Equipment	1,100,000
Vehicles	35,000
Total	$1,535,000

Accounts	Debit	Credit
Land and Improvements	400,000	
Equipment	1,100,000	
Vehicles	35,000	
Cash		1,535,000

Transaction JE08.07—The following assets were sold during the year. The cash proceeds were $340,000:

	Original Cost	Accumulated Depreciation
Equipment	$ 730,000	$420,000
Vehicles	12,000	9,000
Total	$ 742,000	$429,000

Accounts	Debit	Credit
Cash	340,000	
Accumulated depreciation—equipment	420,000	
Accumulated depreciation—vehicles	9,000	
Equipment		730,000
Vehicles		12,000
Miscellaneous revenue—gain on sale of assets		27,000

Transaction JE08.08—During the year, additional notes of $3,200,000 were issued and interest expense of $97,000 was paid. All notes are related to capital-asset transactions:

Accounts	Debit	Credit
Cash	3,103,000	
Interest expense	97,000	
Notes payable		3,200,000

Transaction JE08.09—Compensated absences of $2,000 were paid during the year and additional costs of $5,000 were accrued:

Accounts	Debit	Credit
Personal services expenses	5,000	
Compensated absences liability		3,000
Cash		2,000

Transaction JE08.10—Claims and judgements of $3,000 were paid during the year and additional costs of $10,000 were accrued:

Accounts	Debit	Credit
Insurance claims and expenses	10,000	
Claims and judgements payable		7,000
Cash		3,000

Transaction JE08.11—Depreciation expense recognized during the year was as follows:

Buildings	$220,000
Equipment	1,700,000
Vehicles	7,000
Total	$1,927,000

Accounts	Debit	Credit
Depreciation expense	1,927,000	
Accumulated depreciation—buildings		220,000
Accumulated depreciation—equipment		1,700,000
Accumulated depreciation—vehicles		7,000

Transaction JE08.12—An operating grant of $200,000 and a capital grant of $450,000 were received from the state government:

Accounts	Debit	Credit
Cash	650,000	
Operating grants and contributions		200,000
Capital grants and contributions		450,000

Transaction JE08.13—Other operating revenues earned and received during the year amounted to $10,000 and other operating expenses incurred and paid during the year amounted to $5,000:

Accounts	Debit	Credit
Cash	10,000	
Operating revenues—miscellaneous		10,000
Operating expenses—miscellaneous	5,000	
Cash		5,000

GAAP notes that an important element of the statement of revenues, expenses, and changes in fund net assets is that there must be a differentiation between operating revenues and nonoperating revenues, and operating expenses and nonoperating expenses based on policies established by the governmental entity. Those policies should be disclosed in the entity's summary of significant accounting policies and must be applied consistently from period to period. GASB-34 states that, in general, differentiations between operating and nonoperating transactions should follow the broad guidance established by GASB-9 (Reporting Cash Flows of Proprietary and Nonexpendable Trust Funds and Governmental Entities that Use Proprietary Fund Accounting). For example, transactions related to (1) capital and related financing activities, (2) noncapital financing activities, (3) investing activities, and (4) nonexchange revenues, such as tax revenues, generally are to be considered nonoperating transactions for purposes of preparing the statement of revenues, expenses, and changes in net assets (GASB-34, par. 102).

Transaction JE08.14—A transfer of $40,000 was received from the General Fund:

Accounts	Debit	Credit
Cash	40,000	
Transfers in—General Fund		40,000

Transaction JE08.15—Inventories of $9,000 were on hand at the end of the year:

Accounts	Debit	Credit
Inventories	2,000	
Other supplies and expenses		2,000

After the transactions for the year are posted, the year-end trial balance (June 30, 20X2) for the CTSC appears as follows:

	Adjusted Trial Balance	
Accounts	**Debit**	**Credit**
Cash	$946,000	
Interest receivable	1,000	
Due from other funds—General Fund	170,000	
Due from other funds—Centerville Municipal Airport	85,000	
Due from other funds—Centerville Utilities Authority	35,000	
Due from other funds—Centerville Parking Authority	17,000	
Due from other funds—Centerville Toll Bridge	18,000	
Temporary investments	15,000	
Inventories	9,000	
Land and improvements	2,700,000	
Buildings	1,400,000	
Accumulated depreciation—buildings		$570,000
Equipment	5,870,000	
Accumulated depreciation—equipment		2,480,000
Vehicles	143,000	
Accumulated depreciation—vehicles		53,000
Accounts payable and accrued expenses		50,000
Compensated absences liability		7,000
Claims and judgements payable		19,000
Notes payable		4,700,000
Net assets		6,590,000
Charges for services		5,500,000
Interest and investment revenue		5,000
Miscellaneous revenue—gain on sale of assets		27,000
Operating grants and contributions		200,000
Capital grants and contributions		450,000
Operating revenues—miscellaneous		10,000
Personal services expenses	4,805,000	
Contractual services expenses	1,300,000	

Accounts	Adjusted Trial Balance	
	Debit	Credit
Repairs and maintenance expenses	1,100,000	
Other supplies and expenses	48,000	
Insurance claims and expenses	10,000	
Depreciation expense	1,927,000	
Interest expense	97,000	
Operating expenses—miscellaneous	5,000	
Transfers in—General Fund		40,000
Totals	$20,701,000	$20,701,000

The worksheet that summarizes the journal entries for the CTSC Internal Service Fund for the year-end trial balance is presented in Appendix 8A.

Fleet Management Unit

The Fleet Management Unit (FMU) provides a motor pool to all of the City's governmental funds and to some other governmental units that are not part of the City's reporting entity. The FMU provides no services to Enterprise Funds. The fund's trial balance for the beginning of the fiscal year is as follows:

Accounts	Trial Balance	
	Debit	Credit
Cash	$805,000	
Interest receivable	4,500	
Due from other funds—General Fund	22,000	
Due from other governments—County Fire District	7,000	
Due from other governments—Regional Pollution Control District	3,000	
Temporary investments	19,000	
Inventories	4,000	
Land and improvements	50,000	
Buildings	1,600,000	
Accumulated depreciation—buildings		$450,000
Equipment	1,200,000	
Accumulated depreciation—equipment		770,000
Vehicles	7,400,000	
Accumulated depreciation—vehicles		4,300,000
Accounts payable and accrued expenses		90,000
Compensated absences liability		5,000
Claims and judgements payable		10,000
Notes payable		4,000,000
Net assets		1,489,500
Totals	$11,114,500	$11,114,500

This section presents illustrative transactions and entries for the FMU during the fiscal year ended June 30, 20X2.

Transaction JE08.16—Accounts payable and accrued expenses of $90,000 from the previous year were paid:

Accounts	Debit	Credit
Accounts payable and accrued expenses	90,000	
Cash		90,000

Transaction JE08.17—Accrued interest receivable from the previous year was received:

Accounts	Debit	Credit
Cash	4,500	
Interest receivable		4,500

Transaction JE08.18—During the year, the following billings and cash collections were made from the various funds serviced by the FMU:

Fund Name	Billings	Cash Collections
General Fund	$4,700,000	$4,650,000
County Fire District	200,000	190,000
Regional Pollution Control District	100,000	75,000
Total	$5,000,000	$4,915,000

Accounts	Debit	Credit
Cash	4,915,000	
Due from other funds—General Fund	50,000	
Due from other governments—County Fire District	10,000	
Due from other governments—Regional Pollution Control District	25,000	
Charges for services		5,000,000

Transaction JE08.19—The following operating expenses were incurred during the year, of which $1,825,000 was paid in cash:

Personal services	$1,200,000
Contractual services	400,000
Repairs and maintenance	200,000
Other supplies and expenses	150,000
Total	$1,950,000

Accounts	Debit	Credit
Personal services expenses	1,200,000	
Contractual services expenses	400,000	

Accounts	Debit	Credit
Repairs and maintenance expenses	200,000	
Other supplies and expenses	150,000	
Cash		1,825,000
Accounts payable and accrued expenses		125,000

Transaction JE08.20—During the year, interest and investment revenue of $5,000 was earned, of which $3,000 was received in cash:

Accounts	Debit	Credit
Cash	3,000	
Interest receivable	2,000	
Interest and investment revenue		5,000

Transaction JE08.21—The following capital assets were purchased during the year for cash:

Equipment	$ 350,000	
Vehicles	2,600,000	
Total	$2,950,000	

Accounts	Debit	Credit
Equipment	350,000	
Vehicles	2,600,000	
Cash		2,950,000

Transaction JE08.22—The following assets were sold or abandoned during the year. The cash proceeds were $410,000:

	Original Cost	Accumulated Depreciation
Equipment	$ 220,000	$ 195,000
Vehicles	1,800,000	1,350,000
Total	$2,020,000	$1,545,000

Accounts	Debit	Credit
Cash	410,000	
Accumulated depreciation—equipment	195,000	
Accumulated depreciation—vehicles	1,350,000	
Miscellaneous expenses—loss on sale of assets	65,000	
Equipment		220,000
Vehicles		1,800,000

Transaction JE08.23—During the year, notes of $1,000,000 were paid along with interest expense of $180,000. All notes are related to capital-asset transactions:

Accounts	Debit	Credit
Notes payable	1,000,000	
Interest expense	180,000	
Cash		1,180,000

Transaction JE08.24—Compensated absences of $3,000 were paid during the year and additional costs of $6,000 were accrued:

Accounts	Debit	Credit
Personal services expenses	6,000	
Compensated absences liability		3,000
Cash		3,000

Transaction JE08.25—Claims and judgements of $4,000 were paid during the year and additional costs of $7,000 were accrued:

Accounts	Debit	Credit
Insurance claims and expenses	7,000	
Claims and judgements payable		3,000
Cash		4,000

Transaction JE08.26—Depreciation expense recognized during the year was as follows:

Buildings		$ 370,000
Equipment		310,000
Vehicles		1,850,000
Total		$2,530,000

Accounts	Debit	Credit
Depreciation expense	2,530,000	
Accumulated depreciation—buildings		370,000
Accumulated depreciation—equipment		310,000
Accumulated depreciation—vehicles		1,850,000

Transaction JE08.27—An operating grant of $100,000 was received from the state government:

Accounts	Debit	Credit
Cash	100,000	
Operating grants and contributions		100,000

Transaction JE08.28—Other operating revenues earned and received during the year amounted to $4,000 and other operating expenses incurred and paid during the year amounted to $2,000:

Accounts	Debit	Credit
Cash	4,000	
Operating revenues—miscellaneous		4,000

Accounts	Debit	Credit
Operating expenses—miscellaneous	2,000	
Cash		2,000

Transaction JE08.29—A transfer of $50,000 was made from the FMU to the General Fund:

Accounts	Debit	Credit
Transfers out—General Fund	50,000	
Cash		50,000

Transaction JE08.30—Inventories of $7,000 were on hand at the end of the year:

Accounts	Debit	Credit
Inventories	3,000	
Other supplies and expenses		3,000

After the transactions for the year are posted, the year-end trial balance (June 30, 20X2) for the FMU appears as follows:

Accounts	Adjusted Trial Balance Debit	Credit
Cash	$137,500	
Interest receivable	2,000	
Due from other funds—General Fund	72,000	
Due from other governments—County Fire District	17,000	
Due from other governments—Regional Pollution Control District	28,000	
Temporary investments	19,000	
Inventories	7,000	
Land and improvements	50,000	
Buildings	1,600,000	
Accumulated depreciation—buildings		$820,000
Equipment	1,330,000	
Accumulated depreciation—equipment		885,000
Vehicles	8,200,000	
Accumulated depreciation—vehicles		4,800,000
Accounts payable and accrued expenses		125,000
Compensated absences liability		8,000
Claims and judgements payable		13,000
Notes payable		3,000,000
Net assets		1,489,500
Charges for services		5,000,000
Interest and investment revenue		5,000
Operating grants and contributions		100,000
Operating revenues—miscellaneous		4,000

Accounts	Adjusted Trial Balance	
	Debit	Credit
Personal services expenses	1,206,000	
Contractual services expenses	400,000	
Repairs and maintenance expenses	200,000	
Other supplies and expenses	147,000	
Insurance claims and expenses	7,000	
Depreciation expense	2,530,000	
Interest expense	180,000	
Operating expenses—miscellaneous	2,000	
Miscellaneous expenses—loss on sale of assets	65,000	
Transfers out—General Fund	50,000	
Totals	$16,249,500	$16,249,500

The worksheet that summarizes the journal entries for the FMU for the year-end trial balance is presented in Appendix 8B.

Special Services Support Center

The Special Services Support Center (SSSC) provides services exclusively for the Centerville Municipal Airport. The fund's trial balance for the beginning of the fiscal year is as follows:

Accounts	Trial Balance	
	Debit	Credit
Cash	$ 503,000	
Interest receivable	9,000	
Due from other funds—Centerville Municipal Airport	77,000	
Temporary investments	12,000	
Inventories	16,000	
Land and improvements	1,400,000	
Buildings	1,600,000	
Accumulated depreciation—buildings		$450,000
Equipment	2,300,000	
Accumulated depreciation—equipment		1,300,000
Vehicles	1,800,000	
Accumulated depreciation—vehicles		650,000
Accounts payable and accrued expenses		35,000
Compensated absences liability		14,000
Claims and judgements payable		22,000
Notes payable		450,000
Net assets		4,796,000
Totals	$7,717,000	$7,717,000

This section presents illustrative transactions and entries for the SSSC during the fiscal year ended June 30, 20X2.

Transaction JE08.31—Accounts payable and accrued expenses of $35,000 from the previous year were paid:

Accounts	Debit	Credit
Accounts payable and accrued expenses	35,000	
Cash		35,000

Transaction JE08.32—Accrued interest receivable from the previous year was received:

Accounts	Debit	Credit
Cash	9,000	
Interest receivable		9,000

Transaction JE08.33—During the year, billings of $2,950,000 and cash collections of $2,600,000 were made by the CTSC:

Accounts	Debit	Credit
Cash	2,600,000	
Due from other funds— Centerville Municipal Airport	350,000	
Charges for services		2,950,000

Transaction JE08.34—The following operating expenses were incurred during the year, of which $1,750,000 was paid in cash:

Personal services	$ 900,000
Contractual services	400,000
Repairs and maintenance	350,000
Other supplies and expenses	175,000
Total	$1,825,000

Accounts	Debit	Credit
Personal services expenses	900,000	
Contractual services expenses	400,000	
Repairs and maintenance expenses	350,000	
Other supplies and expenses	175,000	
Cash		1,750,000
Accounts payable and accrued expenses		75,000

Transaction JE08.35—During the year, interest and investment revenue of $15,000 was earned, of which $14,000 was received in cash:

Accounts	Debit	Credit
Cash	14,000	
Interest receivable	1,000	
Interest and investment revenue		15,000

Transaction JE08.36—The following capital assets were purchased during the year for cash:

	Debit	Credit
Land and improvements	$ 350,000	
Equipment	780,000	
Vehicles	425,000	
Total	$1,555,000	

Accounts	Debit	Credit
Land and improvements	350,000	
Equipment	780,000	
Vehicles	425,000	
Cash		1,555,000

Transaction JE08.37—The following assets were sold during the year. The cash proceeds were $95,000:

	Original Cost	Accumulated Depreciation
Equipment	$120,000	$ 90,000
Vehicles	230,000	195,000
Total	$350,000	$285,000

Accounts	Debit	Credit
Cash	95,000	
Accumulated depreciation—equipment	90,000	
Accumulated depreciation—vehicles	195,000	
Equipment		120,000
Vehicles		230,000
Miscellaneous revenue—gain on sale of assets		30,000

Transaction JE08.38—During the year, additional notes of $200,000 were issued and interest expense of $32,000 was paid. Also, notes of $100,000 were paid off. All notes are related to capital-asset transactions:

Accounts	Debit	Credit
Cash	168,000	
Interest expense	32,000	
Notes payable		200,000
Notes payable	100,000	
Cash		100,000

Transaction JE08.39—Compensated absences of $12,000 were paid during the year and additional costs of $15,000 were accrued:

Accounts	Debit	Credit
Personal services expenses	15,000	
Compensated absences liability		3,000
Cash		12,000

Transaction JE08.40—Claims and judgements of $13,000 were paid during the year and additional costs of $12,000 were accrued:

Accounts	Debit	Credit
Insurance claims and expenses	12,000	
Claims and judgements payable	1,000	
Cash		13,000

Transaction JE08.41—Depreciation expense recognized during the year was as follows:

Buildings	$375,000
Equipment	175,000
Vehicles	575,000
Total	$1,125,000

Accounts	Debit	Credit
Depreciation expense	1,125,000	
Accumulated depreciation—buildings		375,000
Accumulated depreciation—equipment		175,000
Accumulated depreciation—vehicles		575,000

Transaction JE08.42—An operating grant of $70,000 and a capital grant of $40,000 were received from the state government:

Accounts	Debit	Credit
Cash	110,000	
Operating grants and contributions		70,000
Capital grants and contributions		40,000

Transaction JE08.43—Other operating revenues earned and received during the year amounted to $3,000 and other operating expenses incurred and paid during the year amounted to $15,000:

Accounts	Debit	Credit
Cash	3,000	
Operating revenues—miscellaneous		3,000
Operating expenses—miscellaneous	15,000	
Cash		15,000

Transaction JE08.44—Inventories of $20,000 were on hand at the end of the year:

Accounts	Debit	Credit
Inventories	4,000	
Other supplies and expenses		4,000

After the transactions for the year are posted, the year-end trial balance (June 30, 20X2) for the SSSC appears as follows:

Accounts	Adjusted Trial Balance	
	Debit	Credit
Cash	$22,000	
Interest receivable	1,000	
Due from other funds—Centerville Municipal Airport	427,000	
Temporary investments	12,000	
Inventories	20,000	
Land and improvements	1,750,000	
Buildings	1,600,000	
Accumulated depreciation—buildings		$825,000
Equipment	2,960,000	
Accumulated depreciation—equipment		1,385,000
Vehicles	1,995,000	
Accumulated depreciation—vehicles		1,030,000
Accounts payable and accrued expenses		75,000
Compensated absences liability		17,000
Claims and judgements payable		21,000
Notes payable		550,000
Net assets		4,796,000
Charges for services		2,950,000
Interest and investment revenue		15,000
Miscellaneous revenue—gain on sale of assets		30,000
Operating grants and contributions		70,000
Capital grants and contributions		40,000
Operating revenues—miscellaneous		3,000
Personal services expenses	915,000	
Contractual services expenses	400,000	
Repairs and maintenance expenses	350,000	
Other supplies and expenses	171,000	
Insurance claims and expenses	12,000	
Depreciation expense	1,125,000	
Interest expense	32,000	
Operating expenses—miscellaneous	15,000	
Totals	$11,807,000	$11,807,000

The worksheet that summarizes the journal entries for the SSSC for the year-end trial balance is presented in Appendix 8C.

FUND FINANCIAL STATEMENTS

At the fund financial statement level, Internal Service Fund balances and activities are combined into a single column and placed on the proprietary fund financial statements to the right of the financial statements of Enterprise Funds. Proprietary funds must prepare a statement of net assets (or balance sheet), statement of revenues, expenses, and changes in fund net assets or fund equity and statement of cash flows. Based on the adjusted trial balances created above, the following financial statements reflect the balances and activities of the three Internal Service Funds (see Appendix 8D).

In the preparation of the statement of net assets, notes payable were assumed to be associated with the acquisition of capital assets and the current and noncurrent portions of certain liabilities were assumed:

Internal Service Funds
Statement of Net Assets
June 30, 20X2

	Communications and Technology Support Center	Fleet Management	Special Services Support Center	Total
ASSETS				
Current assets:				
Cash	$ 946,000	$ 137,500	$ 22,000	$1,105,500
Interest receivable	1,000	2,000	1,000	4,000
Due from other funds	325,000	72,000	427,000	824,000
Due from other governments	—	45,000	—	45,000
Temporary investments	15,000	19,000	12,000	46,000
Inventories	9,000	7,000	20,000	36,000
Total current assets	1,296,000	282,500	482,000	2,060,500
Noncurrent assets:				
Land and improvements	2,700,000	50,000	1,750,000	4,500,000
Buildings	1,400,000	1,600,000	1,600,000	4,600,000
Equipment	5,870,000	1,330,000	2,960,000	10,160,000
Vehicles	143,000	8,200,000	1,995,000	10,338,000
Less accumulated depreciation	(3,103,000)	(6,505,000)	(3,240,000)	(12,848,000)
Total non-current assets	7,010,000	4,675,000	5,065,000	16,750,000
Total assets	8,306,000	4,957,500	5,547,000	18,810,500
LIABILITIES				
Current liabilities:				
Accounts payable and accrued expenses	50,000	125,000	75,000	250,000
Compensated absences	3,000	2,000	5,000	10,000
Claims and judgments	4,000	2,000	7,000	13,000
Notes payable	—	1,500,000	200,000	1,700,000
Total current liabilities	57,000	1,629,000	287,000	1,973,000
Noncurrent liabilities:				
Compensated absences	4,000	6,000	12,000	22,000
Claims and judgements	15,000	11,000	14,000	40,000

	Communications and Technology Support Center	Fleet Management	Special Services Support Center	Total
Notes payable	4,700,000	1,500,000	350,000	6,550,000
Total non-current liabilities	4,719,000	1,517,000	376,000	6,612,000
Total liabilities	4,776,000	3,146,000	663,000	8,585,000

NET ASSETS

Invested in capital assets, net of related debt	2,310,000	1,675,000	4,515,000	8,500,000
Unrestricted	1,220,000	136,500	369,000	1,725,500
Total net assets	$3,530,000	$1,811,500	$4,884,000	$10,225,500

Internal Service Funds
Statement of Revenues, Expenses, and Changes in Fund Net Assets
For the Year Ended June 30, 20X2

	Communications and Technology Support Center	Fleet Management	Special Services Support Center	Total
OPERATING REVENUES				
Charges for services	$5,500,000	$5,000,000	$2,950,000	$13,450,000
Miscellaneous	10,000	4,000	3,000	17,000
Total operating revenues	5,510,000	5,004,000	2,953,000	13,467,000
OPERATING EXPENSES				
Personal services	4,805,000	1,206,000	915,000	6,926,000
Contractual services	1,300,000	400,000	400,000	2,100,000
Repairs and maintenance	1,100,000	200,000	350,000	1,650,000
Other supplies and expenses	48,000	147,000	171,000	366,000
Insurance claims and expenses	10,000	7,000	12,000	29,000
Depreciation	1,927,000	2,530,000	1,125,000	5,582,000
Miscellaneous	5,000	2,000	15,000	22,000
Total operating expenses	9,195,000	4,492,000	2,988,000	16,675,000
Operating income (loss)	(3,685,000)	512,000	(35,000)	(3,208,000)
NONOPERATING REVENUES (EXPENSES)				
Interest and investment revenue	5,000	5,000	15,000	25,000
Interest	(97,000)	(180,000)	(32,000)	(309,000)
Operating grants and contributions	200,000	100,000	70,000	370,000
Miscellaneous	27,000	(65,000)	30,000	(8,000)

	Communications and Technology Support Center	Fleet Management	Special Services Support Center	Total
Total nonoperating revenue (expenses)	135,000	(140,000)	83,000	78,000
Income (loss) before capital contributions and transfers	(3,550,000)	372,000	48,000	(3,130,000)
Capital contributions	450,000	—	40,000	490,000
Transfers in	40,000	—	—	40,000
Transfers out	—	(50,000)	—	(50,000)
Change in net assets	(3,060,000)	322,000	88,000	(2,650,000)
Total net assets—beginning	6,590,000	1,489,500	4,796,000	12,875,500
Total net assets—ending	$3,530,000	$1,811,500	$4,884,000	$10,225,500

Internal Service Funds
Statement of Cash Flows
For the Year Ended June 30, 20X2

	Communications and Technology Support Center	Fleet Management	Special Services Support Center	Total
CASH FLOWS FROM OPERATING ACTIVITIES				
Receipts from customers	$5,296,000	$4,915,000	$2,600,000	$12,811,000
Payments to suppliers	(2,435,000)	(815,000)	(935,000)	(4,185,000)
Payments to employees	(4,782,000)	(1,103,000)	(862,000)	(6,747,000)
Other receipts (payments)	2,000	(2,000)	(25,000)	(25,000)
Net cash provided by operating activities	(1,919,000)	2,995,000	778,000	1,854,000
CASH FLOWS FROM NONCAPITAL FINANCING ACTIVITIES				
Operating subsidies and transfers from (to) other funds	240,000	50,000	70,000	360,000
CASH FLOWS FROM CAPITAL AND RELATED FINANCING ACTIVITIES				
Proceeds from the issuance of capital debt	3,200,000	—	200,000	3,400,000
Capital contributions	450,000	—	40,000	490,000
Acquisitions of capital assets	(1,535,000)	(2,950,000)	(1,555,000)	(6,040,000)
Proceeds from sale of capital assets	340,000	410,000	95,000	845,000
Principal paid on capital debt	—	(1,000,000)	(100,000)	(1,100,000)
Interest paid on capital debt	(97,000)	(180,000)	(32,000)	(309,000)

	Communications and Technology Support Center	Fleet Management	Special Services Support Center	Total
Net cash (used) by capital and related financing activities	2,358,000	(3,720,000)	(1,352,000)	(2,714,000)
CASH FLOWS FROM INVESTING ACTIVITIES				
Interest and dividends	7,000	7,500	23,000	37,500
Net increase (decrease) in cash	686,000	(667,500)	(481,000)	(462,500)
Balances—beginning of year	260,000	805,000	503,000	1,568,000
Balances—end of year	$946,000	$137,500	$22,000	$1,105,500
Reconciliation of operating income (loss) to net cash provided (used) by operating activities:				
Operating income (loss)	$(3,685,000)	$ 512,000	$(35,000)	$(3,208,000)
Adjustments:				
Depreciation expense	1,927,000	2,530,000	1,125,000	5,582,000
Change in assets and liabilities:				
Receivables, net	$ (204,000)	$ (85,000)	$(350,000)	$ (639,000)
Inventories	(2,000)	(3,000)	(4,000)	(9,000)
Accounts and accrued liabilities	45,000	41,000	42,000	128,000
Net cash provided (used) by operating activities	$(1,919,000)	$2,995,000	$ 778,000	$1,854,000

The combined financial statements for the Internal Service Funds are used later, in Chapter 13, "Developing Information for Fund Financial Statements."

CONVERTING TO GOVERNMENT-WIDE FINANCIAL STATEMENTS

Government-wide financial statements are reported on the accrual basis of accounting. Generally, most governments work from their proprietary fund financial statements and through the use of worksheet entries convert to accrual based financial statements. Proprietary funds are presented on an accrual basis. Therefore, there often is no need to make worksheet entries to convert the information from a fund basis to a government-wide basis; however, the residual balances and the activities of Internal Service Funds must be analyzed to determine how they are to be merged into the government-wide financial statements (see Appendix 8E).

Determining the Allocation Base

As noted earlier in this chapter, any profit or loss from an Internal Service Fund must be allocated to governmental and/or business-type activities in order to reduce or increase the operating activities of the fund to break-even amounts. However, the following items are generally not used to determine the allocation of operating results of an Internal Service Fund:

- Interest and investment revenue
- Interest expense
- Transfers in/out
- Billings to external parties

Interest and Investment Revenue

A fundamental concept in the formatting of the statement of activities is the identification of resource inflows to the governmental entities that are related to specific programs and those that are general in nature. GAAP notes that governmental activities are generally financed from the following sources of resource inflows:

- Parties who purchase, use, or directly benefit from goods and services provided through the program (for example, fees for public transportation and licenses)
- Outside parties (other governments and nongovernmental entities or individuals) who provide goods and services to the governmental entity (for example, a grant to a local government from a state government)
- The reporting government's constituencies (for example, property taxes)
- The governmental entity (for example, investment income)

The first source of resources is always program revenue. The second source is program revenue if it is restricted to a specific program; otherwise the item is considered general revenue. The third source is always general revenue, even when restricted. The fourth source of resources, which includes investment income, is usually general revenue.

Based on the nature of an Internal Service Fund, investment income will usually be considered general revenue and reported in the lower section of the statement of activities. Therefore, when an Internal Service Fund has investment income, only the *net profit or loss before investment income* should be allocated to the operating programs. Because none of the interest and investment income is restricted, the amount should be combined with other unrestricted income and presented as a separate line item in the statement of activities for both governmental activities and business-type activities.

Interest Expense

Generally, interest expense on debt issued by an Internal Service Fund is considered an indirect expense and should not be allocated as a direct expense to specific functional categories that appear on the statement of activities but rather should be presented as a single line item, appropriately labeled. For this reason, when an Internal Service Fund has interest expense, only the *profit or loss before interest charges* should be allocated to the governmental operating programs. The interest expense should be combined with other interest expense related to governmental activities and the single amount should be presented on the statement of activities.

When interest expense is incurred by an Internal Service Fund that services only Enterprise Funds, the interest is directly related to business-type activities. That is, the funds could have been borrowed by the Internal Service Fund or directly by the Enterprise Funds. For this reason, interest expense under this circumstance should be used in determining the amount of net profit or loss incurred by the Internal Service Fund that should be allocated to business-type activities.

Transfers In and Out

GAAP states that transfers in and out are nonreciprocal transactions and represent interfund activities whereby the two parties to the events do not receive equivalent cash, goods, or services. Governmental funds should report transfers of this nature in their fund operating statements as other financing uses and other financial sources of funds. Proprietary funds should report this type of transfer in their activity statements after nonoperating revenues and nonoperating expenses. Based on the nature of transfers in and out as defined in GASB-34, these transfers should not be considered when determining the amount of net profit or loss that must be allocated back to the various programs reported on the statement of activities.

Billings to External Parties

A governmental entity may establish an Internal Service Fund that has its predominant activities with other units of the reporting entity but for simplicity purposes also makes sales (of an immaterial amount) to external parties. Under this circumstance, the external sales and related cost of sales should not be used to determine the net profit or loss amount that is the basis for adjusting the expenses incurred in the governmental column of the statement of activities.

Based on the guidance provided above, the basis used to allocate the results of operations of the three Internal Service Funds is computed as follows:

	Communications and Technology Support Center	Fleet Management Unit	Special Services Support Center
Change in net assets as reported in the statement of revenues, expenses, and changes in fund net assets	$(3,060,000)	$322,000	$ 88,000
Less interest and investment revenue	(5,000)	(5,000)	(15,000)
Add interest expense	97,000	180,000	—
Less transfers in	(40,000)	—	—
Add transfers out	—	50,000	—

	Communications and Technology Support Center	Fleet Management Unit	Special Services Support Center
Less profit on external sales*	—	(30,000)	—
Net amount to be allocated to governmental/ business-type activities	$(3,008,000)	$517,000	$ 73,000

* The Fleet Management Unit provides services to two external governments (County Fire District and Regional Pollution Control District). The billings for the year to these external parties totaled $300,000 and the estimated cost of providing these services was $270,000. Thus, the profit on external sales was $30,000 ($300,000–$270,000). As shown later in this chapter (based on the assumed nature of the activities), the external sales are reported as "program revenues—charges for services (general government)" and the related expenses are reported as "expenses—general government" in the statement of activities (a government-wide financial statement).

Communications and Technology Support Center

The CTSC supports all of the City's governmental and proprietary funds. The billings to each of these activities were as follows during the year:

Fund Name	Billings	Percentage of Total Billings	Amount of Operating Loss ($3,008,000) Allocated
General Fund	$4,500,000	81.8%	$2,460,544
Centerville Municipal Airport	600,000	10.9	327,872
Centerville Utilities Authority	220,000	4.0	120,320
Centerville Parking Authority	100,000	1.8	54,144
Centerville Toll Bridge	80,000	1.5	45,120
Total	$5,500,000	100.0%	$3,008,000

Based on the above analysis, the following worksheet entries are made in order to adjust the expenses reported on the statement of activities and allocate the net assets of the Internal Service Fund to the governmental activities column of the statement of net assets:

	Accounts	Debit	Credit
JE08.45	Cash	946,000	
	Interest receivable	1,000	
	Due from other funds	325,000	
	Temporary investments	15,000	
	Inventories	9,000	
	Land and improvements	2,700,000	
	Buildings	1,400,000	
	Equipment	5,870,000	
	Vehicles	143,000	

Accounts	Debit	Credit
Expenses—general government ($2,460,544 × 60%)*	1,476,326	
Expenses—public safety ($2,460,544 × 20%)*	492,109	
Expenses—streets ($2,460,544 × 10%)*	246,055	
Expenses—recreation and parks ($2,460,544 × 5%)*	123,027	
Expenses—health and welfare ($2,460,544 × 5%)*	123,027	
Internal balances		547,456
Interest expense	97,000	
Accumulated depreciation		3,103,000
Accounts payable and accrued expenses		50,000
Compensated absences—current		3,000
Claims and judgements—current		4,000
Compensated absences—noncurrent		4,000
Claims and judgements—noncurrent		15,000
Notes payable—noncurrent		4,700,000
Interest and investment revenue		5,000
Transfers in		40,000
Net assets		6,590,000
(To merge balances of the Communications and Technology Support Center Internal Service Fund with governmental activities)		

* The allocation to the General Fund is distributed to the various program activities based on the following assumption:

General government	60%
Public safety	20%
Streets	10%
Recreation and Parks	5%
Health and Welfare	5%
Total	100%

In addition, the following worksheet entry is made in order to adjust the expenses reported on the statement of activities and to allocate the net assets of the Internal Service Fund to the business-type activities column of the statement of net assets:

	Accounts	Debit	Credit
JE08.46	Expenses—Centerville Municipal Airport	327,872	
	Expenses—Centerville Utilities Authority	120,320	
	Expenses—Centerville Parking Authority	54,144	
	Expenses—Centerville Toll Bridge	45,120	

Accounts	Debit	Credit
Internal balances		547,456
(To merge balances of the Communications and Technology Support Center Internal Service Fund with business-type activities)		

The two entries made above are taken forward to Chapter 14, "Developing Information for Government-Wide Financial Statements."

The internal balance account (which appears on the statement of net assets) represents the net receivable/payable between governmental activities and business-type activities of the primary government. In effect, the account represents the degree to which one set of activities (say, governmental activities) subsidizes the other set of activities (say, the business-type activities). The two balances are mirror images of one another. That is, if the governmental activities balance is a receivable, the business-type activities balance is a payable of the same amount. Although the two are presented on the statement of net assets, they are eliminated when the total column for the reporting entity is presented because the balance represents an interentity balance. In the current example the adjustment is made only to the extent of the effects of the current period's operations. In practice a record of the net cumulative adjustments from previous periods (from the date that GASB-34 was implemented) must be maintained, and that amount is the basis for an additional adjustment. In the current example, for simplicity, it is assumed that prior to the current year the operations in the Internal Service Funds have been at a net cumulative break-even point.

The activities of an Internal Service Fund must be analyzed to determine whether account balances and transactions of the fund must be reported as a governmental activity or a business-type activity on the government-wide financial statements. The GASB's *Comprehensive Implementation Guide* raises the issue of how the activities of a state board (accounted for as an Internal Service Fund) that manages investments for several state funds (Pension Trust Funds, Internal Service Funds, Enterprise Funds, and governmental funds) should be reported in the government-wide financial statements. The state board's activities are financed exclusively by a fee that is charged to each participant. The GASB's *Guide* points out that the activities of the state board should be reported in the governmental activities column in the government-wide financial statements. The fact that a high percentage of the state board's activity involves pension funds is irrelevant even though fiduciary fund financial statements are not presented at the government-wide financial statement level. The criterion to determine where to include an Internal Service Fund's balances is based on whether the fund services governmental funds or Enterprise Funds. Only if Enterprise Funds are the predominant—or only—participants in the state board's activities would the balances be presented in the business-type activities column.

An Internal Service Fund may be used to account for a governmental entity's risk financing activities and, furthermore, the amount charged to participating funds may include "a reasonable provision for future catastrophic losses," as allowed in GASB-10 (par. 66c). The GASB's *Comprehensive Implementation Guide* addresses the issue of how the additional charge for future catastrophic losses and the accumulation of the related resources should be presented at the government-wide financial statement level. The general look-back adjustment applies to all Internal Service Funds, including those used to account for risk financing activities of a governmental entity. Thus, the provision for future catastrophic losses, when billed, creates additional net profit for the Internal Service Fund because, by definition, future losses do not meet the conditions for the recognition of a loss contingency (probable that a liability has been incurred and a reasonable estimate of the liability can be made) and no expense for those future losses will be provided for in the Internal Service Fund. The GASB's *Guide* notes that when the look-back adjustment is made in the preparation of the government-wide financial statements to eliminate the net profit of the Internal Service, that technique reduces the expenses of the participating funds to an amount consistent with the nature of a loss contingency. The accumulated resources arising from the strategy to provide resources for future catastrophic losses (along with other net resources of the Internal Service Fund) are folded into the governmental activities column of the statement of net assets.

Fleet Management

The FMU provides a motor pool to all of the City's governmental funds and to some other governmental units that are not part of the City's reporting entity. The FMU provides no services to other proprietary funds.

Based on the above analysis, the following worksheet entry is made in order to adjust the expenses reported on the statement of activities and allocate the net assets of the Internal Service Fund to the governmental activities column of the statement of net assets:

	Accounts	Debit	Credit
JE08.47	Cash	137,500	
	Interest receivable	2,000	
	Due from other funds	72,000	
	Due from other governments	45,000	
	Temporary investments	19,000	
	Inventories	7,000	
	Land and improvements	50,000	
	Buildings	1,600,000	
	Equipment	1,330,000	
	Vehicles	8,200,000	
	Interest expense	180,000	
	Transfers out	50,000	
	Expenses—general government [($517,000 × 60%) − $270,000]		40,200
	Expenses—public safety ($517,000 × 20%)		103,400
	Expenses—streets ($517,000 × 10%)		51,700

Accounts	Debit	Credit
Expenses—recreation and parks ($517,000 × 5%)		25,850
Expenses—health and welfare ($517,000 × 5%)		25,850
Accumulated depreciation		6,505,000
Accounts payable and accrued expenses		125,000
Compensated absences—current		2,000
Claims and judgements—current		2,000
Notes payable—current		1,500,000
Compensated absences—noncurrent		6,000
Claims and judgements—noncurrent		11,000
Notes payable—noncurrent		1,500,000
Interest and investment revenue		5,000
Program revenues—charges for services (general government)		300,000
Net assets		1,489,500
(To merge balances of the Fleet Management Unit Internal Service Fund with governmental activities)		

The entry made above is taken forward to Chapter 14, "Developing Information for Government-Wide Financial Statements."

Special Services Support Center

The SSSC provides services exclusively for the Centerville Municipal Airport; therefore, all of the residual balances and the adjustment for the operating profit for the year are allocated to the airport (business-type activities) in the following worksheet entry:

Accounts	Debit	Credit
JE08.48 Cash	22,000	
Interest receivable	1,000	
Due from other funds	427,000	
Temporary investments	12,000	
Inventories	20,000	
Land and improvements	1,750,000	
Buildings	1,600,000	
Equipment	2,960,000	
Vehicles	1,995,000	
Expenses—Centerville Municipal Airport		73,000
Accumulated depreciation		3,240,000

Accounts	Debit	Credit
Accounts payable and accrued expenses		75,000
Compensated absences—current		5,000
Claims and judgements—current		7,000
Notes payable—current		200,000
Compensated absences—noncurrent		12,000
Claims and judgements—noncurrent		14,000
Notes payable—noncurrent		350,000
Interest and investment revenue		15,000
Net assets		4,796,000
(To merge balances of the Special Services Support Center Internal Service Fund with business-type activities)		

The above entry is taken forward to Chapter 14, "Developing Information for Government-Wide Financial Statements."

APPENDIX 8A: WORKSHEET FOR SUMMARIZING CURRENT TRANSACTIONS: COMMUNICATIONS AND TECHNOLOGY SUPPORT CENTER

Accounts	Trial Balance Debit	Trial Balance Credit	Adjustments Debit (ref)	Adjustments Debit	Adjustments Credit (ref)	Adjustments Credit	Adjusted Trial Balance Debit	Adjusted Trial Balance Credit	Operating Statement Debit	Operating Statement Credit	Balance Sheet Debit	Balance Sheet Credit
Cash	260,000	—	JE08.02	3,000	JE08.01	15,000	946,000	—	—	—	946,000	—
			JE08.03	5,296,000	JE08.04	7,200,000						
			JE08.05	4,000	JE08.06	1,535,000						
			JE08.07	340,000		—						
			JE08.12	650,000	JE08.09	2,000						
			JE08.13	10,000	JE08.10	3,000						
			JE08.14	40,000	JE08.13	5,000						
			JE08.08	3,103,000		—						
Interest receivable	3,000	—	JE08.05	1,000	JE08.02	3,000	1,000	—	—	—	1,000	—
Due from other funds—General Fund	70,000	—	JE08.03	100,000		—	170,000	—	—	—	170,000	—
Due from other funds—Centerville Municipal Airport	25,000	—	JE08.03	60,000		—	85,000	—	—	—	85,000	—
Due from other funds—Centerville Utilities Authority	15,000	—	JE08.03	20,000		—	35,000	—	—	—	35,000	—

Account	Trial Balance Dr	Trial Balance Cr	Ref.	Adjustments Dr	Ref.	Adjustments Cr	Balance Dr	Balance Cr
Due from other funds—Centerville Parking Authority	7,000	—	JE08.03	10,000	—	—	17,000	—
Due from other funds—Centerville Toll Bridge	4,000	—	JE08.03	14,000	—	—	18,000	—
Temporary investments	15,000	—	—	—	—	—	15,000	—
Inventories	7,000	—	JE08.15	2,000	—	—	9,000	—
Land and improvements	2,300,000	—	JE08.06	400,000	—	—	2,700,000	—
Buildings	1,400,000	—	—	—	—	—	1,400,000	—
Accumulated depreciation—buildings	—	350,000	—	—	JE08.11	220,000	—	570,000
Equipment	5,500,000	—	JE08.06	1,100,000	JE08.07	730,000	5,870,000	—
Accumulated depreciation—equipment	—	1,200,000	JE08.07	420,000	JE08.11	1,700,000	—	2,480,000
Vehicles	120,000	—	JE08.06	35,000	JE08.07	12,000	143,000	—
Accumulated depreciation—vehicles	—	55,000	JE08.07	9,000	JE08.11	7,000	—	53,000
Accounts payable and accrued expenses	—	15,000	JE08.01	15,000	JE08.04	50,000	—	50,000
Compensated absences liability	—	4,000	—	—	JE08.09	3,000	—	7,000

Account								
Claims and judgements payable	12,000	—	7,000	JE08.10	19,000	—	19,000	—
Notes payable	1,500,000	—	3,200,000	JE08.08	4,700,000	—	4,700,000	—
Net assets	6,590,000	—	—	—	6,590,000	—	6,590,000	—
Charges for services	—	—	5,500,000	JE08.03	5,500,000	—	5,500,000	—
Interest and investment revenue	—	—	5,000	JE08.05	5,000	—	5,000	—
Miscellaneous revenue—gain on sale of assets	—	—	27,000	JE08.07	27,000	—	27,000	—
Operating grants and contributions	—	—	200,000	JE08.12	200,000	—	200,000	—
Capital grants and contributions	—	—	450,000	JE08.12	450,000	—	450,000	—
Operating revenues—miscellaneous	—	—	10,000	JE08.13	10,000	—	10,000	—
Personal services expenses	4,800,000	JE08.04	4,805,000		4,805,000	—	—	—
	5,000	JE08.09	—		—	—	—	—
Contractual services expenses	1,300,000	JE08.04	1,300,000		1,300,000	—	—	—
Repairs and maintenance—expenses	1,100,000	JE08.04	1,100,000		1,100,000	—	—	—

Other supplies and expenses	—	JE08.04 50,000	2,000	48,000	JE08.15 48,000	—	—	—
Insurance claims and expenses	—	JE08.10 10,000	—	10,000	10,000	—	—	—
Depreciation expense	—	JE08.11 1,927,000	—	1,927,000	1,927,000	—	—	—
Interest expense	—	JE08.08 97,000	—	97,000	97,000	—	—	—
Operating expenses—miscellaneous	—	JE08.13 5,000	—	5,000	5,000	—	—	—
Transfers in—General Fund	—	—	—	JE08.14 40,000	—	40,000	—	—
Totals	9,726,000	20,926,000	20,926,000	20,701,000	9,292,000	6,232,000	11,409,000	14,469,000
Net increase (decrease)	9,726,000				(3,060,000) 6,232,000	6,232,000	11,409,000	(3,060,000) 11,409,000

APPENDIX 8B: WORKSHEET FOR SUMMARIZING CURRENT TRANSACTIONS: FLEET MANAGEMENT

Accounts	Trial Balance Debit	Trial Balance Credit	Adjustments Ref (Debit)	Adjustments Debit	Adjustments Ref (Credit)	Adjustments Credit	Adjusted Trial Balance Debit	Adjusted Trial Balance Credit	Operating Statement Debit	Operating Statement Credit	Balance Sheet Debit	Balance Sheet Credit
Cash	805,000	—	JE08.17	4,500	JE08.16	90,000	137,500	—	—	—	137,500	—
		—	JE08.18	4,915,000	JE08.19	1,825,000	—	—	—	—	—	—
		—	JE08.20	3,000	JE08.21	2,950,000	—	—	—	—	—	—
		—	JE08.22	410,000	JE08.23	1,180,000	—	—	—	—	—	—
		—	JE08.27	100,000	JE08.24	3,000	—	—	—	—	—	—
		—	JE08.28	4,000	JE08.25	4,000	—	—	—	—	—	—
		—		—	JE08.28	2,000	—	—	—	—	—	—
		—		—	JE08.29	50,000	—	—	—	—	—	—
Interest receivable	4,500	—	JE08.20	2,000	JE08.17	4,500	2,000	—	—	—	2,000	—
Due from other funds—General Fund	22,000	—	JE08.18	50,000		—	72,000	—	—	—	72,000	—
Due from other governments—County Fire District	7,000	—	JE08.18	10,000		—	17,000	—	—	—	17,000	—
Due from other governments—Regional Pollution Control District	3,000	—	JE08.18	25,000		—	28,000	—	—	—	28,000	—

	Debit	Credit	Ref	Debit	Credit	Ref	Debit	Credit	Debit	Credit
Temporary investments	19,000	—		—	—		—	—	19,000	—
Inventories	4,000	—	JE08.30	3,000	—		—	—	7,000	—
Land and improvements	50,000	—		—	—		—	—	50,000	—
Buildings	1,600,000	—		—	—		—	—	1,600,000	—
Accumulated depreciation—buildings	—	450,000		—	—	JE08.26	—	370,000	—	820,000
Equipment	1,200,000	—	JE08.21	350,000	—	JE08.22	—	220,000	1,330,000	—
Accumulated depreciation—equipment	—	770,000	JE08.22	195,000	—	JE08.26	—	310,000	—	885,000
Vehicles	7,400,000	—	JE08.21	2,600,000	—	JE08.22	—	1,800,000	8,200,000	—
Accumulated depreciation—vehicles	—	4,300,000	JE08.22	1,350,000	—	JE08.26	—	1,850,000	—	4,800,000
Accounts payable and accrued expenses	—	90,000	JE08.16	90,000	—	JE08.19	—	125,000	—	125,000
Compensated absences liability	—	5,000		5,000	—		—	—	—	—
Claims and judgements payable	—	—		—	5,000	JE08.24	—	3,000	—	8,000
Notes payable	—	10,000		—	—	JE08.25	—	3,000	—	13,000
Notes payable	—	4,000,000	JE08.23	1,000,000	—		—	—	—	3,000,000
Net assets	—	1,489,500		—	—		—	—	—	1,489,500
Charges for services	—	—		—	—	JE08.18	—	5,000,000	—	5,000,000

Account			Dr. Ref.	Dr. Amount	Cr. Ref.	Cr. Amount	Bal. 1 Dr.	Bal. 1 Cr.	Bal. 2 Dr.	Bal. 2 Cr.	Bal. 3 Dr.	Bal. 3 Cr.		
Interest and investment revenue	—	—	—	—	JE08.20	5,000	—	5,000	—	5,000	—	5,000	—	—
Operating grants and contributions	—	—	—	—	JE08.27	100,000	—	100,000	—	100,000	—	100,000	—	—
Operating revenues—miscellaneous	—	—	—	—	JE08.28	4,000	—	4,000	—	4,000	—	4,000	—	—
Personal services expenses	—	—	JE08.19 JE08.24	1,200,000 6,000	—	—	1,206,000	—	1,206,000	—	1,206,000	—	—	—
Contractual services expenses	—	—	JE08.19	400,000	—	—	400,000	—	400,000	—	400,000	—	—	—
Repairs and maintenance expenses	—	—	JE08.19	200,000	—	—	200,000	—	200,000	—	200,000	—	—	—
Other supplies and expenses	—	—	JE08.19	150,000	JE08.30	3,000	147,000	—	147,000	—	147,000	—	—	—
Insurance claims and expenses	—	—	JE08.25	7,000	—	—	7,000	—	7,000	—	7,000	—	—	—
Depreciation expense	—	—	JE08.26	2,530,000	—	—	2,530,000	—	2,530,000	—	2,530,000	—	—	—
Interest expense	—	—	JE08.23	180,000	—	—	180,000	—	180,000	—	180,000	—	—	—
Operating expenses—miscellaneous	—	—	JE08.28	2,000	—	—	2,000	—	2,000	—	2,000	—	—	—

Miscellaneous expenses—loss on sale of assets	—	—	JE08.22	65,000	—	65,000	—	65,000	—	—	—
Transfers out—General Fund	—	—	JE08.29	50,000	—	50,000	—	50,000	—	—	—
Totals	11,114,500	11,114,500		15,901,500	15,901,500	16,249,500	16,249,500	4,787,000	5,109,000	11,462,500	11,140,500
Net increase (decrease)								322,000	—	—	322,000
								5,109,000	5,109,000	11,462,500	11,462,500

APPENDIX 8C: WORKSHEET FOR SUMMARIZING CURRENT TRANSACTIONS: SPECIAL SERVICES SUPPORT CENTER

Accounts	Trial Balance Debit	Trial Balance Credit	Adjustments Debit (Ref)	Adjustments Debit	Adjustments Credit (Ref)	Adjustments Credit	Adjusted Trial Balance Debit	Adjusted Trial Balance Credit	Operating Statement Debit	Operating Statement Credit	Balance Sheet Debit	Balance Sheet Credit
Cash	503,000	—	JE08.32 JE08.33 JE08.35 JE08.37 JE08.38 JE08.42 JE08.43	9,000 2,600,000 14,000 95,000 168,000 110,000 3,000	JE08.31 JE08.34 JE08.36 JE08.38 JE08.39 JE08.40 JE08.43	35,000 1,750,000 1,555,000 100,000 12,000 13,000 15,000	22,000	—	—	—	22,000	—
Interest receivable	9,000	—	JE08.35	1,000	JE08.32	9,000	1,000	—	—	—	1,000	—
Due from other funds—Centerville Municipal Airport	77,000	—	JE08.33	350,000		—	427,000	—	—	—	427,000	—
Temporary investments	12,000	—		—		—	12,000	—	—	—	12,000	—
Inventories	16,000	—	JE08.44	4,000		—	20,000	—	—	—	20,000	—
Land and improvements	1,400,000	—	JE08.36	350,000		—	1,750,000	—	—	—	1,750,000	—
Buildings	1,600,000	—		—		—	1,600,000	—	—	—	1,600,000	—
Accumulated depreciation—buildings	—	450,000		—	JE08.41	375,000	—	825,000	—	—	—	825,000

Equipment	2,300,000	—	JE08.36	780,000	JE08.37	120,000	2,960,000	—	—	—	2,960,000	—
Accumulated depreciation—equipment	—	1,300,000	JE08.37	90,000	JE08.41	175,000	—	1,385,000	—	—	—	1,385,000
Vehicles	1,800,000	—	JE08.36	425,000	JE08.37	230,000	1,995,000	—	—	—	1,995,000	—
Accumulated depreciation—vehicles	—	650,000	JE08.37	195,000	JE08.41	575,000	—	1,030,000	—	—	—	1,030,000
Accounts payable and accrued expenses	—	35,000	JE08.31	35,000	JE08.34	75,000	—	75,000	—	—	—	75,000
Compensated absences liability	—	14,000	—	—	JE08.39	3,000	—	17,000	—	—	—	17,000
Claims and judgements payable	—	22,000	JE08.40	1,000	—	—	—	21,000	—	—	—	21,000
Notes payable	—	450,000	JE08.38	100,000	JE08.38	200,000	—	550,000	—	—	—	550,000
Net assets	—	4,796,000	—	—	—	—	—	4,796,000	—	—	—	4,796,000
Charges for services	—	—	—	—	JE08.33	2,950,000	—	2,950,000	—	2,950,000	—	—
Interest and investment revenue	—	—	—	—	JE08.35	15,000	—	15,000	—	15,000	—	—
Miscellaneous revenue—gain on sale of assets	—	—	—	—	JE08.37	30,000	—	30,000	—	30,000	—	—

Account											
Operating grants and contributions	—	—	—	JE08.42	70,000	—	70,000	—	70,000	—	—
Capital grants and contributions	—	—	—	JE08.42	40,000	—	40,000	—	40,000	—	—
Operating revenues—miscellaneous	—	—	—	JE08.43	3,000	—	3,000	—	3,000	—	—
Personal services expenses	—	JE08.34	900,000	—	—	915,000	—	915,000	—	—	—
	—	JE08.39	15,000	—	—						
Contractual services expenses	—	JE08.34	400,000	—	—	400,000	—	400,000	—	—	—
Repairs and maintenance expenses	—	JE08.34	350,000	—	—	350,000	—	350,000	—	—	—
Other supplies and expenses	—	JE08.34	175,000	JE08.44	4,000	171,000	—	171,000	—	—	—
Insurance claims and expenses	—	JE08.40	12,000	—	—	12,000	—	12,000	—	—	—
Depreciation expense	—	JE08.41	1,125,000	—	—	1,125,000	—	1,125,000	—	—	—
Interest expense	—	JE08.38	32,000	—	—	32,000	—	32,000	—	—	—
Operating expenses—miscellaneous	—	JE08.43	15,000	—	—	15,000	—	15,000	—	—	—
Totals	7,717,000		8,354,000		8,354,000	11,807,000	11,807,000	3,020,000	3,108,000	8,787,000	8,699,000
Net increase (decrease)	—		—		—	—	—	88,000	—	—	88,000
	7,717,000		8,354,000		8,354,000	11,807,000	11,807,000	3,108,000	3,108,000	8,787,000	8,787,000

APPENDIX 8D: INTERNAL SERVICE FUNDS: STATEMENT OF NET ASSETS; STATEMENT OF REVENUES, EXPENSES, AND CHANGES IN FUND NET ASSETS; AND STATEMENT OF CASH FLOWS

Internal Service Funds
Statement of Net Assets
June 30, 20X2

	Communications and Technology Support Center	Fleet Man-agement	Special Services Support Center	Total
ASSETS				
Current assets:				
Cash	$ 946,000	$ 137,500	$ 22,000	$1,105,500
Interest receivable	1,000	2,000	1,000	4,000
Due from other funds	325,000	72,000	427,000	824,000
Due from other governments	—	45,000	—	45,000
Temporary investments	15,000	19,000	12,000	46,000
Inventories	9,000	7,000	20,000	36,000
Total current assets	1,296,000	282,500	482,000	2,060,500
Noncurrent assets:				
Land and improvements	2,700,000	—	1,750,000	4,450,000
Buildings	1,400,000	1,650,000	1,600,000	4,650,000
Equipment	5,870,000	1,330,000	2,960,000	10,160,000
Vehicles	143,000	8,200,000	1,995,000	10,338,000
Less accumulated depreciation	(3,103,000)	(6,505,000)	(3,240,000)	(12,848,000)
Total noncurrent assets	7,010,000	4,675,000	5,065,000	16,750,000
Total assets	8,306,000	4,957,500	5,547,000	18,810,500
LIABILITIES				
Current liabilities:				
Accounts payable and accrued expenses	50,000	125,000	75,000	250,000
Compensated absences	3,000	2,000	5,000	10,000
Claims and judgements	4,000	2,000	7,000	13,000
Notes payable	—	1,500,000	200,000	1,700,000
Total current liabilities	57,000	1,629,000	287,000	1,973,000
Noncurrent liabilities:				
Compensated absences	4,000	6,000	12,000	22,000
Claims and judgements	15,000	11,000	14,000	40,000
Notes payable	4,700,000	1,500,000	350,000	6,550,000
Total noncurrent liabilities	4,719,000	1,517,000	376,000	6,612,000
Total liabilities	4,776,000	3,146,000	663,000	8,585,000

	Communications and Technology Support Center	Fleet Man- agement	Special Services Support Center	Total
NET ASSETS				
Invested in capital assets, net of related debt	$2,310,000	$1,675,000	$4,515,000	$8,500,000
Unrestricted	1,220,000	136,500	369,000	1,725,500
Total net assets	$3,530,000	$1,811,500	$4,884,000	$10,225,500

Internal Service Funds
Statement of Revenues, Expenses, and Changes in Fund Net Assets
For the Year Ended June 30, 20X2

	Communications and Technology Support Center	Fleet Man- agement	Special Services Support Center	Total
OPERATING REVENUES				
Charges for services	$5,500,000	$5,000,000	$2,950,000	$13,450,000
Miscellaneous	10,000	4,000	3,000	17,000
Total operating revenues	5,510,000	5,004,000	2,953,000	13,467,000
OPERATING EXPENSES				
Personal services	4,805,000	1,206,000	915,000	6,926,000
Contractual services	1,300,000	400,000	400,000	2,100,000
Repairs and maintenance	1,100,000	200,000	350,000	1,650,000
Other supplies and expenses	48,000	147,000	171,000	366,000
Insurance claims and expenses	10,000	7,000	12,000	29,000
Depreciation	1,927,000	2,530,000	1,125,000	5,582,000
Miscellaneous	5,000	2,000	15,000	22,000
Total operating expenses	9,195,000	4,492,000	2,988,000	16,675,000
Operating income (loss)	(3,685,000)	512,000	(35,000)	(3,208,000)
NONOPERATING REVENUES (EXPENSES)				
Interest and investment revenue	5,000	5,000	15,000	25,000
Interest	(97,000)	(180,000)	(32,000)	(309,000)
Operating grants and contributions	200,000	100,000	70,000	370,000
Miscellaneous	27,000	(65,000)	30,000	(8,000)
Total nonoperating revenue (expenses)	135,000	(140,000)	83,000	78,000
Income (loss) before capital contributions and transfers	(3,550,000)	372,000	48,000	(3,130,000)
Capital contributions	450,000	—	40,000	490,000
Transfers in	40,000	—	—	40,000
Transfers out	—	(50,000)	—	(50,000)
Change in net assets	(3,060,000)	322,000	88,000	(2,650,000)
Total net assets—beginning	6,590,000	1,489,500	4,796,000	12,875,500
Total net assets—ending	$3,530,000	$1,811,500	$4,884,000	$10,225,500

Internal Service Funds
Statement of Cash Flows
For the Year Ended June 30, 20X2

	Communications and Technology Support Center	Fleet Man-agement	Special Services Support Center	Total
CASH FLOWS FROM OPERATING ACTIVITIES				
Receipts from customers	$ 5,296,000	$ 4,915,000	$2,600,000	$12,811,000
Payments to suppliers	(2,435,000)	(815,000)	(935,000)	(4,185,000)
Payments to employees	(4,782,000)	(1,103,000)	(862,000)	(6,747,000)
Other receipts (payments)	2,000	(2,000)	(25,000)	(25,000)
Net cash provided by operating activities	(1,919,000)	2,995,000	778,000	1,854,000
CASH FLOWS FROM NON CAPITAL FINANCING ACTIVITIES				
Operating subsidies and transfers from (to) other funds	240,000	50,000	70,000	360,000
CASH FLOWS FROM CAPITAL AND RELATED FINANCING ACTIVITIES				
Proceeds from the issuance of capital debt	3,200,000	—	200,000	3,400,000
Capital contributions	450,000	—	40,000	490,000
Acquisitions of capital assets	(1,535,000)	(2,950,000)	(1,555,000)	(6,040,000)
Proceeds from sale of capital assets	340,000	410,000	95,000	845,000
Principal paid on capital debt		(1,000,000)	(100,000)	(1,100,000)
Interest paid on capital debt	(97,000)	(180,000)	(32,000)	(309,000)
Net cash (used) by capital and related financing activities	2,358,000	(3,720,000)	(1,352,000)	(2,714,000)
CASH FLOWS FROM INVESTING ACTIVITIES				
Interest and dividends	7,000	7,500	23,000	37,500
Net increase (decrease) in cash	686,000	(667,500)	(481,000)	(462,500)
Balances—beginning of year	260,000	805,000	503,000	1,568,000
Balances—end of year	$946,000	$137,500	$22,000	$1,105,500
Reconciliation of operating income (loss) to net cash provided (used) by operating activities:				
Operating income (loss)	$(3,685,000)	$ 512,000	$(35,000)	$(3,208,000)
Adjustments:				
Depreciation expense	1,927,000	2,530,000	1,125,000	5,582,000
Change in assets and liabilities:				
Receivables, net	$(204,000)	$(85,000)	$(350,000)	$(639,000)
Inventories	(2,000)	(3,000)	(4,000)	(9,000)
Accounts and accrued liabilities	45,000	41,000	42,000	128,000
Net cash provided (used) by operating activities	$(1,919,000)	$ 2,995,000	$ 778,000	$ 1,854,000

APPENDIX 8E: MERGING INTERNAL SERVICE FUNDS INTO THE GOVERNMENT-WIDE FINANCIAL STATEMENTS

Proprietary funds are presented on an accrual basis. Therefore, there often is no need to make worksheet entries to convert the information from a fund basis to a government-wide basis; however, the residual balances and the activities of Internal Service Funds must be analyzed to determine how they are to be merged into the government-wide financial statements.

PART IV.
FIDUCIARY FUNDS

CHAPTER 9
PENSION (AND OTHER EMPLOYEE BENEFITS) TRUST FUNDS

CONTENTS

NATURE OF PENSION (AND OTHER EMPLOYEE BENEFITS) TRUST FUNDS

GASB-25 (Financial Reporting for Defined Benefit Pension Plans and Notes Disclosures for Defined Contribution Plans) characterizes "defined pension benefit plans" as "having terms that specify the amount of pension benefits to be provided at a future date or after a certain period of time; the amount specified usually is a function of one or more factors such as age, years of service, and compensation." A public employee retirement system (PERS) may be established to hold assets and pay benefits earned by governmental employees and their beneficiaries under a defined pension benefit plan; however, GASB-25 notes that the term "public employee retirement system" refers to "a state or local governmental fiduciary entity entrusted with administering a plan (or plans) and not to the plan itself."

The standards established by GASB-25 apply to a particular pension plan and not to the PERS that administers the plan. However, when a PERS presents separate financial statements of a defined pension plan in its financial report, the standards established by GASB-25 must be observed. If the financial statements of more than one defined benefits pension plan is included in the PERS report, the standards must be applied separately to each plan. The financial statements for each plan should be presented separately in the combining financial statements of the PERS, along with the appropriate schedules and other disclosures required by GASB-25. This chapter illustrates a Pension Trust Fund that is part of a PERS but that is also reported in the financial statements of the plan sponsor (The City of Centerville).

PRACTICE ALERT: The GASB has released an exposure draft, titled "Financial Reporting for Defined Benefit Pension Plans and Note Disclosures for Defined Contribution Plans—an Amendment of GASB Statement No. 25," which seeks to amend GASB-25 as follows:

1. Financial statements for defined benefit pension plans will be a Statement of Plan Net Position and a Statement of Changes in Plan Net Position. These will be very similar to the current Statement of Plan Net Assets and Statement of Changes in Plan Net Assets except for the inclusion of deferred inflows and outflows of resources. These deferred inflows and outflows of resources will be created by the unamortized balances of the difference between projected investment earnings and actual investment earnings in the plan. Those differences would be amortized in a "closed" manner over five years, meaning that year 1 would be amortized in years 1, 2, 3, 4, and 5, with a following year adding a new layer to the amortization.

2. Additions and deductions to plan net assets would largely include employer and employee contributions, net investment income/losses, and administrative and benefit payments.

3. Notes to the basic financial statements of a plan are proposed to be very similar to what is required by GASB-25. However, allocated insurance contracts that are not included as part of plan net assets will also be disclosed in the notes to the basic financial statements. Single employers and cost-sharing multiple employers would also have notes similar to what is currently required.

4. Any plan net pension liability (net of plan assets at fair value and actuarially accrued liabilities) would inure to the primary government or member governments that are part of a plan in proportion to their contributions. This is because the nexus between employer and employee has been rationalized by the GASB as not in existence at the plan level. Any net pension liability is created and reduced by actions of the employer(s). Therefore the actuarial information at the plan level is largely note disclosure. However, at the employer level, a net pension asset or liability would be declared and presented on the face of the statement of plan net position.

5. In calculation of the liability, the discount rate used is proposed to be the long-term rate of return on plan investments blended with the "AA" 30 year or higher tax-exempt bond index rate. Details of this discount rate calculation will be disclosed in the notes to the basic financial statements. Other elements of the actuarial valuation will also be disclosed in the notes. Proposed changes in the actuarial valuation include a requirement to use the "entry age normal" method of attribution and amortization of the liability, any changes to the plan would be

amortized over the estimated remaining service lives of active members and cost-of-living adjustments whether automatic or ad hoc with a pattern of award would be included in service costs.

6. Defined contribution plans are proposed to have minimal changes from current note disclosure. Upon final deliberation, the defined contribution pension standards contained within GASB-26 may be rescinded.

The proposed effective date is for periods beginning after June 15, 2014, with prior periods adjusted. Required supplementary information would need to be included for the most recent 10 valuations. Therefore, those disclosures will need to be restated, as would any statistical information. Further details on this and the companion exposure draft for employers and agent multiple employer plans can be found in CCH's *Governmental GAAP Guide*. Post-employment benefits other than pensions will likely have an omnibus exposure draft released within a short time frame after the closure of deliberations on these two exposure drafts.

MEASUREMENT FOCUS AND BASIS OF ACCOUNTING

For the most part, a Pension Trust (and Other Employee Benefits) Fund accounts for its assets on an accrual basis; however, liabilities are generally reported on essentially a modified accrual basis. A pension plan invests in a variety of instruments, including equity securities, debt securities, various types of mutual funds, and perhaps derivatives. Most investments held by a pension plan are reported at fair value rather than historical cost. Operating assets, such as buildings, equipment, and leasehold improvements used in the operations of a pension plan, are reported at historical cost. The specific accounting and reporting standards that are followed by a pension plan are established by GASB-31 (Accounting and Financial Reporting for Certain Investments and for External Investment Pools).

No single accounting basis is applicable to the measurement of a pension plan's liabilities. Liabilities related to administrative and investment activities should be reported on an accrual basis, but liabilities related to the plan's obligation for employee benefits should be reported when due and payable as required by the terms of the pension plan.

GASB-26 (Financial Reporting for Postemployment Healthcare Plans Administered by Defined Benefit Pension Plans) addressed financial reporting issues related to postemployment health-care benefits, which included medical, dental, vision, and other health-related benefits provided to terminated employees, retired employees, dependents, and beneficiaries. In general the standards established by GASB-25 were followed for postemployment health-care plans defined in GASB-26.

GASB-43 (Financial Reporting for Postemployment Benefit Plans Other Than Pension (OPEB) Plans) establishes uniform financial reporting standards for OPEB plans and superseded the interim guidance in GASB-26. The standards apply for OPEB trust funds of a plan sponsor or governmental unit employer as well as for stand-alone reports of OPEB plans.

PRACTICE ALERT: GASB-57 (OPEB Measurements by Agent Employers and Agent Multiple-Employer Plans) was issued to clarify certain issues faced by small plans (that have the ability to use the alternative measurement method stipulated in GASB-43). Originally, GASB-43 required that a defined benefit OPEB plans obtain an actuarial valuation. Defined benefit OPEB plans with a total membership of 200 or more are required to obtain an actuarial valuation at least every other year, and plans with a total membership of fewer than 200 or more are required to obtain an actuarial valuation at least every third year. GASB-43 permitted defined benefit OPEB plans with fewer than 100 total plan members to use an alternative measurement method (using mathematics and standard tables) to produce OPEB measures at least every third year. GASB-57 amends those provisions and allows an agent multiple-employer OPEB plan to report an aggregation of results of actuarial valuations of the individual-employer OPEB plans or measurements resulting from use of the alternative measurement method for individual-employer OPEB plans that are eligible. GASB-57 also stipulates that those plans' employers have the same actuarial valuation date. For these provisions, GASB-57 is effective for periods beginning after June 15, 2011, and earlier implementation is encouraged.

FINANCIAL REPORTING AT THE FUND LEVEL

Unlike governmental funds and proprietary funds, the major fund reporting concept does not apply to Pension Trust (and Other Employee Benefits) Funds. GASB-34 requires that fiduciary funds be reported in an entity's financial statements by fund type (Pension [and Other Employee Benefit] Trust Funds, Investment Trust Funds, Private-Purpose Trust Funds, and Agency Funds). If there is more than one pension plan, individual pension plans are presented in the notes to the financial statements unless separate financial statements have been issued. In the latter case, the notes should include information as to how the separate reports may be obtained.

The balances and activities of Pension Trust (and Other Employee Benefits) Funds are presented in the following financial statements at the fund financial statement level:

- Statement of plan net assets

- Statement of changes in plan net assets

The statement of plan net assets reports the pension plan's assets and liabilities; however, there is no need to divide net assets into the three categories (invested in capital assets (net of related debt), restricted net assets, and unrestricted net assets) that must be used in the government-wide financial statements. The equity section of the statement of plan net assets is simply identified as "net assets held in trust for pension benefits."

A pension plan's statement of changes in plan net assets is formatted in a manner to identify (1) additions in net assets, (2) deductions from net assets, and (3) the net increase or decrease in the plan's net assets for the year.

PRACTICE ALERT: GASB:CS-4, introduced deferred inflows and deferred outflows of resources to governmental accounting in June 2007. Deferred inflows and outflows of resources are either acquisitions or consumptions of resources, respectively, that are applicable to future periods. The GASB has issued an exposure draft titled "Financial Reporting of Deferred Outflows of Resources, Deferred Inflows of Resources, and Net Position" that proposes a Statement of Net Position (instead of a Statement of Net Assets), which would incorporate the Deferred Outflows and Inflows of Resources. Net position would include three elements: (1) net investment in capital assets, (2) restricted net position, and (3) unrestricted net position. A new accounting equation would also be implemented. Net Position would be the sum of assets and deferred outflows of resources reduced by liabilities and deferred inflows of resources (deferred positions presented separately from assets and liabilities). If it is approved, the statement would be effective for periods beginning after June 15, 2011. It is likely that upon final deliberation, the GASB will present pension plan information similarly.

FINANCIAL REPORTING AT THE GOVERNMENT-WIDE LEVEL

Financial statements of fiduciary funds are not presented in the government-wide financial statements, because resources of these funds cannot be used to finance a governmental entity's activities. The financial statements are included in the fund financial statements because a governmental entity is financially accountable for those resources even though they belong to other parties (GASB-34, par. 13).

ILLUSTRATIVE TRANSACTIONS

In order to illustrate accounting and financial reporting standards that are observed for Pension Trust (and Other Employee Benefits) Funds (and similar funds), assume that the City of Centerville has the following funds, all of which are administered by the state:

- State Public General Employees Retirement Fund (SPGERF)
- State Public Safety Officers Retirement Fund (SPSORF)
- State Postemployment Healthcare Benefits Fund (SPHBF)

The following entries are made by the state, which administers the funds, but the resulting financial statements must appear in the City's fiduciary fund financial statement section of its financial report.

State Public General Employees Retirement Fund

The City's defined benefits pension agreements for nonpublic safety officers are administered by the State Public General Employees Retirement Fund (SPGERF). The trust fund's trial balance for the beginning of the fiscal year is as follows:

	Trial Balance	
Accounts	Debit	Credit
Cash	$720,000	
Investment in debt securities	5,400,000	
Investment in marketable equity securities	13,200,000	
Accrued interest receivable	11,400	
Accounts payable		$ 12,600
Refunds payable and other liabilities		17,400
Fund balance/net assets		19,301,400
Total	$19,331,400	$19,331,400

This section presents illustrative transactions and entries for the SPGERF during the fiscal year ended June 30, 20X2.

Transaction JE09.01—Refunds payable of $17,400 and accounts payable of $12,600 from the previous year were paid:

Accounts	Debit	Credit
Refunds payable and other liabilities	17,400	
Accounts payable	12,600	
Cash		30,000

Transaction JE09.02—Accrued interest receivable of $11,400 from the previous year was collected:

Accounts	Debit	Credit
Cash	$11,400	
Accrued interest receivable		$11,400

Transaction JE09.03—During the year, contributions of $4,200,000 and $1,620,000 were received from the City of Centerville and employees, respectively:

Accounts	Debit	Credit
Cash	5,820,000	
Contributions—City of Centerville		4,200,000
Contributions—plan members		1,620,000

Transaction JE09.04—During the year, interest and investment revenue of $192,000 was earned and received:

Accounts	Debit	Credit
Cash	192,000	
Interest and investment revenue		192,000

Transaction JE09.05—The following expenditures were paid during the year:

Benefits to retirees and beneficiaries	$2,520,000
Administrative expenses	192,000
Total	$2,712,000

Accounts	Debit	Credit
Benefits paid	2,520,000	
Administrative expenses	192,000	
Cash		2,712,000

Transaction JE09.06—Refunds of $46,200 were made to employees who were terminated and were not vested in the plan:

Accounts	Debit	Credit
Refunds	46,200	
Cash		46,200

Transaction JE09.07—Additional investments in the marketable equity securities portfolio of $1,200,000 were made:

Accounts	Debit	Credit
Investment in marketable equity securities	1,200,000	
Cash		1,200,000

Transaction JE09.08—Additional investments in the debt securities portfolio of $450,000 were made:

Accounts	Debit	Credit
Investment in debt securities	450,000	
Cash		450,000

Transaction JE09.09—An investment in the marketable equity securities portfolio that had a carrying value of $198,000 was sold for $240,000:

Accounts	Debit	Credit
Cash	240,000	
Investment in marketable equity securities		198,000
Interest and investment revenue		42,000

Transaction JE09.10—Administrative expenses of $17,400 and refunds due to terminated employees of $13,800 accrued at the end of the year:

Accounts	Debit	Credit
Administrative expenses	17,400	
Refunds	13,800	
Accounts payable		17,400
Refunds payable and other liabilities		13,800

Transaction JE09.11—Accrued interest at the end of the year was $18,600:

Accounts	Debit	Credit
Accrued interest receivable	18,600	
Interest and investment revenue		18,600

Transaction JE09.12—The net appreciation in the fair value of the marketable equities portfolio was $25,800 and the marketable debt portfolio was $13,200 at the end of the year:

Accounts	Debit	Credit
Investment in marketable equity securities	25,800	
Investment in debt securities	13,200	
Interest and investment revenue		39,000

After the transactions for the year are posted, the year-end trial balance (June 30, 20X2) for the SPGERF appears as follows:

	Adjusted Trial Balance	
Accounts	Debit	Credit
Cash	$ 2,545,200	
Investment in debt securities	6,613,200	
Investment in marketable equity securities	13,477,800	
Accrued interest receivable	18,600	
Accounts payable		$17,400
Refunds payable and other liabilities		13,800
Fund balance/net assets		19,301,400
Interest and investment revenue		291,600
Contributions—City of Centerville		4,200,000
Contributions—plan members		1,620,000
Administrative expenses	209,400	
Refunds	60,000	
Benefits paid	2,520,000	
Totals	$25,444,200	$25,444,200

The worksheet that summarizes the journal entries for the SPGERF for the year-end trial balance is presented in Appendix 9A.

State Public Safety Officers Retirement Fund

The City's defined benefits pension agreements for public safety officers are administered by the State Public Safety Officers Retirement Fund (SPSORF). The trust fund's trial balance for the beginning of the fiscal year is as follows:

	Trial Balance	
Accounts	Debit	Credit
Cash	$ 360,000	
Investment in debt securities	2,700,000	
Investment in marketable equity securities	6,600,000	
Accrued interest receivable	5,700	
Accounts payable		$ 6,300
Refunds payable and other liabilities		8,700
Fund balance/net assets		9,650,700
Totals	$9,665,700	$9,665,700

This section presents illustrative transactions and entries for the SPSORF during the fiscal year ended June 30, 20X2.

Transaction JE09.13—Refunds payable of $8,700 and accounts payable of $6,300 from the previous year were paid:

Accounts	Debit	Credit
Refunds payable and other liabilities	8,700	
Accounts payable	6,300	
Cash		15,000

Transaction JE09.14—Accrued interest receivable of $5,700 from the previous year was collected:

Accounts	Debit	Credit
Cash	5,700	
Accrued interest receivable		5,700

Transaction JE09.15—During the year contributions of $2,100,000 and $810,000 were received from the City of Centerville and employees, respectively:

Accounts	Debit	Credit
Cash	2,910,000	
Contributions—City of Centerville		2,100,000
Contributions—plan members		810,000

Transaction JE09.16—During the year interest and investment revenue of $96,000 was earned and received:

Accounts	Debit	Credit
Cash	96,000	
Interest and investment revenue		96,000

Transaction JE09.17—The following expenditures were made during the year:

Benefits to retirees and beneficiaries	$1,260,000
Administrative expenses	96,000
Total	$1,356,000

Accounts	Debit	Credit
Benefits paid	1,260,000	
Administrative expenses	96,000	
Cash		1,356,000

Transaction JE09.18—Refunds of $23,100 were made to employees who were terminated and were not vested in the plan:

Accounts	Debit	Credit
Refunds	23,100	
Cash		23,100

Transaction JE09.19—Additional investments in the marketable equity securities portfolio of $600,000 were made:

Accounts	Debit	Credit
Investment in marketable equity securities	600,000	
Cash		600,000

Transaction JE09.20—Additional investments in the debt securities portfolio of $225,000 were made:

Accounts	Debit	Credit
Investment in debt securities	225,000	
Cash		225,000

Transaction JE09.21—An investment in the marketable equity securities portfolio that had a carrying value of $99,000 was sold for $120,000:

Accounts	Debit	Credit
Cash	120,000	
Investment in marketable equity securities		99,000
Interest and investment revenue		21,000

Transaction JE09.22—Administrative expenses of $8,700 and refunds due to terminated employees of $6,900 were accrued at the end of the year:

Accounts	Debit	Credit
Administrative expenses	8,700	
Refunds	6,900	
Accounts payable		8,700
Refunds payable and other liabilities		6,900

Transaction JE09.23—Accrued interest at the end of the year was $9,300:

Accounts	Debit	Credit
Accrued interest receivable	9,300	
Interest and investment revenue		9,300

Transaction JE09.24—The net appreciation in the fair value of the marketable equities portfolio was $12,900 and the marketable debt portfolio was $6,600 at the end of the year:

Accounts	Debit	Credit
Investment in marketable equity securities	12,900	
Investment in debt securities	6,600	
Interest and investment revenue		19,500

After the transactions for the year are posted, the year-end trial balance (June 30, 20X2) for the SPSORF appears as follows:

Accounts	Adjusted Trial Balance Debit	Credit
Cash	$1,272,600	
Investment in debt securities	3,306,600	
Investment in marketable equity securities	6,738,900	

Accounts	Adjusted Trial Balance	
	Debit	Credit
Accrued interest receivable	9,300	
Accounts payable		$8,700
Refunds payable and other liabilities		6,900
Fund balance/net assets		9,650,700
Interest and investment revenue		145,800
Contributions—City of Centerville		2,100,000
Contributions—plan members		810,000
Administrative expenses	104,700	
Refunds	30,000	
Benefits paid	1,260,000	
Totals	$12,722,100	$12,722,100

The worksheet that summarizes the journal entries for the SPSORF for the year-end trial balance is presented in Appendix 9B.

State Postemployment Healthcare Benefits Fund (SPHBF)

The City's postemployment health-care benefit plans are administered by the State Postemployment Healthcare Benefits Fund (SPHBF). The trust fund's trial balance for the beginning of the fiscal year is as follows:

Accounts	Trial Balance	
	Debit	Credit
Cash	$ 120,000	
Investment in debt securities	900,000	
Investment in marketable equity securities	2,200,000	
Accrued interest receivable	1,900	
Accounts payable		$ 2,100
Refunds payable and other liabilities		2,900
Fund balance/net assets		3,216,900
Totals	$3,221,900	$3,221,900

Transaction JE09.25—Refunds payable of $2,700 and accounts payable of $2,100 from the previous year were paid:

Accounts	Debit	Credit
Refunds payable and other liabilities	2,700	
Accounts payable	2,100	
Cash		4,800

Transaction JE09.26—Accrued interest receivable of $1,900 from the previous year was collected:

Accounts	Debit	Credit
Cash	1,900	
Accrued interest receivable		1,900

Transaction JE09.27—During the year contributions of $700,000 and $270,000 were received from the City of Centerville and employees, respectively:

Accounts	Debit	Credit
Cash	970,000	
Contributions—City of Centerville		700,000
Contributions—plan members		270,000

Transaction JE09.28—During the year interest and investment revenue of $32,000 was earned and received:

Accounts	Debit	Credit
Cash	32,000	
Interest and investment revenue		32,000

Transaction JE09.29—The following expenditures were made during the year:

Benefits to retirees and beneficiaries	$420,000
Administrative expenses	32,000
Total	$452,000

Accounts	Debit	Credit
Benefits paid	420,000	
Administrative expenses	32,000	
Cash		452,000

Transaction JE09.30—Refunds of $7,700 were made to employees who were terminated and were not vested in the plan:

Accounts	Debit	Credit
Refunds	7,700	
Cash		7,700

Transaction JE09.31—Additional investments in the marketable equity securities portfolio of $200,000 were made:

Accounts	Debit	Credit
Investment in marketable equity securities	200,000	
Cash		200,000

Transaction JE09.32—Additional investments in the debt securities portfolio of $75,000 were made:

Accounts	Debit	Credit
Investment in debt securities	75,000	
Cash		75,000

Transaction JE09.33—An investment in the marketable equity securities portfolio that had a carrying value of $33,000 was sold for $40,000:

Accounts	Debit	Credit
Cash	40,000	
Investment in marketable equity securities		33,000
Interest and investment revenue		7,000

Transaction JE09.34—Administrative expenses of $2,900 and refunds due to terminated employees of $2,300 were accrued at the end of the year:

Accounts	Debit	Credit
Administrative expenses	2,900	
Refunds	2,300	
Accounts payable		2,900
Refunds payable and other liabilities		2,300

Transaction JE09.35—Accrued interest at the end of the year was $3,100:

Accounts	Debit	Credit
Accrued interest receivable	3,100	
Interest and investment revenue		3,100

Transaction JE09.36—The net appreciation in the fair value of the marketable equities portfolio was $4,300 and the marketable debt portfolio was $2,200 at the end of the year:

Accounts	Debit	Credit
Investment in marketable equity securities	4,300	
Investment in debt securities	2,200	
Interest and investment revenue		6,500

After the transactions for the year are posted the year-end trial balance (June 30, 20X2) for the SPHBF appears as follows:

Accounts	Adjusted Trial Balance Debit	Credit
Cash	$ 424,400	
Investment in debt securities	1,102,200	
Investment in marketable equity securities	2,246,300	
Accrued interest receivable	3,100	
Accounts payable		$ 2,900
Refunds payable and other liabilities		2,500
Fund balance/net assets		3,216,900
Interest and investment revenue		48,600
Contributions—City of Centerville		700,000
Contributions—plan members		270,000
Administrative expenses	34,900	
Refunds	10,000	
Benefits paid	420,000	
Totals	$4,240,900	$4,240,900

The worksheet that summarizes the journal entries for the SPHBF for the year-end trial balance is presented in Appendix 9C.

Medicare Part D Payments

GASB Technical Bulletin No. 2006-1 (Accounting and Financial Reporting by Employers and OPEB Plans for Payments from the Federal Government Pursuant to the Retiree Drug Subsidy Provisions of Medicare Part D) clarifies the proper reporting of payments that an employer or a defined benefit other postemployment benefit (OPEB) plan receives from the federal government under Medicare Part D. Medicare Part D is a federal program that provides prescription drug benefits to eligible Medicare recipients.

A Medicare Part D payment from the federal government to the employer is a "voluntary nonexchange transaction" (as discussed in Chapter 17, "Revenues: Nonexchange and Exchange Transactions," of CCH's *Governmental GAAP Guide*). Accordingly, the employer should recognize an asset and revenue for the payment received following the applicable recognition requirements for voluntary nonexchange transactions. The payment is a transaction that is separate from the exchange of services for salaries and benefits (including postemployment prescription drug benefits) between employer and employees, for which the accounting is addressed in GASB-45. Therefore, a sole or agent employer should apply the measurement requirements of GASB-45 to determine the actuarial accrued liabilities, the annual required contribution of the employer (ARC), and the annual OPEB cost *without reduction* for Medicare Part D payments. In addition, the nonexchange transaction does not affect accounting for employer contributions or the financial reporting presentation by a defined benefit OPEB plan in which an employer participates. A defined benefit OPEB plan administered by a qualifying trust should apply the measurement requirements of GASB-43, as discussed in this chapter, to determine the actuarial accrued liabilities, the ARC, and the annual OPEB cost without reduction for Medicare Part D payments.

A Medicare Part D payment from the federal government to the plan is considered an on-behalf payment for fringe benefits (as discussed in Chapter 17, "Revenues: Nonexchange and Exchange Transactions," of CCH's *Governmental GAAP Guide*). The employer should recognize revenue and expense or expenditures for the payment in accordance with the recognition and measurement requirements for such on-behalf payments, pertaining to an employer that is legally responsible for contributions to the OPEB plan. That is, the employer "should follow accounting standards for that type of transaction to recognize expenditures or expenses and related liabilities or assets."

In the statement of changes in plan net assets, the OPEB plan should separately display contributions from the employer(s) and the on-behalf payment from the federal government. In the schedule of employer contributions, the OPEB plan should include the Medicare Part D payment as on-behalf contributions from the federal government and titling the schedule as the schedule of contributions from the employer(s) and other contributing entities. The plan should present the ARC without reduction for the Medicare Part D payment.

FUND FINANCIAL STATEMENTS

At the fund financial statement level a governmental fund must prepare a statement of fiduciary net assets and a statement of changes in fiduciary net assets; however, fiduciary funds are not subject to the major fund reporting concept but, rather, must be reported by fund type. Based on the adjusted trial balances created above, the following combined trial balance is prepared for the three funds. This adjusted trial balance is used to prepare the fund financial statements illustrated in Chapter 13, "Developing Information for Fund Financial Statements":

	Trial Balances			
Accounts	SPGERF	SPSORF	SPHBF	Total
Cash	$ 2,545,200	$ 1,272,600	$ 424,400	$ 4,242,200
Investment in debt securities	6,613,200	3,306,600	1,102,200	11,022,000
Investment in marketable equity securities	13,477,800	6,738,900	2,246,300	22,463,000
Accrued interest receivable	18,600	9,300	3,100	31,000
Accounts payable	(17,400)	(8,700)	(2,900)	(29,000)
Refunds payable and other liabilities	(13,800)	(6,900)	(2,500)	(23,200)
Fund balance/net assets	(19,301,400)	(9,650,700)	(3,216,900)	(32,169,000)
Interest and investment revenue	(291,600)	(145,800)	(48,600)	(486,000)
Contributions—City of Centerville	(4,200,000)	(2,100,000)	(700,000)	(7,000,000)
Contributions—plan members	(1,620,000)	(810,000)	(270,000)	(2,700,000)
Administrative expenses	209,400	104,700	34,900	349,000
Refunds	60,000	30,000	10,000	100,000
Benefits paid	2,520,000	1,260,000	420,000	4,200,000
Totals	$0	$0	$0	$0

GOVERNMENT-WIDE FINANCIAL STATEMENTS

Fiduciary financial statements are presented only at the fund financial statement level (see Appendix 9D).

APPENDIX 9A: WORKSHEET FOR SUMMARIZING CURRENT TRANSACTIONS: STATE PUBLIC GENERAL EMPLOYEES RETIREMENT FUND (SPGERF)

Accounts	Trial Balance Debit	Trial Balance Credit	Adjustments Debit		Adjustments Credit		Adjusted Trial Balance Debit	Adjusted Trial Balance Credit	Operating Statement Debit	Operating Statement Credit	Balance Sheet Debit	Balance Sheet Credit
Cash	720,000	—	JE09.02	11,400	JE09.01	30,000	2,545,200	—	—	—	2,545,200	—
		—	JE09.03	5,820,000	JE09.05	2,712,000	—	—	—	—	—	—
		—	JE09.04	192,000	JE09.06	46,200	—	—	—	—	—	—
		—	JE09.09	240,000	JE09.07	1,200,000	—	—	—	—	—	—
				—	JE09.08	450,000						
Investment in debt securities	5,400,000	—	JE09.07	1,200,000		—	6,613,200	—	—	—	6,613,200	—
			JE09.12	13,200		—						
Investment in marketable equity securities	13,200,000	—	JE09.08	450,000	JE09.09	198,000	13,477,800	—	—	—	13,477,800	—
			JE09.12	25,800		—						
Accrued interest receivable	11,400	—	JE09.11	18,600	JE09.02	11,400	18,600	—	—	—	18,600	—
Accounts payable	—	12,600	JE09.01	12,600	JE09.10	17,400	—	17,400	—	—	—	17,400

Account	Trial Balance Dr	Trial Balance Cr	Adjustments Dr	(JE)	Adjustments Cr	(JE)	Statement of Changes in Fiduciary Net Assets Dr	Statement of Changes in Fiduciary Net Assets Cr	Statement of Fiduciary Net Assets Dr	Statement of Fiduciary Net Assets Cr
Refunds payable and other liabilities	—	17,400	17,400	JE09.01	13,800	—	—	—	—	13,800
Fund balance/net assets	—	19,331,400	—	—	—	—	—	—	—	19,301,400
Interest and investment revenue	—	—	—	—	192,000	JE09.04	—	291,600	—	—
	—	—	—	—	42,000	JE09.09	—	—	—	—
	—	—	—	—	18,600	JE09.11	—	—	—	—
	—	—	—	—	39,000	JE09.12	—	—	—	—
Contributions— City of Centerville	—	—	—	—	4,200,000	JE09.03	—	4,200,000	—	—
Contributions— plan members	—	—	—	—	1,620,000	JE09.03	—	1,620,000	—	—
Administrative expenses	—	—	17,400	JE09.10	—	—	209,400	—	209,400	—
Refunds	—	—	192,000	JE09.05	—	—	—	—	—	—
	—	—	46,200	JE09.06	—	—	60,000	—	60,000	—
	—	—	13,800	JE09.10	—	—	—	—	—	—
Benefits paid	—	—	2,520,000	JE09.05	—	—	2,520,000	—	2,520,000	—
Totals	19,331,400	19,331,400	10,790,400		10,790,400		25,444,200	25,444,200	2,789,400	6,111,600
									19,332,600	22,654,800
Net increase (decrease)								3,322,200	3,322,200	
								6,111,600	6,111,600	22,654,800	22,654,800

APPENDIX 9B: WORKSHEET FOR SUMMARIZING CURRENT TRANSACTIONS: STATE PUBLIC SAFETY OFFICERS RETIREMENT FUND (SPSORF)

Accounts	Trial Balance Debit	Trial Balance Credit	Adjustments (ref) Debit	Adjustments Debit	Adjustments (ref) Credit	Adjustments Credit	Adjusted Trial Balance Debit	Adjusted Trial Balance Credit	Operating Statement Debit	Operating Statement Credit	Balance Sheet Debit	Balance Sheet Credit
Cash	360,000	—	JE09.14	5,700	JE09.13	15,000	1,272,600	—	—	—	1,272,600	—
			JE09.15	2,910,000	JE09.17	1,356,000						
			JE09.16	96,000	JE09.18	23,100						
			JE09.21	120,000	JE09.19	600,000						
					JE09.20	225,000						
Investment in debt securities	2,700,000	—	JE09.19	600,000		—	3,306,600	—	—	—	3,306,600	—
			JE09.24	6,600								
Investment in marketable equity securities	6,600,000	—	JE09.20	225,000	JE09.21	99,000	6,738,900	—	—	—	6,738,900	—
			JE09.24	12,900								
Accrued interest receivable	5,700	—	JE09.23	9,300	JE09.14	5,700	9,300	—	—	—	9,300	—
Accounts payable	—	6,300	JE09.13	6,300	JE09.22	8,700	—	8,700	—	—	—	8,700
Refunds payable and other liabilities	—	8,700	JE09.13	8,700	JE09.22	6,900	—	6,900	—	—	—	6,900
Fund balance/net assets	—	9,650,700		—		—	—	9,650,700	—	—	—	9,650,700

Interest and investment revenue	—	—	—	—	JE09.16	96,000	—	145,800	—	145,800	—
	—	—	—	—	JE09.21	21,000	—	—	—	—	—
	—	—	—	—	JE09.23	9,300	—	—	—	—	—
	—	—	—	—	JE09.24	19,500	—	—	—	—	—
Contributions—City of Centerville	—	—	—	—	JE09.15	2,100,000	—	2,100,000	—	2,100,000	—
Contributions—plan members	—	—	—	—	JE09.15	810,000	—	810,000	—	810,000	—
Administrative expenses	—	—	JE09.22	8,700	—	—	104,700	—	104,700	—	—
	—	—	JE09.17	96,000	—	—	—	—	—	—	—
Refunds	—	—	JE09.18	23,100	—	—	30,000	—	30,000	—	—
	—	—	JE09.22	6,900	—	—	—	—	—	—	—
Benefits paid	—	—	JE09.17	1,260,000	—	—	1,260,000	—	1,260,000	—	—
Totals	9,665,700	9,665,700	—	5,395,200	—	5,395,200	12,722,100	12,722,100	1,394,700	3,055,800	11,327,400 / 9,666,300
Net increase (decrease)	—	—	—	—	—	—	—	—	1,661,100	—	1,661,100
									3,055,800	3,055,800	11,327,400 / 11,327,400

APPENDIX 9C: WORKSHEET FOR SUMMARIZING CURRENT TRANSACTIONS: STATE POSTEMPLOYMENT HEALTHCARE BENEFITS FUND (SPPHBF)

Accounts	Trial Balance Debit	Trial Balance Credit	Adjustments Debit (ref)	Adjustments Debit	Adjustments Credit (ref)	Adjustments Credit	Adjusted Trial Balance Debit	Adjusted Trial Balance Credit	Operating Statement Debit	Operating Statement Credit	Balance Sheet Debit	Balance Sheet Credit
Cash	120,000	—	JE09.26	1,900	JE09.25	4,800	424,400	—	—	—	424,400	—
			JE09.27	970,000	JE09.29	452,000	—	—	—	—	—	—
			JE09.28	32,000	JE09.30	7,700	—	—	—	—	—	—
			JE09.33	40,000	JE09.31	200,000	—	—	—	—	—	—
				—	JE09.32	75,000	—	—	—	—	—	—
Investment in debt securities	900,000	—	JE09.31	200,000		—	1,102,200	—	—	—	1,102,200	—
			JE09.36	2,200		—	—	—	—	—	—	—
Investment in marketable equity securities	2,200,000	—	JE09.32	75,000	JE09.33	33,000	2,246,300	—	—	—	2,246,300	—
			JE09.36	4,300		—	—	—	—	—	—	—
Accrued interest receivable	1,900	—	JE09.35	3,100	JE09.26	1,900	3,100	—	—	—	3,100	—
Accounts payable	—	2,100	JE09.25	2,100	JE09.34	2,900	—	2,900	—	—	—	2,900
Refunds payable and other liabilities	—	2,900	JE09.25	2,700	JE09.34	2,300	—	2,500	—	—	—	2,500
Fund balance/net assets	—	3,216,900		—		—	—	3,216,900	—	—	—	3,216,900
	3,216,900	3,216,900										

Account	TB Dr	TB Cr	Adj. Ref	Adj. Dr	Adj. Ref	Adj. Cr	Adj. TB Dr	Adj. TB Cr	SC Dr	SC Cr	NP Dr	NP Cr
Interest and investment revenue	—	—	—	—	JE09.28	32,000	—	48,600	—	48,600	—	—
					JE09.33	7,000						
					JE09.35	3,100						
					JE09.36	6,500						
Contributions—City of Centerville	—	—	—	—	JE09.27	700,000	—	700,000	—	700,000	—	—
Contributions—plan members	—	—	—	—	JE09.27	270,000	—	270,000	—	270,000	—	—
Administrative expenses	—	—	JE09.34	2,900	—	—	34,900	—	34,900	—	—	—
			JE09.29	32,000								
Refunds	—	—	JE09.30	7,700	—	—	10,000	—	10,000	—	—	—
			JE09.34	2,300								
Benefits paid	—	—	JE09.29	420,000	—	—	420,000	—	420,000	—	—	—
Totals	3,221,900	3,221,900		1,798,200		1,798,200	4,240,900	4,240,900	464,900	1,018,600	3,776,000	3,222,300
Net increase (decrease)	—	—		—		—	—	—	553,700	—	—	553,700
									1,018,600	1,018,600	3,776,000	3,776,000

APPENDIX 9D: PENSION TRUST FUNDS: GOVERNMENT-WIDE FINANCIAL STATEMENTS

Fiduciary financial statements are presented only at the fund financial statement level.

CHAPTER 10
PRIVATE-PURPOSE TRUST FUNDS

CONTENTS

NATURE OF PRIVATE-PURPOSE TRUST FUNDS

Governmental entities often establish fiduciary relationships between themselves and other parties. Transactions and balances that arise from these relationships are accounted for in fiduciary funds. There are four types of fiduciary funds: (1) Pension Trust Funds (or similar funds), (2) Investment Trust Funds, (3) Private-Purpose Trust Funds, and (4) Agency Funds. In general, these fund types are used to report activities related to resources held and administered (except for an Agency Fund) by a governmental entity when it is acting in a fiduciary capacity for individuals, private organizations, or other governments. GASB-34 notes that if it is not appropriate to account for the resources related to a fiduciary relationship in a Pension Trust Fund, Investment Trust Fund, or Agency Fund, then a Private-Purpose Trust Fund should be used to account for "all other trust arrangements under which principal and income benefit individuals, private organizations, or other governments."

MEASUREMENT FOCUS AND BASIS OF ACCOUNTING

The accrual basis of accounting and the flow of economic resources are used to prepare the financial statements of Private-Purpose Trust Funds. Under the flow of economic resources measurement focus and accrual basis of accounting, revenues are recognized when earned and expenses are recorded when incurred if these activities are related to exchange and exchange-like activities. In addition, long-lived assets (such as buildings and equipment), if held by the fund, are capitalized and depreciated over their estimated economic lives (GASB-34, par. 16).

As discussed in Chapter 7, "Enterprise Funds," Enterprise Funds can follow either Alternative 1 or Alternative 2 as described in GASB-20 (Accounting and Financial Reporting for Proprietary Funds and Other Governmental Entities That Use Proprietary Fund Accounting). Even though fiduciary funds—including Private-Purpose Trust Funds—use the same accounting basis as Enterprise Funds, they are not allowed to use the two-alternative approach established in GASB-20 (GASB-34, par. 423).

PRACTICE ALERT: GASB-62 (Codification of Accounting and Financial Reporting Guidance Contained in Pre-November 30, 1989 FASB and AICPA Pronouncements) is an omnibus statement that supersedes the provisions of GASB-20 by incorporating into GASB's literature all FASB Statements and Interpretations, APB Opinions, and ARBs no matter when issued except those that conflict with a GASB pronouncement. GASB-62 would also incorporate all AICPA pronouncements. It is effective for periods beginning after December 15, 2011. All the provisions of the aforementioned standards are incorporated into CCH's *Governmental GAAP Guide*; so, little if any change from this edition is expected due to any upcoming promulgation. However, certain items such as governmental combinations that have guidance contained in APB Opinion No. 16, are being researched by GASB and were not included in GASB-62.

FINANCIAL REPORTING AT FUND LEVEL

Unlike governmental funds and proprietary funds, the *major fund* reporting concept does not apply to Private-Purpose Trust Funds. GAAP requires that fiduciary funds be reported in an entity's financial statements by fund type (Pension [and Other Employee Benefit] Trust Funds, Investment Trust Funds, Private-Purpose Trust Funds, and Agency Funds). If there is more than one Private-Purpose Trust Fund, there is no requirement to report the individual funds in combining financial statements.

The GASB's *Comprehensive Implementation Guide* states that when resources or an activity benefits both the government and private parties, two separate funds (Special Revenue Fund and Private-Purpose Trust Fund) should be used unless one of the two activities is a nonmajor activity, in which case the predominant activity would determine which fund type would be used. In some circumstances, a fund's principal or income benefits a discretely presented component unit. The GASB's *Comprehensive Implementation Guide* points out that a discretely presented component unit is part of the financial reporting entity, so it is not an "individual, private organization or other government"; therefore, the resources should be reported in a Special Revenue Fund.

The balances and activities of Private-Purpose Trust Funds are presented in the following financial statements at the fund financial statement level:

- Statement of net assets

- Statement of changes in net assets

The statement of net assets reports the trust fund's assets and liabilities; however, there is no need to divide net assets into the three categories (invested in capital assets [net of related debt], restricted net assets, and unrestricted net assets) that must be used in the government-wide financial statements. The equity section of the statement of net assets is simply identified as "net assets held in trust for" an identified third party.

PRACTICE ALERT: GASB:CS-4 introduced deferred inflows and deferred outflows of resources to governmental accounting in June 2007. Deferred inflows and outflows of resources are either acquisitions or consumptions of resources, respectively, that are applicable to future periods. The GASB has issued an exposure draft titled "Financial Reporting of Deferred Outflows of Resources, Deferred Inflows of Resources, and Net Position," which proposes a Statement of Net Position (instead of a Statement of Net Assets) that would incorporate the Deferred Outflows and Inflows of Resources. Net position would include three elements: (1) net investment in capital assets, (2) restricted net position, and (3) unrestricted net position. A new accounting equation would also be implemented. Net Position would be the sum of assets and deferred outflows of resources reduced by liabilities and deferred inflows of resources (deferred positions presented separately from assets and liabilities). If approved, the statement would be effective for periods beginning after June 15, 2011.

A Private-Purpose Trust Fund's statement of changes in net assets is formatted in a manner to identify (1) additions in net assets, (2) deductions from net assets, and (3) the net increase or decrease in the fund's net assets for the year.

GASB-37 (Basic Financial Statements—and Management's Discussion and Analysis—for State and Local Governments: Omnibus) requires generally that escheat property be reported in the governmental or proprietary fund that ultimately will receive the escheat property. Escheat property that is held for individuals, private organizations, or another government is reported in either (1) a Private-Purpose Trust Fund, (2) an Agency Fund, or (3) the governmental or proprietary fund that reports escheat property. An Agency Fund rather than a Private-Purpose Trust Fund is used when the property holding period is expected to be brief. Escheat property that is reported in a Private-Purpose Trust Fund is reported as an *addition* in the statement of changes in fiduciary net assets and any balance remaining at the end of the accounting period is reported as "held in trust for trust beneficiaries" in the statement of fiduciary net assets. When the escheat property is reported in an Agency Fund, only a statement of fiduciary net assets is prepared. Consistent with the basic standards established by GASB-34, escheat property reported in a Private-Purpose Trust Fund or an Agency Fund is not reported in the entity's government-wide financial statements.

The GASB's *Comprehensive Implementation Guide* raises a question about a governmental unit (sheriff's department) that charges inmates to use pay telephones and uses the proceeds to finance inmate expenditures, such as meals, uniforms, and so forth. The GASB's *Guide* points out that this relationship is not one that would suggest that a Private-Purpose Trust Fund should be used to account for the receipts and the expenditures. Furthermore, if a separate fund is used, it should be a Special Revenue Fund.

FINANCIAL REPORTING AT GOVERNMENT-WIDE LEVEL

Financial statements of fiduciary funds are not presented in the government-wide financial statements, because resources of these funds cannot be used to finance a governmental entity's activities. The financial statements are included in the fund financial statements because a governmental entity is financially accountable for those resources even though they belong to other parties (GASB-34, par. 13).

ILLUSTRATIVE TRANSACTIONS

In order to illustrate accounting and financial reporting standards that are observed for Private-Purpose Trust Funds, assume that the City of Centerville agreed to administer, through an appropriate City Ordinance, the following funds:

- Scholarship Trust Fund
- Emergency Workers' Relief Fund
- Historical Pike Fund

Scholarship Trust Fund

The Scholarship Trust Fund was created several years ago by a group of local educators. Only the investment earnings from the permanent endowment can be used to finance scholarships awarded to deserving students. The fund's trial balance for the beginning of the fiscal year is as follows:

Accounts	Trial Balance	
	Debit	Credit
Cash	$ 2,400	
Investment in debt securities	270,000	
Accounts payable and accrued expenses		$ 3,000
Net assets		269,400
Totals	$272,400	$272,400

This section presents illustrative transactions and entries for the Private-Purpose Trust Fund during the fiscal year ended June 30, 20X2.

Transaction JE10.01—Accounts payable of $3,000 from the previous year were paid:

Accounts	Debit	Credit
Accounts Payable and Accrued Expenses	3,000	
Cash		3,000

Transaction JE10.02—During the year, interest and investment revenue of $24,000 was earned and received:

Accounts	Debit	Credit
Cash	24,000	
Interest and Investment Revenue		24,000

Transaction JE10.03—Scholarships of $31,200 were paid during the year. Approved tuition payments due at the end of the year but unpaid were $3,000:

Accounts	Debit	Credit
Benefits Paid—Scholarship Costs	34,200	
Cash		31,200
Accounts Payable and Accrued Expenses		3,000

Transaction JE10.04—Additional contributions of $24,000 to the permanent endowment of the fund were received from local educators ($18,000) and the City of Centerville (through its General Fund) ($6,000) during the year:

Accounts	Debit	Credit
Cash	24,000	
Contributions—Individuals		18,000
Contributions—City of Centerville		6,000

Transaction JE10.05—Additional investments of $15,000 in bonds for the year were made:

Accounts	Debit	Credit
Investments in Debt Securities	15,000	
Cash		15,000

Transaction JE10.06—At the end of the year, the portfolio of debt securities had increased in value by $5,400:

Accounts	Debit	Credit
Investments in Debt Securities	5,400	
Interest and Investment Revenue		5,400

After the transactions for the year are posted, the year-end trial balance (June 30, 20X2) for the Scholarship Trust Fund appears as follows:

	Adjusted Trial Balance	
Accounts	Debit	Credit
Cash	$ 1,200	
Investment in Debt Securities	290,400	
Accounts payable and accrued expenses		$ 3,000
Net assets		269,400

Accounts	Adjusted Trial Balance	
	Debit	Credit
Interest and investment revenue		29,400
Benefits paid—scholarship costs	34,200	
Contributions—individuals		18,000
Contributions—City of Centerville		6,000
Totals	$325,800	$325,800

The worksheet that summarizes the journal entries for the Scholarship Trust Fund for the year-end trial balance is presented in Appendix 10A.

Emergency Workers' Relief Fund

The Emergency Workers' Relief Fund was created for the benefit of emergency workers who have been killed or injured in the line of duty and their immediate family members. Expenses of the fund are financed by voluntary contributions from the City, local businesses, and citizens of the community. The fund's trial balance for the beginning of the fiscal year is as follows:

Accounts	Trial Balance	
	Debit	Credit
Cash	$ 1,200	
Investment in Debt Securities	135,000	
Accounts payable and accrued expenses		$ 1,500
Net assets		134,700
Totals	$136,200	$136,200

Transaction JE10.07—Accounts payable of $1,500 from the previous year were paid:

Accounts	Debit	Credit
Accounts Payable and Accrued Expenses	1,500	
Cash		1,500

Transaction JE10.08—During the year interest and investment revenue of $12,000 was earned and received:

Accounts	Debit	Credit
Cash	12,000	
Interest and Investment Revenue		12,000

Transaction JE10.09—Emergency relief payments of $15,600 were paid during the year. Approved relief payments due at the end of the year but unpaid were $1,500:

Accounts	Debit	Credit
Benefits Paid—Relief Costs	17,100	
Cash		15,600
Accounts Payable and Accrued Expenses		1,500

Transaction JE10.10—Additional contributions of $12,000 to the permanent endowment of the fund were received from local businesses and other contributors ($9,000) and the City of Centerville (through its General Fund) ($3,000) during the year:

Accounts	Debit	Credit
Cash	12,000	
Contributions—Individuals		9,000
Contributions—City of Centerville		3,000

Transaction JE10.11—Additional investments of $7,500 in bonds for the year were made:

Accounts	Debit	Credit
Investments in Debt Securities	7,500	
Cash		7,500

Transaction JE10.12—At the end of the year, the portfolio of debt securities had increased in value by $2,700:

Accounts	Debit	Credit
Investments in Debt Securities	2,700	
Interest and Investment Revenue		2,700

After the transactions for the year are posted, the year-end trial balance (June 30, 20X2) for the Emergency Workers' Relief Fund appears as follows:

	Adjusted Trial Balance	
Accounts	Debit	Credit
Cash	$ 600	
Investment in Debt Securities	145,200	
Accounts payable and accrued expenses		$ 1,500
Net assets		134,700
Interest and investment revenue		14,700
Benefits paid—relief costs	17,100	
Contributions—individuals		9,000
Contributions—City of Centerville		3,000
Totals	$162,900	$162,900

The worksheet that summarizes the journal entries for the Emergency Workers' Relief Fund for the year-end trial balance is presented in Appendix 10B.

Historical Pike Fund

The Historical Pike Fund was created to preserve and beautify the portion of Old Pike Road that passes through the southeastern corner of the City. Expenses of the fund are financed by voluntary contributions from the City and the local historical society, a not-for-profit organization. The fund's trial balance for the beginning of the fiscal year is as follows:

	Trial Balance	
Accounts	**Debit**	**Credit**
Cash	$ 400	
Investment in Debt Securities	45,000	
Accounts payable and accrued expenses		$ 500
Net assets		44,900
Totals	$45,400	$45,400

This section presents illustrative transactions and entries for the Historical Pike Fund during the fiscal year ended June 30, 20X2.

Transaction JE10.13—Accounts payable of $500 from the previous year were paid:

Accounts	**Debit**	**Credit**
Accounts Payable and Accrued Expenses	500	
Cash		500

Transaction JE10.14—During the year, interest and investment revenue of $4,000 was earned and received:

Accounts	**Debit**	**Credit**
Cash	4,000	
Interest and Investment Revenue		4,000

Transaction JE10.15—Beautification expenses of $5,200 were paid during the year. Approved payments due at the end of the year but unpaid were $500:

Accounts	**Debit**	**Credit**
Benefits Paid—Beautification Costs	5,700	
Cash		5,200
Accounts Payable and Accrued Expenses		500

Transaction JE10.16—Additional contributions of $4,000 to the permanent endowment of the fund were received from the local historical society ($3,000) and the City of Centerville (through its General Fund) ($1,000) during the year:

Accounts	**Debit**	**Credit**
Cash	4,000	
Contributions—Individuals		3,000
Contributions—City of Centerville		1,000

Transaction JE10.17—Additional investments of $2,500 in bonds for the year were made:

Accounts	Debit	Credit
Investments in Debt Securities	2,500	
Cash		2,500

Transaction JE10.18—At the end of the year, the portfolio of debt securities had increased in value by $900:

Accounts	Debit	Credit
Investments in Debt Securities	900	
Interest and Investment Revenue		900

After the transactions for the year are posted, the year-end trial balance (June 30, 20X2) for the Historical Pike Fund appears as follows:

	Adjusted Trial Balance	
Accounts	Debit	Credit
Cash	$ 200	
Investment in Debt Securities	48,400	
Accounts payable and accrued expenses		$ 500
Net assets		44,900
Interest and investment revenue		4,900
Benefits paid—relief costs	5,700	
Contributions—individuals		3,000
Contributions—City of Centerville		1,000
Totals	$54,300	$54,300

The worksheet that summarizes the journal entries for the Historical Pike Fund for the year-end trial balance is presented in Appendix 10C.

FUND FINANCIAL STATEMENTS

Based on the adjusted trial balance created above, the following financial statements are prepared for the three Private-Purpose Trust Funds (see Appendix 10D):

City of Centerville
Statement of Changes in Fiduciary Net Assets
For the Year Ended June 30, 20X2

	Scholarship Trust Fund	Emergency Workers' Relief Fund	Historical Pike Fund	Total
ADDITIONS				
Contributions by:				
External parties	$18,000	$ 9,000	$3,000	$30,000
City of Centerville	6,000	3,000	1,000	10,000
Total Contributions	24,000	12,000	4,000	40,000

City of Centerville
Statement of Changes in Fiduciary Net Assets
For the Year Ended June 30, 20X2

	Scholarship Trust Fund	Emergency Workers' Relief Fund	Historical Pike Fund	Total
Interest and investment revenue	29,400	14,700	4,900	49,000
Total Additions	53,400	26,700	8,900	89,000
DEDUCTIONS				
Benefits paid	34,200	17,100	5,700	57,000
Change in net assets	19,200	9,600	3,200	32,000
Net assets—beginning of the year	269,400	134,700	44,900	449,000
Net assets—end of the year	$288,600	$144,300	$48,100	$481,000

City of Centerville
Statement of Fiduciary Net Assets
June 30, 20X2

	Scholarship Trust Fund	Emergency Workers' Relief Fund	Historical Pike Fund	Total
ASSETS				
Cash	$1,200	$600	$200	$2,000
Investments in debt securities	290,400	145,200	48,400	484,000
Total Assets	291,600	145,800	48,600	486,000
LIABILITIES				
Accounts payable and accrued expenses	3,000	1,500	500	5,000
Total Liabilities	3,000	1,500	500	5,000
NET ASSETS				
Held in trust for external parties	$288,600	$144,300	$48,100	$481,000

The financial statements for the three Private-Purpose Trust Funds are used later, in Chapter 13, "Developing Information for Fund Financial Statements."

GOVERNMENT-WIDE FINANCIAL STATEMENTS

Fiduciary fund financial statements are presented only at the fund financial statement level (see Appendix 10E).

APPENDIX 10A: WORKSHEET FOR SUMMARIZING CURRENT TRANSACTIONS: PRIVATE-PURPOSE TRUST FUND (SCHOLARSHIP FUND)

Accounts	Trial Balance Debit	Trial Balance Credit	Adjustments Debit	Adjustments Credit	Adjusted Trial Balance Debit	Adjusted Trial Balance Credit	Operating Statement Debit	Operating Statement Credit	Balance Sheet Debit	Balance Sheet Credit
Cash	2,400	—	JE10.02 24,000; JE10.04 24,000	JE10.01 3,000; JE10.03 31,200; JE10.05 15,000	1,200	—	—	—	1,200	—
Investment in debt securities	270,000	—	JE10.05 15,000; JE10.06 5,400	—	290,400	—	—	—	290,400	—
Accounts payable and accrued expenses	—	3,000	JE10.01 3,000	JE10.03 3,000	—	3,000	—	—	—	3,000
Net assets	—	269,400	—	—	—	269,400	—	—	—	269,400
Interest and investment revenue	—	—	—	JE10.02 24,000; JE10.06 5,400	—	29,400	—	29,400	—	—
Benefits paid—scholarships	—	—	JE10.03 34,200	—	34,200	—	34,200	—	—	—
Contributions—individuals	—	—	—	JE10.04 18,000	—	18,000	—	18,000	—	—
Contributions—City of Centerville	—	—	—	JE10.04 6,000	—	6,000	—	6,000	—	—
Totals	272,400	272,400	105,600	105,600	325,800	325,800	34,200	53,400	291,600	272,400
Net increase (decrease)							19,200	—	—	19,200
							53,400	53,400	291,600	291,600

APPENDIX 10B: WORKSHEET FOR SUMMARIZING CURRENT TRANSACTIONS: PRIVATE-PURPOSE TRUST FUND (EMERGENCY WORKERS' RELIEF FUND)

Accounts	Trial Balance Debit	Trial Balance Credit	Adjustments (ref)	Adjustments Debit	Adjustments (ref)	Adjustments Credit	Adjusted Trial Balance Debit	Adjusted Trial Balance Credit	Operating Statement Debit	Operating Statement Credit	Balance Sheet Debit	Balance Sheet Credit
Cash	1,200	—	JE10.08	12,000	JE10.07	1,500	600	—	—	—	600	—
			JE10.10	12,000	JE10.09	15,600						
				—	JE10.11	7,500						
Investment in debt securities	135,000	—	JE10.11	7,500		—	145,200	—	—	—	145,200	—
			JE10.12	2,700								
Accounts payable and accrued expenses	—	1,500	JE10.07	1,500	JE10.09	1,500	—	1,500	—	—	—	1,500
Net assets	—	134,700		—		—	—	134,700	—	—	—	134,700
Interest and investment revenue	—	—		—	JE10.08	12,000	—	14,700	—	14,700	—	—
				—	JE10.12	2,700						
Benefits paid—relief costs	—	—	JE10.09	17,100		—	17,100	—	17,100	—	—	—
Contributions—external parties	—	—		—	JE10.10	9,000	—	9,000	—	9,000	—	—
Contributions—City of Centerville	—	—		—	JE10.10	3,000	—	3,000	—	3,000	—	—
Totals	136,200	136,200		52,800		52,800	162,900	162,900	17,100	26,700	145,800	136,200
Net increase (decrease)									9,600		—	9,600
									26,700	26,700	145,800	145,800

APPENDIX 10C: WORKSHEET FOR SUMMARIZING CURRENT TRANSACTIONS: PRIVATE-PURPOSE TRUST FUND (HISTORICAL PIKE FUND)

Accounts	Trial Balance Debit	Trial Balance Credit	Adjustments Debit Ref	Adjustments Debit	Adjustments Credit Ref	Adjustments Credit	Adjusted Trial Balance Debit	Adjusted Trial Balance Credit	Operating Statement Debit	Operating Statement Credit	Balance Sheet Debit	Balance Sheet Credit
Cash	400	—	JE10.14 JE10.16	4,000 4,000	JE10.13 JE10.15 JE10.17	500 5,200 2,500	200	—	—	—	200	—
Investment in debt securities	45,000	—	JE10.17 JE10.18	2,500 900		—	48,400	—	—	—	48,400	—
Accounts payable and accrued expenses	—	500	JE10.13	500	JE10.15	500	—	500	—	—	—	500
Net assets	—	44,900		—		—	—	44,900	—	—	—	44,900
Interest and investment revenue	—	—		—	JE10.14 JE10.18	4,000 900	—	4,900	—	4,900	—	—
Benefits paid— beautification costs	—	—	JE10.15	5,700		—	5,700	—	5,700	—	—	—
Contributions—external parties	—	—		—	JE10.16	3,000	—	3,000	—	3,000	—	—
Contributions—City of Centerville	—	—		—	JE10.16	1,000	—	1,000	—	1,000	—	—
Totals	45,400	45,400		17,600		17,600	54,300	54,300	5,700	8,900	48,600	45,400
Net increase (decrease)									3,200			3,200
									8,900	8,900	48,600	48,600

APPENDIX 10D: PRIVATE-PURPOSE TRUST FUNDS: STATEMENT OF FIDUCIARY NET ASSETS AND CHANGES IN FIDUCIARY NET ASSETS

City of Centerville
Statement of Changes in Fiduciary Net Assets
For the Year Ended June 30, 20X1

	Scholarship Trust Fund	Emergency Workers' Relief Fund	Historical Pike Fund	Total
ADDITIONS				
Contributions by:				
External parties	$ 18,000	$ 9,000	$ 3,000	$ 30,000
City of Centerville	6,000	3,000	1,000	10,000
Total Contributions	24,000	12,000	4,000	40,000
Interest and investment revenue	29,400	14,700	4,900	49,000
Total additions	53,400	26,700	8,900	89,000
DEDUCTIONS				
Benefits paid	34,200	17,100	5,700	57,000
Change in net assets	19,200	9,600	3,200	32,000
Net assets—beginning of the year	269,400	134,700	44,900	449,000
Net assets—end of the year	$288,600	$144,300	$48,100	$481,000

City of Centerville
Statement of Fiduciary Net Assets
June 30, 20X1

	Scholarship Trust Fund	Emergency Workers' Relief Fund	Historical Pike Fund	Total
ASSETS				
Cash	$ 1,200	$ 600	$ 200	$ 2,000
Investments in debt securities	290,400	145,200	48,400	484,000
Total Assets	291,600	145,800	48,600	486,000
LIABILITIES				
Accounts payable and accrued expenses	3,000	1,500	500	5,000
Total Liabilities	3,000	1,500	500	5,000
NET ASSETS				
Held in trust for external parties	$288,600	$144,300	$48,100	$481,000

APPENDIX 10E: PRIVATE-PURPOSE TRUST FUNDS: GOVERNMENT-WIDE FINANCIAL STATEMENTS

Fiduciary fund financial statements are presented only at the fund financial statement level.

CHAPTER 11
INVESTMENT TRUST FUNDS AND INDIVIDUAL INVESTMENT ACCOUNTS

CONTENTS

NATURE OF INVESTMENT TRUST FUNDS

A governmental entity may pool resources into a single pool for investment purposes. The participants in the investment activity may include internal participants or external participants or both. If the participants include only internal parties, the arrangement is referred to as an internal investment pool, which is defined as follows:

> An arrangement that commingles (pools) the moneys of more than one fund or component unit of a reporting entity. (Investment pools that include participation by legally separate entities that are not part of the same reporting entity as the pool sponsor are not internal investments pools, but rather are external investment pools.)

If participants include only external parties, the arrangement is referred to as an external investment pool, which is defined as

> An arrangement that commingles (pools) the moneys of more than one legally separate entity and invests, on the participants' behalf, in an investment portfolio; one or more of the participants is not part of the sponsor's reporting entity. An external investment pool can be sponsored by an individual gov-

ernment, jointly by more than one government, or by a nongovernmental entity. An investment pool that is sponsored by an individual state or local government is an external investment pool if it includes participation by a legally separate entity that is not part of the same reporting entity as the sponsoring government. If a government-sponsored pool includes only the primary government and its component units, it is an internal investment pool and not an external investment pool.

A governmental entity may pool funds from governmental units that make up its financial reporting entity (internal portion of the pool) and from governmental units that are not part of its financial reporting entity (external portion of the pool). The internal portion of each governmental external investment pool should be allocated to the various funds and component units that make up the financial reporting entity, based on each fund or component unit's equity interest in the investment pool. A sponsoring government should report the external portion of each governmental external investment pool in an Investment Trust Fund.

Individual Investment Accounts

In addition to organizing external investment pools, a governmental entity may create individual investment accounts, which are defined as follows:

> An investment service provided by a governmental entity for other, legally separate entities that are not part of the same reporting entity. With individual investment accounts, specific investments are acquired for individual entities and the income from and changes in the value of those investments affect only the entity for which they were acquired.

Governmental entities that provide individual investment accounts should report those accounts in a separate Investment Trust Fund(s) in a manner similar to the presentation of the external portion of an external investment pool described earlier. However, note disclosures that apply to external investment pools do not apply to individual investment accounts.

When a governmental entity offers an entity an individual investment account service as an alternative (or supplement) to participation in an external investment pool, the individual investment account should be reported in a trust fund separate from that used to report the investment pool.

PRACTICE ALERT: Elements of GASB-59 (Financial Instruments Omnibus) amend activities of investment pools. GASB-31, paragraph 12, is amended by GASB-59, aligning current SEC practice with governmental external investment pool practice with regard to so-called 2a-7-like pools. A 2a7-like pool is an external investment pool that operates in conformity with the Securities and Exchange Commission's (SEC) Rule 2a7 as promulgated under the Investment Company Act of 1940, as amended. Investments in 2a7-like pools are measured at the net asset value per share provided by the pool. The net asset value per share is usually calculated on a basis other than fair value, such as by the "amortized cost" method that provides a net asset value per share that approximates fair value. To qualify as a 2a7-like pool, the pool should satisfy all SEC requirements of Rule 2a7, including that a group of individuals fulfills the functions of a board of directors. If the pool has a principal executive officer of the pool, who can be an elected official, who has the power to enter into contracts and make personnel decisions, however, the investment policies are not set by a separate group of individuals that fulfills the functions of a board of directors or the pool is required to register with the SEC, then the pool is precluded from being considered 2a7-like.

This chapter discusses both external and internal investment pools and individual investment accounts.

MEASUREMENT FOCUS AND BASIS OF ACCOUNTING

The financial statements for fiduciary funds should be based on the flow of economic resources measurement focus and the accrual basis of accounting. The flow of economic resources refers to all of the assets available to the Investment Trust Fund for the purpose of fulfilling its responsibilities to the other parties in the fiduciary relationship. When the flow of economic resources and the accrual basis of accounting are combined, they provide the foundation for generally accepted accounting principles as used by business enterprises in that essentially all assets and liabilities, both current and long-term, are presented in the statement of fiduciary net assets.

An Investment Trust Fund invests in a variety of instruments, including equity securities, debt securities, various types of mutual funds, and perhaps derivatives. These investments should be reported at fair value as described in GASB-31 (Accounting and Financial Reporting for Certain Investments and for External Investment Pools).

FINANCIAL REPORTING AT THE FUND LEVEL

Unlike governmental funds and proprietary funds the major fund reporting concept does not apply to Investment Trust Funds. GASB-34 requires that fiduciary funds be reported in an entity's financial statements by fund type (Pension [and Other Employee Benefit] Trust Funds, Investment Trust Funds, Private-Purpose Trust Funds and Agency Funds).

The balances and activities of Investment Trust Funds are presented in the following financial statements at the fund financial statement level:

- Statement of fiduciary net assets
- Statement of changes in fiduciary net assets

The statement of fiduciary net assets reports the external portion of the trust fund's assets and liabilities; however, there is no need to divide net assets into the three categories (invested in capital assets [net of related debt], restricted net assets, and unrestricted net assets) that must be used in the government-wide financial statements. The equity section of the statement of fiduciary net assets is simply identified as "net assets held in trust for pool participants' benefits."

An Investment Trust Fund's statement of changes in fiduciary net assets is formatted in a manner to identify (1) additions in net assets, (2) deductions from net assets, and (3) the net increase or decrease in the fund's net assets for the year.

PRACTICE POINT: Because these are not governmental funds, GASB-54 does not require analysis as to the level of restricted, committed, assigned, or unrestricted fund balances. Fiduciary funds are inherently restricted net assets.

PRACTICE ALERT: GASB:CS-4, introduced deferred inflows and deferred outflows of resources to governmental accounting in June 2007. Deferred inflows and outflows of resources are either acquisitions or consumptions of resources, respectively, that are applicable to future periods. GASB has issued an exposure draft titled "Financial Reporting of Deferred Outflows of Resources, Deferred Inflows of Resources, and Net Position," which proposes a Statement of Net Position (instead of a Statement of Net Assets) that would incorporate the Deferred Outflows and Inflows of Resources. Net position would include three elements: (1) net investment in capital assets, (2) restricted net position and (3) unrestricted net position. A new accounting equation would also be implemented. Net Position would be the sum of assets and deferred outflows of resources reduced by liabilities and deferred inflows of resources (deferred positions presented separately from assets and liabilities). If it is approved, the statement would be effective for periods beginning after June 15, 2011.

FINANCIAL REPORTING AT THE GOVERNMENT-WIDE LEVEL

Financial statements of fiduciary funds are not presented in the government-wide financial statements, because the resources of these funds cannot be used to finance a governmental entity's activities. The financial statements are included in the fund financial statements because a governmental entity is financially accountable for those resources even though they belong to other parties (GASB-34, par. 13).

ILLUSTRATIVE TRANSACTIONS

In order to illustrate accounting and financial reporting standards that are observed for an Investment Trust Fund, assume that the City of Centerville has the following Investment Trust Funds:

- Equity Investment Pool (EIP)
- Short-Term Fixed Income Investment Pool (STFIIP)
- Reclamation Investment Fund (RIF)

Equity Investment Pool

The EIP has an investment strategy for participants that wish to invest their funds for an intermediate period (1 to 5 years). The investment pool has both an internal participant (through the General Fund) and external participants. The external participants are not part of the City's reporting entity. The trial balance for this fund, including both the internal portion and the external portion, at the beginning of the fiscal year is as follows:

Accounts	Trial Balance	
	Debit	Credit
Cash	$2,000,000	
Investment in short-term instruments	150,000	
Investments in equity securities	2,423,000	
Dividends receivable	4,000	
Interest receivable	1,000	
Other receivables	6,000	
Other assets	3,000	
Accounts payable		$ 12,000
Demand loan payable to bank		75,000
Fund balance/net assets		4,500,000
Totals	$4,587,000	$4,587,000

At the beginning of the year, the internal equity interest in the fund balance at the beginning of the year is $1,800,000 ($4,500,000 × 40%), which is based on a 40% interest in the net assets of the fund. The equity interest is reported in the trial balance of the General Fund (Interest in Equity Investment Pool) in Chapter 2, "The General Fund."

This section presents illustrative transactions and entries for the EIP during the fiscal year ended June 30, 20X2.

Transaction JE11.01—Accounts payable of $12,000 from the previous year were paid:

Accounts	Debit	Credit
Accounts payable	12,000	
Cash		12,000

Transaction JE11.02—Dividends receivable ($4,000) and interest receivable ($1,000) from the previous year were received:

Accounts	Debit	Credit
Cash	5,000	
Dividends receivable		4,000
Interest receivable		1,000

Transaction JE11.03—The following expenses were incurred during the period, of which $230,000 were paid:

Investment advisory fees	$ 120,000
Professional fees	80,000
Custodian and transfer agent fees	45,000
Interest	7,000
Total	$ 252,000

Accounts	Debit	Credit
Investment advisory fees expense	120,000	
Professional fees expense	80,000	
Custodian and transfer agent fees expense	45,000	
Interest expense	7,000	
Cash		230,000
Accounts payable		22,000

Transaction JE11.04—During the year additional investments of $200,000 were received from the General Fund:

Accounts	Debit	Credit
Cash	200,000	
Principal contributions from internal participants		200,000

Transaction JE11.05—During the year additional investments of $300,000 were received from the external participants in the investment fund:

Accounts	Debit	Credit
Cash	300,000	
Principal contributions from external participants		300,000

Transaction JE11.06—The following revenue was earned during the period, of which dividends of $45,000 and interest of $7,000 were received in cash:

Dividends	$52,000
Interest	9,000
Total	$61,000

Accounts	Debit	Credit
Cash	52,000	
Dividends receivable	7,000	
Interest receivable	2,000	
Dividend income		52,000
Interest income		9,000

Transaction JE11.07—Additional equity securities of $3,500,000 were acquired during the year:

Accounts	Debit	Credit
Investment in equity securities	3,500,000	
Cash		3,500,000

Transaction JE11.08—Equity securities with a carrying value of $3,000,000 were sold for $3,400,000:

Accounts	Debit	Credit
Cash	3,400,000	
Investment in equity securities		3,000,000
Change in fair value of investments (revenue)		400,000

PRACTICE POINT: Alternatively, the credit to change in fair value of investments could be credited to "realized investment gains and losses," "investment revenue," or something similar that segregates realized gains and losses from unrealized gains and losses (market value adjustments). For simplicity, most management discussions and analyses portray unrealized and realized amounts as "net investment income (loss)."

Transaction JE11.09—Additional short-term investments of $220,000 were made during the year:

Accounts	Debit	Credit
Investment in short-term instruments	220,000	
Cash		220,000

Transaction JE11.10—Short-term investments of $350,000 matured and were collected during the year:

Accounts	Debit	Credit
Cash	350,000	
Investment in short-term instruments		350,000

Transaction JE11.11—Withdrawals of $550,000 were made through the General Fund during the year:

Accounts	Debit	Credit
Withdrawals by internal participants	550,000	
Cash		550,000

Sometimes a fund overdraws its position in an internal investment pool. Under this circumstance, the AICPA's *State and Local Governments—Audit and Accounting Guide* requires that the fund that overdraws its position report an interfund payable and the fund that is assumed (based on management's discretion) to have funded the overdraft reports an interfund receivable. The accounting for the overdraft and assumed coverage of the overdraft is the same no matter which fund types are involved. For example, an overdraft between two funds of the governmental fund category would be treated the same way as an overdraft between funds that do not belong to the same fund category (for example, the General Fund may fund an overdraft by an Enterprise Fund). The interfund loan is not eliminated when the fund financial statements are prepared; however, the treatment of the interfund loan at the government-wide financial statement level would depend on the fund categories involved. For example, an interfund loan between two governmental funds would be eliminated; however, if the interfund loan was between a governmental fund and an Enterprise Fund, the amounts would be reported as part of the internal balance presented on the statement of net assets. The AICPA Audit Guide points out that care must be taken so that an overdraft funding arrangement does not violate a prohibition established by the governmental entity against such actions.

Transaction JE11.12—Withdrawals of $825,000 were made by the external participants during the year:

Accounts	Debit	Credit
Withdrawals by external participants	825,000	
Cash		825,000

Transaction JE11.13 (Adjustment)—The equity investment portfolio held by the pool has a net increase in fair value of $476,000 at the end of the year:

Accounts	Debit	Credit
Investment in equity securities	476,000	
Change in fair value of investments (revenue)		476,000

Transaction JE11.14 (Adjustment)—The short-term investment portfolio held by the pool has a net increase in fair value of $40,000 at the end of the year:

Accounts	Debit	Credit
Investment in short-term instruments	40,000	
Change in fair value of investments (revenue)		40,000

PRACTICE POINT: Alternatively, the credit to change in fair value of investments could be credited in the case of JE11.13 and JE11.14 to "unrealized investment gains and losses."

After the transactions for the year are posted, the year-end trial balance (June 30, 20X2) for the EIP appears as follows:

	Adjusted Trial Balance	
Accounts	Debit	Credit
Cash	$ 970,000	
Investment in short-term instruments	60,000	
Investment in equity securities	3,399,000	
Dividends receivable	7,000	
Interest receivable	2,000	
Other receivables	6,000	
Other assets	3,000	
Accounts payable		$ 22,000
Demand loan payable to bank		75,000
Fund balance/net assets		4,500,000
Dividend income		52,000
Interest income		9,000
Change in fair value of investments		916,000
Principal contributions from internal participants		200,000
Principal contributions from external participants		300,000
Investment advisory fees expenses	120,000	
Professional fees expense	80,000	
Custodial and transfer agent fees expenses	45,000	
Interest expense	7,000	
Withdrawals by internal participants	550,000	

Accounts	Adjusted Trial Balance	
	Debit	Credit
Withdrawals by external participants	825,000	
Totals	$6,074,000	$6,074,000

The following financial statements are prepared for the fund, which is based on the assumption that the equity interest in the fund by the internal participant is 40%:

PRACTICE POINT: For simplicity, transactions during the year are based on a 40%–60% split between the internal participants and the external participants. In practice, the equity interest would be based on the specific valuation procedures and transactions for all participants.

City of Centerville
Statement of Changes in Fiduciary
Net Assets
for the Year Ended June 30, 20X2

	Total	Internal Portion 40%	External Portion 60%
ADDITIONS			
Principal contributions from internal participants	$ 200,000	$ 200,000	
Principal contributions from external participants	300,000		$300,000
Total contributions from participants	500,000	200,000	300,000
Investment earnings:			
Increase in fair value of investments	916,000	366,400	549,600
Dividend income	52,000	20,800	31,200
Interest income	9,000	3,600	5,400
Total investment earnings	977,000	390,800	586,200
Less: Investment expenses	245,000	98,000	147,000
Net investment earnings	732,000	292,800	439,200
Total Additions	1,232,000	492,800	739,200
DEDUCTIONS			
Withdrawals by internal participants	550,000	550,000	
Withdrawals by external participants	825,000		825,000
Interest expenses	7,000	2,800	4,200
Total Deductions	1,382,000	552,800	829,200
Change in net assets	(150,000)	(60,000)	(90,000)
Net assets—beginning of the year	4,500,000	1,800,800	2,700,000
Net assets—end of the year	$4,350,000	$1,740,000	$2,610,000

City of Centerville
Statement of Fiduciary Net Assets
June 30, 20X2

	Total	Internal Portion 40%	External Portion 60%
ASSETS			
Cash	$970,000	$388,000	$582,000
Investment in short-term instruments	60,000	24,000	36,000
Investments in equity securities	3,399,000	1,359,600	2,039,400
Dividends receivable	7,000	2,800	4,200
Interest receivable	2,000	800	1,200
Other receivable	6,000	2,400	3,600
Other assets	3,000	1,200	1,800
Total Assets	4,447,000	1,778,800	2,668,200
LIABILITIES			
Accounts payable	22,000	8,800	13,200
Demand loan payable to bank	75,000	30,000	45,000
Total Liabilities	97,000	38,800	58,200
NET ASSETS			
Internal portion	1,740,000	1,740,800	
External portion	2,610,000		2,610,000
Total Net Assets	$4,350,000	$1,740,000	$2,610,000

As noted earlier, the internal portion of the fund must be allocated back to the internal participants (only the General Fund in this illustration) and the external portion of the fund is reported in the fund financial statements. In order to merge the information into the General Fund the following entry is made (this entry is repeated from JE02.34, in Chapter 2, "The General Fund"):

Accounts	Debit	Credit
Cash	388,000	
Investment in short-term instruments	24,000	
Investments in equity securities	1,359,600	
Dividends receivable	2,800	
Interest receivable	800	
Other receivables	2,400	
Other assets	1,200	
Expenditures—general government	98,000	
Interest expense	2,800	
Accounts payable		8,800
Demand loan payable to bank		30,000
Increase in fair value of investments		366,400
Dividend income		20,800

Accounts	Debit	Credit
Interest income		3,600
Interest in Equity Investment Pool		1,450,000

The worksheet that summarizes the journal entries for the year-end trial balance is presented in Appendix 11A.

Short-Term Fixed Income Investment Pool

The STFIIP offers an investment strategy for participants that wish to invest their funds for a short-term period (less than one year). The investment pool has a single internal participant, and all receipts and disbursements are through the General Fund. The trial balance for the STFIIP at the beginning of the fiscal year is as follows:

Accounts	Trial Balance Debit	Trial Balance Credit
Cash	$125,000	
Investment in short-term instruments	1,400,000	
Interest receivable	7,000	
Other receivable	12,000	
Other assets	4,000	
Accounts payable		$ 3,000
Demand loan payable to bank		45,000
Fund balance		1,500,000
Totals	$1,548,000	$1,548,000

This section presents illustrative transactions and entries for the STFIIP during the fiscal year ended June 30, 20X2.

Transaction JE11.15—Accounts payable of $3,000 from the previous year were paid:

Accounts	Debit	Credit
Accounts payable	3,000	
Cash		3,000

Transaction JE11.16—Interest receivable ($7,000) from the previous year was received:

Accounts	Debit	Credit
Cash	7,000	
Interest receivable		7,000

Transaction JE11.17—The following expenses were incurred during the period, of which $25,000 were paid:

Investment advisory fees	$20,000
Professional fees	3,000
Custodian and transfer agent fees	2,000

	Debit	Credit
Interest	3,000	
Total	$28,000	

Accounts	Debit	Credit
Investment advisory fees expense	20,000	
Professional fees expense	3,000	
Custodian and transfer agent fees expense	2,000	
Interest expense	3,000	
Cash		25,000
Accounts payable		3,000

Transaction JE11.18—During the year additional investments of $500,000 were received from the General Fund:

Accounts	Debit	Credit
Cash	500,000	
Principal contributions from internal participants		500,000

Transaction JE11.19—Interest income of $122,000 was earned during the year, of which $108,000 was received in cash:

Accounts	Debit	Credit
Cash	108,000	
Interest receivable	14,000	
Interest income		122,000

Transaction JE11.20—Additional short-term investments of $220,000 were made during the year:

Accounts	Debit	Credit
Investment in short-term instruments	220,000	
Cash		220,000

Transaction JE11.21—Short-term investments of $225,000 matured and were collected during the year:

Accounts	Debit	Credit
Cash	225,000	
Investment in short-term instruments		225,000

Transaction JE11.22—Withdrawals of $20,000 were made through the General Fund during the year:

Accounts	Debit	Credit
Withdrawals by internal participants	20,000	
Cash		20,000

Transaction JE11.23 (Adjustment)—The short-term investment portfolio held by the pool has a net decrease in fair value of $94,000 at the end of the year:

Accounts	Debit	Credit
Change in fair value of investments (revenue)	94,000	
Investment in short-term instruments		94,000

PRACTICE POINT: Alternatively, the credit to change in fair value of investments could be credited to "realized investment gains and losses," "investment revenue," or something similar that segregates realized gains and losses from unrealized gains and losses (market value adjustments).

After the transactions for the year are posted, the year-end trial balance (June 30, 20X2) for the STFIIP appears as follows:

Accounts	Adjusted Trial Balance	
	Debit	Credit
Cash	$697,000	
Investment in short-term instruments	1,301,000	
Interest receivable	14,000	
Other receivables	12,000	
Other assets	4,000	
Accounts payable		$ 3,000
Demand loan payable to bank		45,000
Fund balance/net assets		1,500,000
Interest income		122,000
Change in fair value of investments	94,000	
Principal contributions from internal participants		500,000
Investment advisory fees expenses	20,000	
Professional fees expense	3,000	
Custodial and transfer agent fees expense	2,000	
Interest expense	3,000	
Withdrawals by internal participants	20,000	
Totals	$2,170,000	$2,170,000

The worksheet that summarizes the journal entries for the year-end trial balance is presented in Appendix 11B.

The following financial statements are prepared for the fund:

City of Centerville
Statement of Changes in Fiduciary
Net Assets
for the Year Ended June 30, 20X2

ADDITIONS

Principal contributions from internal participants	$ 500,000
Total contributions from participants	500,000
Investment earnings:	
Decrease in fair value of investments	(94,000)

City of Centerville
Statement of Changes in Fiduciary
Net Assets
for the Year Ended June 30, 20X2

Interest income	122,000
Total investment earnings (loss)	28,000
Less: Investment expenses	25,000
Net investment earnings (loss)	3,000
Total Additions	503,000
DEDUCTIONS	
Withdrawals by internal participants	20,000
Interest expenses	3,000
Total Deductions	23,000
Change in net assets	480,000
Net assets—beginning of the year	1,500,000
Net assets—end of the year	$1,980,000

City of Centerville
Statement of Fiduciary Net Assets
June 30, 20X2

ASSETS	
Cash	$697,000
Investments in short-term instruments	1,301,000
Interest receivable	14,000
Other receivable	12,000
Other assets	4,000
Total Assets	2,028,000
LIABILITIES	
Accounts payable	3,000
Demand loan payable to bank	45,000
Total Liabilities	48,000
NET ASSETS	
Internal portion	1,980,000
Total Net Assets	$1,980,000

Because there are no external participants in the fund, all of the accounts of the fund are merged into the General Fund. In order to merge the information into the General Fund the following entry is made (this entry is repeated from JE02.34, in Chapter 2, "The General Fund"):

Accounts	Debit	Credit
Cash	697,000	
Investment in short-term instruments	1,301,000	
Interest receivable	14,000	
Other receivable	12,000	
Other assets	4,000	
Expenditures—general government	25,000	
Interest expense	3,000	
Change in fair value of investments	94,000	
Accounts payable		3,000
Demand loan payable to bank		45,000
Interest income		122,000
Interest in short-term fixed income investment pool		1,980,000

Reclamation Investment Fund

The RIF is an individual investment account that is managed exclusively for the benefit of the Centerville Reclamation and Environmental Agency, which is not part of the City's reporting entity. The trial balance for this fund at the beginning of the fiscal year is as follows:

Accounts	Trial Balance	
	Debit	Credit
Cash	$ 26,000	
Investment in short-term instruments	115,000	
Investment in equity securities	1,400,000	
Dividends receivable	2,000	
Interest receivable	3,000	
Other receivables	2,000	
Other assets	5,000	
Accounts payable		$ 1,000
Demand loan payable to bank		12,000
Fund balance/net assets		1,540,000
Totals	$1,553,000	$1,553,000

This section presents illustrative transactions and entries for the RIF during the fiscal year ended June 30, 20X2.

Transaction JE11.24—Accounts payable of $1,000 from the previous year were paid:

Accounts	Debit	Credit
Accounts payable	1,000	
Cash		1,000

Transaction JE11.25—Dividends receivable ($2,000) and interest receivable ($3,000) from the previous year were received:

Accounts	Debit	Credit
Cash	5,000	
Dividends receivable		2,000
Interest receivable		3,000

Transaction JE11.26—The following expenses were incurred during the period, of which $20,000 was paid:

Investment advisory fees	$11,000
Professional fees	7,000
Custodian and transfer agent fees	5,000
Interest	1,000
Total	$24,000

Accounts	Debit	Credit
Investment advisory fees expense	11,000	
Professional fees expense	7,000	
Custodian and transfer agent fees expense	5,000	
Interest expense	1,000	
Cash		20,000
Accounts payable		4,000

Transaction JE11.27—During the year, additional investments of $50,000 were received from the Centerville Reclamation and Environmental Agency:

Accounts	Debit	Credit
Cash	50,000	
Principal contributions from external participants		50,000

Transaction JE11.28—The following revenue was earned during the period, of which dividends of $83,000 and interest of $2,000 were received in cash:

Dividends	$85,000
Interest	3,000
Total	$88,000

Accounts	Debit	Credit
Cash	85,000	
Dividends receivable	2,000	
Interest receivable	1,000	
Dividend income		85,000
Interest income		3,000

Transaction JE11.29—Additional equity securities of $250,000 were acquired during the year:

Accounts	Debit	Credit
Investment in equity securities	250,000	
Cash		250,000

Transaction JE11.30—Equity securities with a carrying value of $300,000 were sold for $320,000:

Accounts	Debit	Credit
Cash	320,000	
Investment in equity securities		300,000
Change in fair value of investments (revenue)		20,000

Transaction JE11.31—Additional short-term investments of $5,000 were made during the year:

Accounts	Debit	Credit
Investment in short-term instruments	5,000	
Cash		5,000

Transaction JE11.32—Short-term investments of $10,000 matured and were collected during the year:

Accounts	Debit	Credit
Cash	10,000	
Investment in short-term instruments		10,000

Transaction JE11.33—Withdrawals of $200,000 were made by the Centerville Reclamation and Environmental Agency:

Accounts	Debit	Credit
Withdrawals by external participants	200,000	
Cash		200,000

Transaction JE11.34 (Adjustment)—The equity investment portfolio held by the fund had a net increase in fair value of $11,000 at the end of the year:

Accounts	Debit	Credit
Investment in equity securities	11,000	
Change in fair value of investments (revenue)		11,000

Transaction JE11.35 (Adjustment)—The short-term investment portfolio held by the pool has a net increase in fair value of $2,000 at the end of the year:

Accounts	Debit	Credit
Investment in short-term instruments	2,000	
Change in fair value of investments (revenue)		2,000

After the transactions for the year are posted, the year-end trial balance (June 30, 20X2) for the RIF appears as follows:

	Adjusted Trial Balance	
Accounts	Debit	Credit
Cash	$ 20,000	
Investment in short-term instruments	112,000	

Accounts	Adjusted Trial Balance	
	Debit	Credit
Investment in equity securities	1,361,000	
Dividends receivable	2,000	
Interest receivable	1,000	
Other receivables	2,000	
Other assets	5,000	
Accounts payable		$ 4,000
Demand loan payable to bank		12,000
Fund balance/net assets		1,540,000
Dividend income		85,000
Interest income		3,000
Change in fair value of investments		33,000
Principal contributions from external participants		50,000
Investment advisory fees expenses	11,000	
Professional fees expense	7,000	
Custodial and transfer agent fees expense	5,000	
Interest expense	1,000	
Withdrawals by external participants	200,000	
Totals	$1,727,000	$1,727,000

The worksheet that summarizes the journal entries for the year-end trial balance is presented in Appendix 11C.

The following financial statements are prepared for the fund:

City of Centerville
Statement of Changes in Fiduciary
Net Assets
for the Year Ended June 30, 20X2

	Total
ADDITIONS	
Principal contributions from external participants	$50,000
Total contributions from participants	50,000
Investment earnings:	
Increase in fair value of investments	33,000
Dividend income	85,000
Interest income	3,000
Total investment earnings	121,000
Less: Investment expenses	23,000
Net investment earnings	98,000
Total Additions	148,000

DEDUCTIONS

Withdrawals by external participants	200,000
Interest expenses	1,000
Total Deductions	201,000
Change in net assets	(53,000)
Net assets—beginning of the year	1,540,000
Net assets—end of the year	$1,487,000

City of Centerville
Statement of Fiduciary Net Assets
June 30, 20X2

ASSETS

Cash	$ 20,000
Investments in short-term instruments	112,000
Investments in equity securities	1,361,000
Dividends receivable	2,000
Interest receivable	1,000
Other receivable	2,000
Other assets	5,000
Total Assets	1,503,000

LIABILITIES

Accounts payable	4,000
Demand loan payable to bank	12,000
Total Liabilities	16,000

NET ASSETS

External portion	1,487,000
Total Net Assets	$1,487,000

FUND FINANCIAL STATEMENTS

At the fund financial statement level fiduciary funds are combined by fund type. The statements include a statement of fiduciary net assets and changes in fiduciary net assets.

The Investment Trust Funds (by fund type) include the following components:

- Equity Investment Pool (External Portion)

- Reclamation Investment Fund (Individual Investment Account)

Based on the information developed in this chapter, the following financial statements are created for the two funds:

City of Centerville
Statement of Changes in Fiduciary
Net Assets
for the Year Ended June 30, 20X2

	EIP (External Portion)	RIF
ADDITIONS		
Principal contributions from external participants	$300,000	$50,000
Total contributions from participants	300,000	50,000
Investment earnings:		
Increase in fair value of investments	549,600	33,000
Dividend income	31,200	85,000
Interest income	5,400	3,000
Total investment earnings	586,200	121,000
Less: Investment expenses	147,000	23,000
Net investment earnings	439,200	98,000
Total Additions	739,200	148,000
DEDUCTIONS		
Withdrawals by external participants	825,000	200,000
Interest expenses	4,200	1,000
Total Deductions	829,200	201,000
Change in net assets	(90,000)	(53,000)
Net assets—beginning of the year	2,700,000	1,540,000
Net assets—end of the year	$2,610,000	$1,487,000

City of Centerville
Statement of Fiduciary Net Assets
June 30, 20X2

	EIP (External Portion)	RIF
ASSETS		
Cash	$582,000	$20,000
Investments in short-term instruments	36,000	112,000
Investments in equity securities	2,039,400	1,361,000
Dividends receivable	4,200	2,000
Interest receivable	1,200	1,000
Other receivable	3,600	2,000
Other assets	1,800	5,000
Total Assets	2,668,200	1,503,000
LIABILITIES		
Accounts payable	13,200	4,000
Demand loan payable to bank	45,000	12,000
Total Liabilities	58,200	16,000

City of Centerville
Statement of Fiduciary Net Assets
June 30, 20X2

ASSETS	EIP (External Portion)	RIF
NET ASSETS		
Held in trust for pool participants	2,610,000	1,487,000
Total Net Assets	$2,610,000	$1,487,000

PRACTICE POINT: Notice, above, that there are no total columns that add the fund activity across. If a total column is included, it must be marked as "memorandum," because totals imply that *all* net assets are commingled and available for spending by any fund. That is not the case.

GOVERNMENT-WIDE FINANCIAL STATEMENTS

Fiduciary financial statements are presented only at the fund financial statement level.

APPENDIX 11A: WORKSHEET FOR SUMMARIZING CURRENT TRANSACTIONS: EQUITY INVESTMENT POOL (EIP)

Accounts	Trial Balance Debit	Trial Balance Credit	Adjustments Debit		Adjustments Credit		Adjusted Trial Balance Debit	Adjusted Trial Balance Credit	Operating Statement Debit	Operating Statement Credit	Balance Sheet Debit	Balance Sheet Credit
Cash	2,000,000	—	JE11.02	5,000	JE11.01	12,000	970,000	—	—	—	970,000	—
			JE11.04	200,000	JE11.07	3,500,000						
			JE11.05	300,000	JE11.09	220,000						
			JE11.06	52,000	JE11.03	230,000						
			JE11.08	3,400,000	JE11.11	550,000						
			JE11.10	350,000	JE11.12	825,000						
Investment in short-term instruments	150,000	—	JE11.09	220,000	JE11.10	350,000	60,000	—	—	—	60,000	—
			JE11.14	40,000								
Investments in equity securities	2,423,000	—	JE11.07	3,500,000	JE11.08	3,000,000	3,399,000	—	—	—	3,399,000	—
			JE11.13	476,000								
Dividends receivable	4,000	—	JE11.06	7,000	JE11.02	4,000	7,000	—	—	—	7,000	—
Interest receivable	1,000	—	JE11.06	2,000	JE11.02	1,000	2,000	—	—	—	2,000	—
Other receivables	6,000	—		—		—	6,000	—	—	—	6,000	—
Other assets	3,000	—		—		—	3,000	—	—	—	3,000	—
Accounts payable	—	12,000	JE11.01	12,000	JE11.03	22,000	—	22,000	—	—	—	22,000
Demand loan payable to bank	—	75,000		—		—	—	75,000	—	—	—	75,000
Fund balance/net assets	—	4,500,000		—		—	—	4,500,000	—	—	—	4,500,000

Accounts	Trial Balance Debit	Trial Balance Credit	Adjustments Ref	Adjustments Debit	Adjustments Ref	Adjustments Credit	Adjusted Trial Balance Debit	Adjusted Trial Balance Credit	Operating Statement Debit	Operating Statement Credit	Balance Sheet Debit	Balance Sheet Credit
Dividend income	—	—		—	JE11.06	52,000	—	52,000	—	52,000	—	—
Interest income	—	—		—	JE11.06	9,000	—	9,000	—	9,000	—	—
Change in fair value of investments	—	—		—	JE11.08	400,000	—	916,000	—	916,000	—	—
					JE11.13	476,000						
					JE11.14	40,000						
Principal contributions from internal participants	—	—		—	JE11.04	200,000	—	200,000	—	200,000	—	—
Principal contributions from external participants	—	—		—	JE11.05	300,000	—	300,000	—	300,000	—	—
Investment advisory fees expenses	—	—	JE11.03	120,000		—	120,000	—	120,000	—	—	—
Professional fees expense	—	—	JE11.03	80,000		—	80,000	—	80,000	—	—	—
Custodial and transfer agent fees expense	—	—	JE11.03	45,000		—	45,000	—	45,000	—	—	—
Interest expense	—	—	JE11.03	7,000		—	7,000	—	7,000	—	—	—
Withdrawals by internal participants	—	—	JE11.11	550,000		—	550,000	—	550,000	—	—	—
Withdrawals by external participants	—	—	JE11.12	825,000		—	825,000	—	825,000	—	—	—
Totals	4,587,000	4,587,000		10,191,000		10,191,000	6,074,000	6,074,000	1,627,000	1,477,000	4,447,000	4,597,000
Net increase (decrease)									(150,000)			(150,000)
									1,477,000	1,477,000	4,447,000	4,447,000

APPENDIX 11B: WORKSHEET FOR SUMMARIZING CURRENT TRANSACTIONS: SHORT-TERM FIXED INCOME INVESTMENT POOL (STFIIP)

Accounts	Trial Balance Debit	Trial Balance Credit	Adjustments Debit		Adjustments Credit		Adjusted Trial Balance Debit	Adjusted Trial Balance Credit	Operating Statement Debit	Operating Statement Credit	Balance Sheet Debit	Balance Sheet Credit
Cash	125,000	—	JE11.16	7,000	JE11.15	3,000	697,000	—	—	—	697,000	—
			JE11.18	500,000	JE11.17	25,000						
			JE11.19	108,000	JE11.20	220,000						
			JE11.21	225,000	JE11.22	20,000						
Investment in short-term instruments	1,400,000	—	JE11.20	220,000	JE11.21	225,000	1,301,000	—	—	—	1,301,000	—
					JE11.23	94,000						
Interest receivable	7,000	—	JE11.19	14,000	JE11.16	7,000	14,000	—	—	—	14,000	—
Other receivables	12,000	—					12,000	—	—	—	12,000	—
Other assets	4,000	—					4,000	—	—	—	4,000	—
Accounts payable		3,000	JE11.15	3,000	JE11.17	3,000	—	3,000	—	—	—	3,000
Demand loan payable to bank		45,000					—	45,000	—	—	—	45,000
Fund balance/net assets		1,500,000					—	1,500,000	—	—	—	1,500,000
Interest income					JE11.19	122,000	—	122,000	—	122,000	—	—
Change in fair value of investments			JE11.23	94,000			94,000	—	94,000	—	—	—
Principal contributions from internal participants					JE11.18	500,000	—	500,000	—	500,000	—	—

Accounts	Trial Balance Debit	Trial Balance Credit		Adjustments Debit	Adjustments Credit	Adjusted Trial Balance Debit	Adjusted Trial Balance Credit	Operating Statement Debit	Operating Statement Credit	Balance Sheet Debit	Balance Sheet Credit
Investment advisory fees expenses	—	—	JE11.17	20,000	—	20,000	—	20,000	—	—	—
Professional fees expense	—	—	JE11.17	3,000	—	3,000	—	3,000	—	—	—
Custodial and transfer agent fees expense	—	—	JE11.17	2,000	—	2,000	—	2,000	—	—	—
Interest expense	—	—	JE11.17	3,000	—	3,000	—	3,000	—	—	—
Withdrawals by internal participants	—	—	JE11.20	20,000	—	20,000	—	20,000	—	—	—
Totals	1,548,000	1,548,000		1,219,000	1,219,000	2,170,000	2,170,000	142,000	622,000	2,028,000	1,548,000
Net increase (decrease)								480,000	—	—	480,000
								622,000	622,000	2,028,000	2,028,000

APPENDIX 11C: WORKSHEET FOR SUMMARIZING CURRENT TRANSACTIONS: RECLAMATION INVESTMENT FUND (RIF)

Accounts	Trial Balance Debit	Trial Balance Credit	Adjustments (Dr ref)	Adjustments Debit	Adjustments (Cr ref)	Adjustments Credit	Adjusted Trial Balance Debit	Adjusted Trial Balance Credit	Operating Statement Debit	Operating Statement Credit	Balance Sheet Debit	Balance Sheet Credit
Cash	26,000	—	JE11.25	5,000	JE11.24	1,000	20,000	—	—	—	20,000	—
			JE11.27	50,000	JE11.26	20,000	—	—	—	—	—	—
			JE11.28	85,000	JE11.29	250,000	—	—	—	—	—	—
			JE11.30	320,000	JE11.31	5,000	—	—	—	—	—	—
			JE11.32	10,000	JE11.33	200,000	—	—	—	—	—	—
Investment in short-term instruments	115,000	—	JE11.31	5,000	JE11.32	10,000	112,000	—	—	—	112,000	—
			JE11.35	2,000		—	—	—	—	—	—	—
Investments in equity securities	1,400,000	—	JE11.29	250,000	JE11.30	300,000	1,361,000	—	—	—	1,361,000	—
			JE11.34	11,000		—	—	—	—	—	—	—
Dividends receivable	2,000	—	JE11.28	2,000	JE11.25	2,000	2,000	—	—	—	2,000	—
Interest receivable	3,000	—	JE11.28	1,000	JE11.25	3,000	1,000	—	—	—	1,000	—
Other receivables	2,000	—		—		—	2,000	—	—	—	2,000	—
Other assets	5,000	—		—		—	5,000	—	—	—	5,000	—
Accounts payable	—	1,000	JE11.24	1,000	JE11.26	4,000	—	4,000	—	—	—	4,000
Demand loan payable to bank	—	12,000		—		—	—	12,000	—	—	—	12,000
Fund balance/net assets	—	1,540,000		—		—	—	1,540,000	—	—	—	1,540,000

Accounts	Trial Balance Debit	Trial Balance Credit	Adjustments Ref (Dr)	Adjustments Debit	Adjustments Ref (Cr)	Adjustments Credit	Adjusted Trial Balance Debit	Adjusted Trial Balance Credit	Operating Statement Debit	Operating Statement Credit	Balance Sheet Debit	Balance Sheet Credit
Dividend income	—	—		—	JE11.28	85,000	—	85,000	—	85,000	—	—
Interest income	—	—		—	JE11.28	3,000	—	3,000	—	3,000	—	—
Change in fair value of investments	—	—		—	JE11.30	20,000	—	33,000	—	33,000	—	—
					JE11.34	11,000						
					JE11.35	2,000						
Principal contributions from external participants	—	—		—	JE11.27	50,000	—	50,000	—	50,000	—	—
Investment advisory fees expenses	—	—	JE11.26	11,000		—	11,000	—	11,000	—	—	—
Professional fees expense	—	—	JE11.26	7,000		—	7,000	—	7,000	—	—	—
Custodial and transfer agent fees expense	—	—	JE11.26	5,000		—	5,000	—	5,000	—	—	—
Interest expense	—	—	JE11.26	1,000		—	1,000	—	1,000	—	—	—
Withdrawals by external participants	—	—	JE11.33	200,000		—	200,000	—	200,000	—	—	—
Totals	1,553,000	1,553,000		966,000		966,000	1,727,000	1,727,000	224,000	171,000	1,503,000	1,556,000
Net increase (decrease)									(53,000)			(53,000)
									171,000	171,000	1,503,000	1,503,000

CHAPTER 12
AGENCY FUNDS

CONTENTS

NATURE OF AGENCY FUNDS

Generally, an Agency Fund is created to act as a custodian for private entities or other governmental units. Assets are recorded by the Agency Fund, held for a period of time as determined by legal contract or circumstances, and then returned to their owners or to some other party that is entitled to receive the resources.

MEASUREMENT FOCUS AND BASIS OF ACCOUNTING

The accrual basis of accounting and the flow of economic resources are used to prepare the financial statements of an Agency Fund. Under the flow of economic resources measurement focus and the accrual basis of accounting as applied to an Agency Fund, resources are recognized when they are required to be provided to the governmental entity and reductions to resources are recorded when resources are actually distributed to the appropriate party under agency agreement (GASB-34, par. 16).

GASB-37 (Basic Financial Statements—and Management's Discussion and Analysis—for State and Local Governments: Omnibus) requires generally that escheat property be reported in the governmental or proprietary fund that ultimately will receive the escheat property. Escheat property that is held for individuals, private organizations, or another government is reported in either

(1) a Private-Purpose Trust Fund, (2) an Agency Fund, or (3) the governmental or proprietary fund that reports escheat property. An Agency Fund rather than a Private-Purpose Trust Fund is used when the property-holding period is expected to be brief. Escheat property that is reported in a Private-Purpose Trust Fund is reported as an *addition* in the statement of changes in fiduciary net assets and any balance remaining at the end of the accounting period is reported as "held in trust for trust beneficiaries" in the statement of fiduciary net assets. When the escheat property is reported in an Agency Fund, only a statement of fiduciary net assets is prepared. Consistent with the basic standards established by GASB-34, escheat property reported in a Private-Purpose Trust Fund or an Agency Fund is not reported in the entity's government-wide financial statements.

FINANCIAL REPORTING AT FUND LEVEL

Unlike governmental funds and proprietary funds, the *major fund* reporting concept does not apply to Agency Funds. GASB-34 requires that fiduciary funds be reported in an entity's financial statements by fund type (Pension [and Other Employee Benefit] Trust Funds, Investment Trust Funds, Private-Purpose Trust Funds, and Agency Funds). If there is more than one Agency Fund, there is no requirement to report the individual funds in combining financial statements.

A governmental entity may issue bonds that it is responsible for repaying but whose proceeds finance the construction of a capital asset for a component unit. If at the end of the accounting period there are unspent bond proceeds that will subsequently be transferred to the component unit to pay future construction costs, the unspent amount should not be reported in an Agency Fund. The GASB's *Comprehensive Implementation Guide* states that the financial arrangement between the governmental entity and its component unit is similar to an expenditure-driven grant whereby the amounts transferred during the year and unreimbursed costs at the end of the year represent the amount of the grant for the year and the unspent portion is the "unearned portion" of the grant, which, therefore, should be reported as an asset of the governmental entity.

The balances of an Agency Fund are presented in a statement of net assets. An Agency Fund is not required to prepare a statement of changes in net assets like other fiduciary funds are.

The statement of net assets reports the Agency Fund's assets and liabilities; however, there is no net asset balance (equity balance) in an Agency Fund since all of the assets are distributable to third parties.

PRACTICE ALERT: GASB-54 redefines Capital Projects Funds as those funds that are used to account for and report financial resources that are restricted, committed, or assigned to expenditure for capital outlays, including the acquisition or construction of capital facilities and other capital assets. Capital projects funds exclude those types of capital-related outflows financed by proprietary funds or assets that will be held in trust for individuals, private organizations, or other governments. Large governments may fund and build capital projects for smaller governments, deeding the project over to the smaller government upon completion. Because a capital asset is not being constructed that would ultimately be recorded on the larger government's books, either an agency fund (or a special revenue fund) may be used (if funded by federal grants or bonds, a special revenue fund may be preferable). The smaller government may use a capital projects fund on their books if they send monies to the larger government and receive the capital asset in exchange.

FINANCIAL REPORTING AT GOVERNMENT-WIDE LEVEL

Financial statements of fiduciary funds are not presented in the government-wide financial statements, because resources of these funds cannot be used to finance a governmental entity's activities. The financial statements are included in the fund financial statement, because a governmental entity is financially accountable for those resources even though they belong to other parties (GASB-34, par. 13).

ILLUSTRATIVE TRANSACTIONS

In order to illustrate accounting and financial reporting standards that are observed for Agency Funds, assume that the City of Centerville administers, as required by state law, the following funds:

- Community Support Trust Fund
- County Fire District Trust Fund
- County Homeland Security District Trust Fund

Community Support Trust Fund

The Community Support Trust Fund distributes certain state grants to various not-for-profit organizations. Currently, the not-for-profit organizations that are eligible for state funding are Reading Is Fundamental, Inc.; Food For All, Inc.; and Basic Heating Program, Inc. All of the state grants are accounted for in a single fund. The fund's trial balance for the beginning of the fiscal year is as follows:

Accounts	Trial Balance	
	Debit	Credit
Cash	$4,000	
Accounts Payable		$4,000
Totals	$4,000	$4,000

This section presents illustrative transactions and entries for the Community Support Trust Fund during the fiscal year ended June 30, 20X2.

Transaction JE12.01—The following amounts due to not-for-profit organizations from the previous year were paid:

Reading Is Fundamental, Inc.	$20,000
Food For All, Inc.	4,000
Basic Heating Program, Inc.	7,000
Total	$31,000

Accounts	Debit	Credit
Accounts Payable—Reading Is Fundamental, Inc.	20,000	
Accounts Payable—Food For All, Inc.	4,000	
Accounts Payable—Basic Heating Program, Inc.	7,000	
Cash		31,000

Transaction JE12.02—During the year, the following state grants were received in the name of the not-for-profit organizations:

Reading Is Fundamental, Inc.	$230,000
Food For All, Inc.	120,000
Basic Heating Program, Inc.	90,000
Total	$440,000

Accounts	Debit	Credit
Cash	440,000	
Accounts Payable—Reading Is Fundamental, Inc.		230,000
Accounts Payable—Food For All, Inc.		120,000
Accounts Payable—Basic Heating Program, Inc.		90,000

   In some instances, an Agency Fund distributes more cash than it has or has more liabilities than assets. The AICPA's *Audit and Accounting Guide State and Local Governments* notes that if the governmental entity that reports the Agency Fund in its fund financial statements is responsible for the shortfall, an interfund payable should be established by the fund responsible for the shortfall and the Agency Fund should report an interfund receivable. The interfund loan would not be eliminated in the preparation of the fund financial statements and the government-wide financial statements. Financial information of Agency Funds is not incorporated into the government-wide financial statements.

Transaction JE12.03—During the year, the following amounts from the current-year grants were distributed to the not-for-profit organizations:

Reading Is Fundamental, Inc.	$225,000
Food For All, Inc.	100,000
Basic Heating Program, Inc.	80,000
Total	$405,000

Accounts	Debit	Credit
Accounts Payable—Reading Is Fundamental, Inc.	225,000	
Accounts Payable—Food For All, Inc.	100,000	

Accounts	Debit	Credit
Accounts Payable—Basic Heating Program, Inc.	80,000	
Cash		405,000

After the transactions for the year are posted, the year-end trial balance (June 30, 20X2) for the Agency Fund appears as follows:

	Adjusted Trial Balance	
Accounts	Debit	Credit
Cash	$8,000	
Accounts Payable		$8,000
Totals	$8,000	$8,000

The worksheet that summarizes the journal entries for the Community Support Fund for the year-end trial balance is presented in Appendix 12A.

County Fire District Trust Fund

The County Fire District Trust Fund is administered, as required by state law, by the City of Centerville for the benefit of several small fire districts that operate in the same county as Centerville. The role of the City is to collect property taxes related to the fire district services and remit them to various districts. The fund's trial balance for the beginning of the fiscal year is as follows:

	Trial Balance	
Accounts	Debit	Credit
Cash	$ 3,000	
Property taxes receivable	30,000	
Allowance for uncollectible property taxes		$23,000
Due to other tax districts		10,000
Totals	$33,000	$33,000

This section presents illustrative transactions and entries for the County Fire District Trust Fund during the fiscal year ended June 30, 20X2.

Transaction JE12.04—Property taxes receivable of $7,000 at the beginning of the year were collected and the balance ($23,000) was written off:

Accounts	Debit	Credit
Cash	7,000	
Allowance for Uncollectible Property Taxes	23,000	
Property taxes receivable		30,000

Transaction JE12.05—The fire districts levied property taxes of $250,000. It is expected that 10% of the amount levied will be uncollectible:

Accounts	Debit	Credit
Property Taxes Receivable	250,000	
Due to other taxing districts		225,000
Allowance for uncollectible property taxes		25,000

Transaction JE12.06—During the year, the amounts due to the various fire districts from the previous year were paid:

Accounts	Debit	Credit
Due to Other Tax Districts	10,000	
Cash		10,000

Transaction JE12.07—Property taxes of $220,000 were collected by the City for the various fire districts:

Accounts	Debit	Credit
Cash	220,000	
Property Taxes Receivable		220,000

Transaction JE12.08—During the year, $200,000 of property tax receipts were distributed to the various fire districts:

Accounts	Debit	Credit
Due to Other Tax Districts	200,000	
Cash		200,000

After the transactions for the year are posted the year-end trial balance (June 30, 20X2) for the County Fire District Trust Fund appears as follows:

Accounts	Adjusted Trial Balance Debit	Credit
Cash	$20,000	
Property taxes receivable	30,000	
Allowance for uncollectible property taxes		$25,000
Due to other tax districts		25,000
Totals	$50,000	$50,000

The worksheet that summarizes the journal entries for the County Fire District Trust Fund year-end trial balance is presented in Appendix 12B.

County Homeland Security District Trust Fund

The County Homeland Security District Trust Fund is administered, as required by state law, by the City of Centerville for the benefit of county residents. The role of the City is to collect transfer taxes on certain transactions executed in the county and remit them to the county Homeland Security Board. These resources are used by the Board to provide security for high-risk public assets. The fund's trial balance for the beginning of the fiscal year is as follows:

Accounts	Trial Balance	
	Debit	Credit
Cash	$ 10,000	
Due to Other Tax Districts		$10,000
Totals	$10,000	$10,000

This section presents illustrative transactions and entries for the County Homeland Security District Trust Fund during the fiscal year ended June 30, 20X2.

Transaction JE12.09—During the year, the amounts due to the various fire districts from the previous year were paid:

Accounts	Debit	Credit
Due to Other Tax Districts	10,000	
Cash		10,000

Transaction JE12.10—Franchise taxes of $550,000 were collected by the City for the Board:

Accounts	Debit	Credit
Cash	550,000	
Due to Other Tax Districts		550,000

Transaction JE12.11—During the year, $530,000 of franchise tax receipts were distributed to the board:

Accounts	Debit	Credit
Due to Other Tax Districts	530,000	
Cash		530,000

After the transactions for the year are posted, the year-end trial balance (June 30, 20X2) for the County Homeland Security District Trust Fund appears as follows:

Accounts	Adjusted Trial Balance	
	Debit	Credit
Cash	$20,000	
Due to other tax districts		$20,000
Totals	$20,000	$20,000

FUND FINANCIAL STATEMENTS

Based on the adjusted trial balances created above, the following financial statement is prepared for the three Agency Trust Funds (see Appendix 12D):

City of Centerville
Agency Funds
Statement of Fiduciary Net Assets
June 30, 20X2

	Community Support Trust Fund	County Fire District Fund	County Homeland Security District Trust Fund	Total
ASSETS				
Cash	$8,000	$20,000	$20,000	$48,000
Property taxes receivable (net)		5,000		5,000
Total assets	$8,000	$25,000	$20,000	$53,000
LIABILITIES				
Accounts payable	$8,000			$ 8,000
Due to other taxing districts		$25,000	$20,000	45,000
Total liabilities	$8,000	$25,000	$20,000	$53,000

The financial statement for the Agency Fund is used later, in Chapter 13, "Developing Information for Fund Financial Statements."

GOVERNMENT-WIDE FINANCIAL STATEMENTS

Fiduciary financial statements are presented only at the fund financial statement level (see Appendix 12E).

APPENDIX 12A: WORKSHEET FOR SUMMARIZING CURRENT TRANSACTIONS: COMMUNITY SUPPORT TRUST FUND

Accounts	Trial Balance Debit	Credit	Adjustments Debit		Credit		Adjusted Trial Balance Debit	Credit	Balance Sheet Debit	Credit
Cash	4,000	—	JE12.02	440,000	JE12.01	31,000	8,000	—	8,000	—
	—	—		—	JE12.03	405,000	—	—	—	—
Accounts payable	—	4,000	JE12.01	31,000	JE12.02	440,000	—	8,000	—	8,000
	—	—	JE12.03	405,000		—	—	—	—	—
Totals	4,000	4,000		876,000		876,000	8,000	8,000	8,000	8,000
Net increase (decrease)										0
Totals									8,000	8,000

APPENDIX 12B: WORKSHEET FOR SUMMARIZING CURRENT TRANSACTIONS: COUNTY FIRE DISTRICT TRUST FUND

Accounts	Trial Balance Debit	Trial Balance Credit	Adjustments Debit	Adjustments Credit	Adjusted Trial Balance Debit	Adjusted Trial Balance Credit	Balance Sheet Debit	Balance Sheet Credit
Cash	3,000	—	JE12.04 7,000	JE12.06 10,000	20,000	—	20,000	—
			JE12.07 220,000	JE12.08 200,000				
Property taxes receivable	30,000	—	JE12.04 250,000	JE12.04 30,000	30,000	—	30,000	—
			—	JE12.07 220,000				
Allowance for uncollectible property taxes	—	23,000	JE12.05 23,000	JE12.05 25,000	—	25,000	—	25,000
Due to other tax districts	—	10,000	JE12.06 10,000	JE12.05 225,000	—	25,000	—	25,000
			JE12.08 200,000	—				
Totals	33,000	33,000	710,000	710,000	50,000	50,000	50,000	50,000
Net increase (decrease)							0	—
Totals							50,000	50,000

APPENDIX 12C: WORKSHEET FOR SUMMARIZING CURRENT TRANSACTIONS: COUNTY HOMELAND SECURITY DISTRICT TRUST FUND

Accounts	Trial Balance Debit	Trial Balance Credit	Adjustments Debit		Adjustments Credit		Adjusted Trial Balance Debit	Adjusted Trial Balance Credit	Balance Sheet Debit	Balance Sheet Credit
Cash	10,000	—	JE12.10	550,000	JE12.09	10,000	20,000	—	20,000	—
	—	—	JE12.11	—	JE12.11	530,000	—	—	—	—
Due to other taxing districts	—	10,000	JE12.09	10,000	JE12.10	20,000	—	20,000	—	20,000
	—	—	JE12.11	530,000		—	—	—	—	—
Totals	10,000	10,000		1,090,000		1,090,000	20,000	20,000	20,000	20,000
Net increase (decrease)									0	—
Totals									20,000	20,000

APPENDIX 12D: AGENCY FUNDS: STATEMENT OF FIDUCIARY NET ASSETS

City of Centerville
Agency Funds
Statement of Fiduciary Net Assets
June 30, 20X2

	Community Support Trust Fund	County Fire District Fund	County Homeland Security District Trust Fund	Total
ASSETS				
Cash	$8,000	$20,000	$20,000	$48,000
Property taxes receivable (net)		5,000		5,000
Total assets	$8,000	$25,000	$20,000	$53,000
LIABILITIES				
Accounts payable	$8,000			$ 8,000
Due to other taxing districts		$25,000	$20,000	45,000
Total liabilities	$8,000	$25,000	$20,000	$53,000

APPENDIX 12E: AGENCY FUNDS: GOVERNMENT-WIDE FINANCIAL STATEMENTS

Fiduciary financial statements are presented only at the fund financial statement level.

PART V.
THE CONSOLIDATION AND
CONVERSION PROCESS

CHAPTER 13
DEVELOPING INFORMATION FOR FUND FINANCIAL STATEMENTS

CONTENTS

INTRODUCTION

Fund-based financial statements are included in a governmental entity's financial statements in order to demonstrate that restrictions imposed by statutes, regulations, or contracts have been followed. The fund financial statements are built around (1) governmental funds (General Fund, Special Revenue Funds, Capital Projects Funds, Debt Service Funds, and Permanent Funds), (2) proprietary funds (Enterprise Funds and Internal Service Funds), and (3) fiduciary funds (Pension Trust Funds [and similar benefit funds], Investment Trust Funds, Private-Purpose Trust Funds, and Agency Funds). Governmental funds and Enterprise Funds are reported based on the *major fund concept*. The major fund concept does not apply to Internal Service Funds and fiduciary funds. All Internal Service Funds are combined into a single column and presented on the proprietary fund financial statements (to the right of Enterprise Funds). Fiduciary funds are presented by fund-type. These concepts are illustrated in this chapter.

IDENTIFYING A MAJOR FUND

GASB-34 requires that a governmental fund or Enterprise Fund be presented in a separate column in the fund financial statements if the fund is considered a major fund. A major fund is one that satisfies *both* of the following criteria (GASB-34, pars. 75 and 76, as amended by GASB-37, par. 15):

A. 10% Threshold—Total assets, liabilities, revenues and other financing sources, or expenditures/expenses and other financing uses of the govern-mental/enterprise fund are equal to or greater than 10% of the corresponding element total (assets, liability, and so forth) for all funds that are considered governmental funds/enterprise funds.

B. 5% Threshold—The same element that met the 10% criterion in (A) is at least 5% of the corresponding element total for all governmental and Enter-prise Funds combined.

In establishing major fund criteria, the GASB intended that a major fund arises when a particular element (assets, for example) of a fund meets both the 10% threshold and the 5% threshold. Some preparers read the requirement as originally stated in GASB-34 to mean that a major fund arises when one element (assets, for example) satisfies the 10% threshold and another element (revenues, for example) satisfies the 5% threshold. GASB-37 (Basic Financial Statements— and Management's Discussion and Analysis—for State and Local Governments: Omnibus) clarifies the GASB's original intent. That is, a single element of a particular fund must satisfy *both* criteria in order for that fund to be considered a major fund.

In some instances a governmental entity accounts for all of its activities in only governmental funds or alternatively uses only Enterprise Funds. Under either of these two circumstances the GASB's *Comprehensive Implementation Guide* states that only the 10% test is relevant because if the 10% test is satisfied, obviously the 5% test will also be satisfied.

Extraordinary items are not included in total revenues and expenditures/ expenses in identifying a major fund.

The General Fund is always considered a major fund and, therefore, must be presented in a separate column. GASB-34, par. 76, affords governments the ability to decide that even if a fund does not satisfy the conditions described above, the fund can still be presented as a major fund if the governmental entity believes it is important to do so. All other funds that are not considered major funds must be combined in a separate column and labeled as nonmajor funds.

10% Threshold

The following summarization is used to determine which individual funds (governmental and Enterprise Funds) discussed in previous chapters pass the 10% threshold:

10% Threshold Governmental Funds	Total Assets	%	Total Liabilities	%	Total Revenues / Other Financing Sources	%	Total Expenditures/ Expenses / Other Financing Uses	%
General Fund	16,264,400	77.8	3,693,800	94.3	115,389,400	92.2	110,600,013	81.8
Special Revenue Fund—Center City Special Services District	89,500	0.4	60,000	1.5	2,688,000	2.1	2,750,000	2.0
Special Revenue Fund—Local Fuel Tax Fund	44,000	0.2	25,000	0.6	4,506,000	3.6	4,200,000	3.1
Capital Projects Fund—Easely Street Bridge Project	824,956	3.9	95,000	2.4	1,280,000	1.0	11,595,000	8.6
Capital Projects Fund—Bland Street Drainage Project	220,000	1.1	27,000	0.7	754,000	0.6	1,597,000	1.2
Capital Projects Fund—West End Recreation Center	**2,941,000**	**14.1**	5,000	0.1	452,000	0.4	1,325,000	1.0
Debt Service Fund—Senior Citizens' Center Bonds	60,000	0.3	2,000	0.1	4,000	0.0	1,259,000	0.9
Debt Service Fund—Easely Street Bridge Bonds	45,000	0.2	3,000	0.1	1,000	0.0	211,000	0.2
Debt Service Fund—Bland Bonds	129,000	0.6	3,000	0.1	3,000	0.0	1,009,000	0.7
Debt Service Fund—West End Recreation Center Bonds	43,000	0.2	1,000	0.0	1,000	0.0	687,000	0.5
Permanent Fund—Centerville Cemetery	247,000	1.2	4,000	0.1	56,000	0.0	35,000	0.0
Total	**20,907,856**	**100.0**	**3,918,800**	**100.0**	**125,134,400**	**100.0**	**135,268,013**	**100.0**
Centerville Toll Bridge	2,405,500	1.5	213,000	0.5	5,157,000	1.9	4,661,000	1.8
Centerville Utilities Authority	**28,075,000**	**17.4**	**12,678,000**	**31.7**	**37,660,000**	**13.7**	**38,282,000**	**15.2**
Centerville Parking Authority	3,728,000	2.3	649,000	1.6	1,533,000	0.6	6,038,000	2.4
Centerville Municipal Airport	**126,813,000**	**78.8**	**26,440,000**	**66.1**	**230,260,000**	**83.8**	**203,495,000**	**80.6**
Total	**161,021,500**	**100.0**	**39,980,000**	**100.0**	**274,610,000**	**100.0**	**252,476,000**	**100.0**

PRACTICE ALERT: GASB-54 fund balance changes should not affect the 10% or the 5% calculation.

Based on the above analysis, the following funds pass the 10% threshold test:

- Governmental Fund—Capital Projects Fund—West End Recreation Center (14% of total assets)

- Enterprise Fund—Centerville Utilities Authority (17% of total assets, 32% of total liabilities, 14% of total revenues and 15% of total expenses)

- Enterprise Fund—Centerville Municipal Airport (79% of total assets, 66% of total liabilities, 84% of total revenues, and 81% of total expenses)

5% Threshold

The following summarization is used to determine which of the three funds that passed the 10% threshold also pass the 5% threshold:

10% Threshold Governmental Funds	Total Assets	%	Total Liabilities	%	Total Revenues	%	Total Expenditures/ Expenses	%
Capital Projects Fund—West End Recreation Center	2,941,000	2	5,000	n/a	452,000	n/a	1,325,000	n/a
Centerville Utilities Authority	**28,075,000**	**15**	**12,678,000**	**29**	**37,660,000**	**9**	**38,282,000**	**10**
Centerville Municipal Airport	**126,813,000**	**70**	**26,440,000**	**60**	**230,360,000**	**58**	**203,495,000**	**52**
Total for governmental funds (1)	20,907,856		3,918,800		125,134,400		135,268,013	
Total for enterprise funds (2)	161,021,500		39,980,000		274,610,000		252,476,000	
Total [(1) + (2)]	181,929,356		43,898,800		399,744,400		387,744,013	

n/a-These computations are not applicable, because the element did not pass the 10% threshold.

The Capital Projects Fund (West End Recreation Center) does not pass the 5% threshold. The two Enterprise Funds (Centerville Utilities and Centerville Municipal Airport) pass all four of the criteria thresholds and, therefore, must be reported as major funds.

As noted earlier, a government may consider a fund to be a major fund, even if it does not satisfy the 10% and 5% thresholds. For presentation purposes, it is assumed that the City of Centerville believes that the Special Revenue Fund—Local Fuel Tax Fund (for consistency reasons) and Capital Projects Fund—West End Recreation Center (for public interest reasons) are major funds, even though they do not satisfy the 10% and 5% thresholds. Thus, the following five funds are considered to be major funds:

1. General Fund (always considered a major fund)
2. Special Revenue Fund—Local Fuel Tax Fund (does not pass both of the threshold criteria but for consistency is considered a major fund)
3. Capital Projects Fund—West End Recreation Center (does not pass both of the threshold criteria but for public interest reasons is considered a major fund)
4. Enterprise Fund—Centerville Utilities Authority (passes both of the threshold criteria)
5. Enterprise Fund—Centerville Municipal Airport (passes both of the threshold criteria)

A governmental entity applying the major fund criteria to its activities (governmental or Enterprise Funds) might determine that all of its funds are major funds except one. For example, it might have a single Special Revenue Fund that is a major fund, a single Capital Projects Fund that is a major fund, a General Fund (which is always a major fund), and a remaining Permanent Fund that is not a major fund. Based on the reporting requirements established by GASB-34 there needs to be a separate column that reports the Permanent Fund even though it is not a major fund; however, the GASB's *Comprehensive Implementation Guide* states that the financial statements must "clearly distinguish between major and nonmajor funds." This could be accomplished by providing a (1) superheading labeled "Major Funds" (under which appear separate columns for the General Fund, the Special Revenue Fund, and the Capital Projects Fund) and (2) superheading labeled "Other Fund" (under which appears a single separate column for the Permanent Fund).

The GASB's *Guide* points out that Internal Service Funds cannot be presented as major funds. They should be aggregated and presented in a separate column on the face of the proprietary fund financial statements, just to the right of the total column for Enterprise Funds. If a governmental entity wants to present additional detail about Internal Service Funds, that information can be presented in combining statements. However, those statements are optional and not considered part of the general purpose external financial statements; they are part of the CAFR.

GOVERNMENTAL FUNDS FINANCIAL STATEMENTS

At the fund financial statement level, a statement of revenues, expenditures, and changes in fund balances and a balance sheet are prepared for governmental funds. Based on the adjusted trial balances (modified accrual basis) created in previous chapters, this chapter illustrates how the previously created information is used to prepare the fund financial statements for governmental funds.

PRACTICE POINT: In auditing the funds, auditors will want to know the major funds both at the beginning of the audit based on the prior-year results to develop an audit plan and potential "opinion units" and at the end of the audit to make sure that all major funds have been audited. Care must be taken in calculating these amounts, and frequently the auditor will ask the preparer to represent that they are responsible for this calculation. The concept of opinion units is more thoroughly discussed in CCH's *Knowledge Based Audits*™ *of State and Local Governments with Single Audits* and other related titles.

Combining Trial Balances for Nonmajor Funds

The governmental funds in Exhibit 13-1 were illustrated in previous chapters and constitute the City of Centerville's nonmajor governmental funds.

Exhibit 13-1: City of Centerville's Nonmajor Governmental Funds

Nonmajor Governmental Funds	Chapter Reference
Center City Special Services District	Chapter 3: Special Revenue Funds
Easely Street Bridge Project	Chapter 4: Capital Projects Funds
Bland Street Drainage Project	Chapter 4: Capital Projects Funds
Senior Citizens' Center Bonds	Chapter 5: Debt Service Funds
Easely Street Bridge Bonds	Chapter 5: Debt Service Funds
Bland Street Drainage Bonds	Chapter 5: Debt Service Funds
West End Recreation Center Bonds	Chapter 5: Debt Service Funds
Centerville Cemetery	Chapter 6: Permanent Funds

Based on the information developed in the previous chapters, the following combining trial balance (modified accrual basis) is prepared for the nonmajor funds:

	Special Services District (SRF) (Chapter 3) Debits (Credits)	Easely Street Bridge Project (CPF) (Chapter 4) Debits (Credits)	Bland Street Bridge Project (CPF) (Chapter 4) Debits (Credits)	Debt Service Funds (See Note) (Chapter 5) Debits (Credits)	Centerville Cemetery Fund (PF) (Chapter 6) Debits (Credits)	Nonmajor Funds Total Debits (Credits)
Cash	$ 26,500	$129,956	$158,000	$210,000	$ 3,000	$527,456
Interest receivable						
Temporary investments	—	695,000	62,000	67,000	—	824,000
Property taxes receivable	108,000	—	—	—	—	108,000
Allowance for uncollectible property taxes	(60,000)	—	—	—	—	(60,000)
Other receivables	15,000	—	—	—	—	15,000
Intergovernmental grants receivable	—	—	—	—	—	—
Investments in marketable debt securities	—	—	—	—	244,000	244,000
Investments in marketable equity securities	—	—	—	—	—	—
Inventories	—	—	—	—	—	—
Accounts payable	(50,000)	(95,000)	(27,000)	(9,000)	(4,000)	(185,000)
Deferred revenue— property taxes	(10,000)	—	—	—	—	(10,000)
Due to other funds— Internal Service Fund— Communications and Technology Support Center	—	—	—	—	—	—
Due to other funds— Internal Service Fund—Fleet Management Unit	—	—	—	—	—	—

	Special Services District (SRF) (Chapter 3) Debits (Credits)	Easely Street Bridge Project (CPF) (Chapter 4) Debits (Credits)	Bland Street Bridge Project (CPF) (Chapter 4) Debits (Credits)	Debt Service Funds (See Note) (Chapter 5) Debits (Credits)	Centerville Cemetery Fund (PF) (Chapter 6) Debits (Credits)	Nonmajor Funds Total Debits (Credits)
Due to other funds— Enterprise Fund— Centerville Utilities Authority	—	—	—	—	—	—
Due to other funds— Enterprise Fund— Centerville Municipal Airport	—	—	—	—	—	—
Fund balance assigned	(16,500)	(716,000)	(136,000)	—	—	(868,500)
Fund balance— restricted – debt service	—	—	—	(105,000)	—	(105,000)
Fund balance— nonspendable –permanent funds	—	—	—	—	(222,000)	(222,000)
Program revenues— charges for services (general government)	—	—	—	—	—	—
Program revenues— operating grants (recreation and parks)	—	—	—	—	—	—
Program revenues— charges for services (recreation and parks)	—	—	—	—	—	—
Program revenues— charges for services (health and welfare)	—	—	—	—	—	—

	Special Services District (SRF) (Chapter 3) Debits (Credits)	Easely Street Bridge Project (CPF) (Chapter 4) Debits (Credits)	Bland Street Bridge Project (CPF) (Chapter 4) Debits (Credits)	Debt Service Funds (See Note) (Chapter 5) Debits (Credits)	Centerville Cemetery Fund (PF) (Chapter 6) Debits (Credits)	Nonmajor Funds Total Debits (Credits)
Program revenues— operating contributions (health and welfare)	—	—	—	—	—	—
Program revenues— charges for services (streets)	—	—	—	—	—	—
Program revenues— capital grants (streets)	—	(1,250,000)	(750,000)	—	—	(2,000,000)
Program revenues— capital grants (public safety)	—	—	—	—	—	—
Program revenues— charges for services (public safety)	—	—	—	—	—	—
General revenues— property taxes	(2,670,000)	—	—	—	—	(2,670,000)
General revenues— franchise taxes	—	—	—	—	—	—
General revenues— unrestricted grants	—	—	—	—	—	—
Miscellaneous revenue	(18,000)	—	—	—	—	(18,000)
Interest and investment revenue	—	(30,000)	(4,000)	(9,000)	—	(43,000)
Revenue— change in fair value of investments	—	—	—	—	—	—

	Special Services District (SRF) (Chapter 3) Debits (Credits)	Easely Street Bridge Project (CPF) (Chapter 4) Debits (Credits)	Bland Street Bridge Project (CPF) (Chapter 4) Debits (Credits)	Debt Service Funds (See Note) (Chapter 5) Debits (Credits)	Centerville Cemetery Fund (PF) (Chapter 6) Debits (Credits)	Nonmajor Funds Total Debits (Credits)
Interest and investment revenue (program revenue— operating grants and contributions [general government])	—	—	—	—	(34,000)	(34,000)
Expenditures— general government	550,000	495,000	97,000	42,000	35,000	1,219,000
Expenditures— public safety	—	—	—	—	—	—
Expenditures— streets	2,200,000	—	—	—	—	2,200,000
Expenditures— recreation and parks	—	—	—	—	—	—
Expenditures— health and welfare	—	—	—	—	—	—
Encumbrances	—	—	—	—	—	—
Expenditures— education (component unit)	—	—	—	—	—	—
Expenditures— capital outlays	—	11,100,000	1,500,000	—	—	12,600,000
Expenditures— principal	—	—	—	1,950,000	—	1,950,000
Expenditures— interest	—	—	—	1,174,000	—	1,174,000
Revenue— permanent endowment additions	—	—	—	—	(22,000)	(22,000)
Other financing sources— long-term debt issued	—	(10,000,000)	—	—	—	(10,000,000)
Other financing uses— discount on long-term debt issued	—	671,044	—	—	—	671,044

	Special Services District (SRF) (Chapter 3) Debits (Credits)	Easely Street Bridge Project (CPF) (Chapter 4) Debits (Credits)	Bland Street Bridge Project (CPF) (Chapter 4) Debits (Credits)	Debt Service Funds (See Note) (Chapter 5) Debits (Credits)	Centerville Cemetery Fund (PF) (Chapter 6) Debits (Credits)	Nonmajor Funds Total Debits (Credits)
Other financing sources— capitalized leases	—	—	—	—	—	—
Transfers in	(75,000)	(1,000,000)	(900,000)	(3,320,000)	—	(5,295,000)
Transfers out	—	—	—	—	—	—
Total	$ 0	$ 0	$ 0	$ 0	$ 0	$ 0

PRACTICE ALERT: GASB-54 (Fund Balance Reporting and Governmental Fund Type Definitions), effective for periods beginning after June 15, 2010, makes significant changes to fund balance classifications as well as clarifies and makes changes to the definitions of governmental fund types. The new definitions in GASB-54 provide that governmental funds of a particular type either should be used (i.e., required) or are used (i.e., discretionary) for all activities that meet its criteria. If use of a fund type is generally discretionary, specific situations under which a fund of that type should be used are identified either in the definitions in GASB-54 (i.e., debt service funds) or by requirements established in other authoritative pronouncements (i.e., special revenue and capital projects funds). The fund balance classification section of GASB-54 defines the terminology "restricted," "committed," and "assigned."

For the details of the four Debt Service Funds see Chapter 5, "Debt Service Funds."

If a fund does not meet the definitions of a major fund as defined in GASB-54, paragraph 75, it can still be presented as a major fund if the governmental entity believes it is important to do so. Under this circumstance, the fund is considered a major fund, not a nonmajor fund. All other funds that are not considered major funds must be aggregated in a separate column and labeled as nonmajor funds. The GASB's *Comprehensive Implementation Guide* states that more than one column cannot be used to present nonmajor funds, for example, by fund type.

Combining Trial Balances for All Governmental Funds

After the trial balance for the nonmajor funds is prepared, that information can be combined with the trial balances for the General Fund, and the two other major governmental funds (Special Revenue Fund—Local Fuel Tax Fund and Capital Projects Fund—West End Recreation Center) in order to create a combined trial balance for all governmental funds as follows:

	General Fund (Chapter 2) Debits (Credits)	Local Fuel Tax Fund (SRF) (Chapter 3) Debits (Credits)	West End Recreation Center Fund (CPF) (Chapter 4) Debits (Credits)	Nonmajor Funds Debits (Credits)	Total Governmental Funds Debits (Credits)
Cash	$10,045,000	$42,000	$ 19,000	$527,456	$10,633,456
Interest receivable	37,800	—	—	—	37,800
Temporary investments	—	—	2,922,000	824,000	3,746,000
Property taxes receivable	2,355,000	—	—	108,000	2,463,000
Allowance for uncollectible property taxes	(2,000,000)	—	—	(60,000)	(2,060,000)
Other receivables	29,800	2,000	—	15,000	46,800
Intergovernmental grants receivable	—	—	—	—	—
Investment in short-term instruments	1,325,000	—	—	—	1,325,000
Investments in marketable debt securities	650,000	—	—	244,000	894,000
Investments in marketable equity securities	3,799,600	—	—	—	3,799,600
Inventories	17,000	—	—	—	17,000
Other assets	5,200	—	—	—	5,200
Accounts payable	(676,800)	(25,000)	(5,000)	(185,000)	(891,800)
Demand loans payable	(75,000)	—	—	—	(75,000)
Deferred revenue— property taxes	(300,000)	—	—	(10,000)	(310,000)
Due to other funds	(2,642,000)	—	—	—	(2,642,000)
Fund balance	—	—	—	—	—
Fund balance— nonspendable	(12,000)	—	—	(222,000)	(234,000)
Fund balance— Restricted –Health and Welfare	(240,000)	—	—	—	(240,000)
Fund balance— Restricted –Parks and Recreation	(80,000)	—	—	—	(80,000)
Fund balance— Restricted –Education (component unit)	(55,000)	—	—	—	(55,000)
Fund balance— Restricted –Debt Service	—	—	—	(105,000)	(105,000)
Fund balance— Committed – Economic Stabilization	(210,000)	—	—	—	(210,000)

	General Fund (Chapter 2) Debits (Credits)	Local Fuel Tax Fund (SRF) (Chapter 3) Debits (Credits)	West End Recreation Center Fund (CPF) (Chapter 4) Debits (Credits)	Nonmajor Funds Debits (Credits)	Total Governmental Funds Debits (Credits)
Fund balance— Committed –Public Safety	(110,000)	—	—	—	(110,000)
Fund balance— Committed – Education (component unit)	(50,000)	—	—	—	(50,000)
Fund balance— Committed –Health and Welfare	(75,000)	—	—	—	(75,000)
Fund balance— Assigned –Parks and Recreation	(50,000)	—	—	—	(50,000)
Fund balance— Assigned –General Government	(10,000)	—	—	—	(10,000)
Fund balance— Assigned –Local Fuel Tax Fund	—	(13,000)	—	—	(13,000)
Fund balance— Assigned –West End Recreation Center Capital Projects Fund	—	—	(509,000)	—	(509,000)
Fund balance— Assigned –Special Revenue Funds	—	—	—	(868,500)	(868,500)
Fund balance— Unassigned	(11,883,000)	—	—	—	(11,883,000)
Program revenues— charges for services (general government)	—	—	—	—	—
Program revenues— operating grants (recreation and parks)	—	—	—	—	—
Program revenues— charges for services (recreation and parks)	—	—	—	—	—
Program revenues— charges for services (health and welfare)	—	—	—	—	—
Program revenues— operating contributions (health and welfare)	—	—	—	—	—
Program revenues— charges for services (streets)	—	—	—	—	—

	General Fund (Chapter 2) Debits (Credits)	Local Fuel Tax Fund (SRF) (Chapter 3) Debits (Credits)	West End Recreation Center Fund (CPF) (Chapter 4) Debits (Credits)	Nonmajor Funds Debits (Credits)	Total Governmental Funds Debits (Credits)
Program revenues— capital grants (streets)	—	—	—	(2,000,000)	(2,000,000)
Program revenues— operating grants (streets)	—	(4,500,000)	—	—	(4,500,000)
Program revenues— capital grants (public safety)	—	—	—	—	—
Program revenues— charges for services (public safety)	—	—	—	—	—
Program revenues— capital grants and contributions (recreation and parks)	—	—	(450,000)	—	(450,000)
General revenues— property taxes	(87,600,000)	—	—	(2,670,000)	(90,270,000)
General revenues— franchise taxes	(1,300,000)	—	—	—	(1,300,000)
General revenues— unrestricted grants	—	—	—	—	—
Intergovernmental grants	(20,500,000)	—	—	—	(20,500,000)
Charges for services	(537,600)	—	—	—	(537,600)
Contributions	(50,000)	—	—	—	(50,000)
Miscellaneous revenue	—	—	—	(18,000)	(18,000)
Interest and investment revenue	(239,400)	(6,000)	(2,000)	(43,000)	(290,400)
Change in fair value of investments	(362,400)	—	—	—	(362,400)
Interest and investment revenue (program revenue—operating grants and contributions [general government])	—	—	—	(34,000)	(34,000)
Expenditures—general government	33,824,098	210,000	25,000	1,219,000	35,278,098
Expenditures—public safety	18,036,628	—	—	—	18,036,628
Expenditures—streets	11,863,314	3,990,000	—	2,200,000	18,053,314
Expenditures— recreation and parks	6,481,657	—	—	—	6,481,657
Expenditures—health and welfare	8,076,657	—	—	—	8,076,657

	General Fund (Chapter 2) Debits (Credits)	Local Fuel Tax Fund (SRF) (Chapter 3) Debits (Credits)	West End Recreation Center Fund (CPF) (Chapter 4) Debits (Credits)	Nonmajor Funds Debits (Credits)	Total Governmental Funds Debits (Credits)
Encumbrances	—	—	—	—	—
Expenditures— education (component unit)	32,000,000	—	—	—	32,000,000
Expenditures—capital outlays	—	—	1,300,000	12,600,000	13,900,000
Expenditures—principal	—	—	—	1,950,000	1,950,000
Expenditures—interest	317,659	—	—	1,174,000	1,491,659
Revenues—permanent endowment additions	—	—	—	(22,000)	(22,000)
Other financing sources—disposition of capital assets	(4,800,000)	—	—	—	(4,800,000)
Other financing sources—long-term debt issued	—	—	(3,000,000)	(10,000,000)	(13,000,000)
Other financing uses— discount on long-term debt issued	—	—	—	671,044	671,044
Other financing source—capitalized leases	(431,213)	—	—	—	(431,213)
Transfers in	(50,000)	—	(300,000)	(5,295,000)	(5,645,000)
Transfers out	5,475,000	300,000	—	—	5,775,000
Totals	$ 0	$ 0	$ 0	$ 0	$ 0

The information for the General Fund, the Local Fuel Tax Fund (Special Revenue Fund), and the West End Recreation Center Fund (Capital Projects Fund) is taken from previous chapters.

Identification of Nonspendable, Restrictions, Commitments, Assignments, and Unassigned Amounts

The equity of a governmental fund (total assets minus total liabilities) should be identified as nonspendable, restricted, committed, assigned, or unassigned amounts, based on the standards established in GASB-54. The fund balances of the combined nonmajor funds must be presented in appropriate detail to inform the reader of the nature of the reservation and to identify the amount of net unreserved current financial resources that are available for future appropriation. For example, the fund balance for nonmajor Debt Service Funds may be described as restricted for debt service. In addition, assigned fund balances for nonmajor special revenue, capital projects debt service, and permanent funds may be either aggregated by fund type on the face of the balance sheet per GASB-54 or disaggregated by function or program. If aggregation is chosen by the preparer to be presented on the face of the balance sheet, then disaggregated amounts must be presented in the notes to the basic financial statements.

The AICPA's Audit and Accounting Guide *State and Local Governments* points out that a contractual commitment to a third party that is not reported as a liability is an example of an amount that is legally segregated for a specific purpose; nonappropriable amounts include balances related to "inventories, prepaid items, noncurrent receivables that are not offset by deferred revenue, and the noncurrent portion of interfund receivables." In addition, GASB-33, footnote 13, states that a restriction should be reported for time restrictions (both permanent and for specific time periods) and purpose restrictions for as long as the restriction exists.

During the year, amounts will be added and removed from restricted, committed, assigned, and unassigned amounts depending on the City's policies, procedures, and normal course of business. Nonspendable amounts may be changed by additions or reductions to permanent funds, inventory changes and other items. The following is an analysis of nonspendable, restricted, committed, assigned, and unassigned fund balances (many of the amounts are assumed) for the City of Centerville's governmental funds as of the end of the year:

	Total Fund Balance	Nonspendable-Inventories	Restricted for Debt Service	Nonspendable for Permanent Fund	Restricted for Capital Projects	Assigned for Other Purposes	Unassigned General Fund
MAJOR FUNDS:							
General Fund	12,570,600	17,000	—	—	—	25,000	12,528,600
Special Revenue Fund—Local Fuel Tax Fund	19,000	—	—	—	—	19,000	—
Capital Projects Fund—West End Recreation Center	2,936,000	—	—	—	2,450,000[a]	486,000	—
NONMAJOR FUNDS:							
Special Revenue Fund—Center City Special Services District	29,500	—	—	—	—	29,500	—
Capital Projects Fund—Easely Street Bridge Project	729,956	—	—	—	478,956[a]	251,000	—
Capital Projects Fund—Bland Street Drainage Project	193,000	—	—	—	150,000[a]	43,000	—
Debt Service Fund—Senior Citizens' Center Bonds	58,000	—	58,000	—	—	—	—
Debt Service Fund—Easely Street Bridge Bonds	42,000	—	42,000	—	—	—	—
Debt Service Fund—Bland Street Drainage Bonds	126,000	—	126,000	—	—	—	—
Debt Service Fund—West End Recreation Center Bonds	42,000	—	42,000	—	—	—	—

	Total Fund Balance	Nonspendable—Inventories	Restricted for Debt Service	Nonspendable for Permanent Fund	Restricted for Capital Projects	Assigned for Other Purposes	Unassigned General Fund
Permanent Fund—Centerville Cemetery	243,000	—	—	243,000	—	—	—
	16,989,056	17,000	268,000	243,000	3,078,956	853,500	12,528,600

a The fund balance presentation is pursuant to the requirements of NCGA-1. Effective for periods beginning after June 15, 2010, the provisions of GASB-54 will be effective and will change these fund balance classifications. See Chapter 2, "The General Fund," for discussion of GASB-54.

Governmental Fund Financial Statements

The governmental fund financial statements include the following:

- Balance sheet

- Statement of revenues, expenditures, and changes in fund balances

Based on the trial balance presented above, the balance sheet and the statement of revenues, expenditures, and changes in fund balances for the City of Centerville are as follows:

Governmental Funds Balance Sheet June 30, 20X2

	General Fund (Chapter 2)	Local Fuel Tax Fund (Chapter 3)	West End Recreation Center Fund (Chapter 5)	Other Governmental Funds	Total Governmental Funds
ASSETS					
Cash	$10,045,000	$42,000	$ 19,000	$ 527,456	$10,633,456
Temporary investments	1,325,000	—	2,922,000	824,000	5,071,000
Property taxes receivable (net)	355,000	—	—	48,000	403,000
Other receivables	67,600	2,000	—	15,000	84,600
Investments	4,449,600	—	—	244,000	4,693,600
Inventories	17,000	—	—	—	17,000
Other assets	5,200	—	—	—	5,200
Total Assets	**$16,264,400**	**$44,000**	**$2,941,000**	**$1,658,456**	**$20,907,856**
LIABILITIES AND FUND BALANCES					
Liabilities:					
Accounts payable	$ 676,800	$25,000	$ 5,000	$ 185,000	$ 891,800
Demand loans payable	75,000	—	—	—	75,000
Due to other funds	2,642,000	—	—	—	2,642,000
Deferred revenue	300,000	—	—	10,000	310,000
Total Liabilities	**3,693,800**	**25,000**	**5,000**	**195,000**	**3,918,800**
Fund balances:					
Nonspendable for:					
Inventories	17,000	—	—	—	17,000
Permanent Funds	—	—	—	243,000	243,000
Restricted for:					
Debt service	—	—	—	268,000	268,000
Capital Projects	—	—	2,450,000	628,956	3,078,956
Assigned to:					
General Fund	25,000	—	—	—	25,000
Special Revenue Funds	—	19,000	—	29,500	48,500
Capital Projects Funds	—	—	486,000	294,000	780,000
Unassigned	12,528,600				

Governmental Funds Balance Sheet June 30, 20X2

	General Fund (Chapter 2)	Local Fuel Tax Fund (Chapter 3)	West End Recreation Center Fund (Chapter 5)	Other Governmental Funds	Total Governmental Funds
Total Fund Balances	12,570,600	19,000	2,936,000	1,463,456	16,989,056
Total Liabilities and Fund Balances	$16,264,400	$44,000	$2,941,000	$1,658,456	$20,907,856

Note: Commitments are not presented, because no assumptions of legislative or other highest level of decision making authority committing fund balances is being made. Had there been such activity, unassigned and assigned amounts would have been reclassed to commitments.

Governmental Funds
Statement of Revenues, Expenditures, and
Changes in Fund Balances
June 30, 20X2

	General Fund (Chapter 2)	Local Fuel Tax Fund (Chapter 3)	West End Recreation Center Fund (Chapter 5)	Other Governmental Funds	Total Governmental Funds
REVENUES					
Property taxes	$87,600,000	—	—	$2,670,000	$90,270,000
Franchise taxes	1,300,000	—	—	—	1,300,000
Intergovernmental grants	20,500,000	$4,500,000	$450,000	2,000,000	27,450,000
Charges for services	537,600	—	—	—	537,600
Contributions	50,000	—	—	—	50,000
Interest and investment revenue	601,800	6,000	2,000	77,000	686,800
Miscellaneous revenue	—	—	—	40,000	40,000
Total Revenue	110,589,400	4,506,000	452,000	4,787,000	120,334,400
EXPENDITURES					
Current:					
General government	33,824,098	210,000	25,000	1,219,000	35,278,098
Public safety	18,036,628	—	—	—	18,036,628
Streets	11,863,314	3,990,000	—	2,200,000	18,053,314
Recreation and parks	6,481,657	—	—	—	6,481,657
Health and welfare	8,076,657	—	—	—	8,076,657
Education (component unit)	32,000,000	—	—	—	32,000,000
Debt service:					
Principal	—	—	—	1,950,000	1,950,000
Interest	317,659	—	—	1,174,000	1,491,659

Governmental Funds
Statement of Revenues, Expenditures, and
Changes in Fund Balances
June 30, 20X2

	General Fund (Chapter 2)	Local Fuel Tax Fund (Chapter 3)	West End Recreation Center Fund (Chapter 5)	Other Governmental Funds	Total Governmental Funds
Capital outlays	—	—	1,300,000	12,600,000	13,900,000
Total Expenditures	**110,600,013**	**4,200,000**	**1,325,000**	**19,143,000**	**135,268,013**
Excess (deficiency) of revenues over expenditures	(10,613)	306,000	(873,000)	(14,356,000)	(14,933,613)
OTHER FINANCING SOURCES (USES):					
Disposition of capital assets	4,800,000	—	—	—	4,800,000
Long-term debt issued	—	—	3,000,000	10,000,000	13,000,000
Discount on long-term debt issued	—	—	—	(671,044)	(671,044)
Execution of capital leases	431,213	—	—	—	431,213
Transfers in	50,000	—	300,000	5,295,000	5,645,000
Transfers out	(5,475,000)	(300,000)	—	—	(5,775,000)
Total other financing sources and uses	**(193,787)**	**(300,000)**	**3,300,000**	**14,623,956**	**17,430,169**
Net change in fund balances	**(204,400)**	**6,000**	**2,427,000**	**267,956**	**2,496,556**
Fund balances— beginning	12,775,000	13,000	509,000	1,195,500	14,492,500
Fund balances— ending	**$12,570,600**	**$ 19,000**	**$2,936,000**	**$1,463,456**	**$16,989,056**

PRACTICE ALERT: GASB-54 does not require the presentation of deseg-regated fund balances in the statement of revenues, expenditures, and changes in fund balances. To do so would not be GAAP and, furthermore, would probably cause separate columns for separate classes of fund balances similar to not-for-profit financial statements. All surplus or deficit closes to Fund balance—unas-signed in the General Fund and Fund balance—assigned in Special Revenue, Capital Projects, Debt Service, and Permanent Funds.

Reconciliations

GASB-34 requires a summary reconciliation between the governmental fund financial statements and the governmental activities column of the government-wide financial statements. These reconciliations are illustrated in Chapter 16, "Basic Financial Statements."

PROPRIETARY FUNDS FINANCIAL STATEMENTS

At the fund financial statement level, a statement of net assets (or balance sheet), statement of revenues, expenses, and changes in fund net assets or fund equity, and a statement of cash flows are prepared for proprietary funds. Based on the adjusted trial balances created in previous chapters, this chapter illustrates how the previously created information is used to prepare the fund financial statements for proprietary funds.

Combining Trial Balances for Non-major Enterprise Funds

The following governmental funds are illustrated in Chapter 7, "Enterprise Funds," and constitute the City of Centerville's nonmajor Enterprise Funds:

- Centerville Toll Bridge
- Centerville Parking Authority

Based on the information developed in Chapter 14, the following combining trial balance (accrual basis) is prepared for the nonmajor Enterprise Funds:

	Centerville Toll Bridge (Chapter 7) Debits (Credits)	Centerville Parking Authority (Chapter 7) Debits (Credits)	Nonmajor Funds Total Debits (Credits)
Cash	$739,500	$764,000	$1,503,500
Interest receivable	3,000	3,000	6,000
Temporary investments	58,000	5,000	63,000
Inventories	32,000	24,000	56,000
Construction in progress	70,000	15,000	85,000
Land and improvements	140,000	1,780,000	1,920,000
Superstructure	1,400,000	—	1,400,000
Buildings	330,000	2,400,000	2,730,000
Equipment	55,000	140,000	195,000
Vehicles	835,000	102,000	937,000
Accumulated depreciation	(1,257,000)	(1,505,000)	(2,762,000)
Accounts payable and accrued expenses	(50,000)	(90,000)	(140,000)
Due to other funds	(18,000)	(17,000)	(35,000)
Compensated absences	(8,000)	(5,000)	(13,000)
Claims and judgements	(27,000)	(7,000)	(34,000)
Notes payable	(30,000)	(30,000)	(60,000)
Bonds payable	(80,000)	(500,000)	(580,000)
Net assets	(1,646,500)	(3,994,000)	(5,640,500)
Charges for services	(4,750,000)	(1,500,000)	(6,250,000)
Miscellaneous revenues	(20,000)	(22,000)	(42,000)
Expenses—personal services	2,402,000	5,402,000	7,804,000
Expenses—contractual services	1,280,000	400,000	1,680,000

	Centerville Toll Bridge (Chapter 7) Debits (Credits)	Centerville Parking Authority (Chapter 7) Debits (Credits)	Nonmajor Funds Total Debits (Credits)
Expenses—repairs and maintenance	400,000	50,000	450,000
Expenses—other supplies and expenses	194,000	36,000	230,000
Expenses—insurance claims and expenses	10,000	3,000	13,000
Expenses—depreciation	339,000	117,000	456,000
Expenses—miscellaneous	30,000	3,000	33,000
Interest and investment revenue	(30,000)	(10,000)	(40,000)
Interest expense	6,000	27,000	33,000
Operating grants and contributions	(100,000)	—	(100,000)
Nonoperating miscellaneous expenses (revenues)	(7,000)	(1,000)	(8,000)
Capital contributions	(250,000)	—	(250,000)
Transfers in	(50,000)	(90,000)	(140,000)
Special item—gain on sale of parking lot	—	(3,500,000)	(3,500,000)
Total	$ 0	$ 0	$ 0

Combining Trial Balances for All Proprietary Funds

After the trial balance for the nonmajor Enterprise Funds is prepared, that information is presented with the trial balances for the two major Enterprise Funds (Centerville Utilities Authority and Centerville Municipal Airport) and all Internal Service Funds in order to create a combined trial balance for all Enterprise Funds as shown below. (The information for the Internal Service Fund column was created in Chapter 8, "Internal Service Funds.")

	Centerville Utilities Authority (Chapter 7) Debit (Credit)	Centerville Municipal Airport (Chapter 7) Debit (Credit)	Other Enterprise Funds (Chapter 7) Debit (Credit)	Total Debit (Credit)	Internal Service Funds (Chapter 8) Debit (Credit)
Cash	$ 230,000	$10,963,000	$1,503,500	$12,696,500	$1,105,500
Interest receivable	50,000	200,000	6,000	256,000	4,000
Accounts receivable (net)	7,550,000	18,000,000	—	25,550,000	—
Due from other funds	2,000,000	400,000	—	2,400,000	824,000
Due from other governments	100,000	300,000	—	400,000	45,000
Temporary investments	55,000	10,050,000	63,000	10,168,000	46,000
Inventories	75,000	55,000	56,000	186,000	36,000
Construction in progress	200,000	23,500,000	85,000	23,785,000	—
Land and improvements	5,200,000	13,200,000	1,920,000	20,320,000	4,450,000
Superstructure	—	—	1,400,000	1,400,000	—
Distribution and collection systems	46,300,000	—	—	46,300,000	—

	Centerville Utilities Authority (Chapter 7) Debit (Credit)	Centerville Municipal Airport (Chapter 7) Debit (Credit)	Other Enterprise Funds (Chapter 7) Debit (Credit)	Total Debit (Credit)	Internal Service Funds (Chapter 8) Debit (Credit)
Runways and tarmacs	—	27,500,000	—	27,500,000	—
Buildings	14,450,000	33,200,000	2,730,000	50,380,000	4,650,000
Equipment	4,600,000	7,200,000	195,000	11,995,000	10,160,000
Vehicles	1,660,000	2,500,000	937,000	5,097,000	10,338,000
Accumulated depreciation	(54,395,000)	(20,255,000)	(2,762,000)	(77,412,000)	(12,848,000)
Accounts payable and accrued expenses	(4,300,000)	(3,900,000)	(140,000)	(8,340,000)	(250,000)
Due to other funds	(35,000)	(512,000)	(35,000)	(582,000)	—
Compensated absences	(84,000)	(133,000)	(13,000)	(230,000)	(32,000)
Claims and judgements	(229,000)	(195,000)	(34,000)	(458,000)	(53,000)
Notes payable	(330,000)	(7,700,000)	(60,000)	(8,090,000)	(8,250,000)
Revenue bonds— Terminal A	—	(10,000,000)	—	(10,000,000)	—
Revenue bonds— Terminal B	—	(4,000,000)	—	(4,000,000)	—
Bonds payable	(7,700,000)	—	(580,000)	(8,280,000)	—
Net assets	(16,019,000)	(73,608,000)	(5,640,500)	(95,267,500)	(12,875,500)
Charges for services	(36,000,000)	(175,000,000)	(6,250,000)	(217,250,000)	(13,450,000)
Charges for services— rental income— security for Terminal A revenue bonds	—	(30,000,000)	—	(30,000,000)	—
Charges for services— rental income— security for Terminal B revenue bonds	—	(22,000,000)	—	(22,000,000)	—
Miscellaneous revenues	(10,000)	(60,000)	(42,000)	(112,000)	(17,000)
Expenses—personal services	22,022,000	161,025,000	7,804,000	190,851,000	6,926,000
Expenses—contractual services	11,220,000	33,550,000	1,680,000	46,450,000	2,100,000
Expenses—repairs and maintenance	700,000	2,100,000	450,000	3,250,000	1,650,000
Expenses—other supplies and expenses	729,000	1,795,000	230,000	2,754,000	366,000
Expenses—insurance claims and expenses	21,000	100,000	13,000	134,000	29,000
Expenses— depreciation	3,025,000	3,370,000	456,000	6,851,000	5,582,000
Expenses— miscellaneous	5,000	70,000	33,000	108,000	22,000
Interest and investment revenue	(400,000)	(1,200,000)	(40,000)	(1,640,000)	(25,000)
Interest expense	450,000	1,220,000	33,000	1,703,000	309,000

	Centerville Utilities Authority (Chapter 7) Debit (Credit)	Centerville Municipal Airport (Chapter 7) Debit (Credit)	Other Enterprise Funds (Chapter 7) Debit (Credit)	Total Debit (Credit)	Internal Service Funds (Chapter 8) Debit (Credit)
Operating grants and contributions	—	—	(100,000)	(100,000)	(370,000)
Non-operating miscellaneous expenses (revenues)	110,000	265,000	(8,000)	367,000	8,000
Capital contributions	(1,250,000)	(2,000,000)	(250,000)	(3,500,000)	(490,000)
Transfers in	—	—	(140,000)	(140,000)	(40,000)
Transfers out	—	—	—	—	50,000
Special item—gain on sale of parking lot	—	—	(3,500,000)	(3,500,000)	—
Total	$ 0	$ 0	$ 0	$ 0	$ 0

Proprietary Fund Financial Statements

The proprietary fund financial statements include the following:

- Statement of net assets (or balance sheet)
- Statement of revenues, expenses, and changes in fund net assets or fund equity
- Statement of cash flows

Based on the trial balance presented above, the statement of net assets (or balance sheet), statement of revenues, expenses, and changes in fund net assets or fund equity and statement of cash flows for the City of Centerville's proprietary funds are as follows:

Proprietary Funds
Statement of Net Assets
June 30, 20X2

	Centerville Utilities Authority (Chapter 7)	Centerville Municipal Airport (Chapter 7)	Other Enterprise Funds (Chapter 7)	Total	Internal Service Funds (Chapter 8)
ASSETS					
Current assets:					
Cash	$ 230,000	$10,963,000	$1,503,500	$12,696,500	$1,105,500
Interest receivable	50,000	200,000	6,000	256,000	4,000
Accounts receivable (net)	7,550,000	18,000,000	—	25,550,000	—
Due from other funds	2,000,000	400,000	—	2,400,000	824,000
Due from other governments	100,000	300,000	—	400,000	45,000
Temporary investments	55,000	10,050,000	63,000	10,168,000	46,000
Inventories	75,000	55,000	56,000	186,000	36,000

Proprietary Funds
Statement of Net Assets
June 30, 20X2

	Centerville Utilities Authority (Chapter 7)	Centerville Municipal Airport (Chapter 7)	Other Enterprise Funds (Chapter 7)	Total	Internal Service Funds (Chapter 8)
Total current assets	10,060,000	39,968,000	1,628,500	51,656,500	2,060,500
Noncurrent assets:					
Construction in progress	200,000	23,500,000	85,000	23,785,000	—
Land and improvements	5,200,000	13,200,000	1,920,000	20,320,000	4,450,000
Superstructure	—	—	1,400,000	1,400,000	—
Distribution and collection systems	46,300,000	—	—	46,300,000	—
Runways and tarmacs	—	27,500,000	—	27,500,000	—
Buildings	14,450,000	33,200,000	2,730,000	50,380,000	4,650,000
Equipment	4,600,000	7,200,000	195,000	11,995,000	10,160,000
Vehicles	1,660,000	2,500,000	937,000	5,097,000	10,338,000
Less accumulated depreciation	(54,395,000)	(20,255,000)	(2,762,000)	(77,412,000)	(12,848,000)
Total noncurrent assets	18,015,000	86,845,000	4,505,000	109,365,000	16,750,000
Total assets	28,075,000	126,813,000	6,133,500	161,021,500	18,810,500
LIABILITIES					
Current liabilities:					
Accounts payable and accrued expenses	4,300,000	3,900,000	140,000	8,340,000	250,000
Due to other funds	35,000	512,000	35,000	582,000	—
Compensated absences	21,000	15,000	5,000	41,000	10,000
Claims and judgements	17,000	25,000	9,000	51,000	13,000
Notes payable	70,000	—	40,000	110,000	1,700,000
Revenue bonds—Terminal A	—	2,000,000	—	2,000,000	—
Revenue bonds—Terminal B	—	500,000	—	500,000	—
Bonds payable	850,000	—	20,000	870,000	—
Total current liabilities	5,293,000	6,952,000	249,000	12,494,000	1,973,000

Proprietary Funds
Statement of Net Assets
June 30, 20X2

	Centerville Utilities Authority (Chapter 7)	Centerville Municipal Airport (Chapter 7)	Other Enterprise Funds (Chapter 7)	Total	Internal Service Funds (Chapter 8)
Noncurrent liabilities:					
Compensated absences	63,000	118,000	8,000	189,000	22,000
Claims and judgements	212,000	170,000	25,000	407,000	40,000
Notes payable	260,000	7,700,000	20,000	7,980,000	6,550,000
Revenue bonds— Terminal A	—	8,000,000	—	8,000,000	—
Revenue bonds— Terminal B	—	3,500,000	—	3,500,000	—
Bonds payable	6,850,000	—	560,000	7,410,000	—
Total noncurrent liabilities	7,385,000	19,488,000	613,000	27,486,000	6,612,000
Total liabilities	**12,678,000**	**26,440,000**	**862,000**	**39,980,000**	**8,585,000**
NET ASSETS					
Invested in capital assets, net of related debt	9,985,000	69,145,000	3,865,000	82,995,000	8,500,000
Restricted:					
Capital projects	2,000,000	17,000,000	1,000,000	20,000,000	—
Debt service	500,000	1,450,000	50,000	2,000,000	—
Other	2,750,000	12,445,000	167,000	15,362,000	—
Unrestricted	162,000	333,000	189,500	684,500	1,725,500
Total net assets	**$15,397,000**	**$100,373,000**	**$5,271,500**	**$121,041,500**	**$10,225,500**

Proprietary Funds
Statement of Revenues, Expenses, and
Changes in Fund Net Assets
For the Year Ended June 30, 20X2

	Centerville Utilities Authority (Chapter 7)	Centerville Municipal Airport (Chapter 7)	Other Enterprise Funds (Chapter 7)	Total	Internal Service Funds (Chapter 8)
OPERATING REVENUES					
Charges for services	$36,000,000	$175,000,000	$6,250,000	$217,250,000	$13,450,000
Charges for services— rental income— security for Terminal A revenue bonds	—	30,000,000	—	30,000,000	—
Charges for services— rental income— security for Terminal B revenue bonds	—	22,000,000	—	22,000,000	—

Proprietary Funds
Statement of Revenues, Expenses, and
Changes in Fund Net Assets
For the Year Ended June 30, 20X2

	Centerville Utilities Authority (Chapter 7)	Centerville Municipal Airport (Chapter 7)	Other Enterprise Funds (Chapter 7)	Total	Internal Service Funds (Chapter 8)
Miscellaneous	10,000	60,000	42,000	112,000	17,000
Total operating revenues	**36,010,000**	**227,060,000**	**6,292,000**	**269,362,000**	**13,467,000**
OPERATING EXPENSES					
Personal services	22,022,000	161,025,000	7,804,000	190,851,000	6,926,000
Contractual services	11,220,000	33,550,000	1,680,000	46,450,000	2,100,000
Repairs and maintenance	700,000	2,100,000	450,000	3,250,000	1,650,000
Other supplies and expenses	729,000	1,795,000	230,000	2,754,000	366,000
Insurance claims and expenses	21,000	100,000	13,000	134,000	29,000
Depreciation	3,025,000	3,370,000	456,000	6,851,000	5,582,000
Miscellaneous	5,000	70,000	33,000	108,000	22,000
Total operating expenses	**37,722,000**	**202,010,000**	**10,666,000**	**250,398,000**	**16,675,000**
Operating income (loss)	(1,712,000)	25,050,000	(4,374,000)	18,964,000	(3,208,000)
NON-OPERATING REVENUES (EXPENSES)					
Interest and investment revenue	400,000	1,200,000	40,000	1,640,000	25,000
Interest	(450,000)	(1,220,000)	(33,000)	(1,703,000)	(309,000)
Operating grants and contributions	—	—	100,000	100,000	370,000
Miscellaneous	(110,000)	(265,000)	8,000	(367,000)	(8,000)
Total non-operating revenue (expenses)	**(160,000)**	**(285,000)**	**115,000**	**(330,000)**	**78,000**
Income (loss) before capital contributions and transfers	(1,872,000)	24,765,000	(4,259,000)	18,634,000	(3,130,000)
Capital contributions	1,250,000	2,000,000	250,000	3,500,000	490,000
Transfers in	—	—	140,000	140,000	40,000
Transfers out	—	—	—	—	(50,000)
Special item—gain on sale of parking lot	—	—	3,500,000	3,500,000	—
Change in net assets	**(622,000)**	**26,765,000**	**(369,000)**	**25,774,000**	**(2,650,000)**

Proprietary Funds
Statement of Revenues, Expenses, and
Changes in Fund Net Assets
For the Year Ended June 30, 20X2

	Centerville Utilities Authority (Chapter 7)	Centerville Municipal Airport (Chapter 7)	Other Enterprise Funds (Chapter 7)	Total	Internal Service Funds (Chapter 8)
Total net assets— beginning	16,019,000	73,608,000	5,640,500	95,267,500	12,875,500
Total net assets— ending	$15,397,000	$100,373,000	$5,271,500	$121,041,500	$10,225,500

Proprietary Funds
Statement of Cash Flows
For the Year Ended June 30, 20X2

	Centerville Utilities Authority (Chapter 7)	Centerville Municipal Airport (Chapter 7)	Other Enterprise Funds (Chapter 7)	Total	Internal Service Funds (Chapter 8)
CASH FLOWS FROM OPERATING ACTIVITIES					
Receipts from customers	$34,000,000	$214,000,000	$6,250,000	$254,250,000	$12,811,000
Payments to suppliers	(12,112,000)	(36,425,000)	(2,151,000)	(50,688,000)	(4,185,000)
Payments to employees	(19,013,000)	(158,017,000)	(7,732,000)	(184,762,000)	(6,747,000)
Internal activity— payments to other funds	(200,000)	(3,140,000)	(156,000)	(3,496,000)	—
Other receipts payments	5,000	(10,000)	1,000	(4,000)	(25,000)
Net cash provided by operating activities	2,680,000	16,408,000	(3,788,000)	15,300,000	1,854,000
CASH FLOWS FROM NON-CAPITAL FINANCING ACTIVITIES					
Subsidies and transfers from (to) other funds and state government	—	—	240,000	240,000	360,000
CASH FLOWS FROM CAPITAL AND RELATED FINANCING ACTIVITIES					
Proceeds from the issuance of capital debt	2,120,000	3,200,000	—	5,320,000	3,400,000
Capital contributions	1,250,000	1,700,000	280,000	3,230,000	490,000
Acquisitions of capital assets	(5,350,000)	(8,800,000)	(590,000)	(14,740,000)	(6,040,000)
Proceeds from sale of capital assets	500,000	420,000	5,055,000	5,975,000	845,000
Principal paid on capital debt	(1,740,000)	(2,500,000)	(40,000)	(4,280,000)	(1,100,000)
Interest paid on capital debt	(450,000)	(1,220,000)	(33,000)	(1,703,000)	(309,000)
Net cash (used) by capital and related financing activities	(3,670,000)	(7,200,000)	4,672,000	(6,198,000)	(2,714,000)

Proprietary Funds
Statement of Cash Flows
For the Year Ended June 30, 20X2

	Centerville Utilities Authority (Chapter 7)	Centerville Municipal Airport (Chapter 7)	Other Enterprise Funds (Chapter 7)	Total	Internal Service Funds (Chapter 8)
CASH FLOWS FROM INVESTING ACTIVITIES					
Loans to other funds	(2,000,000)	(400,000)	—	(2,400,000)	—
Loans to other governments	(100,000)	—	—	(100,000)	—
Interest and dividends	365,000	1,055,000	39,500	1,459,500	37,500
Purchase of investments	(15,000)	(50,000)	(30,000)	(95,000)	—
Net cash provided (used) by investing activities	**(1,750,000)**	**605,000**	**9,500**	**(1,135,500)**	**37,500**
Net increase (decrease) in cash	**(2,740,000)**	**9,813,000**	**1,133,500**	**8,206,500**	**(462,500)**
Balances—beginning of year	2,970,000	1,150,000	370,000	4,490,000	1,568,000
Balances—end of year	**$ 230,000**	**$10,963,000**	**$1,503,500**	**$12,696,500**	**$1,105,500**
Reconciliation of operating income (loss) to net cash provided (used) by operating activities:					
Operating income (loss)	**$(1,712,000)**	**$25,050,000**	**$(4,374,000)**	**$18,964,000**	**$(3,208,000)**
Adjustments:					
Depreciation expense	3,025,000	3,370,000	456,000	6,851,000	5,582,000
Change in assets and liabilities:					
Receivables, net	(1,850,000)	(13,000,000)	—	(14,850,000)	(639,000)
Inventories	(21,000)	(5,000)	(10,000)	(36,000)	(9,000)
Accounts and accrued liabilities	3,238,000	993,000	140,000	4,371,000	128,000
Net cash provided (used) by operating activities	**$2,680,000**	**$16,408,000**	**$(3,788,000)**	**$15,300,000**	**$1,854,000**

Reconciliations

GASB-34 requires a summary reconciliation between the columns for the total Enterprise Fund balances and the business-type activities column of the government-wide financial statements. These reconciliations are illustrated in Chapter 16, "Basic Financial Statements."

FIDUCIARY FUND FINANCIAL STATEMENTS

Assets held by a governmental entity for other parties (either as a trustee or as an agent) and that cannot be used to finance the governmental entity's own operating programs are reported in the entity's fiduciary fund financial statement category. The financial statements for fiduciary funds are based on the flow of economic resources measurement focus and the accrual basis of accounting (with the exception of certain liabilities of defined benefit pension plans and certain post-employment health-care plans). Fiduciary fund financial statements are not reported by major fund (which is required for governmental funds and proprietary funds as illustrated earlier in this chapter) but must be reported based on the following fund types (GASB-34, pars. 106 and 107):

- Pension (and other employee benefit) Trust Funds
- Private-Purpose Trusts
- Investment Trust Funds
- Agency Funds
- Component Units (that are fiduciary in nature)

The following financial statements should be included for fiduciary funds:

- Statement of fiduciary net assets
- Statement of changes in fiduciary net assets

Only a statement of fiduciary net assets is prepared for an Agency Fund.

Statement of Fiduciary Net Assets

The assets, liabilities, and net assets of fiduciary funds are presented in the statement of fiduciary net assets. There is no need to divide net assets into the three categories (invested in capital assets [net of related debt], restricted net assets, and unrestricted net assets) that must be used in the government-wide financial statements.

The following statement of fiduciary net assets reflects the fiduciary funds illustrated in previous chapters:

City of Centerville
Statement of Fiduciary Net Assets
Fiduciary Funds
June 30, 20X2

	Employee Retirement Fund (Chapter 9)	Investment Trust Fund (Chapter 11)	Individual Investment Account (Chapter 11)	Private-Purpose Trust Fund (Chapter 10)	Agency Fund (Chapter 12)
ASSETS					
Cash	$ 4,244,000	$582,000	$ 20,000	$ 27,000	$48,000
Other receivables	31,000	9,000	5,000	—	—
Investments in debt securities	11,022,000	36,000	112,000	459,000	5,000

City of Centerville
Statement of Fiduciary Net Assets
Fiduciary Funds
June 30, 20X2

	Employee Retirement Fund (Chapter 9)	Investment Trust Fund (Chapter 11)	Individual Investment Account (Chapter 11)	Private-Purpose Trust Fund (Chapter 10)	Agency Fund (Chapter 12)
Investment in marketable equity securities	22,463,000	2,039,400	1,361,000	—	—
Other assets	—	1,800	5,000	—	—
Total Assets	**37,760,000**	**2,668,200**	**1,503,000**	**486,000**	**53,000**
LIABILITIES					
Accounts payable and accrued expenses	29,000	13,200	4,000	5,000	8,000
Due to other taxing authorities	—	—	—	—	45,000
Refunds payable and other liabilities	25,000	45,000	12,000	—	—
Total Liabilities	**54,000**	**58,200**	**16,000**	**5,000**	**53,000**
NET ASSETS					
Held in trust for pension benefits and other purposes	$37,706,000	$2,610,000	$1,487,000	$481,000	

Statement of Changes in Fiduciary Net Assets

The statement of changes in fiduciary net asset summarizes the additions to, deductions from, and net increase or decrease in net assets for the year. In addition, GASB-34 requires that the statement provide information "about significant year-to-year changes in net assets":

City of Centerville
Statement of Changes in Fiduciary Net Assets
Fiduciary Funds
For the Year Ended June 30, 20X2

	Employee Retirement Fund (Chapter 9)	Investment Trust Fund (Chapter 11)	Individual Investment Account (Chapter 11)	Private-Purpose Trust Fund (Chapter 10)
ADDITIONS				
Contributions by:				
City of Centerville	$ 7,000,000	—	—	$ 10,000
Plan members/external parties	2,700,000	$ 300,000	$ 50,000	30,000
Total Contributions	**9,700,000**	**300,000**	**50,000**	**40,000**
Interest and investment revenue	486,000	439,000	98,000	49,000

City of Centerville
Statement of Changes in Fiduciary Net Assets
Fiduciary Funds
For the Year Ended June 30, 20X2

	Employee Retirement Fund (Chapter 9)	Investment Trust Fund (Chapter 11)	Individual Investment Account (Chapter 11)	Private-Purpose Trust Fund (Chapter 10)
Total additions	10,186,000	739,200	148,000	89,000
DEDUCTIONS				
Benefits paid	4,200,000	825,000	200,000	57,000
Refunds of contributions	100,000	—	—	—
Administrative expenses	349,000	4,200	1,000	—
Total deductions	4,649,000	829,200	201,000	57,000
Change in net assets	5,537,000	(90,000)	(53,000)	32,000
Net assets—beginning of the year	32,169,000	2,700,000	1,540,000	449,000
Net assets—end of the year	$37,706,000	$2,610,000	$1,487,000	$481,000

CHAPTER 14
DEVELOPING INFORMATION FOR GOVERNMENT-WIDE FINANCIAL STATEMENTS

CONTENTS

INTRODUCTION

The flow of economic resources measurement focus and accrual accounting (which are the concepts upon which commercial enterprises prepare their financial statements) are the basis upon which government-wide financial statements are prepared. Generally, under the flow of economic resources measurement focus and accrual basis of accounting, revenues are recognized when earned and expenses are recorded when incurred when these activities are related to exchange and exchange-like activities. In addition, long-lived assets (such as buildings and equipment) are capitalized and depreciated, and all debt is reported in the fund (GASB-34, par. 16).

Government-wide financial statements are formatted to identify a separate column for governmental activities and business-type activities.

GOVERNMENTAL ACTIVITIES

GASB-34 notes that governmental activities "generally are financed through taxes, intergovernmental revenues, and other nonexchange revenues (and) are usually reported in governmental funds and Internal Service Funds." The information presented in governmental funds is accounted for under the modified accrual basis of accounting and must be converted to an accrual basis. Internal Service Fund information is prepared on an accrual basis, but must be merged into governmental fund financial information that has been converted to an accrual basis. The conversion process was begun in previous chapters, and the accrual balances created in those chapters for governmental funds and Internal Service Funds are consolidated in this chapter.

The prime focus of this reclassification and reorganization is to minimize the possibility of doubling revenues, expenses, assets, and liabilities when combining internal service operations with governmental and business-type activities. There are three main types of eliminations or reclassifications:

1. Receivables and payables between governmental business-type activities and fiduciary funds are not internal balances. Rather, they are receivables from and payables to external parties.

2. Receivables and payables between governmental and business-type activities are either reclassified to internal balances that offset each other when totaled or offset through an adjustment column that shows the elimination before a total column.

3. Amounts that are due to or from funds *within* a governmental or business-type activity are eliminated in between the fund presentation and the statement of net assets. Amounts that are due to or from funds within a group of internal service funds are also eliminated.

The following worksheet consolidates all of the accrual trial balances for governmental funds that were developed in previous chapters:

	General Fund (Ch. 2) (Accrual Based) Debits (Credits)	Special Revenue Funds (Ch. 3) (Accrual Based) Debits (Credits)	Capital Projects Funds (Ch. 4) (Accrual Based) Debits (Credits)	Debt Service Funds (Ch. 5) (Accrual Based) Debits (Credits)	Permanent Fund (Ch. 6) (Accrual Based) Debits (Credits)	Governmental Funds Accrual Basis Total
Cash	$ 10,045,000	$ 68,500	$ 306,956	$210,000	$ 3,000	$ 10,633,456
Temporary investments	—	—	3,679,000	67,000	—	3,746,000
Property taxes receivable (net)	1,755,000	48,000	—	—	—	1,803,000
Other receivables	76,000	17,000	—	—	—	93,000
Investments	5,774,600	—	—	—	244,000	6,018,600
Inventories	17,000	—	—	—	—	17,000
Other assets	5,200	—	—	—	—	5,200
Intergovernmental grants receivable	6,000,000	70,000	—	—	—	6,070,000
Land and improvements	125,000,000	—	—	—	—	125,000,000
Construction in progress	2,050,000	—	13,900,000	—	—	15,950,000
Buildings	213,000,000	—	—	—	—	213,000,000
Equipment	22,300,000	—	—	—	—	22,300,000
Vehicles	73,220,000	—	—	—	—	73,220,000
Leased capital assets	8,249,753	—	—	—	—	8,249,753
Infrastructure assets	20,000,000	—	—	—	—	20,000,000
Accumulated depreciation	(163,619,947)	—	—	—	—	(163,619,947)
Accounts payable	(676,800)	(75,000)	(127,000)	(9,000)	(4,000)	(891,800)
Demand loans payable to bank	(75,000)	—	—	—	—	(75,000)
Interest payable	(24,290)	—	—	(525,000)	—	(549,290)

	General Fund (Ch. 2) (Accrual Based) Debits (Credits)	Special Revenue Funds (Ch. 3) (Accrual Based) Debits (Credits)	Capital Projects Funds (Ch. 4) (Accrual Based) Debits (Credits)	Debt Service Funds (Ch. 5) (Accrual Based) Debits (Credits)	Permanent Fund (Ch. 6) (Accrual Based) Debits (Credits)	Governmental Funds Accrual Basis Total
Due to other funds	(2,642,000)	—	—	—	—	(2,642,000)
Deferred revenue	(300,000)	(10,000)	—	—	—	(310,000)
Claims payable	(1,900,000)	—	—	—	—	(1,900,000)
Compensated absences payable	(4,660,000)	—	—	—	—	(4,660,000)
Lease obligation payable	(4,340,724)	—	—	—	—	(4,340,724)
Revenue bonds payable	—	—	—	(9,250,000)	—	(9,250,000)
Bonds payable	—	—	(12,328,956)	(5,785,359)	—	(18,114,315)
Fund balances/ net assets	(314,445,888)	(29,500)	(1,361,000)	16,859,791	(222,000)	(299,198,597)
General revenue— property taxes	(89,000,000)	(2,670,000)	—	—	—	(91,670,000)
Franchise taxes	(1,300,000)	—	—	—	—	(1,300,000)
Intergovernmental grants—general revenues— unrestricted grants	(26,500,000)	—	—	—	—	(26,500,000)
Program revenues/ charges for services (general government)	(55,000)	—	—	—	—	(55,000)
Program revenues— operating grants and contributions (general government)	—	—	—	—	(34,000)	(34,000)
Program revenues/ charges for services (recreations and parks)	(135,000)	—	—	—	—	(135,000)
Program revenues— capital grants and contributions (recreation and parks)	—	—	(450,000)	—	—	(450,000)
Program revenues/ charges for services (public safety)	(202,000)	—	—	—	—	(202,000)

	General Fund (Ch. 2) (Accrual Based) Debits (Credits)	Special Revenue Funds (Ch. 3) (Accrual Based) Debits (Credits)	Capital Projects Funds (Ch. 4) (Accrual Based) Debits (Credits)	Debt Service Funds (Ch. 5) (Accrual Based) Debits (Credits)	Permanent Fund (Ch. 6) (Accrual Based) Debits (Credits)	Governmental Funds Accrual Basis Total
Program revenues/ charges for services (health and welfare)	(4,000)	—	—	—	—	(4,000)
Program revenues/ charges for services (streets)	(150,000)	—	—	—	—	(150,000)
Program revenues— operating grants (streets)	—	(4,570,000)	—	—	—	(4,570,000)
Program revenues— capital grants (streets)	—	—	(2,000,000)	—	—	(2,000,000)
Contributions	(50,000)	—	—	—	—	(50,000)
Interest and investment revenue	(239,400)	(6,000)	(36,000)	(9,000)	—	(290,400)
Miscellaneous revenue	—	(18,000)	—	—	—	(18,000)
Investment revenue— change in fair value of investments	(362,400)	—	—	—	—	(362,400)
General government expenditures/ expenses	51,164,503	760,000	617,000	42,000	35,000	52,618,503
Public safety expenditures/ expenses	22,448,222	—	—	—	—	22,448,222
Streets expenditures/ expenses	14,803,278	6,190,000	—	—	—	20,993,278
Recreation and parks expenditures/ expenses	7,524,694	—	—	—	—	7,524,694
Health and welfare expenditures/ expenses	9,482,250	—	—	—	—	9,482,250
Interest expense	341,949	—	—	1,719,568	—	2,061,517
Education (component unit)	32,000,000	—	—	—	—	32,000,000
Revenues— permanent endowment additions	—	—	—	—	(22,000)	(22,000)

	General Fund (Ch. 2) (Accrual Based) Debits (Credits)	Special Revenue Funds (Ch. 3) (Accrual Based) Debits (Credits)	Capital Projects Funds (Ch. 4) (Accrual Based) Debits (Credits)	Debt Service Funds (Ch. 5) (Accrual Based) Debits (Credits)	Permanent Fund (Ch. 6) (Accrual Based) Debits (Credits)	Governmental Funds Accrual Basis Total
Extraordinary item—donation of land by the state	(20,000,000)	—	—	—	—	(20,000,000)
Transfers in	(50,000)	(75,000)	(2,200,000)	(3,320,000)		(5,645,000)
Transfers out	5,475,000	300,000	—	—	—	5,775,000
Total	$ 0	$ 0	$ 0	$ 0	$ 0	$ 0

In order to convert the combined totals for all governmental funds restated on an accrual basis presented in the above consolidated trial balance to the trial balance for governmental activities, the following items are considered:

- Integration of Internal Service Fund account balances

- Reclassification of account balances

Merging Internal Service Funds into Governmental Activities

As described in Chapter 8, "Internal Service Funds," at the government-wide financial statement level, activities related to Internal Service Funds are eliminated to avoid doubling-up expenses and revenues in the presentation of the governmental activities and business-type activities columns in the statement of activities. The effect of this approach is to adjust activities in an Internal Service Fund to a break-even balance. That is, if the Internal Service Fund had a "net profit" for the year, there is a pro rata reduction in the charges made to the funds that used the Internal Service Fund's services for the year. Likewise, a net loss requires a pro rata adjustment that increases the charges made to the various participating funds. After making these eliminations, any residual balances related to the Internal Service Fund's assets and liabilities are reported in either the government activities column or the business-type activities column.

The City of Centerville has the following Internal Service Funds:

- Communications and Technology Support Center (provides a variety of communication and computer support services to all of the City's governmental and proprietary funds)

- Fleet Management (provides a motor pool to all of the City's governmental funds and to some other governmental units that are not part of the City's reporting entity; it provides no service to Enterprise Funds)

- Special Services Support Center (provides services exclusively for the Centerville Municipal Airport)

Based on the nature of each Internal Service Fund, the Communications and Technology Support Center balances are allocated to both governmental activities and business-type activities, the Fleet Management Fund is allocated exclusively to governmental activities, and the Special Services Support Center is allocated exclusively to business-type activities.

The previous consolidated trial balance of all governmental funds reported on an accrual basis is adjusted in the following to reflect the first two Internal Service Funds.

Prior to the issuance of GASB-34, Internal Service Funds were presented by fund type and were not merged into governmental funds or Enterprise Funds.

	Governmental Funds Accrual Basis Total	Communications And Technology Support Center* (Chapter 8)	Preliminary Fleet Management Unit** (Chapter 8)	Governmental Activities Total
Cash	10,633,456	946,000	137,500	11,716,956
Temporary investments	3,746,000	15,000	19,000	3,780,000
Property taxes receivable (net)	1,803,000	—	—	1,803,000
Other receivables	93,000	1,000	2,000	96,000
Due from other funds	—	325,000	72,000	397,000
Investments	6,018,600	—	—	6,018,600
Inventories	17,000	9,000	7,000	33,000
Other assets	5,200	—	—	5,200
Due from other governments	—	—	45,000	45,000
Intergovernmental grants receivable	6,070,000	—	—	6,070,000
Internal balances	—	547,456	—	547,456
Land and improvements	125,000,000	2,700,000	50,000	127,750,000
Construction in progress	15,950,000	—	—	15,950,000
Buildings	213,000,000	1,400,000	1,600,000	216,000,000
Equipment	22,300,000	5,870,000	1,330,000	29,500,000
Vehicles	73,220,000	143,000	8,200,000	81,563,000
Leased capital assets	8,249,753	—	—	8,249,753
Infrastructure assets	20,000,000	—	—	20,000,000
Accumulated depreciation	(163,619,947)	(3,103,000)	(6,505,000)	(173,227,947)
Accounts payable	(891,800)	(50,000)	(125,000)	(1,066,800)
Demand loans payable to bank	(75,000)	—	—	(75,000)
Interest payable	(549,290)	—	—	(549,290)
Due to other funds	(2,642,000)	—	—	(2,642,000)
Deferred revenue	(310,000)	—	—	(310,000)
Claims payable	(1,900,000)	(19,000)	(13,000)	(1,932,000)
Compensated absences payable	(4,660,000)	(7,000)	(8,000)	(4,675,000)
Notes payable	—	(4,700,000)	(3,000,000)	(7,700,000)
Lease obligation payable	(4,340,724)	—	—	(4,340,724)
Revenue bonds payable	(9,250,000)	—	—	(9,250,000)
Bonds payable	(18,114,315)	—	—	(18,114,315)
Fund balances/net assets	(299,198,597)	(6,590,000)	(1,489,500)	(307,278,097)
General revenue—property taxes	(91,670,000)	—	—	(91,670,000)
Franchise taxes	(1,300,000)	—	—	(1,300,000)
Intergovernmental grants—general revenues—unrestricted grants	(26,500,000)	—	—	(26,500,000)
Program revenues/charges for services (general government)	(55,000)	—	(300,000)	(355,000)
Program revenues—operating grants and contributions (general government)	(34,000)	—	—	(34,000)

	Governmental Funds Accrual Basis Total	Communications And Technology Support Center* (Chapter 8)	Preliminary Fleet Management Unit** (Chapter 8)	Governmental Activities Total
Program revenues/charges for services (recreations and parks)	(135,000)	—	—	(135,000)
Program revenues—capital grants and contributions (recreation and parks)	(450,000)	—	—	(450,000)
Program revenues/charges for services (public safety)	(202,000)	—	—	(202,000)
Program revenues/charges for services (health and welfare)	(4,000)	—	—	(4,000)
Program revenues/charges for services (streets)	(150,000)	—	—	(150,000)
Program revenues—operating grants (streets)	(4,570,000)	—	—	(4,570,000)
Program revenues—capital grants (streets)	(2,000,000)	—	—	(2,000,000)
Contributions	(50,000)	—	—	(50,000)
Interest and investment revenue	(290,400)	(5,000)	(5,000)	(300,400)
Miscellaneous revenue	(18,000)	—	—	(18,000)
Investment revenue—change in fair value of investments	(362,400)	—	—	(362,400)
General government expenditures/ expenses	52,618,503	1,476,326	(40,200)	54,054,629
Public safety expenditures/ expenses	22,448,222	492,109	(103,400)	22,836,931
Streets expenditures/expenses	20,993,278	246,055	(51,700)	21,187,633
Recreation and parks expenditures/ expenses	7,524,694	123,027	(25,850)	7,621,871
Health and welfare expenditures/ expenses	9,482,250	123,027	(25,850)	9,579,427
Interest expense	2,061,517	97,000	180,000	2,338,517
Education (component unit)	32,000,000	—	—	32,000,000
Revenues—permanent endowment additions	(22,000)	—	—	(22,000)
Extraordinary item—donation of land by the state	(20,000,000)	—	—	(20,000,000)
Transfers in	(5,645,000)	(40,000)	—	(5,685,000)
Transfers out	5,775,000	—	50,000	5,825,000
Total	$ 0	$ 0	$ 0	$ 0

* This column is based on worksheet entry JE08.45, which was made in Chapter 8, "Internal Service Funds."
** This column is based on worksheet entry JE08.47, which was made in Chapter 8, "Internal Service Funds."

Reclassification of Account Balances

In order to reclassify a variety of accounts that appear in the consolidated totals for governmental activities as presented in the above trial balance, the following reclassification entries are made:

	Accounts	Debit	Credit
JE14.01	Investments	3,780,000	
	Temporary investments		3,780,000

Accounts	Debit	Credit
(To reclassify temporary investments)		
JE14.02 Receivables (net)	8,014,000	
Intergovernmental grants receivable		6,070,000
Property taxes receivable (net)		1,803,000
Due from other governments		45,000
Other receivables		96,000
(To reclassify various receivables)		
JE14.03 Due to other funds	242,000	
Internal balances	155,000	
Due from other funds		397,000
(To eliminate amounts due to and due from funds that make up governmental activities (amounts due from the General Fund to Communications and Technology Support Center ($170,000) and Fleet Management ($72,000) and to reclassify the amounts due to the Enterprise Funds ($155,000) as an internal balance)		
JE14.04 Due to other funds	2,400,000	
Internal balances		2,400,000
(To reclassify amounts due from the General Fund to Enterprise Funds [Utilities Authority $2,000,000 and Municipal Airport $400,000] as an Internal Balance)		
JE14.05 Land, improvements, and construction in progress	143,700,000	
Construction in progress		15,950,000
Land and improvements		127,750,000
(To reclassify capital assets not subject to depreciation)		
JE14.06 Other capital assets (net)	182,084,806	
Accumulated depreciation	173,227,947	
Buildings		216,000,000
Equipment		29,500,000
Vehicles		81,563,000
Leased capital assets		8,249,753
Infrastructure assets		20,000,000
(To reclassify accumulated depreciation and capital assets subject to depreciation)		
JE14.07 Accounts payable	1,066,800	
Interest payable	549,290	
Accounts payable and accrued expenses		1,616,090
(To reclassify various payables)		
JE14.08 Compensated absences payable	4,675,000	
Claims and judgements payable	1,932,000	
Notes payable	7,700,000	
Lease obligation payable	4,340,724	
Revenue bonds payable	9,250,000	
Bonds payable	18,114,315	
Long-term liabilities—due within one year		4,658,932
Long-term liabilities—due in more than one year		41,353,107

Accounts	Debit	Credit
(To reclassify debt into due within one year and beyond one year)		
JE14.09 Contributions	50,000	
Program revenues—operating grants and contributions (health and welfare)		50,000
(To reclassify corporate contributions)		
JE14.10 Interest and investment revenue	300,400	
Investment revenue—change in fair value of investments	362,400	
Unrestricted investment earnings		662,800
(To reclassify interest and investment revenue as unrestricted investment earnings)		
JE14.11 Interest on long-term debt	2,338,517	
Payments to school district	32,000,000	
Interest expense		2,338,517
Education (component unit)		32,000,000
(To reclassify various expenses)		
JE14.12 Revenue—permanent endowment additions	22,000	
Contributions to permanent funds		22,000
(To reclassify addition to endowment)		
JE14.13 Transfers in	5,685,000	
Transfers out		5,685,000
(To eliminate transfers within governmental activities)		

After posting the entries for reclassifying various accounts, the trial balance for governmental activities appears as follows:

	Preliminary Governmental Activities Total Debit (Credit)		Reclassifications and Adjustments Debit (Credit)	Government-Wide Financial Statements Debit (Credit)
Cash	$ 11,716,956		—	$ 11,716,956
Internal Balances	547,456	JE14.04	$ (2,400,000)	(1,697,544)
	—	JE14.03	155,000	—
Temporary investments	3,780,000	JE14.01	(3,780,000)	—
Receivables (net)	—	JE14.02	8,014,000	8,014,000
Property taxes receivable (net)	1,803,000	JE14.02	(1,803,000)	—
Other receivables	96,000	JE14.02	(96,000)	—
Due from other funds	397,000	JE14.03	(397,000)	—
Investments	6,018,600	JE14.01	3,780,000	9,798,600
Inventories	33,000		—	33,000
Other Assets	5,200		—	5,200
Due from other governments	45,000	JE14.02	(45,000)	—
Intergovernmental grants receivable	6,070,000	JE14.02	(6,070,000)	—
Land, improvements, and construction in progress	—	JE14.05	143,700,000	143,700,000
Land and improvements	127,750,000	JE14.05	(127,750,000)	—
Construction in progress	15,950,000	JE14.05	(15,950,000)	—
Other capital assets (net)	—	JE14.06	182,084,806	182,084,806
Buildings	216,000,000	JE14.06	(216,000,000)	—
Equipment	29,500,000	JE14.06	(29,500,000)	—

	Preliminary Governmental Activities Total Debit (Credit)		Reclassifications and Adjustments Debit (Credit)	Government-Wide Financial Statements Debit (Credit)
Vehicles	81,563,000	JE14.06	(81,563,000)	—
Leased capital assets	8,249,753	JE14.06	(8,249,753)	—
Infrastructure assets	20,000,000	JE14.06	(20,000,000)	—
Accumulated depreciation	(173,227,947)	JE14.06	173,227,947	—
Accounts payable and accrued expenses	—	JE14.07	(1,616,090)	(1,616,090)
Accounts payable	(1,066,800)	JE14.07	1,066,800	—
Demand loans payable to bank	(75,000)	JE14.07	—	(75,000)
Interest payable	(549,290)	JE14.07	549,290	—
Due to other funds	(2,642,000)	JE14.03	242,000	—
		JE14.04	2,400,000	
Deferred revenue	(310,000)		—	(310,000)
Long-term liabilities—due within one year	—	JE14.08	(4,658,932)	(4,658,932)
Long-term liabilities—due in more than one year	—	JE14.08	(41,353,107)	(41,353,107)
Claims payable	(1,932,000)	JE14.08	1,932,000	—
Compensated absences payable	(4,675,000)	JE14.08	4,675,000	—
Notes payable	(7,700,000)	JE14.08	7,700,000	—
Lease obligation payable	(4,340,724)	JE14.08	4,340,724	—
Revenue bonds payable	(9,250,000)	JE14.08	9,250,000	—
Bonds payable	(18,114,315)	JE14.08	18,114,315	—
Fund balance/net assets	(307,278,097)		—	(307,278,097)
General revenue—property taxes	(91,670,000)		—	(91,670,000)
Franchise taxes	(1,300,000)		—	(1,300,000)
Intergovernmental grants—general revenues—unrestricted grants	(26,500,000)		—	(26,500,000)
Program revenues/charges for services (general government)	(355,000)		—	(355,000)
Program revenues—operating grants and contributions (general government)	(34,000)		—	(34,000)
Program revenues/charges for services (recreations and parks)	(135,000)		—	(135,000)
Program revenues—capital grants and contributions (recreation and parks)	(450,000)		—	(450,000)
Program revenues/charges for services (public safety)	(202,000)		—	(202,000)
Program revenues/charges for services (health and welfare)	(4,000)		—	(4,000)
Program revenues—operating grants and contributions (health and welfare)	—	JE14.09	(50,000)	(50,000)
Program revenues/charges for services (streets)	(150,000)		—	(150,000)
Program revenues—operating grants and contributions (streets)	(4,570,000)		—	(4,570,000)
Program revenues—capital grants and contributions (streets)	(2,000,000)		—	(2,000,000)

	Preliminary Governmental Activities Total Debit (Credit)		Reclassifications and Adjustments Debit (Credit)	Government-Wide Financial Statements Debit (Credit)
Contributions	(50,000)	JE14.09	50,000	—
Unrestricted investment earnings	—	JE14.10	(662,800)	(662,800)
Interest and investment revenue	(300,400)	JE14.10	300,400	—
Miscellaneous revenue	(18,000)		—	(18,000)
Investment revenue—change in fair value of investments	(362,400)	JE14.10	362,400	—
General government expenses	54,054,629		—	54,054,629
Public safety expenses	22,836,931		—	22,836,931
Streets expenditures/expenses	21,187,633		—	21,187,633
Recreation and parks expenses	7,621,871		—	7,621,871
Health and welfare expenses	9,579,427		—	9,579,427
Interest on long-term debt	—	JE14.11	2,338,517	2,338,517
Payments to school district	—	JE14.11	32,000,000	32,000,000
Interest expense	2,338,517	JE14.11	(2,338,517)	—
Contributions to permanent funds	—	JE14.12	(22,000)	(22,000)
Education (component unit)	32,000,000	JE14.11	(32,000,000)	—
Revenues—permanent endowment additions	(22,000)	JE14.12	22,000	
Extraordinary item—donation of land by the state	(20,000,000)		—	(20,000,000)
Transfers in	(5,685,000)	JE14.13	5,685,000	—
Transfers out	5,825,000	JE14.13	(5,685,000)	140,000
Total	$ 0		$ 0	$ 0

The last column in the above worksheet is the basis for preparing the governmental activities column in the government-wide financial statements.

GASB-34 introduced the concept of an "internal balance" between governmental funds and proprietary funds. Internal balances are presented on the face of the statement of net assets for both the governmental activities and the business-type activities, but they offset (net to zero) when totals are extended to the "reporting entity column" on the statement.

GASB-34 requires that program revenues be classified and reported as (1) charges for services, (2) operating grants and contributions, and (3) capital grants and contributions. During the implementation process for GASB-34, questions arose about how revenues raised by one function/activity but used by another function/activity should be classified in the statement of activities. For example, if revenue generated by a state lottery (a separately reported function/activity) must be used to finance education (another function/activity), should the proceeds from the lottery be reported as revenue for the lottery or for education? GASB-37 (Basic Financial Statements—and Management's Discussion and Analysis—for State and Local Governments: Omnibus) states that the following factors are to be used to determine which revenue should be related to a program: (1) for charges for services the determining factor is which function generates the revenue and (2) for grants and contributions the determining factor is the function the revenue is restricted to. Thus, in the lottery example, the proceeds from the lottery are reported as charges for services of the lottery activity because the educational activity used the resources but did not create the proceeds from lottery activities.

A governmental entity that classifies its expenses by function may receive a state grant (which meets the definition of program revenue) that is to be used for specified programs. The GASB's *Comprehensive Implementation Guide* states that the fact that the grant is based on one classification scheme and a governmental entity's statement of activities is based on another does not change the original character of the revenue. That is, the grant is classified as program revenue (not general revenue) even though it must be allocated to a variety of functions in the statement of activities.

PRACTICE POINT: Some governments that allocate their indirect expenses or central service (overhead) costs to its functions prefer to be present these allocations separately, although GASB-34 does not require separate presentation for these allocations. By doing so, a more accurate picture of the cost of individual services may be presented. If a government prefers to present allocations separately, a separate column is presented to the right of the program expenses so that direct expenses can be seen easily, segregated from indirect expenses, and users can infer that the total of the two columns (not required to be added together) signifies total functional costs. GASB-34, Appendix B-2, depicts this version of the Statement of Activities. Should this extra column be added, the total indirect expenses allocation must net to zero and the General Government function must add to zero when taking into account program and other revenues.

The GASB's *Comprehensive Implementation Guide* notes that not all program revenues create restricted net assets. By their nature grants and contributions (both operational and capital) give rise to restricted net assets, but charges for services may be unrestricted, restricted to the program that gave rise to the charge, or restricted to a program that is unrelated to the revenue generated service. On the other hand, the GASB's *Guide* states that tax revenue could be restricted for a particular use (for example, taxes levied specifically to pay debt service) but nonetheless be reported as general revenue, perhaps under a heading that identifies it as restricted for a particular purpose.

The language used in GASB-34 strongly implied that only three categories could be used to identify program revenues, namely: (1) charges for services, (2) operating grants and contributions, and (3) capital grants and contributions. GASB-37 states that the formatting of the statement of activities is more flexible than originally conveyed in GASB-34. For example, more than one column could be included under one of the three program revenue columns. Furthermore, the columnar heading may be modified to be more descriptive. For example, a program revenue column could be labeled "operating grants, contributions, and restricted interest."

With the issuance of GASB-34, some financial statement preparers were unsure about how revenues related to fines and forfeitures should be classified in the statement of activities. GASB-37 modifies GASB-34 by specifically stating that fines and forfeitures are to be classified as charges for services because "they result from direct charges to those who are otherwise directly affected by a program or service, even though they receive no benefit." However, GASB-37 recognizes that there is an element of confusion and arbitrariness in classifying fines and forfeitures as charges for services by noting that the statement of activities could be formatted (1) in order to present a separate column labeled Fines and Forfeitures" under the "Charges for Services" column or (2) by captioning the column "Charges for Services, Fees, Fines, and Forfeitures."

GASB-38 (Certain Financial Statement Note Disclosures) requires that a governmental entity present in the notes to its financial statements the details of receivables and payables reported on the statements of net assets and balance sheets "when significant components have been obscured by aggregation." In addition, significant receivable balances that are not expected to be collected within one year of the date of the financial statements should be disclosed.

BUSINESS-TYPE ACTIVITIES

GASB-34 notes that business-type activities "are financed in whole or in part by fees charged to external parties for goods or services [and] these activities are usually reported in Enterprise Funds." The information presented in Enterprise Funds is accounted for using the accrual basis of accounting and, therefore, the balances that appeared on the fund financial statements for Enterprise Funds do not have to be adjusted before they are reported in the business-type activities column of the government-wide financial statements. However, because of the unique format of the government-wide financial statements, it is necessary to combine and reclassify some of the accounts that were reported in the Enterprise Funds at the fund financial statement level. In some instances, it may also be necessary to merge Internal Service Fund balances with Enterprise Funds. To begin this process, the following consolidating trial balance for all Enterprise Funds is presented below and is based on the information developed in Chapter 7, "Enterprise Funds."

	Centerville Toll Bridge (Chapter 7) Debit (Credit)	Centerville Utilities Authority (Chapter 7) Debit (Credit)	Centerville Parking Authority (Chapter 7) Debit (Credit)	Centerville Municipal Airport (Chapter 7) Debit (Credit)	Combined Totals For Enterprise Funds Debit (Credit)
Cash	$ 739,500	$ 230,000	$ 764,000	$10,963,000	$12,696,500
Interest receivable	3,000	50,000	3,000	200,000	256,000
Accounts receivable (net)	—	7,550,000	—	18,000,000	25,550,000
Due from other funds	—	2,000,000	—	400,000	2,400,000
Due from other governments	—	100,000	—	300,000	400,000
Temporary investments	58,000	55,000	5,000	10,050,000	10,168,000
Inventories	32,000	75,000	24,000	55,000	186,000
Construction in progress	70,000	200,000	15,000	23,500,000	23,785,000
Land and improvements	140,000	5,200,000	1,780,000	13,200,000	20,320,000
Superstructure	1,400,000	—	—	—	1,400,000
Distribution and collection systems	—	46,300,000	—	—	46,300,000
Runways and tarmacs	—	—	—	27,500,000	27,500,000
Buildings	330,000	14,450,000	2,400,000	33,200,000	50,380,000

	Centerville Toll Bridge (Chapter 7) Debit (Credit)	Centerville Utilities Authority (Chapter 7) Debit (Credit)	Centerville Parking Authority (Chapter 7) Debit (Credit)	Centerville Municipal Airport (Chapter 7) Debit (Credit)	Combined Totals For Enterprise Funds Debit (Credit)
Equipment	55,000	4,600,000	140,000	7,200,000	11,995,000
Vehicles	835,000	1,660,000	102,000	2,500,000	5,097,000
Accumulated depreciation	(1,257,000)	(54,395,000)	(1,505,000)	(20,255,000)	(77,412,000)
Accounts payable and accrued expenses	(50,000)	(4,300,000)	(90,000)	(3,900,000)	(8,340,000)
Due to other funds	(18,000)	(35,000)	(17,000)	(512,000)	(582,000)
Compensated absences	(8,000)	(84,000)	(5,000)	(133,000)	(230,000)
Claims and judgments	(27,000)	(229,000)	(7,000)	(195,000)	(458,000)
Notes payable	(30,000)	(330,000)	(30,000)	(7,700,000)	(8,090,000)
Revenue bonds—Terminal A	—	—	—	(10,000,000)	(10,000,000)
Revenue bonds—Terminal B	—	—	—	(4,000,000)	(4,000,000)
Bonds payable	(80,000)	(7,700,000)	(500,000)	—	(8,280,000)
Net assets	(1,646,500)	(16,019,000)	(3,994,000)	(73,608,000)	(95,267,500)
Charges for services	(4,750,000)	(36,000,000)	(1,500,000)	(175,000,000)	(217,250,000)
Charges for services—rental income—security for Terminal A revenue bonds	—	—	—	(30,000,000)	(30,000,000)
Charges for services—rental income—security for Terminal B revenue bonds	—	—	—	(22,000,000)	(22,000,000)
Miscellaneous revenues	(20,000)	(10,000)	(22,000)	(60,000)	(112,000)
Expenses—personal services	2,402,000	22,022,000	5,402,000	161,025,000	190,851,000
Expenses—contractual services	1,280,000	11,220,000	400,000	33,550,000	46,450,000
Expenses—repairs and maintenance	400,000	700,000	50,000	2,100,000	3,250,000
Expenses—other supplies and expenses	194,000	729,000	36,000	1,795,000	2,754,000
Expenses—insurance claims and expenses	10,000	21,000	3,000	100,000	134,000
Expenses—depreciation	339,000	3,025,000	117,000	3,370,000	6,851,000
Expenses—miscellaneous	30,000	5,000	3,000	70,000	108,000
Interest and investment revenue	(30,000)	(400,000)	(10,000)	(1,200,000)	(1,640,000)
Interest expense	6,000	450,000	27,000	1,220,000	1,703,000
Operating grants and contributions	(100,000)	—	—	—	(100,000)
Non-operating miscellaneous expenses (revenues)	(7,000)	110,000	(1,000)	265,000	367,000
Capital contributions	(250,000)	(1,250,000)	—	(2,000,000)	(3,500,000)
Transfers in	(50,000)	—	(90,000)	—	(140,000)
Transfers out	—	—	—	—	0
Special item—gain on sale of parking lot	—	—	(3,500,000)	—	(3,500,000)
Total	$ 0	$ 0	$ 0	$ 0	$ 0

In order to convert the combined totals for all Enterprise Funds as presented in the above trial balance to the trial balance for business-type activities, the following items are considered:

- Integration of Internal Service Fund account balances

- Reclassification of account balances

Merging Internal Service Funds into Business-Type Activities

Based on the nature of each Internal Service Fund, the Communications and Technology Support Center balances are allocated to both governmental activities (which was done earlier) and business-type activities, and the Special Services Support Center balances are allocated exclusively to business-type activities. This analysis was made in Chapter 8, "Internal Service Funds," and resulted in the following entries:

	Accounts	Debit	Credit
JE08.46	Expenses—Centerville Municipal Airport	327,872	
	Expenses—Centerville Utilities Authority	120,320	
	Expenses—Centerville Parking Authority	54,144	
	Expenses—Centerville Toll Bridge	45,120	
	Internal balances		547,456

	Accounts	Debit	Credit
JE08.48	Cash	22,000	
	Interest receivable	1,000	
	Due from other funds	427,000	
	Temporary investments	12,000	
	Inventories	20,000	
	Land and improvements	1,750,000	
	Buildings	1,600,000	
	Equipment	2,960,000	
	Vehicles	1,995,000	
	Expenses—Centerville Municipal Airport		73,000
	Accumulated depreciation		3,240,000
	Accounts payable and accrued expenses		75,000
	Compensated absences		17,000
	Claims and judgments		21,000
	Notes payable		550,000
	Interest and investment revenue		15,000
	Net assets		4,796,000

Entry JE08.46 merges the appropriate balances from the Communications and Technology Support Center and Entry JE08.48 merges the balances from the Special Services Support Center. These entries are combined with the reclassification entries in the following section.

Reclassification of Account Balances

On the statement of net assets, only totals for business activities are presented. That is, a single balance for cash (for business-type activities) is presented rather than cash for each Enterprise Fund. In this illustration, the following account titles are used to prepare the statement of net assets:

- Cash
- Interest receivable
- Temporary investments
- Internal balances

- Receivables (net)
- Inventories
- Land, improvements, and construction in progress
- Other capital assets (net)
- Accounts payable and accrued expenses
- Long-term liabilities—due in one year
- Long-term liabilities—due in more than one year
- Net assets (the three components of net assets are added later in the chapter)

On the statement of activities, generally only the following nominal accounts are presented for business-type activities (not all of these accounts are used in this illustration):

- Charges for services—Centerville Toll Bridge
- Charges for services—Centerville Parking Authority
- Charges for services—Centerville Utilities Authority
- Charges for services—Centerville Municipal Airport
- Operating grants and contributions—Centerville Toll Bridge
- Operating grants and contributions—Centerville Parking Authority
- Operating grants and contributions—Centerville Utilities Authority
- Operating grants and contributions—Centerville Municipal Airport
- Capital grants and contributions—Centerville Toll Bridge
- Capital grants and contributions—Centerville Parking Authority
- Capital grants and contributions—Centerville Utilities Authority
- Capital grants and contributions—Centerville Municipal Airport
- Expenses—Centerville Toll Bridge
- Expenses—Centerville Utilities Authority
- Expenses—Centerville Parking Authority
- Expenses—Centerville Municipal Airport
- Unrestricted investment earnings
- Miscellaneous revenue
- Extraordinary items
- Special items

The format for the government-wide statement of activities as established by GASB-34 is significantly different from any prior operating statement used in governmental financial reporting. To some, the statement of activities is the most important statement issued by a state or local government. The focus of the statement of activities is on the *net cost* of various activities provided by the governmental entity. The statement begins with a column that identifies the cost of each governmental activity. Another column identifies the revenues that are specifically related to the classified governmental activities. The difference between the expenses and revenues related to specific activities computes the net cost or benefits of the activities, which "identifies the extent to which each function of the government draws from the general revenues of the government or is self-financing through fees and intergovernmental aid" (GASB-34, pars. 38–40).

The GASB's *Comprehensive Implementation Guide* points out that generally the difference between activities in the goods, services, or programs provided is obvious, but in some circumstances professional judgment must be used to determine when activities should be reported separately. For example, the GASB's *Guide* states that a city that uses a single fund to account for water and electric utilities should report these two activities as separate functions or programs in the statement of activities. On the other hand, a city that uses four separate funds to report its four separate water districts may (but does not have to) combine the four sets of accounts and report a single separate activity or function on its statement of activities.

The liquidity of assets is determined by their ability to be converted to cash and the absence of any restriction that might limit their conversion to cash. If an asset is restricted, the nature of the restriction must be evaluated to determine the appropriate location within the asset classification. The GASB's *Comprehensive Implementation Guide* provides the following examples of how restrictions affect asset presentation: (1) cash restricted for the servicing of debt: If the cash is expected to be used to pay "current maturities," the cash could be reported with unrestricted cash, (2) permanently restricted assets: If assets are permanently restricted, they are not available to pay a governmental entity's expenses and are therefore as illiquid as capital assets, and (3) term restrictions: The term of the restriction determines where assets subject to term restrictions are presented. If the restriction ends within a short period after the date of the financial statements, the assets are relatively liquid. On the other hand, if the time restriction is longer than one year, the assets are as illiquid as long-term receivables that have a similar "maturity" date.

In order to reclassify a variety of accounts that appear in the consolidated totals for Enterprise Funds as presented in the above trial balance, the following reclassification entries are made. (The amounts that are reclassified reflect the consolidated amounts in the trial balance for all Enterprise Funds and the two entries made to integrate Internal Service Fund balances [represented by amounts in parentheses].)

	Accounts	Debit	Credit
JE14.14	Investments	10,180,000	
	Temporary investments ($10,050,000 + 5,000 + 55,000 + 58,000)		10,180,000
	(To reclassify temporary investments)		
JE14.15	Receivable (net)	26,207,000	
	Interest receivable ($256,000 + $1,000)		257,000
	Accounts receivable (net)		25,550,000
	Due from other governments		400,000
	(To reclassify various receivables)		
JE14.16	Internal balances	2,400,000	

Accounts	Debit	Credit
Due from other funds		2,400,000
(To reclassify amounts due from the General Fund as an internal balance)		
JE14.17 Land, improvements, and construction in progress	45,855,000	
Construction in progress		23,785,000
Land and improvements ($20,320,000 + $1,750,000)		22,070,000
(To reclassify capital assets not subject to depreciation)		
JE14.18 Other capital assets (net)	68,575,000	
Accumulated depreciation ($77,412,000 + $3,240,000)	80,652,000	
Superstructure		1,400,000
Distribution and collection systems		46,300,000
Runways and tarmacs		27,500,000
Buildings ($50,380,000 + $1,600,000)		51,980,000
Equipment ($11,995,000 + $2,960,000)		14,955,000
Vehicles ($5,097,000 + $1,995,000)		7,092,000
(To reclassify accumulated depreciation and capital assets subject to depreciation)		
JE14.19 Due to other funds	582,000	
Internal balances		155,000
Due from other funds		427,000
(To eliminate the intra-fund receivable/payable ($427,000) and to reclassify the amount due to the Communication and Technology Support Center—Internal Service Fund that was merged with the governmental activities [$155,000])		
JE14.20 Compensated absences	247,000	
Claims and judgements	479,000	
Notes payable	8,640,000	
Revenue bonds—Terminal A	10,000,000	
Revenue bonds—Terminal B	4,000,000	
Bonds payable	8,280,000	
Long-term liabilities—due within one year		3,784,000
Long-term liabilities—due in more than one year		27,862,000
(To reclassify debt into due within one year and beyond one year)		
JE14.21 Charges for services	217,250,000	
Charges for services—rental income—security for Terminal A revenue bonds	30,000,000	
Charges for services—rental income—security for Terminal B revenue bonds	22,000,000	
Miscellaneous revenue	112,000	
Charges for services—Centerville Toll Bridge		4,770,000
Charges for services—Centerville Parking Authority		1,522,000
Charges for services—Centerville Utilities Authority		36,010,000
Charges for services—Centerville Municipal Airport		227,060,000
(To reclassify charges for services to specific activities)		
JE14.22 Operating grants and contributions	100,000	
Capital contributions	3,500,000	
Operating grants and contributions—Centerville Toll Bridge		100,000
Capital grants and contributions—Centerville Toll Bridge		250,000

	Accounts	Debit	Credit
	Capital grants and contributions—Centerville Utilities Authority		1,250,000
	Capital grants and contributions—Centerville Municipal Airport		2,000,000
	(To reclassify grants and contributions to specific activities)		
JE14.23	Expenses—Centerville Municipal Airport	202,010,000	
	Expenses—Centerville Utilities Authority	37,722,000	
	Expenses—Centerville Parking Authority	6,011,000	
	Expenses—Centerville Toll Bridge	4,655,000	
	Expenses—personal services		190,851,000
	Expenses—contractual services		46,450,000
	Expenses—repairs and maintenance		3,250,000
	Expenses—other supplies and expenses		2,754,000
	Expenses—insurance claims and expenses		134,000
	Expenses—depreciation		6,851,000
	Expenses—miscellaneous		108,000
	(To reclassify operating expenses to specific activities)		
JE14.24	Expenses—Centerville Municipal Airport	1,220,000	
	Expenses—Centerville Utilities Authority	450,000	
	Expenses—Centerville Parking Authority	27,000	
	Expenses—Centerville Toll Bridge	6,000	
	Interest expense		1,703,000
	(To reclassify interest expense to specific activities)		
JE14.25	Expenses—Centerville Municipal Airport	110,000	
	Expenses—Centerville Utilities Authority	265,000	
	Expenses—Centerville Parking Authority		1,000
	Expenses—Centerville Toll Bridge		7,000
	Non-operating miscellaneous expenses (revenues)		367,000
	(To reclassify gains and losses on the sale of assets to specific activities)		
JE14.26	Interest and Investment Revenue ($1,640,000 + $15,000)	1,655,000	
	Unrestricted Investment Earnings		1,655,000
	(To reclassify interest and investment revenue as unrestricted investment earnings)		

After posting the entries to merge the balances of the Internal Service Fund and to reclassify various accounts, the trial balance for business-type activities appears below is as follows:

	Combined Totals For Enterprise Funds Debit (Credit)		Reclassifications and Adjustments Debit (Credit)	Government-Wide Financial Statements Debit (Credit)
Cash	$12,696,500	JE08.48	$22,000	$12,718,500
Internal Balances	—	JE08.46	(547,456)	1,697,544
	—	JE14.16	2,400,000	
	—	JE14.19	(155,000)	
Receivables (net)	—	JE14.15	26,207,000	26,207,000
Interest receivable	256,000	JE08.48	1,000	0
	—	JE14.15	(257,000)	

	Combined Totals For Enterprise Funds Debit (Credit)		Reclassifications and Adjustments Debit (Credit)	Government-Wide Financial Statements Debit (Credit)
Accounts receivable (net)	25,550,000	JE14.15	(25,550,000)	0
Due from other funds	2,400,000	JE08.48	427,000	0
	—	JE14.16	(2,400,000)	
	—	JE14.19	(427,000)	
Due from other governments	400,000	JE14.15	(400,000)	0
Temporary investments	10,168,000	JE08.48	12,000	0
	—	JE14.14	(10,180,000)	
Investments	—	JE14.14	10,180,000	10,180,000
Inventories	186,000	JE08.48	20,000	206,000
Land, improvements, and construction in progress	—	JE14.17	45,855,000	45,855,000
Construction in progress	23,785,000	JE14.17	(23,785,000)	0
Land and improvements	20,320,000	JE08.48	1,750,000	0
	—	JE14.17	(22,070,000)	
Other capital assets (net)	—	JE14.18	68,575,000	68,575,000
Superstructure	1,400,000	JE14.18	(1,400,000)	0
Distribution and collection systems	46,300,000	JE14.18	(46,300,000)	0
Runways and tarmacs	27,500,000	JE14.18	(27,500,000)	0
Buildings	50,380,000	JE08.48	1,600,000	0
	—	JE14.18	(51,980,000)	
Equipment	11,995,000	JE08.48	2,960,000	0
	—	JE14.18	(14,955,000)	
Vehicles	5,097,000	JE08.48	1,995,000	
	—	JE14.18	(7,092,000)	
Accumulated depreciation	(77,412,000)	JE08.48	(3,240,000)	0
	—	JE14.18	80,652,000	
Accounts payable and accrued expenses	(8,340,000)	JE08.48	(75,000)	(8,415,000)
Due to other funds	(582,000)	JE14.19	582,000	0
Long-Term Liabilities—Due within one year	—	JE14.20	(3,784,000)	(3,784,000)
Long-Term Liabilities—Due in more than one year	—	JE14.20	(27,862,000)	(27,862,000)
Compensated absences	(230,000)	JE08.48	(17,000)	0
	—	JE14.20	247,000	
Claims and judgments	(458,000)	JE08.48	(21,000)	0
	—	JE14.20	479,000	
Notes payable	(8,090,000)	JE08.48	(550,000)	0
	—	JE14.20	8,640,000	
Revenue bonds—Terminal A	(10,000,000)	JE14.20	10,000,000	0
Revenue bonds—Terminal B	(4,000,000)	JE14.20	4,000,000	0
Bonds payable	(8,280,000)	JE14.20	8,280,000	0
Net assets	(95,267,500)	JE08.48	(4,796,000)	(100,063,500)
Charges for services—Centerville Toll Bridge	—	JE14.21	(4,770,000)	(4,770,000)
Charges for services—Centerville Parking Authority	—	JE14.21	(1,522,000)	(1,522,000)

	Combined Totals For Enterprise Funds Debit (Credit)		Reclassifications and Adjustments Debit (Credit)	Government-Wide Financial Statements Debit (Credit)
Charges for services—Centerville Utilities Authority	—	JE14.21	(36,010,000)	(36,010,000)
Charges for services—Centerville Municipal Airport	—	JE14.21	(227,060,000)	(227,060,000)
Charges for services	(217,250,000)	JE14.21	217,250,000	0
Charges for services—rental income—security for Terminal A revenue bonds	(30,000,000)	JE14.21	30,000,000	0
Charges for services—rental income—security for Terminal B revenue bonds	(22,000,000)	JE14.21	22,000,000	0
Miscellaneous revenues	(112,000)	JE14.21	112,000	0
Expenses—personal services	190,851,000	JE14.23	(190,851,000)	0
Expenses—contractual services	46,450,000	JE14.23	(46,450,000)	0
Expenses—repairs and maintenance	3,250,000	JE14.23	(3,250,000)	0
Expenses—other supplies and expenses	2,754,000	JE14.23	(2,754,000)	0
Expenses—insurance claims and expenses	134,000	JE14.23	(134,000)	0
Expenses—depreciation	6,851,000	JE14.23	(6,851,000)	0
Expenses—miscellaneous	108,000	JE14.23	(108,000)	0
Expenses—Centerville Municipal Airport	—	JE08.46	327,872	203,594,872
	—	JE08.48	(73,000)	
	—	JE14.23	202,010,000	
	—	JE14.24	1,220,000	
	—	JE14.25	110,000	
Expenses—Centerville Utilities Authority	—	JE08.46	120,320	38,557,320
	—	JE14.23	37,722,000	
	—	JE14.24	450,000	
	—	JE14.25	265,000	
Expenses—Centerville Parking Authority	—	JE08.46	54,144	6,091,144
	—	JE14.23	6,011,000	
	—	JE14.24	27,000	
	—	JE14.25	(1,000)	
Expenses—Centerville Toll Bridge	—	JE08.46	45,120	4,699,120
	—	JE14.23	4,655,000	
	—	JE14.24	6,000	
	—	JE14.25	(7,000)	
Unrestricted investment earnings	—	JE14.26	(1,655,000)	(1,655,000)
Interest and investment revenue	(1,640,000)	JE08.48	(15,000)	0
	—	JE14.26	1,655,000	
Interest expense	1,703,000	JE14.24	(1,703,000)	0
Operating grants and contributions—Centerville Toll Bridge	—	JE14.22	(100,000)	(100,000)

	Combined Totals For Enterprise Funds Debit (Credit)		Reclassifications and Adjustments Debit (Credit)	Government-Wide Financial Statements Debit (Credit)
Capital grants and contributions— Centerville Toll Bridge	—	JE14.22	(250,000)	(250,000)
Capital grants and contributions— Centerville Utilities Authority	—	JE14.22	(1,250,000)	(1,250,000)
Capital grants and contributions— Centerville Municipal Airport	—	JE14.22	(2,000,000)	(2,000,000)
Operating grants and contributions	(100,000)	JE14.22	100,000	0
Non-operating miscellaneous expenses (revenues)	367,000	JE14.25	(367,000)	0
Capital contributions	(3,500,000)	JE14.22	3,500,000	0
Transfers in	(140,000)		—	(140,000)
Transfers out Special item—gain on sale of parking lot	(3,500,000)		—	(3,500,000)
Total	$ 0		$ 0	$ 0

The information on the foregoing worksheet is brought forward to Chapter 16, "Basic Financial Statements."

Components of Net Assets

The above illustrations present only a single amount for net assets. GASB-34 requires that the statement of net assets identify the components of net assets, namely (1) invested in capital assets, net of related debt, (2) restricted net assets, and (3) unrestricted net assets. The method used to identify these three components is illustrated in Chapter 16, "Basic Financial Statements."

GASB-34 introduced the concept of "net assets," which represents the difference between a governmental entity's total assets and its total liabilities.

The *GASB's Comprehensive Implementation Guide* specifically notes that other terms, such as "equity," "net worth," and "fund balance" should not be used in the statement of net assets.

The GASB's *Guide* makes the following observations about investments in capital assets (net of related debt): (1) All capital assets, irrespective of any restrictions (for example, federal surplus property), must be considered in the computation of net assets invested in capital assets (net of related debt). The GASB's *Guide* notes that the purpose of identifying net assets as "restricted" and "unrestricted" is to provide insight into the availability of *financial*, not capital, resources. (2) Net assets invested in capital assets (net of related debt) is the difference between (a) capital assets, net of accumulated depreciation and (b) liabilities "attributable to the acquisition, construction, or improvement of those assets." When debt has been issued to finance the acquisition, construction, or improvement of capital assets and all or part of the cash has not been spent by the end of the fiscal year, the unspent portion of the debt should not be used to determine the amount of invested capital assets (net or related debt) amount. The portion of the unspent debt "should be included in the same net assets component as the unspent proceeds—for example, *restricted for capital projects*." (3) Many governmental entities create (a) a Capital Projects Fund to account for capital debt proceeds to be used to acquire, construct, or improve infrastructure assets and buildings (including land) and (b) specific accounts in the General Fund or other funds for capital debt proceeds to be used to acquire capital assets other than infrastructure assets. When these approaches are used, it is relatively simple to identify the unspent portion of capital debt proceeds. For those governmental entities that do not use these two approaches and commingle funds, the GASB's *Guide* states that they must "use their best estimates—in a manner that can be documented—to determine the unspent portion." (4) A governmental entity is not expected to determine whether all of the proceeds of capital debt are used to acquire capital assets. However, if a significant portion of the proceeds is not used to acquire capital assets, then that portion should not be used to determine the net assets invested in capital assets (net of related debt) component. In this area, the GASB's *Guide* attempts to apply the concept of materiality to the required standard. (5) When debt is issued to refund existing capital-related debt, the newly issued debt is considered capital-related and would be used to compute the net assets invested in capital assets (net of related debt) component. (6) When a governmental entity has capital assets but no related debt, the net asset component should be simply identified as "net assets invested in capital assets." And (7) when a general purpose government issues bonds to construct school buildings for its independent school districts and the repayment of the bonds is the responsibility of the general purpose government, because the debt was not used to acquire, construct, or improve capital assets for the governmental entity, the outstanding debt is not capital-related and would not be used to compute the amount of net assets invested in capital assets (net of related debt) of the general purpose government. The effect would be to reduce unrestricted net assets. The GASB's *Guide* notes that if doing so has a significant effect on the unrestricted net assets component, the circumstances may be further explained in a note to the financial statements.

The GASB's *Guide* states that GASB-34 requires that information supporting details of restricted net assets be presented in the body of the financial statements, not in the notes to the financial statements.

The GASB's *Guide* takes the position that the recognition of interest on deep-discount capital debt should generally reduce the invested in capital assets (net of related debt) component of net assets. On the other hand, if a sinking fund is being used to fund the retirement of the debt, the accretion (interest expenses recognition) should be reported as a reduction to the same component of net assets as that identified with the sinking fund resources.

The GASB's *Guide* states that the disclosure related to the policy regarding the use of restricted resources (paragraph 115h) requires the governmental entity to explain when restricted resources are used. That is, whether restricted resources are used only after unrestricted resources have been spent for a particular purpose or restricted resources are assumed to be spent first.

CHAPTER 15
COMPONENT UNITS

CONTENTS

NATURE OF COMPONENT UNITS

The governmental financial reporting consists of a primary government and its component units. Component units can be governmental and certain nongovernmental organizations. A component unit cannot be a primary government. GASB-14, as amended by GASB-39 and, further, by GASB-61, requires that three separate approaches be applied to an entity to determine whether it is a component unit of the primary government. These three approaches are summarized in the following table:

	Approach	Method of Integration	GASB Statement Reference
1.	The primary government is financially accountable for the other organization	Blending or discrete presentation	GASB-14, pars. 20–40 (as amended by GASB-61, pars. 4(b)–(c) and 6)
2.	The nature and significance of the relationship between the primary government and the other organization	Discrete presentation only	GASB-14, par. 40a (as amended by GASB-39)
3.	The other organization is closely related to, or financially integrated with the primary government	Blending or discrete presentation	GASB-14, par. 41 (as amended by GASB-39 and, further, by GASB-61, par. 5)

GASB-39 states that the financial statements of governmental and nongovernmental organizations for which a primary government (or the primary government's component units) is not financially accountable should, under certain circumstances, be included in the primary government's financial statements. This determination is based on "the nature and significance of the relationship between the primary government and the potential component unit, including the latter's ongoing financial support of the primary government and its other component units." Although that concept is broad, GASB-39 states that a legally separate, tax-exempt organization's financial statements are to be included in the primary government's financial statements if all of the following conditions exist: (1) the economic resources received or held by the separate organization are entirely or almost entirely for the direct benefit of the primary government, its component units, or its constituents, (2) the primary government is entitled to, or has the ability to otherwise access, a majority of the economic resources received or held by the separate organization, and (3) the economic resources received or held by an individual organization that the specific primary government or its component units is entitled to or has the ability to otherwise access are significant to that primary government. In addition, the GASB recognizes that the foregoing three conditions might be too constrictive in that certain organizations that do not satisfy them could nonetheless be an important component unit of a primary government. For this reason, GASB-39 states that professional judgment should be used to identify those organizations that "are closely related to, or financially integrated with the primary government" and that they should be reported as component units by the primary government.

PRACTICE ALERT: GASB-61 clarifies GASB-14 and GASB-39 by modifying the requirements for inclusion of component units in the financial reporting entity. For organizations that previously were required to be included as component units by meeting the criterion of fiscal dependency, a financial benefit or burden relationship also would need to be present between the primary government and that organization for it to be included in the reporting entity as a component unit. Furthermore, for organizations that *do not* meet the financial accountability criteria for inclusion as component units but should be included because the primary government's management determines that it would be misleading to exclude them, GASB-61 clarifies the manner in which that determination should be made and the types of relationships that generally should be considered in making the determination.

GASB-61 also amends the criteria for reporting blending component units in certain circumstances. For component units that currently are blended based on the "substantively the same governing body" test, GASB-61 additionally requires that (1) the primary government and the component unit have a financial benefit or burden relationship *or* (2) management (below the level of the elected officials) of the primary government have operational responsibility (as defined in paragraph 8a) for the activities of the component unit. GASB-61 adds a requirement to blend component units whose total debt outstanding is expected to be repaid entirely *or almost entirely* with resources of the primary government. The blending provisions are amended to clarify that funds of a blended component unit have the same financial reporting requirements as a fund of the primary government. Lastly, additional reporting guidance is provided for blending a component unit if the primary government is a business-type activity that uses a single-column presentation for financial reporting.

GASB-61 also clarifies the reporting of equity interests in legally separate organizations. It requires a primary government to report its equity interest in a component unit as an asset. Finally, GASB-61 clarifies joint venture reporting. GASB-61 is effective for financial statements for periods beginning after June 15, 2012.

OBSERVATION: The provisions of GASB-61 may result in some component units currently presented discretely to be not presented if no fiscal dependency exists and vice versa. Furthermore certain discretely presented component units may be blended if they entail financing mechanisms on behalf of primary governments.

This chapter illustrates governmental entities that are component units of the primary government based on financial accountability (the first approach). When a governmental unit is considered to be a component unit of a primary government, its financial activities and balances must be incorporated into the reporting entity's financial statements either through blending or by discrete presentation.

BLENDED COMPONENT UNITS

When the blending method is used, transactions of a component unit are presented as if they were executed directly by the primary government. That is, the funds for the blended component units are evaluated as either major or nonmajor funds and reported accordingly, just like all other funds (except Fiduciary Funds) of the primary government. The balances and activities of the blended component units cannot be distinguished from those of the primary government. In a similar manner, balances in a component unit's financial statements are merged with similar balances of the primary government in the preparation of the government-wide financial statements. The two circumstances that require the blending of a component unit's financial statements with those of the primary government relate to (1) similar governing bodies and (2) scope of services. GASB-61 adds a third criterion: if the component units debts (of all types) are paid entirely or almost entirely by a primary government, then blending is required. Included in the illustrations of the City of Centerville CAFR are two blended component units:

1. Centerville Utilities Authority

2. Centerville Parking Authority

These component units are blended into the CAFR as Enterprise Funds of the City of Centerville primary government. See Chapter 7, "Enterprise Funds," for the financial statement presentation of the blended component units.

DISCRETELY PRESENTED COMPONENT UNITS

When the discrete presentation method is used, there is a clear distinction between the balances and activities of the primary government and discretely presented component units. This distinction is achieved by presenting information for the discrete component units only in the government-wide financial statements using one of the following approaches:

- Present each major component unit in a separate column in the government-wide financial statements

- Present combining statements

- Present condensed financial statements in a note to the financial statements

This chapter illustrates the financial reporting of discretely presented component units.

The GASB's *Comprehensive Implementation Guide* states that if a discretely presented component unit does not issue a separate financial report, the reporting entity's CAFR must include fund financial statements for the component unit (major fund reporting format). This information is presented as supplementary information. This requirement is based on GASB-14 (paragraph 50); however, GASB-34 requires that the fund financial statements be focused on major funds of the component unit rather than its fund types. Furthermore, if a component unit does not issue separate financial statements and that unit uses proprietary fund accounting, then the reporting entity must include in its CAFR (as supplementary information) a statement of cash flows for the unit.

The GASB's *Guide* states that a condensed statement of cash flows is not required when segment disclosures are made for major discretely presented component units. Paragraph 122d does require a segment to present a condensed statement of cash flows; however, the GASB's *Guide's* statement is based on the reasoning that "cash flow reporting is not required for component units anywhere else—not in the government-wide statements and not in the major component unit information."

IMPLEMENTATION GUIDANCE: The GASB's *Guide* states that if a discretely presented component unit has component units of its own but does not present a reporting entity total column, GASB-34 as amended states that the component unit financial data that are incorporated into a reporting entity's financial statements should include the data from all of its component units. Therefore, the data that should be taken from the discretely presented component unit's financial statements are the amounts that would be in its entity total column if one had been presented. Ideally, the discretely presented component unit should present a total column to easily present a total entity in the primary government (GASB-34, par. 126; GASB-14, par. 43).

NON-GOVERNMENTAL COMPONENT UNITS

The financial statement preparer needs to be constantly aware that GASB pronouncements apply to financial reports of all state and local governmental entities, including general purpose governments, public benefit corporations and authorities, public employee retirement systems, public utilities, hospitals and other health-care providers, and colleges and universities, unless otherwise specified.

These primary governments in evaluating potential component units need to be reminded that GASB-39 should be applied to non-governmental component units when they are included in a governmental financial reporting entity. GASB-39 establishes additional guidance on the application of existing standards for the assessment of potential component units in determining the financial reporting entity. In addition GASB-39 applies to financial reporting by primary governments and other stand-alone governments, and to the separately issued financial statements of governmental component units as defined in paragraph 9 of GASB-14.

Most of the organizations that meet the criteria in GASB-39 have unique and significantly different characteristics from most component units as defined by GASB-14. The noted common differences relating to potential non-governmental component units seemed to be as follows:

- The organizations generally are not created or organized by the primary government.

- The organizations generally do not provide services to the public.

- The organizations' activities are usually restricted to providing financial resources to the government.

GASB recognized that there may be rare circumstances where the relationship between an organization and a primary government is such that it warrants inclusion. GASB-14 enables this by allowing the exercise of professional judgment. GASB-39 requires the discrete presentation of all organizations that meet its criteria. The application of professional judgment to ensure that readers are not misled is no longer permissible in many situations.

The GASB's *Comprehensive Implementation Guide* states that many organizations that GASB-39 requires to be included in a government's reporting entity as discretely presented component units are non-governmental and follow FASB standards in their separately issued financial statements. It further discusses whether the financial statements of a non-governmental component unit should be converted to comply with GASB standards. This newly updated GASB's *Guide* responds to this question by stating that there are no requirements to change the recognition, measurement, or disclosure standards applied in a nongovernmental component unit's separate financial statements. However, other discussions contained in the GASB's *Guide* state additional provisions of GASB-14 should be applied to the financial statements of a non-governmental component unit when those statements are incorporated into a governmental financial reporting entity. Based on specific criteria contained in GASB-14, a non-governmental component unit should include component units of its own. Additionally, the non-governmental component unit's financial statements may need to be reformatted to comply with the classification and display requirements in GASB-34.

PRACTICE ALERT: GASB-61 clarifies guidance for those entities where an equity interest is owned by a government. If a government owns a majority of the equity interest in a legally separate organization (for example, through acquisition of its voting stock), the government's intent for owning the equity interest should determine whether the organization should be presented as a component unit or an investment of the primary government. If the government's intent for owning a majority equity interest is to directly enhance its ability to provide governmental services, the organization should be reported as a component unit. When such a component unit is discretely presented, the equity interest should be reported as an asset of the fund that has the equity interest. When such a component unit is blended, in the period of acquisition the purchase typically should be reported as an outflow of the fund that provided the resources for the acquisition and, in that and subsequent reporting periods, the component unit should be reported pursuant to the blending requirements. If, however, the government owns the equity interest for the purpose of obtaining income or profit rather than to directly enhance its ability to provide governmental services, it should report its equity interest as an investment, regardless of the extent of its ownership.

Measurement Focus and Basis of Accounting

Component units may use either Governmental Funds or Proprietary Funds (depending on the nature of their operations) to account for their activities and therefore their financial statements may be prepared based on the modified accrual basis and flow of current financial resources or the accrual basis of accounting and the flow of economic resources, respectively.

OBSERVATION: The requirement for major component unit information does not apply to component units that are fiduciary in nature.

Financial Reporting at the Fund Level

The financial statements of discretely presented component units are not presented in the primary government's fund financial statements.

Financial Reporting of Discretely Presented Component Units at the Government-Wide Level

As noted earlier there are three ways that the financial statements of component units can be presented in the government-wide financial statements.

Separate Column Presentation

Each major component unit may be presented in a separate column on the face of the government-wide financial statements. Under this presentation format all nonmajor component units are combined and presented in a single column. These financial statements should provide a total column for governmental activities and business-type activities (the primary government), and a total column for the reporting entity is optional.

GASB-34 does not provide a definition of a major component unit, but GASB-14 states that "consideration should be given to each component unit's significance relative to the other component units and the nature and significance of its relationship to the primary government" in identifying a major component unit.

The GASB's *Comprehensive Implementation Guide* points out that the reporting governmental entity cannot combine as a single function (for example, higher education) related information of the primary government and a discretely presented component unit, because GASB-14 requires that the financial statements of the reporting entity distinguish between the accounts and transactions of the primary government and its discretely presented component units.

Combining Financial Statements Presentation

All component units may be combined and presented in a single column in the government-wide financial statements, with combining financial statements presenting the detail for the major component units (separate columns) and nonmajor component units (an aggregate column).

When the approach of presenting combining statements is used, paragraph 126 of GASB-34 states that the "aggregated total component unit information, as discussed in GASB-14, should be taken from the total columns in the component units' statements of net assets and activities so that the details support the totals reported in the reporting entity's government-wide statements." When this guidance is followed, a question arises concerning which "total" should be taken from the combining statements. Standards established by GASB-37 make it clear that when a component unit also has component units but does not present a reporting entity total column, the totals that should be brought to the reporting entity's financial statements should be the total for the component unit and all of its component units, even if the component unit does not present a total column for the reporting entity as a whole. Ideally, a component unit that has a component unit present totaled amounts.

The combining statements presentation method is illustrated in this chapter and Chapter 16, "Basic Financial Statements."

Note Disclosure Presentation

If the note-disclosure method is used, the following disclosures must be made:

- Condensed statement of net assets

    - *Total assets* Distinguishing between capital assets and other assets. Amounts receivable from the primary government or from other component units of the same reporting entity should be reported separately.

- — *Total liabilities* Distinguishing between long-term debt outstanding and other liabilities. Amounts payable to the primary government or to other component units of the same reporting entity should be reported separately.
- — *Total net assets* Distinguishing between restricted, unrestricted, and amounts invested in capital assets, net of related debt.
- Condensed statement of activities
  - — Expenses, with separate identification of depreciation expense and amortizations of long-lived assets
  - — Program revenues (by type)
  - — Net program (expense) revenue
  - — Tax revenues
  - — Other nontax general revenues
  - — Contributions to endowments and permanent fund principal
  - — Extraordinary and special items
  - — Change in net assets
  - — Beginning and ending net assets

PRACTICE ALERT: GASB-61 clarifies guidance on for discretely presented component unit presentation. Funds of a blended component unit have the same financial reporting requirements as a fund of the primary government. In addition, in the instance where a blended component unit exists if the primary government is a business-type activity that reports in a single column, then condensed combining information in the notes to the financial statements is presented. The condensed combining information should include the following details, at a minimum:

(1) Condensed statement of net assets:

    (a) Total assets—distinguishing between current assets, capital assets, and other assets. Amounts receivable from the primary government or other component units should be reported separately.

    (b) Total liabilities—distinguishing between current and long-term amounts. Amounts payable to the primary government or other component units should be reported separately.

    (c) Total net assets—distinguishing among amounts invested in capital assets, net of related debt; restricted (separately reporting expendable and nonexpendable components); and unrestricted.

(2) Condensed statement of revenues, expenses, and changes in net assets:

    (a) Operating revenues (by major source).

    (b) Operating expenses—identifying depreciation (including any amortization) separately.

    (c) Operating income (loss).

    (d) Nonoperating revenues (expenses)—with separate reporting of major revenues and expenses.

    (e) Capital contributions and additions to permanent and term endowments.

    (f) Special and extraordinary items.

    (g) Transfers.

    (h) Change in net assets.

    (i) Beginning net assets.

    (j) Ending net assets.

(3) Condensed statement of cash flows:

    (a) Net cash provided (used) by:

        (i) Operating activities.

        (ii) Noncapital financing activities.

        (iii) Capital and related financing activities.

        (iv) Investing activities.

    (b) Beginning cash and cash equivalent balances.

    (c) Ending cash and cash equivalent balances.

According to GASB-34's existing guidance on fiduciary component units, they should be included only in the fund financial statements with the primary government's fiduciary funds.

Illustrative Financial Information: Discretely Presented Component Units

In order to illustrate accounting and financial reporting standards that are observed for discretely presented component units, assume that the City of Centerville has the following discretely presented component units:

- Centerville Public School System (considered to be a major component unit by the City)

- Centerville Parks District (considered to be a nonmajor component unit by the City)

- Centerville Regional Transit System (considered to be a major component unit by the City)

- Centerville Sports Authority (considered to be a nonmajor component unit by the City)

Each of the component units prepares separate, stand-alone financial statements that are available for distribution to the public.

Unlike previous chapters this chapter does not present basic transactions and a summary accounting worksheet, because a component unit uses one or more of the funds described and illustrated in previous chapters. The assumption is that the component unit has prepared its financial statements in a manner consistent with what has been described and illustrated in the previous chapters.

Centerville Public School System (Major Component Unit)

The Centerville Public School System provides education for students from kindergarten through 12th grade but also administers outreach programs that include adult education and adult remedial educational programs. The system uses governmental funds, proprietary funds, and fiduciary funds and has prepared the following district-wide financial statements based on these funds (with the exception of its fiduciary funds). The system has no component units.

Centerville Public School System Statement of Activities
for the Year ended June 30, 20X2

		Program Revenues			Net (Expense) Revenues and Changes in Net Assets		
Functions:	Expenses	Charges for Services	Operating Grants and Contributions	Capital Grants and Contributions	Governmental Activities	Business-Type Activities	Total
Primary government:							
Governmental activities:							
Instruction	$43,500,000	$2,750,000	—	$13,700,000	$(27,050,000)	—	$(27,050,000)
Special education	4,530,000	640,000	$2,300,000	770,000	(820,000)	—	(820,000)
Academic support	1,650,000	—	—	—	(1,650,000)	—	(1,650,000)
Other educational programs	2,300,000	125,000	—	—	(2,175,000)	—	(2,175,000)
General administration	3,750,000	7,400	—	—	(3,742,600)	—	(3,742,600)
School administration	1,250,000	—	720,000	—	(530,000)	—	(530,000)
Transportation	3,660,000	12,500	1,800,000	550,000	(1,297,500)	—	(1,297,500)
Interest on long-term debt	1,200,000	—	—	—	(1,200,000)	—	(1,200,000)
Total governmental activities	61,840,000	3,534,900	4,820,000	15,020,000	(38,465,100)	—	(38,465,100)
Business-type activities:							
Adult education	2,650,000	2,100,000	120,000	55,000		$ (375,000)	(375,000)
Remedial education	1,870,000	1,470,000	350,000	—		(50,000)	(50,000)
Food services	5,450,000	4,100,000	1,500,000	110,000		260,000	260,000
Special certification programs	1,350,000	1,700,000	—	—		350,000	350,000

| | Program Revenues | | | | Net (Expense) Revenues and Changes in Net Assets | | |
	Expenses	Charges for Services	Operating Grants and Contributions	Capital Grants and Contributions	Governmental Activities	Business-Type Activities	Total
Total business-type activities	11,320,000	9,370,000	1,970,000	165,000	—	185,000	185,000
Total primary government	$73,160,000	$12,904,900	$6,790,000	$15,185,000	(38,465,100)	185,000	(38,280,100)
General revenues:							
Payment from the City of Centerville					32,000,000	—	32,000,000
Taxes:							
Property taxes					2,750,000	—	2,750,000
Other					105,000	—	105,000
Grants and contributions not restricted to specific programs					2,300,000	—	2,300,000
Unrestricted investment earnings					27,000	15,000	42,000
Miscellaneous					55,000	—	55,000
Special item—gain on sale of land					120,000	—	120,000
Transfers					(22,000)	22,000	—
Total general revenues, special items, and transfers					37,335,000	37,000	37,372,000
Change in net assets					(1,130,100)	222,000	(908,100)
Net assets—beginning					306,771,989	125,156,044	431,928,033
Net assets—ending					$305,641,889	$125,378,044	$431,019,933

Centerville Public School System
Statement of Net Assets June 30, 20X2

	Primary Government		
	Governmental Activities	Business-Type Activities	Total
ASSETS			
Cash	$ 11,716,956	$ 12,718,500	$ 24,435,456
Internal balances	(1,697,544)	1,697,544	—
Receivables (net)	8,014,000	26,207,000	34,221,000
Investments	9,798,600	10,180,000	19,978,600
Inventories	33,000	206,000	239,000
Other assets	5,200	—	5,200
Capital assets:			
Land, improvements, and construction in progress	143,700,000	45,855,000	189,555,000
Other capital assets, net of depreciation	182,084,806	68,575,000	250,659,806
Total Assets	353,655,018	165,439,044	519,094,062
LIABILITIES			
Accounts payable and accrued expenses	1,616,090	8,415,000	10,031,090
Demand loans payable to bank	75,000	—	75,000
Deferred revenue	310,000	—	310,000
Long-term liabilities:			
Due within one year	4,658,932	3,784,000	8,442,932
Other capital assets, net of depreciation	41,353,107	27,862,000	69,215,107
Total Liabilities	48,013,129	40,061,000	88,074,129
NET ASSETS			
Invested in capital assets, net of related debt	$286,400,335	$ 87,510,000	$373,910,335
Restricted for:			
Capital projects	3,858,956	20,000,000	23,858,956
Debt service	268,000	2,000,000	2,268,000
Other purposes	118,500	15,362,000	15,480,500
Other purposes (nonexpendable)	243,000	—	243,000
Unrestricted (deficit)	14,753,098	506,044	15,259,142
Total Net Assets	$305,641,889	$125,378,044	$431,019,933

Centerville Parks District (Nonmajor Component Unit)

The Centerville Parks District provides an extensive, multipurpose park system that includes facilities within the City as well as properties administered and maintained in various locations in Centerville County. The district's activities are coordinated with the City's Recreation and Parks Department but are presented as a discrete component unit rather than as a blended component unit because they do not share a governing body and the district does not provide exclusive or almost exclusive benefits to the City. The district uses Governmental Funds and Proprietary Funds and has prepared the following park-wide financial statements based on these funds. The park district has no component units.

Centerville Parks District Statement of Activities
for the Year ended June 30, 20X2

Functions:	Expenses	Program Revenues			Net (Expense) Revenues and Changes in Net Assets		
		Charges for Services	Operating Grants and Contributions	Capital Grants and Contributions	Governmental Activities	Business-Type Activities	Total
Primary government:							
Governmental activities:							
General administration	$ 2,200,000	$ 120,000	$ 50,000	$ 17,000	$ (2,013,000)	—	$ (2,013,000)
Educational and civic activities	6,800,000	2,350,000	1,700,000	1,400,000	(1,350,000)	—	(1,350,000)
Maintenance	3,800,000	—	1,250,000	2,660,000	110,000	—	110,000
Athletic activities	3,450,000	125,000	27,000	155,000	(3,143,000)	—	(3,143,000)
Culture events	1,750,000	277,000	350,000	220,000	(903,000)	—	(903,000)
Interest on long-term debt	2,727,000	—	—	—	(2,727,000)	—	(2,727,000)
Total governmental activities	20,727,000	2,872,000	3,377,000	4,452,000	(10,026,000)	—	(10,026,000)
Business-type activities:							
Corporate activities	1,300,000	1,700,000	22,000	45,000		$ 467,000	467,000
Athletic events	2,770,000	2,650,000	350,000	—		230,000	230,000
Food services	4,500,000	5,100,000	34,000	20,000		654,000	654,000
Retail sales and services	5,140,000	6,150,000	—	45,000		1,055,000	1,055,000
Total business-type activities	13,710,000	15,600,000	406,000	110,000		2,406,000	2,406,000
Total primary government	$34,437,000	$18,472,000	$3,783,000	$4,562,000	(10,026,000)	2,406,000	(7,620,000)

	Program Revenues			Net (Expense) Revenues and Changes in Net Assets		
Expenses	Charges for Services	Operating Grants and Contributions	Capital Grants and Contributions	Governmental Activities	Business-Type Activities	Total
General revenues:						
Taxes:						
Property taxes				5,990,000	—	5,990,000
Other				105,000	—	105,000
Grants and contributions not restricted to specific programs				3,050,000	—	3,050,000
Unrestricted investment earnings				600,000	22,000	622,000
Miscellaneous				32,000	—	32,000
Transfers				40,000	(40,000)	—
Total general revenues, special items, and transfers				9,817,000	(18,000)	9,799,000
Change in net assets				(209,000)	2,388,000	2,179,000
Net assets—beginning				325,981,000	7,665,000	333,646,000
Net assets—ending				$325,772,000	$10,053,000	$335,825,000

**Centerville Parks District
Statement of Net Assets
June 30, 20X2**

	Primary Government		
	Governmental Activities	Business-Type Activities	Total
ASSETS			
Cash	$ 4,500,000	$ 2,350,000	$ 6,850,000
Internal balances	(405,000)	405,000	—
Receivables (net)	1,350,000	4,005,000	5,355,000
Investments	7,500,000	350,000	7,850,000
Inventories	17,000	2,670,000	2,687,000
Other assets	12,000	18,000	30,000
Capital assets:			
Land, improvements, and construction in progress	320,000,000	1,460,000	321,460,000
Other capital assets, net of depreciation	152,000,000	2,700,000	154,700,000
Total Assets	484,974,000	13,958,000	498,932,000
LIABILITIES			
Accounts payable and accrued expenses	750,000	1,430,000	2,180,000
Demand loans payable to bank	—	—	—
Deferred revenue	402,000	—	402,000
Long-term liabilities:			
Due within one year	13,050,000	175,000	13,225,000
Due in more than one year	145,000,000	2,300,000	147,300,000
Total Liabilities	159,202,000	3,905,000	163,107,000
NET ASSETS			
Invested in capital assets, net of related debt	313,950,000	1,685,000	315,635,000
Restricted for:			
Capital projects	2,750,000	250,000	3,000,000
Debt service	300,000	22,000	322,000
Other purposes	34,000	—	34,000
Other purposes (nonexpendable)	105,000	42,000	147,000
Unrestricted (deficit)	8,633,000	8,054,000	16,687,000
Total Net Assets	$325,772,000	$10,053,000	$335,825,000

Centerville Regional Transit System (Major Component Unit)

The Centerville Regional Transit System provides transportation services to the City and several smaller communities that are contiguous to the City. The system uses only a single Enterprise Fund, and following the guidance established by GASB-34 (paragraph 138) only the financial statements required for an Enterprise Fund are prepared, which are presented below. The system has no component units.

Centerville Regional Transit System
Statement of Net Assets June 30, 20X2

ASSETS

Current assets:

Cash	$ 4,437,000
Interest receivable	18,000
Temporary investments	348,000
Supplies	192,000
Total current assets	4,995,000

Noncurrent assets:

Land and improvements	7,660,000
Buildings	3,980,000
Equipment	330,000
Vehicles	5,010,000
Less accumulated depreciation	(7,542,000)
Total noncurrent assets	9,438,000
Total assets	14,433,000

LIABILITIES

Current liabilities:

Accounts payable and accrued expenses	300,000
Due to other funds	108,000
Compensated absences	18,000
Claims and judgments	30,000
Notes payable	60,000
Bonds payable	120,000
Total current liabilities	636,000

Noncurrent liabilities:

Compensated absences	30,000
Claims and judgments	132,000
Notes payable	120,000
Bonds payable	360,000
Total noncurrent liabilities	642,000
Total liabilities	1,278,000

NET ASSETS

Invested in capital assets, net of related debt	8,778,000
Restricted	3,732,000
Unrestricted	645,000
Total net assets	$13,155,000

Centerville Regional Transit System
Statement of Revenues, Expenses, and Changes
in Fund Net Assets
for the Year Ended June 30, 20X2

OPERATING REVENUES

Charges for services	$28,500,000
Miscellaneous	120,000
Total operating revenues	28,620,000

OPERATING EXPENSES

Personal services	14,412,000
Contractual services	7,680,000
Repairs and maintenance	2,400,000
Other supplies and expenses	1,164,000
Insurance claims and expenses	60,000
Depreciation	2,034,000
Miscellaneous	180,000
Total operating expenses	27,930,000
Operating income (loss)	690,000

NONOPERATING REVENUES (EXPENSES)

Interest and investment revenue	180,000
Interest	(36,000)
Operating grants and contributions	600,000
Miscellaneous	42,000
Total nonoperating revenue (expenses)	786,000
Income (loss) before capital contributions and transfers	1,476,000
Capital contributions	1,800,000
Change in net assets	3,276,000
Total net assets—beginning	9,879,000
Total net assets—ending	$13,155,000

Centerville Regional Transit System
Statement of Cash Flows
for the Year Ended June 30, 20X2

CASH FLOWS FROM OPERATING ACTIVITIES

Receipts from customers	$ 28,500,000
Payments to suppliers	(10,836,000)
Payments to employees	(14,226,000)
Internal activity—payments to other funds	
Other receipts (payments)	(504,000)
Net cash provided by operating activities	2,934,000

CASH FLOWS FROM NONCAPITAL FINANCING ACTIVITIES

Subsidies and transfers from (to) other funds and state government	600,000

CASH FLOWS FROM CAPITAL AND RELATED FINANCING ACTIVITIES

Capital contributions	1,800,000
Acquisitions of capital assets	(2,340,000)
Proceeds from sale of capital assets	300,000
Principal paid on capital debt	(180,000)
Interest paid on capital debt	(36,000)
Net cash (used) by capital and related financing activities	(456,000)

CASH FLOWS FROM INVESTING ACTIVITIES

Interest and dividends	189,000
Purchase of investments	(150,000)
Net cash provided (used) by investing activities	39,000
Net increase (decrease) in cash	3,117,000
Balances—beginning of year	1,320,000
Balances—end of year	$ 4,437,000

Reconciliation of operating income (loss) to net cash provided (used) by operating activities:

Operating income (loss)	$ 690,000
Adjustments:	
Depreciation expense	2,034,000
Change in assets and liabilities:	
Inventories	(36,000)
Accounts and accrued liabilities	246,000
Net cash provided (used) by operating activities	$2,934,000

Centerville Sports Authority (Nonmajor Component Unit)

The Centerville Sports Authority hosts a variety of sporting, entertainment, and other events. The Authority uses only a single Enterprise Fund, and following the guidance established by GASB-34 (par. 138) only the financial statements required for an Enterprise Fund are prepared, which are presented below. The Authority has no component units.

**Centerville Sports Authority
Statement of Net Assets
June 30, 20X2**

ASSETS
Current assets:

Cash	$1,996,650
Interest receivable	8,100
Temporary investments	156,600
Supplies	86,400
Total current assets	2,247,750

Noncurrent assets:

Land and improvements	2,347,000
Buildings	891,000
Equipment	148,500
Vehicles	4,254,500
Less accumulated depreciation	(3,393,900)
Total noncurrent assets	4,247,100
Total assets	6,494,850

LIABILITIES
Current liabilities:

Accounts payable and accrued expenses	135,000
Compensated absences	8,100
Claims and judgments	13,500
Notes payable	27,000
Bonds payable	54,000
Total current liabilities	237,600

Noncurrent liabilities:

Compensated absences	13,500
Claims and judgments	59,400
Notes payable	102,600
Bonds payable	162,000
Total noncurrent liabilities	337,500
Total liabilities	575,100

NET ASSETS

Invested in capital assets, net of related debt	$3,950,100
Restricted	1,679,400
Unrestricted	290,250
Total net assets	$5,919,750

Centerville Sports Authority
Statement of Revenues, Expenses, and Changes
in Fund Net Assets
for the Year Ended June 30, 20X2

OPERATING REVENUES

Charges for services	$12,825,000
Miscellaneous	54,000
Total operating revenues	12,879,000

OPERATING EXPENSES

Personal services	6,485,400
Contractual services	3,456,000
Repairs and maintenance	1,080,000
Other supplies and expenses	523,800
Insurance claims and expenses	27,000
Depreciation	915,300
Miscellaneous	81,000
Total operating expenses	12,568,500
Operating income (loss)	310,500

NONOPERATING REVENUES (EXPENSES)

Interest and investment revenue	81,000
Interest	(16,200)
Operating grants and contributions	270,000
Miscellaneous	18,900
Total nonoperating revenue (expenses)	353,700
Income (loss) before capital contributions and transfers	664,200
Capital contributions	810,000
Change in net assets	1,474,200
Total net assets—beginning	4,445,550
Total net assets—ending	$ 5,919,750

**Centerville Sports Authority Statement
of Cash Flows for the Year Ended June 30, 20X2**

CASH FLOWS FROM OPERATING ACTIVITIES

Receipts from customers	$12,825,000
Payments to suppliers	(4,876,200)
Payments to employees	(6,401,700)
Other receipts (payments)	(226,800)
Net cash provided by operating activities	1,320,300

CASH FLOWS FROM NONCAPITAL FINANCING ACTIVITIES

Subsidies and transfers from (to) other funds and state government	540,000

CASH FLOWS FROM CAPITAL AND RELATED FINANCING ACTIVITIES

Capital contributions	675,000
Acquisitions of capital assets	(1,188,000)
Proceeds from sale of capital assets	135,000
Principal paid on capital debt	(81,000)
Interest paid on capital debt	(16,200)
Net cash (used) by capital and related financing activities	(475,200)

CASH FLOWS FROM INVESTING ACTIVITIES

Interest and dividends	85,050
Purchase of investments	(67,500)
Net cash provided (used) by investing activities	17,550
Net increase (decrease) in cash	1,402,650
Balances—beginning of year	594,000
Balances—end of year	$ 1,996,650

Reconciliation of operating income (loss) to net cash provided (used) by operating activities:

Operating income (loss)	$ 310,500
Adjustments:	
Depreciation expense	915,300
Change in assets and liabilities:	
Inventories	(16,200)
Accounts and accrued liabilities	110,700
Net cash provided (used) by operating activities	$1,320,300

Fund Financial Statements

As noted earlier in this chapter, the fund financial statements for discretely presented component units are not presented in the primary government's financial statements.

Converting to Government-Wide Financial Statements

The financial statements of discretely presented component units are presented on an accrual basis in the government-wide financial statements of the primary government. The previous illustrations in this chapter assumed that component units had prepared their own stand-alone financial statements and submitted them to the primary government for inclusion in the primary government's basic external financial statements. For this reason the starting point for folding the component units' financial statements into the primary government's financial statements is the component's "unit-wide" (school district-wide, system-wide, etc.) financial statements. If the component unit had not prepared separate, stand-alone financial statements or information, it would be necessary to convert the financial information from fund-based financial data to unit-wide financial data (which is illustrated in previous chapters).

As discussed earlier, once the financial information for component units has been converted to an accrual basis the information may be included in the primary government's financial statements in one of the following three ways:

1. Present each major component unit in a separate column in the government-wide financial statements

2. Present combining statements

3. Present condensed financial statements in a note to the financial statements

This text illustrates the second alternative (combining financial statements), whereby the City of Centerville's government-wide financial statements include a single column that includes the aggregated financial information for all component units. Under this approach the first step is to combine the two minor component units (Centerville Parks District and the Centerville Sports Authority) as shown below. The first worksheet combines the statement of net assets information and the second worksheet combines the statement of activities information for the two minor component units.

	Centerville Parks District	Centerville Sports Authority	Total
Cash	$ 6,850,000	$ 1,996,650	$ 8,846,650
Property taxes receivable (net)	5,355,000	—	5,355,000
Other receivables	—	8,100	8,100
Investments	7,850,000	156,600	8,006,600
Inventories and supplies	2,687,000	86,400	2,773,400
Land, improvements and construction in progress	321,460,000	2,347,000	323,807,000
Other capital assets, net of depreciation	154,700,000	1,900,100	156,600,100
Other assets	30,000	—	30,000
Accounts payable and accrued expenses	(2,180,000)	(135,000)	(2,315,000)
Deferred revenue	(402,000)	—	(402,000)
Long-term liabilities— due within one year	(13,225,000)	(102,600)	(13,327,600)
Long-term liabilities— due in more than one year	(147,300,000)	(337,500)	(147,637,500)
Net assets—invested in capital assets, net of related debt	(315,635,000)	(3,950,100)	(319,585,100)
Net assets—restricted for capital projects	(3,000,000)	—	(3,000,000)
Net assets—restricted for debt service	(322,000)	—	(322,000)
Net assets—restricted for other purposes	(34,000)	(1,679,400)	(1,713,400)
Net assets restricted for other purposes (nonexpendable)	(147,000)	(290,250)	(437,250)
Net assets— unrestricted	(16,687,000)	—	(16,687,000)
Total	$ 0	$ 0	$ 0

	Centerville Parks District	Centerville Sports Authority	Total
General revenues— property taxes	$ (5,990,000)	$ —	$ (5,990,000)
General revenues— other taxes	(105,000)	—	(105,000)
Grants and contributions not restricted to specific programs	(3,050,000)	(810,000)	(3,860,000)
Unrestricted investment earnings	(622,000)	(81,000)	(703,000)
Miscellaneous revenues	(32,000)	(72,900)	(104,900)
Program revenues— charges for services	(18,472,000)	(12,825,000)	(31,297,000)
Program revenues— operating grants and contributions	(3,783,000)	(270,000)	(4,053,000)
Program revenues— capital grants and contributions	(4,562,000)	—	(4,562,000)
Program expenses	34,437,000	12,584,700	47,021,700
Change in net assets	$ (2,179,000)	$ (1,474,200)	$ (3,653,200)

The Centerville Public School System and the Centerville Regional Transit System are considered by the primary government to be major component units. However, they are formatted differently in the combining financial statements. The Centerville Public School System has both governmental and business-type activities, and this information is presented so that the net (expenses) revenues are identified for each functional activity of the system. The Centerville Regional Transit System has only business-type activities (originally presented as a single Enterprise Fund) and is reported in the combining financial statements only as a single activity.

The combining financial statements for all of the component units are as follows:

City of Centerville Statement of Net Assets
Component Units June 30, 20X2

	Centerville Public School System	Centerville Regional Transit System	Other Component Units	Total
ASSETS				
Cash	$ 24,435,456	$ 4,437,000	$ 8,846,650	$37,719,106
Receivables (net)	34,221,000	18,000	5,363,100	39,602,100
Other assets	5,200	—	30,000	35,200
Investments	19,978,600	348,000	8,006,600	28,333,200
Inventories and supplies	239,000	192,000	2,773,400	3,204,400
Capital assets:				
Land, improvements, and construction in progress	189,555,000	7,660,000	323,807,000	521,022,000
Other capital assets, net of depreciation	250,659,806	1,778,000	156,600,100	409,037,906
Total assets	519,094,062	14,433,000	505,426,850	1,038,953,912
LIABILITIES				
Accounts payable and accrued expenses	10,031,090	300,000	2,315,000	12,646,090
Demand loans payable to bank	75,000	—	—	75,000
Deferred revenue	310,000	—	402,000	712,000
Long-term liabilities				
Due within one year	8,442,932	228,000	13,327,600	21,998,532
Due in more than one year	69,215,107	750,000	147,637,500	217,602,607
Total liabilities	88,074,129	1,278,000	163,682,100	253,034,229
Net assets—invested in capital assets, net of related debt	373,910,335	8,778,000	319,585,100	702,273,435
Net assets—restricted for capital projects	23,858,956	—	3,000,000	26,858,956
Net assets—restricted for debt service	2,268,000	—	322,000	2,590,000
Net assets—restricted for other purposes	15,480,500	3,732,000	1,713,400	20,925,900
Net assets—restricted for other purposes (nonexpendable)	243,000	—	437,250	680,250
Net assets—unrestricted	15,259,142	645,000	16,687,000	32,591,142
Total net assets	$431,019,933	$13,155,000	$341,744,750	$785,919,683

City of Centerville Statement of Activities
Component Units for the Year Ended June 30, 20X2

		Program Revenues			Net Revenue (Expense) and Changes in Net Assets			
	Expenses	Charges for Services	Operating Grants and Contributions	Capital Grants and Contributions	Centerville Public School System	Centerville Regional Transit System	Other Component Units	Total
Centerville Public School System								
Instruction	$43,500,000	$2,750,000	—	$13,700,000	$(27,050,000)	—	—	$(27,050,000)
Special education	4,530,000	640,000	$2,300,000	770,000	(820,000)	—	—	(820,000)
Academic Support	1,650,000	—	—	—	(1,650,000)	—	—	(1,650,000)
Other educational programs	2,300,000	125,000	—	—	(2,175,000)	—	—	(2,175,000)
General administration	3,750,000	7,400	—	—	(3,742,600)	—	—	(3,742,600)
School administration	1,250,000	—	720,000	—	(530,000)	—	—	(530,000)
Transportation	3,660,000	12,500	1,800,000	550,000	(1,297,500)	—	—	(1,297,500)
Business-type activities	11,320,000	9,370,000	1,970,000	165,000	185,000	—	—	185,000
Interest on long-term debt	1,200,000	—	—	—	(1,200,000)	—	—	(1,200,000)
Total—Public School System	73,160,000	12,904,900	6,790,000	15,185,000	(38,280,100)	—	—	(38,280,100)
Centerville Regional Transit system	27,966,000	28,500,000	600,000	—		$1,134,000		1,134,000
Other Component Units	47,021,700	31,297,000	4,053,000	4,562,000			$(7,109,700)	(7,109,700)
Total Component Units	$148,147,700	$72,701,900	$11,443,000	$19,747,000				(44,255,800)
General revenues:								
Payment from the City of Centerville					32,000,000			32,000,000
Taxes:								
Property taxes					2,750,000		5,990,000	8,740,000
Other					105,000		105,000	210,000

| | Expenses | Program Revenues | | | Net Revenue (Expense) and Changes in Net Assets | | | |
		Charges for Services	Operating Grants and Contributions	Capital Grants and Contributions	Centerville Public School System	Centerville Regional Transit System	Other Component Units	Total
Grants and contributions not restricted to specific programs					2,300,000	1,800,000	3,860,000	7,960,000
Unrestricted investment earnings					42,000	180,000	703,000	925,000
Miscellaneous					55,000	162,000	104,900	321,900
Special item—gain on sale of land					120,000	—	—	120,000
Total general revenues, special items, and transfers					37,372,000	2,142,000	10,762,900	50,276,900
Change in net assets					(908,100)	3,276,000	3,653,200	6,021,100
Net assets—beginning					431,928,033	9,879,000	338,091,550	779,898,583
Net assets—ending					$431,019,933	$13,155,000	$341,744,750	$785,919,683

This information is used in Chapter 16, "Basic Financial Statements."

PART VI.
THE FINANCIAL STATEMENTS
AND RELATED DISCLOSURES

CHAPTER 16
BASIC FINANCIAL STATEMENTS

CONTENTS

INTRODUCTION

The basic financial statements include two financial statement components: (1) fund financial statements and (2) government-wide financial statements. This type of reporting model may lead financial statements readers to wonder which set is *correct*. In order to help readers understand the relationship between the two sets of financial statements, GAAP requires summary reconciliations between the fund financial statements and the government-wide financial statements. The nature of the reconciliations can be divided into the following categories:

- Reconciliations for governmental activities
- Reconciliations for business-type activities

Reconciliations for Governmental Activities

The totals in the fund financial statements for governmental funds will not equal totals in the governmental activities columns of the government-wide financial statements, because different measurement focuses and bases of accounting are used to prepare the two different sets of financial statements. (The totals may not equal because of the merging of balances from Internal Service Funds.) For this reason, GAAP requires that at the bottom of the fund financial statements or in a separate schedule there be a summary reconciliation between the fund financial statements and the government-wide financial statements. That is, the amount shown as the "total fund balances" in the "total governmental funds" column on the fund balance sheets is reconciled to the "net assets" for governmental activities presented on the statement of net assets. Also, the amount shown as "net changes in fund balance" in the "total governmental funds" column on the statement of revenues, expenditures, and change in fund balances is reconciled to the "change in net assets" for governmental activities presented on the statement of activities.

Based on the illustration developed in previous chapters of this book, the balances to be reconciled are as follows:

	Fund Balances/Net Assets	Change in Fund Balances/Net Assets
Total balances for governmental funds*	$ 16,989,056	$ 2,496,556
Total balances for governmental activities**	$305,641,889	$(1,636,208)

---

* These balances are from the governmental fund financial statements presented later in this chapter.
** These balances are from the government-wide financial statements (governmental activities) presented later in this chapter.

GASB-54's implementation will not change this reconciliation. In order to explain the differences between the two sets of financial statements' balances, the worksheet entries—made to convert from a modified accrual basis to an accrual basis and to merge the balances of Internal Service Funds—are as follows:

	Debit	Credit	Effects on Balances Fund Balances/ Net Assets	Change in Fund Balances/ Net Assets
Per Governmental Fund Financial Statements	—	—	$16,989,056	$2,496,556
General Fund:	—	—		
JE02.51A				
Other financing sources— capitalized leases	431,213			(431,213)
Expenditures—general government		431,213		431,213
Leased capital assets	431,213		431,213	
Lease obligation payable		431,213	(431,213)	
Lease obligation payable	100,000		100,000	
Expenditures—general government		100,000		100,000
Expenses—general government	79,058		(79,058)	(79,058)
Accumulated depreciation—leased capital assets		79,058		
Interest expenses	24,290		(24,290)	(24,290)
Interest payable		24,290		
JE02.51B				
Lease obligation payable	1,188,141		1,188,141	1,188,141
Expenditures—general government		712,885		
Expenditures—public safety		237,628		
Expenditures—streets		118,814		
Expenditures—recreation and parks		59,407		
Expenditures—health and welfare		59,407		
JE02.52				
Intergovernmental grants receivable	6,000,000		6,000,000	
General revenues— unrestricted grants		6,000,000		6,000,000
JE02.53A				
Vehicles	900,000		900,000	900,000
Expenditures—general government		100,000		
Expenditures—public safety		300,000		
Expenditures—streets		400,000		

			Effects on Balances	
	Debit	**Credit**	**Fund Balances/ Net Assets**	**Change in Fund Balances/ Net Assets**
Expenditures—recreation and parks		100,000		
JE02.53B				
Expenses—general government	19,445		(175,000)	(175,000)
Expenses—public safety	58,333			
Expenses—streets	*77,778*			
Expenses—recreation and parks	19,444			
Accumulated depreciation—vehicles		175,000		
JE02.53C				
Vehicles	520,000		520,000	520,000
Expenditures—public safety		520,000		
Expenses—public safety	28,889		(28,889)	(28,889)
Accumulated depreciation—vehicles		28,889		
JE02.53D				
Equipment	4,700,000		4,700,000	4,700,000
Expenditures—general government		2,000,000		
Expenditures—public safety		1,300,000		
Expenditures—streets		700,000		
Expenditures—recreation and parks		500,000		
Expenditures—health and welfare		200,000		
Expenses—general government	170,000		(437,000)	(437,000)
Expenses—public safety	110,000			
Expenses—streets	95,000			
Expenses—recreation and parks	40,000			
Expenses—health and welfare	22,000			
Accumulated depreciation— equipment		437,000		
JE02.54				
Accumulated depreciation— buildings	2,000,000		(5,600,000)	(5,600,000)
Accumulated depreciation— equipment	1,000,000			

			Effects on Balances	
	Debit	Credit	Fund Balances/ Net Assets	Change in Fund Balances/ Net Assets
Accumulated depreciation—vehicles	3,000,000			
Other financing sources—disposition of capital assets	4,800,000			
Expenses—general government	700,000			
Expenses—public safety	100,000			
Buildings		7,000,000		
Equipment		1,400,000		
Vehicles		3,200,000		
JE02.55				
Expenses—general government	19,620,000		(33,400,000)	(33,400,000)
Expenses—public safety	6,540,000			
Expenses—streets	3,970,000			
Expenses—recreation and parks	1,635,000			
Expenses—health and welfare	1,635,000			
Accumulated depreciation—buildings		8,000,000		
Accumulated depreciation—equipment		1,500,000		
Accumulated depreciation—vehicles		22,000,000		
Accumulated depreciation—leased capital assets		1,200,000		
Accumulated depreciation—infrastructure assets		700,000		
JE02.56				
Land	20,000,000		20,000,000	20,000,000
Extraordinary item—donation of land by the state		20,000,000		
JE02.57A				
Expenses—public safety	300,000		(300,000)	(300,000)
Claims payable		300,000		
Expenses—general government	132,000		(220,000)	(220,000)
Expenses—public safety	44,000			
Expenses—streets	22,000			

	Debit	Credit	Effects on Balances	
			Fund Balances/ Net Assets	Change in Fund Balances/ Net Assets
Expenses—recreation and parks	11,000			
Expenses—health and welfare	11,000			
Compensated absences payable		220,000		
JE02.57B				
Claims payable	400,000		400,000	400,000
Expenditures—public safety		400,000		
JE02.57C				
Compensated absences payable	60,000		60,000	60,000
Expenditures—general government		36,000		
Expenditures—public safety		12,000		
Expenditures—streets		6,000		
Expenditures—recreation and parks		3,000		
Expenditures—health and welfare		3,000		
JE02.58				
Property taxes receivable	1,400,000		1,400,000	1,400,000
General revenues— property taxes		1,400,000		
JE02.59				
Other receivables	8,400		8,400	8,400
Program revenues— charges for services (recreation and parks)		4,000		
Program revenues— charges for services (public safety)		800		
Program revenues— charges for services (health and welfare)		1,600		
Program revenues— charges for services (general government)		2,000		
JE02.60				
Land and improvements	105,000,000		313,368,540	
Construction in progress	2,050,000			
Buildings	220,000,000			
Equipment	19,000,000			

	Debit	Credit	Effects on Balances	
			Fund Balances/ Net Assets	Change in Fund Balances/ Net Assets
Vehicles	75,000,000			
Leased capital assets	7,818,540			
Infrastructure assets	20,000,000			
Accumulated depreciation—buildings		75,000,000		
Accumulated depreciation—equipment		7,000,000		
Accumulated depreciation—vehicles		39,000,000		
Accumulated depreciation—leased capital assets		2,500,000		
Accumulated depreciation—infrastructure assets		12,000,000		
Net assets		313,368,540		
JE02.61				
Net assets	5,197,652		(5,197,652)	
Lease obligations payable		5,197,652		
JE02.62				
Net assets	6,500,000		(6,500,000)	
Compensated absences payable		4,500,000		
Claims and judgments payable		2,000,000		
Special Revenue Funds:				
JE03.19				
Intergovernmental receivables	50,000		50,000	50,000
General revenues—unrestricted grants		50,000		
JE03.20				
Intergovernmental receivables	20,000		20,000	20,000
General revenues—unrestricted grants		20,000		
Capital Projects Funds:				
JE04.3				
Construction-in-progress	11,100,000		11,100,000	11,100,000
Expenditures—capital outlays (streets)		11,100,000		
JE04.26				

	Debit	Credit	Effects on Balances Fund Balances/ Net Assets	Change in Fund Balances/ Net Assets
Long-term debt issued (other sources of financial resources)	10,000,000		(9,328,956)	(9,328,956)
Discount on long-term debt issued (other uses of financial resources)		671,044		
Bonds payable		9,328,956		
JE04.27				
Construction-in-progress	1,500,000		1,500,000	1,500,000
Expenditures—capital outlays (streets)		1,500,000		
JE04.28				
Construction-in-progress	1,300,000		1,300,000	1,300,000
Expenditures—capital outlays (recreation and parks)		1,300,000		
JE04.29				
Long-term debt issued (other sources of financial resources)	3,000,000		(3,000,000)	(3,000,000)
Bonds payable		3,000,000		
Debt Service Funds:				
JE05.3				
Fund balance restricted— Senior Citizens' Center bonds	10,000,000		(16,964,791)	
Fund balance restricted— Easely Street Bridge bonds	2,064,791			
Fund balance restricted— Bland Street Drainage bonds	4,900,000			
Revenue bonds payable (Senior Citizens' Center bonds)		10,000,000		
Bonds payable (Easely Street Bridge bonds)		2,064,791		
Bonds payable (Bland Street Drainage bonds)		4,900,000		
JE05.26				
Revenue bonds payable	750,000		750,000	750,000
Expenditures—principal		750,000		
JE05.27				
Bonds payable	14,169		14,169	14,169
Interest expense		14,169		

			Effects on Balances	
	Debit	Credit	Fund Balances/ Net Assets	Change in Fund Balances/ Net Assets
JE05.28				
Interest expense	559,737		(559,737)	(559,737)
Interest payable		525,000		
Bonds payable		34,737		
JE05.29				
Bonds payable	700,000		700,000	700,000
Expenditures—principal		700,000		
JE05.30				
Bonds payable	500,000		500,000	500,000
Expenditures—principal		500,000		
Internal Service Funds:				
JE08.45				
Cash	946,000		6,590,000	(2,512,544)
Interest receivable	1,000		(2,512,544)	
Due from other funds	325,000			
Temporary investments	15,000			
Inventories	9,000			
Land and improvements	2,700,000			
Buildings	1,400,000			
Equipment	5,870,000			
Vehicles	143,000			
Expenses—general government	1,476,326			
Expenses—public safety	492,109			
Expenses—streets	246,055			
Expenses—recreation and parks	123,027			
Expenses—health and welfare	123,027			
Internal balances	547,456			
Interest expense	97,000			
Accumulated depreciation		3,103,000		
Accounts payable and accrued expenses		50,000		
Compensated absences—current		3,000		
Claims and judgments— current		4,000		
Compensated absences—noncurrent		4,000		
Claims and judgments— noncurrent		15,000		

	Debit	Credit	Fund Balances/ Net Assets	Change in Fund Balances/ Net Assets
			Effects on Balances	
Notes payable—noncurrent		4,700,000		
Interest and investment revenue		5,000		
Transfers in		40,000		
Net assets		6,590,000		
JE08.47				
Cash	137,500		1,489,500	322,000
Interest receivable	2,000		322,000	
Due from other funds	72,000			
Due from other governments	45,000			
Temporary investments	19,000			
Inventories	7,000			
Land and improvements	50,000			
Buildings	1,600,000			
Equipment	1,330,000			
Vehicles	8,200,000			
Interest expense	180,000			
Transfers out	50,000			
Expenses—general government		40,200		
Expenses—public safety		103,400		
Expenses—streets		51,700		
Expenses—recreation and parks		25,850		
Expenses—health and welfare		25,850		
Accumulated depreciation		6,505,000		
Accounts payable and accrued expenses		125,000		
Compensated absences—current		2,000		
Claims and judgments—current		2,000		
Notes payable—current		1,500,000		
Compensated absences—noncurrent		6,000		
Claims and judgment—noncurrent		11,000		
Notes payable—noncurrent		1,500,000		
Interest and investment revenue		5,000		

	Debit	Credit	Effects on Balances Fund Balances/ Net Assets	Change in Fund Balances/ Net Assets
Program revenues— charges for services (general government)		300,000		
Net assets		1,489,500		
Per Government-Wide Financial Statement			$ 305,641,889	$ (1,636,208)

Each of the foregoing worksheet entries is taken from a previous chapter. For example, "JE02.51A" refers to a worksheet entry ("51A") discussed in Chapter 2, "General Fund."

It is also necessary to categorize each reconciling item so that the items can be presented in the reconciliation in a manageable way. The categorization scheme shown in Exhibits 16-1 and 16-2 is used for the balance sheet and the statement of changes in revenues, expenditures, and changes in fund balances. (The focus of the explanations in Exhibits 16-1 and 16-2 is from the fund financial statements to the government-wide financial statements.)

Exhibit 16-1: Categorization Scheme.

Categories for Balance Sheet	Type of Reconciling Item
A	Capital assets are not reported in this fund financial statement because they are not current financial resources, but they are reported in the statement of net assets.
B	Certain long-term assets are not reported in this fund financial statement because they are not available to pay current-period expenditures, but they are reported as assets in the statement of net assets.
C	Certain liabilities (such as bonds payable and accrued expenses) are not reported in this fund financial statement because they are not due and payable, but they are presented as liabilities in the statement of net assets.
D	Assets and liabilities of certain Internal Service Funds related to governmental programs are not reported in this fund financial statement because they are presented on a different accounting basis, but they are presented as assets and liabilities in the statement of net assets.

Exhibit 16-2: Categorization Scheme.

Categories for Statements of Revenues, Expenditures, and Changes in Fund Balances	Type of Reconciling Item
AA	Capital outlays are reported as expenditures in this fund financial statement because they use current financial resources, but they are presented as assets in the statement of activities and depreciated over their estimated economic lives. The amount by which capital outlays ($20,019,000), which is made up of capital outlays reported in Capital Projects Funds of $13,900,000 and $6,120,000 of capital outlays reported in the Genera Fund, exceeds depreciation ($33,419,947) for the year.
BB	Revenues that are not available to pay current obligations are not reported in this fund financial statement, but t hey are presented as revenues in the statement of activities.
CC	The proceeds from the issuance of bonds provide current financial resources and are reported in this fund financial statement, but they are presented as liabilities in the statement of net assets.
DD	The net revenues (expenses) of certain Internal Service Funds related to governmental programs are not reported in this fund financial statement because they are presented on a different accounting basis (in the proprietary fund financial statements), but they are presented in the statement of activities.
EE	Generally expenditures recognized in this fund's financial statements are limited to only those that use current financial resources but expenses are recognized in the statement of activities when they are incurred.
FF	Gains and losses are not presented in this financial statement because they do not provided or use current financial resources, but they are presented in the statement of activities.

Using the classification scheme in Exhibits 16-1 and 16-2, the specific worksheet entries presented earlier in this chapter are classified for the fund balance sheet reconciliation disclosure as follows:

Fund balances per governmental funds financial statements					$16,989,056
Entries	A	B	C	D	
JE02.51A	$ 352,155	—	$ (355,503)	—	(3,348)
JE02.51B	—	—	1,188,141	—	1,188,141
JE02.52	—	$6,000,000	—	—	6,000,000
JE02.53	5,479,111	—	—	—	5,479,111
JE02.54	(5,600,000)	—	—	—	(5,600,000)

Entries	A	B	C	D
JE02.55	(33,400,000)	—	—	— (33,400,000)
JE02.56	20,000,000	—	—	— 20,000,000
JE02.57A	—	—	(520,000)	— (520,000)
JE02.57B	—	—	400,000	— 400,000
JE02.57C	—	—	60,000	— 60,000
JE02.58	—	1,400,000	—	— 1,400,000
JE02.59	—	8,400	—	— 8,400
JE02.60	313,368,540	—	—	— 313,368,540
JE02.61	—	—	(5,197,652)	— (5,197,652)
JE02.62	—	—	(6,500,000)	— (6,500,000)
JE03.19	—	50,000	—	— 50,000
JE03.20	—	20,000	—	— 20,000
JE04.3	11,100,000	—	—	— 11,100,000
JE04.26	—	—	(9,328,956)	— (9,328,956)
JE04.27	1,500,000	—	—	— 1,500,000
JE04.28	1,300,000	—	—	— 1,300,000
JE04.29	—	—	(3,000,000)	— (3,000,000)
JE05.3	—	—	(16,964,791)	— (16,964,791)
JE05.26	—	—	750,000	— 750,000
JE05.27	—	—	14,169	— 14,169
JE05.28	—	—	(559,737)	— (559,737)
JE05.29	—	—	700,000	— 700,000
JE05.30	—	—	500,000	— 500,000
JE08.45	—	—	—	$4,077,456 4,077,456
JE08.47	—	—	—	1,811,500 1,811,500
Net difference	$314,099,806	$7,478,400	$(38,814,329)	$5,888,956 288,652,833

Net assets per government-wide financial statements $305,641,889

The specific worksheet entries presented earlier in this chapter are classified for the statement of revenues, expenditures, and changes in fund balances classifications as follows:

Change in fund balances per statement of revenues, expenditures and changes in fund balances $2,496,556

Entries	AA	BB	CC	DD	EE	FF	
JE02.51A	$ (79,058)	—	—	—	$75,710	—	(3,348)
JE02.51B	—	—	—	—	1,188,141	—	1,188,141
JE02.52	—	$6,000,000	—	—	—	—	6,000,000
JE02.53	5,479,111	—	—	—	—	—	5,479,111
JE02.54	—	—	—	—	—	$(5,600,000)	(5,600,000)

Entries	AA	BB	CC	DD	EE	FF	
JE02.55	(33,400,000)	—	—	—	—	—	(33,400,000)
JE02.56	—	—	—	—	—	20,000,000	20,000,000
JE02.57A	—	—	—	—	(520,000)	—	(520,000)
JE02.57B	—	—	—	—	400,000	—	400,000
JE02.57C	—	—	—	—	60,000	—	60,000
JE02.58	—	1,400,000	—	—	—	—	1,400,000
JE02.59	—	8,400	—	—	—	—	8,400
JE02.60	—	—	—	—	—	—	—
JE02.61	—	—	—	—	—	—	—
JE02.62	—	—	—	—	—	—	—
JE03.19	—	50,000	—	—	—	—	50,000
JE03.20	—	20,000	—	—	—	—	20,000
JE04.3	11,100,000	—	—	—	—	—	11,100,000
JE04.26	—	—	(9,328,956)	—	—	—	(9,328,956)
JE04.27	1,500,000	—	—	—	—	—	1,500,000
JE04.28	1,300,000	—	—	—	—	—	1,300,000
JE04.29	—	—	(3,000,000)	—	—	—	(3,000,000)
JE05.3	—	—	—	—	—	—	—
JE05.26	—	—	—	750,000	—	—	750,000
JE05.27	—	—	—	14,169	—	—	14,169
JE05.28	—	—	—	(559,737)	—	—	(559,737)
JE05.29	—	—	—	700,000	—	—	700,000
JE05.30	—	—	—	500,000	—	—	500,000
JE08.45	—	—	$(2,512,544)	—	—	—	(2,512,544)
JE08.47	—	—	322,000	—	—	—	322,000
Net difference	$(14,099,947)	$7,478,400	$(12,328,956)	$(2,190,544)	$2,608,283	$14,400,000	(4,132,764)

| Change in net assets per statement of activities | | | | | | | $(1,636,208) |

These foregoing balances by categories are used in the presentation of the fund financial statements presented later in this chapter.

Reconciliations for Business-Type Activities

Often the totals in the business-type activities columns of the government-wide financial statements will be equal to the totals in the fund financial statements for Enterprise Funds, because the accrual basis of accounting is used to prepare the two different sets of financial statements. However, if balances related to an Internal Service Fund(s) are reflected in the government-wide financial statements, there must be a summary reconciliation between the fund financial statements and the government-wide financial statements. That is, the amount shown as the "total net assets" in the "total for Enterprise Funds" column on the fund balance sheets are reconciled to the "net assets" for business-type activities presented on the statement of net assets. Also, the amount shown as "change in net assets" in the total column for Enterprise Funds on the statement of revenues, expenses, and changes in fund net assets is reconciled to the "change in net assets" for business-type activities presented on the statement of activities.

Often there are no reconciling items between the business-type activities as they appear on the government-wide financial statements and the fund financial statements, because both are prepared on the accrual basis of accounting. However, the GASB's *Comprehensive Implementation Guide* states that generally, only the following could arise as reconciling items: (1) When Enterprise Funds are the only or predominant participants in an Internal Service Fund, the balances related to the Internal Service Fund must be included in the business-type activities column (not the governmental activities column, which is the typical presentation). Because Internal Service Funds are not included in the totals of the Enterprise Funds (but rather presented in a column to the right of those funds) in the fund financial statements, a reconciling item arises. (2) When Enterprise Funds participate in an Internal Service Fund and the Internal Service Fund is not at a "break even" position, a look-back adjustment must modify the expenses in the business-type activities column. This creates a difference between the expenses as presented in the fund financial statements and the expenses presented in the government-wide financial statements. Or (3) When a governmental activity is performed in an Enterprise Fund (or vice versa), the results of the activity are presented in an Enterprise Fund financial statement. However, those same results must be presented in the governmental-activity column of the government-wide financial statements. This creates a difference between the two financial statements.

The GASB's *Guide* states that indirect expenses could be allocated to business-type activities as well as governmental activities, assuming there is a reasonable basis for doing so. However, if those expenses are allocated to business-type activities, the allocation creates an additional item that must be disclosed as a reconciling item between the fund financial statements and the government-wide financial statements.

Based on the continuing illustration used in this book, the balances to be reconciled are as follows:

	Net Assets	Change in Net Assets
Total balances for Enterprise Funds*	$121,041,500	$25,774,000
Total balances for business-type activities**	$125,378,044	$25,314,544

* These balances are from the proprietary fund financial statements presented later in this chapter.
** These balances are from the government-wide financial statements (business-type activities) presented later in this chapter

In order to explain the differences between the two sets of financial statements balances, the worksheet entries made to merge the balances of Internal Service Funds are as follows:

	Debit	Credit	Effects on Balances	
			Net Assets	Change in Net Assets
Net asset balance per Enterprise Fund financial statements			$121,041,500	$25,774,000
JE08.46				
Expenses— Centerville Municipal Airport	327,872			
Expenses— Centerville Utilities Authority	120,320			
Expenses— Centerville Parking Authority	54,144			
Expenses— Centerville Toll Bridge	45,120			
Internal balances		547,456	(547,456)	(547,456)
JE08.48				
Cash	22,000			
Interest receivable	1,000			
Due from other funds	427,000			
Temporary investments	12,000			
Inventories	20,000			
Land and improvements	1,750,000			
Buildings	1,600,000			
Equipment	2,960,000			
Vehicles	1,995,000			
Expenses—Centerville Municipal Airport		73,000	73,000	73,000
Accumulated depreciation		3,240,000		
Accounts payable and accrued expenses		75,000		
Compensated absences		17,000		
Claims and judgements		21,000		
Notes payable		550,000		
Interest and investment revenue		15,000	15,000	15,000
Net assets		4,796,000	4,796,000	

			Effects on Balances	
	Debit	Credit	Net Assets	Change in Net Assets
Net adjustment to reconcile			4,336,544	(459,456)
Net asset balance per government-wide financial statements			**$125,378,044**	**$25,314,544**

Each of the above worksheet entries is taken from Chapter 8, "Internal Service Funds." In addition, each of the worksheet entries is classified to identify the nature of the worksheet entry based on the classification scheme discussed earlier in this chapter for governmental activities. The reconciling items for the Enterprise Funds are all related to Internal Service Fund categories (D and DD).

These balances by categories are used in the presentation of the fund financial statements presented later in this chapter.

The GASB's *Comprehensive Implementation Guide* emphasizes that expenses and revenues should be reported gross on the statement of activities.

Components of Net Assets: Governmental Activities

Net assets represent the difference between a governmental entity's total assets and its total liabilities. The statement of net assets must identify the components of net assets, namely (1) invested in capital assets, net of related debt, (2) restricted net assets, and (3) unrestricted net assets.

The GASB's *Guide* states that an equity interest in a joint venture is represented by unrestricted net assets because the investment does not reflect (1) capital assets held directly by the governmental entity or (2) "restricted" as defined in paragraph 34 of GASB-34. The unrestricted net asset category is the default category. If an item does not qualify for classification as invested in capital assets (net of related debt) or restricted net assets, then it must be classified as unrestricted net assets.

PRACTICE ALERT: GASB-61 states that in an organization that has several participants, if one participating government appoints a voting majority of the organization's governing body (and joint control is precluded because that participant has the power to make decisions unilaterally), the organization is either a component unit or a related organization of that participating government and should be reported in that participating government's financial statements as either a discretely presented or blended component unit (as applicable) or as a related organizations. However, the other (minority) governmental participants should report their participation in the organization at cost if it is a proprietary fund or as a net investment in a joint venture in a governmental fund. The organization itself, when included as a component unit in the majority participant's financial reporting entity, should report any equity interests of the minority participants as "restricted net assets, nonexpendable." In addition, there may be instances where a jointly controlled organization (such as a regional government) is considered a component unit of one of the participating governments because it is fiscally dependent on and has a financial benefit or burden relationship with that participating government. This type of organization should be reported, by all participants as either a component unit, a related organization or as a net investment in a joint venture. When permanent endowments, permanent fund principal amounts, or minority interest in a component unit are included, "restricted net assets" should be displayed in two additional components—expendable and nonexpendable. Nonexpendable net assets are those that are required to be retained in perpetuity or that represent minority interests in component units.

Invested in capital assets (net of related debt) is the difference between (1) capital assets, net of accumulated depreciation, and (2) liabilities "attributable to the acquisition, construction, or improvement of those assets." Restricted net assets arise if either of the following conditions exists:

- Externally imposed by creditor (such as through debt covenants), grantors, contributors, or laws or regulations of other governments; or

- Imposed by law through constitutional provisions or enabling legislation.

IMPLEMENTATION GUIDANCE: Under some circumstances a governmental entity reports capital debt but not the capital asset that was purchased with the debt proceeds. For example, a so-called Phase 3 government is encouraged but does not have to report major general infrastructure asset retroactively, but the related debt must be reported. Under this circumstance, the question arises of whether the capital debt should be considered in determining the amount to be reported as net assets invested in capital assets (net of related debt). The GASB's *Comprehensive Implementation Guide* states that the capital debt must be used to compute the amount of net assets invested in capital assets (net of related debt) even though the related capital asset is not reported in the statement of net assets. Furthermore if the total capital debt is greater than the reported capital assets, the net assets invested in capital assets (net of related debt) will have a negative (debit) balance; however, that negative amount must nonetheless be reported in the governmental entity statement of net assets. Large general purpose governments that bond for construction of assets that are subsequently delivered to other governments could have total debt could be greater than capital assets because those constructed assets are not capital assets. In that instance case, net assets invested in capital assets (net of related debt) have a negative (debit) balance that is reported in the governmental entity's statement of net assets. Another possibility for a debit balance in invested in capital assets net of related debt could be for the government to have a policy of depreciating capital assets faster than debt principal is paid. If that is the case, the accounting policy should be reviewed by the government.

In some instances a governmental entity specifically restricts assets that are to be used to pay the current portion of bonds that were issued to finance the acquisition of capital assets. Even though the restricted assets are used to determine the amount of restricted net assets, the GASB's *Comprehensive Implementation Guide* states that the related current portion of the maturing debt must be used to determine the amount of net assets invested in capital assets (net of related debt) rather than restricted net assets.

Restricted net assets should be identified based on major categories that make up the restricted balance. These categories could include items such as net assets restricted for capital projects and for debt service. In some instances, net assets may be restricted on a permanent basis (in perpetuity). Under this circumstance, the restricted net assets are subdivided into expendable and nonexpendable restricted net assets.

The statement of net assets illustrated in this chapter is unclassified. Alternatively, GASB-34 notes that assets and liabilities may be presented in the statement of net assets using a classified financial statement format whereby accounts are grouped in current and noncurrent categories similar to the presentation used by business enterprises. When a governmental entity presents a classified statement of net assets, the question arises regarding whether the amount that represents restricted net assets (in the equity section) requires that specific assets be identified as restricted *assets* (in the asset section). In preparing financial statements there is no general requirement that specific net asset (equity) accounts be traceable to specific assets. Therefore, when a classified statement of net assets is presented there is no need to establish a subcategory of assets identified as restricted; however, a financial statement preparer should carefully evaluate the ramifications of restrictions to determine whether they are determinant in categorizing an asset as current or noncurrent. ARB-43 (Restatement and Revision of Accounting Research Bulletins) notes that current assets should not include "cash and claims to cash that are restricted as to withdrawal or use for other than current operations, are designated for expenditure in the acquisition or construction of noncurrent assets, or are segregated for the liquidation of long-term debt." The GASB's *Comprehensive Implementation Guide* states that "resources accounted for in the General Fund, Special Revenue Funds, and Debt Service Funds are generally expected to be used in current operations or to liquidate current obligations and thus generally would be considered current assets." On the other hand, cash presented in a Capital Projects Fund or a Permanent Fund, due to the nature of each fund, should be evaluated to determine whether the amount or a portion of the amount should be reported as a current or noncurrent asset.

The GASB's *Comprehensive Implementation Guide* reiterates that restricted net assets cannot be reported as a negative amount within any category of restricted net assets. If liabilities that relate to specific restricted assets exceed those assets, no restricted net asset balance should be reported—the net negative amount should reduce unrestricted net assets. The related "shortfall," defined as related liabilities exceeding the assets on hand, by default is covered by unrestricted assets.

The AICPA Audit and Accounting Guide *State and Local Governments* addresses the issue of how "assets restricted for debt retirement [that] include amounts due from other funds" should be reported in the statement of net assets. For example, the assets of a Debt Service Fund may include an amount due from the General Fund. When all governmental funds are consolidated to create the government activities column in the statement of net assets, the interfund receivable and payable are eliminated, however, care must be taken that the implied restriction on cash for debt retirement is considered when a classified statement of net assets is prepared (differentiating between current and noncurrent assets) and when an unclassified statement of net assets is prepared (listing assets based on their liquidity).

In some instances a state statute requires that revenues derived from a fee or charge shall not be used for any purpose other than that for which the fee or charge was imposed. The GASB's *Comprehensive Implementation Guide* states that if a local government has imposed such a fee or charge (for example for the replacement of infrastructure assets), the unspent resources accumulated from the fee or charge represent a restricted net asset.

A state legislature may change an existing law that previously restricted the use of tax revenue to a particular type of expenditure. The GASB's *Comprehensive Implementation Guide* points out that although "the new restriction is not established by the original enabling legislation," the net assets arising from the changed legislation are nonetheless restricted for purposes of financial statement disclosure even though the new tax revenues are to be used for a purpose different from that identified in the original legislation.

Assets that are not classified as invested in capital assets (net of related debt) or restricted are included in the category unrestricted net assets. Portions of the entity's net assets may be identified by management to reflect tentative plans or commitments of governmental resources. The *tentative* plans or commitments may be related to items, such as plans to retire debt at some future date or to replace infrastructure or specified capital assets. Designated amounts are not the same as restricted amounts because designations represent planned actions, not actual commitments. For this reason, designated amounts should not be classified with restricted net assets, but rather should be reported as part of the unrestricted net asset component. In addition, designations cannot be disclosed as such on the face of the statement of net assets.

A restricted fund (for example, a Special Revenue Fund) might include an asset balance that exceeds the requirements of the related restriction. The GASB's *Comprehensive Implementation Guide* states that under this circumstance the excess amount should be used to compute the amount of unrestricted net assets.

PRACTICE ALERT: The new definitions in GASB-54 provide that governmental funds of a particular type either should be used (i.e., required) or are used (i.e., discretionary) for all activities that meet its criteria. If use of a fund type is generally discretionary, specific situations under which a fund of that type should be used are identified either in the definitions in GASB-54 (i.e., debt service funds) or by requirements established in other authoritative pronouncements (i.e., special revenue and capital projects funds). The fund balance classification section of GASB-54 defines the terminology "restricted," "committed," and "assigned." GASB-54 modified the definitions of governmental fund types. Specifically, special revenue funds are defined as those funds used to account for and report the proceeds of specific revenue sources that are restricted or committed to expenditure for specified purposes other than debt service or capital projects.

Therefore, a stabilization arrangement would meet the criteria to be reported as a separate special revenue fund only if the fund's resources are derived from a specific restricted or committed revenue source, specifically restricted or committed for that stabilization purpose.

The basic concept of restricted net assets is that the restrictions are not unilaterally established by the reporting government itself and cannot be removed without consent of those imposing the restrictions (externally imposed restrictions) or through formal due process (internally imposed restrictions). These concepts are formulated within GASB-46 (Net Assets Restricted by Enabling Legislation—an Amendment of GASB Statement No. 34).

"Externally imposed restrictions" are commonly found in the form of

- Laws and regulations of another government that has jurisdiction over the reporting government
- Debt covenants of the government's creditors
- Requirements contained in grant agreements with grantors
- Contractual agreements with donors or other contributors

"Legally imposed restrictions" are commonly found in the form of

- The reporting government's constitution or similar document (such as a municipal charter)
- Enabling legislation (such as state laws for a state and municipal ordinances for a municipality) that creates a new resource and imposes legally enforceable restrictions on the use of the new resource

---

OBSERVATION: It is important to note that the earmarking of an existing resource or revenue for a specific use by the reporting government does not result in the reporting of restricted net assets from the earmarking. Question 7.24.11 of the GASB's *Comprehensive Implementation Guide* states that "earmarking existing revenue is not equivalent to enabling legislation." The earmarking of an existing resource is similar to a designation of the government's intent and is not the same as a legal restriction established at the time the revenue was created.

Common errors made by financial statement preparers related to reporting restricted net assets include the following:

- Inappropriately classifying all reserved fund balances of governmental funds as restricted net assets of governmental activities
- Inappropriately believing that all assets reported as restricted will also be reported as restricted net assets
- Failing to reduce restricted assets by the liabilities payable from those restricted assets or the liabilities that were incurred to generate the restricted assets

The components for net assets for the City of Centerville for governmental activities are determined in the following analysis:

Fund Balances	Restricted for				Invested in Capital Assets Net of Related Debt	Total
	Capital Projects	Debt Service	Other Purposes	Unrestricted		
General Fund	—	—	—	$12,570,600	—	$12,570,600
Major funds:						
Local Fuel Tax	—	—	$ 19,000	—	—	19,000
West End Recreation Center	$2,936,000	—	—	—	—	2,936,000
Nonmajor funds:						
Special Services District	—	—	29,500	—	—	29,500
Easely Street Bridge Project	729,956	—	—	—	—	729,956
Bland Street Drainage Project	193,000	—	—	—	—	193,000
All Debt Service Funds	—	$268,000	—	—	—	268,000
Cemetery Fund	—	—	243,000	—	—	243,000
Total fund balances	3,858,956	268,000	291,500	12,570,600	—	16,989,056
Accrual adjustments:						
JE02.51A	—	—	—	(24,290)	$ 20,942	(3,348)
JE02.51B	—	—	—	—	1,188,141	1,188,141
JE02.52	—	—	—	6,000,000	—	6,000,000
JE02.53	—	—	—	—	5,479,111	5,479,111
JE02.54	—	—	—	—	(5,600,000)	(5,600,000)
JE02.55	—	—	—	—	(33,400,000)	(33,400,000)
JE02.56	—	—	—	—	20,000,000	20,000,000
JE02.57A	—	—	—	(520,000)	—	(520,000)
JE02.57B	—	—	—	400,000	—	400,000
JE02.57C	—	—	—	60,000	—	60,000
JE02.58	—	—	—	1,400,000	—	1,400,000
JE02.59	—	—	—	8,400	—	8,400
JE02.60	—	—	—	—	313,368,540	313,368,540
JE02.61	—	—	—	—	(5,197,652)	(5,197,652)
JE02.62	—	—	—	(6,500,000)	—	(6,500,000)
JE03.19	—	—	50,000	—	—	50,000
JE03.20	—	—	20,000	—	—	20,000
JE04.15	—	—	—	—	11,100,000	11,100,000
JE04.26	—	—	—	—	(9,328,956)	(9,328,956)
JE04.27	—	—	—	—	1,500,000	1,500,000
JE04.28	—	—	—	—	1,300,000	1,300,000
JE04.29	—	—	—	—	(3,000,000)	(3,000,000)
JE05.15	—	—	—	—	(16,964,791)	(16,964,791)
JE05.26	—	—	—	—	750,000	750,000
JE05.27	—	—	—	14,169	—	14,169
JE05.28	—	—	—	(559,737)	—	(559,737)
JE05.29	—	—	—	—	700,000	700,000
JE05.30	—	—	—	—	500,000	500,000
JE08.45	—	—	—	1,767,456	2,310,000	4,077,456
JE08.47	—	—	—	136,500	1,675,000	1,811,500
Net assets	$3,858,956	$268,000	$361,500	$14,753,098	$286,400,335	$305,641,889

In the above analysis, interest accrued on capital debt and the amortization of discount and premium (see JE02.51A, JE05.17, and JE05.28) are not related to "net assets invested in capital assets, net of related debt." Also, part of the balance identified as "restricted for other purposes" includes the net assets of the Cemetery Fund (Permanent Fund), which are nonexpendable. The statement of net asset must identify any restricted net assets that are nonexpendable.

The GASB's *Comprehensive Implementation Guide* makes the following observations about restricted net assets: (1) paragraph 34 of GASB-34 is the starting point for determining whether or not net assets are restricted. In addition, the GASB's *Guide* points out that, in order to be considered restricted net assets, the restriction must be narrower than the "reporting unit in which it is reported." For example, if the resources are restricted to "public safety," then they are considered to be restricted. On the other hand, if the resources are to be used "for the benefit of the citizens," that restriction is as broad as the governmental entity; there is effectively no restriction on net assets. (2) The requirements of paragraph 35 apply only to permanent endowments and permanent fund principal because restrictions imposed on term endowments will at some point be expendable. (3) The liabilities related to restricted assets must be considered in determining restricted net assets. For example, the statement of net assets usually identifies net assets restricted for capital projects. The starting point in determining that amount is to identify total net assets in all Capital Projects Funds. Of course, the total net assets in these funds are computed by subtracting total liabilities from total assets. Additionally, because a Capital Projects Fund is on the modified accrual basis and the statement of net assets is on the accrual basis, it is necessary to take into consideration any "conversion" adjustments that increase or decrease the liabilities in the Capital Projects Funds. Thus, restricted assets as reported in the statement of net assets do take into consideration related liabilities. A negative (deficit) balance in restricted net assets cannot be displayed on the statement of net assets. Any negative amount is used to reduce the unrestricted net asset balance. And (4) "earmarking" an existing revenue source is not the same as enabling legislation. The enabling legislation criterion is satisfied only when the same law that creates a tax or other source of revenue also sets the restrictions on how the resulting resources may be used.

GASB-46 (Net Assets Restricted by Enabling Legislation) addresses issues related to reporting restrictions on net assets resulting from provisions in enabling legislation. GASB-34 requires that limitations on the use of net assets imposed by enabling legislation be reported as restricted net assets. Essentially, for net assets to be restricted by enabling legislation, GASB-34 restrictions had to be "legally enforceable."

Prior to GASB-46 (Net Assets Restricted by Enabling Legislation), there existed considerable confusion and inconsistent interpretation of the concept of legal enforceability. GASB-46 clears up this confusion and accomplishes the following three primary objectives related to reporting restricted net assets:

1. It clarifies that a legally enforceable enabling legislation restriction is one that a party external to the government can compel a government to honor.

2. It provides for the accounting and financial reporting requirements if new enabling legislation replaces existing enabling legislation or if legal enforceability is reevaluated.

3. It requires governments to disclose the portion of total net assets restricted by enabling legislation.

Components of Net Assets: Business-Type Activities

The components of net assets for Enterprise Funds (as reported on the fund financial statements) are generally equal to the same components as reported on the statement of net assets. However, in the current illustration, the effects of merging an Internal Service Fund (Special Services Support Center) must be taken into consideration. The component for net assets for the City of Centerville for business-type activities is determined in the following analysis:

NET ASSETS	Total Enterprise Fund	Internal Service Fund	Total
Invested in capital assets, net of related debt	$82,995,000	$4,515,000	$87,510,000
Restricted	37,362,000	—	37,362,000
Unrestricted	684,500	(178,456)	506,044
Total net assets	**$121,041,500**	**$4,336,544**	**$125,378,044**

Component Units

The manner by which component units are folded into the financial statements of a primary government is discussed in Chapter 15, "Component Units," in which the following four component units of the City of Centerville are illustrated:

1. Centerville Public School System (considered to be a major component unit by the City)

2. Centerville Parks District (considered to be a minor component unit by the City)

3. Centerville Regional Transit System (considered to be a major component unit by the City)

4. Centerville Sports Authority (considered to be a minor component unit by the City)

These four component units are reported in the City of Centerville's financial statements as discretely presented component units. When the discrete presentation method is used, there is a clear distinction between the balances and activities of the primary government and the discretely presented component units. This distinction is achieved by presenting information for the discrete component units only in the government-wide financial statements using one of the following approaches:

- Present each major component unit in a separate column in the government-wide financial statements
- Present combining statements

- Present condensed financial statements in a note to the financial statements

This text illustrates the combining financial statements alternative, whereby the City of Centerville's government-wide financial statements include a single column that includes the aggregated financial information for all component units. The component unit information is found in the last column in Exhibits 16-3 and 16-4. That columnar information is based on the information found in Exhibit 16-14 and Exhibit 16-15. The information in Exhibits 16-14 and 16-15 is developed in Chapter 15, "Component Units."

FINANCIAL STATEMENTS

Using the illustrations developed in this and in previous chapters, the City of Centerville presents the following financial statements:

- Statement of Net Assets (Exhibit 16-3)
- Statement of Activities (Exhibit 16-4)
- Balance Sheet: Governmental Funds (Exhibit 16-5) (with fund balance aggregated, assuming disaggregated amounts will be presented in the notes to the basic financial statements)
- Reconciliation of the Balance Sheet of Governmental Funds to the Statement of Net Assets (Exhibit 16-6)
- Statement of Revenues, Expenditures, and Changes in Fund Balances: Governmental Funds (Exhibit 16-7)
- Reconciliation of the Statement of Revenues, Expenditures, and Changes in Fund Balances of Governmental Funds to the Statement of Activities (Exhibit 16-8)
- Statement of Net Assets-Proprietary Funds (Exhibit 16-9)
- Statement of Revenues, Expenses, and Changes in Fund Net Assets: Proprietary Funds (Exhibit 16-10)
- Statement of Cash Flows (Exhibit 16-11)
- Statement of Fiduciary Net Assets (Exhibit 16-12)
- Statement of Changes in Fiduciary Net Assets (Exhibit 16-13)
- Statement of Net Assets: Component Units (Exhibit 16-14)
- Statement of Activities: Component Units (Exhibit 16-15)

The GASB's *Comprehensive Implementation Guide* points out that GASB-34 does not require that comparative prior-year data be presented but that it may be presented. For this reason, GASB-34 provides no guidelines for the presentation of prior-year data. Presenting comparative data in governmental financial statements, as opposed to corporate financial statements, is very problematic because of the complicated structure of governmental statements. For example, reporting a comparative statement of net assets for many governmental entities would require eight columns or more, and trying to format a statement of activities for many governmental entities would probably be too unwieldy. If a governmental entity is not a complex reporting entity (for example, it may have only governmental activities and no component units), presenting prior-year data might not be cumbersome. The GASB's *Guide* points out that, for more complicated reporting entities, the best way to present prior-year data may be by reproducing the prior-year financial statements in the current-year's financial statements.

The GASB's *Guide* emphasizes that a fiduciary fund that a governmental entity believes is particularly important cannot be presented in a separate column in the fund financial statements. If a governmental entity wants to present additional detail about its fiduciary funds, that information can be presented in combining statements. However, those statements are optional and not considered part of the general-purpose external financial statements; they are part of the CAFR.

GASB Concepts Statement No. 4 (GASB:CS-4) (Elements of Financial Statements) provides new definitions for seven elements of historically based financial statements of state and local governments:

- Elements of the Statement of Financial Position

  1. Assets
  2. Liabilities
  3. Deferred Outflow of Resources
  4. Deferred Inflow of Resources
  5. Net Position

- Elements of the Resources Flow Statements

  6. Inflow of Resources
  7. Outflow of Resources

The GASB definitions of the elements are based upon the inherent characteristics of each element, and they are linked by a common definition feature in that they are based on the concept of measuring and reporting *resources.* The definitions of the elements apply to an entity that is a governmental unit (that is, a legal entity) and are applicable to any measurement focus under which financial statements may be prepared, for example, economic resources, current financial resources, and cash resources measurement focuses.

PRACTICE ALERT: GASB has issued an exposure draft titled "Financial Reporting of Deferred Outflows of Resources, Deferred Inflows of Resources, and Net Position," which proposes a Statement of Net Position (instead of a Statement of Net Assets) that would incorporate the Deferred Outflows and Inflows of Resources. Net position would include three elements: (1) net investment in capital assets, (2) restricted net position, and (3) unrestricted net position. A new accounting equation would also be implemented. Net Position would be the sum of assets and deferred outflows of resources reduced by liabilities and deferred inflows of resources (deferred positions presented separately from assets and liabilities). If it is approved, the statement would be effective for periods beginning after June 15, 2011. However, for governments that have deferred inflows and outflows of resources associated with hedging derivatives, implementation of the standard upon approval may provide more clarity.

Exhibit 16-3: Statement of Net Assets.

City of Centerville
Statement of Net Assets
June 30, 20X2
Primary Government

	Governmental Activities	Business-Type Activities	Total	Component Units
ASSETS				
Cash	$11,716,956	$12,718,500	$24,435,456	$37,719,106
Internal balances	(1,697,544)	1,697,544		
Receivables (net)	8,014,000	26,207,000	34,221,000	39,602,100
Investments	9,798,600	10,180,000	19,978,600	28,333,200
Inventories	33,000	206,000	239,000	3,204,400
Other assets	5,200		5,200	35,200
Capital assets:				
Land, improvements, and construction in progress	143,700,000	45,855,000	189,555,000	521,022,000
Other capital assets, net of depreciation	182,084,806	68,575,000	250,709,806	33,900,000
Total assets	$353,655,018	$165,439,044	$519,094,062	$1,038,953,912
LIABILITIES				
Accounts payable and accrued expenses	$1,616,090	$8,415,000	$10,031,090	$12,646,090
Demand loans payable to bank	75,000		75,000	75,000
Deferred revenue	310,000		310,000	712,000
Long-term liabilities:				
Due within one year	4,658,932	3,784,000	8,442,932	21,998,532

City of Centerville
Statement of Net Assets
June 30, 20X2
Primary Government

	Governmental Activities	Business-Type Activities	Total	Component Units
Due in more than one year	41,353,107	27,862,000	69,215,107	217,602,607
Total liabilities	$48,013,129	$40,061,000	$88,074,129	$253,034,229
NET ASSETS				
Invested in capital assets, net of related debt	286,400,335	87,510,000	373,910,335	702,273,435
Restricted for:				
Capital projects	3,858,956	20,000,000	23,858,956	26,858,956
Debt service	268,000	8,0002,000	2,268,000	2,590,000
Other purposes	118,500	15,362,000	15,480,500	20,925,900
Other purposes (non-expendable)	243,000		243,000	680,250
Unrestricted (deficit)	14,753,098	506,044	15,259,142	32,591,142
Total net assets	$305,641,889	$125,378,044	$431,019,933	$785,919,683

Exhibit 16-4: Statement of Activities.

CITY OF CENTERVILLE
STATEMENT OF ACTIVITIES
FOR THE YEAR ENDED JUNE 30, 20X2

Functions:	Expenses	Program Revenues			Net (Expense) Revenue and Chain Net Assets Primary Government			Component Units
		Charges For Services	Operating Grants and Contributions	Capital Grants and Contributions	Governmental Activities	Business-Type Activities	Total	
Primary government:								
Governmental activities:								
General government	$54,054,629	$ 355,000	$ 34,000	—	$(53,665,629)	—	$(53,665,629)	—
Public safety	22,836,931	202,000	—	—	(22,634,931)	—	(22,634,931)	—
Streets	21,187,633	150,000	4,570,000	$2,000,000	(14,467,633)	—	(14,467,633)	—
Recreation and parks	7,621,871	135,000	—	450,000	(7,036,871)	—	(7,036,871)	—
Health and welfare	9,579,427	4,000	50,000	—	(9,525,427)	—	(9,525,427)	—
Payment to school district	32,000,000	—	—	—	(32,000,000)	—	(32,000,000)	—
Interest on long-term debt	2,338,517	—	—	—	(2,338,517)	—	(2,338,517)	—
Total governmental activities	149,619,008	846,000	4,654,000	2,450,000	(141,669,008)	—	(141,669,008)	—
Business-type activities:								
Airport	203,594,872	227,060,000	—	2,000,000		$25,465,128	25,465,128	—
Utilities	38,557,320	36,010,000	—	1,250,000		(1,297,320)	(1,297,320)	—
Parking	6,091,144	1,522,000	—	—		(4,569,144)	(4,569,144)	—
Toll bridge	4,699,120	4,770,000	100,000	250,000		420,880	420,880	—
Total business-type activities	252,942,456	269,362,000	100,000	3,500,000		20,019,544	20,019,544	—
Total primary government	$402,561,464	$270,208,000	$4,754,000	$5,950,000	(141,669,008)	20,019,544	(121,649,464)	—
Component units:								
Centerville Public School System	$73,160,000	$12,904,900	$6,790,000	$15,185,000	—	—	—	$(38,280,100)
Centerville Regional Transit System	27,966,000	28,500,000	600,000	—	—	—	—	1,134,000
Other component units	47,021,700	31,297,000	4,053,000	4,562,000	—	—	—	(7,109,700)

	Expenses	Program Revenues — Charges For Services	Program Revenues — Operating Grants and Contributions	Program Revenues — Capital Grants and Contributions	Net (Expense) Revenue and Chain Net Assets — Primary Government — Governmental Activities	Net (Expense) Revenue and Chain Net Assets — Primary Government — Business-Type Activities	Net (Expense) Revenue and Chain Net Assets — Primary Government — Total	Net (Expense) Revenue and Chain Net Assets — Component Units
Total component units	$148,147,700	$72,701,900	$11,443,000	$19,747,000	—	—	—	(44,255,800)
General revenues: Taxes:								
Property taxes					91,670,000	—	91,670,000	8,740,000
Franchise taxes					1,300,000	—	1,300,000	210,000
Contributions to permanent funds					22,000	—	22,000	—
Payment to school district								32,000,000
Grants and contributions not restricted to specific programs					26,500,000	—	26,500,000	7,960,000
Unrestricted investment earnings					662,800	1,655,000	2,317,800	925,000
Miscellaneous					18,000	—	18,000	321,900
Special item—gain on sale of nondepreciable capital assets					—	3,500,000	3,500,000	120,000
Extraordinary gain—donation of land from state					20,000,000	—	20,000,000	—
Transfers					(140,000)	140,000	—	—
Total general revenues, special items, extraordinary items and transfers					140,032,800	5,295,000	145,327,800	50,276,900
Change in net assets					(1,636,208)	25,314,544	23,678,336	6,021,100
Net assets—beginning					307,278,097	100,063,500	407,341,597	779,898,583
Net assets—ending					$305,641,889	$125,378,044	$431,019,933	$785,919,683

Exhibit 16-5: Balance-Sheet: Governmental Funds.

Governmental Funds
Balance Sheet
June 30, 20X2

	General Fund	Local Fuel Tax Fund	West End Recreation Center Project Fund	Other Governmental Funds	Total Governmental Funds
ASSETS					
Cash	$10,045,000	$42,000	$ 19,000	$527,456	$10,633,456
Temporary investments	1,325,000	—	2,922,000	824,000	5,071,000
Property taxes receivable (net)	355,000	—	—	48,000	403,000
Other receivables	67,600	2,000	—	15,000	84,600
Investments	4,449,600	—	—	244,000	4,693,600
Inventories	17,000	—	—	—	17,000
Other assets	5,200	—	—	—	5,200
Total assets	$16,264,400	$44,000	$2,941,000	$1,658,456	$20,907,856
LIABILITIES AND FUND BALANCES					
Liabilities:					
Accounts payable	$ 676,800	$25,000	$5,000	$ 185,000	$ 891,800
Demand loans payable	75,000	—	—	—	75,000
Due to other funds	2,642,000	—	—	—	2,642,000
Deferred revenue	300,000	—	—	10,000	310,000
Total liabilities	3,693,800	25,000	5,000	195,000	3,918,800
Fund balances:					
Nonspendable	17,000	—	—	243,000	260,000
Restricted	—	—	2,450,000	268,000	2,726,000
Assigned	25,000	19,000	486,000	323,500	853,500
Unassigned	12,528,600	—	—	—	12,528,600
Total fund balances	12,570,600	19,000	2,936,000	1,463,456	16,989,056
Total liabilities and fund balances	$16,264,400	$44,000	$2,941,000	$1,658,456	$20,907,856

NOTE: Committed amounts do not appear in fund balances because the author has not made an assumption as to whether or not the highest decision-making authority had committed funds. If funds were committed, an additional category would be added above assigned noted as committed.

Exhibit 16-6: Reconciliation of the Balance Sheet of Governmental Funds to the Statement of Net Assets.

City of Centerville
Reconciliation of the Balance Sheet
of Governmental Funds
To the Statement of Net Assets
June 30, 20X2

Total fund balances per fund financial statements	$16,989,056
Amounts reported for governmental activities in the statement of net assets are different because:	
Capital assets are not reported in this fund financial statement because they are not current financial resources, but they are reported in the statement of net assets.	314,099,806
Certain long-term assets are not reported in this fund financial statement because they are not available to pay current-period expenditures, but they are reported in the statement of net assets.	7,478,400
Certain liabilities (such as bonds payable and accrued expenses) are not reported in this fund financial statement because they are not due and payable, but they are presented in the statement of net assets.	(38,814,329)
Assets and liabilities of certain Internal Service Funds related to governmental programs are not reported in this fund financial statement because they are presented on a different accounting basis, but they are presented in the statement of net assets.	5,888,956
Net assets for governmental activities	$305,641,889

Exhibit 16-7: Statement of Revenues, Expenditures, and Changes in Fund Balances: Governmental Funds.

Governmental Funds
Statement of Revenues, Expenditures,
and Changes in Fund Balances
June 30, 20X2

	General Fund	Local Fuel Tax Fund	West End Recreation Center Project Fund	Other Governmental Funds	Total Governmental Funds
REVENUES					
Property taxes	$ 87,600,000	—	—	$ 2,670,000	$ 90,270,000
Franchise taxes	1,300,000	—	—	—	1,300,000
Intergovernmental grants	20,500,000	$4,500,000	$4,500,000	4,500,000	27,450,000
Charges for services	537,600	—	—	—	537,600
Contributions	50,000	—	—	—	50,000
Interest and investment revenue	601,800	6,000	2,000	77,000	686,800
Miscellaneous revenue	—	—	—	40,000	40,000
Total revenue	110,589,400	4,506,000	452,000	4,787,000	120,334,400
EXPENDITURES					
Current:					
General government	33,824,098	210,000	25,000	1,219,000	35,278,098
Public safety	18,036,628	—	—	—	18,036,628
Streets	11,863,314	3,990,000	—	2,200,000	18,053,314
Recreation and parks	6,481,657	—	—	—	6,481,657
Health and welfare	8,076,657	—	—	—	8,076,657
Education (component unit)	32,000,000	—	—	—	32,000,000
Debt service:					
Principal	—	—	—	1,950,000	1,950,000
Interest	317,659	—	—	1,174,000	1,491,659
Capital outlays	—	—	1,300,000	12,600,000	13,900,000
Total expenditures	110,600,013	4,200,000	1,325,000	19,143,000	135,268,013

Governmental Funds
Statement of Revenues, Expenditures,
and Changes in Fund Balances
June 30, 20X2

	General Fund	Local Fuel Tax Fund	West End Recreation Center Project Fund	Other Governmental Funds	Total Governmental Funds
Excess (deficiency) of revenues over expenditures	(10,613)	306,000	(873,000)	(14,356,000)	(14,933,613)
OTHER FINANCING SOURCES (USES):					
Disposition of capital assets	4,800,000	—	—	—	4,800,000
Long-term debt issued	—	—	3,000,000	10,000,000	13,000,000
Discount on long-term debt issued	—	—	—	(671,044)	(671,044)
Execution of capital leases	431,213	—	—	—	431,213
Transfers in	50,000	—	300,000	5,295,000	5,645,000
Transfers out	(5,475,000)	(300,000)	—	—	(5,775,000)
Total other financing sources and uses	(193,787)	(300,000)	3,300,000	14,623,956	17,430,169
Net change in fund balances	(204,400)	6,000	2,427,000	267,956	2,496,556
Fund balances— beginning	12,775,000	13,000	509,000	1,195,500	14,492,500
Fund balances— ending	$12,570,600	$19,000	$2,936,000	$1,463,456	$16,989,056

Exhibit 16-8: Reconciliation of the Statement of Revenues, Expenditures, and Changes in Fund Balances of Governmental Funds to the Statement of Activities.

City of Centerville
Reconciliation of the Statement of Revenues, Expenditures,
and Changes in Fund Balances of Governmental Funds
To the Statement of Activities
For the Year Ended June 30, 20X2

Net change in total fund balances per fund financial statements	$ 2,496,556
Amounts reported for governmental activities in the statement of activities are different because:	
Capital outlays are reported as expenditures in this fund financial statement because they use current financial resources, but they are presented as assets in the statement of activities and depreciated over their estimated economic lives. The amount by which capital outlays ($20,019,000), which is made up of capital outlays reported in Capital Projects Funds of $13,900,000 and $6,120,000 of capital outlays reported in the General Fund exceeds depreciation ($33,419,947) for the year.	(14,099,947)
Revenues that are not available to pay current obligations are not reported in this fund financial statement, but they are presented in the statement of activities.	7,478,400
The proceeds from the issuance of bonds provide current financial resources and are reported in this fund financial statement, but they are presented as liabilities in the statement of net assets.	(12,328,956)
The net revenues (expenses) of certain Internal Service Funds related to governmental programs are not reported in this fund financial statement because they are presented on a different accounting basis, but they are presented in the statement of activities.	(2,190,544)
Generally expenditures recognized in this fund's financial statements are limited to only those that use current financial resources, but expenses are recognized in the statement of activities when they are incurred.	2,608,283
Gains or losses are not presented in this financial statement because they do not provided or use current financial resources, but they are presented in the statement of activities.	14,400,000
Change in net assets of governmental activities	$ (1,636,208)

Exhibit 16-9: Statement of Net Assets: Proprietary Funds.

Proprietary Funds
Statement of Net Assets
June 30, 20X2

	Centerville Utilities Authority	Centerville Municipal Airport	Other Enterprise Funds	Total	Internal Service Funds
ASSETS					
Current assets:					
Cash	$ 230,000	$10,963,000	$1,503,500	$12,696,500	$12,696,500
Interest receivable	50,000	200,000	6,000	256,000	4,000
Accounts receivable (net)	7,550,000	18,000,000	—	25,550,000	—
Due from other funds	2,000,000	400,000	—	2,400,000	824,000
Due from other governments	100,000	300,000	—	400,000	45,000
Temporary investments	55,000	10,050,000	63,000	10,168,000	46,000
Inventories	75,000	55,000	56,000	186,000	36,000
Total current assets	10,060,000	39,968,000	1,628,500	51,656,500	2,060,500
Noncurrent assets:					
Construction in progress	200,000	23,500,000	85,000	23,785,000	—
Land and improvements	5,200,000	13,200,000	1,920,000	200,000	4,500,000
Superstructure	—	—	1,400,000	1,400,000	—
Distribution and collection Systems	46,300,000	—	—	46,300,000	—
Runways and tarmacs	—	27,500,000	—	27,500,000	—
Buildings	14,450,000	33,200,000	2,730,000	50,380,000	4,600,000
Equipment	4,600,000	7,200,000	195,000	11,995,000	10,160,000
Vehicles	1,660,000	2,500,000	937,000	5,097,000	10,338,000
Less accumulated depreciation	(54,395,000)	(20,255,000)	(2,762,000)	(77,412,000)	(12,848,000)
Total noncurrent assets	18,015,000	86,845,000	4,505,000	109,365,000	16,750,000
Total assets	28,075,000	126,813,000	6,133,500	161,021,500	18,810,500
LIABILITIES					

**Proprietary Funds
Statement of Net Assets
June 30, 20X2**

	Centerville Utilities Authority	Centerville Municipal Airport	Other Enterprise Funds	Total	Internal Service Funds
Current liabilities:					
Accounts payable and accrued expenses	4,300,000	3,900,000	140,000	8,340,000	250,000
Due to other funds	35,000	512,000	35,000	582,000	—
Compensated absences	21,000	15,000	5,000	41,000	10,000
Claims and judgments	17,000	25,000	9,000	51,000	13,000
Notes payable	70,000		40,000	110,000	1,700,000
Revenue bonds— Terminal A	—	2,000,000	—	2,000,000	—
Revenue bonds— Terminal B	—	500,000	—	500,000	—
Bonds payable	850,000	—	20,000	870,000	—
Total current liabilities	5,293,000	6,952,000	249,000	12,494,000	1,973,000
Noncurrent liabilities:					
Compensated absences	63,000	118,000	8,000	189,000	22,000
Claims and judgments	212,000	170,000	40,000	407,000	40,000
Notes payable	260,000	7,700,000	260,000	7,980,000	6,550,000
Revenue bonds— Terminal A	—	8,000,000	—	8,000,000	—
Revenue bonds— Terminal B	—	3,500,000	—	3,500,000	—
Bonds payable	6,850,000	—	560,000	7,410,000	—
Total noncurrent liabilities	7,385,000	19,488,000	613,000	27,486,000	6,612,000
Total liabilities	12,678,000	26,440,000	862,000	39,980,000	8,585,000
NET ASSETS					
Invested in capital assets, net of related debt	9,985,000	69,145,000	3,865,000	82,995,000	8,500,000

Proprietary Funds
Statement of Net Assets
June 30, 20X2

	Centerville Utilities Authority	Centerville Municipal Airport	Other Enterprise Funds	Total	Internal Service Funds
Restricted:					
Capital projects	2,000,000	17,000,000	1,000,000	20,000,000	—
Debt service	500,000	1,450,000	500,000	2,000,000	—
Other	2,750,000	12,445,000	167,000	15,362,000	—
Unrestricted	162,000	333,000	189,500	684,500	1,725,500
Total net assets	$15,397,000	$100,373,000	$5,271,500	121,041,500	$10,225,500

Some amounts reported for business-type activities in the statement of net assets are different because certain Internal Service Fund assets and liabilities are included with business-type activities 4,336,544

Net assets of business-type activities $125,378,044

Exhibit 16-10: Statement of Revenues, Expenses, and Changes in Fund Net Assets: Proprietary Funds.

Proprietary Funds
Statement of Revenues, Expenses, and
Changes In Fund Net Assets
For the Year Ended June 30, 20X2

	Centerville Utilities Authority	Centerville Municipal Airport	Other Enterprise Funds	Total	Internal Service Funds
OPERATING REVENUES					
Charges for services	$36,000,000	$175,000,000	$6,250,000	$217,250,000	$13,450,000
Charges for services— rental income— security for Terminal A revenue bonds	—	30,000,000	—	30,000,000	—
Charges for services— rental income— security for Terminal B revenue bonds	—	22,000,000	—	22,000,000	—
Miscellaneous	10,000	60,000	42,000	112,000	17,000
Total operating revenues	36,010,000	227,060,000	6,292,000	269,362,000	13,467,000
OPERATING EXPENSES					
Personal services	22,022,000	161,025,000	7,804,000	190,851,000	6,926,000
Contractual services	11,220,000	33,550,000	1,680,000	46,450,000	2,100,000
Repairs and maintenance	700,000	2,100,000	450,000	3,250,000	1,650,000
Other supplies and expenses	729,000	1,795,000	230,000	2,754,000	366,000
Insurance claims and expenses	21,000	100,000	13,000	134,000	29,000
Depreciation	3,025,000	3,370,000	456,000	6,851,000	5,582,000
Miscellaneous	5,000	70,000	33,000	108,000	22,000
Total operating expenses	37,722,000	202,010,000	10,666,000	250,398,000	16,675,000
Operating income (loss)	(1,712,000)	25,050,000	(4,374,000)	18,964,000	(3,208,000)
NONOPERATING REVENUES (EXPENSES)					

Proprietary Funds
Statement of Revenues, Expenses, and
Changes In Fund Net Assets
For the Year Ended June 30, 20X2

	Centerville Utilities Authority	Centerville Municipal Airport	Other Enterprise Funds	Total	Internal Service Funds
Interest and investment revenue	400,000	1,200,000	400,000	1,640,000	25,000
Interest	(450,000)	(1,220,000)	(33,000)	(1,703,000)	(309,000)
Operating grants and contributions	—		100,000	100,000	370,000
Miscellaneous	(110,000)	(265,000)	8,000	(367,000)	(8,000)
Total nonoperating revenue (expenses)	(160,000)	(285,000)	115,000	(330,000)	78,000
Income (loss) before capital contributions and transfers	(1,872,000)	24,765,000	(4,259,000)	18,634,000	(3,130,000)
Capital contributions	1,250,000	2,000,000	250,000	3,500,000	490,000
Transfers in	—	—	140,000	140,000	40,000
Transfers out	—	—	—	—	(50,000)
Special item— gain on sale of parking lot	—	—	3,500,000	3,500,000	—
Change in net assets	(622,000)	26,765,000	(369,000)	25,774,000	(369,000)
Total net assets— beginning	16,019,000	73,608,000	5,640,500		12,875,500
Total net assets— ending	$15,397,000	$100,373,000	$5,271,500		$10,225,500

Some amounts reported for business-type activities in the statement of activities are different because the net revenue (expense) of certain Internal Service Funds is reported with business-type activities.   (459,456)

Change in net assets of business-type activities $25,314,544

Exhibit 16-11: Statement of Cash Flows: Proprietary Funds.

Proprietary Funds
Statement of Cash Flows
For the Year Ended June 30, 20X2

	Centerville Utilities Authority	Centerville Municipal Airport	Other Enterprise Funds	Total	Internal Service Funds
CASH FLOWS FROM OPERATING ACTIVITIES					
Receipts from customers	$34,000,000	$214,000,000	$6,250,000	$254,250,000	$12,811,000
Payments to suppliers	(12,112,000)	(36,425,000)	(2,151,000)	(50,688,000)	(4,185,000)
Payments to employees	(19,013,000)	(158,017,000)	(7,732,000)	(184,762,000)	(6,747,000)
Internal activity-payments to other funds	(200,000)	(3,140,000)	(156,000)	(3,496,000)	—
Other receipts (payments)	5,000	(10,000)	1,000	(4,000)	(25,000)
Net cash provided by operating activities	2,680,000	16,408,000	(3,788,000)	15,300,000	1,854,000
CASH FLOWS FROM NONCAPITAL FINANCING ACTIVITIES					
Subsidies and transfers from (to) other funds and state government	—	—	240,000	240,000	360,000
CASH FLOWS FROM CAPITAL AND RELATED FINANCING ACTIVITIES					
Proceeds from the issuance of capital debt	2,120,000	3,200,000	—	5,320,000	3,400,000
Capital contributions	1,250,000	1,700,000	280,000	3,230,000	490,000
Acquisitions of capital assets	(5,350,000)	(8,800,000)	(590,000)	(14,740,000)	(6,040,000)
Proceeds from sale of capital assets	500,000	420,000	5,055,000	5,975,000	845,000
Principal paid on capital debt	(1,740,000)	(2,500,000)	(40,000)	(4,280,000)	(1,100,000)
Interest paid on capital debt	(450,000)	(1,220,000)	(33,000)	(1,703,000)	(309,000)

Proprietary Funds
Statement of Cash Flows
For the Year Ended June 30, 20X2

	Centerville Utilities Authority	Centerville Municipal Airport	Other Enterprise Funds	Total	Internal Service Funds
Net cash (used) by capital and related financing activities	(3,670,000)	(7,200,000)	4,672,000	(6,198,000)	(2,714,000)
CASH FLOWS FROM INVESTING ACTIVITIES					
Loans to other funds	(2,000,000)	(400,000)	—	(2,400,000)	—
Loans to other governments	(100,000)	—	—	(100,000)	—
Interest and dividends	365,000	1,055,000	39,500	1,459,500	37,500
Purchase of investments	(15,000)	(50,000)	(30,000)	(95,000)	—
Net cash provided (used) by investing activities	(1,750,000)	605,000	9,500	(1,135,500)	37,500
Net increase (decrease) in cash	(2,740,000)	9,813,000	1,133,500	8,206,500	(462,500)
Balances—beginning of year	2,970,000	1,150,000	370,000	4,490,000	1,568,000
Balances—end of year	$ 230,000	$10,963,000	$1,503,500	$12,696,500	$1,105,500
Reconciliation of operating income (loss) to net cash provided (used) by operating activities					
Operating income (loss)	$(1,712,000)	$25,050,000	$(4,374,000)	$18,964,000	$(3,208,000)
Adjustments:					
Depreciation expense	3,025,000	3,370,000	456,000	6,851,000	5,582,000
Change in assets and liabilities:					
Receivables, net	(1,850,000)	(13,000,000)	—	(14,850,000)	(639,000)

Proprietary Funds
Statement of Cash Flows
For the Year Ended June 30, 20X2

	Centerville Utilities Authority	Centerville Municipal Airport	Other Enterprise Funds	Total	Internal Service Funds
Inventories	(21,000)	(5,000)	(10,000)	(36,000)	(9,000)
Accounts and accrued liabilities	3,238,000	993,000	140,000	4,371,000	128,000
Net cash provided (used) by operating activities	$ 2,680,000	$16,408,000	$(3,788,000)	$15,300,000	$ 1,854,000

Exhibit 16-12: Statement of Fiduciary Net Assets.

City of Centerville
Statement of Fiduciary Net Assets
Fiduciary Funds
June 30, 20X2

	Employee Retirement and Postretirement Health Care Benefits Fund (Chapter 9)	Investment Trust Fund (Chapter 10)	Individual Investment Account (Chapter 10)	Private Purpose Trust Funds (Chapter 11)	Agency Fund (Chapter 12)
ASSETS					
Cash	$4,244,000	$ 582,000	$ 20,000	$ 27,000	$48,000
Other receivables (net)	31,000	9,000	5,000	—	5,000
Investments in debt securities	11,022,000	36,000	112,000	459,000	—
Investment in marketable equity securities	22,463,000	2,039,400	1,361,000	—	—
Other assets	—	1,800	5,000	—	—
Total Assets	37,760,000	2,668,200	1,503,000	486,000	53,000
LIABILITIES					
Accounts payable and accrued expenses	29,000	13,200	4,000	5,000	8,000
Due to other taxing districts	—	—	—	—	45,000
Refunds payable and other liabilities	25,000	45,000	12,000	—	—
Total Liabilities	54,000	58,200	16,000	5,000	53,000
NET ASSETS					
Held in trust for pension benefits and other purposes	$37,706,000	$2,610,000	$1,487,000	$481,000	

Exhibit 16-13: Statement of Changes in Fiduciary Net Assets.

City of Centerville
Statement of Changes in Fiduciary Net Assets
Fiduciary Funds
For the Year Ended June 30, 20X2

	Employee Retirement and Postretirement Health Care Benefits Fund (Chapter 9)	Investment Trust Fund (Chapter 11)	Individual Investment Account (Chapter 11)	Private Purpose Trust Funds (Chapter 10)
ADDITIONS				
Contributions by: City of Centerville	$ 7,000,000	—	—	$ 10,000
Plan members/ external parties	2,700,000	$ 300,000	$ 50,000	30,000
Total Contributions	9,700,000	300,000	50,000	40,000
Interest and investment revenue (net of expenses)	486,000	439,000	98,000	49,000
Total additions	10,186,000	739,200	148,000	89,000
DEDUCTIONS				
Benefits paid/withdrawals	4,200,000	825,000	200,000	57,000
Refunds of contributions	100,000	—	—	—
Administrative expenses	349,000	4,200	1,000	—
Total deductions	4,649,000	829,200	201,000	57,000
Change in net assets	5,537,000	(90,000)	(53,000)	32,000
Net assets—beginning of the year	32,169,000	2,700,000	1,540,000	449,000
Net assets—end of the year	$37,706,000	$2,610,000	$1,487,000	$481,000

Exhibit 16-14: Statement of Net Assets: Component Units.

City of Centerville
Statement of Net Assets
Component Units
June 30, 20X2

	Centerville Public School System	Centerville Regional Transit System	Other Component Units	Total
ASSETS				
Cash	$ 24,435,456	$ 4,437,000	$ 8,846,650	$37,719,106
Receivables (net)	34,221,000	18,000	5,363,100	39,602,100
Other assets	5,200	—	30,000	35,200
Investments	19,978,600	348,000	8,006,600	28,333,200
Inventories and supplies	239,000	192,000	2,773,400	3,204,400
Capital assets:				
Land, improvements and construction in progress	189,555,000	7,660,000	323,807,000	521,022,000
Other capital assets, net of depreciation	250,659,806	1,778,000	156,600,100	409,037,906
Total assets	519,094,062	14,433,000	505,426,850	1,038,953,912
LIABILITIES				
Accounts payable and accrued expenses	10,031,090	300,000	2,315,000	12,646,090
Demand loans payable to bank	75,000	—	—	75,000
Deferred revenue	310,000	—	402,000	712,000
Long-term liabilities				
Due within one year	8,442,932	228,000	13,327,600	21,998,532
Due in more than one year	69,215,107	750,000	147,637,500	217,602,607
Total liabilities	88,074,129	1,278,000	163,682,100	253,034,229
Net assets—invested in capital assets, net of related debt	373,910,335	8,778,000	319,585,100	702,273,435
Net assets—restricted for capital projects	23,858,956	—	3,000,000	26,858,956
Net assets—restricted for debt service	2,268,000	—	322,000	2,590,000
Net assets—restricted for other purposes	15,480,500	3,732,000	1,713,400	20,925,900

City of Centerville
Statement of Net Assets
Component Units
June 30, 20X2

	Centerville Public School System	Centerville Regional Transit System	Other Component Units	Total
Net assets restricted for other purposes (nonexpendable)	243,000	—	437,250	680,250
Net assets— unrestricted	15,259,142	645,000	16,687,000	32,591,142
Total net assets	$431,019,933	$13,155,000	$341,744,750	$785,919,683

Exhibit 16-15: Statement of Activities: Component Units.

City of Centerville
Statement of Activities
Component Units
for the Year Ended I June 30, 20X2

		Program Revenues			Net (Expense) Revenues and Changes in Net Assets			
	Expenses	Charges For Services	Operating Grants and Contributions	Capital Grants and Contributions	Centerville Public School System	Centerville Regional Transit System	Other Component Units	Total
Centerville Public School System								
Instruction	$43,500,000	$ 2,750,000	—	$13,700,000	($27,050,000)	—	—	($27,050,000)
Special education	4,530,000	640,000	$ 2,300,000	770,000	(820,000)	—	—	(820,000)
Academic support	1,650,000	—	—	—	(1,650,000)	—	—	(1,650,000)
Other educational programs	2,300,000	125,000	—	—	(2,175,000)	—	—	(2,175,000)
General administration	3,750,000	7,400	—	—	(3,742,600)	—	—	(3,742,600)
School administration	1,250,000	—	720,000	—	(530,000)	—	—	(530,000)
Transportation	3,660,000	12,500	1,800,000	550,000	(1,297,500)	—	—	(1,297,500)
Business-type activities	11,320,000	9,370,000	1,970,000	185,000	185,000	—	—	185,000
Interest on long-term debt	1,200,000	—	—	—	(1,200,000)	—	—	(1,200,000)
Total—Public School System	73,160,000	12,904,900	6,790,000	15,185,000	(38,280,100)	—	—	(38,280,100)
Centerville Regional Transit System	27,966,000	28,500,000	600,000	—		$1,134,000		1,134,000
Other component units	47,021,700	31,297,000	4,053,000	4,562,000			($7,109,700)	($7,109,700)
Total component units	$148,147,700	$72,701,900	$11,443,000	$19,747,000				(44,255,800)

General revenues:

City of Centerville
Statement of Activities
Component Units
for the Year Ended I June 30, 20X2

		Program Revenues			Net (Expense) Revenues and Changes in Net Assets			
	Expenses	Charges For Services	Operating Grants and Contributions	Capital Grants and Contributions	Centerville Public School System	Centerville Regional Transit System	Other Component Units	Total
Payment from the City of Centerville					32,000,000	—	—	32,000,000
Taxes:								
Property taxes					2,750,000	—	5,990,000	8,740,000
Other					105,000	—	105,000	210,000
Grants and contributions not restricted to specific programs					2,300,000	1,800,000	3,860,000	7,960,000
Unrestricted investment earnings					42,000	180,000	703,000	925,000
Miscellaneous					55,000	162,000	104,900	321,900
Special item—gain on sale of land					120,000	—	—	120,000
Total general revenues, special items, and transfers					37,372,000	2,142,000	10,762,900	50,276,900
Change in net assets					(908,100)	3,276,000	3,653,200	6,021,100
Net assets—beginning					431,928,033	9,879,000	338,091,550	779,898,583
Net assets—ending					$431,019,933	$13,155,000	$341,744,750	$785,919,683

CHAPTER 17
NOTES TO THE FINANCIAL STATEMENTS

CONTENTS

INTRODUCTION

The basic financial statements for state and local governments comprise three essential elements: the government-wide financial statements, the fund financial statements, and the notes to the financial statements. The notes to the financial statements should communicate information essential for fair presentation of the financial statements that is not displayed on the face of the financial statements. As such, the notes are an integral part of the basic financial statements.

GASB Concepts Statement No. 3 (GASB:CS-3) (Communication Methods in General Purpose External Financial Reports That Contain Basic Financial Statements) defines the communication methods commonly used in general-purpose external financial reports, develops criteria for each communication method, and provides a hierarchy for their use. The definitions, criteria, and hierarchy should help the GASB and all government financial statement preparers determine the appropriate methods to use to communicate an item of information. A primary goal of GASB:CS-3 is to provide greater consistency and comparability among governments in the use of communication methods, ultimately resulting in more efficient and effective use of financial reports.

Once an item of information is considered appropriate for inclusion within general-purpose external financial reports, the appropriate communication method (placement) to be used to convey particular financial information should be determined. GASB:CS-3 states that this placement decision should be based on a hierarchy in the following order:

1. Recognition in basic financial statements
2. Disclosure in notes to basic financial statements
3. Presentation as required supplementary information (RSI)
4. Presentation as supplementary information (SI)

FOCUS OF NOTE DISCLOSURES

The notes to the financial statements are an integral part of the financial statements and are essential to a user's understanding of the reporting unit's financial position and inflows and outflows of resources. The criteria for reporting financial information within the notes to the financial statements are as follows:

- Information that has a clear and demonstrable relationship to information in the financial statements

- Information that is essential to a user's understanding of the statements

GASB:CS-3 states that the notes should not include either subjective assessments of the effects of reported information on the reporting unit's future financial position or predictions about the effects of future events on future financial position.

The notes to the financial statements should focus on the primary government (which includes its blended component units) and support the information in the government-wide financial statements and the fund financial statements (GASB-34, par. 113).

Note disclosures related to discretely blended component units should be presented based on the requirements established by GASB-14, paragraph 63.

REQUIRED NOTE DISCLOSURES

Note disclosures required for state and local government financial statements were originally introduced in NCGAI-6 (Notes to the Financial Statements Disclosure). Note disclosures established by GASB-34, as amended by GASB-38, modify but do not replace the disclosures required by NCGAI-6. (Note: Appendix 20B of the CCH's *Governmental GAAP Guide* provides a governmental entity presentation and disclosure checklist.)

When NCGAI-6 was amended and codified as GASB Codification Section 2300, the following were listed as essential notes to the fair presentation of the basic financial statements:

A. Summary of significant accounting policies:

- A description of the government-wide financial statements, noting that neither fiduciary funds nor component units that are fiduciary in nature are included.

- A brief description of the component units of the financial reporting entity and their relationships to the primary government. This should include a discussion of the criteria for including component units in the financial reporting entity and how the component units are reported. Also include information about how the separate financial statements for the individual component units may be obtained.

- A description of the activities accounted for in each of the following columns—major funds, internal service funds, and fiduciary funds types—presented in the basic financial statements.

- The measurement focus and basis of accounting used in the government-wide statements, and the revenue recognition policies used in fund financial statements.

- The length of time used to define "available" for purposes of revenue recognition in the governmental fund financial statements.

- The policy for eliminating internal activity in the government-wide statement of activities.

- The policy for capitalizing assets and for estimating the useful lives of those assets. Governments that use the modified approach for eligible infrastructure assets should describe that approach.

- A description of the types of transactions included in program revenues and the policy for allocating indirect expenses to functions in the statement of activities.

- The policy for defining operating and nonoperating revenues of proprietary funds.

- The policy for applying FASB pronouncements issued after November 30, 1989 to business-type activities and to enterprise funds of the primary government (only to be used until GASB-62 is implemented for periods beginning after December 15, 2011).

- The definition of cash equivalents used in the statement of cash flows for proprietary fund types.

- The government's policy regarding whether to first apply restricted or unrestricted resources when an expense is incurred for purposes for which both restricted and unrestricted net assets are available.

PRACTICE ALERT: In implementing GASB-54, governments should disclose any formally adopted a minimum fund-balance policy (for example, in lieu of separately setting aside stabilization amounts) and describe in the notes to its financial statements the policy established by the government that sets forth the minimum amount. It is also a best practice (although not required) to disclose what entity is the highest decision-making authority with the ability to commit fund balances. For assigned fund balances, disclosure should include (1) the body or official authorized to assign amounts to a specific purpose and (2) the policy established by the governing body pursuant to which that authorization is given.

B. Cash deposits with financial institutions

C. Investments

D. Significant contingent liabilities

E. Encumbrances outstanding: In implementing GASB-54, governments should disclose encumbrance balances by major funds and nonmajor funds in the aggregate in conjunction with required disclosures about other significant commitments.

F. Significant effects of subsequent events

G. Annual pension cost and net pension obligations

H. Annual OPEB costs and net OPEB obligations

I. Significant violations of finance-related legal or contractual provisions and actions taken to address such violations

J. Debt service requirement to maturity

K. Commitments under operating leases

L. Construction and other significant commitments

M. Required disclosures about capital assets

N. Required disclosures about long-term liabilities

O. Deficit fund balance or net assets of individual funds

P. Interfund balances and transfers

Q. Significant transactions between major discretely presented component units and with the primary government

R. Disclosures about donor-restricted endowments

In addition, GASB Codification Section 2300 points out that the above notes to the financial statements are not the only disclosures required and that additional disclosures, such as the following, should be made:

A. Entity risk management activities

B. Property taxes

C. Segment information for Enterprise Funds

D. Condensed financial statements for major discretely presented component units

E. Short-term debt instruments and liquidity

F. Related party transactions

G. The nature of the primary government's accountability for related organizations

H. Capital leases

I. Joint ventures and jointly governed organizations

J. Debt refundings

K. Nonexchange transactions, including grants, entitlements, and shared revenues that are not recognized because they are not measurable

L. Reserves (in pension and OPEB plans)

M. Interfund eliminations in fund financial statements not apparent from headings

N. Pension plans—in both separately issued plan financial statements and employer statements

O. OPEB plans—in both separately issued plan financial statements and employer statements

P. Bond, tax, or revenue anticipation notes excluded from fund or current liabilities (proprietary funds)

Q. Nature and amount of inconsistencies in financial statements caused by transactions between component units having different fiscal year-ends or changes in component unit fiscal year-ends

R. In component unit separate reports, identification of the primary government in whose financial report the component unit is included and a description of its relationship to the primary government

S. Reverse repurchase and dollar reverse repurchase agreements

T. Securities lending transactions

U. Special assessment debt and related activities

V. Demand bonds

W. Landfill closure and post-closure care

X. On-behalf payments for fringe benefits and salaries

Y. Entity involvement in conduit debt obligations

Z. Sponsoring government disclosures about external investment pools reported as Investment Trust Funds

AA. The amount of interest expense included in direct expenses

BB. Significant transactions or other events that are either unusual or infrequent but not within the control of management

CC. Nature of individual elements of a particular reconciling item between the fund and government-wide financial statements if obscured in the aggregated information

DD. Discounts and allowances that reduce gross revenues, when not reported on the face of the financial statements

EE. Disaggregation of receivables and payables and fund balances

FF. Impairment losses, idle impaired capital assets, and insurance recoveries, when not apparent from the face of the financials statements

GG. The amount of the primary government's net assets at period end that are restricted by enabling legislation

HH. Termination benefits

II. Future revenues that are pledged or sold.

The disclosures listed above are not all-inclusive. Professional judgment must be used to determine whether additional disclosures should be made in the financial statements. See GASB Codification Section 2300 for note disclosure guidance.

PRACTICE POINT: With each new GASB statement, note disclosures to the basic financial statements are added, removed, or modified. Care must be taken in the implementation of new statements to make sure that all changes to the note disclosures to the basic financial statements are implemented.

Paragraph 11a of GASB-34 requires that the MD&A provide a brief discussion of the basic financial statements; paragraph 115a requires a description of the government-wide financial statements in the summary of significant accounting policies. The GASB's *Comprehensive Implementation Guide* notes that the difference between these two requirements is that paragraph 115a focuses on a description and scope of the government-wide financial statements and paragraph 11a requires a discussion of both government-wide and fund financial statements.

The GASB's *Comprehensive Implementation Guide* states that the disclosure related to the policy regarding the use of restricted resources (paragraph 115h) requires the governmental entity to explain when restricted resources are used. That is, are restricted resources used only after unrestricted resources have been spent for a particular purpose or are restricted resources assumed to be spent first?

Required Note Disclosures about Fund Types and Activities of Funds

The appendix to NCGAI-6 originally recommended that the financial statements include a description of fund categories and generic fund types; however, in practice there is some question about whether these descriptions provide an adequate explanation of the activities performed by a governmental entity. In addition, GASB-34 requires, for the most part, that the focus of fund financial statements be directed away from fund types to major funds, aggregated nonmajor governmental and proprietary funds, the internal service fund type, and fiduciary fund types. With the implementation of the standards established by GASB-34, it is likely that the disclosure requirements recommended by NCGAI-6 will be even less useful to those readers of the financial statements who want a clear understanding of the activities provided by a particular governmental entity.

In order to address this issue, GASB-38 requires that the summary of significant accounting policies include a description of the activities accounted for in the following columns of fund financial statements presented in the basic financial statements, assuming the columnar titles used in the fund financial statements are not sufficiently descriptive of the activities accounted for in a specific fund or fund type (GASB-38, par. 6):

- Major funds (governmental and proprietary funds)
- Internal Service Funds
- Fiduciary Fund Types (Pension [and other employee benefit]Trust Funds, Investment Trust Funds, Private-Purpose Trust Funds, and Agency Funds).

The description should not focus on the definition of the fund type used to account for the activity but, rather, describe the nature of the activities specifically accounted for in the fund. For example, if a restricted grant is accounted for in a Special Revenues Fund, the description should not simply present the definition of a Special Revenue Fund as provided by NCGA-1 but, rather, describe the source, purpose, and the restrictive nature of the grant. Because the Internal Service Fund column and the columns for each of the four fiduciary fund types could be made up of two or more separate funds, the description should include the major activities combined in each of these financial statement columns.

Based on the standards established by GASB-34, the General Fund is always considered a major fund. Because of the nature of a General Fund, its description could be limited to a general statement such as "this fund is the municipality's primary operating fund and it is used to account for all financial resources of the general government except those required to be accounted for in another fund." However, in some instances a governmental entity may decide the title (General Fund) is sufficiently descriptive and provide no description of the fund in the summary of significant accounting policies.

Required Note Disclosures about Capital Assets and Long-Term Liabilities

In order to support information included in a governmental entity's statement of net assets prepared on a government-wide basis, disclosures related to capital assets and long-term liabilities should be included in the governmental entity's notes. The disclosures should observe the following guidance (GASB-34, par. 116):

- The presentations should be based on major classes of capital assets and long-term liabilities.
- Capital assets and long-term liabilities should be segregated into governmental activities and business-type activities.
- Nondepreciable capital assets, such as land, must be presented separately from depreciable capital assets.

Capital Asset Disclosures

Disclosures that relate to capital assets should include the following information (GASB-34, par. 117):

- Beginning and year-end balances (regardless of whether prior-year data are presented on the face of the government-wide financial statements), with accumulated depreciation separately identified
- Capital acquisitions for the period
- Sales or other dispositions for the period
- Current-period depreciation expense, supported by identifying amounts allocated to each functional expense presented in the statement of activities

If a governmental entity chooses not to capitalize collection items, the following disclosures should be made (GASB-34, par. 118):

- A description of the capital assets not capitalized
- The reason the assets are not capitalized

If collections (historical treasures, art, etc.) are capitalized, the disclosures that apply to all other capital assets must be observed.

Long-Term Liabilities Disclosures

The disclosures related to long-term debt should encompass both long-term debt instruments (such as bonds, loans, and capitalized leases) and other long-term liabilities (such as estimated liabilities related to compensated absences and claims and judgments). These disclosures should include the following information (GASB-34, par. 119):

- Beginning and year-end balances (regardless of whether prior-year data are presented on the face of the government-wide perspective financial statements)
- Increases and decreases (separately presented) for the period
- The part of each liability that is due within one year
- The governmental fund that has generally been used to pay other long-term liabilities (that is, items such as compensated absences and claims and judgments)

The GASB's *Comprehensive Implementation Guide* states that if a governmental entity has changed its policy concerning which governmental fund has been used in the past to liquidate certain long-term liabilities, that change should be disclosed in the financial statements.

Disclosures about Interfund Balances and Transfers

Various interfund transfers occur within most governmental reporting entities. For example, an interfund balance may arise from the sale of goods or services, the reimbursement of expenditures or expenses, or the provision of operating capital. These transfers can be an important resource for governmental services performed, and for this reason an analysis of interfund balances and transfers can provide insight into the viability of a particular governmental activity. GASB-38 requires that the following information for interfund balances included in fund financial statements be disclosed in a note to the financial statements:

- Identification of the amounts due from other funds by (1) individual major funds, (2) aggregated nonmajor governmental funds, (3) aggregated nonmajor Enterprise Funds, (4) aggregated Internal Service Funds, and (5) fiduciary fund types.
- The purpose for interfund balances.
- Interfund balances that are not expected to be repaid within one year of the date of the balance sheet.

The presentation should include interfund balances that are considered material. Those that are immaterial should be aggregated and presented as a single amount. However, the total of all balances should agree with the total interfund balances presented in the statements of net assets/balance sheet for governmental funds and proprietary funds.

The focus of the aforementioned analysis is on the debtor fund rather than the creditor fund because the GASB believes that it is important for readers to be able to assess the likelihood that a particular interfund loan can be repaid. On the other hand, the explanations for interfund balances that are not expected to be paid within a year can alert readers of the financial statements to loan arrangements that are more or less long-term in nature, recurring, or unusual.

GASB-38 also requires that interfund activity for the year be summarized in a note to the financial statements that includes the following:

- Disclosure of amounts transferred from other funds by (1) individual major funds, (2) aggregated nonmajor governmental funds, (3) aggregated nonmajor Enterprise Funds, (4) aggregated Internal Service Funds, and (5) fiduciary fund types.

- General description of the principal reasons for the government's interfund transfers.

- The purpose and amount of significant transfers that satisfy either or both of the following criteria:

  — Do not occur on a routine basis

  — Are inconsistent with the activities of the fund making the transfer

The focus of the disclosure of interfund transfers for the period is on the fund that provides the resources to another fund. The GASB believes that this focus is justified because it will help readers to determine whether the provider fund has the ability to continue to make subsidies to the recipient fund. However, the scope of the disclosure is limited in that there is no requirement to disclose the nature of all interfund transfers except in general terms. For example, the principal reasons for interfund transfers could include subsidy strategies, debt service requirements, and the need to match grants received from other governmental entities. However, if during the year there has been an interfund transfer that is not routine, financial statements readers should be informed of the size and nature of the transfer. In a similar fashion, when an interfund transfer is not consistent with the nature of the provider fund, readers should also be informed of that matter. For example, if a Debt Service Fund makes a transfer to an Enterprise Fund, that interfund transfer usually must be explained.

The presentation should include transfers that are considered material. Those that are immaterial should be aggregated and presented as a single amount. However, the total of all transfers should agree with the total transfers presented in the financial statements of governmental funds and proprietary funds.

In the past, certain accounting and financial reporting guidance contained within AICPA Statements on Auditing Standards and discussed in the Audit and Accounting Guide *State and Local Governments* represented issues not yet addressed by the GASB. This guidance was considered Level B GAAP applicable to state and local governments. This guidance included accounting, reporting, and disclosure standards for related-party transactions, subsequent events, going-concern considerations, and materiality considerations. GASB-56 (Codification of Accounting and Financial Reporting Guidance Contained in AICPA Statements on Auditing Standards), issued in March 2009, incorporated the AICPA guidance on related-party transactions, subsequent events, and going-concern considerations into GASB authoritative standards. These topics are discussed in further detail in Chapter 1, "Foundation and Overview of Governmental Generally Accepted Accounting Principles," of CCH's *Governmental GAAP Guide.*

CHAPTER 18
MANAGEMENT'S DISCUSSION AND ANALYSIS AND OTHER REQUIRED SUPPLEMENTARY INFORMATION

CONTENTS

INTRODUCTION

GAAP requires that the following information be presented in a governmental entity's financial statements:

- Management's Discussion and Analysis Information (GASB-34, pars. 8–11)

- Budgetary Comparison Schedules (GASB-34, pars. 130–131)

- Certain notes to the financial statements related to capital assets and long-term debt (GASB-34, pars. 116–117)

Other required supplementary information contained in GAAP includes the following:

- Ten-year revenue and claims development data for public entity risk pools.
- Schedules of funding progress and employer contributions for defined benefit pension and other post-employment benefit plans (most recent actuarial valuations and two preceding valuations).

These items are further discussed in the *Governmental GAAP Guide*.

MANAGEMENT'S DISCUSSION AND ANALYSIS

One of the requirements established by GASB-34 is the introduction of management's discussion and analysis (MD&A) as an integral part of an entity's financial report. The purpose of this section is to discuss and illustrate the MD&A requirements established by the GASB. Although the SEC has required public companies to present MD&A for many years, the GASB's requirement for a similar presentation was first introduced new to governmental financial reporting as part of GASB-34.

IMPLEMENTATION GUIDANCE: The GASB's *Comprehensive Implementation Guide* notes that although paragraph 9 of GASB-34 encourages the use of charts and graphs in MD&A, comparison of condensed financial information should not be provided with charts and graphs; however, charts and graphs may be used to elaborate on the presentation of the condensed information.

Nature and Structure of MD&A

GAAP requires that a governmental entity's basic financial statements be preceded by MD&A, which the GASB identifies as required supplementary information (RSI). The purpose of MD&A is to "provide an objective and easily readable analysis of the government's financial activities based on currently known facts, decisions, or conditions." "Currently known facts" are "information that management is aware of as of the date of the auditor's report."

PRACTICE ALERT: Many governments are focusing on fiscal sustainability measures as part of overall operations. The main drivers of fiscal non-sustainability are currently debt levels and the costs of pension and other post-employment benefits. All three of these items are "currently known facts" that are disclosed primarily in the notes to the basic financial statements (with the exception of debt) under current GAAP. However, GASB is studying how fiscal sustainability measures should be presented. An alternative could be in an MD&A. A reminder though that current GAAP require a minimum *and* a maximum of items to be presented in an MD&A as outlined in paragraph 11 (a–h) of GASB-34.

Paragraph 11a of GASB-34 requires that MD&A provide a brief discussion of the basic financial statements; however, paragraph 115a requires a description of the government-wide financial statements in the summary of significant accounting policies. The GASB's *Comprehensive Implementation Guide* notes that the difference between these two requirements is that paragraph 115a focuses on a description and scope of the government-wide financial statements, whereas paragraph 11a requires a discussion of both government-wide and fund financial statements.

The GASB's *Guide* points out that GASB-34 does not address specifically whether MD&A should be placed before or after the letter of transmittal, but simply states that it must precede the financial statements; however, the GASB's *Guide* suggests that (1) MD&A should be presented as part of the financial section of the CAFR and (2) the letter of transmittal should be part of the introductory section of the CAFR. In addition, it would not be advisable to place the letter of transmittal between MD&A and the audited (basic) financial statements, because there may be confusion about whether the auditor's opinion applies to the letter of transmittal.

PRACTICE ALERT: In 2010, the AICPA's Auditing Standards Board released two statements on auditing standards (SAS-119 (AU 551) (Supplementary Information in Relation to the Financial Statements as a Whole), and SAS-120 (AU 558) (Required Supplementary Information)) that directly influence the audit of the MD&A and other required supplementary information. These standards increase the auditor's testing for required information and analytical review for supplementary information. The effective date for all three is for audits of financial statements for periods beginning on or after December 15, 2010, with early application permitted. Auditors will have to describe in the report the RSI that is presented and communicate whether or not the RSI was presented in accordance with GAAP. Auditors will ask management about the sources of information for the RSI and whether or not there were any changes from prior periods. Management will also represent that they are responsible for the RSI. If the auditor cannot confirm this information, then a qualified opinion may occur if there is a material departure from GAAP.

MD&A should portray a broad analysis of a governmental entity's short-term and long-term activities, based on information presented in the financial report and fiscal policies that have been adopted by the governmental entity. Although the analysis provided by management should be directed to current-year results in comparison with the previous year's results, the emphasis should be on the current year. In an attempt to make the information understandable to constituents, the governmental entities should consider using graphs, multicolor presentations, or other presentation strategies.

The GASB's *Comprehensive Implementation Guide* states that a government with both governmental and business-type activities may present comparative data (for example, total reporting entity columns for the current and a previous year) in its basic financial statements. MD&A is not required for the previous year's presentation, because that presentation does not constitute a complete set of financial statements (basic financial statements, notes and RSI). On the other hand, most governmental entities do not present comparative financial statements (basic financial statements, notes, and RSI for two years), because of the space requirements needed for such presentations. However, if comparative financial statements are presented, MD&A must be presented for each year. That does not mean that there must be two completely separate MD&A presentations. For example, condensed financial information in MD&A for both years could be presented on a comparative basis and the analysis of the overall financial position and results of operations for each year could be included in the same paragraph or section. Governmental entities that might have the space to present comparative financial statements include governments with a single program or a business-type activities only entity.

The MD&A should focus on the primary government's activities (both governmental and business-type activities) and distinguish between its activities and its discretely presented component units. The GASB emphasizes that management of the governmental entity should see the MD&A section of the financial report as an opportunity to communicate with interested parties and warns against preparing boilerplate material that adds little insight into the financial position and activity of the government.

GASB-34 requires that MD&A include relevant information about the following categories:

- Brief discussion of the basic financial statements
- Presentation of condensed financial information
- Analysis of the overall financial position and results of operations
- Analysis of balances and transactions of individual funds
- Analysis of significant budget variations
- Discussion of significant capital assets and long-term debt activity
- Description of currently known facts

In order to achieve the objectives of MD&A, GASB-34 requires that "at a minimum, MD&A should include" information about the above broad components. Some readers interpreted this requirement to mean that MD&A had to include at least these eight components but that a financial statement preparer was free to add other components. GASB-37 (Basic Financial Statements—and Management's Discussion and Analysis—for State and Local Governments: Omnibus) points out that the language in paragraph 11 should have been interpreted to mean that "the information presented should be confined to the topics discussed in a through h."

The GASB's *Comprehensive Implementation Guide* notes that the GASB encourages governmental entities not to report information in the letter of transmittal of the CAFR that is included in the MD&A section of the basic financial statements. The GASB's *Guide* notes that duplication can be minimized by making a brief reference to an item in the letter of transmittal with an appropriate reference to the further discussion of the item in MD&A. A governmental entity has significant flexibility in determining what should be included in the letter of transmittal because there are no GAAP rules that apply to the letter.

The MD&A illustration in Appendix 18 is based on the example developed in the previous chapters.

GAAP also requires that MD&A include a discussion of the modified depreciation approach if that approach is employed by a governmental entity. This illustration assumes that a governmental entity does not use the modified depreciation approach, but rather records depreciation expense on all infrastructure assets.

The GASB's *Guide* notes that currently known facts must be based on events that have taken place. For example, the enactment of a new sales tax is a currently known fact and should be included in MD&A. The prediction of how much tax receipts will increase if there is an economic upturn is not a known fact, and such a discussion is inappropriate in MD&A. Also, the GASB's *Guide* points out that some currently known facts that are discussed in MD&A could also be included in the notes to the financial statements. Under this circumstance, the MD&A presentation should only highlight the information included in the note. The GASB's *Guide* also states that the discussion of currently known facts, decisions, or conditions should focus separately on both governmental and business-type activities.

PRACTICE POINT: The preparer of the MD&A should strive to not use boilerplate or a previous period's language trued-up to current-year presentation. The MD&A to some may be the only portion of the basic financial statements that is read and it should be in a language tailored to the average user and contain as current information as possible and as allowable under GAAP.

BUDGETARY COMPARISON SCHEDULES

GAAP requires that a budgetary comparison schedules for the General Fund and each major Special Revenue Fund that has a legally adopted annual budget be presented as RSI. The schedule should include columns for the following:

- The original budget
- The final appropriated budget
- Actual results (presented on the government's budgetary basis as defined in NCGA-1, paragraph 154)

Prior to the issuance of GASB-34, NCGA-1 (Governmental Accounting and Financial Reporting Principles) required that a governmental entity present a "combined statement of revenues, expenditures and changes in fund balances—budget and actual" for each governmental fund type that had an annual appropriated budget.

The following budgetary descriptions are established by GAAP:

- *Original budget* The first complete appropriated budget. The original budget may be adjusted by reserves, transfers, allocations, supplemental appropriations, and other legally authorized legislative and executive changes before the beginning of the fiscal year. The original budget should also include the actual appropriation amount automatically carried over from prior years by law.

- *Final budget* The original budget adjusted by all reserves, transfers, allocations, supplemental appropriations and other legally authorized legislative and executive changes applicable to the fiscal year, whenever signed into law or otherwise legally authorized.

- *Appropriated budget* The expenditure authority created by the appropriation bills or ordinances that are signed into law and related estimated revenues.

The GASB's *Comprehensive Implementation Guide* states that governments that budget on a biennial basis must report budgetary comparison information required by GASB-34.

Some governmental entities include in the financial section of their CAFR budgetary comparisons for debt service, capital projects, nonmajor special revenue funds, and other funds that have legally adopted budgets. However, the GASB's *Guide* points out that GASB-34 establishes standards for the basic financial statements, MD&A, and certain RSI, but that its scope does not cover other components of the CAFR. If a governmental entity decides to present budgetary comparison schedules for debt service, capital projects, nonmajor special revenues funds, and other funds, the guidance established by GASB-34 (paragraphs 130 and 131) may, but does not have to be, followed.

The GASB encourages (but does not require) governmental entities to present an additional column that reflects the differences between the final budget and the actual amounts. An additional column may present the differences between the original budget and the final budget.

OBSERVATION: The comparative budgetary information described above can be presented as a basic financial statement rather than as RSI (schedule presentation).

The comparative budgetary information may be presented "using the same format, terminology, and classifications as the budget document, or using the format, terminology, and classifications in a statement of revenues, expenditures, and changes in fund balances." In either case, there must be a reconciliation (presented in a separate schedule or in notes to the RSI) between the budgetary information and the GAAP information (as discussed in NCGAI-10 (State and Local Government Budgetary Reporting)). Any excess of expenditures over appropriations in an individual fund must be disclosed in a note to the RSI as required by NCGAI-6, paragraph 4. If the governmental entity presents the comparative budgetary information as a basic financial statement, the note related to the excess of expenditures over appropriations must be reported as a note to the financial statements rather than as a note to RSI.

The GASB's *Comprehensive Implementation Guide* provides the following guidance for original and final budgets: (1) Some governmental entities initially use an interim budget (for example, three months) that provides temporary spending authority. The original budget (as described above) must cover the entire fiscal period. (2) Paragraph 130a specifically requires that "the original budget include actual appropriation amounts automatically carried over from prior years by law." If prior-year encumbrances are by law rolled forward, the current (original) budget includes those items. The amount of the encumbrances will be known, or a reasonable estimate of them can be made in time to prepare the financial information. And (3) Paragraph 130b specifically states that amendments (such as transfers of appropriations between line items) must be included in the final budget, irrespective of when they are "signed in law or otherwise legally authorized."

The following is an illustration of a budgetary comparison schedule for the General Fund and a reconciliation between the budgetary basis and the GAAP basis:

NOTE: It is assumed that the major Special Revenue Fund (Local Fuel Tax Fund) is not required to have a legally adopted annual budget.

Required Supplementary Information
City of Centerville
Budgetary Comparison Schedule—General Fund
For the Year Ended June 30, 20X1

	Budgetary Amounts Original	Budgetary Amounts Final	Actual Amounts (See Note A)	Variance Budget Positive (Negative)
Budgetary fund balance beginning of year	$13,478,000	$12,748,000	$12,748,000	
Resources (inflows):				
Property taxes	87,000,000	87,100,000	87,600,000	$ 500,000
Franchise taxes	1,300,000	1,400,000	1,300,000	(100,000)
Intergovernmental grants	19,000,000	21,000,000	20,500,000	(500,000)
Charges for services	500,000	550,000	537,600	(12,400)
Contributions	—	—	50,000	50,000
Interest and investment revenue	240,000	250,000	601,800	351,800
Disposition of capital assets	4,800,000	5,000,000	4,800,000	(200,000)
Transfers from other funds	—	—	50,000	50,000
Amounts available for appropriation	126,318,000	128,048,000	128,187,400	139,400
Charges to appropriations (outflows):				
General government	33,500,000	33,302,885	33,412,885	(110,000)
Public safety	18,000,000	18,137,628	18,036,628	101,000
Streets	11,200,000	11,868,814	11,863,314	5,500
Recreation and parks	6,500,000	6,584,407	6,481,657	102,750
Health and welfare	8,000,000	8,084,407	8,076,657	7,750
Interest	311,859	317,659	317,659	0
Education (component unit)	30,000,000	32,000,000	32,000,000	0
Transfers to other funds	5,300,000	5,500,000	5,475,000	25,000
Total charges to appropriations	112,811,859	115,795,800	115,663,800	132,000
Budgetary fund balance, end of year	$ 13,506,141	$ 12,252,200	$ 12,523,600	$ 271,400

Requires Supplementary Information
Budgetary Comparison Schedule
Note to Required Supplementary Information

	General Fund

NOTE A: Explanation of Differences Between Budgetary Inflows and Outflows and GAAP Revenues and Expenditures

Sources/Inflow of Resources:

Actual amounts (budgetary basis) "available for appropriation" from the budgetary comparison schedule Differences—Budget to GAAP:	$128,187,400
The fund balance at the beginning of the year is a budgetary resource but is not a current-year revenue for financial reporting purposes.	(12,748,000)
Transfers from other funds are inflows of budgetary resources but are not revenues for financial reporting purposes.	(50,000)
Total revenues as reported on the statement of revenues, expenditures, and changes in fund balances—governmental funds	$115,389,400

Uses/Outflows of Resources

Actual amounts (budgetary basis) "total charges to appropriations": from the budgetary comparison schedule Differences—Budget to GAAP:	$115,663,800
The city budgets for purchases of inventories on the cash basis, rather than on the modified accrual basis.	(5,000)
Encumbrances for certain contract expenditures ordered but not received are reported in the year the order is placed for budgetary purposes and in the year the resources are received for financial reporting purposes.	(15,000)
Capital leases executed during a year are not reported as expenditures for budgetary purposes, but are reported as program expenditures for financial reporting purposes.	431,213
Transfers to other funds are outflows of budgetary resources but are not expenditures for financial reporting purposes.	(5,475,000)
Total expenditures as reported on the statement of revenues, expenditures, and changes in fund balances—governmental funds	$110,600,013

GASB-34 continued the requirement that there be reconciliation between the budgetary information and the GAAP-based information.

Paragraph 131 of GASB-34 establishes disclosure requirements for budgetary comparison schedules, which are required supplementary information. One of the requirements states that any excess of expenditures over appropriations in an individual fund must be disclosed. The question has arisen as to whether the required disclosure applies to only those funds that are presented in the budgetary comparison schedule. GASB-37 (Basic Financial Statements—and Management's Discussion and Analysis—for State and Local Governments: Omnibus) clarifies the standards established by GASB-34 by limiting the disclosures related to budgetary comparison schedules to the funds that are part of the required supplementary information.

The appendix to NCGAI-6 recommends that the financial statements include a description of general budgetary policies. To comply with this recommendation, some governmental entities disclose their budgetary calendar and the legal level of budgetary control. GASB-38 (Certain Financial Statement Note Disclosures) states that general budget policies are not to be included as part of the appendix to NCGAI-6. The GASB believes that sufficient presentation of budgetary information is achieved by the requirements established by previously NCGA pronouncements and GASB-34. These presentation requirements include (1) budgetary comparison schedules, (2) reconciliation of budgetary information to GAAP information, (3) disclosure of the major provisions of a budgetary basis of accounting, and (4) disclosure of violations of legal provisions.

APPENDIX 18: MD&A: CITY OF CENTERVILLE

Basic Financial Statements

In general, the purpose of financial reporting is to provide external parties that read financial statements with information that will help them to make decisions or draw conclusions about an entity. There are many external parties that read the City of Centerville's financial statements; however, these parties do not always have the same specific objectives. In order to address the needs of as many parties as reasonably possible, the City, in accordance with required reporting standards, presents (1) government-wide financial statements and (2) fund financial statements.

Government-Wide Financial Statements

The focus of government-wide financial statements is on the overall financial position and activities of the City of Centerville. These financial statements are constructed around the concept of a primary government, the City, and its component units, except for fiduciary funds. As described below, the financial statements of the City's fiduciary funds are not included in the government-wide financial statements, because resources of these funds cannot be used to finance the City's activities. However, the financial statements of fiduciary funds are included in the City's financial statements because the City is financially accountable for those resources, even though they belong to other parties.

The City's government-wide financial statements include the statement of net assets and statement of activities, which are prepared using accounting principles that are similar to commercial enterprises. The purpose of the statement of net assets is to attempt to report all of the assets held and liabilities owed by the City. The City reports all of its assets when it acquires ownership over the assets and reports all of its liabilities when they are incurred. For example, the City reports buildings and infrastructure as assets, even though they are not available to pay the obligations incurred by the City. On the other hand, the City reports liabilities, such as litigation claims, even though these liabilities might not be paid until several years into the future.

The difference between the City's total assets and total liabilities is labeled as *net assets* and this difference is similar to the total owners' equity presented by a commercial enterprise. Although the purpose of the City is not to accumulate net assets, in general, as this amount increases it indicates that the financial position of the City is improving over time.

The purpose of the statement of activities is to present the revenues and expenses of the City. Again, the items presented on the statement of activities are measured in a manner similar to the approach used by a commercial enterprise in that revenues are recognized when earned or established criteria are satisfied and expenses are reported when incurred by the City. Thus, revenues are reported even when they may not be collected for several months after the end of the accounting period and expenses are recorded even though they may not have used cash during the current period.

Although the statement of activities looks different from a commercial enterprise's income statement, the financial statements are different only in format, not substance. Whereas the bottom line in a commercial enterprise is its net income, the City reports an amount described as *change in net assets*, essentially the same thing.

The focus of the statement of activities is on the *net cost* of various activities provided by the City. The statement begins with a column that identifies the cost of each of the City's major functions. Another column identifies the revenues that are specifically related to the classified governmental functions. The difference between the expenses and revenues related to specific program/activities computes the net cost or benefits of the program/activities, which identifies the extent to which each function of the City draws from general revenues or is self-financing through fees, intergovernmental aid, and other sources of resources.

The City's government-wide financial statements are divided into the primary government and its component units. The primary government is further divided into governmental activities and business-type activities. Governmental activities are generally financed through taxes, intergovernmental revenues, and other nonexchange revenues, while business-type activities are financed to some degree by charging external parties for the goods or services they acquire from the City. Governmental activities include programs/activities such as general government, public safety, streets, and health and welfare. Business-type activities, an integral part of the City's activities and responsibilities, include the City's Toll Bridge, Utilities Authority, Parking Authority, and airport. Component units are legally separate from the City, but because the City is financially accountable for them, they are reported in the City's financial statements. The City's component units include the Centerville Public School System and the Municipal Transit System.

The City's government-wide financial statements are presented on pages XX-XXX.

Fund Financial Statements

Unlike government-wide financial statements, the focus of fund financial statements is directed to specific activities of the City rather than the city as a whole. Except for the General Fund, a specific fund is established to satisfy managerial control over resources or to satisfy finance-related legal requirements established by external parties or governmental statutes or regulations. The City's fund financial statements are divided into three broad categories, namely, (1) governmental funds, (2) proprietary funds, and (3) fiduciary funds.

Governmental funds. Governmental fund financial statements consist of a balance sheet and statement of revenues, expenditures, and change in fund balances and are prepared on an accounting basis that is significantly different from that used to prepare the government-wide financial statements.

In general, these financial statements have a short-term emphasis and, for the most part, measure and account for cash and other assets that can easily be converted to cash. For example, amounts reported on the balance sheet include items such as cash and receivables collectible within a very short period of time, but do not include capital assets such as land and buildings. Fund liabilities include amounts that are to be paid within a very short period after the end of the fiscal year. The difference between a fund's total assets and total liabilities is labeled as the fund balance, and generally indicates the amount that can be used to finance the next fiscal year's activities. Likewise, the operating statement for governmental funds reports only those revenues and expenditures that were collected in cash or paid with cash, respectively, during the current period or very shortly after the end of the year.

For the most part, the balances and activities accounted for in governmental funds are also reported in the governmental activities columns of the government-wide financial statements; however, because different accounting bases are used to prepare fund financial statements and government-wide financial statements, there are often significant differences between the totals presented in these financial statements. For this reason, there is an analysis at the bottom of the balance sheet that reconciles the total fund balances to the amount of net assets presented in the governmental activities column on the statement of net assets. Also, there is an analysis at the bottom of the statement of revenues, expenditures, and changes in fund balances that reconciles the total change in fund balances for all governmental funds to the change in net assets as reported in the governmental activities column in the statement of activities.

The City presents in separate columns funds that are most significant to the City (major funds) and all other governmental funds are aggregated and reported in a single column (nonmajor funds).

The City's governmental fund financial statements are presented on pages XX-XXX.

Proprietary funds. Proprietary fund financial statements consist of a statement of net assets, statement of revenues, expenses, and changes in fund net assets and statement of cash flows, and are prepared on an accounting basis that is similar to the basis used to prepare the government-wide financial statements. For financial reporting purposes, proprietary funds are grouped into Enterprise Funds and Internal Service Funds.

The City uses Enterprise Funds to account for business-type activities that charge fees to customers for the use of specific goods or services. For the most part, the balances and activities accounted for in the City's Enterprise Funds are also reported in the business-type activities columns of the government-wide financial statements; however, because of the nature of Internal Service Funds, as described below, there are some differences between the totals presented in these financial statements. These differences are presented as reconciling items on the bottom part of the Enterprise Funds' statement of net assets, and statement of revenues, expenses, and changes in fund net assets.

The City uses Internal Service Funds to account for services provided and billed on an internal basis. These services may be billed to either governmental funds or an Enterprise Fund. The balances and activities of Internal Service Funds are presented in the proprietary funds (along with Enterprise Funds), but they are integrated into the government-wide financial statements, depending upon whether a particular Internal Service Fund services a governmental fund or an Enterprise Fund.

The City presents in separate columns Enterprise Funds that are most significant to the City and all other Enterprise Funds are aggregated and reported in a single column. Internal Service Funds are all aggregated and presented in a single column. A statement of cash flows is presented at the fund financial statement level for proprietary funds, but no equivalent statement is presented in the government-wide financial statements for either governmental activities or business-type activities.

The City's proprietary fund financial statements are presented on pages XX-XXX.

Fiduciary funds. Fiduciary fund financial statements consist of a statement of fiduciary net assets and a statement of changes in fiduciary net assets. Assets held by the City for other parties (either as a trustee or as an agent) and that cannot be used to finance the City's own operating programs are reported in the fiduciary funds. The City is responsible for ensuring that the activities reported in fiduciary funds are based on their intended purposes.

As noted earlier, fiduciary funds are presented in the fund financial statements but are not reported in the government-wide financial statements.

The City's fiduciary fund financial statements are presented on pages XX-XXX.

The relationships between the fund financial statements and the government-wide financial statements are summarized in Exhibit 18-1.

Exhibit 18-1: Summary of Government-Wide Financial Statements.

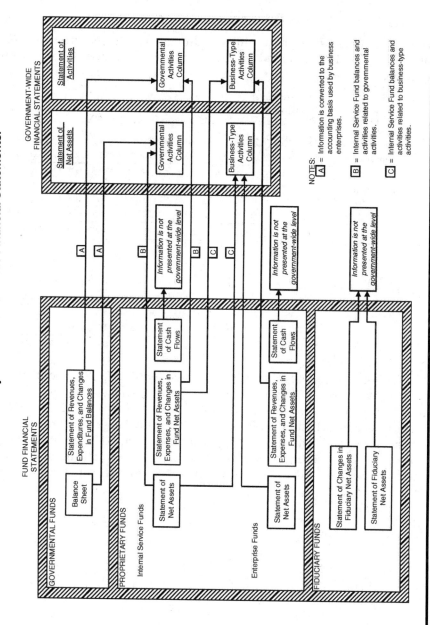

NOTE: The presentation of condensed financial information is illustrated in the following section along with the analysis of the information.

Overview of the City's Financial Position and Operations

The City's overall financial position and operations for the past two years are summarized as follows based on the information included in the government-wide financial statements:

Financial Position	Governmental Activities		Business-Type Activities		Total	
	20X2	20X1	20X2	20X1	20X2	20X1
Current and other assets	$ 27,870,212	$ 26,722,350	$ 51,009,044	$ 49,822,616	$ 78,879,256	$ 76,544,966
Capital assets	325,784,806	325,813,540	114,430,000	109,668,000	440,214,806	435,481,540
Total assets	353,655,018	352,535,890	165,439,044	159,490,616	519,094,062	512,026,506
Long-term liabilities	41,353,107	29,469,133	27,862,000	25,884,000	69,215,107	55,353,133
Other liabilities	6,660,022	15,788,660	12,199,000	33,543,116	18,859,022	49,331,776
Total liabilities	48,013,129	45,257,793	40,061,000	59,427,116	88,074,129	104,684,909
Net assets:						
Invested in capital assets, net of related debt	286,400,335	298,151,097	87,510,000	79,918,000	373,910,335	378,069,097
Restricted	4,488,456	3,412,600	37,362,000	19,745,000	41,850,456	23,157,600
Unrestricted	14,753,098	5,714,400	506,044	400,500	15,259,142	6,114,900
Total net assets	$305,641,889	$307,278,097	$125,378,044	$100,063,500	$431,019,933	$407,341,597

The total net assets of the City increased by $23,678,336 (about 5.8%), from $407,341,597 to $431,019,933. The increase was caused by a decrease of $1,636,208 in the net assets of governmental activities and an increase of $25,314,544 related to business-type activities. Although some of the increase in net assets is related to increases in capital assets, most of the increase is liquid in that it is unrelated to capital assets. However, few of the net assets related to business-type activities are transferable to governmental activities because of restrictions imposed by statutes or contracts.

Operations	Governmental Activities		Business-Type Activities		Total	
	20X2	20X1	20X2	20X1	20X2	20X1
Revenues						
Program revenues:						
Charges for services	$ 846,000	$ 805,000	$269,362,000	$245,550,000	$270,208,000	$246,355,000
Operating grants and contributions	4,584,000	9,505,000	100,000	250,000	4,684,000	9,755,000
Capital grants and contributions	2,450,000	3,500,000	3,500,000	4,000,000	5,950,000	7,500,000
General revenues:						
Property taxes	91,670,000	89,340,000	—	—	91,670,000	89,340,000
Franchise taxes	1,300,000	1,050,000	—	—	1,300,000	1,050,000
Unrestricted grants and contributions	26,570,000	29,505,000	—	—	26,570,000	29,505,000
Other general revenues	702,800	220,000	1,655,000	1,855,000	2,357,800	2,075,000
Total revenues	128,122,800	133,925,000	274,617,000	251,655,000	402,739,800	385,580,000
Program expenses:						
General	54,054,629	49,220,000	—	—	54,054,629	49,220,000
Public safety	22,836,931	21,003,000	—	—	22,836,931	21,003,000
Streets	21,187,633	19,200,000	—	—	21,187,633	19,200,000
Recreation and parks	7,621,871	5,400,000	—	—	7,621,871	5,400,000
Health and welfare	9,579,427	8,100,000	—	—	9,579,427	8,100,000
School district	32,000,000	29,500,000	—	—	32,000,000	29,500,000
Interest	2,338,517	1,856,000	—	—	2,338,517	1,856,000
Airport	—	—	203,594,872	189,770,000	203,594,872	189,770,000
Utilities	—	—	38,557,320	35,333,000	38,557,320	35,333,000
Parking	—	—	6,091,144	5,400,000	6,091,144	5,400,000
Toll Bridge	—	—	4,699,120	4,100,000	4,699,120	4,100,000
Total expenses	149,619,008	134,279,000	252,942,456	234,603,000	402,561,464	368,882,000
Change in net assets before other items	(21,496,208)	(354,000)	21,674,544	17,052,000	178,336	16,698,000
Special item—gain on sale of parking lot	—	—	3,500,000	—	3,500,000	—
Extraordinary item—donation of land from state	20,000,000	—	—	—	20,000,000	—
Transfers	(140,000)	(220,000)	140,000	220,000	—	—
Increase (decrease) in net assets	$(1,636,208)	$ (574,000)	$25,314,544	$17,272,000	$23,678,336	$16,698,000

There was a significant decrease ($16,519,664) in the change in *net assets before other items* for the City as a whole when operations for the current year are compared with those of the previous year. This occurred because even though total revenue during the year increased by $17,159,800, that increase was not sufficient to offset the increase in total expenses of $33,679,464. However, due to two irregular items that occurred during the year, the overall increase in net assets rose from $16,698,000 to $23,678,336. These changes are more fully explained below.

Governmental Activities

Last year there was a decrease in net assets related to governmental activities of $574,000; however, this year, there was a decrease of $1,636,208. If irregular items are excluded from operating activities, there was a decrease in net assets of $21,496,208 during the year ended June 30, 20X2. Last year, there was a decrease of $354,000 for the change in net assets before irregular items. The reason for the significant deterioration in operations during the current year and related fiscal policies that the City has implemented to address these issues are summarized as follows:

- The current year's total revenues decreased by $5,802,200, a 4.3% decline. Most of this decrease occurred because intergovernmental operating and capital grants fell $8,906,000, because both the state and federal governments reduced certain types of grants to governmental entities. In order to address the revenue shortfall, property tax rates have been increased by 8% for the year 20X3 and property tax ratables for the same year have increased by 5%. The 20X3 budget reflects these changes and budgeted property tax revenues are projected to increase accordingly.

- During the current year, expenses related to overtime pay increased by approximately $4,200,000; however, the City recently signed new agreements with all of its unions. New provisions in the contracts will significantly reduce the cost of overtime pay. These new work rules are consistent with rules implemented by most municipalities that are of a size similar to the City and the financial implication of these revised rules have been reflected in the 20X3 city budget.

- A hiring freeze and other cost containment strategies have been adopted and a $7,000,000 reduction for operating expenses is reflected in the 20X3 City budget.

- Based on new legislation adopted by the state, the state will begin a program to help fund public education. The statue is applicable to the 20X3 budgetary period and the state has authorized a payment of $6,000,000 to the City to help fund the public school system.

A comparison of revenue sources related to governmental activities for the two-year period is summarized in Exhibit 18-2, "Governmental Activities Revenue Sources: 20X2 versus 20X1."

A comparison of expenses related to government activities for the two-year period is summarized in Exhibit 18-3, "Governmental Activities Expenses: 20X2 versus 20X1."

Exhibit 18-2: Governmental Activities Revenue Sources: 20X2 versus 20X1.

	20X2	20X1
Operating grants and contributions	$ 4,584,000	$ 9,505,000
Capital grants and contributions	2,450,000	3,500,000
Property taxes	91,670,000	89,340,000
Unrestricted grants and contributions	26,570,000	29,505,000
Charges, franchise taxes and other revenues	2,848,800	2,075,000

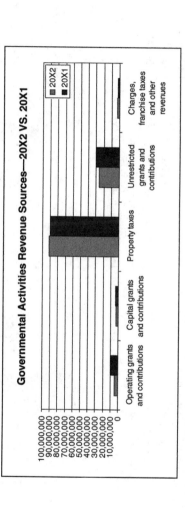

Governmental Activities Revenue Sources—20X2 VS. 20X1

Exhibit 18-3: Governmental Activities Expenses: 20X2 versus 20X1.

	20X2	20X1
General	$54,054,629	$49,220,000
Public safety	22,836,931	21,003,000
Streets	21,187,633	19,200,000
Recreation and parks	7,621,871	5,400,000
Health and welfare	9,579,427	8,100,000
School district	32,000,000	29,500,000
Interest	2,338,517	1,856,000

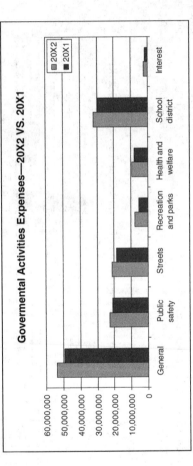

Govermental Activities Expenses—20X2 VS. 20X1

Business-Type Activities

The combined change in net assets before irregular items for business-type activities increased by 27% ($4,622,544) from the previous year. Most of that change was due to the activities of the City airport. Recent runway additions and the expansion of retail shops at the airport have resulted in significant growth in revenues and a general consensus that the facility is becoming an attractive regional alternative to the two major airports that are within a 60-mile radius.

While the airport growth had a positive impact on overall business-type activities, the combined numbers somewhat obscure the poorer operating results for the Parking Authority and Utility Authority. These two operating units had a 7% and 5% drop in changes in net assets before irregular items when compared to the previous year. During the year, the Parking Authority sold one of its parking lots that had minor revenues but significant fixed costs. The sale of the parking lot generated a one-time gain of $3,500,000. Also, parking fees were increased by 25% as of July 1, 20X2, the first rate increased in almost five years. In addition, The State Utility Board has approved a new method for determining utility rates that better reflects the market cost of natural gas and other fossil fuels. This new pricing mechanism goes into effect on January 1, 20X3.

Analysis of Balances and Transactions of Individual Funds

The City's combined fund balances as of the end of the current year for governmental funds, presented on page XX, were $17 million. This balance represent an increase of $2.3 million (16%) over last year's ending balance. Although this was a significant increase in the fund balance for the year, that net amount for the most part comprised a $204,000 deficit in the General Fund, which was offset by a $2.4 million increase in the West End Recreation Center Capital Project.

The primary reasons for the General Fund deficit were discussed previously in the section titled "An Overview of the City's Financial Position and Operations." In addition, approximately $2.1 million of resources were transferred from the General Fund for the construction of capital assets ($1.9 million), and to support activities included in other funds. While capital assets expenditures do reduce the overall fund balance for governmental funds, those expenditures create long-term assets that will benefit the community for many years to come. Total transfers from the General Fund amounted to $5.5 million.

On the other hand, the increase in the fund balance for the West End Recreation Center Capital Project was mainly due to the issuance of $3,300,000 of serial bonds for the year. The bond proceeds at the end of the year were placed in temporary investments, but they will be used during the next fiscal year to finish construction on the Center. The proceeds represent a liability of the City, and the bonds will have to be paid off over the next six years.

Also during the year, significant resources were received and expended by the Easely Street Bridge Project. Bond proceeds and capital grants amounted to $10.6 million and capital expenditures on the bridge totaled $11.1 million. When completed, the bridge will relieve much of the downtown congestion for the foreseeable future. The bonds will be paid off over a 10-year period.

General Fund Budgetary Highlights

The original budget passed by the City Council anticipated an increase in the budgetary fund balance during the year of $28,141; however, the final budgetary amounts expected a decrease of $495,800, a net unfavorable change of $523,941. The change from the original budget to the final budget was mainly due to the expected position of the budgetary fund balance that was brought forward from the 20X0 fiscal year. It was anticipated that budgetary resources of $13.5 million dollars would be brought forward from the previous year but this amount was subsequently changed to $12.7 million.

There were minor differences between the final budgetary amounts and the actual budgetary figures. The anticipated budgetary fund balance as of June 30, 20X2 was expected to be $12.3 million and the actual results were $132,000 more than the anticipated amount. Exhibit 18-4 compares final budgetary figures and the actual budgetary figures for revenues.

The budgetary figures and actual budgetary amounts for expenditures are compared in Exhibit 18-5.

Exhibit 18-4: Comparison of Final Budgetary Resources and Actual Budgetary Resources: 20X2.

	Budget	Actual
Property taxes	$87,100,000	$87,600,000
Intergovernmental grants	21,000,000	20,500,000
Other revenues	7,200,000	7,339,400

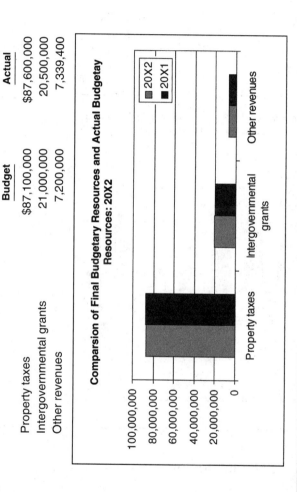

Comparsion of Final Budgetary Resources and Actual Budgetay Resources: 20X2

Exhibit 18-5: Comparison of Final Budgetary Appropriations and Actual Budgetary Appropriations: 20X2.

	Budget	Actual
General government	$33,302,885	$33,412,885
Public safety	18,137,628	18,036,628
Streets	11,868,814	11,863,314
Recreation and parks	6,584,407	6,481,657
Health and welfare	8,084,407	8,076,657
Education (component unit)	32,000,000	32,000,000
Transfers to other funds	5,500,000	5,475,000

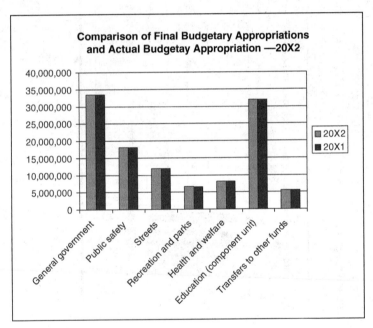

Capital Asset and Debt Administration

Capital Assets

The City has invested $440 million in capital assets (net of depreciation). Approximately 81% of this investment is related to governmental activities and includes infrastructure, buildings, equipment, and land. Governmental capital assets have declined slightly from the previous year, while capital assets held for business-type activities have increased by about 5%. Capital assets held by the City at the end of the current and previous year are summarized as follows:

Capital Assets (net of depreciation)

Operations	Governmental Activities		Business-Type Activities		Total	
	20X2	20X1	20X2	20X1	20X2	20X1
Land, improvements and construction in progress	$143,700,000	$109,400,000	$ 45,855,000	$ 45,190,000	$189,555,000	$154,590,000
Buildings	140,610,000	147,200,000	31,045,000	27,960,000	171,655,000	175,160,000
Equipment and vehicles	34,174,806	61,213,540	13,008,000	10,618,000	47,182,806	71,831,540
Infrastructure assets	7,300,000	8,000,000	24,522,000	25,250,000	31,822,000	33,250,000
Totals	$325,784,806	$325,813,540	$114,430,000	$109,018,000	$440,214,806	$434,831,540

During the current year, major capital additions for governmental activities were as follows:

- Construction costs for the Easely Street Bridge Project $11,100,000
- Construction costs for the Bland Street Drainage Project   1,500,000
- Construction costs for the West End Recreation Center Project   1,300,000
- Acquisitions of equipment and vehicles   6,551,213
- Gift of land from the state   20,000,000

The overall amount of capital assets related to governmental activities remained about the same, because assets with a net cost basis of about $6 million were sold and depreciation expense for the year was $38.5 million.

In addition, the following major acquisitions were made by for business-type activities:

- Construction costs for distribution and collection systems (Centerville Utilities Authority) $ 1,500,000
- Construction costs for runways and tarmacs (Centerville Municipal Airport)   500,000
- Investments in buildings, equipment and vehicles   12,330,000

Additional information about the City's capital assets is presented in the financial statements.

Long-Term Obligations

At the end of the current year, the City had long-term debt related to governmental activities of $39.4 million, which was an increase from the previous year of $11.7 million. Of the amount of debt outstanding as of the end of 20X2, about 77% was backed by the full faith and credit of the government and the balance was secured by various revenue sources. The total amount of debt related to business-type activities remained stable from the end of 20X1 to 20X2. Approximately 55% of this debt was backed by the full faith and credit of the government.

The debt position of the City is summarized below and is more fully analyzed in the financial statements.

	Governmental Activities		Business-Type Activities		Total	
	20X2	20X1	20X2	20X1	20X2	20X1
General obligation debt backed by the City	$30,155,039	$17,662,443	$16,920,000	$13,250,000	$47,075,039	$30,912,443
Revenue bonds backed by specific sources of revenues	9,250,000	10,000,000	14,000,000	16,500,000	23,250,000	26,500,000
Totals	$39,405,039	$27,662,443	$30,920,000	$29,750,000	$70,325,039	$57,412,443

During the current year, major debt changes for governmental activities were as follows:

- Bonds issued to support construction of Easely Street Bridge $9,363,693
- Bonds issued to support construction of West End Recreation Center 3,000,000
- Execution of capital leases for general government purposes 431,213

Also during the year, approximately $3.3 million was paid to reduce the City's debt position.

In addition, the following major debt changes for business-type activities were as follows:

- Debt issued to finance the construction of assets for the Centerville Municipal Airport $3,200,000
- Debt issued to finance the construction of assets for the Utilities Authority 2,100,000

Also during the year, approximately $4.5 million was paid to reduce the debt outstanding related to business-type activities.

The City also has long-term liabilities related to compensated absences and claims and judgements. These liabilities, for both governmental activities and business-type activities, increased by less than $200,000 during the current year.

The credit rating for the City's general obligation bonds is the third highest rating possible. That rate has not changed over the last several years.

Relevant Current Economic Factors, Decisions, and Conditions

Regional economic trends that affect the financial conditions of the City are generally favorable. The unemployment rate for the second quarter of 20X2 in the Centerville Metropolitan Area is approximately 2.1%, which is significantly lower than either the rate for the state (2.9%) or the nation (3.1%). The metropolitan region's retail sales and new construction continue to grow at a rate that is significantly greater than that experienced by the United States as a whole. During the last several years, the region's higher growth rate has tended to increase the inflation rate (as measured by the Consumer Price Index) slightly higher than either the state or the nation. For example, the inflation rate for the year ended December 31, 20X1 in the metropolitan area (3.9%) was slightly higher than the rate for either the state (3.7%) or the nation (3.6%). Recent estimates of current inflation trends reconfirm the region's experience for the past few years.

All of these factors, as well as others referred to elsewhere in this MD&A, were taken into consideration in preparing the budget for the General Fund for the year ended June 30, 20X3. The City's property tax base has increased by approximately 5% because of the continued new construction in both the downtown and residential areas. Over the past few years, property tax rates have essentially remained stable but the 20X3 budget reflects a rate increase of 8%. Even with this rate increase, the overall tax rate for the City is approximately 20–25% less than the tax rate assessed by other cities of the approximate same size within a 25-mile radius. These budgetary changes are expected to offset declines in certain grants that have been traditionally made by the state and federal governments. However, one important development during the past year was the state's legislative action to begin to increase its commitment to public education. During the 20X3 budgetary year, the state has pledged to fund approximately 15% of total public education expenditures and over the next three years that percentage will grow to 33%.

In addition to increases in revenue sources, the City has implemented a plan to better control operating expenditures for the next budgetary period. These strategies, which were discussed earlier, include a hiring freeze, cost reduction strategies for most departments, and new provisions in all of the union contracts that are expected to significantly reduce the cost of overtime pay.

If the strategies and estimates described above are realized, the City's budgetary fund balance for the General Fund is expected to increase by approximately 3% by the end of the 20X3 fiscal year.

Overall, the business-type activities conducted by the City are expected to continue to improve. Most of these favorable results are expected to be related to the operations of the Municipal Airport. Toward the end of the 20X2 fiscal year, the management of the airport signed several new contracts with retail stores located in the airport concourses. The new rental rates, which will take effect on January 1, 20X3, represent an overall increase of approximately 21% in rental rates spread evenly over a three-year period. The activities of the Centerville Toll Bridge are expected to increase modestly and its financial position is not expected to change significantly by the end of the 20X3 fiscal year. The other two business-type activities (parking and utilities) are expected to reverse a downward trend that has been experienced for the past three years. As explained earlier, parking fees have been increased significantly and a new method for determining utility rates will take effect during the next budgetary period.

Request for Information

This financial report is designed to provide various interested parties with a general overview of the City's finances and to show the City's accountability for the money it receives. If you have questions about this report or need additional financial information, contact the City Controller's Office at 856-555-5555, or you may request a copy of the Comprehensive Annual Financial Report at our Web site (http://www.centervillenj.gov).

CHAPTER 19
COMBINING AND INDIVIDUAL FUND FINANCIAL STATEMENT PRESENTATIONS

CONTENTS

INTRODUCTION

NCGA-1 (Governmental Accounting and Financial Reporting Principles) expresses its opinion on the number of funds a governmental entity should use in the following principle of governmental financial reporting:

> Number of Funds—Governmental units should establish and maintain those funds required by law and sound financial administration. Only the minimum number of funds consistent with legal and operating requirements should be established, however, because unnecessary funds result in inflexibility, undue complexity, and inefficient financial administration.

For many governmental entities, size, organizational simplicity, and an awareness of the above principle ensure that a relatively small number of funds can effectively communicate the operational characteristics and financial position of the entity. However, some governmental entities must by necessity create and maintain a significant number of funds which result in a fairly complicated reporting format that requires the use of combining and individual fund financial statements. Prior to the issuance of GASB-34, much of the financial reporting model was based on combining financial statements, generally focused on reporting by fund types. Because GASB-34 changed the focus of fund reporting from reporting by fund type to reporting by major fund, the presentation of combining financial statements has been eliminated or moved from a governmental entity's general purpose external financial statements to the supplementary information section in the entity's Comprehensive Annual Financial Report (CAFR).

This chapter uses material created in previous chapters to illustrate how combining and individual fund financial statements are presented in a governmental entity's financial report, including the CAFR. The reporting formatting issues are discussed in the following sections:

Governmental Funds

- Combining statements for nonmajor governmental funds

Proprietary Funds

- Combining statements for nonmajor enterprise funds
- Combining statements for internal service funds

Fiduciary Funds

- Combining statements for pension (and other employee benefit) trust funds
- Combining statements for private-purpose trust funds
- Combining statements for investment trust funds
- Combining statements for agency funds

Component Units

- Combining statements for nonmajor blended component units
- Combining statements for nonmajor discretely presented component units
- Individual fund financial statements

GOVERNMENTAL FUNDS

The following financial statements are presented for governmental funds (General, Special Revenue, Capital Projects, Debt Service, and Permanent Funds) as part of the general purpose external financial statements (basic financial statements):

- Balance Sheet

- Statement of Revenue, Expenditures, and Changes in Fund Balances

GAAP requires that a governmental fund be presented in a separate column in the fund financial statements if the fund is considered a major fund. A major fund is one that satisfies both of the following criteria:

A. *10% Threshold* Total assets, liabilities, revenues, or expenditures/expenses of the governmental (enterprise) fund are equal to or greater than 10% of the corresponding element total (assets, liability, and so forth) for all funds that are considered governmental funds (enterprise funds)

B. *5% Threshold* The same element that met the 10% criterion in A is at least 5% of the corresponding element total for all governmental and enterprise funds combined.

All nonmajor governmental funds are presented as supplementary information in the governmental entity's CAFR.

Combining Statements for Nonmajor Governmental Funds

The General Fund is always considered a major fund and therefore must be presented in a separate column. If a fund does not satisfy the conditions described above, it can still be presented as a major fund if the governmental entity believes it is important to do so. All other funds that are not considered major funds must be combined in a separate column and labeled as nonmajor funds.

Separate financial statements for each individual nonmajor governmental fund do not have to be presented in the general purpose external financial statements, but they should be presented as supplementary information in the CAFR. The structure of the presentation of the nonmajor combining financial statements generally depends on the number of nonmajor funds.

If there are only a few specific funds that make up the nonmajor fund column in the fund financial statements, the combined financial statements could simply include a column for each nonmajor fund and a total column for all of the nonmajor funds. The amounts in the total column should be traceable to the amounts presented in the nonmajor column in the fund financial statements that include the major governmental funds.

If there are numerous nonmajor funds, it is necessary to have a series of combining statements that eventually are layered together in order to compute totals for all nonmajor funds. For example, a government that has thirty nonmajor Special Revenue Funds could group the funds by broad categories (for example, recreational activities, transportation activities, etc.) and then for each category, present a column for each Special Revenue Fund in that category, along with a total column. The amounts in the total column for each broad category could be brought forward to form combining statements for all Special Revenue Funds, along with a total column. The amounts in the total column for all combining (nonmajor) Special Revenue Funds could be brought forward to form combined statements for all nonmajor governmental funds.

There is no single approach that is mandated by governmental accounting standards except that each individual fund must appear either as part of the general purpose external financial statements (i.e., major funds) or part of combining statements that are part of the entity's CAFR.

In Chapter 13, "Developing Information for Fund Financial Statements," the City of Centerville's governmental funds were evaluated to determine which ones were major funds for financial reporting purposes. Three governmental funds were designated as major funds and therefore are reported in separate columns in the governmental fund financial statements. Exhibit 13-1 lists nonmajor funds.

The structure used to illustrate the nonmajor governmental funds for the City of Centerville is to (1) present the single Special Revenue Fund and the single Permanent Fund separately in the overall combining financial statements for nonmajor governmental funds and (2) present combined totals for the two Capital Projects Funds and the four Debt Service Funds and support these two fund types with combining financial statements for the individual funds grouped by fund type. Based on this approach, the following combining financial statements are presented for the City of Centerville in its CAFR:

Nonmajor Governmental Funds
(by Fund Type)
Combining Balance Sheet
June 30, 20X2

| | Center City Special Services Fund | | | Centerville Cemetery Fund | |
	Special Revenue Fund	Capital Projects Funds	Debt Service Funds	Permanent Fund	Total
Assets					
Cash	$ 26,500	$ 287,956	$ 210,000	$ 3,000	$ 527,456
Temporary Investments	-	757,000	67,000	-	824,000
Property taxes receivable (net)	48,000	-	-	-	48,000
Other receivables	15,000	-	-	-	15,000
Investments	-	-	-	244,000	244,000
Total Assets	$ 89,500	$ 1,044,956	$ 277,000	$ 247,000	$ 1,658,456
Liabilities and Fund Balances					
Liabilities:					
Accounts payable	$ 50,000	$ 122,000	$ 9,000	$ 4,000	$ 185,000
Deferred revenue-property taxes	10,000	-	-	-	10,000
Total Liabilities	60,000	122,000	9,000	4,000	195,000
Fund Balances:					
Restricted - Debt Service Fund	-	-	268,000	-	268,000
Restricted - Permanent Fund	-	-	-	243,000	243,000
Assigned - City Special Services Fund	29,500	-	-	-	29,500
Assigned - Capital Projects Funds	-	922,956	-	-	922,956
Total Fund Balances	29,500	922,956	268,000	243,000	1,463,456
Total Liabilities and Fund Balances	$ 89,500	$ 1,044,956	$ 277,000	$ 247,000	$ 1,658,456

Note: The various levels of fund balances presented in accordance with GASB-54 are based on an analysis in Chapter 13, "Developing Information for Fund Financial Statements."

**Nonmajor Governmental Funds
(by Fund Type)
Combining Statement of Revenues, Expenditures,
and Changes in Fund Balances
June 30, 20X2**

	Center City Special Services Fund			Centerville Cemetery Fund	
	Special Revenue Fund	Capital Projects Funds	Debt Service Funds	Permanent Fund	Total
REVENUES					
Property taxes	$2,670,000	—	—	—	$2,670,000
Intergovernmental grants	—	$2,000,000	—	—	2,000,000
Interest and investment revenue	—	34,000	$ 9,000	$ 34,000	$77,000
Miscellaneous revenue	18,000	—	—	22,000	$40,000
Total revenue	2,688,000	2,034,000	9,000	56,000	$4,787,000
EXPENDITURES					
General government	550,000	592,000	42,000	35,000	1,219,000
Streets	2,200,000	—	—	—	2,200,000
Debt service:					
Principal	—	—	1,950,000	—	1,950,000
Interest and investment revenue	—	—	1,174,000	—	1,174,000
Capital outlays	—	12,600,000	—	—	12,600,000
Total expenditures	2,750,000	13,192,000	3,166,000	35,000	19,143,000
Excess (deficiency) of revenues over expenditures	(62,000)	(11,158,000)	(3,157,000)	21,000	(14,356,000)
OTHER FINANCING SOURCES (USES)					
Long-term debt issued	—	10,000,000	—	—	10,000,000
Discount on long-term debt issued	—	(671,044)	—	—	(671,044)
Transfers in	75,000	1,900,000	3,320,000	—	5,295,000
Total other financing sources and uses	75,000	11,228,956	3,320,000	—	14,623,956
Net change in fund balances	13,000	70,956	163,000	21,000	267,956
Fund balances—beginning	16,500	852,000	105,000	222,000	1,195,500
Fund balances—ending	$29,500	$922,956	$268,000	$243,000	$1,463,456

Nonmajor Capital Projects Funds
Combining Balance Sheet
June 30, 20X2

	Easily Street Bridge Project	Bland Street Drainage Project	Total
Assets			
Cash	$ 129,956	$ 158,000	$ 287,956
Temporary Investments	695,000	62,000	757,000
Total Assets	$ 824,956	$ 220,000	$ 1,044,956
Liabilities and Fund Balances			
Liabilities:			
Accounts payable	$ 95,000	$ 27,000	$ 122,000
Total Liabilities	95,000	27,000	122,000
Fund Balances:			
Assigned - Easily Street Bridge Project	729,956	-	729,956
Assigned - Bland Street Drainage Project	-	193,000	193,000
Total Fund Balances	729,956	193,000	922,956
Total Liabilities and Fund Balances	$ 824,956	$ 220,000	$ 1,044,956

Nonmajor Capital Projects Funds
Combining Statement of Revenues, Expenditures,
and Changes in Fund Balances June 30, 20X2

	Easely Street Bridge Project	Bland Street Drainage Project	Total
REVENUES			
Intergovernmental grants	$1,250,000	$750,000	$2,000,000
Interest	30,000	4,000	34,000
Total revenue	1,280,000	754,000	2,034,000
EXPENDITURES			
General government	495,000	97,000	592,000
Capital outlays	11,100,000	1,500,000	12,600,000
Total Expenditures	11,595,000	1,597,000	13,192,000
Excess (deficiency) of revenues over expenditures	(10,315,000)	(843,000)	(11,158,000)
OTHER FINANCING SOURCES (USES)			
Long-term debt issued	10,000,000	—	10,000,000
Discount on long-term debt issued	(671,044)	—	(671,044)
Transfers in	1,000,000	900,000	1,900,000
Total other financing sources and uses	10,328,956	900,000	11,228,956
Net change in fund balances	13,956	57,000	70,956
Fund balances—beginning	716,000	136,000	852,000
Fund balances—ending	$729,956	$193,000	$922,956

Nonmajor Debt Service Funds
Combining Balance Sheet
June 30, 20X2

	Senior Citizens' Center Bonds	Easely Street Bridge Bonds	Bland Street Drainage Bonds	West End Recreation Center Bonds	Total
ASSETS					
Cash	$40,000	$28,000	$105,000	$37,000	$210,000
Temporary investments	20,000	17,000	24,000	6,000	$ 67,000
Total assets	$60,000	$45,000	$129,000	$43,000	$277,000
LIABILITIES AND FUND BALANCES					
Liabilities:					
Accounts payable	$2,000	$3,000	$3,000	$ 1,000	$9,000
Total liabilities	2,000	3,000	3,000	1,000	9,000
Fund balance-restricted	58,000	42,000	126,000	42,000	268,000
Total liabilities and fund balances	$60,000	$45,000	$129,000	$43,000	$277,000

**Nonmajor Debt Service Funds
Combining Statement of Revenues, Expenditures,
and Changes in Fund Balances
June 30, 20X2**

	Senior Citizens' Center Bonds	Easely Street Bridge Bonds	Bland Street Drainage Bonds	West End Recreation Center Bonds	Total
REVENUES					
Interest	$ 4,000	$ 1,000	$ 3,000	$ 1,000	$ 9,000
Total Revenue	4,000	1,000	3,000	1,000	9,000
EXPENDITURES					
General government	9,000	11,000	15,000	7,000	42,000
Principal	750,000	—	700,000	500,000	1,950,000
Interest	500,000	200,000	294,000	180,000	1,174,000
Total Expenditures	1,259,000	211,000	1,009,000	687,000	3,166,000
Excess (deficiency) of revenues over expenditures	(1,255,000)	(210,000)	(1,006,000)	(686,000)	(3,157,000)
OTHER FINANCING SOURCES (USES)					
Transfers in	1,300,000	220,000	1,100,000	700,000	3,320,000
Total other financing sources and uses	1,300,000	220,000	1,100,000	700,000	3,320,000
Net change in fund balances	45,000	10,000	94,000	14,000	163,000
Fund balances— beginning	13,000	32,000	32,000	28,000	105,000
Fund balances— ending	$ 58,000	$ 42,000	$ 126,000	$ 42,000	$ 268,000

PROPRIETARY FUNDS

The following financial statements are presented for proprietary funds (Enterprise Funds and Internal Service Funds) as part of the general purpose external financial statements:

- Statement of Net Assets (or Balance Sheet)

- Statement of Revenues, Expenses, and Changes in Fund Net Assets (or Fund Equity)

- Statement of Cash Flows

The presentation of proprietary funds in the general purpose external financial statements depends on whether a specific proprietary fund is an Enterprise Fund or an Internal Service Fund.

Combining Statements for Nonmajor Enterprise Funds

In Chapter 13, "Developing Information for Fund Financial Statements," the City of Centerville's Enterprise Funds were evaluated to determine which ones were major funds for financial reporting purposes. Two Enterprise Funds were designated as major funds (Centerville Utilities Authority and Centerville Municipal Airport) and therefore are reported in separate columns in the proprietary fund financial statements. Other alternatives for presenting combining statements of nonmajor Enterprise Funds are discussed in the previous section, titled "Combining Statements for Nonmajor Governmental Funds." The Centerville Toll Bridge and Centerville Parking Authority were identified as nonmajor funds and therefore are aggregated and reported in a single column in the proprietary fund financial statements. The structure used to illustrate the combining financial statements for the nonmajor Enterprise Funds for the City of Centerville is to combine the two funds and create a total column in a single set of financial statements. Based on this approach the following combining financial statements are presented for the City of Centerville:

Enterprise Funds
Combining Statement of Net Assets June 30, 20X2

	Centerville Toll Bridge	Centerville Parking Authority	Total
ASSETS			
Current assets:			
Cash	$739,500	$764,000	$1,503,500
Interest receivable	3,000	3,000	6,000
Temporary investments	58,000	5,000	63,000
Supplies	32,000	24,000	56,000
Total current assets	832,500	796,000	1,628,500
Noncurrent assets:			
Construction in progress	70,000	15,000	85,000
Land and improvements	140,000	1,780,000	1,920,000
Superstructure	1,400,000	—	1,400,000
Buildings	330,000	2,400,000	2,730,000
Equipment	55,000	140,000	195,000
Vehicles	835,000	102,000	937,000
Less accumulated depreciation	(1,257,000)	(1,505,000)	(2,762,000)
Total noncurrent assets	1,573,000	2,932,000	4,505,000
Total assets	2,405,500	3,728,000	6,133,500
LIABILITIES			
Current liabilities:			
Accounts payable and accrued expenses	50,000	90,000	140,000
Due to other funds	18,000	17,000	35,000
Compensated absences	3,000	2,000	5,000
Claims and judgments	5,000	4,000	9,000
Notes payable	10,000	30,000	40,000
Bonds payable	20,000	—	20,000
Total current liabilities	106,000	143,000	249,000
Noncurrent liabilities:			
Compensated absences	5,000	3,000	8,000
Claims and judgments	22,000	3,000	25,000
Notes payable	20,000	—	20,000
Bonds payable	60,000	500,000	560,000
Total noncurrent liabilities	107,000	506,000	613,000
Total liabilities	213,000	649,000	862,000
NET ASSETS			
Invested in capital assets, net of related debt	1,463,000	2,402,000	3,865,000
Restricted	622,000	595,000	1,217,000
Unrestricted	107,500	82,000	189,500
Total net assets	$2,192,500	$3,079,000	$5,271,500

Enterprise Funds
Combining Statement of Revenues, Expenses,
and Changes in Fund Net Assets
for the Year Ended
June 30, 20X2

	Centerville Toll Bridge	Centerville Parking Authority	Total
OPERATING REVENUES			
Charges for services	$4,750,000	$1,500,000	$6,250,000
Miscellaneous	20,000	22,000	42,000
Total operating revenues	4,770,000	1,522,000	6,292,000
OPERATING EXPENSES			
Personal services	2,402,000	5,402,000	7,804,000
Contractual services	1,280,000	400,000	1,680,000
Repairs and maintenance	400,000	50,000	450,000
Other supplies and expenses	194,000	36,000	230,000
Insurance claims and expenses	10,000	3,000	13,000
Depreciation	339,000	117,000	456,000
Miscellaneous	30,000	3,000	33,000
Total operating expenses	4,655,000	6,011,000	10,666,000
Operating income (loss)	115,000	(4,489,000)	(4,374,000)
NONOPERATING REVENUES (EXPENSES)			
Interest and investment revenue	30,000	10,000	40,000
Interest	(6,000)	(27,000)	(33,000)
Operating grants and contributions	100,000	—	100,000
Miscellaneous	7,000	1,000	8,000
Total nonoperating revenue (expenses)	131,000	(16,000)	115,000
Income (loss) before capital contributions and transfers	246,000	(4,505,000)	(4,259,000)
Capital contributions	250,000	—	250,000
Transfers in	50,000	90,000	140,000
Special item—gain on sale of parking lot	—	3,500,000	3,500,000
Change in net assets	546,000	(915,000)	(369,000)
Total net assets—beginning	1,646,500	3,994,000	5,640,500
Total net assets—ending	$2,192,500	$3,079,000	$5,271,500

Enterprise Funds
Combining Statement of Cash Flows
for the Year Ended June 30, 20X2

	Centerville Toll Bridge	Centerville Parking Authority	Total
CASH FLOWS FROM OPERATING ACTIVITIES			
Receipts from customers	$4,750,000	$1,500,000	$6,250,000
Payments to suppliers	(1,806,000)	(345,000)	(2,151,000)
Payments to employees	(2,371,000)	(5,361,000)	(7,732,000)
Internal activity—payments to other funds	(66,000)	(90,000)	(156,000)
Other receipts (payments)	(18,000)	19,000	1,000
Net cash provided (used) by operating activities	489,000	(4,277,000)	(3,788,000)
CASH FLOWS FROM NONCAPITAL FINANCING ACTIVITIES			
Subsidies and transfers from (to) other funds and state government	150,000	90,000	240,000
CASH FLOWS FROM CAPITAL AND RELATED FINANCING ACTIVITIES			
Capital contributions	250,000	30,000	280,000
Acquisitions of capital assets	(390,000)	(200,000)	(590,000)
Proceeds from sale of capital assets	50,000	5,005,000	5,055,000
Principal paid on capital debt	(30,000)	(10,000)	(40,000)
Interest paid on capital debt	(6,000)	(27,000)	(33,000)
Net cash provided (used) by capital and related financing activities	(126,000)	4,798,000	4,672,000
CASH FLOWS FROM INVESTING ACTIVITIES			
Interest and dividends	31,500	8,000	39,500
Purchase of investments	(25,000)	(5,000)	(30,000)
Net cash provided (used) by investing activities	6,500	3,000	9,500
Net increase (decrease) in cash	519,500	614,000	1,133,500
Balances—beginning of year	220,000	150,000	370,000
Balances—end of year	$739,500	$764,000	$1,503,500
Reconciliation of operating income (loss) to net cash provided (used) by operating activities:			
Operating income (loss) Adjustments:	$115,000	$(4,489,000)	$(4,374,000)
Depreciation expense	339,000	117,000	456,000
Change in assets and liabilities:			
Inventories	(6,000)	(4,000)	(10,000)
Accounts and accrued liabilities	41,000	99,000	140,000
Net cash provided (used) by operating activities	$489,000	$(4,277,000)	$(3,788,000)

Combining Statements for Internal Service Funds

The major-fund reporting concept does not apply to the presentation of Internal Service Funds. Thus, at the fund financial statement level, Internal Service Fund balances and activities are combined into a single column and placed on the proprietary fund financial statements to the right of the totals column for Enterprise Funds. The details for the individual Internal Service Funds presented in the aggregated column of the proprietary fund financial statements are presented in combining statements as part of the CAFR.

The City of Centerville has the following Internal Service Funds:

- Communications and Technology Support Center
- Fleet Management Unit
- Special Services Support Center

Separate financial statements for each individual Internal Service Fund do not have to be presented in the general purpose external financial statements, but they should be presented as supplementary information in the CAFR. The structure of the presentation of the nonmajor combining financial statements generally depends on the number of Internal Service Funds (as explained in the previous discussion of governmental funds). The structure used to illustrate the combining financial statements for Internal Service Funds for the City of Centerville is to combine the three funds and create a total column in a single set of financial statements.

The details for these funds are developed in Chapter 8, "Internal Service Funds." The combining financial statements are as follows:

Internal Service Funds
Combining Statement of Net Assets
June 30, 20X2

	Communications and Technology Support Center	Fleet Management	Special Services Support Center	Total
ASSETS				
Current assets:				
Cash	$ 946,000	$ 137,500	$ 22,000	$1,105,500
Interest receivable	1,000	2,000	1,000	4,000
Due from other funds	325,000	72,000	427,000	824,000
Due from other governments	—	45,000	—	45,000
Temporary investments	15,000	19,000	12,000	46,000
Inventories	9,000	7,000	20,000	36,000
Total current assets	1,296,000	282,500	482,000	2,060,500
Noncurrent assets:				
Land and improvements	2,700,000	50,000	1,750,000	4,500,000
Buildings	1,400,000	1,600,000	1,600,000	4,600,000
Equipment	5,870,000	1,330,000	2,960,000	10,160,000
Vehicles	143,000	8,200,000	1,995,000	10,338,000
Less accumulated depreciation	(3,103,000)	(6,505,000)	(3,240,000)	(12,848,000)
Total noncurrent assets	7,010,000	4,675,000	5,065,000	16,750,000
Total assets	8,306,000	4,957,500	5,547,000	18,810,500
LIABILITIES				
Current liabilities:				
Accounts payable and accrued expenses	50,000	125,000	75,000	250,000
Compensated absences	3,000	2,000	5,000	10,000
Claims and judgments	4,000	2,000	7,000	13,000
Notes payable	—	1,500,000	200,000	1,700,000
Total current liabilities	57,000	1,629,000	287,000	1,973,000
Noncurrent liabilities:				
Compensated absences	4,000	6,000	12,000	22,000
Claims and judgments	15,000	11,000	14,000	40,000
Notes payable	4,700,000	1,500,000	350,000	6,550,000
Total noncurrent liabilities	4,719,000	1,517,000	376,000	6,612,000
Total liabilities	4,776,000	3,146,000	663,000	8,585,000
NET ASSETS				
Invested in capital assets, net of related debt	2,310,000	1,675,000	4,515,000	8,500,000
Unrestricted	1,220,000	136,500	369,000	1,725,500
Total net assets	$3,530,000	$1,811,500	$4,884,000	$10,225,500

**Internal Service Funds
Combining Statement of Revenues, Expenses,
and Changes in Fund Net Assets
For the Year Ended June 30, 20X2**

	Communications and Technology Support Center	Fleet Management	Special Services Support Center	Total
OPERATING REVENUES				
Charges for services	$5,500,000	$5,000,000	$2,950,000	$13,450,000
Miscellaneous	10,000	4,000	3,000	17,000
Total operating revenues	5,510,000	5,004,000	2,953,000	13,467,000
OPERATING EXPENSES				
Personal services	4,805,000	1,206,000	915,000	6,926,000
Contractual services	1,300,000	400,000	400,000	2,100,000
Repairs and maintenance	1,100,000	200,000	350,000	1,650,000
Other supplies and expenses	48,000	147,000	171,000	366,000
Insurance claims and expenses	10,000	7,000	12,000	29,000
Depreciation	1,927,000	2,530,000	1,125,000	5,582,000
Miscellaneous	5,000	2,000	15,000	22,000
Total operating expenses	9,195,000	4,492,000	2,988,000	16,675,000
Operating income (loss)	(3,685,000)	512,000	(35,000)	(3,208,000)
NONOPERATING REVENUES (EXPENSES)				
Interest and investment revenue	5,000	5,000	15,000	25,000
Interest	(97,000)	(180,000)	(32,000)	(309,000)
Operating grants and contributions	200,000	100,000	70,000	370,000
Miscellaneous	27,000	(65,000)	30,000	(8,000)
Total nonoperating revenue (expenses)	135,000	(140,000)	83,000	78,000
Income (loss) before capital contributions and transfers	(3,550,000)	372,000	48,000	(3,130,000)
Capital contributions	450,000	—	40,000	490,000
Transfers in	40,000	—	—	40,000
Transfers out	—	(50,000)	—	(50,000)
Change in net assets	(3,060,000)	322,000	88,000	(2,650,000)
Total net assets— beginning	6,590,000	1,489,500	4,796,000	12,875,500
Total net assets— ending	$3,530,000	$1,811,500	$4,884,000	$10,225,500

Internal Service Funds
Combining Statement of Cash Flows
For the Year Ended June 30, 20X2

	Communications and Technology Support Center	Fleet Management	Special Services Support Center	Total
CASH FLOWS FROM OPERATING ACTIVITIES				
Receipts from customers	$5,296,000	$4,915,000	$2,600,000	$12,811,000
Payments to suppliers	(2,435,000)	(815,000)	(935,000)	(4,185,000)
Payments to employees	(4,782,000)	(1,103,000)	(862,000)	(6,747,000)
Other receipts (payments)	2,000	(2,000)	(25,000)	(25,000)
Net cash provided (used) by operating activities	(1,919,000)	2,995,000	778,000	1,854,000
CASH FLOWS FROM NONCAPITAL FINANCING ACTIVITIES				
Operating subsidies and transfers from (to) other funds	240,000	50,000	70,000	360,000
CASH FLOWS FROM CAPITAL AND RELATED FINANCING ACTIVITIES				
Proceeds from the issuance of capital debt	3,200,000	—	200,000	3,400,000
Capital contributions	450,000	—	40,000	490,000
Acquisitions of capital assets	(1,535,000)	(2,950,000)	(1,555,000)	(6,040,000)
Proceeds from sale of capital assets	340,000	410,000	95,000	845,000
Principal paid on capital debt	—	(1,000,000)	(100,000)	(1,100,000)
Interest paid on capital debt	(97,000)	(180,000)	(32,000)	(309,000)
Net cash provided (used) by capital and related financing activities	2,358,000	(3,720,000)	(1,352,000)	(2,714,000)
CASH FLOWS FROM INVESTING ACTIVITIES				
Interest and dividends	7,000	7,500	23,000	37,500
Net increase (decrease) in cash	686,000	(667,500)	(481,000)	(462,500)
Balances—beginning of year	260,000	805,000	503,000	1,568,000
Balances—end of year	$946,000	$137,500	$22,000	$1,105,500
Reconciliation of operating income (loss) to net cash provided (used) by operating activities:				
Operating income (loss)	$(3,685,000)	$512,000	$(35,000)	$(3,208,000)
Adjustments:				
Depreciation expense	1,927,000	2,530,000	1,125,000	5,582,000
Change in assets and liabilities:				
Receivables, net	(204,000)	(85,000)	(350,000)	(639,000)
Inventories	(2,000)	(3,000)	(4,000)	(9,000)
Accounts and accrued liabilities	45,000	41,000	42,000	128,000
Net cash provided (used) by operating activities	$(1,919,000)	$2,995,000	$ 778,000	$1,854,000

FIDUCIARY FUND FINANCIAL STATEMENTS

The following financial statements are presented for fiduciary funds (Pension and Other Employee Benefit Trust Funds, Investment Trust Funds, Private-Purpose Trust Funds, and Agency Funds) as part of the general purpose external financial statements:

- Statement of Fiduciary Net Assets
- Statement of Changes in Fiduciary Net Assets (except for Agency Funds as explained below)

The major-fund reporting concept does not apply to the presentation of fiduciary funds. Thus, at the fund financial statement level, fiduciary funds of a particular fund type are combined into a single column for financial reporting purposes. The details for the individual funds presented in the aggregated columns by fund type are presented in combining statements as part of the entity's CAFR.

COMBINING STATEMENTS FOR PENSION (AND OTHER EMPLOYEE BENEFIT) TRUST FUNDS

The City of Centerville participates in the following Pension Trust Funds and Other Employee Benefit Trust Funds:

- State Public General Employees Retirement Fund (SPGERF)
- State Public Safety Officers Retirement Fund (SPSORF)
- State Postemployment Healthcare Benefits Fund (SPHBF)

The structure of the presentation of combining financial statements for these funds generally depends on their number (as explained in the previous discussion of governmental funds). The structure used to illustrate the combining financial statements for Pension Trust Funds and Other Employee Benefit Trust Funds for the City of Centerville is to combine the three funds and create a total column in a single set of financial statements.

The details for these funds are developed in Chapter 9, "Pension (and Other Employee Benefits) Trust Funds." The combining financial statements are as follows:

City of Centerville
Combining Statement of Fiduciary Net Assets
Pension and Other Employee Benefit Trust Funds
June 30, 20X2

	State Public General Employees Retirement Fund	State Public Safety Officers Retirement Fund	State Post- Employment Healthcare Benefits Fund	Total
ASSETS				
Cash	$ 2,546,400	$ 1,273,200	$ 424,400	$ 4,244,000
Other receivables	18,600	9,300	3,100	31,000
Investments in debt securities	6,613,200	3,306,600	1,102,200	11,022,000
Investment in market- able equity securities	13,477,800	6,738,900	2,246,300	22,463,000
Total assets	22,656,000	11,328,000	3,776,000	37,760,000
LIABILITIES				
Accounts payable and accrued expenses	17,400	8,700	2,900	29,000
Refunds payable and other liabilities	15,000	7,500	2,500	25,000
Total liabilities	32,400	16,200	5,400	54,000
NET ASSETS				
Held in trust for pension benefits and other purposes.	$22,623,600	$11,311,800	$3,770,600	$37,706,000

City of Centerville
Combining Statement of Fiduciary Net Assets
Pension and Other Employee Benefit Trust Funds
June 30, 20X2

	State Public General Employees Retirement Fund	State Public Safety Officers Retirement Fund	State Post-Employment Healthcare Benefits Fund	Total
ADDITIONS				
Contributions by:				
City of Centerville	$4,200,000	$2,100,000	$700,000	$7,000,000
Plan members	1,620,000	810,000	270,000	2,700,000
Total contributions	5,820,000	2,910,000	970,000	9,700,000
Interest and investment revenue	291,600	145,800	48,600	486,000
Total additions	6,111,600	3,055,800	1,018,600	10,186,000
DEDUCTIONS				
Benefits paid	2,520,000	1,260,000	420,000	4,200,000
Refunds	60,000	30,000	10,000	100,000
Administrative expenses	209,400	104,700	34,900	349,000
Total deductions	2,789,400	1,394,700	464,900	4,649,000
Change in net assets	3,322,200	1,661,100	553,700	5,537,000
Net assets—beginning of the year	19,301,400	9,650,700	3,216,900	32,169,000
Net assets—end of the year	$22,623,600	$11,311,800	$3,770,600	$37,706,000

Combining Statements for Private-Purpose Trust Funds

The City of Centerville participates in the following Private-Purpose Trust Funds:

- Scholarship Trust Fund
- Emergency Workers' Relief Fund
- Historical Pike Fund

The structure of the presentation of the individual Private-Purpose Trust Funds in combining financial statements generally depends on the number of funds in this fund type category. The structure used to illustrate the combining financial statements for Private-Purpose Trust Funds for the City of Centerville is to combine the three funds and create a total column in a single set of financial statements.

The details for these funds are developed in Chapter 10, "Private-Purpose Trust Funds." The combining financial statements are as follows:

City of Centerville
Private-Purpose Trust Funds
Combining Statement of Changes in Fiduciary Net Assets
For the Year Ended June 30, 20X2

	Scholarship Trust Fund	Emergency Workers' Relief Fund	Historical Pike Fund	Total
ADDITIONS				
Contributions by:				
External parties	$ 18,000	$ 9,000	$ 3,000	$ 30,000
City of Centerville	6,000	3,000	1,000	10,000
Total contributions	24,000	12,000	4,000	40,000
Interest and investment revenue	29,400	14,700	4,900	49,000
Total additions	53,400	26,700	8,900	89,000
DEDUCTIONS				
Benefits paid	34,200	17,100	5,700	57,000
Change in net assets	19,200	9,600	3,200	32,000
Net assets—beginning of the year	269,400	134,700	44,900	449,000
Net assets—end of the year	$288,600	$144,300	$48,100	$481,000

City of Centerville
Combining Statement of Changes in Fiduciary Net Assets
Investment Trust Funds For the Year Ended June 30, 20X2

	Scholarship Trust Fund	Emergency Workers' Relief Fund	Historical Pike Fund	Total
ASSETS				
Cash	$ 1,200	$ 600	$ 200	$ 2,000
Investments in debt securities	290,400	145,200	48,400	484,000
Total assets	291,600	145,800	48,600	486,000
LIABILITIES				
Accounts payable and accrued expenses	3,000	1,500	500	5,000
Total liabilities	3,000	1,500	500	5,000
NET ASSETS				
Held in trust for external parties	$288,600	$144,300	$48,100	$481,000

Combining Statements for Investment Trust Funds

The City of Centerville participates in the following Investment Trust Funds:

- Equity Investment Pool (EIP)
- Short-Term Fixed Income Investment Pool (STFIIP)
- Reclamation Investment Fund (RIF)

The Short-Term Fixed Income Investment Pool (as explained in Chapter 11, "Investment Trust Funds and Individual Investment Accounts") is not an external investment pool and therefore its financial statements are not reported separately either as part of the general purpose external financial statements or as supplementary information in the CAFR.

The structure of the presentation of the individual Investment Trust Funds in combining financial statements generally depends on the number of funds in this fund type category. The structure used to illustrate the combining financial statements for Investment Trust Funds for the City of Centerville is to combine the two funds and create a total column in a single set of financial statements.

The details for these funds are developed in Chapter 11, "Investment Trust Funds and Individual Investment Accounts." The combining financial statements are as follows:

City of Centerville
Combining Statement of Changes in Fiduciary Net Assets
Investment Trust Funds
For the Year Ended June 30, 20X2

	Reclamation Equity Investment Pool (External Portion)	Investment Fund (Individual Investment Account)
ADDITIONS		
Principal contributions from external participants	$300,000	$50,000
Total contributions from participants	300,000	50,000
Investment earnings:		
Increase in fair value of investments	549,600	33,000
Dividend income	31,200	85,000
Interest income	5,400	3,000
Total investment earnings	586,200	121,000
Less: Investment expenses	147,000	23,000
Net investment earnings	439,200	98,000
Total additions	739,200	148,000
DEDUCTIONS		
Withdrawals by external participants	825,000	200,000
Interest expenses	4,200	1,000
Total deductions	829,200	201,000
Change in net assets	(90,000)	(53,000)
Net assets—beginning of the year	2,700,000	1,540,000
Net assets—end of the year	$2,610,000	$1,487,000

City of Centerville
Agency Funds Combining
Statement of Fiduciary Net Assets
June 30, 20X2

ASSETS		
Cash	$ 582,000	$ 20,000
Investment in short-term instruments	36,000	112,000
Investments in equity securities	2,039,400	1,361,000
Dividends receivable	4,200	2,000
Interest receivable	1,200	1,000
Other receivables	3,600	2,000
Other assets	1,800	5,000
Total assets	2,668,200	1,503,000
LIABILITIES		
Accounts payable	13,200	4,000
Demand loan payable to bank	45,000	12,000
Total liabilities	58,200	16,000
NET ASSETS		
Held in trust for pool participants	2,610,000	1,487,000
Total net assets	$2,610,000	$1,487,000

Combining Statements for Agency Funds

The City of Centerville participates in the following Agency Funds:

- Community Support Trust Fund
- County Fire District Trust Fund County
- Homeland Security District Trust Fund

At the fund financial statement level, Agency Funds are required to present a statement of net assets but not a statement of changes in net assets (unlike other fiduciary funds); however, Agency Funds must present a combining statement of changes in assets and liabilities by individual fund in the supplementary information of the CAFR as part of the combining financial statements.

The structure of the presentation of combining financial statements for these funds generally depends on their number (as explained in the previous discussion of governmental funds). The structure used to illustrate the combining financial statements for Agency Funds is to combine the three funds and create a total column in a single set of financial statements.

The details for these funds are developed in Chapter 12, "Agency Funds." The combining financial statements are as follows:

City of Centerville
Agency Funds
Combining Statement of Fiduciary Net Assets
June 30, 20X2

	Community Support Trust Fund	County Fire District Fund	County Homeland Security District Trust Fund	Total
ASSETS				
Cash	$8,000	$20,000	$20,000	$48,000
Property taxes receivable (net)	—	5,000	—	5,000
Total assets	8,000	25,000	20,000	53,000
LIABILITIES				
Accounts payable	8,000	—	—	8,000
Due to other taxing districts	—	25,000	20,000	45,000
Total liabilities	$8,000	$25,000	$20,000	$53,000

City of Centerville
Agency Funds
Combining Statement of Changes in Assets and Liabilities
For the Year Ended June 30, 20X2

	Balance July 1, 20X0	Additions	Deductions	Balance June 30, 20X1
COMMUNITY SUPPORT TRUST FUND				
ASSETS				
Cash	$4,000	$440,000	$436,000	$8,000
Total assets	$4,000	$440,000	$436,000	$8,000
LIABILITIES				
Accounts payable	$4,000	$440,000	$436,000	$8,000
Total liabilities	$4,000	$440,000	$436,000	$8,000
COUNTY FIRE DISTRICT TRUST FUND				
ASSETS				
Cash	$ 3,000	$227,000	$210,000	$20,000
Property taxes receivable (net)	7,000	225,000	227,000	5,000
Total assets	$10,000	$452,000	$437,000	$25,000
LIABILITIES				
Due to other tax districts	$10,000	$225,000	$210,000	$25,000
Total liabilities	$10,000	$225,000	$210,000	$25,000
COUNTY HOMELAND SECURITY DISTRICT TRUST FUND				
Cash	$10,000	$550,000	$540,000	$20,000
Total assets	$10,000	$550,000	$540,000	$20,000
LIABILITIES				
Due to other tax districts	$10,000	$550,000	$540,000	$20,000
Total liabilities	$10,000	$550,000	$540,000	$20,000
TOTALS—ALL AGENCY FUNDS				
ASSETS				
Cash	$17,000	$1,217,000	$1,186,000	$48,000
Property taxes receivable (net)	7,000	225,000	227,000	5,000
Total assets	$24,000	$1,442,000	$1,413,000	$53,000
LIABILITIES				
Accounts payable	$ 4,000	$ 440,000	$ 436,000	$ 8,000
Due to other tax districts	20,000	775,000	750,000	45,000
Total liabilities	$24,000	$1,215,000	$1,186,000	$53,000

COMPONENT UNITS

A basic strategy of GASB-14 (The Financial Reporting Entity) is to present financial information for component units separately from the financial information for the primary government. This strategy is achieved through the use of the discrete-presentation method, which is described in Chapter 15, "Component Units." However, in some circumstances the GASB believes that it is more appropriate to use the blending method to incorporate the financial information of a component unit into the primary government's financial statements.

Combining Statements for Nonmajor Blended Component Units

When the blending method is used, transactions of a component unit are presented as if they were executed directly by the primary government. That is, the funds for the blended component units are evaluated as either major or nonmajor funds and reported accordingly, just like all other funds (governmental funds and proprietary funds, but not fiduciary funds) of the primary government. The balances and activities of the blended component units are not distinguishable from those of the primary government. In a similar manner, balances in a component unit's financial statements are merged with similar balances of the primary government in the preparation of the government-wide financial statements. For example, assume that a primary government has a component unit (that is to be incorporated into its financial statements by the blending method) that had the following funds:

- General Fund
- Three Special Revenue Funds
- Two Enterprise Funds
- Three Internal Service Funds

The General Fund is considered a Special Revenue Fund for the primary government, and as a Special Revenue Fund it is categorized as either a major fund or nonmajor fund based on the criteria established by GASB-34 (discussed earlier in this chapter). If the fund is considered a major fund, it is reported in a separate column in the governmental fund financial statements. If the fund is considered a nonmajor fund, it is (1) aggregated and presented with all other nonmajor governmental funds and (2) its individual statements are presented in the combining financial statements. In the latter case, the nonmajor Special Revenue Fund would be presented as supplementary information (combining financial statements) in the CAFR along with all the other nonmajor governmental funds of the primary government.

The major fund criteria would also be applied to the three Special Revenue Funds of the component units. For example, if one of the three funds is a major fund, it would be presented as such in the financial statements for governmental funds and the other two Special Revenue Funds would be presented in the combining financial statements for governmental funds.

Again, the major fund criteria would be applied to the two Enterprise Funds and, for example, if one of the funds is a major fund, its financial statements would be presented as such in the financial statements for proprietary funds and the financial statements of the other Enterprise Fund would be aggregated with all other nonmajor Enterprise Funds and presented in a single column in the financial statements for proprietary funds. The component unit's nonmajor Enterprise Fund would also be presented as supplementary information (combining financial statements) in the CAFR along with all the other nonmajor Enterprise Funds of the primary government.

The component unit's three Internal Service Funds would be presented in a manner similar to the treatment of the primary government's other Internal Service Funds. That is, the three Internal Service Funds would be aggregated with all of the primary government's other Internal Service Funds and presented (in a single column) on the financial statements for proprietary funds. The component unit's three Internal Service Funds would also be presented as supplementary information (combining financial statements) in the CAFR along with all of the Internal Service Funds of the primary government.

The City of Centerville has two component units that are incorporated into the financial statements by the use of the blending method. The two blended component units are as follows:

1. Centerville Utilities Authority
2. Centerville Parking Authority

Combining Statements for Nonmajor Discretely Presented Component Units

The following financial statements are presented for discretely presented component units:

- Statement of net assets
- Statement of activities

In order to provide a clear distinction between the balances and activities of the primary government and its discretely presented component units, one of the following formats should be used in preparing the reporting entity's government-wide financial statements:

- Present each major component unit in a separate column in the government-wide financial statements
- Present combining statements as part of the basic financial statements
- Present condensed financial statements in a note to the financial statements

For each of the three formats, every major component unit has a separate column and all nonmajor component units are aggregated into a single column. Thus, for each of the format presentations the financial statements of a major component unit (either in detail or in condensed form) are presented as part of the general purpose external financial statements. All nonmajor discretely presented component units are presented as supplementary information in the governmental entity's CAFR.

OBSERVATION: GASB-34 does not provide a definition of a "major component unit," but states that "consideration should be given to each component unit's significance relative to the other component units and the nature and significance of its relationship to the primary government." GASB-61 also does not fully define a "major component unit." Rather, it focuses on amended note disclosure for major component units in general.

In Chapter 15, "Component Units," the City of Centerville's discretely presented component units are identified as major and nonmajor component units as described as follows:

- Centerville Public School System (major component unit)
- Centerville Regional Transit System (major component unit)
- Centerville Parks District (nonmajor component unit)
- Centerville Sports Authority (nonmajor component unit)

The City of Centerville elects the second formatting strategy (presenting combining statements as part of the basic financial statements). Based on this approach, the following combining financial statements for the nonmajor component units are presented for the City of Centerville:

City of Centerville
Combining Statement of Net Assets
Nonmajor Component Units
June 30, 20X2

	Centerville Parks District	Centerville Sports Authority	Total
ASSETS			
Cash	$6,850,000	$1,996,650	$8,846,650
Receivables (net)	5,355,000	8,100	5,363,100
Other assets	30,000	—	30,000
Investments	7,850,000	156,600	8,006,600
Inventories and supplies	2,687,000	86,400	2,773,400
Capital assets:			
Land, improvements, and construction in progress	321,460,000	2,347,000	323,807,000
Other capital assets, net of depreciation	154,700,000	1,900,100	156,600,100
Total assets	498,932,000	6,494,850	505,426,850
LIABILITIES			
Accounts payable and accrued expenses	2,180,000	135,000	2,315,000
Deferred revenue	402,000	—	402,000
Long-term liabilities:			
Due within one year	13,225,000	102,600	13,327,600
Due in more than one year	147,300,000	337,500	147,637,500
Total liabilities	163,107,000	575,100	163,682,100
NET ASSETS			
Net assets—invested in capital assets, net of related debt	315,635,000	3,950,100	319,585,100
Net assets—restricted for capital projects	3,000,000	—	3,000,000
Net assets—restricted for debt service	322,000	—	322,000
Net assets—restricted for other purposes	34,000	1,679,400	1,713,400
Net assets restricted for other purposes (nonexpendable)	147,000	290,250	437,250
Net assets—unrestricted	16,687,000	—	16,687,000
Total net assets	$335,825,000	$5,919,750	$341,744,750

City of Centerville
Combining Statement of Activities
Nonmajor Component Units
For the Year Ended June 30, 20X2

		Program Revenues			Net (Expense) Revenues and Changes in Net Assets		
	Expenses	Charges for Services	Operating Grants and Contributions	Capital Grants and Contributions	Centerville Parks District	Centerville Sports Authority	Total
FUNCTIONS							
Centerville Parks District	$34,437,000	$18,472,000	$3,783,000	$4,562,000	$(7,620,000)	—	$(7,620,000)
Centerville Sports Authority	12,584,700	12,825,000	270,000	—	—	$510,300	510,300
Total	$47,021,700	$31,297,000	$4,053,000	$4,562,000	(7,620,000)	510,300	$(7,109,700)
General revenues—							
property taxes					5,990,000	—	5,990,000
General revenues—other taxes					105,000	—	105,000
Grants and contributions not restricted to specific programs					3,050,000	810,000	3,860,000
Unrestricted investment earnings					622,000	81,000	703,000
Miscellaneous revenues					32,000	72,900	104,900
Total general revenues					9,799,000	963,900	10,762,900
Change in net assets					2,179,000	1,474,200	3,653,200
Net assets—beginning					333,646,000	4,445,550	338,091,550
Net assets—ending					$335,825,000	$5,919,750	$341,744,750

In most instances, a discretely presented component unit publishes separate financial statements that are available to the public. If the component unit's financial statements are not available, fund information for a major component unit should be presented as supplementary information in the reporting entity's (for example, the City of Centerville) CAFR; however, there is no requirement to present similar information in the reporting entity's CAFR for nonmajor discretely presented component units.

INDIVIDUAL FUND FINANCIAL STATEMENTS

The reporting strategy in preparing a governmental entity's financial statements is to report each fund in a separate column somewhere in the CAFR. This general strategy may be accomplished either by reporting a separate column for a fund in the reporting entity's basic financial statements or in the supplementary information section of its CAFR. The latter reporting strategy can be achieved by presenting either combining fund financial statements or individual fund financial statements. The first part of this chapter focused on the presentation of combining financial statements. This section summarizes the reporting circumstances under which it would be appropriate to prepare individual fund financial statements.

Fund-Type of Fund Grouping with a Single Fund

As described earlier, a major governmental fund is presented in a separate column in the fund financial statements, and all nonmajor governmental funds (Special Revenue Funds, Capital Projects Funds, Debt Service Funds, and Permanent Funds) are aggregated into a single column and presented in the same financial statements. However, if a governmental entity has only a single nonmajor fund in this fund grouping (governmental funds), then there is no need to present the single nonmajor fund in the governmental entity's supplementary information section of the CAFR. That is, not only would it make no sense to prepare a combining statement of only one fund but also there is no need to report the single fund as part of the supplementary information, because its financial statement is in effect reported as a single column in the basic financial statements. For example, if a governmental entity has a Special Revenue Fund that is its only nonmajor fund, the fund's individual financial statements would be presented as a separate column in the governmental fund's financial statements (part of the basic financial statements); that presentation would serve as the fund's individual fund financial statements. However, care must be taken to label the Special Revenue Fund as a nonmajor fund in the fund financial statements.

A governmental entity might have only one nonmajor Enterprise Fund or one Internal Service Fund and, for reasons similar to those described above, it would be unnecessary to present the single non-major Enterprise Fund or Internal Service Fund's financial statements as part of a combining financial statements or as a separate individual fund in the supplementary information section of the CAFR. Care must be taken in the case of the Enterprise Fund to label the nonmajor Enterprise Fund as a nonmajor fund in the proprietary fund financial statements. This type of labeling would not be appropriate for the single Internal Service Fund, because the major fund reporting concept does not apply to this fund type.

Fiduciary funds are reported by fund type rather than by major fund. A governmental entity may have a single fund in one of the fiduciary fund types (Pension or Other Employee Benefit Trust Funds, Private-Purpose Trust Funds, Investment Trust Funds, or Agency Funds). If there is only a single fund in each fiduciary fund type, there is no need to prepare combining financial statements or individual fund financial statements as part of supplementary information. For example, if a governmental entity has a single Pension Trust Fund to report, its balances and activities are reported as a separate column in the basic financial statements (fiduciary fund financial statements) and its separate column presentation serves as its individual financial statements.

Finally, when a governmental entity has only a single nonmajor discretely presented component unit, there is no need to present its balances and activities as part of a combining financial statements or as individual financial statements. It will be recalled that discretely presented major component units are reported in the entity's basic financial statements in one of the following ways:

- Present each major component unit in a separate column in the government-wide financial statements
- Present combining statements as part of the basic financial statements
- Present condensed financial statements in a note to the financial statements

If the entity has a single nonmajor discretely presented component unit, its financial information would be reported as a separate column (appropriately labeled as a nonmajor component unit) either on the face of the government-wide financial statements, in the combining financial statements (which are part of the basic financial statements rather than supplementary information), or in a note to the financial statements.

Budgetary Information Not Part of the General Purpose External Financial Statements

Budgetary comparison schedules (part of required supplementary information) or budgetary comparison financial statements (part of the basic financial statements) must be presented for the General Fund and each major Special Revenue Fund that that has a legally adopted annual budget. In addition, budgetary comparison information must be presented as part of the supplementary information in the CAFR for any of the following funds that have legally adopted annual budgets:

- Nonmajor Special Revenue Funds
- Capital Projects Funds
- Debt Service Funds
- Permanent Funds

In addition, the GASB states that "more comprehensive budget presentations are generally to be preferred over the minimum standards," and for this reason some governmental entities present budgetary information not only for governmental funds but also for proprietary funds and trust funds whether or not budgetary information is based on an appropriated budget.

Individual fund financial statements (presented as supplementary information) may be used to present the budgetary information described above.

Additional Level of Budgetary Detail Requested

Budgetary information is generally presented at the functional level for the General Fund and major Special Revenue Funds that have a legally adopted annual budget; however, this presentation might not be at a level that demonstrates compliance with the legally adopted budget. A governmental entity may demonstrate such compliance by preparing individual budgetary financial statements that are included as supplementary information in the CAFR.

Comparative Financial Information

In most instances, because of their multicolumn presentation format, it is difficult to construct governmental financial statements (including combining financial statements) in a manner that compares current financial statements with those of the previous year. Alternatively, comparative financial statements (including comparative budgetary information) may be presented for an individual fund as part of the supplementary information in the CAFR. For example, a governmental entity could present comparative financial information for its General Fund for a two-year period as an individual financial statement in the supplementary information.

Demonstration of Finance-Related Contractual Compliance

When financial statements are formatted as part of the basic financial statements or as part of combining financial statements, their detail accounts are often combined or described in a manner that diminishes their descriptiveness. Although that lack of description might be advantageous from an overall perspective, it might not enable a particular fund to demonstrate its compliance with finance-related contractual requirements. Such compliance may be achieved by presenting individual financial statements (generally for a governmental fund, such as a Capital Projects Fund, or an Enterprise Fund) that are formatted to demonstrate compliance with finance-related contractual requirements.

CHAPTER 20
STATISTICAL SECTION

CONTENTS

INTRODUCTION

GASB-44 (Economic Condition Reporting: The Statistical Section—an amendment of NCGA Statement) established new reporting requirements for a government's statistical section of its annual report *when a statistical section is presented.* The GASB recommends that state and local governments prepare a CAFR that includes a statistical section; however, governments are not required to prepare a CAFR. Therefore, a statistical section is not required *unless the government presents its basic financial statements within a CAFR.* GASB-44 addresses three shortcomings identified in the statistical section of the report that have existed since NCGA-1 (Governmental Accounting and Financial Reporting Principles) was issued in 1979:

1. NCGA-1 listed 15 required schedules but provided no explanation of the nature of the information they were to contain.

2. The statistical section required schedules to be oriented toward general-purpose governments and did not provide guidance for special-purpose governments.

3. The NCGA-1 requirements for the statistical section were obviously not developed with GASB-34 (Basic Financial Statements—and Management's Discussion and Analysis—for State and Local Governments) government-wide information in mind.

These shortcomings often caused incomplete and inconsistent application of the standards resulting in diminished usefulness and comparability of statistical information.

With the issuance of GASB-44, GASB redefined the objectives of reporting statistical section information as follows: "To provide financial statement users with additional historical perspective, context, and detail to assist in using the information in the financial statements, notes to financial statements, and required supplementary information to understand and assess a government's economic condition."

PRACTICE ALERT: GASB-44 is only an initial assessment of economic condition. The GASB is in the midst of studying how to best portray the economic condition of a government and whether or not a government has programs and services that are fiscally sustainable. There is a possibility that aspects of intergovernmental fiscal dependency will also be included in the project. A due-process document is not expected until late in 2011.

ANALYSIS AND IMPLEMENTATION

Governments that include their basic financial statements in a CAFR, and therefore are required to prepare a statistical section, will be significantly affected by the changes resulting from GASB-44. In an effort to resolve the shortcomings of NCGA-1 regarding CAFR statistical sections, the GASB categorized the required statistical information into five categories that describe the nature of the required information:

Financial trends information This information is intended to assist users in understanding and assessing how a government's financial position has changed over time. Examples for general purpose governments include:

— Net assets by component, last 10 fiscal years;

— Changes in net assets, last 10 fiscal years

— Fund balances, governmental funds, last 10 fiscal years; and

— Changes in fund balances, governmental funds, last 10 fiscal years.

Revenue capacity information This information is intended to assist users in understanding and assessing the factors affecting a government's ability to generate its own-source revenues. Examples for general purpose governments include:

— Assessed and actual values of taxable property, last 10 fiscal years;

— Direct and overlapping property tax rates, last 10 fiscal years;

— Principal property taxpayers, current year and nine years ago; and

— Property tax levies and collections, last 10 fiscal years.

Debt capacity information This information is intended to assist users in understanding and assessing a government's debt burden and its ability to issue additional debt. Examples for general purpose governments include:

— Ratios of outstanding debt by type, last 10 fiscal years;

— Ratios of general bonded debt outstanding, last 10 fiscal years;

— Direct and overlapping governmental activities debt as of current year end;

— Legal debt margin, last 10 fiscal years; and

— Pledged revenue coverage, last 10 fiscal years.

Demographic and economic information This information is intended to assist users in understanding the socioeconomic environment within which a government operates and to provide information that facilitates comparisons among governments over time. Examples for general purpose governments include

— Demographic and economic statistics, last 10 calendar years; and

— Principal employers, current year and nine years ago.

Operating information This information is intended to provide contextual data about a government's operations and resources to aid users in understanding and assessing economic condition. Examples for general purpose governments include:

— Full-time equivalent employees by function/program, last 10 fiscal years;

— Operating indicators by function/program, last 10 fiscal years; and

— Capital asset statistics by function/program, last 10 fiscal years. . . .

Appendix C to GASB-44 provides comprehensive illustrated examples of the various statistical schedules. These illustrations provide example schedules for both general purpose governments and special purpose governments within the five categories discussed previously. For example, revenue capacity information for a water utility would include such historical schedules as

- Water sold by type of customer, last 10 fiscal years; and
- Water rates, last 10 fiscal years.

By providing example schedules for special purpose governments in relation to the five categories of required statistical information, the GASB has improved the likelihood of usefulness and comparability of statistical information in the CAFR for these types of entities. . . .

The statistical section requirements of GASB-44 includes 10 year trend information about net assets and changes in net assets as produced in the GASB-44 government-wide financial statements. This is likely the most significant addition to the statistical section resulting from the new requirements of GASB-44. In addition, debt information within the statistical section will be more comprehensive and include the expanded information from the government-wide statements and notes.

PRACTICE POINT: Governments that prepare or are planning to prepare a CAFR should get an early start on gathering the information for the new and revised information for the statistical section. In addition to new and revised schedules, GASB-44 also requires the schedules to include narrative information about the sources, assumptions, and methodologies used in presenting the information. The schedules should also contain explanations for atypical and anomalous data that is needed for sufficient understanding of the schedules.

APPENDIX 20A: ILLUSTRATIONS ON STATISTICAL SECTION

This appendix illustrates the display and disclosure requirements of GASB-44. It is presented for illustrative purposes only and is non-authoritative. These sample statistical section schedules are presented to assist the reader of this Statement in understanding its requirements and alternatives. Amounts are not reflected in the statistical section in order to concentrate on the specific requirements and/or specific formatting.

This appendix presents a cover sheet (Exhibit 20A-1) that presents information explaining each category and illustrates of all the required schedules. It is organized by category of statistical section information. For example, Exhibits 20A-2 through 20A-5 illustrates the schedules of financial trends information of a typical city. A complete set of statistical section schedules for this illustrative city government (City of Centerville) is as follows:

Schedule number	Type of schedule
20A-1	Statistical Section Cover Sheet
20A-2, 20A-3, 20A-4, 20A-5	Financial trends schedules
20A-6, 20A-7, 20A-8, 20A-9	Revenue capacity schedules
20A-10, 20A-11, 20A-12, 20A-13, 20A-14	Debt capacity schedules
20A-15, 20A-16	Demographic and economic schedules
20A-17, 20A-18, 20A-19	Operating schedules

Governments should use the format that is most appropriate and useful for their situation, based on the requirements set forth in GASB-44 and the needs of their financial statement users.

Most of the illustrations are limited to a single page. Matters of presentation and formatting, unless specifically addressed by this GASB-44, are left to the judgment of the government financial statement preparer. Some governments may wish to present some of these schedules on two or more pages to improve the readability and usefulness of the schedules.

Schedules of Financial Trends Information

GASB-44 states that the objective of the financial trends information is "to assist users in understanding and assessing how a government's financial position has changed over time." Governments are required to present schedules with the following two types of information:

1. Net assets

2. Changes in net assets

Governments that report modified accrual information for governmental funds are also required to present schedules with information about fund balances and changes in fund balances. GASB-44 encourages, but does not require, governments to implement the schedules containing government-wide information retroactively to the year they implemented GASB-34.

GASB-44 states that financial statement preparers should consider the following:

> if a government did not previously prepare one or more of the governmental funds schedules, it may implement them prospectively and is not required to retroactively report years prior to the implementation date of [GASB-44]. However, governments are encouraged to report retroactively if the information is readily available.

> Furthermore, if a government prepared such a schedule prior to implementation but presented information that is different from what [GASB-44] now requires, the government is encouraged but not required to restate prior years. If a government does not restate prior years, it should explain on the face of the schedule how the information prior to implementation differs from the information following implementation. If a government previously prepared any of these schedules with greater detail than is illustrated in these exhibits, it does not need to change or reduce the level of detail unless specifically required to do so.

Exhibit 20A-1 illustrates the cover of a government's statistical section of its annual report when a statistical section is presented.

Exhibit 20A-1: Cover of a Government's Statistical Section of Its Annual Report.

Statistical Section

This part of the City of Centerville's comprehensive annual financial report presents detailed information as a context for understanding what the information in the financial statements, note disclosures, and required supplementary information says about the city's overall financial health.

Contents	Page
Financial Trends	XXX

These schedules contain trend information to help the reader understand how the city's financial performance and well-being have changed over time.

Revenue Capacity   XXX

These schedules contain information to help the reader assess the city's most significant local revenue source, the property tax.

Debt Capacity   XXX

These schedules present information to help the reader assess the affordability of the city's current levels of outstanding debt and the city's ability to issue additional debt in the future.

Demographic and Economic Information   XXX

These schedules offer demographic and economic indicators to help the reader understand the environment within which the city's financial activities take place.

Contents	Page
Operating Information	XXX

These schedules contain service and infrastructure data to help the reader understand how the information in the city's financial report relates to the services the city provides and the activities it performs.

Sources: Unless otherwise noted, the information in these schedules is derived from the comprehensive annual financial reports for the relevant year. The city implemented GASB Statement 34 in 20X1; schedules presenting government-wide information include information beginning in that year.

Exhibit 20A-2, Exhibit 20A-3, Exhibit 20A-4, and Exhibit 20A-5 are illustrations of the required schedules of financial trends information.

Exhibit 20A-2: Net Assets by Component, Last Ten Fiscal Years.

Schedule 1
City of Centerville
Net Assets by
Component,
Last Ten Fiscal
Years

	Fiscal Year	
	20X1	20X2
Governmental activities		
Invested in capital assets, net of related debt	$ xxx,xxx,xxx	$ xxx,xxx,xxx
Restricted	xx,xxx,xxx	xx,xxx,xxx
Unrestricted	xx,xxx,xx	xx,xxx,xxx
Total governmental activities net assets	$ xxx,xxx,xxx	$ xxx,xxx,xxx
Business-type activities		
Invested in capital assets, net of related debt	$ xxx,xxx,xxx	$ xxx,xxx,xxx
Unrestricted	xx,xxx,xxx	xx,xxx,xxx
Total business-type activities net assets	$ xxx,xxx,xxx	$ xxx,xxx,xxx
Primary government		
Invested in capital assets, net of related debt	$ xxx,xxx,xxx	$ xxx,xxx,xxx
Restricted	xx,xxx,xxx	xx,xxx,xxx
Unrestricted	xxx,xxx,xxx	xxx,xxx,xxx
Total primary government net assets	$ xxx,xxx,xxx	$ xxx,xxx,xxx

Exhibit 20A-3: Changes in Net Assets, Last Ten Fiscal Years.

Schedule 2
City of Centerville
Changes in Net Assets, Last Ten Fiscal Years

	Fiscal Year	
	20X1	**20X2**
Expenses		
Governmental activities:		
General government	$ xx,xxx,xxx	$ xx,xxx,xxx
Police	xx,xxx,xxx	xx,xxx,xxx
Fire	xx,xxx,xxx	xx,xxx,xxx
Refuse collection	xx,xxx,xxx	xx,xxx,xxx
Other public works	xx,xxx,xxx	xx,xxx,xxx
Redevelopment	xx,xxx,xxx	xx,xxx,xxx
Parks and recreation	xx,xxx,xxx	xx,xxx,xxx
Library	xx,xxx,xxx	xx,xxx,xxx
Interest on long-term debt	xx,xxx,xxx	xx,xxx,xxx
Total governmental activities expenses	xxx,xxx,xxx	xxx,xxx,xxx
Business-type activities:		
Water	xx,xxx,xxx	xx,xxx,xxx
Wastewater	xx,xxx,xxx	xx,xxx,xxx
Transit	xxx,xxx	xxx,xxx
Total business-type activities expenses	xx,xxx,xxx	xx,xxx,xxx
Total primary government expenses	$ xxx,xxx,xxx	$ xxx,xxx,xxx
Program Revenues		
Governmental activities:		
Charges for services:		
Refuse collection	$ x,xxx,xxx	$ x,xxx,xxx
Other public works	x,xxx,xxx	x,xxx,xxx
Parks and recreation	x,xxx,xxx	x,xxx,xxx
Other activities	x,xxx,xxx	x,xxx,xxx
Operating grants and contributions	x,xxx,xxx	x,xxx,xxx
Capital grants and contributions	x,xxx,xxx	x,xxx,xxx
Total governmental activities program revenues	xx,xxx,xxx	xx,xxx,xxx
Business-type activities:		
Charges for services:		
Water	xx,xxx,xxx	xx,xxx,xxx
Wastewater	x,xxx,xxx	x,xxx,xxx
Other activities	xxx,xxx	xxx,xxx

	Fiscal Year	
	20X1	**20X2**
Operating grants and contributions	xx,xxx,xxx	xx,xxx,xxx
Capital grants and contributions	xxx,xxx	xxx,xxx
Total business-type activities program revenues	xx,xxx,xxx	xx,xxx,xxx
Total primary government program revenues	$ xx,xxx,xxx	$ xx,xxx,xxx

Net (Expense)/Revenue

Governmental activities	$ (xx,xxx,xxx)	$ (xx,xxx,xxx)
Business-type activities	xxx,xxx	x,xxx,xxx
Total primary government net expense	$ (xx,xxx,xxx)	$ (xx,xxx,xxx)

General Revenues and Other Changes in Net Assets

Governmental activities:

Taxes		
Property taxes	$ xx,xxx,xxx	$ xx,xxx,xxx
Franchise taxes	x,xxx,xxx	x,xxx,xxx
Sales taxes	xx,xxx,xxx	xx,xxx,xxx
Other taxes	x,xxx,xxx	x,xxx,xxx
Unrestricted grants and contributions	x,xxx,xxx	x,xxx,xxx
Payments in lieu of taxes	xx,xxx,xxx	x,xxx,xxx
Investment earnings	x,xxx,xxx	x,xxx,xxx
Miscellaneous	x,xxx,xxx	x,xxx,xxx
Transfers	x,xxx,xxx	(x,xxx,xxx)
Total governmental activities	xx,xxx,xxx	xx,xxx,xxx

Business-type activities:

Investment earnings	x,xxx,xxx	x,xxx,xxx
Transfers	(x,xxx,xxx)	x,xxx,xxx
Total business-type activities	x,xxx,xxx	x,xxx,xxx
Total primary government	$ xx,xxx,xxx	$ xx,xxx,xxx

Change in Net Assets

Governmental activities	$ xx,xxx,xxx	$ xx,xxx,xxx
Business-type activities	x,xxx,xxx	x,xxx,xxx
Total primary government	$ xx,xxx,xxx	$ xx,xxx,xxx

Exhibit 20A-4: Fund Balances, Governmental Funds, Last Ten Fiscal Years.

Schedule 3
City of Centerville
Fund Balances, Governmental Funds,
Last Ten Fiscal Years
(modified accrual basis of accounting)

	Fiscal Year									
	20X0	20X1	20X2	20X3	20X4	20X5	20X6	20X7	20X8	20X9
General Fund										
Reserved	$ x,xxx,xxx	$ x,xxx,xxx	$ x,xxx,xxx	$ x,xxx,xxx	$ x,xxx,xxx	$ x,xxx,xxx	$ x,xxx,xxx	$ x,xxx,xxx	$ x,xxx,xxx	$ x,xxx,xxx
Unreserved	xx,xxx,xxx	xx,xxx,xxx	xx,xxx,xxx	xx,xxx,xxx	xx,xxx,xxx	xx,xxx,xxx	xx,xxx,xxx	xx,xxx,xxx	xx,xxx,xxx	xx,xxx,xxx
Total general fund	$ xx,xxx,xxx	$ xx,xxx,xxx	$ xx,xxx,xxx	$ xx,xxx,xxx	$ xx,xxx,xxx	$ xx,xxx,xxx	$ xx,xxx,xxx	$ xx,xxx,xxx	$ xx,xxx,xxx	$ xx,xxx,xxx
All Other Governmental Funds										
Reserved	$ xx,xxx,xxx	$ xx,xxx,xxx	$ xx,xxx,xxx	$ xx,xxx,xxx	$ xx,xxx,xxx	$ xx,xxx,xxx	$ xx,xxx,xxx	$ xx,xxx,xxx	$ xx,xxx,xxx	$ xx,xxx,xxx
Unreserved, reported in:										
Special revenue funds	x,xxx,xxx	x,xxx,xxx	x,xxx,xxx	x,xxx,xxx	x,xxx,xxx	x,xxx,xxx	x,xxx,xxx	x,xxx,xxx	x,xxx,xxx	x,xxx,xxx
Capital projects funds	x,xxx,xxx	x,xxx,xxx	x,xxx,xxx	x,xxx,xxx	x,xxx,xxx	x,xxx,xxx	x,xxx,xxx	x,xxx,xxx	x,xxx,xxx	x,xxx,xxx
Debt service funds	x,xxx,xxx	x,xxx,xxx	x,xxx,xxx	x,xxx,xxx	x,xxx,xxx	x,xxx,xxx	x,xxx,xxx	x,xxx,xxx	x,xxx,xxx	x,xxx,xxx
Total all other governmental funds	$ xx,xxx,xxx	$ xx,xxx,xxx	$ xx,xxx,xxx	$ xx,xxx,xxx	$ xx,xxx,xxx	$ xx,xxx,xxx	$ xx,xxx,xxx	$ xx,xxx,xxx	$ xx,xxx,xxx	$ xx,xxx,xxx

NOTE ON EXHIBIT 20A-4, Schedule 3: GASB-54, paragraph 36 stipulates that fund balance reclassifications made to conform to the provisions of GASB-54 should be applied retroactively by restating fund balance for all prior periods presented. Changes to the fund balance information presented in a statistical section may be made prospectively, although retroactive application is *encouraged*. If the information for previous years is not restated, governments should explain the nature of the differences from the prior information. For this reason, two alternatives of presentation emerge. The government can restate all ten years of this exhibit as follows:

General Fund:

Nonspendable	$XXXX
Restricted	XXXX
Committed	XXXX
Assigned	XXXX
Unassigned	XXXX
Total General Fund	$XXXX

All Other Governmental Funds Combined

Nonspendable	$XXXX
Restricted	XXXX
Committed	XXXX
Assigned	XXXX
Unassigned	XXXX (only if negative and no assigned balances)
Total Governmental Funds	$XXXX

The second alternative is to present the existing schedule until it "ages" out over ten years and the schedule that is compliant with GASB-54 starting with periods beginning after June 15, 2010 and forward. The schedule would be as follows:

	Periods ending 2010 and before (present each year)	Periods ending 2011 and after (present each year)
General Fund		
Reserved	$XXXX	
Unreserved	XXXX	
Nonspendable		XXXX
Restricted		XXXX
Committed		XXXX
Assigned		XXXX
Unassigned		XXXX
Total general fund	XXXX	
All Other Governmental Funds		
Reserved	XXXX	

Unreserved, reported in:
    Special revenue funds   XXXX
    Capital projects funds   XXXX
    Debt service funds   XXXX
Nonspendable   XXXX
Restricted   XXXX
Committed   XXXX
Assigned   XXXX

Total all other governmental funds   XXXX

Exhibit 20A-5: Changes in Fund Balances, Governmental Funds, Last Ten Fiscal Years.

Schedule 4
City of Centerville
Changes in Fund Balances, Governmental Funds,
Last Ten Fiscal Years
(modified accrual basis of accounting)

	Fiscal Year									
	20X0	20X1	20X2	20X3	20X4	20X5	20X6	20X7	20X8	20X9
Revenues										
Taxes	$ xx,xxx,xxx	$ xx,xxx,xxx	$ xx,xxx,xxx	$ xx,xxx,xxx	$ xx,xxx,xxx	$ xx,xxx,xxx	$ xx,xxx,xxx	$ xx,xxx,xxx	$ xx,xxx,xxx	$ xx,xxx,xxx
Licenses, fees and permits	x,xxx,xxx	x,xxx,xxx	x,xxx,xxx	x,xxx,xxx	x,xxx,xxx	xx,xxx,xxx	x,xxx,xxx	xx,xxx,xxx	x,xxx,xxx	xx,xxx,xxx
Fines and penalties	xxx,xxx	xxx,xxx	xxx,xxx	xxx,xxx	xxx,xxx	xxx,xxx	xxx,xxx	xxx,xxx	x,xxx,xxx	x,xxx,xxx
Charges for services	x,xxx,xxx	x,xxx,xxx	x,xxx,xxx	x,xxx,xxx	x,xxx,xxx	x,xxx,xxx	x,xxx,xxx	x,xxx,xxx	xx,xxx,xxx	xx,xxx,xxx
Special assessments	xx,xxx,xxx	xx,xxx,xxx	xx,xxx,xxx	x,xxx,xxx	x,xxx,xxx	x,xxx,xxx	xx,xxx,xxx	x,xxx,xxx	x,xxx,xxx	x,xxx,xxx
Intergovernmental	xx,xxx,xxx	xx,xxx,xxx	xx,xxx,xxx	x,xxx,xxx	xx,xxx,xxx	xx,xxx,xxx	xx,xxx,xxx	xx,xxx,xxx	xx,xxx,xxx	xx,xxx,xxx
Investment earnings	xx,xxx,xxx	xx,xxx,xxx	xx,xxx,xxx	x,xxx,xxx	xx,xxx,xxx	xx,xxx,xxx	x,xxx,xxx	xx,xxx,xxx	x,xxx,xxx	xx,xxx,xxx
Other revenues	x,xxx,xxx	x,xxx,xxx	x,xxx,xxx	x,xxx,xxx	xx,xxx,xxx	xx,xxx,xxx	xx,xxx,xxx	xx,xxx,xxx	xx,xxx,xxx	xx,xxx,xxx
Total revenues	xx,xxx,xxx	xx,xxx,xxx	xx,xxx,xxx	xx,xxx,xxx	xx,xxx,xxx	xx,xxx,xxx	xx,xxx,xxx	xxx,xxx,xxx	xxx,xxx,xxx	xxx,xxx,xxx
Expenditures										
General government	x,xxx,xxx	x,xxx,xxx	x,xxx,xxx	x,xxx,xxx	x,xxx,xxx	x,xxx,xxx	x,xxx,xxx	xx,xxx,xxx	xx,xxx,xxx	xx,xxx,xxx
Police	xx,xxx,xxx	xx,xxx,xxx	xx,xxx,xxx	xx,xxx,xxx	xx,xxx,xxx	xx,xxx,xxx	xx,xxx,xxx	xx,xxx,xxx	xx,xxx,xxx	xx,xxx,xxx
Fire	x,xxx,xxx	x,xxx,xxx	x,xxx,xxx	x,xxx,xxx	x,xxx,xxx	xx,xxx,xxx	xx,xxx,xxx	xx,xxx,xxx	xx,xxx,xxx	xx,xxx,xxx
Refuse collection	x,xxx,xxx	x,xxx,xxx	x,xxx,xxx	x,xxx,xxx	x,xxx,xxx	x,xxx,xxx	x,xxx,xxx	x,xxx,xxx	x,xxx,xxx	x,xxx,xxx
Other public works	xx,xxx,xxx	x,xxx,xxx	x,xxx,xxx	xx,xxx,xxx	x,xxx,xxx	x,xxx,xxx	x,xxx,xxx	x,xxx,xxx	x,xxx,xxx	x,xxx,xxx
Parks and recreation	x,xxx,xxx	x,xxx,xxx	x,xxx,xxx	x,xxx,xxx	x,xxx,xxx	x,xxx,xxx	x,xxx,xxx	x,xxx,xxx	x,xxx,xxx	xx,xxx,xxx

Fiscal Year

	20X0	20X1	20X2	20X3	20X4	20X5	20X6	20X7	20X8	20X9
Library	x,xxx,xxx	x,xxx,xxx	x,xxx,xxx	x,xxx,xxx	x,xxx,xxx	x,xxx,xxx	x,xxx,xxx	x,xxx,xxx	x,xxx,xxx	x,xxx,xxx
Capital outlay	xx,xxx,xxx	xx,xxx,xxx	xx,xxx,xxx	xx,xxx,xxx	xx,xxx,xxx	xx,xxx,xxx	xx,xxx,xxx	xx,xxx,xxx	xx,xxx,xxx	xx,xxx,xxx
Debt service										
Interest	xx,xxx,xxx	xx,xxx,xxx	xx,xxx,xxx	xx,xxx,xxx	xx,xxx,xxx	xx,xxx,xxx	xx,xxx,xxx	xx,xxx,xxx	xx,xxx,xxx	xx,xxx,xxx
Principal	x,xxx,xxx	x,xxx,xxx	x,xxx,xxx	x,xxx,xxx	x,xxx,xxx	x,xxx,xxx	x,xxx,xxx	x,xxx,xxx	x,xxx,xxx	x,xxx,xxx
Total expenditures	xx,xxx,xxx	xx,xxx,xxx	xx,xxx,xxx	xx,xxx,xxx	xx,xxx,xxx	xx,xxx,xxx	xx,xxx,xxx	xx,xxx,xxx	xx,xxx,xxx	xx,xxx,xxx
Excess of revenues over (under) expenditures	(xx,xxx,xxx)	(xx,xxx,xxx)	(xx,xxx,xxx)	(xx,xxx,xxx)	(x,xxx,xxx)	x,xxx,xxx	(x,xxx,xxx)	x,xxx,xxx	x,xxx,xxx	(x,xxx,xxx)
Other Financing Sources (Uses)										
Proceeds from borrowing	—	—	xx,xxx,xxx	—	x,xxx,xxx	—	—	—	—	x,xxx,xxx
Proceeds from refunding	—	—	—	—	—	—	—	xx,xxx,xxx	—	xx,xxx,xxx
Payments to escrow agent								(xx,xxx,xxx)		(xx,xxx,xxx)
Transfers in	xx,xxx,xxx	xx,xxx,xxx	xx,xxx,xxx	xx,xxx,xxx	xx,xxx,xxx	x,xxx,xxx	x,xxx,xxx	xx,xxx,xxx	xx,xxx,xxx	x,xxx,xxx
Transfers out	(x,xxx,xxx)	(x,xxx,xxx)	(x,xxx,xxx)	(x,xxx,xxx)	(x,xxx,xxx)	(x,xxx,xxx)	(x,xxx,xxx)	(x,xxx,xxx)	(x,xxx,xxx)	(x,xxx,xxx)
Total other financing sources (uses)	xx,xxx,xxx	xx,xxx,xxx	xx,xxx,xxx	xx,xxx,xxx	xx,xxx,xxx	xx,xxx,xxx	x,xxx,xxx	x,xxx,xxx	x,xxx,xxx	x,xxx,xxx
Net change in fund balances	$ (x,xxx,xxx)	$(x,xxx,xxx)	$(x,xxx,xxx)	$ x,xxx,xxx	$ x,xxx,xxx	$xxx,xxx	$(x,xxx,xxx)	$ xx,xxx,xxx	$ x,xxx,xxx	$ x,xxx,xxx
Debt service as a percentage of noncapital expenditures	xx.x%	xx.x%	xx.x%	xx.x%	xx.x%	xx.x%	xx.x%	xx.x%	xx.x%	xx.x%

Schedules of Revenue Capacity Information

GASB-44 states that the objective of revenue capacity information is "to assist users in understanding and assessing the factors affecting a government's ability to generate its own-source revenues." Governments are required to present schedules with the following three types of information:

1. Revenue base
2. Revenue rates
3. Principal revenue payers

If a government presents revenue capacity information about a property tax, it should also present information about property tax levies and collections.

Exhibit 20A-6, Exhibit 20A-7, Exhibit 20A-8, and Exhibit 20A-9 are illustrations of the required schedules of revenue capacity information.

Exhibit 20A-6 assumes that property is assessed at actual value; therefore, separate assessed and actual data are not presented.

With regard to Exhibit 20A-7, state governments are not required to present information about the revenue rates of the overlapping governments within their borders. Regional governments are encouraged, but not required, to present overlapping rate information.

With regard to Exhibit 20A-8, governments should present a schedule of principal payers of the own-source revenue presented in its schedules of revenue base and rate information. See also Exhibit 20A-9.

Exhibit 20A-6: Assessed Value and Actual Value of Taxable Property, Last Ten Fiscal Years.

Schedule 5
City of Centerville
Assessed Value and Actual Value of Taxable Property,
Last Ten Fiscal Years
(in thousands of dollars)

Fiscal Year Ended December 31,	Residential Property	Commercial Property	Industrial Property	Less: Tax-Exempt Property	Total Taxable Assessed Value	Total Direct Tax Rate
20X0	$ x,xxx,xxx	$ x,xxx,xxx	$ x,xxx,xxx	$ xxx,xxx	$ x,xxx,xxx	$ x.xx
20X1	x,xxx,xxx	x,xxx,xxx	x,xxx,xxx	xxx,xxx	x,xxx,xxx	x.xx
20X2	x,xxx,xxx	x,xxx,xxx	x,xxx,xxx	xxx,xxx	x,xxx,xxx	x.xx
20X3	x,xxx,xxx	x,xxx,xxx	x,xxx,xxx	xxx,xxx	x,xxx,xxx	x.xx
20X4	x,xxx,xxx	x,xxx,xxx	x,xxx,xxx	xxx,xxx	x,xxx,xxx	x.xx
20X5	x,xxx,xxx	x,xxx,xxx	x,xxx,xxx	xxx,xxx	x,xxx,xxx	x.xx
20X6	x,xxx,xxx	x,xxx,xxx	x,xxx,xxx	xxx,xxx	x,xxx,xxx	x.xx
20X7	x,xxx,xxx	x,xxx,xxx	x,xxx,xxx	x,xxx,xxx	x,xxx,xxx	x.xx
20X8	x,xxx,xxx	x,xxx,xxx	x,xxx,xxx	x,xxx,xxx	x,xxx,xxx	x.xx
20X9	x,xxx,xxx	x,xxx,xxx	x,xxx,xxx	x,xxx,xxx	x,xxx,xxx	x.xx

Source: Centerville County Board of Equalization and Assessment.

Note: Property in the city is reassessed each year. Property is assessed at actual value; therefore, the assessed values are equal to actual value. Tax rates are per $1,000 of assessed value.

Exhibit 20A-7: Direct and Overlapping Property Tax Rates, Last Ten Fiscal Years.

Schedule 6
City of Centerville
Direct and Overlapping Property Tax Rates,
Last Ten Fiscal Years
(rate per $1,000 of assessed value)

| Fiscal Year | Basic Rate | City Direct Rates | | | | Overlapping Rates[a] | | |
		General Obligation Debt Service	Redevelopment Debt Service	Redevelopment Program	Total Direct	Centerville School District	Centerville Flood Control District	Centerville County
20X0	$x.xx	$ x.xx	$ x.xx	$ x.xx	$ x.xx	$ x.xx	$ x.xx	$ x.xx
20X1	x.xx	x.xx	x.xx	x.xx	x.xx	x.xx	x.xx	x.xx
20X2	x.xx	x.xx	x.xx	x.xx	x.xx	x.xx	x.xx	x.xx
20X3	x.xx	x.xx	x.xx	x.xx	x.xx	x.xx	x.xx	x.xx
20X4	x.xx	x.xx	x.xx	x.xx	x.xx	x.xx	x.xx	x.xx
20X5	x.xx	x.xx	x.xx	x.xx	x.xx	x.xx	x.xx	x.xx
20X6	x.xx	x.xx	x.xx	x.xx	x.xx	x.xx	x.xx	x.xx
20X7	x.xx	x.xx	x.xx	x.xx	x.xx	x.xx	x.xx	x.xx
20X8	x.xx	x.xx	x.xx	x.xx	x.xx	x.xx	x.xx	x.xx
20X9	x.xx	x.xx	x.xx	x.xx	x.xx	x.xx	x.xx	x.xx

Source: Centerville County Board of Equalization and Assessment.

Note: The city's basic property tax rate may be increased only by a majority vote of the city's residents. Rates for debt service are set based on each year's requirements.

[a] Overlapping rates are those of local and county governments that apply to property owners within the City of Centerville. Not all overlapping rates apply to all Centerville property owners; for example, although the county property tax rates apply to all city property owners, the Flood Control District rates apply only to the approximately one-third of city property owners whose property is located within that district's geographic boundaries.

Exhibit 20A-8: Principal Property Tax Payers, Current Year and Nine Years Ago.

Schedule 7
City of Centerville
Principal Property Tax Payers,
Current Year and Nine Years Ago

Taxpayer	20X9 Taxable Assessed Value	20X9 Rank	20X9 Percentage of Total City Taxable Assessed Value	20X0 Taxable Assessed Value	20X0 Rank	20X0 Percentage of Total City Taxable Assessed Value
Soy Farmers of America, Inc.	$ xxx,xxx,xxx	1	x.xx%	$ xx,xxx,xxx	1	x.xx%
Starwood Health First, Inc.	xx,xxx,xxx	2	x.xx	xx,xxx,xxx	4	x.xx
MP Energy Partners Ltd.	xx,xxx,xxx	3	x.xx	—		—
New Start Laboratories	xx,xxx,xxx	4	x.xx	xx,xxx,xxx	3	x.xx
Cross Car Fresheners	xx,xxx,xxx	5	x.xx	x,xxx,xxx	7	x.xx
Oklahoma First Power	xx,xxx,xxx	6	x.xx	—		—
Willow Box Corp.	xx,xxx,xxx	7	x.xx	—		—
Dreamland Properties Limited	xx,xxx,xxx	8	x.xx	xx,xxx,xxx	6	x.xx
AmericaFirst, Inc.	xx,xxx,xxx	9	x.xx	—		—
Crawford Industries	xx,xxx,xxx	10	x.xx	xx,xxx,xxx	2	x.xx
Loyd Energy Partners Ltd.	—		—	xx,xxx,xxx	5	x.xx
Backwoods Country Ltd.	—		—	xx,xxx,xxx	8	x.xx
Billy Bob Acres Ltd.	—		—	x,xxx,xxx	9	x.xx
Blackjack Wood Farms	—		—	x,xxx,xxx	10	x.xx
Chautauqua Foundries	—		—	x,xxx,xxx		x.xx
Total	$ xxx,xxx,xxx		x.xx%	$ xxx,xxx,xxx		x.xx%

Source: County Board of Equalization and Assessment.

Exhibit 20A-9: Property Tax Levies and Collections, Last Ten Fiscal Years.

Schedule 8
City of Centerville
Property Tax Levies and Collections,
Last Ten Fiscal Years

Fiscal Year Ended December 31,	Taxes Levied for the Fiscal Year	Collected within the Fiscal Year of the Levy		Collections In Subsequent Years	Total Collections to Date	
		Amount	Percentage of Levy		Amount	Percentage of Levy
20X0	$ xx,xxx,xxx	$ xx,xxx,xxx	xx.xx%	$ x,xxx,xxx	$ xx,xxx,xxx	xx.xx%
20X1	xx,xxx,xxx	xx,xxx,xxx	xx.xx	x,xxx,xxx	xx,xxx,xxx	xx.xx
20X2	xx,xxx,xxx	xx,xxx,xxx	xx.xx	x,xxx,xxx	xx,xxx,xxx	xx.xx
20X3	xx,xxx,xxx	xx,xxx,xxx	xx.xx	x,xxx,xxx	xx,xxx,xxx	xx.xx
20X4	xx,xxx,xxx	xx,xxx,xxx	xx.xx	x,xxx,xxx	xx,xxx,xxx	xx.xx
20X5	xx,xxx,xxx	xx,xxx,xxx	xx.xx	x,xxx,xxx	xx,xxx,xxx	xx.xx
20X6	xx,xxx,xxx	xx,xxx,xxx	xx.xx	x,xxx,xxx	xx,xxx,xxx	xx.xx
20X7	xx,xxx,xxx	xx,xxx,xxx	xx.xx	x,xxx,xxx	xx,xxx,xxx	xx.xx
20X8	xx,xxx,xxx	xx,xxx,xxx	xx.xx	xxx,xxx	xx,xxx,xxx	xx.xx
20X9	xx,xxx,xxx	xx,xxx,xxx	xx.xx	—	xx,xxx,xxx	xx.xx

Sources: Centerville County Board of Equalization and Assessment and Centerville County Department of Finance.

Schedules of Debt Capacity Information

GASB-44 states that the objectives in providing debt capacity information is "to assist users in understanding and assessing a government's debt burden and ability to issue additional debt." Governments are required to present schedules with the following four types of information:

1. Ratios of outstanding debt
2. Direct and overlapping debt
3. Debt limitations
4. Pledged-revenue coverage

Governments that have outstanding general obligation debt or other bonded debt financed with general governmental resources should provide additional information about ratios of general bonded debt.

Exhibit 20A-10, Exhibit 20A-11, Exhibit 20A-12, Exhibit 20A-13, and Exhibit 20A-14 are illustrations of the required debt capacity information.

With regard to Exhibit 20A-11, if a government has resources that are restricted to the repayment of the principal of general bonded debt outstanding, these amounts are to be shown in a schedule titled "Ratios of net general bonded debt outstanding."

State governments are not required to prepare the schedule shown in Exhibit 20A-12; however, county and regional governments are encouraged, but not required, to prepare this schedule.

The schedule in Exhibit 20A-13 requires presentation of the legal debt margin calculation for the most recent year; and the debt limit, debt applicable to the limit, legal debt margin, and a debt limit ratio for each of the last ten years.

GASB-44 requires that the schedule in Exhibit 20A-14 include all debt backed by pledged revenues, not just debt identified as "revenue bonds." Special assessment bonds should be included in the pledged-revenue-coverage schedule.

Exhibit 20A-10: Ratios of Outstanding Debt by Type, Last Ten Fiscal Years.

Schedule 9
City of Statistical
Ratios of Outstanding Debt by Type,
Last Ten Fiscal Years
(dollars in thousands, except per capita)

| | Governmental Activities | | | | | Business-Type Activities | | | | | | |
Fiscal Year	General Obligation Bonds	Redevelopment Bonds	Sales Tax Increment Bonds	Lease Revenue Bonds[a]	Special Assessment Bonds	Water Bonds	Term Loan Payable	Certificates of Participation	Capital Leases	Total Primary Government	Percentage of Personal Income[b]	Per Capita[b]
20X0	$ xx,xxx	$ —	$ x,xxx	$ xx,xxx	$ xx,xxx	$ —	$ —	$ —	$ x,xxx	$ xx,xxx	x.xx %	$ xxx
20X1	xx,xxx	—	x,xxx	xx,xxx	xx,xxx	—	—	—	x,xxx	xx,xxx	x.xx	xxx
20X2	x,xxx	xx,xxx	x,xxx	xx,xxx	xx,xxx	—	—	—	xxx	xxx,xxx	x.xx	x,xxx
20X3	x,xxx	xx,xxx	x,xxx	xx,xxx	xx,xxx	—	—	—	xxx	xxx,xxx	x.xx	x,xxx
20X4	x,xxx	xx,xxx	x,xxx	xx,xxx	xx,xxx	—	—	—	xxx	xxx,xxx	x.xx	x,xxx
20X5	x,xxx	xx,xxx	x,xxx	xx,xxx	xx,xxx	—	—	x,xxx	xxx	xxx,xxx	x.xx	x,xxx
20X6	x,xxx	xx,xxx	x,xxx	xx,xxx	xx,xxx	xx,xxx	—	x,xxx	xxx	xxx,xxx	x.xx	x,xxx
20X7	x,xxx	xx,xxx	x,xxx	xx,xxx	xx,xxx	xx,xxx	xx,xxx	x,xxx	xxx	xxx,xxx	x.xx	x,xxx
20X8	x,xxx	xx,xxx	x,xxx	xx,xxx	xx,xxx	xx,xxx	xx,xxx	x,xxx	xxx	xxx,xxx	x.xx	x,xxx
20X9	x,xxx	xx,xxx	x,xxx	xx,xxx	xx,xxx	xx,xxx	xx,xxx	x,xxx	xxx	xxx,xxx	x.xx	x,xxx

Note: Details regarding the city's outstanding debt can be found in the notes to the financial statements.

[a] In addition to $xx.x million of refunding lease revenue bonds, the city issued over $x million of new lease revenue bonds in 20X9.

[b] See Schedule 15 (Exhibit 20A-14) for personal income and population data. These ratios are calculated using personal income and population for the prior calendar year.

Exhibit 20A-11: Ratios of General Bonded Debt Outstanding, Last Ten Fiscal Years.

Schedule 10
City of Centerville
Ratios of General Bonded Debt Outstanding,
Last Ten Fiscal Years
(dollars in thousands, except per capita)

	General Bonded Debt Outstanding			Percentage of Actual Taxable Value[a] of Property	Per Capita[b]
Fiscal Year	General Obligation Bonds	Redevelopment Bonds	Total		
20X0	$ xx,xxx	$ —	$ xx,xxx	x.xx%	$ xxx.xx
20X1	xx,xxx	—	xx,xxx	x.xx	xxx.xx
20X2	x,xxx	xx,xxx	xx,xxx	x.xx	xxx.xx
20X3	x,xxx	xx,xxx	xx,xxx	x.xx	xxx.xx
20X4	x,xxx	xx,xxx	xx,xxx	x.xx	xxx.xx
20X5	x,xxx	xx,xxx	xx,xxx	x.xx	xxx.xx
20X6	x,xxx	xx,xxx	xx,xxx	x.xx	xxx.xx
20X7	x,xxx	xx,xxx	xx,xxx	x.xx	xxx.xx
20X8	x,xxx	xx,xxx	xx,xxx	x.xx	xxx.xx
20X9	x,xxx	xx,xxx	xx,xxx	x.xx	xxx.xx

Note: Details regarding the city's outstanding debt can be found in the notes to the financial statements.
[a] See Schedule 5 (Exhibit 20A-6) for property value data.
[b] Population data can be found in Schedule 14 (Exhibit 20A-15).

Exhibit 20A-12: Direct and Overlapping Governmental Activities Debt as of December 31, 20X2.

Schedule 11
City of Centerville
Direct and Overlapping Governmental Activities Debt
As of December 31, 20X9
(dollars in thousands)

Governmental Unit	Debt Outstanding	Estimated Percentage Applicable[a]	Estimated Share of Overlapping Debt
Debt repaid with property taxes			
Centerville School District	$ xx,xxx	xx.xxx%	$ xx,xxx
Centerville School District Facilities District #x	x,xxx	xxx.xxx%	x,xxx
Centerville School District Facilities District #x	x,xxx	xx.xxx%	x,xxx
Centerville School District Facilities District #x	x,xxx	xx.xxx%	x,xxx
Centerville County General Obligation Debt	xxx,xxx	xx.xxx%	xx,xxx
Other debt			
Centerville County Capital Leases	xx,xxx	xx.xxx%	x,xxx
Centerville County Economic Development Bonds	xx,xxx	x.xxx%	x,xxx

Governmental Unit	Debt Outstanding	Estimated Percentage Applicable[a]	Estimated Share of Overlapping Debt
Centerville County Loan: State Environmental Revolving Fund	xx,xxx	xx.xxx%	x,xxx
Centerville County—other debt	xx,xxx	xx.xxx%	x,xxx
Subtotal, overlapping debt			xxx,xxx
City direct debt			xx,xxx
Total direct and overlapping debt			$ xxx,xxx

Sources: Assessed value data used to estimate applicable percentages provided by the Centerville County Board of Equalization and Assessment. Debt outstanding data provided by each governmental unit.

Note: Overlapping governments are those that coincide, at least in part, with the geographic boundaries of the city. This schedule estimates the portion of the outstanding debt of those overlapping governments that is borne by the residents and businesses of Centerville. This process recognizes that, when considering the city's ability to issue and repay long-term debt, the entire debt burden borne by the residents and businesses should be taken into account. However, this does not imply that every taxpayer is a resident, and therefore responsible for repaying the debt, of each overlapping government.

[a] For debt repaid with property taxes, the percentage of overlapping debt applicable is estimated using taxable assessed property values. Applicable percentages were estimated by determining the portion of another governmental unit's taxable assessed value that is within the city's boundaries and dividing it by each unit's total taxable assessed value. This approach was also used for Centerville County's capital lease, loan, and other debt. The applicable percentage of Centerville County Economic Development Bonds, which are backed by county sales taxes, was estimated by dividing the city's retail sales by the county's retail sales.

Exhibit 20A-13: Legal Debt Margin Information, Last Ten Fiscal Years.

Schedule 12
City of Centerville
Legal Debt Margin Information,
Last Ten Fiscal Years
(dollars in thousands)

Legal Debt Margin Calculation for Fiscal Year xxXx

Assessed value	$ x,xxx,xxx
Debt limit (xx% of assessed value)	x,xxx,xxx
Debt applicable to limit:	
General obligation bonds	x,xxx
Less: Amount set aside for repayment of general obligation debt	(x,xxx)
Total net debt applicable to limit	x,xxx
Legal debt margin	$ x,xxx,xxx

Fiscal Year

	20X0	20X1	20X2	20X3	20X4	20X5	20X6	20X7	20X8	20X9
Debt limit	$ xxx,xxx	$ xxx,xxx	$ xxx,xxx	$ xxx,xxx	$ xxx,xxx	$ xxx,xxx	$ xxx,xxx	$ x,xxx,xxx	$ x,xxx,xxx	$ x,xxx,xxx
Total net debt applicable to limit	x,xxx	x,xxx	x,xxx	x,xxx	x,xxx	x,xxx	x,xxx	x,xxx	x,xxx	x,xxx
Legal debt margin	$ xxx,xxx	$ xxx,xxx	$ xxx,xxx	$ xxx,xxx	$ xxx,xxx	$ xxx,xxx	$ xxx,xxx	$ x,xxx,xxx	$ x,xxx,xxx	$ x,xxx,xxx
Total net debt applicable to the limit as a percentage of debt limit	x.xx%	x.xx%	x.xx%	x.xx%	x.xx%	x.xx%	x.xx%	x.xx%	x.xx%	x.xx%

Note: Under state finance law, the city's outstanding general obligation debt should not exceed xx percent of total assessed property value. However, the city has established a more conservative internal limit of no more than x percent. By law, the general obligation debt subject to the limitation may be offset by amounts set aside for repaying general obligation bonds.

Exhibit 20A-14: Pledged-Revenue Coverage, Last Ten Fiscal Years.

Schedule 13
City of Centerville
Pledged-Revenue Coverage,
Last Ten Fiscal Years
(dollars in thousands)

| Fiscal Year | Water Revenue Bonds | | | | | | Special Assessment Bonds | | | | Sales Tax Increment Bonds[a] | | | |
	Utility Service Charges	Less: Operating Expenses	Net Available Revenue	Debt Service Principal	Debt Service Interest	Coverage	Special Assessment Collections	Debt Service Principal	Debt Service Interest	Coverage	Sales Tax Increment	Debt Service Principal	Debt Service Interest	Coverage
20X0	$ —	$ —	$ —	$ —	$ —	—	$ x,xxx	$ x,xxx	$ x,xxx	x.xx	$ xxx	$ xxx	$ xxx	x.xx
20X1	—	—	—	—	—	—	x,xxx	x,xxx	x,xxx	x.xx	xxx	xxx	xxx	x.xx
20X2	—	—	—	—	—	—	x,xxx	x,xxx	x,xxx	x.xx	xxx	xxx	xxx	x.xx
20X3	—	—	—	—	—	—	x,xxx	x,xxx	x,xxx	x.xx	x,xxx	xxx	xxx	x.xx
20X4	—	—	—	—	—	—	x,xxx	x,xxx	x,xxx	x.xx	x,xxx	xxx	xxx	x.xx
20X5	—	—	—	—	—	—	x,xxx	x,xxx	x,xxx	x.xx	x,xxx	xxx	xxx	x.xx
20X6	xx,xxx	xx,xxx	xx,xxx	xxx	x,xxx	x.xx	x,xxx	x,xxx	x,xxx	x.xx	x,xxx	xxx	xxx	x.xx
20X7	xx,xxx	xx,xxx	xx,xxx	xxx	x,xxx	x.xx	x,xxx	x,xxx	x,xxx	x.xx	x,xxx	xxx	xxx	x.xx
20X8	xx,xxx	xx,xxx	xx,xxx	xxx	x,xxx	x.xx	x,xxx	x,xxx	x,xxx	x.xx	x,xxx	xxx	xxx	x.xx
20X9	xx,xxx	xx,xxx	xx,xxx	xxx	x,xxx	x.xx	x,xxx	x,xxx	x,xxx	x.xx	x,xxx	xxx	xxx	x.xx

Note: Details regarding the city's outstanding debt can be found in the notes to the financial statements. Operating expenses do not include interest, depreciation, or amortization expenses.

a Sales tax increment bonds are backed by the sales tax revenue produced by the sales tax rate in effect when the bonds were issued (x.x percent) applied to the increase in retail sales in the Commons shopping area since that time.

Schedules of Demographic and Economic Information

The objectives of demographic and economic information are stated by GASB-44 as follows: "(1) to assist users in understanding the socioeconomic environment within which a government operates and (2) to provide information that facilitates comparisons of financial statement information over time and among governments." Governments are required to present one or more of the following five schedules containing, at a minimum:

1. Population
2. Total personal income (if not presented in the debt capacity schedules)
3. Per-capita personal income
4. Unemployment rate
5. Principal employers

The GASB has delivered guidance that "Governments may include any other demographic information they deem relevant to their individual circumstances and useful to the readers of their financial reports. Common examples of other demographic and economic information presented by governments include school enrollment, median age, education level, personal income by industry, retail sales, employment by industry, and construction activity. If the required indicators are not relevant to a particular special-purpose government, relevant alternative indicators should be presented instead."

Exhibit 20A-15 and Exhibit 20A-16 are illustrations of the required schedules of demographic and economic information.

Schedules of Operating Information

The GASB states that the objective of operating information is "to provide contextual information about a government's operations and resources to assist readers in using financial statement information to understand and assess a government's economic condition." Governments are required to present schedules with the following three kinds of information:

1. Numbers of government employees
2. Operating indicators
3. Capital asset information

Exhibit 20A-15: Demographic and Economic Statistics, Last Ten Calendar Years.

Schedule 14
City of Centerville
Demographic and Economic Statistics,
Last Ten Calendar Years

Year	Population	Personal Income (thousands of dollars)	Per Capita Personal Income	Median Age	Education Level in Years of Schooling	School Enrollment	Unemployment Rate
20X0	xx,xxx	$ x,xxx,xxx	$ xx,xxx	xx.x	xx.x	xx,xxx	x.x%
20X1	xx,xxx	x,xxx,xxx	xx,xxx	xx.x	xx.x	xx,xxx	x.x%
20X2	xx,xxx	x,xxx,xxx	xx,xxx	xx.x	xx.x	xx,xxx	x.x%
20X3	xx,xxx	x,xxx,xxx	xx,xxx	xx.x	xx.x	xx,xxx	x.x%
20X4	xx,xxx	x,xxx,xxx	xx,xxx	xx.x	xx.x	xx,xxx	x.x%
20X5	xxx,xxx	x,xxx,xxx	xx,xxx	xx.x	xx.x	xx,xxx	x.x%
20X6	xxx,xxx	x,xxx,xxx	xx,xxx	xx.x	xx.x	xx,xxx	x.x%
20X7	xxx,xxx	x,xxx,xxx	xx,xxx	xx.x	xx.x	xx,xxx	x.x%
20X8	xxx,xxx	x,xxx,xxx	xx,xxx	xx.x	xx.x	xx,xxx	x.x%
20X9	xxx,xxx	x,xxx,xxx	xx,xxx	xx.x	xx.x	xx,xxx	x.x%

Sources: Population, median age, and education level information provided by the State Department of Planning. Personal income and unemployment data provided by the State Department of Commerce and Labor. School enrollment data provided by the Centerville Independent School District.

Note: Population, median age, and education level information are based on surveys conducted during the last quarter of the calendar year. Personal income information is a total for the year. Unemployment rate information is an adjusted yearly average. School enrollment is based on the census at the start of the school year.

Exhibit 20A-16: Principal Employers, Current Year and Nine Years Ago.

Schedule 15
City of Centerville
Principal Employers,
Current Year and Nine Years Ago

Employer	20X9			20X0		
	Employees	Rank	Percentage of Total City Employment	Employees	Rank	Percentage of Total City Employment
New Start Laboratories	x,xxx	1	x.xx%	x,xxx	1	x.xx%
Cross Car Fresheners	xxx	2	x.xx%	xxx	2	x.xx%
City of Centerville	xxx	3	x.xx%	xxx	4	x.xx%
Starwood Health First, Inc.	xxx	4	x.xx%	xxx	3	x.xx%
Really Big Chain Store	xxx	5	x.xx%	—		—
Crawford Industries	xxx	6	x.xx%	xxx	6	x.xx%
Puffin-Oak Partners LLP	xxx	7	x.xx%	—		—
Deanwood Properties	xxx	8	x.xx%	xxx	7	x.xx%
Bronson, Brunson & Branson	xxx	9	x.xx%	—		—
Megagoogleplex Cinemas	xxx	10	x.xx%	—		—
Willow Container Corp.	—		—	xxx	5	x.xx%
Puffin LLP	—		—	xxx	8	x.xx%
Inward Outreach	—		—	xxx	9	x.xx%
Loyd Energy Partners Ltd.	—		—	xx	10	x.xx%
Total	x,xxx		x.xx%	x,xxx		x.xx%

Source: City Economic Development Division.

Exhibit 20A-17: Full-time Equivalent City Government Employees by Function/Program, Last Ten Fiscal Years.

Schedule 16
City of Centerville
Full-time Equivalent City Government Employees by Function/Program,
Last Ten Fiscal Years

Full-time Equivalent Employees as of December 31

Function/Program	20X0	20X1	20X2	20X3	20X4	20X5	20X6	20X7	20X8	20X9
General government
Management services	xx	xx	xx	xx	xx	xx	xx	xx	xx	xx
Finance	xx	xx	xx	xx	xx	xx	xx	xx	xx	xx
Planning	xx	xx	xx	xx	xx	xx	xx	xx	xx	xx
Building	xx	xx	xx	xx	xx	xx	xx	xx	xx	xx
Other	x	x	x	x	x	x	x	x	x	x
Police
Officers[a]	xxx	xxx	xxx	xxx	xxx	xxx	xxx	xxx	xxx	xxx
Civilians	xx	xx	xx	xx	xx	xx	xx	xx	xx	xx
Fire
Firefighters and officers	xx	xx	xx	xx	xx	xx	xx	xx	xx	xx
Civilians	xx	xx	xx	xx	xx	xx	xx	xx	xx	xx
Refuse collection	xx	xx	xx	xx	xx	xx	xx	xx	xx	xx

Full-time Equivalent Employees as of December 31

Function/Program	20X0	20X1	20X2	20X3	20X4	20X5	20X6	20X7	20X8	20X9
Other public works										
Engineering[b]	xx	xx	xx	xx	xx	xx	xx	xx	xx	xx
Other	xx	xx	xx	xx	xx	xx	xx	xx	xx	xx
Redevelopment	xx	xx	xx	xx	xx	xx	xx	xx	xx	xx
Parks and recreation	xx	xx	xx	xx	xx	xx	xx	xx	xx	xx
Library	xx	xx	xx	xx	xx	xx	xx	xx	xx	xx
Water[b]	xx	xx	xx	xx	xx	xx	xx	xx	xx	xx
Wastewater	xx	xx	xx	xx	xx	xx	xx	xx	xx	xx
Transit	x	x	x	x	x	x	x	x	x	x
Total	xxx	xxx	xxx	xxx	xxx	xxx	xxx	xxx	xxx	xxx

Source: City Budget Office.

[a] The police department began the hiring of additional police officers in 20X7 to staff community policing positions.

[b] The city has added additional engineering and water staff in recent years in connection with several infrastructure improvement initiatives.

Exhibit 20A-18: Operating Indicators by Function/ Program, Last Ten Fiscal Years.

Schedule 17
City of Centerville
Operating Indicators by Function/Program,
Last Ten Fiscal Years

Function/Program	Fiscal Year									
	20X0	20X1	20X2	20X3	20X4	20X5	20X6	20X7	20X8	20X9
Police										
Physical arrests	xx,xxx	xx,xxx	xx,xxx	xx,xxx	xx,xxx	xx,xxx	xx,xxx	xx,xxx	xx,xxx	xx,xxx
Parking violations	xx,xxx	xx,xxx	xx,xxx	xx,xxx	xx,xxx	xx,xxx	xx,xxx	xx,xxx	xx,xxx	xx,xxx
Traffic violations	xx,xxx	xx,xxx	xx,xxx	xx,xxx	xx,xxx	xx,xxx	xx,xxx	xx,xxx	xx,xxx	xx,xxx
Fire										
Emergency responses	xx,xxx	xx,xxx	xx,xxx	xx,xxx	xx,xxx	xx,xxx	xx,xxx	xx,xxx	xx,xxx	xx,xxx
Fires extinguished	x,xxx	x,xxx	x,xxx	x,xxx	x,xxx	x,xxx	x,xxx	x,xxx	x,xxx	x,xxx
Inspections	xx,xxx	xx,xxx	xx,xxx	xx,xxx	xx,xxx	xx,xxx	xx,xxx	xx,xxx	xx,xxx	xx,xxx
Refuse collection[a]										
Refuse collected (tons per day)	xxx.x	xxx.x	xxx.x	xxx.x	xxx.x	xxx.x	xxx.x	xxx.x	xxx.x	xxx.x
Recyclables collected (tons per day)	xx.x	xx.x	xx.x	xx.x	xx.x	xx.x	xx.x	xx.x	xx.x	xx.x
Other public works										
Street resurfacing (miles)	xx.x	xx.x	xx.x	xx.x	xx.x	xx.x	xx.x	xx.x	xx.x	xx.x
Potholes repaired	xxx	xxx	xxx	xxx	xxx	xxx	xxx	x,xxx	x,xxx	x,xxx
Parks and recreation										
Athletic field permits issued[b]	x,xxx	x,xxx	x,xxx	x,xxx	x,xxx	x,xxx	x,xxx	x,xxx	x,xxx	x,xxx
Community center admissions	xxx,xxx	xxx,xxx	xxx,xxx	xxx,xxx	xxx,xxx	xxx,xxx	xxx,xxx	xxx,xxx	xxx,xxx	xxx,xxx

Fiscal Year

Function/Program	20X0	20X1	20X2	20X3	20X4	20X5	20X6	20X7	20X8	20X9
Library										
Volumes in collection	xxx,xxx	xxx,xxx	xxx,xxx	xxx,xxx	xxx,xxx	xxx,xxx	xxx,xxx	xxx,xxx	xxx,xxx	xxx,xxx
Total volumes borrowed	xxx,xxx	xxx,xxx	xxx,xxx	xxx,xxx	xxx,xxx	xxx,xxx	xxx,xxx	xxx,xxx	xxx,xxx	xxx,xxx
Water										
New connections	xxx	xxx	xxx	xxx	xxx	xxx	xxx	xxx	xxx	xxx
Water mains breaks	x	x	x	x	xx	xx	x	x	xx	xx
Average daily consumption (thousands of gallons)	x,xxx	x,xxx	x,xxx	x,xxx	x,xxx	x,xxx	x,xxx	x,xxx	x,xxx	x,xxx
Peak daily consumption (thousands of gallons)	x,xxx	x,xxx	x,xxx	x,xxx	x,xxx	x,xxx	x,xxx	x,xxx	x,xxx	x,xxx
Wastewater										
Average daily sewage treatment (thousands of gallons)	x,xxx	x,xxx	x,xxx	x,xxx	x,xxx	x,xxx	x,xxx	x,xxx	x,xxx	x,xxx
Transit										
Total route miles	xx,xxx	xx,xxx	xx,xxx	xx,xxx	xx,xxx	xx,xxx	xx,xxx	xx,xxx	xx,xxx	xx,xxx
Passengers	xxx,xxx	xxx,xxx	xxx,xxx	xxx,xxx	xxx,xxx	xxx,xxx	xxx,xxx	xxx,xxx	xxx,xxx	xxx,xxx

Sources: Various city departments.

Note: Indicators are not available for the general government function.

[a] The Department of Sanitation implemented a recycling initiative in 20X5.

[b] The twelve athletic fields in Paradise Park were out of service during most of 20X5 while they were rehabilitated.

Exhibit 20A-19: Capital Asset Statistics by Function/Program, Last Ten Fiscal Years.

Schedule 18
City of Centerville
Capital Asset Statistics by Function/Program,
Last Ten Fiscal Years

Function/Program	Fiscal Year									
	20X0	20X1	20X2	20X3	20X4	20X5	20X6	20X7	20X8	20X9
Police										
Stations	x	x	x	x	x	x	x	x	x	x
Zone offices	x	x	x	x	x	x	x	x	x	x
Patrol units	xx	xx	xx	xx	xx	xx	xx	xx	xx	xx
Fire stations	x	x	x	x	x	x	x	x	x	x
Refuse collection										
Collection trucks	x	x	x	x	x	x	x	x	x	x
Other public works										
Streets (miles)	xxx.x	xxx.x	xxx.x	xxx.x	xxx.x	xxx.x	xxx.x	xxx.x	xxx.x	xxx.x
Highways (miles)[a]	xx.x	xx.x	xx.x	xx.x	xx.x	xxx.x	xxx.x	xxx.x	xxx.x	xxx.x
Streetlights	x,xxx	x,xxx	x,xxx	x,xxx	x,xxx	x,xxx	x,xxx	x,xxx	x,xxx	x,xxx
Traffic signals	xx	xx	xx	xx	xx	xxx	xxx	xxx	xxx	xxx
Parks and recreation										
Acreage	xxx	xxx	xxx	xxx	xxx	xxx	xxx	xxx	xxx	xxx
Playgrounds	xx	xx	xx	xx	xx	xx	xx	xx	xx	xx

	Fiscal Year									
Function/Program	**20X0**	**20X1**	**20X2**	**20X3**	**20X4**	**20X5**	**20X6**	**20X7**	**20X8**	**20X9**
Baseball/softball diamonds[b]	xx	xx	xx	xx	xx	xx	xx	xx	xx	xx
Soccer/football fields[b]	xx	xx	xx	xx	xx	xx	xx	xx	xx	xx
Community centers	x	x	x	x	x	x	x	x	x	x
Water										
Water mains (miles)	xxx.x	xxx.x	xxx.x	xxx.x	xxx.x	xxx.x	xxx.x	xxx.x	xxx.x	xxx.x
Fire hydrants	x,xxx	x,xxx	x,xxx	x,xxx	x,xxx	x,xxx	x,xxx	x,xxx	x,xxx	x,xxx
Storage capacity (thousands of gallons)	x,xxx	x,xxx	x,xxx	x,xxx	x,xxx	x,xxx	x,xxx	x,xxx	x,xxx	x,xxx
Wastewater										
Sanitary sewers (miles)	xxx.x	xxx.x	xxx.x	xxx.x	xxx.x	xxx.x	xxx.x	xxx.x	xxx.x	xxx.x
Storm sewers (miles)	xxx.x	xxx.x	xxx.x	xxx.x	xxx.x	xxx.x	xxx.x	xxx.x	xxx.x	xxx.x
Treatment capacity (thousands of gallons)	x,xxx	x,xxx	x,xxx	x,xxx	x,xxx	x,xxx	x,xxx	x,xxx	x,xxx	x,xxx
Transit-minibuses	x	x	x	x	x	x	x	x	x	x

Sources: Various city departments.

Note: No capital asset indicators are available for the general government or library function.

[a] The Crawford Memorial Highway opened in 20X5.

[b] The twelve athletic fields in Paradise Park were out of service during most of 20X5 while they were rehabilitated.

Accounting Resources on the Web

Presented here are World Wide Web URLs of interest to practitioners. Because of the constantly changing nature of the Internet, addresses change and new resources become available every day. To find additional resources, use search engines such as Google (http://www.google.com), the Open Directory Project (http://www.dmoz.org), and Yahoo! (http://www.yahoo.com).

"Agreed-Upon Procedures and Results Assessment of Federal Audit Clearinghouse Database Fiscal Year 1998 Audit Reports" http://www.oig.doc.gov/Pages/Agreed-UponProceduresandResultsAssessmentofFederalAuditClearinghouseDatabaseFiscalYear1998AuditRepor.aspx

"Choosing an External Auditor" http://www.auditforum.org/mid america/midam_exauditor.htm

Accountants World http://www.accountantsworld.com/

Accounting Research Manager http://www.accountingresearchmanager.com/

Accounting Resources on the Internet http://accounting.rutgers.edu

Action Without Borders—Idealist Org http://www.idealist.org

AICPA http://www.aicpa.org

AICPA International Financial Reporting Standards Resources http://www.ifrs.com

AICPA Library Service http://www.olemiss.edu/depts/general_library/aicpa

American Accounting Association http://www.aaahq.org

American Legal Publishing Corp. http://amlegal.com/library

Association of Certified Fraud Examiners (ACFE) http://www.acfe.org/

Association of College and University Auditors (ACUA) http://www.acua.org

Association of Government Accountants (AGA) http://www.agacgfm.org

Association of Local Government Auditors (ALGA) http://www.GovernmentAuditors.org/

Association of School Business Officials http://www.asbointl.org/

Automated Clearing House http://www.fms.treas.gov/ach/

BoardSource http://www.boardsource.org/

Bureau of Labor Statistics http://www.bls.gov/

Cash Management Improvement Act http://www.fms.treas.gov/cmia/

Catalog of Federal Domestic Assistance (CFDA) http://www.cfda.gov/

CCH INCORPORATED http://CCHGroup.com/

Code of Federal Regulations http://www.gpoaccess.gov/cfr/

Compliance Assistance Employment Law Guide http://www.dol.gov/compliance/guide/dbra.htm

Compliance Supplement http://www.whitehouse.gov/omb/circulars/a133_compliance_supplement_2010

COSO (Committee of Sponsoring Organizations of the Treadway Commission) http://www.coso.org/

Council of State Governments (CSG) http://www.csg.org/csg/default

Council on Foundations http://www.cof.org/

Data Collection Form http://harvester.census.gov/fac/collect/formoptions.html

Department of Education OIG's Non-Federal Audit Team http://www2.ed.gov/about/offices/list/oig/nonfed/nfteam.html

Electronic Privacy Information Center http://www.epic.org/

Evangelical Council for Financial Accountability (ECFA) http://www.ecfa.org/

FASB http://www.fasb.org/

Federal Agencies Web Locator http://www.lib.lsu.edu/gov/

Federal Audit Clearinghouse http://harvester.census.gov/sac/

Federal Financial Accounting Standards Board (FASAB) http://www.fasab.gov/

Federal Inspectors General (IGnet) http://www.ignet.gov/

Federal Register http://www.gpoaccess.gov/fr/index.html

FEDSTATS http://www.fedstats.gov/

Forensic Accounting Information http://www.forensic-accounting-information.com/

GASB http://www.gasb.org/

General Services Administration http://www.gsa.gov/

Government Accountability Office http://www.gao.gov/

Government Auditing Standards http://www.gao.gov/yellowbook

Government Finance Officers Association (GFOA) http://www.gfoa.org/

Government Printing Office http://www.gpo.gov/

GSA Forms http://www.gsa.gov/forms

IGnet Federal Inspectors General http://www.ignet.gov/

Infomine government publications http://infomine.ucr.edu/cgi-bin/search?category=govpub

Information about Tax-Exempt Organizations http://www.irs.gov/charities/index.html

Institute of Internal Auditors, The (IIA) http://www.theiia.org/

Institute of Management Accountants (IMA) http://www.imanet.org/

Intergovernmental Audit Forums http://www.auditforum.org/

Internal Audit and Fraud Investigation Articles http://www.mrsciacfe.cjb.net/

International Accounting Standards Board and International Financial Reporting Standards Foundation http://www.ifrs.org/Home.htm

International City/County Management Association http://icma.org/en/icma/home

International Federation of Accountants http://ifac.org

AICPA International Financial Reporting Standards Resources http://www.ifrs.com

International Organization of Securities Commission http://www.iosco.org/about/

IRS Digital Daily http://www.irs.gov/

Legal Information Institute (Cornell Law School) http://www.law.cornell.edu/statutes.html

Legal Services Corporation (LSC) http://www.lsc.gov/

LSU Libraries Government Documents http://www.lib.lsu.edu/govdocs/index.html

National Archives and Records Administration Code of Federal Regulations http://www.gpoaccess.gov/cfr/index.html

National Association of College and University Business Officers (NACUBO) http://www.nacubo.org/

National Association of State Auditors, Comptrollers, and Treasurers (NASACT) http://www.nasact.org/

National Association of State Boards of Accountancy (NASBA) http://www.nasba.org/

National Association of State Budget Officers http://www.nasbo.org/

National Conference of State Legislatures (NCSL) http://www.ncsl.org/

National Labor Relations Board http://www.nlrb.gov/

North American Industry Classification System (NAICS) http://www.census.gov/epcd/www/naics.html

Occupational Employment Statistics http://stats.bls.gov/oes/home.htm

Office of Federal Contract Compliance Programs (OFCCP) http://www.dol.gov/ofccp/regs/compliance/ca_irca.htm

Office of Management and Budget http://www.whitehouse.gov/omb

PCIE Single Audit Guidance http://www.thecre.com/fedlaw/legal3a/psingle.htm

Police List of Resources: Electronic Crime http://police.sas.ab.ca/prl/elect.html

Privacy Foundation http://www.privacyfoundation.org/

Prompt Payment Act Interest Rate http://www.treasurydirect.gov/govt/rates/tcir/tcir_opdprmt2.htm

ProSystem fx http://www.cchgroup.com/webapp/wcs/stores/servlet/category_ProSystem-fx-Suite-Solutions_10151_-1_10053_50005702_10151_N_Y

Public Company Accounting Oversight Board http://www.pcaobus.org

SAB-99 http://www.sec.gov/interps/account/sab99.htm

SAB-101 http://www.sec.gov/interps/account/sab101.htm

Sarbanes-Oxley Act of 2002 http://www.gpo.gov/fdsys/pkg/
PLAW-107publ204/content-detail.html

SEC Edgar Database http://www.sec.gov/edgar.shtml

SEC Staff Accounting Bulletins http://www.sec.gov/interps/account.shtml

Securities and Exchange Commission http://www.sec.gov/

Software and Information Industry Association (SIIA) http://www.siia.net/

State and local links http://www.Statelocal.gov

Sterling Codifiers, Inc. http://www.sterlingcodifiers.com/codesonline.php

The Library of Congress http://www.loc.gov/

Thomas: Legislative Information http://thomas.loc.gov/

Treasury—Financial Management Service http://www.fms.treas.gov/

Uniform CPA Examination http://www.cpa-exam.org/

U.S. Conference of Mayors http://www.usmayors.org/

U.S. Department of Agriculture http://www.usda.gov/

U.S. Department of Commerce http://www.commerce.gov/

U.S. Department of Defense http://www.defense.gov

U.S. Department of Education http://www.ed.gov/

U.S. Department of Education OIG's Non-Federal Audit Team http://
www2.ed.gov/about/offices/list/oig/nonfed/nfteam.html

U.S. Department of Energy http://www.energy.gov/

U.S. Department of Health and Human Services http://www.dhhs.gov/

U.S. Department of Housing and Urban Development http://www.hud.gov/

U.S. Department of Labor http://www.dol.gov/

U.S. Department of Labor Wage and Hour Division http://www.dol.gov/
whd/index.htm

U.S. Department of State http://www.state.gov/

U.S. Department of the Interior http://www.doi.gov/

U.S. Department of the Treasury http://www.treas.gov/

U.S. Departmant of the Treasury Financial Management Service http://
www.fms.treas.gov/

U.S. Department of the Treasury's Listing of Approved Sureties http://
www.fms.treas.gov/c570/c570.html

U.S. Department of Transportation http://www.dot.gov/

U.S. Environmental Protection Agency http://www.epa.gov/

U.S. GAO Bid Protest Decisions http://www.gao.gov/decisions/bidpro/
bidpro.htm

U.S. General Services Administration http://www.gsa.gov/

U.S. Government forms http://www.gsa.gov/forms

U.S. House of Representatives http://www.house.gov/

U.S. House of Representatives Current Floor Proceedings http:// clerk.house.gov/

U.S. HUD Office of Inspector General http://www.hudoig.gov/

U.S. HUD Office of Labor Relations http://www.hud.gov/offices/olr/ index.cfm

U.S. Senate http://www.senate.gov/

U.S. Small Business Administration http://www.sba.gov/

U.S. State & Local Gateway http://www.statelocal.gov/

U.S. Treasury http://www.treas.gov/

University of Michigan Documents Center http://www.lib.umich.edu/ govdocs/

Yellow Book http://www.gao.gov/yellowbook

INDEX